Readings in Political Economy

IO700348

Blackwell Readings for Contemporary Economics

This series presents collections of writings by some of the world's foremost economists on core issues in the discipline. Each volume dovetails with a variety of existing economics courses at the advanced undergraduate, graduate, and MBA levels. The readings, gleaned from a wide variety of classic and contemporary sources, are placed in context by a comprehensive introduction from the editor. In addition, a thorough index facilitates research.

Readings in Political Economy

Edited by
Kaushik Basu

Blackwell
Publishing

© 2003 by Blackwell Publishers Ltd
a Blackwell Publishing company
except for editorial arrangement and introduction © 2003 by Kaushik Basu

350 Main Street, Malden, MA 02148-5018, USA
108 Cowley Road, Oxford OX4 1JF, UK
550 Swanston Street, Carlton, Victoria 3053, Australia
Kurfürstendamm 57, 10707 Berlin, Germany

The right of Kaushik Basu to be identified as the Author of the Editorial Material in this Work has been asserted in accordance with the UK Copyright, Designs, and Patents Act 1988.

All rights reserved. No part of this publication may be reproduced, stored in a retrieval system, or transmitted, in any form or by any means, electronic, mechanical, photocopying, recording or otherwise, except as permitted by the UK Copyright, Designs and Patents Act 1988, without the prior permission of the publisher.

First published 2003 by Blackwell Publishers Ltd

Library of Congress Cataloging-in-Publication Data has been applied for

ISBN 0-631-22332-0 (hbk)
ISBN 0-631-22333-9 (pbk)

A catalogue record for this title is available from the British Library.

Set in 10/11.5 pt Ehrhardt
by Kolam Information Services Pvt. Ltd, Pondicherry, India
Printed and bound in the United Kingdom by T.J. International, Padstow, Cornwall

For further information on
Blackwell Publishing, visit our website:
http://www.blackwellpublishing.com

Contents

Acknowledgments

The editor and publishers gratefully acknowledge the following for permission to reproduce copyright material:

American Economic Association, for Avner Greif (1992), "Institutions and International Trade: Lessons from the Commercial Revolution," in *American Economic Review*, vol. 82; Amartya Sen (1995), "Rationality and Social Choice," in *American Economic Review*, vol. 85; Avinash Dixit (1997), "Power of Incentives in Private versus Public Organizations," in *American Economic Review*, vol. 87; and Torsten Persson and Guido Tabellini (1994), "Is Inequality Harmful for Growth?," in *American Economic Review*, vol. 84.

American Political Science Review, for William H. Riker (1980), "Implications from the Disequilibrium of Majority Rule for the Study of Institutions," in *American Political Science Review*, vol. 74; and Mancur Olson (1993), "Dictatorship, Democracy, and Development," in *American Political Science Review*, vol. 87.

Blackwell Publishers, for Paul R. Milgrom, Douglass C. North, and Barry R. Weingast (1990), "The Role of Institutions in the Revival of Trade: the Law Merchant, Private Judges and the Champagne Fairs," in *Economics and Politics*, vol. 2; Brendan O'Flaherty and Jagdish Bhagwati (1997), "Will Free Trade with Political Science Put Normative Economists out of Work?" in *Economics and Politics*, vol. 9, and Kaushik Basu (1997), "On Misunderstanding Government: an Analysis of the Art of Policy Advice," in *Economics and Politics*, vol. 9.

Elsevier Science, for Oliver Williamson (1996) "Transaction Cost Economics and Organization Theory," in Schmalensee and Willig, *Handbook of Industrial Organization*, vol. 1 (1989).

Macmillan Ltd, for Kenneth J. Arrow (1998), "The Place of Institutions in the Economy: a Theoretical Perspective," in Y. Hayami and M. Aoki (eds.), *The Institutional Foundations of East Asian Economic Development*.

MIT Press, for the extract from Avinash Dixit, *The Making of Economic Policy: A Transaction Cost* (1996).

MIT Press Journals, for Timothy Besley and Stephen Coate (1997), "An Economic Model of Representative Democracy," in *Quarterly Journal of Economics*, vol. 112, copyright © 1997 by the President and Fellows of Harvard College and the Massachusetts Institute of Technology; Alberto Alesina and Dani Rodrik (1994), "Distributive Politics and Economic Growth," in *Quarterly Journal of Economics*, vol. 109, copyright © 1994 by the President and Fellows of Harvard College and the Massachusetts Institute of Technology; Assar Lindbeck, Sten Nyberg, and Jörgen W. Weibull (1999), "Social Norms and Economic Incentives in the Welfare State," in *Quarterly Journal of Economics*, vol. 114. Copyright © 1999 by the President and Fellows of Harvard College and the Massachusetts Institute of Technology.

Natural Resources Journal, for James M. Buchanan (1973), "The Coase Theorem and the Theory of the State," in *Natural Resources Journal*, vol. 13.

Oxford University Press, for Bengt Holstrom and Paul R. Milgrom (1991), "Multitask Principal–Agent Analyses: Incentive Contracts, Asset Ownership, and Job Design," in *Journal of Law, Economics and Organization*, vol. 7; and Jean Tirole (1994), "The Internal Organization of Government," in *Oxford Economic Papers*, vol. 46. Used by permission of Oxford University Press.

Pearson Education Inc., for Anthony Downs, *An Economic Theory of Democracy*, copyright © 1957, 1985 Anthony Downs. Reprinted by permission of Pearson Education Inc.

The publishers apologize for any errors or omissions in the above list and would be grateful to be notified of any corrections that should be incorporated in the next edition or reprint of this book.

Introduction

KAUSHIK BASU*

I

Political economy, as the term has come to be used today, is a broad discipline that studies the interface between economics and politics, using the method of rational choice theory. In traditional economics, "government" was treated as exogenous and beyond the pale of analysis. Political scientists, on the other hand, had their attention directed at government, but they were not, in general, concerned with the rationality of the agents of government, and, when they were, they did not have the tools necessary for a formal analysis of rationality. The new political economy was born out of the economist's realization that for a proper understanding of the economy one needed to endogenize government, and the political scientist's discovery that there was a body of well-developed rational choice theory within economics that could be adapted to the political context.

This confluence of economics and politics has given rise to a profusion of research, great expectations, and some remarkable new insights.

Consider the institution of share tenancy. Standard economic analysis is concerned with questions such as what the equilibrium rent will be, what effect such a system may have on other markets, such as labor and credit, and whether such an institution is efficient or not. Indeed, in this case, a large literature (there are notable exceptions, though) has castigated share tenancy as inefficient.

A typical political economy researcher, however, may ask all the above questions but also ask an additional question, which is germane to his or her analysis: Why does share tenancy exist in the first place? Who formed the interest groups that pushed for this system or, in case the system evolved slowly over a long period, who were the people that resisted attempts to abolish this system? If this system is founded in the law, or its abolition failed to be passed by government, why did the legislators behave the way they did?

At times such inquiry into the political foundations of some simple economic phenomenon can yield revealing insights. Suppose an examination of share tenancy reveals that in certain social and political milieux share tenancy is inevitable, because its survival is founded in vested interests of groups that have political clout. This has major implications for the economist. It shows that the advice "Repeal share tenancy because it is inefficient" may not have much use. Political economy shows that the institution of share tenancy is not a detachable part of our political and social system.

Such analysis can be and has been extended to a variety of economic phenomena: minimum wages (why do we have minimum wages when we do?), progressive taxation, unemployment insurance and the autonomy of the central bank (Persson and Tabellini, 2000; Shepsle and Bonchuk, 1997).

The method of political economy is not without its pitfalls. One mistake is to make a habit of it, and to presume that the analysis of *no* institution is complete unless one asks from where the institution came and why it has persisted. The mistake lies in failing to recognize that there is an infinite regress problem here. If we can explain an institution as an outcome of electoral politics and a certain voting system, the question arises as to why there is electoral politics and why the voting system is the way it is. If one answers this by pointing to the constitution that was implemented a century ago, one can go on to ask why the constitution is the way it is. And the answer to that can be confronted with yet another question. Since, our analysis has to stop somewhere, we surely have to take some institutions as given.[1]

A second mistake (widespread among the new converts to rational choice political science) is to presume that human beings are unfailingly rational. In reality, people often misjudge their own interests and do not consider all the options open to them (Basu, 2000, chapter 11). Hence, the standard economic analysis which shows that a certain institution (for instance, rent control) is inefficient or that it is not in the interest of the people, who defend it, can be of value. It can at times change minds. Political economy analysis has its advantages, but also its limitations.

What I am describing here as "political economy" is quite distinct from its progenitor, the political economy before the rise of neo-classical economics, in the late nineteenth century. The political economy of John Stuart Mill, for instance, also straddled politics, government and economics, but it was not overly concerned with founding it all on a formal rationality calculus. With the rise of neo–classical economics and, in particular, the works of Jevons and Walras, it became necessary to separate the study of economics and politics (and also, within economics, to separate macroeconomics from microeconomics). Economists became increasingly concerned with formalism and intricate deductive systems. Unless something was amenable to formal analysis, economists tended to ignore it. And given the limitations of the tools of traditional economics, it was hard enough to give formal shape to studying purely economic matters; it was therefore not surprising that politics and social norms received scant attention.

What changed all this was the rise of game theory in the 1970s and 1980s.[2] Game theory gave us a mathematically easy, but at the same time rigorous, instrument for broadening the scope of economics. Not surprisingly, the emergence of the (new) political economy and the study of social norms and institutions and their effects on the economy, had to wait for the maturing of game theory.

One hopes that as political economy progresses, this discipline will also learn to take account of the fact of human less-than-rationality (Thaler, 1991; Kahneman, 1994). Its other big task is the modeling of government. At one level, all the papers included in this volume are devoted to this task. Yet this is an activity that is, as I have argued elsewhere (Basu, 2000, 2001) still in its nascency.

The endeavor to understand government goes back several centuries – the most-famous work being Thomas Hobbes's *Leviathan*. Hobbes argued that human beings left to themselves are greedy, grabbing, competitive and glory-seeking. Hence, in the absence of extrinsic control, human beings will tend to be at war with one another. Therefore, the life of man will be, in the famous words of Hobbes (1651, p. 76), "solitary, poor, nasty, brutish and short."

Even in his own life Hobbes was quite terrified of war and anarchy. Unlike many other philosophers who were proud of their courage, Hobbes always exhibited pride in his cowardice. He boasted, for instance, that he was the first Briton to leave England (for France) during the Civil War.

Hobbes' government was born of this fear of anarchy. Government was the Leviathan needed to keep man's vile tendencies under control. Human beings needed a "common power to keep them in awe and to direct their actions to the common benefit." And "the only way to erect such a common power . . . is to confer all their power and strength upon one man or upon one assembly of men" (Hobbes, 1651, p. 109).

Having found the *raison d'être* of government, Hobbes attempted, unlike his predecessors, to scientifically scrutinize government and polity. This is what makes Hobbes' work especially significant and this is what prompts me to present some extracts from his *Leviathan* as the first reading in this collection (chapter 1). As Alan Ryan (1996, p. 212) has argued, "Hobbes's political philosophy was distinctive in its ambition to be a science of politics."

While Hobbes deserves credit for being first, it is David Hume who must be recognized for the depth of his analysis of government. Why will one person obey another just because the latter is king or the head of the state, asked Hume. After all, many a king could be overpowered, physically, by his labor-hardened subjects. So, in the end, we owe our order to self-enforcing discipline – our belief or opinion about what others will do to us if we violate the norms of society. Hume (1739, 1758) marveled how, despite the "infirmities" and infidelity of individuals, the collectivity of human beings, through an intricate web of "opinion," can bring order and progress. Along with Hobbes, I have selected an essay by Hume (chapter 2) as the other entry in the first part of this book, which provides the backdrop for the contemporary research in political economy.

II

Coming to more recent times, one can isolate two core contributions that gave impetus to the simultaneous study of economics and politics: Arrow (1951) and Downs (1957) – see chapters 3 and 15. Arrow's discovery that some simple normative axioms, that we usually take for granted, cannot all be satisfied by *any* voting rule (for example, the majority decision rule; or two-thirds majority or status quo; or the rank order rule, etc.) is one of the most important theorems in the social sciences of the twentieth century. It sparked off an enormous literature, formalizing different sets of normative axioms and investigating their mutual compatibility.

Downs, on the other hand, focused on the subject of political competition. How will two parties trying to choose their political agenda with the ultimate aim of winning an election behave? This is what Downs studied and gave rise to the "median voter" theorem. While this is the best-known result in Downs' book, the book has much more and, in an informal way, anticipates much of the research that was to appear over the next decades.

While Arrow's work is intellectually unparalleled, giving us an algebra that forms the basis of modern political economy, its direct descendant is social choice and not political economy. In the present collection, for reasons of comprehensiveness, I have included two papers which straddle the fringes of political economy and Arrovian social choice theory, one emanating from the discipline of economics and the other from politics – Sen (1995) and Riker (1980).

Given that there is a more direct line from Downs to political economy, I have chosen to include extracts from Downs' classic book – in particular, the section where he derives the median voter theorem – and several subsequent papers which use or extend this result. The paper by Sen (chapter 16), on the other hand, gives what is probably the most elegant proof of Arrow's theorem available and a statement of the connection between individual well-being and the problem of collective decision-making.

It may be useful to give here a brief, Downsian account of voting and agenda selection. Suppose a government has to decide how much public good x to produce, where $x \in [0,1]$. In order to produce a larger amount of public good it has to collect more taxes, so it is conceivable that different citizens have different views as to the ideal amount of public good the government should produce. Let us assume that there are many citizens – for mathematical convenience, a continuum. Let $F(x)$ be the number of citizens whose ideal public good choice is less than or equal to x. Clearly $F(1)$ is the total population of the economy under consideration.

We shall also assume that each individual has strictly quasi-concave preferences, which in effect means that if a person i's ideal point is $x^* \in [0, 1]$ and $x' < x'' \leq x^*$, or $x^* \geq x'' > x'$, then she will prefer x'' to x'.

Now suppose two political parties, A and B, running for government, have to announce their "agenda" for what each will do if they get elected. Since the only problem that a government encounters in our simple polity is to decide how much public good to produce, the agenda of party P (where P is either A or B) is denoted by $x_p \in [0, 1]$. In other words, party A promises that it will produce x_A units of public goods if it wins the election. Likewise for party B.

If each party's aim is to win the election, and the electoral rule followed by the country is that of the majority decision, then it is easy to see what agenda the parties will choose. In answering this problem, I will assume that a citizen, who is indifferent to the agenda of both parties, decides her vote by the toss of an unbiased coin.

Observe that if any party, say party A, announces an agenda x_A which has the property that either (i) $F(x_A) > \frac{1}{2}$, or (ii) $F(x_A) < \frac{1}{2}$, then this party will surely be beaten. In case (i) B will choose x_B immediately to the left of x_A, and in case (ii) B will announce an x_B just to the right of x_A. And by doing this B will get more votes than A. Hence, the only reasonable way for these parties to select their agenda is to set $x_A = x_B = x_M$, where x_M is defined as that value of x for which $F(x) = \frac{1}{2}$. If both parties behave in this way, no party can do better through a unilateral change in its agenda.

It is plain that x_M is the "median agenda" or the ideal point of the "median voter." Hence, what we have established is that in a democratic system, the agenda of different political parties will tend to converge on one another and together they will converge on the median voter's ideal.

For many years after 1957 this became the pivotal model. Other writers motivated their work by citing this model, whether in agreement or disagreement.

III

While a large part of political economy is concerned with voting and the political process, it is also concerned with the larger and, in some ways, more ill-defined idea of "institutions" (Platteau, 2000). The five papers that make up Part II of this collection – Arrow (1998), Williamson (1996), Milgrom, North, and Weingast (1990), Greif (1992), and Riker (1980) – are all attempts to give formal shape to the concept of institutions and the effect of alternative institutions on the functioning of markets and the economy.

Standard economics is written as if institutions and norms do not matter. It is, however, arguable – as Arrow maintains – that an institution-free economics is an illusion. This is because the assumptions that we write down explicitly in our standard models – for example, that individuals have transitive preferences and that they prefer more to less and that firms face diminishing marginal productivity, and so on – are not the only assumptions that we use. Typically, we have other assumptions, which are built into the framework of our model, and therefore escape notice. Observe, for instance, that in writing a model of general equilibrium or trade or markets, we never state the assumption that human beings can speak. Yet it is eminently arguable that trade and exchange between economic agents would not occur as smoothly as our models suggest if the agents could not speak to one another and exchange information (Warneryd, 1995; Basu, 2000, section 4.1). Hence, while we are careful in specifying our assumptions concerning continuity, convexity and so on, we take for granted and leave implicit assumptions such as the fact that human beings can speak and communicate or that they believe in non-violence or that they adhere to the norm of not stealing another agent's property. The bundle of these assumptions, the basic rules of human intercourse that underlie a society, constitutes its "institutions."

The success and failure of economies and markets can depend crucially on the nature of these underlying institutions (Williamson, 1985; North, 1990; Greif, 1992). As several economists have argued (see Greif, 1992, 1993; Milgrom, North, and Weingast, 1990), during the early Middle Ages, when trade began to expand across nations and great distances, much depended on how much entrepreneurs could trust their agents. Hence, the presence of institutions for preventing cheating could be a crucial factor in the prospect of prosperity among a people, community or a nation.

Williamson's (1996) paper, included in this volume (see chapter 4), reviews different interpretations of institutional economics, the role of transactions costs and the elusive concept of trust. He highlights some of the tensions between economics and sociology in this terrain of interdisciplinary research and develops his own scheme for resolving some of these tensions.

Over time, as the institution of the modern state came into being, it unsurped the major responsibility of preventing cheating and keeping order in a society. A paper on institutions that nevertheless belongs to a very different genre is Riker (1980; see chapter 7). Riker's works have been very influential in drawing the attention of political scientists to the development of public choice and social choice theories and, through these, to the new political economy. He made use of location theory to capture the variations of the preference of voters, a technique which is generally accepted today. In the paper included in this collection, Riker surveys some of the early writings in choice theory. He then goes on to show how in some situations the median voter theorem may fail to hold in a rather interesting way: there simply may not exist any equilibrium. He then argues that the non-existence of equilibrium may be fundamental to our understanding of institutions and politics.

By the time economic theory came into its own, the modern state was so well entrenched that it was easy for us to take it for granted. And that is exactly what economists did. The state, as was explained earlier, was treated as a nondescript, exogenous sector. Since it is obviously foolish for us to try to change the endogenous variables of our economy, all the advice of economists was directed at the state. Thus the exogenous state became the *raison d'être* of the policy economist.

But what is the state and what are the motivations that drive the agents of the state? This is the question that concerns the papers that appear in Part III – Buchanan (1973), Olson (1993), O'Flaherty and Bhagwati (1997) and Basu (1997).

Buchanan's paper (chapter 8) is mainly on the Coase theorem. It consists of an analysis of the theorem's validity in unusual institutional settings. In the process, Buchanan is forced to confront the question: what is the state? The same question is asked and answered by Olson (chapter 9), but with greater sophistication – as you would expect after two further decades of research. Olson's paper consists of a searching inquiry into the origins of the state, different kinds of government, and the connection between the nature of the state and economic progress.

This line of research, taken to its logical end, compels us to view government as a fully endogenous organization. The agents of government – the ministers, the judges, and even the head of the state – are, in the final analysis, like a consumer with his wallet in hand trying to decide what to buy, or the entrepreneur of a firm pondering over how to organize the firm and how much to produce. Like the consumer and the entrepreneur, the politician has his own aims and ambitions. Hence, policies which were earlier treated as exogenous, for instance, trade tariffs, now become an endogenous variable in a larger politico-economic system (see Dixit, 1996).[3]

To admit this compels us to confront the question: is it not then futile to give policy advice? If the advisee is a fully determined agent, is not our advice to him like speaking into deaf ears? It is this problem that O'Flaherty and Bhagwati (chapter 10) describe as the "determinacy paradox" and their paper and that of Basu (chapter 11) are studies of ways to break out of the paradox. There is in economics an interesting literature on *why* we speak and on how person i's speech can influence j's *action* (Crawford and Sobel, 1982; Alesina and Cukierman, 1990; Austen-Smith, 1990; Krishna and Morgan, 2000). Basu uses such models to investigate the scope for advising an endogenous government and reaches the conclusion that there is scope for advising government but the advice may have to be given in a very different form from that which is traditionally supposed.

IV

A closely related question to what is the state is: how does government function? For a long time, government was treated as a black box by economists. This was unfortunate and could not but handicap our understanding of the economy, since government is such an important part of modern economic life. The political scientist had, for long, been interested in the structure and functioning of government. But that did not serve the purpose of economists. The same object can be studied in different ways. For example, the taxidermist and the zoologist may both know a lot about the tiger but each may find the other's knowledge of little use.

In economics there has been a growing need to understand the internal workings of government in the same way that economists have inquired and come to understand the internal structure of the firm. There is fortunately a recent literature – albeit brief – that has investigated the internal organization of government. The three papers that constitute Part IV – Holmstrom and Milgrom (1991), Tirole (1994) and Dixit (1997) – are among the most important contributions to this field.

On the face of it, the paper by Holmstrom and Milgrom (chapter 12) has little to do with government. However, by developing a model of incentives within an organization it provided some of the crucial theoretical foundations for the more direct work on government that has occurred in recent times. Essentially what Holmstrom and Milgrom studied was a principal–agent model, in which the principal gives the agent several tasks or one task which has several dimensions. They show how this can lead to incentives being muted within organizations.

Drawing on this and also the work of James Wilson (1989) on bureaucracy, Dixit (1997) addresses more directly the subject of incentives inside government. Dixit focuses on the fact that government bureaucracies are typically answerable to several principals. The department of taxation, for instance, has to respond to the demands not only of the finance minister, but also the commerce minister, the law minister and the prime minister. Hence, a bureaucracy may not only have many tasks to perform but several principals interested in those tasks.

A full description of the internal organization of government is attempted by Tirole (chapter 13; see also Laffont and Tirole, 1993). Tirole also recognizes the multiple objectives of government agencies and the fact that these objectives are often non-measurable. He has studied the lack of adequate incentives inside government, and by constructing a full description of government, he is able to ask other questions, such as how bureaucrats strategically manipulate information and favor some interest groups and why government does not always behave as a coherent entity.

The final part of the book consists of a somewhat motley collection of papers, which study the voting processes (Downs, 1957; Besley and Coate, 1997), their implications for the choice of economic policy (Alesina and Rodrik, 1994; Persson and Tabellini, 1994; Lindbeck, Nyberg and Weibull, 1999) and the connection between political economy, public choice and social choice (Sen, 1995). Starting from a simple Downsian structure, Besley and Coate (chapter 17) construct a more realistic and complex model of the political process in which there are no exogenously specified politicians (that is, in their model any citizen can stand for office), policies can be multi-dimensional and the voters have preference not just for policies but also for politicians *per se*. And likewise, politicians care not just about winning elections but also about the policies that get chosen (see also Alesina and Cukierman, 1990). This yields a variety of new insights, including explanations for why representative democracies may fail to be efficient.

Alesina and Rodrik (chapter 18) consider a fairly standard model of endogenous growth in which policies are not given exogenously, as in economics textbooks, but are chosen by majority voting. This allows them to model the link between inequality of wealth and income in a society and the growth rate of the society (see also Rodrik, 1995). They find that the greater the inequality, the lower the growth rate. The model is then empirically tested and the findings corroborated. A similar relation between inequality and growth is found by Persson and Tabellini (chapter 19), though, unlike the Alesina–Rodrik exercise that focuses on the functional distribution of income, Persson and Tabellini are concerned with the size distribution of income.

Lindbeck, Nyberg and Weibull (chapter 20) also model the formation of policy, pertaining to taxes and transfers in the context of a labor market, but in a sense their concern is larger. Their paper deals with the role of social norms and stigma and how the existence of such norms create the possibility of multiple equilibria. Indeed the occurrence of multiple equilibria becomes in general quite pervasive in market outcomes when we recognize the role of social norms and politics (see, for instance, Hoff, 2000).

It is easy to see this. Suppose we have a society with a given wage distribution such that $F(w)$ is the number of people who earn a wage less than or equal to w. Let t be the proportional income tax rate that prevails in this society. Let u be the utility function that converts a person's income into utility. Hence, a person who earns a wage of w gets a utility of $u[(1 - t)w]$ by going to work. Suppose that government gives an unemployment dole of T to every unemployed person. However, being unemployed entails a "stigma cost," c. It seems reasonable to assume, and Lindbeck, Nyberg and Weibull do assume this (see also Besley and Coate, 1992), that c is inversely related to the number, n, of people who are unemployed. Hence, $c = c(n)$ and $c'(n) < 0$. In other words, it is less embarrassing to be living off the dole in a society where lots of people live off the dole. Hence, if a person chooses to be unemployed he earns a net utility of $u(T) - c(n)$. I am here ignoring the joys of leisure. This is harmless since it can be thought of as subsumed in $c(n)$.

It is now obvious that a person who commands a wage of w will choose to work if and only if $u[(1 - t)w] \geq u(T) - c(n)$. Define w^* as the critical wage at which a person is indifferent to working or not working. Hence,

$$u[(1 - t)w^*] = u(T) - c(n);$$

and we may write this, in turn, as:

$$w^* \equiv w(t, T, n).$$

Since all those who earn a wage of $w < w^*$ will choose not to work, it follows that, given t, T and n, the number of people who will be unemployed is given by $F(w(t, T, n))$. Clearly, if $F(w(t, T, n)) \neq n$, then this cannot be an equilibrium. Hence, n^* may be called an *equilibrium unemployment* if $n^* = F[w(t, T, n^*)]$.

Note that as n rises, $w(t, T, n)$ will rise (since $c'(n) < 0$). Hence, $F[w(t, T, n)]$ will rise. This immediately suggests the possibility of multiple equilibria.

Of course for a study of the full equilibrium we also need to find out the level of t and T that will prevail over time. And this brings in crucial questions of political economy and leads us back to the central theme of this book – to wit, an explanation of how a state chooses its policy variables: taxes, unemployment doles, tariffs and subsidies.

V

As happens with all new directions of research, much more is being written in the field of political economy than will survive the test of time. In the enthusiasm of this new-found direction of research, we are trying to move faster than is possible or realistic to expect. Gradually, once the dust settles, not all that is holding our attention today will survive. But that in no way detracts from the fact that the breach in the boundary between economics and politics has been needed for a long time, and is therefore an event that deserves celebration.

Notes

*   In writing this chapter and editing the book I have had the benefit of discussions with and assistance from Geraint Jones, Gayatri Koolwal and Mandar Oak.
1   Likewise, when we speak of a free market economy we typically take the structure of property rights as given. Some have tried to go a step further and examine the origins of property rights or at least to start from a system where the rights are not pre-specified (e.g. de Meza and Gould, 1992; Muthoo, 2000). But even in such an exercise one has to fall back on other rules and rights that are given. At this stage at least it is not clear if this infinite regress problem is at all solvable.
2   The origins of game theory go back to von Neumann and Morgenstern (1944) and even earlier (see Aumann, 1987, for discussion). But game theory became "accessible" and able to handle dynamics two or three decades after the appearance of von Neumann and Morgenstern's classic book.
3   For a formal model of the endogenous determination of trade policy, especially that pertaining to protection, see Grossman and Helpman (1994).

References

Alesina, A. and Cukierman, A. (1990), "The Politics of Ambiguity," *Quarterly Journal of Economics*, 105.

Alesina, A. and Rodrik, D. (1994). "Distributive Politics and Economic Growth," *Quarterly Journal of Economics*, 109: 465–90. [See chapter 18 of this volume.]

Arrow, K. J. (1951), *Social Choice and Individual Values*. New York: John Wiley.

Arrow, K. J. (1998), "The Place of Institutions in the Economy: a Theoretical Perspective," in Y. Hayami and M. Aoki (eds.), *The Institutional Foundations of East Asian Economic Development*. Basingstoke: Macmillan. [See chapter 3 of this volume.]

Aumann, R. J. (1987), "Game Theory," in J. Eatwell, M. Milgate and P. Newman (eds.), *The New Palgrave*. Basingstoke: Macmillan.

Austen-Smith, D. (1990), "Information Transmission in Debate," *American Journal of Political Science*, 34: 124–52.

Basu, K. (1997), "On Misunderstanding Government: an Analysis of the Art of Policy Advice," *Economics and Politics*, 9: 231–50. [See chapter 11 of this volume.]

Basu, K. (2000), *Prelude to Political Economy: A Study of the Social and Political Foundations of Economics*. Oxford and New York: Oxford University Press.

Basu, K. (2001), "The Role of Norms and Law in Economics: an Essay on Political Economy," in J. Scott and D. Keates (eds.), *Schools of Thought: Twenty-Five Years of Interpretive Social Science*. Princeton, NJ: Princeton University Press.

Besley, T. and Coate, S. (1992), "Understanding Welfare Stigma: Taxpayer Resentment and Statistical Discrimination," *Journal of Public Economics*, 48: 165–83.

Besley, T. and Coate, S. (1997), "An Economic Model of Representative Democracy," *Quarterly Journal of Economics*, 112: 85–114. [See chapter 17 of this volume.]

Buchanan, J. M. (1973), "The Coase Theorem and the Theory of the State," *Natural Resources Journal*, 13: 579–94. [See chapter 8 of this volume.]

Crawford, V. and Sobel, J. (1982), "Strategic Information Transmission," *Econometrica*, 50: 1431–51.

de Meza, D. and Gould, J. R. (1992), "The Social Efficiency of Private Decisions to Enforce Property Rights," *Journal of Political Economy*, 100: 561–80.

Dixit, A. (1996), *The Making of Economic Policy*. Cambridge, MA: MIT Press.

Dixit, A. (1997), "Power of Incentives in Private versus Public Organizations," *American Economic Review*, 87: 378–82. [See chapter 14 of this volume.]

Downs, A. (1957), *An Economic Theory of Democracy*. New York: Harper & Row. [See chapter 15 of this volume.]

Greif, A. (1992), "Institutions and International Trade: Lessons from the Commercial Revolution," *American Economic Review*, 82: 128–33. [See chapter 6 of this volume.]

Greif, A. (1993), "Contract Enforceability and Economic Institutions in Early Trade: the Maghribi Traders' Coalition," *American Economic Review*, 83: 525–48.

Grossman, G. and Helpman, E. (1994), "Protection for Sale," *American Economic Review*, 84: 833–50.

Hobbes, T. (1651), *Leviathan*, 1994 edition. Indianapolis, IN: Hackett. [See chapter 1 of this volume.]

Hoff, K. (2000), "The Logic of Political Constraints and Reform with Applications to Strategies for Privatization," mimeo, World Bank.

Holmstrom, B. and Milgrom, P. (1991), "Multitask Principal–Agent Analyses," *Journal of Law Economics and Organization*, 7: 24–52. [See chapter 12 of this volume.]

Hume, D. (1739), *A Treatise of Human Nature*, 1987 edition, London: Penguin.

Hume, D. (1758), "Of the First Principles of Government," in *Essays: Moral, Political and Literary*, 1987 edition, ed. F. Miller. Indianapolis: Liberty Fund, pp. 32–6. [See chapter 2 of this volume.]

Kahneman, D. (1994), "New Challenges to the Rationality Assumption," *Journal of Institutional and Theoretical Economics*, 150: 18–36.

Krishna, V. and Morgan, J. (2000), "A Model of Expertise," *Quarterly Journal of Economics*, forthcoming.

Laffont, J. J. and Tirole, J. J. (1993), *A Theory of Incentives in Procurement and Regulation*. Cambridge, MA: MIT Press.

Lindbeck, A., Nyberg, S., and Weibull, J. (1999), "Social Norms and Economic Incentives in the Welfare State," *Quarterly Journal of Economics*, 114: 1–35. [See chapter 20 of this volume.]

Milgrom, P. R., North, D., and Weingast, B. R. (1990), "The Role of Institutions in the Revival of Trade: the Law Merchant, Private Judges and the Champagne Fairs," *Economics and Politics*, 2: 1–23. [See chapter 5 of this volume.]

Muthoo, A. (2000), "On the Foundations of Basic Property Rights: a Model of the State of Nature with Two Players," mimeo, University of Essex.

North, D. C. (1990), *Institutions, Institutional Change and Economic Performance*. Cambridge: Cambridge University Press.

O'Flaherty, B. and Bhagwati, J. (1997), "Will Free Trade with Political Science Put Normative Economists out of Work?" *Economics and Politics*, 9: 207–19. [See chapter 10 of this volume.]

Olson, M. (1993), "Dictatorship, Democracy, and Development," *American Political Science Review*, 87: 567–76. [See chapter 9 of this volume.]

Persson, T. and Tabellini, G. (1994), "Is Inequality Harmful for Growth?" *American Economic Review*, 84: 600–21. [See chapter 19 of this volume.]

Persson, T. and Tabellini, G. (2000), *Political Economics: Explaining Economic Policy*. Cambridge, MA: MIT Press.

Platteau, J. P. (2000), *Institutions, Social Norms, and Economic Development*, Harwood Academic Publishers.

Riker, W. H. (1980), "Implications from the Disequilibrium of Majority Rule for the Study of Institutions," *American Political Science Review*, 74: 432–46. [See chapter 7 of this volume.]

Rodrik, D. (1995), "Political Economy of Trade Policy," in G. Grossman and K. Rogoff (eds.), *Handbook of International Economics*, vol. 3. Amsterdam: North-Holland.

Ryan, A. (1996), "Hobbes's Political Philosophy," in T. Sorell (ed.), *The Cambridge Companion to Hobbes*. Cambridge: Cambridge University Press.

Sen, A. (1995), "Rationality and Social Choice," *American Economic Review*, 85: 1–24. [See chapter 16 of this volume.]

Shepsle, K. A. and Bonchuk, M. S. (1997), *Analyzing Politics: Rationality, Behavior and Institutions*. New York: W. W. Norton.

Thaler, R. H. (1991), *Quasi-Rational Economics*. New York: Russell Sage.

Tirole, J. (1994), "The Internal Organization of Government," *Oxford Economic Papers*, 46: 1–29. [See chapter 13 of this volume.]

von Neumann, J. and Morgenstern, O. (1944), *Theory of Games and Economic Behavior*. Princeton, NJ: Princeton University Press.

Warneryd, K. (1995), "Language, Evolution and the Theory of Games," in J. L. Casti, and A. Karlqvist (eds.), *Cooperation and Conflict in General Evolutionary Processes*. New York: John Wiley.

Williamson, O. E. (1985), *The Economic Institutions of Capitalism*. Basingstoke: Macmillan.

Williamson, O. E. (1996), "Transaction Cost Economics and Organization Theory," in O. E. Williamson, *The Mechanisms of Governance*. Oxford: Oxford University Press. [See chapter 4 of this volume.]

Wilson, J. (1989), *Bureaucracy*. New York: Basic Books.

Roots

ONE

Extracts from *Leviathan*

Thomas Hobbes

Source: From Thomas Hobbes, *Leviathan*, ed. Edwin Curley. New York: Hackett, 1994, pp.74–8, 106–10. (Original publication 1651.)

Part I: Of Man

Chapter XIII. Of the Natural Condition of Mankind, As Concerning Their Felicity, and Misery

[1]   Nature hath made men so equal in the faculties of body and mind as that, though there be found one man sometimes manifestly stronger in body or of quicker mind than another, yet when all is reckoned together the difference between man and man is not so considerable as that one man can thereupon claim to himself any benefit to which another may not pretend as well as he. For as to the strength of body, the weakest has strength enough to kill the strongest, either by secret machination, or by confederacy with others that are in the same danger with himself.

[2]   And as to the faculties of the mind – setting aside the arts grounded upon words, and especially that skill of proceeding upon general and infallible rules called science (which very few have, and but in few things), as being not a native faculty (born with us), nor attained (as prudence) while we look after somewhat else – I find yet a greater equality amongst men than that of strength. For prudence is but experience, which equal time equally bestows on all men in those things they equally apply themselves unto. That which may perhaps make such equality incredible is but a vain conceit of one's own wisdom, which almost all men think they have in a greater degree than the vulgar; that is, than all men but themselves and a few others whom, by fame or for concurring with themselves, they approve. For such is the nature of men that howsoever they may acknowledge many others to be more witty, or more eloquent, or more learned, yet they will hardly believe there be many so wise as themselves. For they see their own wit at hand, and other men's at a distance. But this proveth rather that men are in that point equal, than unequal. For there is not ordinarily a greater sign of the equal distribution of anything than that every man is contented with his share.

[3]   From this equality of ability ariseth equality of hope in the attaining of our ends. And therefore, if any two men desire the same thing, which nevertheless they cannot both enjoy, they become enemies; and in the way to their end, which is principally their own

conservation, and sometimes their delectation only, endeavour to destroy or subdue one another. And from hence it comes to pass that, where an invader hath no more to fear than another man's single power, if one plant, sow, build, or possess a convenient seat, others may probably be expected to come prepared with forces united, to dispossess and deprive him, not only of the fruit of his labour, but also of his life or liberty. And the invader again is in the like danger of another.

[4]   And from this diffidence of one another, there is no way for any man to secure himself so reasonable as anticipation, that is, by force or wiles to master the persons of all men he can, so long till he see no other power great enough to endanger him. And this is no more than his own conservation requireth, and is generally allowed. Also, because there be some that taking pleasure in contemplating their own power in the acts of conquest, which they pursue farther than their security requires, if others (that otherwise would be glad to be at ease within modest bounds) should not by invasion increase their power, they would not be able, long time, by standing only on their defence, to subsist. And by consequence, such augmentation of dominion over men being necessary to a man's conservation, it ought to be allowed him.

[5]   Again, men have no pleasure, but on the contrary a great deal of grief, in keeping company where there is no power able to over-awe them all. For every man looketh that his companion should value him at the same rate he sets upon himself, and upon all signs of contempt, or undervaluing, naturally endeavours, as far as he dares (which amongst them that have no common power to keep them in quiet, is far enough to make them destroy each other), to extort a greater value from his contemners, by damage, and from others, by the example.

[6]   So that in the nature of man we find three principal causes of quarrel: first, competition; secondly, diffidence; thirdly, glory.

[7]   The first maketh men invade for gain; the second, for safety; and the third, for reputation. The first use violence to make themselves masters of other men's persons, wives, children, and cattle; the second, to defend them; the third, for trifles, as a word, a smile, a different opinion, and any other sign of undervalue, either direct in their persons, or by reflection in their kindred, their friends, their nation, their profession, or their name.

[8]   Hereby it is manifest that during the time men live without a common power to keep them all in awe, they are in that condition which is called war, and such a war as is of every man against every man. For War consisteth not in battle only, or the act of fighting, but in a tract of time wherein the will to contend by battle is sufficiently known. And therefore, the notion of *time* is to be considered in the nature of war, as it is in the nature of weather. For as the nature of foul weather lieth not in a shower or two of rain, but in an inclination thereto of many days together, so the nature of war consisteth not in actual fighting, but in the known disposition thereto during all the time there is no assurance to the contrary. All other time is Peace.

[9]   Whatsoever therefore is consequent to a time of war, where every man is enemy to every man, the same is consequent to the time wherein men live without other security than what their own strength and their own invention shall furnish them withal. In such condition there is no place for industry, because the fruit thereof is uncertain, and consequently, no culture of the earth, no navigation, nor use of the commodities that may be imported by sea, no commodious building, no instruments of moving and removing such things as require much force, no knowledge of the face of the earth, no account of

time, no arts, no letters, no society, and which is worst of all, continual fear and danger of violent death, and the life of man, solitary, poor, nasty, brutish, and short.

[10] It may seem strange, to some man that has not well weighed these things, that nature should thus dissociate, and render men apt to invade and destroy one another. And he may, therefore, not trusting to this inference made from the passions, desire perhaps to have the same confirmed by experience. Let him therefore consider with himself – when taking a journey, he arms himself, and seeks to go well accompanied; when going to sleep, he locks his doors; when even in his house, he locks his chests; and this when he knows there be laws, and public officers, armed, to revenge all injuries shall be done him – what opinion he has of his fellow subjects, when he rides armed; of his fellow citizens, when he locks his doors; and of his children and servants, when he locks his chests. Does he not there as much accuse mankind by his actions, as I do by my words? But neither of us accuse man's nature in it. The desires and other passions of man are in themselves no sin. No more are the actions that proceed from those passions, till they know a law that forbids them – which till laws be made they cannot know. Nor can any law be made, till they have agreed upon the person that shall make it.

[11] It may peradventure be thought there was never such a time nor condition of war as this; and I believe it was never generally so, over all the world. But there are many places where they live so now. For the savage people in many places of *America* (except the government of small families, the concord whereof dependeth on natural lust) have no government at all, and live at this day in that brutish manner as I said before. Howsoever, it may be perceived what manner of life there would be where there were no common power to fear, by the manner of life which men that have formerly lived under a peaceful government use to degenerate into, in a civil war.

[12] But though there had never been any time wherein particular men were in a condition of war one against another, yet in all times kings and persons of sovereign authority, because of their independency, are in continual jealousies and in the state and posture of gladiators, having their weapons pointing and their eyes fixed on one another, that is, their forts, garrisons, and guns upon the frontiers of their kingdoms, and continual spies upon their neighbours, which is a posture of war. But because they uphold thereby the industry of their subjects, there does not follow from it that misery which accompanies the liberty of particular men.

[13] To this war of every man against every man, this also is consequent: that nothing can be unjust. The notions of right and wrong, justice and injustice, have there no place. Where there is no common power, there is no law; where no law, no injustice. Force and fraud are in war the two cardinal virtues. Justice and injustice are none of the faculties neither of the body, nor mind. If they were, they might be in a man that were alone in the world, as well as his senses and passions. They are qualities that relate to men in society, not in solitude. It is consequent also to the same condition that there be no propriety, no dominion, no *mine* and *thine* distinct, but only that to be every man's that he can get, and for so long as he can keep it. And thus much for the ill condition which man by mere nature is actually placed in, though with a possibility to come out of it, consisting partly in the passions, partly in his reason.

[14] The passions that incline men to peace are fear of death, desire of such things as are necessary to commodious living, and a hope by their industry to obtain them. And reason suggesteth convenient articles of peace, upon which men may be drawn to

agreement. These articles are they which otherwise are called the Laws of Nature, whereof I shall speak more particularly in the two following chapters.

Part II: Of Commonwealth

Chapter XVII: Of the Causes, Generation, and Definition of a Commonwealth

[1]   The final cause, end, or design of men (who naturally love liberty and dominion over others) in the introduction of that restraint upon themselves in which we see them live in commonwealths is the foresight of their own preservation, and of a more contented life thereby; that is to say, of getting themselves out from that miserable condition of war, which is necessarily consequent (as hath been shown) to the natural passions of men, when there is no visible power to keep them in awe, and tie them by fear of punishment to the performance of their covenants and observation of those laws of nature set down in the fourteenth and fifteenth chapters.

[2]   For the laws of nature (as *justice*, *equity*, *modesty*, *mercy*, and (in sum) *doing to others as we would be done to*) of themselves, without the terror of some power to cause them to be observed, are contrary to our natural passions, that carry us to partiality, pride, revenge, and the like. And covenants without the sword are but words, and of no strength to secure a man at all. Therefore notwithstanding the laws of nature (which every one hath then kept, when he has the will to keep them, when he can do it safely), if there be no power erected, or not great enough for our security, every man will, and may lawfully rely on his own strength and art, for caution against all other men. And in all places where men have lived by small families, to rob and spoil one another has been a trade, and so far from being reputed against the law of nature that the greater spoils they gained, the greater was their honour; and men observed no other laws therein but the laws of honour, that is, to abstain from cruelty, leaving to men their lives and instruments of husbandry. And as small families did then, so now do cities and kingdoms (which are but greater families) for their own security enlarge their dominions upon all pretences of danger and fear of invasion or assistance that may be given to invaders, [and] endeavour as much as they can to subdue or weaken their neighbours, by open force and secret arts for want of other caution, justly (and are remembered for it in after ages with honour).

[3]   Nor is it the joining together of a small number of men that gives them this security; because in small numbers, small additions on the one side or the other make the advantage of strength so great as is sufficient to carry the victory; and therefore gives encouragement to an invasion. The multitude sufficient to confide in for our security is not determined by any certain number, but by comparison with the enemy we fear, and is then sufficient, when the odds of the enemy is not of so visible and conspicuous moment, to determine the event of war, as to move him to attempt.

[4]   And be there never so great a multitude, yet if their actions be directed according to their particular judgments and particular appetites, they can expect thereby no defence, nor protection, neither against a common enemy, nor against the injuries of one another. For being distracted in opinions concerning the best use and application of their strength, they do not help, but hinder one another, and reduce their strength by mutual opposition to

nothing; whereby they are easily, not only subdued by a very few that agree together, but also when there is no common enemy, they make war upon each other, for their particular interests. For if we could suppose a great multitude of men to consent in the observation of justice and other laws of nature without a common power to keep them all in awe, we might as well suppose all mankind to do the same; and then there neither would be, nor need to be, any civil government or commonwealth at all, because there would be peace without subjection.

[5]   Nor is it enough for the security, which men desire should last all the time of their life, that they be governed and directed by one judgment for a limited time, as in one battle or one war. For though they obtain a victory by their unanimous endeavour against a foreign enemy, yet afterwards, when either they have no common enemy, or he that by one part is held for an enemy is by another part held for a friend, they must needs by the difference of their interests dissolve, and fall again into a war amongst themselves.

[6]   It is true that certain living creatures (as bees and ants) live sociably one with another (which are therefore by *Aristotle* numbered amongst political creatures), and yet have no other direction than their particular judgments and appetites, nor speech whereby one of them can signify to another what he thinks expedient for the common benefit; and therefore some man may perhaps desire to know why mankind cannot do the same. To which I answer,

[7]   First, that men are continually in competition for honour and dignity, which these creatures are not; and consequently, amongst men there ariseth, on that ground, envy and hatred, and finally war; but amongst these not so.

[8]   Secondly, that amongst these creatures the common good differeth not from the private; and being by nature inclined to their private, they procure thereby the common benefit. But man, whose joy consisteth in comparing himself with other men, can relish nothing but what is eminent.

[9]   Thirdly, that these creatures (having not, as man, the use of reason) do not see, nor think they see, any fault in the administration of their common business; whereas amongst men there are very many that think themselves wiser, and abler to govern the public, better than the rest; and these strive to reform and innovate, one this way, another that way; and thereby bring it into distraction and civil war.

[10]   Fourthly, that these creatures, though they have some use of voice (in making known to one another their desires and other affections), yet they want that art of words by which some men can represent to others that which is good in the likeness of evil, and evil in the likeness of good, and augment or diminish the apparent greatness of good and evil, discontenting men, and troubling their peace at their pleasure.

[11]   Fifthly, irrational creatures cannot distinguish between *injury* and *damage*; and therefore, as long as they be at ease, they are not offended with their fellows, whereas man is then most troublesome, when he is most at ease; for then it is that he loves to shew his wisdom, and control the actions of them that govern the commonwealth.

[12]   Lastly, the agreement of these creatures is natural; that of men is by covenant only, which is artificial; and therefore, it is no wonder if there be somewhat else required (besides covenant) to make their agreement constant and lasting, which is a common power to keep them in awe, and to direct their actions to the common benefit.

[13]   The only way to erect such a common power as may be able to defend them from the invasion of foreigners and the injuries of one another, and thereby to secure them in

such sort as that by their own industry, and by the fruits of the earth, they may nourish themselves and live contentedly, is to confer all their power and strength upon one man, or upon one assembly of men, that may reduce all their wills, by plurality of voices, unto one will, which is as much as to say, to appoint one man or assembly of men to bear their person, and every one to own and acknowledge himself to be author of whatsoever he that so beareth their person shall act, or cause to be acted, in those things which concern the common peace and safety, and therein to submit their wills, every one to his will, and their judgments, to his judgment. This is more than consent, or concord; it is a real unity of them all, in one and the same person, made by covenant of every man with every man, in such manner as if every man should say to every man *I authorise and give up my right of governing myself to this man, or to this assembly of men, on this condition, that thou give up thy right to him, and authorize all his actions in like manner*. This done, the multitude so united in one person is called a COMMONWEALTH, in Latin CIVITAS. This is the generation of that great LEVIATHAN, or rather (to speak more reverently) of that *Mortal God* to which we owe, under the *Immortal God*, our peace and defence. For by this authority, given him by every particular man in the commonwealth, he hath the use of so much power and strength conferred on him that by terror thereof he is enabled to conform the wills of them all to peace at home and mutual aid against their enemies abroad. And in him consisteth the essence of the commonwealth, which (to define it) is *one person, of whose acts a great multitude, by mutual covenants one with another, have made themselves every one the author, to the end he may use the strength and means of them all, as he shall think expedient, for their peace and common defence*.

[14]   And he that carrieth this person is called SOVEREIGN, and said to have *Sovereign Power*; and every one besides, his SUBJECT.

[15]   The attaining to this sovereign power is by two ways. One, by natural force, as when a man maketh his children to submit themselves and their children to his government, as being able to destroy them if they refuse, or by war subdueth his enemies to his will, giving them their lives on that condition. The other is when men agree amongst themselves to submit to some man, or assembly of men, voluntarily, on confidence to be protected by him against all others. This latter may be called a political commonwealth, or commonwealth by *institution*, and the former, a commonwealth by *acquisition*. And first, I shall speak of a commonwealth by institution.

TWO

Of the First Principles of Government

DAVID HUME

Source: From David Hume, *Essays: Moral, Political, and Literary*, ed. Eugene F. Miller. Indianapolis: Liberty Fund, 1987, pp. 32–6. (Original publication 1758.)

Nothing appears more surprising to those, who consider human affairs with a philosophical eye, than the easiness with which the many are governed by the few; and the implicit submission, with which men resign their own sentiments and passions to those of their rulers. When we enquire by what means this wonder is effected, we shall find, that, as Force is always on the side of the governed, the governors have nothing to support them but opinion. It is, therefore, on opinion only that government is founded; and this maxim extends to the most despotic and most military governments, as well as to the most free and most popular. The soldan of Egypt, or the emperor of Rome, might drive his harmless subjects, like brute beasts, against their sentiments and inclination: But he must, at least, have led his *mamalukes*, or *prætorian bands*, like men, by their opinion.

Opinion is of two kinds, to wit, opinion of interest, and opinion of right. By opinion of interest, I chiefly understand the sense of the general advantage which is reaped from government; together with the persuasion, that the particular government, which is established, is equally advantageous with any other that could easily be settled. When this opinion prevails among the generality of a state, or among those who have the force in their hands, it gives great security to any government.

Right is of two kinds, right to power and right to property. What prevalence opinion of the first kind has over mankind may easily be understood, by observing the attachment which all nations have to their ancient government, and even to those names, which have had the sanction of antiquity. Antiquity always begets the opinion of right; and whatever disadvantageous sentiments we may entertain of mankind, they are always found to be prodigal both of blood and treasure in the maintenance of public justice. There is, indeed, no particular, in which, at first sight, there may appear a greater contradiction in the frame of the human mind than the present. When men act in a fraction, they are apt, without shame or remorse, to neglect all the ties of honour and morality, in order to serve their party; and yet, when a faction is formed upon a point of right or principle, there is no occasion where men discover a greater obstinacy, and a more determined sense of justice and equity. The same social disposition of mankind is the cause of these contradictory appearances.

It is sufficiently understood, that the opinion of right to property is of moment in all matters of government. A noted author has made property the foundation of all government;[1] and most of our political writers seem inclined to follow him in that particular. This is carrying the matter too far; but still it must be owned that the opinion of right to property has a great influence in this subject.

Upon these three opinions, therefore, of public *interest*, of *right to power*, and of *right to property*, are all governments founded, and all authority of the few over the many. There are indeed other principles, which add force to these, and determine, limit, or alter their operation; such as *self-interest*, *fear*, and *affection*. But still we may assert, that these other principles can have no influence alone, but suppose the antecedent influence of those opinions above-mentioned. They are, therefore, to be esteemed the secondary, not the original principles of government.

For, *first*, as to *self-interest*, by which I mean the expectation of particular rewards, distinct from the general protection which we receive from government, it is evident that the magistrate's authority must be antecedently established, at least be hoped for, in order to produce this expectation. The prospect of reward may augment his authority with regard to some particular persons; but can never give birth to it, with regard to the public. Men naturally look for the greatest favours from their friends and acquaintance; and therefore, the hopes of any considerable number of the state would never center in any particular set of men, if these men had no other title to magistracy, and had no separate influence over the opinions of mankind. The same observation may be extended to the other two principles of *fear* and *affection*. No man would have any reason to *fear* the fury of a tyrant, if he had no authority over any but from fear; since, as a single man, his bodily force can reach but a small way, and all the farther power he possesses must be founded either on our own opinion, or on the presumed opinion of others. And though *affection* to wisdom and virtue in a *sovereign* extends very far, and has great influence; yet he must antecedently be supposed invested with a public character, otherwise the public esteem will serve him in no stead, nor will his virtue have any influence beyond a narrow sphere.

A Government may endure for several ages, though the balance of power, and the balance of property do not coincide. This chiefly happens where any rank or order of the state has acquired a large share in the property; but from the original constitution of the government, has no share in the power. Under what pretence would any individual of that order assume authority in public affairs? As men are commonly much attached to their ancient government, it is not to be expected, that the public would ever favour such usurpations. But where the original constitution allows any share of power, though small, to an order of men, who possess a large share of the property, it is easy for them gradually to stretch their authority, and bring the balance of power to coincide with that of property. This has been the case with the house of commons in England.

Most writers, that have treated of the British government, have supposed, that, as the lower house represents all the commons of Great Britain, its weight in the scale is proportioned to the property and power of all whom it represents. But this principle must not be received as absolutely true. For though the people are apt to attach themselves more to the house of commons, than to any other member of the constitution; that house being chosen by them as their representatives, and as the public guardians of their liberty; yet are there instances where the house, even when in opposition to the crown, has not been followed by the people; as we may particularly observe of the *tory* house of commons in the reign of king William.[2] Were the members obliged to receive instructions from their constituents, like the Dutch deputies, this would entirely alter the case; and if such immense power and riches, as those of all the commons of Great Britain, were brought into the scale, it is not easy to conceive that the crown could either influence that multitude of people, or withstand that overbalance of property. It is true, the crown has great influence over the collective body in the elections of members; but were this influence, which at present is only exerted once in seven years, to be employed in bringing over the people to every vote, it would soon be wasted; and no skill, popularity, or revenue, could support it. I must, therefore, be of opinion that an alteration in this particular would introduce a total alteration in our government, and would soon reduce it to a pure republic; and, perhaps, to a republic of no inconvenient form. For though the people, collected in a body like the Roman tribes, be quite unfit for government, yet when dispersed in small bodies, they are more susceptible both of reason and order; the force of popular currents and tides is, in a great measure, broken; and the public interest may be pursued with some method and constancy. But it is needless to reason any farther concerning a form of government, which is never likely to have a place in Great Britain, and which seems not to be the aim of any party amongst us. Let us cherish and improve our ancient government as much as possible, without encouraging a passion for such dangerous novelties.

Notes

1   Probably James Harrington (1611–77), author of the *Commonwealth of Oceana* (1656), who maintained that the balance of political power depends upon the balance of property, especially landed property.
2   During the period from 1698 to 1701, the House of Commons, under Tory control, opposed measures taken by William III for the security of Europe against Louis XIV of France. When the county of Kent sent petitioners to London in 1701 to chide the House of Commons for its distrust of the king and its delay in voting supplies, the petitioners were arrested. Public disgust at the treatment of the Kentish petitioners was expressed in a Whig pamphlet called the *Legion Memorial* (1701). The *Kentish Petition* and the *Legion Memorial* proved that popular feeling was on the king's side in this struggle with the Commons.

Institutions, Markets, and Political Power

THREE

The Place of Institutions in the Economy: a Theoretical Perspective

KENNETH J. ARROW

Source: From Y. Hayami and M. Aoki (eds.), *The Institutional Foundations of East Asian Economic Development*. Basingstoke: Macmillan, 1998.

1 Introduction

Standard economic theory is only apparently institution-free. More importantly, the failures of the theory serve as a fruitful way to examine the need for institutions and explain why they emerge. It is, however, less useful, but not entirely useless, in analyzing which institutions will emerge.[1]

By 'standard theory', I mean the world of competitive general equilibrium theory (CGE). It will be argued below that the assumptions of CGE make considerable institutional assumptions. But more importantly, the real economy differs from CGE in significant ways, especially (1) asymmetry of information, (2) market failure, particularly with regard to contingent futures markets, and (3) the possibility of gains through coordination in the presence of externalities and increasing returns. These failures are interrelated. These failures create a value for non-market institutions. Their essence is to coordinate expectations and to enforce incentives.

However, institutions are a form of capital. They cannot operate in general on a completely current basis. Hence, altering them in response to changing conditions (tastes, technologies, political conditions) must take time, just as changing a capital structure takes time. In view of the uncertainty as to the future, this means that institutions at any moment represent adaptations in part to past conditions, not present ones. History therefore matters.

I draw some implications for economic transition as well as for the analysis of economic development in general. I am summarizing and interpreting a considerable body of literature, which goes back at least to Thorstein Veblen (1899, chapter 8) and has been developed in more recent years by Ronald Coase (1937), Douglass North (1973), Oliver Williamson (1975), Paul David (1994), and Brain Arthur (1994), among many others.

2   Institutions in Competitive General Equilibrium Theory

CGE depends on assumptions as to institutional background, and also implies social institutions within it, as already noted by J. S. Mill (1848) under the influence of Auguste Comte. (1) The market is itself described as a social institution, operating according to very definite rules understood by everybody. The institution is designed to guard, even though imperfectly, against departures from its rules. (2) There are assumptions about a legal system which assigns and enforces property rights, including rights in the future and rights contingent upon future information (e.g., residual profits or the ability to buy and sell assets).

1   The fact that we say 'prices are set to equal supply and demand', without saying who sets them implies that the market is being modelled as an institution, not as an economic agent.
2   The competitive system, perfect or imperfect, implies a clear assignment of property rights. Implicit in these rights is the existence of a set of institutions which enforce them and the contracts based on them. In modern societies, this means a legal and judicial system. In earlier societies and even today, other social mechanisms are at work, such as reputation effects and trust based on an implicit social contract. In the absence of these institutions, other social bonds, such as family or the Mafia, become the basis for economic relations, but these contradict the CGE model and undermine economic efficiency.

3   Informational Asymmetries and Institutions

CGE postulates that all agents have the same information. They are, in general, uncertain about the future, but all are conditioning their probabilities on the same observations. Certainly, this assumption is not in fact true. On the contrary, a dispersion of information is a necessary concomitant of a market system. Indeed, a classic defence of markets, from Adam Smith to Friederich von Hayek, is that markets economize on information. Each agent has to know only about a limited range of economically relevant facts, which differ from one individual to another. As Smith emphasized, economic specialization is an important precondition of efficiency, and the very fact of economic specialization creates informational differences.

Modern CGE emphasizes the value of having markets for deliveries of goods (or at least financial payments) contingent on the occurrence of certain events. An insurance policy is a clear example of a contingent market, a common stock a somewhat less obvious one. An informational difference means that an event observed by one individual is not observed by another. Clearly, the two agents cannot both participate in a market contingent on that event (Radner, 1968). Thus, informational differences lead to a failure of contingent markets.

But these markets have a social value. There will be a pressure to replace them by incentive-compatible contracts, which are themselves institutions. Indeed, they are frequently formalized in various ways, long-term contracts (explicit or implicit), firms, and larger business groupings, such as the *keiretsu* or the banker-led aggregations common in the United States around 1900 but subsequently outlawed. These arguments were advanced by Coase (1937) and greatly elaborated by Oliver Williamson (1975). As they showed, markets are advantageously replaced by hierarchies under certain circumstances.

4 Market Failure

Future or contingent markets may fail to exist not only because of informational asymmetry but also because of thinness or of complexity. There may not be enough supply and demand for a particular contingent market to give it the necessary liquidity; for example, a market in the future purchasing power of the dollar was abandoned for this reason. Alternatively, specifying the events on which the market is contingent may be too complex. Real business contracts rarely specify what will happen under all conceivable contingencies, even foreseeable remote possibilities.

As already suggested, the absent contingent markets may be replaced by long-term relations, including hierarchical ones. In any case, the actual futures or contingent price will be replaced by expectations of future prices and quantities. Expectation *per se* can be thought of as an element of individual psychology, but in practice social institutions play a major role in guiding and forming expectations. There are expectations that similar economic and legal systems will be in effect in the future, understandings that others will not exploit every possible short-term profit opportunity, and elaborate financial services networks to provide forecasts and to smooth out temporary difficulties. Labour unions have performed similar functions in the labour market.

The state, through its fiscal powers, and the central bank are expected to carry out stabilization functions, both macroeconomic and microeconomic.

The present trend to marketization and globalization has had the effect of eroding previous expectations, especially in the labour markets. I believe there will be a reaction, for this need to rely on expectations is too important to be neglected.

5 Games and Coordination

The most general way of formulating social interaction is as a game. That is, we specify the strategies of the agents, or *players* as game theorists term them, and then we specify the outcome of the games for each possible choice of strategies by each player. These strategies may be very complex. The game is usually spread out over time, with each player being able to observe the actions of other players and respond to them. Each player may also use the actions of other players to seek to infer aspects of their resources or utility functions not originally known to them.

Formal game theory, like CGE, proceeds by assuming rationality of all players. Without going into details, some of the degrees of inference become incredible. The assumption is that the players have the same degree of understanding as the analyst. But economic analysts themselves have repeatedly revised their theories to see more complexity than they had before, which suggests that the players may have had more knowledge than analysts.

Thus each player is assumed to know what other players would expect him to do. The trouble with this high degree of rationality may be exemplified by the rational analysis of the stock market. Imagine that there is a steady flow of new information, but different players learn different parts of that information. Then, if players differed only in the information they receive, there would be no trade on the market, though the prices would be adjusting so as to reflect all the information available. The volume of trade on the stock market or the foreign exchange market suggests the lack of full rationality.

It therefore cannot be expected that when an institution is created and accepted, the consequences will be as predicted. The ultimate implications may be very different than those expected.

In one kind of game theory analysis, the so-called cooperative game theory, the moves are bargains of any possible type. Von Neumann and Morgenstern (1944, p. 526, equation (56:25)), echoing Edgeworth (1881) before them, argued that whatever else may happen, the outcome of a cooperative game has to be Pareto optimal; intelligent players, they held, would certainly find a bargain which would make everyone better off. This was later repeated by Ronald Coase (1960), though he emphasized that the optimal conclusion would not be reached because of the costs incurred in learning about each other and in the process of bargaining, what he called 'transaction costs'.

Why would we expect there to be gains to a cooperative game which would not be achieved through the market? I have already emphasized the role of asymmetric information. But asymmetric information creates an equal obstacle to the conclusion of bargains. Consider the case of pollution. Suppose, following Coasian principles, we assign property rights. For example, no one can be polluted without his or her consent. A potential polluter would have to buy out the rights of all. But the potential polluter does not know the cost of pollution to individuals. Therefore, it pays anyone in danger of pollution to exaggerate the costs in order to get a higher payment. Even if pollution were efficient, it might not be possible to come to this agreement in these conditions of asymmetric information.

We are led, then, to create special institutions to guard against these failures. The state may decide on policies, using the political process, possibly supplemented by benefit–cost analysis. In some circumstances, the legal system may be used. Damages due to externalities are to be assessed by a court. Other examples of institutions have been voluntary agreements to limit the exploitation of common goods, such as fishing grounds and forests. These are all games, with varying rules. The outcomes are rarely Pareto efficient, but they provide an imperfect substitute for the failure of the market.

The real-life version of the mythical 'tragedy of the commons' (Hardin, 1968) shows how institutions mitigate market failure. In Hardin's fable, the failure to impose a price system on common lands for grazing cattle led to rapid disaster. There are the parallel problems in fishing and forestry. In fact, as well documented, these systems have lasted for long periods of time. What has happened is that alternative mechanisms have arisen for limiting utilization, and these have frequently been very effective (Hanna et al., 1996).

A different form of coordination failure occurs when there are economies of scale. The market provides one kind of solution, that of monopoly or imperfect competition. There will be inefficiencies, but they may be less than under other systems. The games played under imperfect competition belong to the category called non-cooperative games. No direct bargains are struck, but the behaviour of each player has to take into account the behaviour of other players – for example, the prices they charge or the quantities they produce.

There are incentives for rival firms, in those circumstances, to collaborate, as Adam Smith already noted, disapprovingly (Smith, 1776, book I, chapter X, part II, especially p. 145). In the United States and increasingly elsewhere, legal prohibitions against some forms of collaboration have been provided, making the game still more complicated.

Many cases of increasing returns do not admit of any serious competition, even imperfect. Irrigation projects are very ancient in China or the area now known as Iraq and require collective action. On a sufficiently large scale, they have required state action and, it has been argued, have led to the encouragement of despotism. On smaller scales, however, irrigation requires cooperative action of, say, a village, and encourages democracy and local initiative (Ishikawa, 1988).

One must also note provisions for supply of information, most notably with regard to information about safety of products and employment and about the inner workings of firms, to be given to their actual and potential stockholders.

6 The Formation of Institutions

All of these pressures are for the creation of institutions. In order for institutions to operate, they must create reasonably stable expectations. By definition, then, they have to change slowly. The assumption that at any moment the institutions are optimal solutions to market failure is as false as the statement that the current capital structure is optimally adapted to current demands and technology. Expectations change only slowly. Their alteration is a social act, so that changes must be coordinated. Hence, it is reasonable to accept the view of Veblen and sociologists influenced by him that the actual institutions at any moment represent adaptation to past as well as present difficulties (Veblen, 1899, chapter 8; Ogburn, 1950). This problem is reinforced because there is complementarity among different institutions and between institutions and other aspects of the economy. As Paul David (1993) has pointed out, institutions resemble the network externalities found in telecommunications, power, and computing systems. Both David and Veblen (1915) have shown examples of the slowness of institutional adaptation in the presence of complementarities.

Hence, history matters, as Douglass North (1973) has emphasized. An institution adapted to conditions at one moment of time will persist even when no longer fully optimal. The institution will itself have effects on economic development and on future institutional development. We observe that even among advanced capitalist countries with similar technologies, there are widely different financial systems, considerable differences in industrial structure (for example, the importance of business groups larger than firms), and very different labour markets. Each one seems well adapted to its milieu, suggesting the presence of multiple equilibria.

This situation is not surprising in view of the analogous process of biological evolution. The species that exist are not 'optimal'. They carry within them the remains of previous adaptations, which have influenced the course of future developments.

The emergence of institutions indeed follows what Carl Menger (1883) called 'spontaneous order'. But this term may be misleading. In the first instance, every institution is someone's deliberate invention; '[a]n institution is the lengthened shadow of one man'

(Emerson, 1946, p. 148). It may or may not be the result of deliberate legislation. What is true is that when an institution is created, it may or may not survive, just as biological mutations or, to take a closer analogy, technological innovations may or may not survive. The alleged dichotomy between deliberate change and spontaneous emergence of institutions is a fallacy. They are actually the same process.

7   Transition and Development

The rapid change in economic systems in the former Soviet Union, Eastern Europe, and China is virtually without precedent. Among other things, expectations are being falsified at a rapid rate, and institutions are being destroyed and created. In Eastern Europe and the former Soviet Union, these changes have led to a very large economic downturn. For whatever reason, the course of Chinese development is very different.

My own view is that, from a purely economic viewpoint, the change in the former Soviet bloc could have been handled much better, by recognizing the economic value of gradual changes in expectations. It is clear that the process of institution-building is a slow one, and destruction of existing coordination mechanisms may have been too rapid. Whether a slower change was possible politically, however, is more difficult to determine.

Institutions seem to have played distinctive coordinating roles in different developing countries. Conservative and bureaucratic direction has guided the path of India, the coordinated building of the market of Korea. In both cases, the institutions have played their roles, though clearly with differing results. On the other hand, many Latin American countries have exhibited what would appear to be an unwillingness to create expectation-stabilizing institutions, with the consequence of considerable uncertainty.

8   A Speculative Note on 'Culture'

Much is frequently made of the role of 'culture' as a controlling influence on economic development. I want to distinguish an emphasis on institutions as economic mechanisms from the more specific references to culture. The latter notion is by no means clearly defined, but to the extent that it has explanatory power, culture is thought of as an integrated belief system, so that social behaviour in seemingly remote contexts forms a single pattern. Thus, it is held, it is possible to argue from religion to economic behaviour.

This kind of argument is already found in Karl Marx, who, however, held economic or technological institutions to be primary, and explained others, the so-called 'superstructure', in terms of them. Many modern scholars, on the contrary, feel the need to explain economic phenomena, particularly national differences in economic development, in terms of non-economic institutions. The pioneer was the German sociologist–economist Max Weber, famous for his thesis that modern capitalism required the specific ethics and world-viewpoint of Protestantism, especially in its Calvinist form (Weber, 1930). He even explains why the Confucian viewpoint is incompatible with a capitalist, rationalist approach to economic problems (Weber, 1951, especially part VIII).

The more general concept of an integrated culture with mutually dependent sectors has been perhaps most stressed by the cultural anthropologist Franz Boas, and by some of his disciples, most notably Ruth Benedict (1934, 1946) and Margaret Mead (1935). Though they were not especially concerned with economic performance, the difficulty of changing cultures could certainly be interpreted as suggesting the importance of specific cultural background for economic success.

How would an economic theorist make sense of this role of culture? There are several possibilities. One is that the preferences, taken as given by the theorist, are in fact determined by cultural patterns. By itself, this would merely imply a different demand pattern; I understand that the proportion of income spent on food by the French is considerably higher relative to other countries than could easily be explained by differences in prices. But this should hardly affect growth as such, merely the specific direction of resource allocation among final goods.

Another possibility, more in line with the modern economics of information, would be that the culture determines a set of beliefs about the world (prior probabilities in the language of theory) and that some of these beliefs are more productive than others. This is reminiscent of theories, such as that of Benjamin Lee Whorf (1956), about the influence of language on thought. Whorf argued that it was possible to think only through language, so that thinking, and consequently acting, were constrained by the spoken language. Language is an aspect of culture, and the Whorf hypothesis could certainly be extended to argue that other cultural traits, such as religious beliefs, would make certain thoughts and ways of behaviour impossible.

The Whorf hypothesis has been severely criticized. Pinker (1994, chapter 3) has summarized the evidence that thinking ('mentalese', as he calls it) is not limited by the existing language structure. While the influence of culture on economic institutions is an empirical proposition, not a theoretical one, I must record that several decades of reading cultural analyses have not given me much confidence that there are useful implications.

Note

1 I am grateful to Luigi Pasinetti for calling my attention to his paper on the same theme (Pasinetti, 1994). Our understandings of the need for institutions to explain economic growth seem to agree. He then argues that some underlying insights from classical (pre-neoclassical) economics provide a better basis for institutional analysis. I cannot say that I follow his argument on this point, but perhaps I have not fully grasped it.

References

Arthur, B. (1994) *Increasing Returns and Path Dependence in the Economy* (Ann Arbor: University of Michigan Press).

Benedict, R. (1934) *Patterns of Culture* (New York: Houghton Mifflin).

Benedict, R. (1946) *The Chrysanthemum and the Sword: Patterns of Japanese Culture* (New York: Houghton Mifflin).

Coase, R. H. (1937) 'Nature of the Firm', *Economica* (n.s.), vol. 4, pp. 386–405.

Coase, R. H. (1960) 'The Problem of Social Cost', *Journal of Law and Economics*, vol. 3, pp. 1–44.

David, P. (1993) 'Path Dependence and Predictability in Dynamic Systems with Local Network Externalities: a Paradigm for Historical Economics', in D. Foray and C. Freeman (eds), *Technology and the Wealth of Nations* (London: Francis Pinter) pp. 208–31.

David, P. (1994) 'Why are Institutions the "Carriers of History"? Path Dependence and the Evolution of Conventions', *Structural Change and Economic Dynamics*, vol. 5, pp. 205–26.

Edgeworth, F. Y. (1881) *Mathematical Psychics* (London: Kegan, Paul).

Emerson, R. W. (1946) 'Self-Reliance', in C. Bode (ed.), *The Portable Emerson* (New York: Viking) pp. 138–64.

Hanna, S., C. Folke and K.-G. Mäler (eds.) (1996) *Rights to Nature* (Washington, DC, and Covelo, CA: Island Press).

Hardin, G. (1968) 'The Tragedy of the Commons', *Science*, vol. 162, pp. 1243–8.

Ishikawa, S. (1988) 'Problems of Late Industrialization: an Asian Perspective', in K. J. Arrow (ed.), *The Balance between Industry and Agriculture in Economic Development*, vol. 1: *Basic Issues* (Basingstoke and London: Macmillan for the International Economic Association) chapter 6, pp. 85–104.

Mead, M. (1935) *Sex and Temperament in Three Primitive Societies* (New York: W. Morrow).

Menger, C. (1883) *Untersuchungen über die Methode der Sozialwissenschaft und der Politischen Oekonomie insbesondere* (Leipzig: Duncker & Humboldt). English translation (F. J. Nock, tr.), *Investigations into the Method of the Social Sciences with Special Reference to Economics* (New York: New York University Press, 1985).

Mill, J. S. (1848) *Principles of Political Economy*, 1st edn. (London: John W. Paul); new edn. (W. Ashley, ed.) (London: Longmans, Green, 1909).

North, D. and R. P. Thomas (1973) *The Rise of the Western World* (London and New York: Cambridge University Press).

Ogburn, W. F. (1950) *Social Change with Respect to Culture and Original Nature*, new 1950 edition (New York: Viking Press).

Pasinetti, L. (1994) 'Economic Theory and Institutions', in R. Delorme and K. Dopfer (eds), *The Political Economy of Diversity* (London: Edward Elgar) pp. 34–45.

Pinker, S. (1994) *The Language Instinct* (New York: William Morrow).

Radner, R. (1968) 'Competitive Equilibrium under Uncertainty', *Econometrica*, vol. 36, pp. 31–56.

Smith, A. (1776) *Inquiry into the Nature and Causes of the Wealth of Nations* (London: W. Strahan and T. Cadell); Glasgow edition (R. H. Campbell and A. S. Sherman, general eds; W. B. Todd, textual ed.) (Liberty Classics, Indianapolis, 1981).

Veblen, T. (1899) *The Theory of the Leisure Class* (New York: Macmillan).

Veblen, T. (1915) *Imperial Germany and the Industrial Revolution* (New York: Macmillan).

Von Neumann, J. and O. Morgenstern (1944) *Theory of Games and Economic Behavior* (Princeton, NJ: Princeton University Press).

Weber, M. (1930) *The Protestant Ethic and the Spirit of Capitalism*, tr. Talcott Parsons (London: Allen & Unwin).

Weber, M. (1951) *The Religion of China*, tr. and ed. by H. H. Gerth (Glencoe, IL: The Free Press).

Whorf, B. L. (1956) *Language, Thought and Reality* (Cambridge, MA: Technology Press).

Williamson, O. (1975) *Markets and Hierarchies: Analysis and Antitrust Implications* (New York: The Free Press).

FOUR

Transaction Cost Economics and Organization Theory

OLIVER WILLIAMSON

Source: From Oliver Williamson, *The Mechanisms of Governance*. Oxford: Oxford University Press, 1996; reprinted from Schmalensee and Willig, *Handbook of Industrial Organization*, vol. 1. Oxford: Elsevier, 1989.

1 Introduction

Economic and sociological approaches to economic organization have reached a state of healthy tension. That is to be contrasted with an earlier state of affairs in which the two approaches were largely disjunct, hence ignored one another, or described each other's research agendas and research accomplishments with disdain (Swedberg, 1990, p. 4). Healthy tension involves genuine give-and-take. Neither the obsolescence of organization theory, to which Charles Perrow has recently alluded (1992, p. 162), nor the capitulation of economics, about which James March (tongue-in-cheek) remarks,[1] is implied.

A more respectful relation, perhaps even a sense that economics and organization are engaged in a joint venture, is evident in W. Richard Scott's remark that "while important areas of disagreement remain, more consensus exists than is at first apparent" (1992, p. 3), in game theorist David Kreps's contention that "almost any theory of organization which is addressed by game theory will do more for game theory than game theory will do for it" (1992, p. 1), and in my argument that a science of organization is in progress in which law, economics, and organization are joined.[2]

Joint ventures sometimes evolve into mergers and sometimes unravel. I do not expect that either will happen here. That merger is not in prospect is because economics, organization theory, and law have separate as well as combined agendas. A full-blown merger, moreover, would impoverish the evolving science of organization – which has benefited from the variety of insights that are revealed by the use of different lenses. I expect that the joint venture will hold until one of the parties has learned enough from the others to go it alone. Progress attended by controversy is what I project for the remainder of the decade.

This chapter focuses on connections between transaction cost economics and organization theory and argues that a three-part relation is taking shape. The first and most important of these is that transaction cost economics has been (and will continue to be) massively influenced by concepts and empirical regularities that have their origins in organization theory. Secondly, I sketch the key concepts out of which transaction cost economics works to which organization theorists can (and many do) productively relate. But thirdly, healthy tension survives – as revealed by an examination of phenomena for which rival interpretations have been advanced, remain unsolved, and provoke controversy.

I begin this paper with some background on institutional economics, both old and new. A three-level schema for studying economic organization is proposed in section 3. Some of the more important ways in which transaction cost economics has benefited from organization theory are examined in section 4. The key concepts in transaction cost economics are sketched in section 5. Empirical regularities, as discerned through the lens of transaction cost economics, that are pertinent to organization theory are discussed in section 6. Contested terrain is surveyed in section 7. Concluding remarks follow.

2   Institutional Economics

2.1   Older traditions

Leading figures in the older institutional economics movement in the United States were Wesley Mitchell, Thorstein Veblen, and John R. Commons. Although many sociologists appear to be sympathetic with the older tradition, there is growing agreement that the approach was "largely descriptive and historically specific" (DiMaggio and Powell, 1991, p. 2) and was not cumulative (Granovetter, 1988, p. 8). Criticisms of the old institutional economics by economists have been scathing (Stigler, 1983, p. 170; Coase, 1984, p. 230; Matthews, 1986, p. 903).

My general agreement with these assessments notwithstanding, I would make an exception for John R. Commons. Not only is the institutional economics tradition at Wisconsin still very much alive (Bromley, 1989), but also the enormous public policy influence of Commons and his students and colleagues deserves to be credited. Andrew Van de Ven's summary of Commons's intellectual contributions is pertinent to the first of these:

> Especially worthy of emphasis [about Commons] are his (a) dynamic views of institutions as a response to scarcity and conflicts of interest, (b) original formulation of the transaction as the basic unit of analysis, (c) part–whole analysis of how collective action constrains, liberates, and expands individual action in countless numbers of routine and complementary transactions on the one hand, and how individual wills and power to gain control over limiting or contested factors provide the generative mechanisms for institutional change on the other, and (d) historical appreciation of how customs, legal precedents, and laws of a society evolve to construct a collective standard of prudent reasonable behavior for resolving disputes between conflicting parties in pragmatic and ethical ways.   (1993, p. 148)

Albeit in varying degree, transaction cost economics is responsive to Commons in *all four of these respects.*[3]

Commons and his colleagues and students were very influential in politics during and after the Great Depression – in shaping social security, labor legislation, public utility regulation, and, more generally, public policy toward business. Possibly because of its public policy successes, the Wisconsin School was remiss in developing its intellectual foundations. The successive operationalization – from informal into preformal, semiformal, and fully formal modes of analysis – that I associate with transaction cost economics

(Williamson, 1993) never materialized. Instead, the institutional economics of Commons progressed very little beyond the informal stage.

There is also an older institutional economics tradition in Europe. Of special importance was the German Historical School. (Interested readers are advised to consult Terrence Hutchison, 1984, and Richard Swedberg, 1991, for assessments.) And, of course, there were the great works of Karl Marx.

A later German School, the Ordoliberal or Freiburg School, also warrants remark. As discussed by Heinz Grossekettler (1989), this School was inspired by the work of Walter Eucken, whose student Ludwig Erhard was the German Minister of Economics from 1949 to 1963, Chancellor from 1963 to 1966, and is widely credited with being the political father of the "economic miracle" in West Germany. Grossekettler describes numerous parallels between the Ordoliberal program and those of Property Rights Theory, Transaction Cost Economics, and especially Constitutional Economics (1989, pp. 39, 64–7).

The Ordoliberal program proceeded at a very high level of generality (Grossekettler, 1989, p. 47) and featured the application of lawful principles to the entire economy (pp. 46–57). Its great impact on postwar German economic policy notwithstanding, the influence of the School declined after the mid-1960s. Although Grossekettler attributes the decline to the "wide scale of acceptance of the Keynesian theory . . . [among] young German intellectuals" (pp. 69–70), an additional problem is that the principles of Ordoliberal economics were never given operational content. Specific models were never developed; key trade-offs were never identified; the mechanisms remained very abstract. The parallels with the Wisconsin School – great public policy impact, underdeveloped conceptual framework, loss of intellectual influence – are striking.

2.2 The new institutional economics

The new institutional economics comes in a variety of flavors and has been variously defined. The economics of property rights – as developed especially by Coase (1959, 1960), Armen Alchian (1961), and Harold Demsetz (1967) – was an early and influential dissent from orthodoxy. An evolutionary as opposed to a technological approach to economic organization was advanced, according to which new property rights were created and enforced as the economic needs arose, if and as these were cost effective.

The definition of ownership rights advanced by Eirik Furubotn and Svetozar Pejovich is broadly pertinent: "By general agreement, the right of ownership of an asset consists of three elements: (a) the right to use the asset . . . , (b) the right to appropriate the returns from the asset . . . , and (c) the right to change the asset's form and/or substance" (1974, p. 4). Strong claims on behalf of the property rights approach to economic organization were set out by Coase as follows:

> A private enterprise system cannot function unless property rights are created in resources, and when this is done, someone wishing to use a resource has to pay the owner to obtain it. Chaos disappears; and so does the government except that a legal system to define property rights and to arbitrate disputes is, of course, necessary. (1959, p. 14)

As it turns out, these claims overstate the case for the property rights approach. Not only is the definition of property rights sometimes costly – consider the difficult problems of defining intellectual property rights – but also court ordering can be a costly way to proceed. A comparative contractual approach rather than a pure property rights approach, therefore has a great deal to recommend it.

Although the earlier property rights approach and the more recent comparative contractual approach appear to be rival theories of organization, much of that tension is relieved by recognizing that the new institutional economics has actually developed in two complementary parts. One of these parts deals predominantly with background conditions (expanded beyond property rights to include contract laws, norms, customs, conventions, and the like) while the second branch deals with the mechanisms of governance.

What the economics of organization is predominantly concerned with is this: holding these background conditions constant, why organize economic activity one way (e.g., procure from the market) rather than another (e.g., produce to your own needs: hierarchy)?

3   A Three-Level Schema

Transaction cost economics is mainly concerned with the governance of contractual relations. Governance does not, however, operate in isolation. The comparative efficacy of alternative modes of governance varies with the institutional environment on the one hand and the attributes of economic actors on the other. A three-level schema is therefore proposed, according to which the object of analysis, governance, is bracketed by more macro features (the institutional environment) and more micro features (the individual). Feedbacks aside (which are underdeveloped in the transaction cost economics set-up), the institutional environment is treated as the locus of shift parameters, changes in which shift the comparative costs of governance, and the individual is where the behavioral assumptions originate.

Roger Friedland and Robert Alford also propose a three-level schema in which environment, governance, and individual are distinguished, but their emphasis is very different. They focus on the individual and argue that the three levels of analysis are "nested, where organization and institution specify progressively higher levels of constraint and opportunity for individual action" (1991, p. 242).

The causal model proposed here is akin to and was suggested by, but is different from, the causal model recently proposed by W. Richard Scott (1992, p. 45), who is also predominantly concerned with governance. There are three main effects in my schema (see figure 4.1). These are shown by the solid arrows. Secondary effects are drawn as dashed arrows. As indicated, the institutional environment defines the rules of the game. If changes in property rights, contract laws, norms, customs, and the like induce changes in the comparative costs of governance, then a reconfiguration of economic organization is usually implied.

The solid arrow from the individual to governance carries the behavioral assumptions within which transaction cost economics operates, and the circular arrow within the governance sector reflects the proposition that organization, like the law, has a life of its own. The latter is the subject of section 4.

Although behavioral assumptions are frequently scanted in economics, transaction cost economics subscribes to the proposition that economic actors should be described in workably realistic terms (Simon, 1978; Coase, 1984). Interestingly, "outsiders," especially

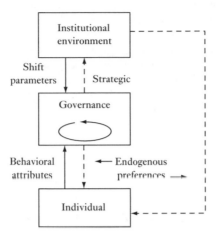

Figure 4.1   A layer schema

physicists, have long been insistent that a better understanding of the actions of human agents requires more self-conscious attention to the study of how men's minds work (Bridgeman, 1955, p. 450; Waldrop, 1992, p. 142). Herbert Simon concurs:

> Nothing is more fundamental in setting our research agenda and informing our research methods than our view of the nature of the human beings whose behavior we are studying. It makes a difference, a very large difference, to our research strategy whether we are studying the nearly omniscient *Homo economicus* of rational choice theory or the boundedly rational *Homo psychologicus* of cognitive psychology. It makes a difference to research, but it also makes a difference for the proper design of political institutions. James Madison was well aware of that, and in the pages of the *Federalist Papers* he opted for this view of the human condition (*Federalist*, No. 55):
>
>> As there is a degree of depravity in mankind which requires a certain degree of circum-spection and distrust, so there are other qualities in human nature which justify a certain portion of esteem and confidence.
>
> – a balanced and realistic view, we may concede, of bounded human rationality and its accom-panying frailties of motive and reason.   (1985, p. 303)

Transaction cost economics expressly adopts the proposition that human cognition is subject to bounded rationality – where this is defined as behavior that is "intendedly rational, but only limitedly so" (Simon, 1957, p. xxiv) – but differs from Simon in its interpretation of the "degree of depravity" to which Madison refers.

Whereas Simon regards the depravity in question as "frailties of motive and reason," transaction cost economics describes it instead as opportunism – to include self-interest seeking with guile. The former is a much more benign interpretation, and many social scientists understandably prefer it. Consider, however, Robert Michels's concluding remarks about oligarchy: "nothing but a serene and frank examination of the oligarchical dangers of democracy will enable us to minimize these dangers" (1962, p. 370). If a serene and frank reference to opportunism alerts us to avoidable dangers which the more benign reference to frailties of motive and reason would not, then there are real hazards in adopting the more benevolent construction. As discussed in section 5, below, the mitigation of opportunism plays a central role in transaction cost economics.

Opportunism can take blatant, subtle, and natural forms. The blatant form is associated with Niccolò Machiavelli. Because he perceived that the economic agents with whom the Prince was dealing were opportunistic, the Prince was advised to engage in reciprocal and even pre-emptive opportunism – to breach contracts with impugnity whenever "the reasons which made him bind himself no longer exist" (1952, p. 92). The subtle form is strategic and has been described elsewhere as "self-interest seeking with guile" (Williamson, 1975 pp. 26–37; 1985, pp. 46–52, 64–7). The natural form involves tilting the system at the margin. The so-called "dollar-a-year" men in the Office of Production Management, of which there were 250 at the beginning of World War II, were of concern to the Senate Special Committee to Investigate the National Defense Program because

> Such corporate executives in high official roles were too inclined to make decisions for the benefit of their corporations. "They have their own business at heart," [Senator] Truman remarked. The report called them lobbyists "in a very real sense," because their presence inevitably meant favoritism, "human nature being what it is." (McCullough, 1992, p. 265)

Michel Crozier's treatment of bureaucracy makes prominent provision for all forms of opportunism, which he describes as "the active tendency of the human agent to take advantage, in any circumstances, of all available means to further his own privileges" (1964, p. 194).

Feedback effects from governance to the institutional environment can be either instrumental or strategic. An example of the former would be an improvement in contract law, brought about at the request of parties who find that extant law is poorly suited to support the integrity of contract. Strategic changes could take the form of protectionist trade barriers against domestic and/or foreign competition. Feedback from governance to the level of the individual can be interpreted as "endogenous preference" formation (Bowles and Gintis, 1993), due to advertising or other forms of "education." The individual is also influenced by the environment, in that endogenous preferences are the product of social conditioning. Although transaction cost economics can often relate to these secondary effects, other modes of analysis are often more pertinent.

More generally, the Friedland and Alford scheme, the Scott scheme, and the variant that I offer are not mutually exclusive. Which to use when depends on the questions being asked. To repeat, the main case approach to economic organization that I have proposed works out of the heavy line causal relations shown in figure 4.1, to which the dashed lines represent refinements.

4   The Value Added of Organization Theory

Richard Swedberg (1987, 1990), Robert Frank (1992), and others have described numerous respects in which economics has been influenced by sociology and organization theory. The value added to which I refer here deals only with those aspects where transaction cost economics has been a direct and significant beneficiary.

The behavioral assumptions to which I refer in section 3 above – bounded rationality and opportunism – are perhaps the most obvious examples of how transaction cost economics has been shaped by organization theory. But the proposition that organization has a life of its own (the circular arrow in the governance box in figure 4.1) is also important. And there are yet additional influences as well.

4.1 Intertemporal process transformations

Describing the firm as a production function invites an engineering approach to organization. The resulting "machine model" of organization emphasizes intended effects to the neglect of unintended effects (March and Simon, 1958, chapter 3). But if organizations have a life of their own, and if the usual economic approach is unable to relate to the intertemporal realities of organization, then – for some purposes at least – an extra-economic approach may be needed.

Note that I do not propose that the economic approach be abandoned. Rather, the "usual" or orthodox economic approach gives way to an augmented or extended economic approach. That is very different from adopting an altogether different approach – as, for example, that of neural networks.

As it turns out, the economic approach is both very elastic and very powerful. Because it is elastic and because increasing numbers of economists have become persuaded of the need to deal with economic organization "as it is," warts and all, all significant regularities whatsoever – intended and unintended alike – come within the ambit. Because it is very powerful, economics brings added value. Specifically, the "farsighted propensity" or "rational spirit" that economics ascribes to economic actors permits the analysis of previously neglected regularities to be taken a step further. Once the unanticipated consequences are understood, those effects will thereafter be anticipated and the ramifications can be folded back into the organizational design. Unwanted costs will then be mitigated, and unanticipated benefits will be enhanced. Better economic performance will ordinarily result.

Unintended effects are frequently delayed and are often subtle. Deep knowledge of the details and intertemporal process transformations that attend organization is therefore needed. Because organization theorists have wider and deeper knowledge of these conditions, economists have much to learn and ought to be deferential. Four specific illustrations are sketched here.

4.1.1 Demands for control
A natural response to perceived failures of performance is to introduce added controls. Such efforts can have both intended and unintended consequences (Merton, 1936; Gouldner, 1954).

One illustration is the employment relation, where an increased emphasis on the reliability of behavior gives rise to added rules (March and Simon, 1958, pp. 38–40). Rules, however, serve not merely as controls but also define minimally acceptable behavior (Cyert and March, 1963). Managers who apply rules to subordinates in a legalistic and mechanical way invite "working to rules," which frustrates effective performance.

These unintended consequences are picked up by the wider peripheral vision of organization theorists. In the spirit of farsighted contracting, however, the argument can be taken yet a step further. Once apprised of the added consequences, the farsighted economist will make allowance for them by factoring these into the original organizational design. (Some organization theorists might respond that this last is fanciful and unrealistic. That can be decided by examining the data.)

4.1.2 Oligarchy

The Iron Law of Oligarchy holds that "It is organization which gives birth to the dominion of the elected over the electors, of the mandatories over the mandators, of the delegates over the delegators. Who says organization, says oligarchy" (Michels, 1962, p. 365). Accordingly, good intentions notwithstanding, the initial leadership (or its successors) will inevitably develop attachments for the office.

One response would be to eschew organization in favor of anarchy, but that is extreme. The better and deeper lesson is to take all predictable regularities into account at the outset, whereupon it may be possible to mitigate foreseeable oligarchical excesses at the initial design stage.[4]

4.1.3 Identity/capability

The proposition that identity matters has been featured in transaction cost economics from the outset. As developed in section 6, below, identity is usually explained by some form of "asset specificity." The "capabilities" view of the firm (Penrose, 1959; Selznick, 1957; Wernerfelt, 1984; Teece et al., 1992) raises related but additional issues.

One way to unpack the "capabilities" view of the firm is to ask what – in addition to an inventory of its physical assets, an accounting for its financial assets, and a census of its workforce – is needed to describe the capabilities of a firm. Features of organization that are arguably important include the following: (i) the communication codes that the firm has developed (Arrow, 1974); (ii) the routines that it employs (Cyert and March, 1963; Nelson and Winter, 1982); (iii) the corporate culture that has taken shape (Kreps, 1990b). What do we make of these?

One response is to regard these as spontaneous features of economic organization. As interpreted by institutional theory in sociology, "organizational structures, procedures, and decisions are *largely ritualistic and symbolic*, especially so when it is difficult or impossible to assess the efficacy of organizational decisions on the basis of their tangible outcomes" (Baron and Hannan, 1992, p. 57, emphasis added).

If, of course, efficiency consequences are impossible to ascertain, then intentionality has nothing to add. Increasingly, however, some of the subtle efficiency consequences of organization are coming to be better understood, whereupon they are (at least partly) subject to strategic determination. If the benefits of capabilities vary with the attributes of transactions, which arguably they do, then the cost effective thing to do is to *shape* culture, *develop* communication codes, and *manage* routines in a deliberative (transaction specific) way. Implementing the intentionality view will require that the microanalytic attributes that define culture, communication codes, and routines be uncovered, which is an ambitious exercise.

4.1.4 Bureaucratization

As compared with the study of market failure, the study of bureaucratic failure is under-developed. It is elementary that a well-considered theory of organization will make provision for failures of all kinds.

Albeit underdeveloped, the bureaucratic failure literature is vast, partly because purported failures are described in absolute rather than comparative terms. Unless, however, a superior and feasible form of organization to which to assign a transaction (or related set of transactions) can be identified, the failure in question is effectively irremediable. One of the tasks of transaction cost economics is to assess purported bureaucratic failures in comparative institutional terms.

The basic argument is this: it is easy to show that a particular hierarchical structure is beset with costs, but that is neither here nor there if all feasible forms of organization are beset with the same or equivalent costs. Efforts to ascertain bureaucratic costs that survive comparative institutional scrutiny are reported elsewhere (Williamson, 1975, chapter 7; 1985, chapter 6), but these are very provisional and preliminary. Although intertemporal transformations and complexity are recurrent themes in the study of bureaucratic failure, much more concerted attention to these matters is needed.

4.2 Adaptation

As described earlier, the economist Friedrich Hayek maintained that the main problem of economic organization was that of adaptation and argued that this was realized spontaneously through the price system. The organization theorist Chester Barnard also held that adaptation was the central problem of organization. But whereas Hayek emphasized autonomous adaptation of a spontaneous kind, Barnard was concerned with cooperative adaptation of an intentional kind.

Transaction cost economics (i) concurs that adaptation is the central problem of economic organization; (ii) regards adaptations of both autonomous and cooperative kinds as important; (iii) maintains that whether adaptations to disturbances ought to be predominantly autonomous, cooperative, or a mixture thereof varies with the attributes of the transactions (especially on the degree to which the investments associated with successive stages of activity are bilaterally or multilaterally dependent); and (iv) argues that each generic form of governance – market, hybrid, and hierarchy – differs systematically in its capacity to adapt in autonomous and cooperative ways. A series of predicted (transaction cost economizing) alignments between transactions and governance structures thereby obtain (Williamson, 1991a), which predications invite and have been subjected to empirical testing (Joskow, 1988; Klein and Shelanski, 1995; Masten, 1982).

4.3 Politics

Terry Moe (1990b) makes a compelling case for the proposition that public bureaucracies are different. Partly that is because the transactions that are assigned to the public sector are different, but Moe argues additionally that public sector bureaucracies are shaped by politics. Democratic politics requires compromises that are different in kind from those posed in the private sector and poses novel expropriation hazards. Added "inefficiencies" arise in the design of public agencies on both accounts.[5]

4.4   Embeddedness and networks

Gary Hamilton and Nicole Biggart take exception with the transaction cost economics interpretation of economic organization because it implicitly assumes that the institutional environment is everywhere the same; namely, that of Western democracies, and most especially that of the United States. They observe that large firms in East Asia differ from United States corporations in significant respects and explain that "organizational practices . . . are fashioned out of pre-existing interactional patterns, which in many cases date to pre-industrial times. Hence, industrial enterprise is a complex modern adaptation of pre-existing patterns of domination to economic situations in which profit, efficiency, and control usually form the very conditions of existence" (1988, p. S54).

The evidence that East Asian corporations differ is compelling. The argument, however, that transaction cost economics does not have application to East Asian economies goes too far.

The correct argument is that the institutional environment matters and that transaction cost economics, in its preoccupation with governance, has been neglectful of that. Treating the institutional environment as a set of shift parameters – changes in which induce shifts in the comparative costs of governance – is, to a first approximation at least, the obvious response (Williamson, 1991a). That is the interpretation advanced above and shown in Figure 4.1.

The objection could nevertheless be made that this is fine as far as it goes, but that comparative statics – which is a once-for-all exercise – does not go far enough. As Mark Granovetter observes, "More sophisticated . . . analyses of cultural influences . . . make it clear that culture is not a once-for-all influence but an *ongoing process*, continuously constructed and reconstructed during interaction. It not only shapes its members but is also shaped by them, in part for their own strategic reasons" (1985, p. 486).

I do not disagree, but I would observe that "more sophisticated analyses" must be judged by their value added. What are the deeper insights? What are the added implications? Are the effects in question really beyond the reach of economizing reasoning?

Consider, with reference to this last, the embeddedness argument that "concrete relations and structures" generate trust and discourage malfeasance of non-economic or extra-economic kinds:

> Better than a statement that someone is known to be reliable is information from a trusted informant that he has dealt with that individual and found him so. Even better is information from one's own past dealings with that person. This is better information for four reasons: (1) it is cheap; (2) one trusts one's own information best – it is richer, more detailed, and known to be accurate; (3) individuals with whom one has a continuing relation have an economic motivation to be trustworthy, so as not to discourage future transactions; and (4) departing from pure economic motives, continuing economic relations often become overlaid with social content that carries strong expectations of trust and abstention from opportunism.
>
> (Granovetter, 1985, p. 490)

This last point aside, the entire argument is consistent with, and much of it has been anticipated by, transaction cost reasoning. Transaction cost economics and embeddedness reasoning are evidently complementary in many respects.

A related argument is that transaction cost economics is preoccupied with dyadic relations, whereupon network relations are given short shift. The former is correct,[6] but the suggestion that network analysis is beyond the reach of transaction cost economics is too strong. For one thing, many of the network effects described by Ray Miles and Charles Snow (1992) correspond very closely to the transaction cost economics treatment of the hybrid form of economic organization (Williamson, 1983, 1991). For another, as the discussion of Japanese economic organization reveals, transaction cost economics can be and has been extended to deal with a richer set of network effects.

4.5 Discrete structural analysis

One possible objection to the use of maximization/marginal analysis is that "Parsimony recommends that we prefer the postulate that men are reasonable to the postulate that they are supremely rational when either of the two assumptions will do our work of inference as well as the other" (Simon, 1978, p. 8). But while one might agree with Simon that satisficing is more reasonable than maximizing, the analytical toolbox out of which satisficing works is, as compared with maximizing apparatus, incomplete and very cumbersome. Thus if one reaches the same outcome through the satisficing postulate as through maximizing, and if the latter is much easier to implement, then economists can be thought of as analytical satisficers: they use a short-cut form of analysis that is simple to implement. Albeit at the expense of realism in assumptions, maximization gets the job done.

A different criticism of marginal analysis is that this glosses over first-order effects of a discrete structural kind. Capitalism and socialism, for example, can be compared in both discrete structural (bureaucratization) and marginal analysis (efficient resource allocation) respects. Recall Oskar Lange's conjectured theory that, as between the two, bureaucratization posed a much more severe danger to socialism than did inefficient resource allocation (1938, p. 109).

That he was sanguine with respect to the latter was because he had derived the rules for efficient resource allocation (mainly of a marginal cost pricing kind) and was confident that socialist planners and managers could implement them. Joseph Schumpeter (1942) and Abram Bergson (1948) concurred. The study of comparative economic systems over the next fifty years was predominantly an allocative efficiency exercise.

Bureaucracy, by contrast, was mainly ignored. Partly that is because the study of bureaucracy was believed to be beyond the purview of economics and belonged to sociology (Lange, 1938, p. 109). Also, Lange held that "monopolistic capitalism" was beset by even more serious bureaucracy problems (p. 110). If, however, the recent collapse of the former Soviet Union is attributable more to conditions of waste (operating inside the frontier) than to inefficient resource allocation (operating at the wrong place on the frontier), then it was cumulative burdens of bureaucracy – goal distortions, slack, maladaptation, technological stagnation – that spelt its demise.

The lesson here is this: always study first-order (discrete structural) effects before examining second-order (marginalist) refinements. Arguably, moreover, that should be obvious: waste is easily a more serious source of welfare losses than are price induced distortions (cf. Harberger, 1954, with Williamson, 1968).

Simon advises similarly. Thus he contends that the main questions are

> Not "how much flood insurance will a man buy?" but "what are the structural conditions that make buying insurance rational or attractive?"
> Not "at what levels will wages be fixed" but "when will work be performed under an employment contract rather than a sales contract?"   (1978, p. 6)

Friedland and Alford's recent treatment of institutions is also of a discrete structural kind. They contend that "Each of the most important institutional orders of contemporary Western societies has a central logic – a set of material practices and symbolic constructions – which constitutes its organizing principles and which is available to organizations and individuals to elaborate" (1991, p. 248). Transaction cost economics concurs. But whereas Friedland and Alford are concerned with discrete structural logics between institutional orders – capitalism, the state, democracy, the family, etc. – transaction cost economics maintains that distinctive logics within institutional orders also need to be distinguished. Within the institutional order of capitalism, for example, each generic mode of governance – market, hybrid, and hierarchy – possesses its own logic and distinctive cluster of attributes. Of special importance is the proposition that each generic mode of governance is supported by a distinctive form of contract law.

5   Transaction Cost Economics: the Strategy

The transaction cost economics program for studying economic organization has been described elsewhere (Williamson, 1975, 1981, 1985, 1988, 1991a; Klein, Crawford, and Alchian, 1978; Alchian and Woodward, 1987; Davis and Powell, 1992). My purpose here is to sketch the general strategy that is employed by transaction cost economics, with the suggestion that organization theorists could adopt (some already have adopted) parts of it.

The five-part strategy that I describe entails (i) a main case orientation (transaction cost economizing), (ii) choice and explication of the unit of analysis, (iii) a systems view of contracting, (iv) rudimentary trade-off apparatus, and (v) a remediableness test for assessing "failures."

5.1   The main case

Economic organization being very complex and our understanding being primitive, there is a need to sort the wheat from the chaff. I propose for this purpose that each rival theory of organization should declare the *main case* out of which it works and develop the *refutable implications* that accrue thereto.

Transaction cost economics holds that economizing on transaction costs is mainly responsible for the choice of one form of capitalist organization over another. It thereupon applies this hypothesis to a wide range of phenomena – vertical integration, vertical market restrictions, labor organization, corporate governance, finance, regulation (and deregulation), conglomerate organization, technology transfer, and, more generally, to any issue that can be posed directly or indirectly as a contracting problem. As it turns out, large numbers of problems which on first examination do not appear to be of a contracting kind turn out to have an underlying contracting structure – the oligopoly problem (Williamson, 1975, chapter 12) and the organization of the company town (Williamson, 1985 pp. 35–8) being examples. Comparisons with other – rival or complementary – main case alternatives are invited.

Three of the older main case alternatives are that economic organization is mainly explained by (i) technology, (ii) monopolization, and (iii) efficient risk bearing. More recent main case candidates are (iv) contested exchange between labor and capital, (v) other types of power arguments (e.g., resource dependency), and (vi) path dependency. My brief responses to the first three are that (i) technological non-separabilities and indivisibilities explain only small groups and, at most, large plants, but explain neither multiplant organization nor the organization of technologically separable groups/activities (which should remain autonomous and which should be joined), (ii) monopoly explanations require that monopoly preconditions be satisfied, but most markets are competitively organized, and (iii) although differential risk aversion may apply to many employment relationships, it has much less applicability to trade between firms (where portfolio diversification is more easily accomplished and where smaller firms ([for incentive intensity and economizing, but not risk bearing, reasons] are often observed to bear inordinate risk). Responses to the last three are developed more fully below. My brief responses are these: (iv) the failures to which contested exchange refers are often irremediable, (v) resource dependency is a truncated theory of contract, and (vi) although path dependency is an important phenomenon, remediable inefficiency is rarely established.

To be sure, transaction cost economizing does not always operate smoothly or quickly. Thus we should "expect [transaction cost economizing] to be most clearly exhibited in industries where entry is [easy] and where the struggle for survival is [keen]" (Koopmans, 1957, p. 141).[7] Transaction cost economics nevertheless maintains that later, if not sooner, inefficiency in the commercial sector invites its own demise – all the more so as international competition has become more vigorous. Politically imposed impediments (tariffs, quotas, subsidies, rules) can and have, however, delayed the reckoning[8] and disadvantaged parties (railroad workers, longshoremen, managers) may also be able to delay changes unless compensated by buyouts.

The economizing to which I refer operates through weak-form selection (Simon, 1983, p. 69)[9] and works through a private net benefit calculus. That suits the needs of positive economics – What's going on out there? – rather well, but public policy needs to be more circumspect. As discussed below, the relevant test of whether public policy intervention is warranted is that of remediableness.

These important qualifications notwithstanding, transaction cost economics maintains that economizing is mainly determinative of private sector economic organization and, as indicated, invites comparsion with rival main case hypotheses.

5.2 Unit of analysis

A variety of units of analysis have been proposed to study economic organization. Simon has proposed that the *decision premise* is the appropriate unit of analysis (1957 pp. xxx–xxxii). "*Ownership*" is the unit of analysis for the economics of property rights. The *industry* is the unit of analysis in the structure–conduct–performance approach to industrial organization (Bain, 1956; Scherer, 1970). The *individual* has been nominated as the unit of analysis by positive agency theory (Jensen, 1983). Transaction cost economics follows John R. Commons (1924, 1934) and takes the *transaction* to be the basic unit of analysis.

Whatever unit of analysis is selected, the critical dimensions with respect to which that unit of analysis differs need to be identified. Otherwise the unit will remain non-operational. Also, a paradigm problem to which the unit of analysis applies needs to be described. Table 4.1 sets out the relevant comparisons.

Table 4.1   Comparison of units of analysis

Unit of analysis	Critical dimensions	Focal problem
Decision premise	Role; information; idiosyncratic[a]	Human problem solving[b]
Ownership	"Eleven characteristics"[c]	Externality
Industry	Concentration: barriers to entry	Price–cost margins
Individual	Undeclared	Incentive alignment
Transaction	Frequency: uncertainty: asset specificity	Vertical integration

[a] Simon (1957) pp. xxx–xxxi.
[b] Newell and Simon (1972).
[c] Bromley (1989) pp. 187–90.

As shown, the representative problem with which transaction cost economics deals is that of vertical integration – when should a firm make rather than buy a good or service? The focal dimension on which much of the predictive content of transaction cost economics relies, moreover, is asset specificity, which is a measure of bilateral dependency. More generally, transaction cost economics is concerned with the governance of contractual relations (which bears a resemblance to the "going concerns" to which Commons referred). As it turns out, economic organization – in intermediate products markets, labor markets, capital markets, regulation, and even the family – involves variations on a few key transaction cost economizing themes. The predictive action turns on the hypothesis of discriminating alignment.

The arguments are familiar and are developed above. Suffice it to observe here that empirical research in organization theory has long suffered from the lack of an appropriate unit of analysis and the operationalization, which is to say, dimensionalization, thereof.

5.3   Farsighted contracting

The preoccupation of economists with direct and intended effects to the neglect of indirect and (often delayed) unintended effects is widely interpreted as a condition of myopia. In fact, however, most economists are actually farsighted. The problem is one of limited peripheral vision.

Tunnel vision is both a strength and a weakness. The strength is that a focused lens, provided that it focuses on core issues, can be very powerful. The limitation is that irregularities which are none the less important will be missed and/or, even worse, dismissed.

Transaction cost economics relates to these limitations by drawing on organization theory. Because organization has a life of its own, transaction cost economics (i) asks to be apprised of the more important indirect effects, whereupon (ii) it asks what, given these prospective effects, are the ramifications for efficient governance. A joinder of unanticipated effects (from organization theory) with farsighted contracting (from economics) thereby obtains.

Lest claims of farsightedness be taken to hyper-rationality extremes, transaction cost economics concedes that all complex contracts are unavoidably incomplete. That has both practical and theoretical significance. The practical lesson is this: all of the relevant contracting action cannot be concentrated in the *ex ante* incentive alignment but some spills over into *ex post* governance. The theoretical lesson is that differences among organization forms lose economic significance under a comprehensive contracting set-up because any form of organization can then replicate any other (Hart, 1990).

Transaction cost economics combines incompleteness with the farsighted contracting by describing the contracting process as one of "incomplete contracting in its entirety." But for incompleteness, the above-described significance of *ex post* governance would vanish. But for farsightedness, transaction cost economics would be denied access to one of the most important "tricks" in the economist's bag, namely the assumption that economic actors have the ability to look ahead, discern problems and prospects, and factor these back into the organizational/contractual design. "Plausible farsightedness," as against hyper-rationality, will often suffice.

Consider, for example, the issue of threats. Threats are easy to make, but which threats are to be believed? If *A* says that it will do *X* if *B* does *Y*, but if after *B* does *Y*, *A*'s best response is to do *Z*, then the threat will not be perceived to be credible to a farsighted *B*. Credible threats are thus those for which a farsighted *B* perceives that *A*'s *ex post* incentives comport with its claims, because, for example, *A* has made the requisite kind and amount of investment to support its threats (Dixit, 1980).

Or consider the matter of opportunism. As described above, Machiavelli worked out of a myopic logic, whereupon he advised his Prince to reply to opportunism in kind (get them before they get you). By contrast, the farsighted Prince is advised to look ahead and, if he discerns potential hazards, to take the hazards into account by redesigning the contractual relation – often by devising *ex ante* safeguards that will deter *ex post* opportunism. Accordingly, the wise Prince is advised to give and receive "credible commitments."

To be sure, it is more complicated to think about a contract as a triple (p, k, s) where p refers to the price at which the trade takes place, k refers to the hazards that are associated with the exchange, s denotes the safeguards within which the exchange is embedded, and price, hazards, and safeguards are determined simultaneously—than as a scalar, where price alone is determinative.

5.4 Trade-offs

The ideal organization adapts quickly and efficaciously to disturbances of all kinds, but actual organizations experience trade-offs. Thus whereas more decentralized forms of organization (e.g., markets) support high-powered incentives and display outstanding adaptive properties to disturbances of an autonomous kind, they are poorly suited in cooperative adaptation respects. Hierarchy, by contrast, has weaker incentives and is comparatively worse at autonomous adaptation but is comparatively better in cooperative adaptation respects.

Simple transactions (for which $k = 0$) – in intermediate product markets, labor, finance, regulation, and the like – are easy to organize. The requisite adaptations here are preponderantly of an autonomous kind and the market-like option is efficacious (so firms buy rather than make, use spot contracts for labor, use debt rather than equity, eschew regulation, etc.). Problems with markets arise as bilateral dependencies, and the need for cooperative adaptations, build up. Markets give way to hybrids which in turn give way to hierarchies (which is the organization form of last resort) as the needs for cooperative adaptations ($k > 0$) build up.

More generally, the point is this: informed choice among alternative forms of organization entails trade-offs. Identifying and explicating trade-offs is the key to the study of comparative economic organization. Social scientists – economists and organization theorists alike – as well as legal specialists, need to come to terms with that proposition.

5.5   Remediableness

As developed elsewhere, the concept of remediableness has special relevances to politics. But it applies quite generally.

Note in this connection that "inefficiency" is unavoidably associated with contractual hazards. The basic market and hierarchy trade-off that is incurred upon taking transactions out of markets and organizing them internally substitutes one form of inefficiency (bureaucracy) for another (maladaptation). Other examples where one form of inefficiency is used to patch up another are (i) decisions by firms to integrate into adjacent stages of production (or distribution) in a weak intellectual property rights regime, thereby to mitigate the leakage of valued know-how (Teece, 1986), (ii) decisions by manufacturers' agents to incur added expenses, over and above those needed to develop the market, if these added expenses strengthen customer bonds in a cost-effective way, thereby to deter manufacturers from entering and expropriating market development investments (Heide and John, 1988), and (iii) the use of costly bonding to deter franchisees from violating quality norms (Klein and Leffler, 1981). Organization also has a bearing on the distribution of rents as well as asset protection. Concern over rent dissipation influenced the decision by the United States automobile industry firms to integrate into parts (Helper and Levine, 1992) and also helps to explain the resistance by oligopolies to industrial unions.

To be sure, any sacrifice of organizational efficiency, for oligopolistic rent protection reasons or otherwise, poses troublesome public policy issues.[10] A remediability test is none the less required to ascertain whether public policy should attempt to upset the oligopoly power in question. The issues are discussed further in relation to path dependency in section 7.

6   Added Regularities

It is evident from the foregoing that the comparative contractual approach out of which transaction cost economics works can be and needs to be informed by organization theory. Transaction cost economics, however, is more than a mere user. It pushes the logic of self-interest seeking to deeper levels, of which the concept of credible commitment is one example. More generally, it responds to prospective dysfunctional consequences by proposing improved *ex ante* designs and/or alternative forms of governance. Also, and what concerns me here, transaction cost economics has helped to discover added regularities that are pertinent to the study of organization. These include (i) the Fundamental Transformation, (ii) the impossibility of selective intervention, (iii) the economics of atmosphere, and (iv) an interpretation of Japanese economic organization.

These will not be repeated here (see, however, Williamson, 1993, pp. 133–7, for a summary). All are important to an understanding of economic organization. ·

7   Unresolved Tensions

The healthy tension to which I referred at the outset has contributed to better and deeper understandings of a variety of phenomena. The matters that concern me here – power, path dependence, the labor-managed enterprise, trust, and tosh – are ones for which differences between transaction cost economics and organization theory are great.

7.1   Power/resource dependence

That efficiency plays such a large role in the economic analysis of organization is because parties are assumed to consent to a contract and do this in a relatively farsighted way. Such voluntarism is widely disputed by sociologists, who "tend to regard systems of exchange as embedded within systems of power and domination (usually regarded as grounded in a class structure in the Marxian tradition) or systems of norms and values" (Baron and Hannan, 1992, p. 14).

The concept of power is very diffuse. Unable to define power, some specialists report that they know it when they see it. That has led others to conclude that power is a "disappointing concept. It tends to become a tautological label for the unexplained variance" (March, 1988, p. 6).

Among the ways in which the term power is used are the following: the power of capital over labor (Bowles and Gintis, 1993); strategic power exercised by established firms in relation to extant and prospective rivals (Shapiro, 1989); special interest power over the political process (Moe, 1990a); and resource dependency. Although all are relevant to economic organization, the last is distinctive to organization theory.[11] I examine it.

Two versions of resource dependency can be distinguished. The weak version is that parties who are subject to dependency will try to mitigate it. That is unexceptionable and is akin to the safeguard argument advanced in section 5, above. There are two significant differences, however: (i) resource dependency nowhere recognizes that price, hazards, and safeguards are determined simultaneously; (ii) resource dependency nowhere remarks that asset specificity (which is the source of contractual hazard) is intentionally chosen because it is the source of productive benefits.

The strong version of resource dependency assumes myopia. The argument here is that myopic parties to contracts are victims of unanticipated and unwanted dependency. Because myopic parties do not perceive the hazards, safeguards will not be provided and the hazards will not be priced out.

Evidence pertinent to the myopic versus farsighted view of contract includes the following. (i) Are suppliers indifferent between two technologies that involve identical investments and have identical (steady state) operating costs, but one of which technologies is much less redeployable than the other? (ii) Is the degree of non-redeployability evident *ex ante* or is it revealed only after an adverse state realization (which includes defection from the spirit of the agreement) has materialized? (iii) Do added *ex ante* safeguards appear as added specificity builds up? (iv) Does contract law doctrine and enforcement reflect one or the other of these concepts of contract? Transaction cost economics answers these queries as follows: (i) the more generic (redeployable) technology will always be used whenever the *cetera* are *paria*; (ii) non-redeployability can be discerned *ex ante* and is recognized as such (Masten, 1984; Palay, 1984, 1985); (iii) added *ex ante* safeguards do appear as asset specificity builds up (Joskow, 1985, 1988); (iv) because truly unusual events are unforeseeable and can have punitive consequences if contracts are enforced literally, various forms of "excuse" are recognized by the law, but excuse is granted sparingly.[12]

7.2   Path dependency

Transaction cost economics not only subscribes to the proposition that history matters but relies on that proposition to explain the differential strengths and weaknesses of alternative forms of governance. The Fundamental Transformation, for example, is a specific manifestation of the proposition that history matters. (Transactions that are not subject to the Fundamental Transformation are much easier to manage contractually.) The bureaucracy problems that afflict internal organization (entrenchment, coalitions) are also the product of experience and illustrate the proposition that history matters. Were it not that systems drifted away from their initial conditions, efforts to replicate markets within hierarchies (or the reverse) and selectively intervene would be much easier – in which event differences between organization forms would diminish.

The benefits that accure to experience are also testimony to the proposition that history matters. Tacit knowledge and its consequences (Polanyi, 1962; Marshak, 1968; Arrow, 1974) attest to that. More generally, firm-specific human assets of both spontaneous (e.g. coding economies) and intentional (e.g. learning) kinds are the product of idiosyncratic experience. The entire institutional environment (laws, rules, conventions, norms, etc.) within which the institutions of governance are embedded is the product of history. And although the social conditioning that operates within governance structures (e.g. corporate culture; Kreps, 1990a) is reflexive and often intentional, this too has accidental and temporal features.

That history matters does not, however, imply that only history matters. Intentionality and economizing explain a lot of what is going on out there. Also, most of the path dependency literature emphasizes technology (e.g. the QWERTY typewriter keyboard) rather than the organizational consequences referred to above, Paul David's paper (1992) being an exception. I am not persuaded that technological, as against organizational, path dependency is as important as much of that literature suggests. Many of the "inefficiencies" to which the technological path dependency literature refers are of an irremediable kind.

7.2.1   Remediable inefficiencies
As described early, transaction cost economics emphasizes remediable inefficiencies; that is, those conditions for which a feasible alternative can be described which, if introduced,

would yield net gains. That is to be distinguished from hypothetical net gains, where the inefficiency in question is judged by comparing an actual alternative with a hypothetical ideal.

To be sure, big disparities between actual and hypothetical sometimes signal opportunities for net gains. The need, however, is to realize real gains. Both public and private ordering are pertinent.

Whether public ordering can do better depends on whether (i) the public sector is better informed about externalities, (ii) the requisite collective action is easier to orchestrate through the public sector (possibly by fiat), and/or (iii) the social net benefit calculus differs from the private in sufficient degree to warrant a different result. Absent *plausible* assumptions that would support a prospective net gain (in either private or social respects), the purported inefficiency is effectively irremediable.

That is regrettable, in that society would have done better if it had better knowledge or if a reorganization could have been accomplished more easily. Hypothetical regrets are neither here nor there. Real costs in relation to real choices is what comparative institutional economics is all about.

7.2.2 Quantitative significance

Path dependency, remediable or not, poses a greater challenge if the effects in question are large and lasting rather than small and temporary. It is not easy to document the quantitative significance of path dependency. Arthur provides a series of examples and emphasizes especially the video cassette recorder (where VHS prevailed over the Beta technology [1990, p. 92]) and nuclear power (where light water reactors prevailed over high-temperature, gas-cooled reactors [1990, p. 99]). But while both are interesting examples of path dependency, it is not obvious that the "winning" technology is significantly inferior to the loser, or even, for that matter, whether the winner is inferior at all.

Much the most widely cited case study is that of the typewriter keyboard. The QWERTY keyboard story has been set out by Paul David (1985, 1986). It illustrates "why the study of economic history is a necessity in the making of good economists" (David, 1986, p. 30).

QWERTY refers to the first six letters on the top row of the standard typewriter keyboard. Today's keyboard layout is the same as that which was devised when the typewriter was first invented in 1870. The early mechanical technology was beset by typebar clashes, which clashes were mitigated by the QWERTY keyboard design.

Subsequent developments in typewriter technology relieved problems with typebar clashes, but the QWERTY keyboard persisted in the face of large (reported) discrepancies in typing speed between it and later keyboard designs. Thus the Dvorak Simplified Keyboard (DSK), which was patented in 1932, was so much faster than the standard keyboard that, according to United States Navy experiments, the "increased efficiency obtained with DSK would amortize the cost of retraining a group of typists within the first ten days of their subsequent full-time employment" (David, 1986, p. 33). More recently, the Apple IIC computer comes with a built-in switch which instantly converts its keyboard from QWERTY to DSK: "If as Apple advertising copy says, DSK 'lets you type 20–40% faster,' why did this superior design meet essentially the same resistance...?" (David, 1986, p. 34).

There are several possibilities. These include non-rational behavior, conspiracy among typewriter firms, and path dependency (David, 1986, pp. 34–46). David makes a strong case for the last, but there is a fourth possibility, subsequently raised and examined by Liebowitz and Margolis (1990): neither the Navy study nor Apple advertising copy can support the astonishing claims made on their behalf. Upon going back to the archives and examining the data, Liebowitz and Margolis conclude that "the standard history of QWERTY versus Dvorak is flawed and incomplete. . . . [The] claims of superiority of the Dvorak keyboard are suspect. The most dramatic claims are traceable to Dvorak himself, and the best documented experiments, as well as recent ergonomic studies, suggest little or no advantage for the Dvorak keyboard" (1990, p. 21). If that assessment stands up, then path dependence has had only modest efficiency effects in the QWERTY keyboard case. Such effects could easily fall below the threshold of remediable inefficiency.

Recent studies of the evolution of particular industries by sociologists also display path dependency. Population ecologists have used the ecological model of density-dependent legitimation and competition to examine the evolutionary process – both in particular industries (e.g. the telephone industry [Barnett and Carroll, 1993]) and in computer simulations. Glenn Carroll and Richard Harrison conclude from the latter that "chance can play a major role in organizational evolution" (1992, p. 26).

Although their simulations do suggest that path dependency has large and lasting effects, Carroll and Harrison do not address the matter of remediableness. Until a feasible reorganization of the decision process for choosing technologies can be described, the effect of which is to yield expected net private or social gains, it seems premature to describe their experiments as a test of the "relative roles of chance and rationality" (Carroll and Harrison, 1992, p. 12). Large but irremediable inefficiencies nevertheless do raise serious issues for modelling economic organization.[13]

7.2.3   Perspectives

David contends and I am persuaded that "there are many more QWERTY worlds lying out there" (1986, p. 47). An unchanged keyboard layout does not, however, strike me as the most important economic attribute of typewriter development from 1870 to the present. What about improvements in the mechanical technology? What about the electric type-writer? What about personal computers and laser printers? Why did these prevail in the face of path dependency? Were other "structurally superior" technologies (as defined by Carroll and Harrison) bypassed? If, with lags and hitches, the more efficient technologies have regularly supplanted less efficient technologies, should not that be featured? Possibly the response is that "everyone knows" that economizing is the main case: "It goes without saying that economizing is the main case to which path dependency, monopolizing, efficient risk bearing, etc. are qualifications."

The persistent neglect of economizing reasoning suggests otherwise. Thus the "inhospitability tradition" in antitrust proceeded with sublime confidence that non-standard and unfamiliar business practices had little or no efficiency rationale but mainly had monopoly purpose and effect. Similarly, the vast inefficiencies that brought down the economies of the Soviet Union and Eastern Europe may now be obvious, but that could never have been gleaned from the postwar literature on comparative economic systems or from CIA intelligence estimates. The preoccupation in the area of business strategy with clever "plans, ploys, and positioning" to the neglect of economizing is likewise testimony to the widespread tendency to disregard efficiency (Williamson, 1991b). And the view that the "effective organization is (1) *garrulous*, (2) *clumsy*, (3) *superstitious*, (4) *hypocritical*, (5) *monstrous*, (6) *octopoid*, (7) *wandering*, and (8) *grouchy*" (Weick, 1977, pp. 193–4, emphasis in original) is reconciled with economizing only with effort. More recent "social construction of industry" arguments reduce economizing to insignificance.[14]

If economizing really does get at the fundamentals, then that condition ought to be continuously featured. Some progress has been made (Zald, 1987), but there is little reason to be complacent.

7.3 Worker-managed enterprises

John Bonin and Louis Putterman define a worker-managed firm as

> a productive enterprise the ultimate decision-making rights over which are held by member-workers, on the basis of equality of those rights regardless of job, skill grade, or capital contribution. A full definition would state that no non-workers have a direct say in enterprising decisions, and that no workers are denied an equal say in those decisions. This definition does not imply that any particular set of decisions must be made by the full working group, nor does it imply a particular choice rule, such as majority voting. It says nothing about financing structures other than that financiers are not accorded direct decision-making powers in the enterprise by virtue of their non-labor contributions, and it does not say anything about how income is distributed among workers. On all of these matters, all that is implied is that ultimate decision-making rights are vested in the workers, and only in the workers. Thus, the basic definition centers on an allocation of governance rights, and is simultaneously economic and political. (1987, p. 2)

This definition does not preclude hierarchical structure, specialized decision-making, a leadership élite, or marginal product payment schemes. It merely stipulates that finance can have no decision rights in the labor-managed enterprise. The question is whether these financial restrictions come at a cost. Putterman evidently believes that they do not, since he elsewhere endorses Roger McCain's proposal that the labor-managed enterprise be financed in part by "risk participation bonds," where these purportedly differ from "ordinary equity" only in that "its owner can have no voting control over enterprise decisions, or over the election of enterprise management" (Putterman, 1984, p. 1989). Since "the labor-managed firm whose objective is to maximize profit-per-worker, having both ordinary and 'risk participation' bonds at its disposal, would 'attain the same allocation of resources as would a capitalist corporation, under comparable circumstances and informationally efficient markets'" (1984, p. 189), Putterman concludes that the labor-managed firm is on a parity.

The argument illustrates the hazards of addressing issues of economic organization within a framework that ignores, hence effectively suppresses, the role of governance. Operating, as he does, out of a firm-as-production-function framework, McCain (1977) is only concerned with examining the marginal conditions that obtain under two different set-ups, under both of which the firm is described as a production function.

Governance issues never arise and hence are not amenable to analysis within this orthodox framework. If, however, a critical – indeed, I would say, the critical – attribute of equity is the ability to exercise contingent control by concentrating votes and taking over the board of directors, then McCain's demonstration that allocative efficiency is identical under standard equity and risk participation bonds is simply inapposite.

Indeed, if risk participation finance is available on more adverse terms than standard equity because holders are provided with less security against mismanagement and expropriation, then the constraints that Bonin and Putterman have built into the worker-managed firm come at a cost. To be sure, the worker-managed firm may be able to offset financial disabilities by offering compensating advantages. If those advantages are not uniform but vary among firms and industries, then the net gains of the worker-managed firm will vary accordingly.

I submit that firms that can be mainly financed with debt are the obvious candidates for worker-management. Thus, if there is little equity-like capital at stake, then there is little reason for equity to ask or expect that preemptive control over the board of directors will be awarded to equity as a contractual safeguard. The question then is what types of firms best qualify for a preponderance of debt financing?

As discussed elsewhere, peer group forms of organization can and do operate well in small enterprises where the membership has been carefully screened and is committed to democratic ideals (Williamson, 1975, chapter 3). Also, the partnership form of organization works well in professional organizations, such as law and accounting firms, where the need for firm-specific physical capital is small (Hansmann, 1988). There being little need for equity capital to support investment in such firms, the control of these firms naturally accrues to those who supply specialized human assets (Williamson, 1989, pp. 24–6). These exceptions aside, "third forms" experience serious incentive disabilities.[15]

7.4   Trust

There is a growing tendency, among economists and sociologists alike, to describe trust in calculative terms: both rational choice sociologists (Coleman, 1990) and game theorists (Dasgupta, 1988) treat trust as a subclass of risk. I concur with Granovetter that to craft credible commitments (through the use of bonds, hostages, information disclosure rules, specialized dispute settlement mechanisms, and the like) is to create functional substitutes for trust (Granovetter, 1985, p. 487). Albeit vitally important to economic organization, such substitutes should not be confused with (real) trust.[16]

That calculativeness plays a larger role in economics than in the other social sciences is evident from my discussion of farsighted contracting. But calculativeness can also be taken to excesses.

7.5   Tosh

The legal philosopher Lon Fuller distinguished between "essentials" and "tosh," where the former involves an examination of the "rational core" (1978, pp. 359–62) and tosh is preoccupied with "superfluous rituals, rules of procedure without clear purpose, [and] needless precautions preserved through habit" (p. 356). According to Fuller, to focus on the latter would "abandon any hope of fruitful analysis" (p. 360).

I think that this last goes too far: a place should be made for tosh, but tosh should be kept in its place.[17] Consider in this connection the Friedland and Alford interpretation of Clifford Geertz's description of Balinese cockfights:

Enormous sums of money can change hands at each match, sums that are *irrational* from an individualistic, utilitarian perspective. The higher the sums, the more *evenly matched* the cocks are arranged to be, and the more likely the odds on which the bet is made are even. The greater the sum of money at stake, the more the decision to bet is not individualistic and utilitarian, but collective – one bets with one's kin or village – and status-oriented.   (1991, pp. 247–8, emphasis added)

That there are social pressures to support one's kin or village is a sociological argument. Absent these pressures, the concentration of bets on evenly matched cocks would be difficult to explain. It does not, however, follow that it is "irrational" to bet enormous sums on evenly matched cocks. Given the social context, it has become non-viable, as a betting matter, to fight unevenly matched cocks.

Thus suppose that the objective odds for a proposed match are 4:1. Considerations of local pride may reduce the effective odds to 3:2. Such a match will not attract much betting because those from the village with the lesser cock who view it from an individualistic, acquisitive perspective will make only perfunctory bets. Accordingly, the only interesting matches are those *where social pressures are relieved by the even odds*.[18] The "symbolic construction of reality" to which Friedland and Alford refer thus has real consequences. It delimits the feasible set within which rationality operates; but rationality is fully operative thereafter.

One interpretation of this is that tosh has discrete structural effects and that rationality, operating through the marginal calculus, applies thereafter. Indeed, that seems to fit the Balinese cockfight rather well. Whether the social construction of reality has such important consequences more generally is then the question. My sense is that it varies with the circumstances.

Tosh is arguably more important in non-commercial circumstances – state, family, religion – than in the commercial sector, although the Hamilton and Biggart (1988) examination of differences in corporate forms in Far East Asia might be offered as a contradiction. Hamilton and Biggart, however, go well beyond tosh (as described by Fuller) to implicate the institutional environment – to include property rights, contract law, politics, and the like.

Thus although both tosh (superfluous rituals) and the institutional environment refer to background conditions, the one should not be confused with the other. Tosh is a source of interesting variety and adds spice to life. Core features of the institutional environment, as defined by North (1986, 1991) and others (Sundaram and Black, 1992), are arguably more important, however, to the study of comparative economic organization.[19]

8   Conclusions

The science of organization to which Barnard made reference (1938, p. 290) over fifty years ago has made major strides in the past ten and twenty years. All of the social sciences have a stake in this, but none more than economics and organization theory.

If the schematic set out in figure 4.1 is an accurate way to characterize much of what is going on, then the economics of governance needs to be informed both from the level of the institutional environment (where sociology has a lot to contribute) and from the level of the individual (where psychology is implicated). The intertemporal process transformations that take place within the institutions of governance (with respect to which organization theory has a lot to say) are also pertinent. The overall schema works out of the rational spirit approach that is associated with economics.[20]

This multilevel approach relieves some, perhaps much, of the strain to which Baron and Hannan refer: "we think it important to understand the different assumptions and forms of reasoning used in contemporary sociology versus economics.... These disciplinary differ-ences...represent major barriers to intellectual trade between economics and sociology" (1992, p. 13). If, however, deep knowledge at several levels is needed and is beyond the competence of any one discipline, and if a systems conception can be devised in which intellectual trade among levels can be accomplished, then some of the worst misunder-standings of the past can be put behind us.

I summarize here what I see to be some of the principal respects in which the healthy tension to which I referred at the outset has supported intellectual trade, of which more is in prospect.

Organization theory supports for transaction cost economics

Behavioral assumptions
Organization theory's insistence on workably realistic, as opposed to analytically conveni-ent, behavioral assumptions is a healthy antidote. Transaction cost economics responds by describing economic actors in terms of bounded rationality and opportunism.

Adaptation
The cooperative adaptation emphasized by Barnard is joined with the autonomous adapta-tion of Hayek, with the result that transaction cost economics makes an appropriate place for both market and hierarchy.

Unanticipated consequences
The subtle and unintended consequences of control and organization need to be uncovered, whereupon provision can be made for these in the *ex ante* organizational design.

Politics
Because property rights in the public arena are shaped by democratic politics, provision needs to be made for these in the *ex ante* organizational design of public sector bureaus.

Embeddedness
The first-order response to the proposition that embeddedness matters is to regard the institutional environment as a locus of shift parameters, changes in which change the comparative costs of governance.

Discrete structural analysis
Each generic form of organization is described as a syndrome of attributes and possesses its own logic. These discreteness features need to be discovered and explicated both within and between sectors.

Transaction cost economics supports for organization theory

Unit of analysis
Any theory of organization that fails to name the unit of analysis out of which it works and thereafter identify the critical dimensions with respect to which that unit of analysis varies is non-operational at best and could be bankrupt.

The main case
All rival theories of organization are asked to nominate the main case, develop the refutable implications that accrue thereto, and examine the data. Economizing on transaction costs is the transaction cost economics candidate.

Farsighted contracting
Looking ahead, recognizing hazards, and folding these back into the design of governance is often feasible and explains a very considerable amount of organizational variety.

Trade-offs
Because each mode of governance is a syndrome of attributes, the move from one mode to another involves trade-offs. The key trade-offs need to be stated and explicated.

Remediableness
Relevant choices among feasible forms of organization are what the analysis of comparative economic organization is all about.

Notes

1 James March advised the Fourth International Conference of the Society for the Advancement of Socio-Economics that economics had been so fully reformed that the audience should "declare victory and go home" (Coughlin, 1992, p. 23).

2 Richard Posner comes out differently. He argues that "organization-theory . . . [adds] nothing to economics that the literature on information economics had not added years earlier" (1993a, p. 84).

3 Briefly, the transaction cost economics responses are: (i) institutions respond to scarcity as economizing devices, (ii) the transaction is expressly adopted as the basic unit of analysis, (iii) conflicts are recognized and relieved by the creation of credible commitments/*ex post* governance apparatus, and (iv) the institutional environment is treated as a set of shift parameters that change the comparative costs of governance. Although these may be incomplete responses, the spirit of the transaction cost economics enterprise nevertheless makes serious contact with Commons's prescription.

4 Oligarchy is usually applied to composite organization, but it applies to subdivisions as well. Whether a firm should make or buy is thus a matter for which oligarchy has a bearing. If the decision to take a transaction out of the market and organize it internally is attended by subsequent information distortions and subgoal pursuit, then that should be taken into account at the outset (Williamson, 1975, chapter 7; 1985 chapter 6). Not only do operating costs rise but also a constituency develops that favors the renewal of internal facilities. An obvious response is to demand high hurdle rates for new projects, thereby to protect against the unremarked but

predictable distortions (added costs; advocacy efforts) to which internal (as compared with market) procurement is differentially subject.

The argument applies to public sector projects as well. Because of the deferred and undisclosed but nevertheless predictable distortions to which "organization" is subject, new projects and regulatory proposals should be required to display large (apparent) net gains.

5 Politics really is different. But it is not as though there is no private, sector counterpart. The more general argument is this: weak property rights regimes – both public and private – invite farsighted parties to provide added protection. The issues are discussed further in conjunction with remediableness (see section 5.5 below).

Note, as a comparative institutional matter, that secure totalitarian regimes can, according to this logic, be expected to design more efficient public agencies. That is neither here nor there if democratic values are held to be paramount – in which event the apparent inefficiencies of agencies under a democracy are simply a cost of this form of governance.

6 Interdependencies among dyadic contracting relations and the possible manipulation thereof have, however, been examined (Williamson, 1985, pp. 318–19).

7 The statement is a weakened variant on Tjalling Koopmans. Where he refers to "profit maximization," "easiest," and "keenest," I have substituted "transaction cost economizing," "easy," and "keen."

8 Joel Mokyr observes that resistance to innovation "occurred in many periods and places but seems to have been neglected by most historians" (1990, p. 178). He nevertheless gives a number of examples in which established interests, often with the use of the political process, set out to defeat new technologies. In the end, however, the effect was not to defeat but to delay machines that pressed pinheads, an improved slide rest lathe, the ribbon loom, the flying shuttle, the use of arabic numerals, and the use of the printing press (Mokyr, 1990, pp. 178–9). That, of course, is not dispositive. There may be many cases in which superior technologies were in fact defeated – of which the typewriter keyboard (see section 7, below) is purportedly an example. Assuming, however, that the appropriate criterion for judging superiority is that of remediableness (see below), I register grave doubts that significance technological or organizational efficiencies can be delayed indefinitely.

9 The Schumpeterian process of "handing on" – which entails "a fall in the price of the product to the new level of costs" (Schumpeter, 1947, p. 155) and purportedly works whenever rivals are alert to new opportunities and are not prevented by purposive restrictions from adopting them – is pertinent. The efficacy of handing on varies with the circumstances. When are rivals *more* alert? What are the underlying information assumptions? Are there other capital market and/or organizational concerns?

10 This has public policy ramifications. As between two oligopolies, one of which engages in rent-protective measures while the other does not, and assuming that they are identical in other respects, the dissolution of the rent-protective oligopoly will yield larger welfare gains.

11 Friedland and Alford identify resource dependency as one of the two dominant theories of organization (the other being population ecology) (1991, p. 235).

12 Because contracts are incomplete and contain gaps, errors, omissions, and the like, and because the immediate parties may not be able to reconcile their differences when an unanticipated disturbance arises, parties to a contract will sometimes ask courts to be excused from performance. Because, moreover, literal enforcement can pose unacceptably severe contractual hazards – the effects of which are to discourage contracting (in favor of vertical integration) and/or to discourage potentially cost-effective investments in specialized assets – some relief from strict enforcement recommends itself. How much relief is then the question. Were excuse to be granted routinely whenever adversity occurred, then incentives to think through contracts, choose technologies judiciously, share risks efficiently, and avert adversity would be impaired. Accordingly, transaction cost economics recommends that (i) provision be made for excuse but

(ii) excuse should be awarded sparingly – which it evidently is (Farnsworth, 1968, p. 885; Buxbaum, 1985).

13 I have argued that dominant firm industries in which chance plays a role do warrant public policy intervention (Williamson, 1975, chapter 11), but whether net gains would really be realized by implementing that proposal (especially as international competition becomes more intensive) is problematic.

14 The "new sociology of organization" holds that "even in identical economic and technical conditions, outcomes may differ dramatically if social structures are different" (Granovetter, 1992, p. 9). The "social construction of industry" argument is developed in a major book by Patrick McGuire, Mark Granovetter, and Michael Schwartz on the origins of the American electric power industry. That book has been described as follows:

> Building on detailed historical research . . . this book treats the origins of the electrical utility industry from a sociological perspective. The idea that industries, like other economic institutions, are "socially constructed", derives from Granovetter's work on "embeddedness" (1985) and presents an alternative to the new institutional economics, which contends that economic institutions should be understood as the efficient solutions to economic problems. . . .
>
> We believe that the way the utility industry developed from its inception in the 1880s was not the only technologically practical one, nor the most efficient. It arose because a set of powerful actors accessed certain techniques and applied them in a highly visible and profitable way. Those techniques resulted from the shared personal understandings, social connections, organizational conditions, and historical opportunities available to these actors. This success, in turn, triggered pressures for uniformity across regions, even when this excluded viable and possibly more efficient alternative technologies and organizational forms.
>
> Our argument resembles that made by economists Paul David and Brian Arthur on the "lock-in" of inefficient technologies (such as the QWERTY keyboard . . .), but draws on the sociology of knowledge and of social structure. (McGuire, Granovetter, and Schwartz, 1992, pp. 1–2)

15 The limits of third forms for organizing *large* enterprises with *variegated* membership are severe in both theory and fact. To be sure, some students of economic organization remain sanguine (Horvat, 1991). The evidence from Eastern Europe has not, however, been supportive. Iwanek (1991, p. 12) remarks of the Polish experience that "except [among] advocates of workers' management, nobody believes that the . . . governance scheme of state-owned enterprises [by workers' management] creates strong incentives"; Hinds (1990, p. 28) concludes that "absenteeism, shirking, and lack of initiative are pervasive in the self-managed firm"; Kornai (1990, p. 144) counsels that "it would be intellectually dishonest to hide the evidence concerning the weakness of third forms".

16 Note that the trust that Granovetter ascribes to ongoing relations can go either way – frequent suggestions to the contrary notwithstanding. That is because experience can be either good (more confidence) or bad (less confidence), which, if contracts of both kinds are renewed, will show up in differential contracting (Crocker and Reynolds, 1993).

17 The evolution of cooperation between opposed armies or gangs that are purportedly engaged in "deadly combat" is illustrated by Robert Axelrod's examination of "The Live-and-Let-Live System in Trench Warfare in World War I" (1984, pp. 73–87). Interesting and important as the live-and-let-live rituals were, these non-violent practices should not be mistaken for the main case. Rather, these rituals were the exception to the main case, which was that British and German troops were at war.

18   Richard M. Coughlin contends that the "essence" of the socio-economic approach proposed by
     Amitai Etzioni is that

> human behavior must be understood in terms of the fusion of individually-based and
> communally-based forces, which Etzioni labels the *I* and *We*. The *I* represents the
> individual acting in pursuit of his or her own pleasure; the *We* stands for the obligations
> and restraints imposed by the collectivity.   (1992, p. 3)

     That is close to the interpretation that I advance here to interpret the Balinese cockfights.
19   This is pertinent, among other things, to the study of the multinational enterprise. As Anant
     Sundaram and J. Stewart Black observe, MNEs "pursue different entry/involvement strategies
     in different markets and for different products at any given time" (1992, p. 740). Their
     argument, that transaction cost economics "is inadequate for explaining simultaneously different
     entry modes because . . . asset specificity . . . [is] largely the same the world over" (p. 740) assumes
     that the governance level operates independently of the institutional environment under a
     transaction cost set-up. This is mistaken.
20   I borrow the term "rational spirit" from Kenneth Arrow (1974, p. 16). The rational spirit
     approach holds that there is a *logic* to organization and that this logic is mainly discerned by the
     relentless application of economic reasoning (subject, however, to cognitive constraints). The
     rational spirit approach is akin to but somewhat weaker (in that it eschews stronger forms of
     utility maximization) than the "rational choice" approach associated with James Coleman (1990).

References

Alchian, Armen (1961) *Some Economics of Property*. RAND D-2316 (Santa Monica, CA: RAND
     Corporation).
Alchian, Armen, and Susan Woodward (1987) "Reflections on the Theory of the Firm." *Journal of
     Institutional and Theoretical Economics*, 143 (March): 110–36.
Arrow, Kenneth (1974) *The Limits of Organization* (New York: W. W. Norton).
Arthur, Brian (1990) "Positive Feedbacks in the Economy." *Scientific American*, February, pp. 92–9.
Axelrod, Robert (1984) *The Evolution of Cooperation* (New York: Basic Books).
Bain, Joe (1956) *Barriers to New Competition* (Cambridge, MA: Harvard University Press).
Barnard, Chester (1938) *The Functions of the Executive* (Cambridge, MA: Harvard University Press).
Barnett, W., and G. Carroll (1993) "How Institutional Constraints Affected the Organization of
     the Early American Telephone Industry." *Journal of Law, Economics, and Organization*, 9 (April):
     98–126.
Baron, J., and M. Hannan (1992) "The Impact of Economics on Contemporary Sociology." Unpub-
     lished manuscript.
Bergson, Abram (1948) "Socialist Economics." In Howard Ellis (ed.), *Survey of Contemporary
     Economies* (Philadelphia: Blakiston) pp. 430–58.
Bonin, John, and Louis Putterman (1987) *Economics of Cooperation and Labor Managed Economies*
     (Cambridge: Cambridge University Press).
Bowles, S. and Gintis, H. (1993) "The Revenge of Homo Economicus: Contested Exchange and the
     Revival of Political Economy." *Journal of Economic Perspectives*, 7 (Winter): 83–102.
Bridgeman, Percy (1955) *Reflections of a Physicist*, 2nd edn. (New York: Philosophical Library).
Bromley, Daniel (1989) *Economic Interests and Institutions* (New York: Basil Blackwell).
Buxbaum, Richard M. (1985) "Modification and Adaptation of Contracts: American Legal Develop-
     ments." *Studies in Transnational Economic Law*, 3: 31–54.
Carroll, G., and J. R. Harrison (1992) "Chance and Rationality in Organizational Evolution."
     Unpublished manuscript.

Coase, R. H. (1959) "The Federal Communications Commission." *Journal of Law and Economics*, 2 (October): 1–40.

Coase, R. H. (1960) "The Problem of Social Costs." *Journal of Law and Economics*, 3 (October): 1–44.

Coase, R. H. (1984) "The New Institutional Economics." *Journal of Institutional and Theoretical Economics*, 140 (March): 229–31.

Coleman, James (1990) *The Foundations of Social Theory* (Cambridge, MA: Harvard University Press).

Commons, John R. (1924) *Legal Foundations of Capitalism* (New York: Macmillan).

Commons, John R. (1934) *Institutional Economics* (Madison: University of Wisconsin Press).

Coughlin, R. (1992) "Interdisciplinary Nature of Socio-Economics." Unpublished manuscript.

Crocker, K., and K. Reynolds (1993) "The Efficiency of Incomplete Contracts: an Empirical Analysis of Air Force Engine Procurement." *RAND Journal of Economics*, 24 (Spring): 126–46.

Crozier, M. (1964) *The Bureaucratic Phenomenon* (Chicago: University of Chicago Press).

Cyert, Richard M., and James G. March (1963) *A Behavioral Theory of the Firm* (Englewood Cliffs, NJ: Prentice-Hall).

Dasgupta, Partha (1988) "Trust as a Commodity." In Diego Gambetta (ed.), *Trust: Making and Breaking Cooperative Relations* (Oxford: Basil Blackwell) pp. 49–72.

David, Paul (1985) "Clio in the Economics of QWERTY." *American Economic Review*, 75 (May): 332–7.

David, Paul (1986) "Understanding the Economics of QWERTY: the Necessity of History." In W. N. Parker (ed.), *Economic History and the Modern Economist* (New York: Basil Blackwell) pp. 30–40.

David, Paul (1992) "Heroes, Herds, and Hysteresis in Technological History." *Industrial and Corporate Change*, 1: 129–80.

Davis, G. F., and W. W. Powell (1992) "Organization–Environment Relations." In M. Dunnette (ed.), *Handbook of Industrial and Organizational Psychology*, vol. 3 (New York: Consulting Psychologists Press) pp. 315–75.

Demsetz, Harold (1967) "Toward a Theory of Property Rights." *American Economic Review*, 57 (May): 347–59.

DiMaggio, P., and W. Powell (1991) "Introduction." In Walter Powell and Paul DiMaggio (eds.), *The New Institutionalism in Organizational Analysis* (Chicago: University of Chicago Press) pp. 1–38.

Dixit, A. (1980) "The Role of Investment in Entry Deterrence." *Economic Journal*, 90 (March): 95–106.

Farnsworth, Edward Allan (1968) "Disputes over Omissions in Contracts." *Columbia Law Review*, 68 (May): 860–91.

Frank, R. (1992) "Melding Sociology and Economics." *Journal of Economic Literature*, 30 (March): 147–70.

Friedland, R., and R. Alford (1991) "Bringing Society Back In: Symbols, Practices, and Institutional Contradictions." In Walter Powell and Paul DiMaggio (eds.), *The New Institutionalism in Organizational Analysis* (Chicago: University of Chicago Press) pp. 232–66.

Fuller, L. (1978) "The Forms and Limits of Adjudication," *Harvard Law Review*, 92: 353–409.

Furubotn, E., and S. Pejovich (1974) *The Economics of Property Rights* (Cambridge, MA: Ballinger).

Gouldner, A. W. (1954) *Industrial Bureaucracy* (Glencoe, IL: Free Press).

Granovetter, Mark (1985) "Economic Action and Social Structure: the Problem of Embeddedness." *American Journal of Sociology*, 91 (November): 481–501.

Granovetter, Mark (1988) "The Sociological and Economic Approaches to Labor Market Analysis." In George Farkas and Paula England (eds.), *Industries, Firms, and Jobs* (New York: Plenum) pp. 187–218.

Granovetter, Mark (1992) "Economic Institutions of Social Construction: a Framework for Analysis." *Acta Sociologica*, 35: 3–11.

Grossekettler, H. (1989) "On Designing and Economic Order: the Contributions of the Freiburg School." In Donald Walker (ed.), *Perspectives on the History of Economic Thought*, vol. 2 (Aldershot: Edward Elgar) pp. 38–84.

Hamilton, Gary, and Nicole Biggart (1988) "Market, Culture, and Authority." *American Journal of Sociology*, (supplement) 94: S52–S94.

Hansmann, H. (1988) "The Ownership of the Firm." *Journal of Law, Economics, and Organization*, 4 (Fall): 267–303.

Harberger, Arnold (1954) "Monopoly and Resource Allocation." *American Economic Review*, 44 (May): 77–87.

Hart, O. (1990) "An Economist's Perspective on the Theory of the Firm." In Oliver Williamson (ed.), *Organization Theory* (New York: Oxford University Press) pp. 154–71.

Heide, Jan, and George John (1988) "The Role of Dependence Balancing in Safeguarding Transaction-Specific Assets in Conventional Channels." *Journal of Marketing*, 52 (January): 20–35.

Helper, Susan, and David Levine (1992) "Long-Term Supplier Relations and Product-Market Structure." *Journal of Law, Economics, and Organization*, 8 (October): 561–81.

Hinds, Manuel (1990) "Issues in the Introduction of Market Forces in Eastern European Socialist Economies." *World Bank Report*, no. IDP-0057.

Horvat, Branko L (1991) "Review of Janos Kornai, the Road to a Free Economy." *Journal of Economic Behavior and Organization*, 15 (May): 408–10.

Hutchison, T. (1984) "Institutional Economics Old and New." *Journal of Institutional and Theoretical Economics*, 140 (March): 20–9.

Iwanek, M. (1991) "Issues of Institutions, Transformations and Ownership Changes in Poland." *Journal of Institutional and Theoretical Economics*, 147: 83–95.

Jensen, Michael (1983) "Organization Theory and Methodology." *Accounting Review*, 50 (April): 319–39.

Joskow, Paul (1985) "Vertical Integration and Long-Term Contracts." *Journal of Law, Economics, and Organization*, 1 (Spring): 33–80.

Joskow, Paul (1988) "Asset Specificity and the Structure of Vertical Relationships: Empirical Evidence." *Journal of Law, Economics, and Organization*, 4 (Spring): 95–117.

Klein, Benjamin, R. A. Crawford, and A. A. Alchian (1978) "Vertical Integration, Appropriable Rents, and the Competitive Contracting Process." *Journal of Law and Economics*, 21 (October): 297–326.

Klein, Benjamin, and Keith B. Leffler (1981) "The Role of Market Forces in Assuring Contractual Performance." *Journal of Political Economy*, 89 (August): 615–41.

Klein, Peter, and Howard Shelanski (1995) "Empirical Work in Transaction Cost Economics." *Journal of Law, Economics, and Organization*, 11 (October).

Koopmans, Tjalling (1957) *Three Essays on the State of Economic Science* (New York: McGraw-Hill).

Kornai, Janos (1990) "The Affinity between Ownership Forms and Coordination Mechanisms: the Common Experience of Reform in Socialist Countries." *Journal of Economic Perspectives*, 4 (Summer): 131–47.

Kreps, David (1990a) "Corporate Culture and Economic Theory." In James Alt and Kenneth Shepsle (eds.), *Perspectives on Positive Political Economy* (Cambridge: Cambridge University Press) pp. 90–143.

Kreps, David (1990b) *A Course in Microeconomic Theory* (Princeton, NJ: Princeton University Press).

Kreps, David (1990c) *Game Theory and Economic Modelling* (Oxford: Clarendon Press).

Kreps, David (1992) "(How) Can Game Theory Lead to a Unified Theory of Organization?" Unpublished manuscript.

Lange, Oskar (1938) "On the Theory of Economic Socialism." In Benjamin Lippincott (ed.), *On the Economic Theory of Socialism* (Minneapolis: University of Minnesota Press) pp. 55–143.

Liebowitz, Stanley J., and Stephen Margolis (1990) "The Fable of the Keys." *Journal of Law and Economics*, 33 (April): 1–26.

Machiavelli, Niccolò (1952) *The Prince* (New York: New American Library).

March, James (1988) *Decisions and Organizations* (Oxford: Basil Blackwell).

March, James, and Herbert A. Simon (1958) *Organizations* (New York: Wiley).

Marshak, Jacob (1968) "Economics of Inquiring, Communicating, Deciding." *American Economic Review*, 58 (May): 1–18.

Masten, Scott (1982) "Transaction Costs, Institutional Choice, and the Theory of the Firm." PhD diss., University of Pennsylvania.

Masten, Scott (1984) "The Organization of Production: Evidence from the Aerospace Industry." *Journal of Law and Economics*, 27 (October): 403–18.

Matthews, R. C. O. (1986) "The Economics of Institutions and the Sources of Economic Growth." *Economic Journal*, 96 (December): 903–18.

McCain, Roger (1977) "On the Optimal Financial Environment for Worker Cooperatives." *Zeitschrift für Nationalökonomie*, 37: 355–84.

McCullough, David (1992) *Truman* (New York: Simon & Schuster).

McGuire, P., M. Granovetter, and M. Schwartz (1992) "The Social Construction of Industry." Book prospectus.

Merton, Robert (1936) "The Unanticipated Consequences of Purposive Social Action." *American Sociological Review*, 1: 894–904.

Michels, Robert (1962) *Political Parties* (Glencoe, IL: Free Press).

Miles, R., and C. Snow (1992) "Causes of Failure in Network Organizations." *California Management Review*, 34 (Summer): 53–72.

Moe, Terry (1990a) "Political Institutions: the Neglected Side of the Story." *Journal of Law Economics, and Organization* (special issues), 6: 213–53.

Moe, Terry (1990b) "The Politics of Structural Choice: toward a Theory of Public Bureaucracy." In Oliver Williamson (ed.), *Organization Theory* (New York: Oxford University Press) pp. 116–53.

Mokyr, Joel (1990) *The Lever of Riches* (New York: Oxford University Press).

Nelson, R., and S. G. Winter (1982) *An Evolutionary Theory of Economic Change* (Cambridge, MA: Harvard University Press).

Newell, A., and H. Simon (1972) *Human Problem Solving* (Englewood Cliffs, NJ: Prentice-Hall).

North, Douglass (1986) "The New Institutional Economics." *Journal of Theoretical and Institutional Economics*, 142: 230–7.

North, Douglass (1991) "Institutions." *Journal of Economic Perspectives*, 5 (Winter): 97–112.

Palay, Thomas (1984) "Comparative Institutional Economics: the Governance of Rail Freight Contracting." *Journal of Legal Studies*, 13 (June): 265–88.

Palay, Thomas (1985) "Avoiding Regulatory Constraints: the Use of Informal Contracts." *Journal of Law, Economics, and Organization*, 1 (Spring): 155–75.

Penrose, Edith (1959) *The Theory of Growth of the Firm* (New York: Wiley).

Perrow, Charles (1992) "Review of the New Competition." *Administrative Science Quarterly*, 37 (March): 162–6.

Polanyi, Michael (1962) *Personal Knowledge: Towards a Post-Critical Philosophy* (New York: Harper & Row).

Posner, Richard (1993) "The New Institutional Economics Meets Law and Economics." *Journal of Institutional and Theoretical Economics*, 149 (March): 73–87.

Putterman, Louis (1984) "On Some Recent Explanations of Why Capital Hires Labor." *Economic Inquiry*, 22: 171–87.

Scherer, F. M. (1970) *Industrial Market Structure and Economic Performance* (Chicago: Rand McNally).

Schumpeter, Joseph A. (1942) *Capitalism, Socialism, and Democracy* (New York: Harper & Row).

Schumpeter, Joseph A. (1947) "The Creative Response in Economic History." *Journal of Economic History*, 7 (November): 149–59.

Scott, W. Richard (1992) "Institutions and Organizations: toward a Theoretical Synthesis." Unpublished manuscript.

Selznick, Philip (1957) *Leadership in Administration* (New York: Harper & Row).

Shapiro, Carl (1989) "The Theory of Business Strategy." *Rand Journal of Economics*, 20 (Spring): 125–37.

Simon, Herbert (1957) *Administrative Behavior*, 2nd edn. (New York: Macmillan).

Simon, Herbert (1978) "Rationality as Process and as Product of Thought." *American Economic Review*, 68 (May): 1–16.

Simon, Herbert (1983) *Reason in Human Affairs*. Stanford, CA: Stanford University Press.

Simon, Herbert (1985) "Human Nature in Politics: the Dialogue of Psychology with Political Science." *American Political Science Review*, 79: 293–304.

Stigler, G. J. (1983) Comments in Edmund W. Kitch (ed.), "The Fire of Truth: a Remembrance of Law and Economics at Chicago, 1932–1970." *Journal of Law and Economics*, 26 (April): 163–234.

Sundaram, A., and J. S. Black (1992) "The Environment and Internal Organization of Multinational Enterprise." *Academy of Management Review*, 17 (October): 729–57.

Swedberg, Richard (1987) "Economic Sociology: Past and Present." *Current Sociology*, 35: 1–221.

Swedberg, Richard (1990) *Economics and Sociology: On Redefining Their Boundaries* (Princeton, NJ: Princeton University Press).

Swedberg, Richard (1991) "Major Traditions of Economic Sociology." *Annual Review of Sociology*, 17: 251–76.

Teece, David J. (1986) "Profiting from Technological Innovation." *Research Policy*, 15 (December): 285–305.

Teece, David J., Richard Rumelt, Giovanni Dosi, and Sidney Winter (1992) "Understanding Corporate Coherence: Theory and Evidence." CCC Working Paper no. 92–6, University of California, Berkeley.

Van de Ven, A. (1993) "The Institutional Theory of John R. Commons: a Review and Commentary." *Academy of Management Review*, 18 (January): 139–52.

Waldrop, M. M. (1992) *Complexity* (New York: Simon & Schuster).

Weick, Karl E. (1977) "Re-Punctuating the Problem." In Paul S. Goodman and Johannes M. Penning (eds.), *New Perspectives on Organizational Effectiveness* (San Francisco: Jossey-Bass) pp. 193–225.

Wernerfelt, B. (1984) "A Resource-Based View of the Firm." *Strategic Management Journal*, 5: 171–80.

Williamson, Oliver E. (1968) "Economies as an Antitrust Defense: the Welfare Tradeoffs." *American Economic Review*, 58 (March): 18–35.

Williamson, Oliver E. (1975) *Markets and Hierarchies: Analysis and Antitrust Implications* (New York: Free Press).

Williamson, Oliver E. (1981) "The Economics of Organization: the Transaction Cost Approach." *American Journal of Sociology*, 87 (November): 548–77.

Williamson, Oliver E. (1983) "Credible Commitments: Using Hostages to Support Exchange." *American Economic Review*, 73 (September): 519–40.

Williamson, Oliver E. (1985) *The Economic Institutions of Capitalism* (New York: Free Press).

Williamson, Oliver E. (1986) "A Microanalytic Assessment of 'the Share Economy'." *Yale Law Journal*, 95: 627–37.

Williamson, Oliver E. (1988) "The Logic of Economic Organization." *Journal of Law, Economics, and Organization*, 4 (Spring): 65–93.

Williamson, Oliver E. (1989) "International Economic Organization." In Oliver E. Williamson, Sven Erik Sjostrand, and Jan Johanson (eds.), *Perspectives on the Economics of Organization* (Lund: Lund University Press) pp. 7–48.

Williamson, Oliver E. (1991a) "Comparative Economic Organization: the Analysis of Discrete Structural Alternatives." *Administrative Science Quarterly*, 36 (June): 269–96.

Williamson, Oliver E. (1991b) "Economic Institutions: Spontaneous and Intentional Governance." *Journal of Law, Economics, and Organization*, 7 (special issue): 159–87.

Williamson, Oliver E. (1993) "Transaction Cost Economics and Organization Theory." *Institutional and Corporate Change*, 2: 107–56.

Zald, Mayer (1987) "Review Essay: the New Institutional Economics." *American Journal of Sociology*, 93 (November): 701–8.

FIVE

The Role of Institutions in the Revival of Trade: the Law Merchant, Private Judges, and the Champagne Fairs

PAUL R. MILGROM, DOUGLASS C. NORTH, AND BARRY R. WEINGAST*

Source: From *Economics and Politics* (1990), 2: 1–23.

How can people promote the trust necessary for efficient exchange when individuals have short run temptations to cheat? The same question arises whether the traders are legislators swapping votes, medieval merchants exchanging goods, or modern businesspeople trading promises about future deliveries. In each of these situations, one of the important ways in which individuals ensure one another's honest behavior is by establishing a continuing relationship. In the language of economics, if the relationship itself is a valuable asset that a party could lose by dishonest behavior, then the relationship serves as a *bond*: a trader would be unwilling to surrender this bond unless the gain from dishonest behavior was large.

Variants on this basic idea are found throughout the literatures of economics (Klein and Leffler, 1981; Shapiro, 1983; Shapiro and Stiglitz, 1984), politics (Axelrod, 1984, 1986; Calvert, 1986) and game theory (Abreu, 1988; Aumann, 1985; Fudenberg and Maskin, 1986). Even in a community in which any particular pair of people meet rarely, it is still possible (as we show) for an individual's reputation in the group as a whole to serve as a bond for his good and honest behavior toward each individual member. This illustrates the important fact that a reputation system may sometimes work only when it encompasses sufficiently many traders and trades, that is, there are economies of scale and scope in reputation systems.

These conclusions about the potential effectiveness of a reputation system, however, leave us with a puzzle: if informal arrangements based on reputations can effectively bond good behavior, then what is the role of formal institutions in helping to support honest exchange? The legal apparatus for enforcing business contracts in many ages and many parts of the world, the suppliers' organizations that negotiate contracting patterns among modern Japanese firms, the complex institutional structure that facilitates agreements among US Congressmen,[1] the notaries that recorded agreements in the Italian city-states in the middle ages, and the organization of international trade via the Champagne Fairs are all examples of institutionalized arrangements to support trade and contracting. All involve the creation of specialized roles which would not be necessary if reputations alone could be an adequate bond for trade. But, why can't a simple system of reputations motivate honest trade in these various settings? And, what role do formal institutions play when simple reputational mechanisms fail?

We embed our study of these questions in the time of the revival of trade in Europe during the early middle ages. At that time, without the benefit of state enforcement of contracts or an established body of commercial law, merchants evolved their own private code of laws (the *Law Merchant*) with disputes adjudicated by a judge who might be a local official or a private merchant. While hearings were held to resolve disputes under the code, the judges had only limited powers to enforce judgments against merchants from distant places. For example, if a dispute arose after the conclusion of the Champagne Fair about the quality of the goods delivered or if agreements made at the Fair for future delivery or for acceptance of future delivery were not honored, no physical sanction or seizure of goods could then be applied.

The evolution and survival for a considerable period of a system of private adjudication raises both particular versions of our general questions and new questions about the details of the mechanism. What was the purpose of the private adjudication system? Was it a substitute for the reputation mechanism that had worked effectively in earlier periods (Greif, 1989)? Also, if there was no state to enforce judgments, how did they have any effect? How could a system of adjudication function without substantial police powers?

The practice and evolution of the Law Merchant in medieval Europe was so rich and varied that no single model can hope to capture all the relevant variations and details. Our simple model is intended to represent certain universal incentive problems that any successful system would have to solve. It abstracts from many of the interesting variations that are found across time and space as well as from other general problems, such as the spatial diversion of traders and trading centers and the interactions among competing trading systems.

We begin in section 1 with a discussion of the medieval Law Merchant and related institutions. We set the theoretical context for our analysis in section 2. It is well known, as we have explained above, that in long-term, frequent bilateral exchange, the value of the relationship itself may serve as an adequate bond to ensure honest behavior and promote trust between the parties. We argue in section 2 that even if no pair of traders come together frequently, if each individual trades frequently enough within the community of traders, then transferable reputations for honesty can serve as an adequate bond for honest behavior *if members of the trading community can be kept informed about each other's past behavior*. Well-informed traders could boycott those who have violated community norms of honesty, only if they knew who the violators were. It is the costliness of generating and communicating information – rather than the infrequency of trade in any particular bilateral relationship – that, we argue, is the problem that the system of private enforcement was designed to overcome.

In section 3, we introduce our basic model of a system of private enforcement and develop our core thesis that the role of the judges in the system, far from being substitutes for the reputation mechanism, is to make the reputation system more effective as a means of promoting honest trade. The formal system is more complex than the simple informal system of reputations that preceded it, but that was a natural outcome of the growing extent of trade. In a large community, we argue, it would be too costly to keep everyone informed about what transpires in all trading relationships, as a simple reputation system might require. So the system of private judges is designed to promote private resolution of disputes and otherwise to transmit *just enough* information to the right people in the right circumstances to enable the reputation mechanism to function effectively for enforcement. In order to succeed, such a system must solve a number of interconnected incentive problems: individual members of the community must be induced to behave honestly, to boycott those who have behaved dishonestly, to keep informed about who has been dishonest, to provide evidence against those who have cheated, and to honor the decisions of the judges. All of these problems can be resolved by the system if certain institutional constraints are satisfied, as we show in section 3. Briefly, the costs of making queries, providing evidence, adjudicating disputes, and making transfer payments must not be too high relative to the frequency and profitability of trade if the system is to function successfully.

Intuitively, the system of private judges accomplishes its objectives by *bundling* the services which are valuable to the individual trader with services that are valuable to the community, so that a trader pursuing his individual interest serves the community's interest as well. Unless a trader makes appropriate queries, he cannot use the system to resolve disputes. The requirement that the traders make queries provides an opportunity for the judge to collect payments for his services even if no actual disputes arise. As applied to the Champagne Fairs, the local lord or his agents could appoint honest judges, register transactions, and tax them.

In section 4, we make a brief digression to assess how *efficiently* the system of private judges accomplishes its task. We argue that no system can restore the effectiveness of the community reputation mechanism without incurring costs that are qualitatively similar to those incurred by the system of private judges, and moreover that the latter system seems to have been designed in a way that kept these transaction costs low.

Our analysis in section 3 gives the judge a passive role only. In section 5, we study the possibility that the judge may threaten to sully the reputations of honest traders unless they pay bribes. We show how the system can survive some such threats, though we do not attempt a comprehensive evaluation of all the kinds of bribes and extortion that might be tried in such a system.

Concluding remarks, relating our model to a broader institutional perspective, are given in section 6.

1   The Medieval Law Merchant

The history of long-distance trade in medieval and early modern Europe is the story of sequentially more complex organization that eventually led to the "Rise of the Western World". In order to capture the gains associated with geographic specialization, a system had to be established that lowered information costs and provided for the enforcement of agreements across space and time. Prior to the revival of trade in the early middle ages, few institutions underpinned commercial activity; there was no state to enforce contracts, let alone to protect merchants from pirates and brigands. In contrast, modern Western economies possess highly specialized systems of enforcing contracts and protecting merchants, resulting in widespread geographic specialization and impersonal exchange. The story of this evolution has been told elsewhere (e.g., Lopez, 1976; North and Thomas, 1973). Our purpose in this section is to suggest the outlines of an important step in this evolution, namely the early development of commercial law prior to the rise of large-scale third-party enforcement of legal codes by the nation-state.

A large number of problems had to be resolved in order to support the expansion of trade. First, as trading communities grew larger, it became harder within each community for merchants to monitor one another's behavior. New institutions were required to mitigate the types of cheating afforded by the new situation. Second, as trade grew among different regions, institutions were needed to prevent reneging by merchants who might cheat in one location, never to be seen again.

In response to these problems, a host of institutions arose and evolved over time. Towns with their own governments became homes for merchants who developed their own law separate from the traditional feudal order (Pirenne, 1925; Rorig, 1967). Merchant guilds arose to provide protection to foreign merchants away from their homes, but also protection to local merchants against fly-by-night foreign merchants who might never be seen again (DeRoover, 1963; Thrupp, 1948). Key to understanding the ability of merchants from widely varying regions to enforce contracts was the evolution of the *Lex Mercatoria* or Law Merchant – the legal codes governing commercial transactions and administered by private judges drawn from the commercial ranks. While practice varied across time and space, by the end of the eleventh century, the Law Merchant came to govern most commercial transactions in Europe, providing a uniform set of standards across large numbers of locations (Benson, 1989). It thereby provided a means for reducing the uncertainty associated with variations in local practices and limited the ability of localities to discriminate against alien merchants (Berman, 1983; Trakman, 1983). Thus, "commercial law can be conceived of as coordinating the self-interested actions of merchants, but perhaps an equally valuable insight is gained by *viewing it as coordinating the actions of people with limited knowledge and trust*" (Benson, 1989, p. 648; emphasis added).

While the governments of towns supported the development of markets and were intimately involved in developing merchant law (Pirenne, 1925; Rorig, 1967), they often could not provide merchants protection outside their immediate area.[2] Nor could they enforce judgments against foreign merchants who had left town prior to a case being heard. Thus, merchant law developed prior to the rise of a geographically extensive nation-state. But this raises a key problem in the theory of enforcement, for what made these judgments credible if they were not backed up by the state? Ostracism played an important role here, for merchants who failed to abide by the decisions of the judges would not be merchants for long (Benson, 1989; DeRoover, 1963; Trakman, 1983).

The Law Merchant and related legal codes evolved considerably over time. In addition to providing a court of law especially suited for merchants, it fostered significant legal developments that reduced the transaction costs of exchange (North, 1990, chapter 13). As agency relationships became common – whether between partners in different locations or between a sedentary merchant who financed a traveling one – a new set of rules governing these agreements was required. The same also held for the new practices of credit agreements and insurance. Here, we note the development of law covering agency relations (DeRoover, 1963; Greif, 1989), bills of exchange, and insurance (North, 1990, chapter 13).

The benefits of all these developments, however, could only be enjoyed as long as merchants obeyed the Law Merchant. Moreover, since disputes arise even among honest merchants, there needed to be a system for hearing and settling these disputes. To see how these feats of coordination might have been accomplished, we develop a game theoretic model of the judicial enforcement system – a model inspired by the Law Merchant and by the Champagne Fairs. The latter played a central role in trade in the twelfth and thirteenth centuries (DeRoover, 1963; North and Thomas, 1973; Verlinden, 1963), and included a legal system in which merchants could bring grievances against their trading partners. However, it is not clear why such a system would be effective. What prevents a merchant from cheating by supplying lower quality goods than promised, and then leaving the Fairs before being detected? In these circumstances the cheated merchant might be able to get a judgment against his supplier, but what good would it do if the supplier never returned to the Fairs? Perhaps ostracism by the other merchants might be an effective way to enforce the payment of judgments. However, if that is so, why was a legal system needed at all?

Another part of the inspiration for our formal model is the system of notaries that was widely used to register the existence of certain types of contracts and obligations. Typically, notaries were used for long-term contracts such as those for apprenticeships, sales of land, and partnerships (Lopez and Raymond, 1955). The extensive use of notaries in certain areas to register agreements suggests that reputation via word of mouth alone was insufficient to support honest behavior and that a third party without any binding authority to enforce obligations was nonetheless quite valuable for promoting honest exchange.

2   Community Enforcement without Institutions

With the exception of barter transactions, in which physical commodities are exchanged on the spot, virtually all economic transactions leave open the possibility of cheating. In the Champagne Fairs, where merchants brought samples of their goods to trade, the quantities they brought were not always sufficient to supply all the potential demand. Then, the merchants sometimes exchanged promises – to deliver goods of like quality at a particular time and place, or to make payment in a certain form. Promises, however, can be broken.

To represent the idea that cheating may be profitable in a simple exchange, we use the Prisoners' Dilemma (PD) game as our model of a single exchange transaction. Although this PD model is too simple to portray the richness of even simple contracts, it has the advantage that it is very well known and its characteristics in the absence of institutions have been thoroughly studied, so that the incremental contribution made by the Law Merchant system will be quite clear. Moreover, the PD game represents in an uncluttered way the basic facts that traders have opportunities and temptations to cheat and that there are gains possible if the traders can suppress these temptations and find a way to cooperate.

The Prisoners' Dilemma game that we employ is shown below, where $\alpha > 1$ and $\alpha - \beta < 2$.

	Honest	Cheat
Honest	1, 1	$-\beta$, α
Cheat	α, $-\beta$	0, 0

Each player can choose to play one of two strategies: Honest or Cheat. As is well known, Honest behavior maximizes the total profits of the two parties. However, a trader profits by cheating an honest partner ($\alpha > 1$) even though cheating imposes a still larger loss on his honest partner ($1 - (-\beta) > \alpha - 1$).

It is clear that if this game is played only once, it is in each player's separate interest to play Cheat, since that play maximizes the player's individual utility regardless of the play chosen by the competitor. Consequently, the only *Nash equilibrium* of the game is for both to play Cheat. Then both are worse off than if they could somehow agree to play Honest.

Now suppose that the players trade repeatedly. Let a_{it} represent the action taken by player i in period t; let $\pi_i(a_{1t}, a_{2t})$ represent the resulting payoff earned by player i in period t; and let δ be the discount factor applied to compute the present value of a stream of payoffs. If trade is frequent, then δ is close to one; if trade occurs only once (or is quite infrequent), then δ is (close to) zero. A player's time weighted average payoff over the whole sequence of trades is given by:

$$\bar{\pi}_i - (1 - \delta) \sum_{t=0}^{\infty} \delta^t \pi_i(a_{1t}, a_{2t}). \tag{1}$$

In this repeated trading relationship, if the players can condition their actions in each period on what has transpired in the past, then they have an instrument to reward past honest behavior and to punish cheating. For the PD game, Axelrod (1984) has shown that for δ close enough to 1 there is a Nash equilibrium in which each player adopts the Tit-for-Tat (TFT) strategy – according to which the player chooses honest play at $t = 0$ and for any later t plays whatever his partner played in the immediately preceding period (that is, at $t - 1$).

The central idea that frequent trading with the same partner, or "clientization," makes it possible to find an equilibrium with efficient trading applies even for more refined solution concepts, such as subgame perfect equilibrium. It has been shown to hold for virtually all repeated games, regardless of the number of players, the number of strategies available to each, or the magnitudes of the payoffs (Fudenberg and Maskin, 1986). What is less fully appreciated is that the same conclusion holds in a community of traders in which players change partners often and cheaters may never again have to face the cheated partner – provided that information about the behavior of the traders is widely shared in the community.

To see this, suppose that there are N traders and that there is some rule M that matches them at each stage. Let h_t be the history of trade through date t and let $M(h_t, i)$ be the identity of the trader who is matched with trader i at date $t + 1$ at history h_t. Consider the Adjusted Tit-for-Tat (ATFT) strategy according to which player i plays Honest at date 0 and then plays Cheat at date $t + 1$ if two conditions hold: (1) i made the play at date t that was specified by his equilibrium strategy, and (2) $M(h_t, i)$ did not make the play at date t that was specified by his equilibrium strategy. If either condition fails, then the ATFT strategy calls for i to play Honest. The ATFT strategy formalizes the idea that a trader who cheats will be punished by the next merchant he meets if that merchant is honest, even if that merchant is not the one who was cheated.

One might wonder what reason the merchant who was not cheated has to carry out the punishment. Within the PD model, the answer is twofold: first, punishing the cheater is directly profitable, because the punishment is delivered by playing Cheat. Second – and this is the reason that applies even in more general models – a merchant who fails to deliver a punishment, say by participating in a boycott, when he is supposed to do so is himself subject to punishment by the community of merchants. The community, in its turn, will carry out the punishment, for the very same reasons. Theorem 1 below verifies that this system is in fact sometimes an equilibrium, that is, no merchant could gain at any time by deviating from its rules provided he expects other merchants to adhere to the rules in all future play.

THEOREM 1   *For δ near enough to one – specifically if*

$$\delta \geq \text{Max}[\beta/(1 + \beta), (\alpha - 1)/(1 + \beta)] \tag{2}$$

– the Adjusted Tit-for-Tat strategies are a subgame perfect equilibrium in the community trading game for any *matching rule* M.

PROOF   By the Optimality Principle of dynamic programming, it suffices to show that there is no point at which player i can make a one-time play different from the equilibrium play that raises his total payoff. By inspection of the strategies, it is clear that the player may face one of four decision situations according to whether condition (1) only is satisfied, condition (2) only is satisfied, or both or neither of (1) and (2) are satisfied. If just condition (1) or condition (2) (not both) is satisfied, then a current period deviation by player i is unprofitable if:

$$(1 - \delta)[\alpha - \delta\beta] + \delta^2 \cdot 1 \leq (1 - \delta) \cdot 1 + \delta \cdot 1 \tag{3}$$

which holds if and only if $\delta \geq (\alpha - 1)/(1 + \beta)$. If (1) and (2) are both satisfied, deviation is unprofitable if:

$$(1 - \delta)[0 - \delta\beta] + \delta^2 \cdot 1 \leq (1 - \delta) \cdot \alpha + \delta \cdot 1 \tag{4}$$

and this is satisfied for all $\delta \geq 0$. If neither (1) nor (2) is satisfied, then deviation is unprofitable if:

$$(1 - \delta)[0 - \delta\beta] + \delta^2 \cdot 1 \leq -(1 - \delta) \cdot \beta + \delta \cdot 1 \tag{5}$$

which holds if and only if $\delta \geq \beta/(1 + \beta)$.   □

Our formal analysis verifies that it is not necessary for any pair of traders to interact frequently – that is, for traders to establish client relationship – in order for the boycott mechanism to be effective. However, that simple conclusion relies on the condition that the members of the community are well enough informed to know whom to boycott. This condition is probably satisfied in some communities, but it is more problematical in others. For example, merchants engaged in long-distance trade could not be expected to know, of their own knowledge, whether another pair of merchants had honored their mutual obligations. Unless social and economic institutions developed to fill in the knowledge gap or unless other means of enforcement were established, honest behavior in a community of self-interested traders could not be maintained. Our model in the next section shows how a particular institution could have resolved this problem.

3   The Law Merchant Enforcement System

We now consider in more detail a model of trade in which outsiders cannot readily observe what has transpired in a given bilateral trade. While "disputes" may arise in which one party accuses the other of cheating, none of the other players has a method of freely verifying the parties' claims. Even if the dispute itself can be observed by others, they cannot costlessly determine whether cheating by one has actually occurred or whether the other is opportunistically claiming that it did.

In our model, we suppose that choices in each bilateral exchange are known only to the trading pair, so that each individual possesses direct information *solely about his own past trading experience.*[3] To capture the idea that traders know little of their partners' past trading behavior, we use an extreme model of matching due to Townsend (1981). In Townsend's matching model, there is an infinity of traders indexed by ij where $i = 1$ or 2 and j is an integer which may be positive or negative. At period t, trader $1j$ is matched with trader 2, $j + t$.[4] In particular, no two traders ever meet twice and no trader's behavior can directly or indirectly influence the behavior of his future trading partners. In the absence of institutions, players possess *no information* about their current partner's past behavior.

Under these conditions, the opportunities available to a player in any period cannot depend in any way on his past behavior. Strategies such as TFT and ATFT become ineffective. So, in our Prisoners' Dilemma game, it can never be in the players' interest to be honest. We have established the following:

THEOREM 2   *In the incomplete information Prisoners' Dilemma with the Townsend matching rule, the outcome at any Nash equilibrium is that each trader plays Cheat at every opportunity.*[5]

With limited information about the past behavior of trading partners and no institution to compensate, there are no incentives for honest behavior. It is evident that incentives could be restored by introducing an institution that provides full information to each trader about how each other has behaved. Such an institution, however, would be costly to operate. Moreover, efficient trade does not require that every trader know the full history of the behavior of each other trader. For example, in the ATFT strategy considered in the preceding section, a trader need only know his own history of behavior and whether his partner has defected in the immediately preceding period to determine his own current behavior. One part of the problem is to arrange that the traders are *adequately* well informed so that they can sanction a Cheater when that is required.

However, there is a second problem that the institutions must overcome: Traders may not find it in their individual interests to participate in punishing those who cheat. As one simple example, if trade is expected to be profitable, a trader will be reluctant to engage in a trade boycott. The institutions must be designed both to keep the traders adequately informed of their responsibilities and to motivate them to do their duties.

In the model we develop below, this second problem has multiple aspects. First, traders must be motivated to execute sanctions against Cheaters when that is a personally costly activity. Second, traders must be motivated to keep well enough informed to know when sanctions are required, even though information-gathering activities may be personally costly and difficult to monitor. In effect, one who keeps informed about who should be punished for past transgressions is supplying a public good; he deters the traders from cheating against *others*. Moreover, in our model, no other trader except his current partner will ever know if a trader does not check his partner's past history, so the trader could avoid supplying the public good without facing any sanction from future traders. Third, traders who are cheated must be motivated to document the episode, even though providing documentation may be personally costly. After all, from the cheated trader's perspective, what's lost is lost, and there may be little point in "throwing good money after bad." But if players who are cheated are unwilling to invest in informing their neighbors, then, just as surely as if the neighbors are unwilling to invest in being informed, the Cheater will profit from his action and Honest trade will suffer. These are the problems that the trading institution in our model must solve.

The institution that we model as the resolution of these problems is based on the presence of a specialized actor – a "judge" or "law merchant" (LM) who serves both as a repository of information and as an adjudicator of disputes. The core version of our model is based on the following assumptions. After any exchange, each party can accuse the other of cheating and appeal to the LM. Any dispute appealed to the LM is perfectly and honestly adjudicated at cost C to the plaintiff. (We consider the case of a dishonest LM later.) The LM's pronouncements include the ability to award damages if the defendant is found to have cheated the plaintiff. However, payment of the damage award is *voluntary* in the sense that there is no state to enforce payment. Finally, we assume that any party can visit the LM prior to finalizing a contract. At that time, for a cost of Q, the party can *query* the LM for the records of previous judgments about any other player. Without querying the LM, players have *no* information about their current partners' trading history.

By structuring this sequence of events around the basic trade transaction, we create an "extended" stage game called the *LM system stage game* with the following sequence of play:

(a) Players may query the LM about their current partner at utility cost $Q > 0$. In response to a query, the LM reports to the traders whether a party has any "unpaid judgments." Whatever transpires at this stage becomes common knowledge among the LM and the two partners.

(b) The two traders play the (Prisoners' Dilemma) game and learn the outcome.

(c) Either may appeal to the LM at personal cost $C > 0$, but only if he has queried the LM.

(d) If either party makes an appeal, then the LM awards a judgment, J, to the plaintiff if he has been Honest and his trading partner has Cheated (we call this a *valid appeal*); otherwise, no award is made.

(e) If a judgment J is awarded, the defendant may pay it, at personal cost $f(J)$, or he may refuse to pay, at cost zero.

(f) Any unpaid judgments are recorded by the LM and become part of the LM's permanent record.

The players' utilities for the extended stage game are determined as the sum of the payments received less those made. For example, a player who queries, plays Honest, is Cheated, and appeals, receives $-Q - \beta + -CJ$ if the other party pays the judgment and $-Q - \beta - C$ if he does not.

The function $f: \mathcal{R}^+ \to \mathcal{R}^+$ represents the utility cost of paying a given judgment. We naturally assume that f is increasing and continuous. Thus, the greater the size of the judgment, the greater the cost to the defendant. We also assume that $f(x) \geq x$: the cost of paying a judgment is never less than the judgment itself. This excludes the possibility that the payment of judgments adds to the total utility of the players.

The desired behavior of the parties in various contingencies under the Law Merchant system is fully described by the *Law Merchant System Strategy* (LMSS) as follows.

At substage (a), a trader queries the Law Merchant if he has no unpaid judgments on record, but not otherwise.

At substage (b), if either player has failed to query the Law Merchant or if the query establishes that at least one player has an outstanding judgment, then both traders play Cheat (which we may interpret as a refusal by the honest trader to trade); otherwise, both play Honest.

At substage (c), if both parties queried at substage (a) and exactly one of the two players Cheated at substage (b), then the victim appeals to the LM; otherwise, no appeal is filed.

At substage (d), if a valid appeal was filed, the LM awards damages of J to the aggrieved party.

At substage (e), the defendant pays the judgment J if and only if he has no other outstanding judgments.

THEOREM 3 *The Law Merchant System Strategy is a symmetric sequential equilibrium strategy of the LM system game if and only if the following inequality holds.*

$$(1 - Q)\delta/(1 - \delta) \geq f(J) \geq \max[(\alpha - 1), f(C)]. \tag{6}$$

If this condition is satisfied, then the average payoff per period for each player (at the equilibrium) is $1 - Q$.

REMARK The condition in Theorem 3 can be satisfied only if $1 - Q$ is positive (because the right-hand-side is at least $\alpha - 1 > 0$).

PROOF To establish that the LMSS is a symmetric sequential equilibrium strategy, we again appeal to the Optimality Principle of Dynamic Programming. If we show that there is no point at which a single change in the trader's current action only (followed by later adherence to the LMSS) can raise the trader's expected payoff at that point, then there is no point at which some more complicated deviation can be profitable, either.

In evaluating his expected payoffs, the player must make certain conjectures about what other players have done in the past in order to forecast what they will do in the future. To verify the equilibrium, we may assume that the trader believes that all other traders have played according to the LMSS in all past plays except those where the trader has actually observed a deviation. We may also assume that the trader believes that all others will adhere to the LMSS in all future plays. To derive the conditions under which the LMSS is an equilibrium strategy, we work backward through a typical extended stage game.

First, we check when it "pays to pay judgments," that is, under what conditions a player will find it more profitable to pay any judgment rendered against him than to refuse to pay. (We ignore the sunk portion of the payoff which is unaffected by later behavior.) Paying the judgment J yields an additional payoff of $-f(J)$ in the current period. In future periods, the player will spend Q to query the LM and earn a trading payoff of 1, for a total of $1 - Q$. In terms of lifetime average payoff, paying the judgment leads to $-(1 - \delta)f(J) + \delta(1 - Q)$. If the trader refuses to pay the judgment, then his current period payoff is zero and, given the system, his payoff is also zero in every subsequent period. Therefore, it "pays to pay judgments" if and only if $-(1 - \delta)f(J) + \delta(1 - Q) \geq 0$, or equivalently,

$$f(J) \leq (1 - Q)\delta/(1 - \delta). \tag{7}$$

Second, does it pay the victim to appeal at substage (c), incurring personal cost C? Given the strategies, the trader expects the judgment to be paid. So he will appeal if and only if $J \geq C$. It is convenient to write this condition as:

$$f(J) \geq f(C). \tag{8}$$

If there are no unpaid judgments and the LM has been queried, does it pay the trader to play Honest? If he does, then his current period payoff will be $1 - Q$. If he Cheats and later adheres to the strategy (which entails paying the judgment), then his payoff will be $-Q + \alpha - f(J)$. Equilibrium requires that the former is larger, that is:

$$f(J) \geq \alpha - 1. \tag{9}$$

Does it pay the trader otherwise to play Cheat? With the given strategy, his future opportunities do not depend on his play in this case, and Cheat always maximizes the payoffs for the current period, so the answer is that it does pay, regardless of parameter values.

Does it pay the players to query the LM if neither has an outstanding judgment? If a player does so, his current period payoff is expected to be $1 - Q$. If not, it will be zero. In both cases, his payoffs per period for subsequent periods are expected to be $1 - Q$. So, it pays if and only if

$$Q \leq 1. \tag{10}$$

However, condition (10) is redundant in view of conditions (7) and (9).

Does it pay a party with an outstanding judgment to query? No, because the party's expected payoff is $-Q$ if he queries and 0 if he does not.

Thus, regardless of the circumstances wrought by past play, there is no situation in which a one-time deviation from the Law Merchant System Strategy that is profitable for a trader provided that conditions (7)–(9) hold. These are the conditions summarized in formula (6). □

COROLLARY   There is a judgment amount J which makes the LMSS a symmetric sequential equilibrium strategy (that is, satisfying formula (6)) if and only if

$$(1 - Q)\delta/(1 - \delta) \geq \max[(\alpha - 1), f(C)]. \tag{11}$$

Conditions (7)–(10) show the relationship among the various parameters for the LM system to support the efficient cooperation. Each corresponds to one of the problems we described in introducing the model. Condition (7) requires that Cheating and then paying a judgment not be profitable; put simply, the judgment must be large enough to deter Cheating. Condition (8) requires that judgments exceed the cost of an appeal, that is, the judgment must also be large enough to encourage the injured party to appeal. Otherwise, information about Cheating will never reach the LM and Cheating will go unpunished. The two previous conditions require that the judgment be large enough, but condition (9) requires that it not be so large that the Cheater would refuse to pay, for then the injured party would not expect to collect, and so would find it unprofitable to appeal. Notice that the feasibility of satisfying all these conditions simultaneously depends on the technology of wealth transfer summarized by f. If the traders live at great distances from one another and if their principal asset holdings are illiquid (such as land and fixed capital, or reputation and family connections), then wealth transfers may be quite costly ($f(J)/J$ may be large) and the fines required by the LM system then will not work.

Finally, condition (10) requires that it be worthile for the traders to query the LM. In our model, this condition is implied by the others, but that need not be true for extensions of the model. If traders do not query the LM, then they will have insufficient information to administer punishments, so once again Cheating will go unpunished. The LM institution encourages queries by making them a condition for appealing to the LM, and, as we have seen, querying deters Cheating. At equilibrium, traders who fail to query are constantly Cheated by their trading partners.

If condition (6) fails, then the LMSS is not an equilibrium strategy. However, the condition is satisfied for a wide range of plausible parameter values. Table 5.1 gives some acceptable values for the parameters. In it, we assume that $f(x) = x/(1 - p)$ where p is the

Table 5.1   Sample Parameters for which the Law Merchant Strategy is a sequential equilibrium strategy

Transaction costs parameters			Temptation to Cheat	Discount factor	Penalty or judgment
Q	C	p	α	δ	J
0.50	0.5	50%	2.0	0.67	1.0
0.50	1.0	50%	3.0	0.80	2.0
0.33	3.0	50%	7.0	0.90	6.0

percentage of value that is lost when assets are transferred. The LMSS is an equilibrium strategy for some J with the given combinations of parameters and for any other combination with lower transaction costs (lower p, Q, and C), less temptation to cheat (lower α), and more frequent trade (higher δ). In the table, $J = C/(1 - p) = \alpha - 1$ is the judgment which is just sufficient to provide the incentives for not cheating and for complaining about being cheated.

For example, in the last line of table 5.1, Cheating is seven times more profitable than playing Honest at each current round, the cost of querying the LM consumes one-third of the profits of Honest ventures, the cost of complaining is three times the profits of the venture, and half of any assets transferred in settlement of a judgment are lost. The judgment itself is six times what the Cheater could expect to earn from Honest trade with his next partner (nine times net of transaction costs). Nevertheless, if the inter-trade discount factor is at least 0.9, the LM system is in equilibrium and supports honest behavior, filing of valid complaints, and payment of judgments.

4   Minimizing Transaction Costs

Theorem 3 shows that the LM system restores cooperation even when the players know little about their partners' histories. There are transaction costs necessary to maintain this system, however: that the average payoff per period is $1 - Q$ reflects the transaction cost of Q per period incurred by each trader to support the Law Merchant system.

Notice that the cost, C, of making and investigating a claim and the cost $f(J) - J$ of making the transfer do not appear in the expression for the average payoff. These costs do appear in condition (6): the Law Merchant system is not viable if the cost of making and investigating a claim or the cost of paying a judgment is too high, for then the traders cannot reasonably expect that the others will make claims and pay judgments when they should. However, once these costs are low enough that the threat to file claims with the Law Merchant is credible, they act only as a deterrent: these costs are never actually incurred at equilibrium in our model of the Law Merchant system.

Is the Law Merchant system the least expensive way to induce Honest behavior from rational traders at every stage? Theoretically, any institution that restores incentives for Honest trading by restoring the effectiveness of decentralized enforcement must inform a player when his partner has cheated in the past. If the temptation to Cheat is small and the value of continued trading is high, then this information need not be perfect, as in our model. So it may be possible to induce honest behavior using a less costly information system – one that costs only $q < Q$ to inform a trader adequately well – and correspondingly to increase the traders' average payoffs from $1 - Q$ to $1 - q$.[6] However, using imperfect information to economize on information costs calls merely for a refinement of the Law Merchant system – not for something fundamentally different. It is not possible to provide correct incentives without incurring some information cost of this kind and, as we have seen, the LM system avoids the unnecessary costs of dispute resolution and loss on transfers.

In operation, the Law Merchant system would appear to be a low-cost way to disseminate information, for two reasons. First, the LM system centralizes the information system so that, for information about any partner, a player need only go to one place. He need not incur costs trying (i) to establish who was his current partner's previous partner, and (ii) to find the partner to make the relevant inquiry. Second, for the Prisoners' Dilemma, it is not sufficient to know only one period's history, but several.[7] The LM system not only centralizes this information but provides it in a very simple form: all that needs to be communicated is whether there are any outstanding judgments. For large communities, locating each of one's partner's previous partners and asking them for information is likely to be more expensive than the centralized record-keeping system of the Law Merchant.

Given the lack of quantitative evidence about the full costs of running different kinds of institutions, it is not possible to write down a convincing formal model to establish that the LM system minimizes costs in the class of feasible institutions. What we can say confidently is that the *kind* of costs incurred by the LM system are inevitable if Honest trade is to be sustained in the face of self-interested behavior and that the system seems well designed to keep those costs as low as possible.

5　Dishonest Law Merchants

Our analysis in section 2 proceeded on the assumption that the Law Merchant has no independent interest in the outcome of his decision. In addition, he is diligent, honest, and fair.

One need not look far in history (or, for that matter, in the modern world) to see that judges are not always so perfect. Within our model, there are many small amendments that could be made to insert opportunities for bribery and extortion. Although we do not provide a systematic treatment of these, we shall give a brief development of one of them to emphasize the simple idea that the Law Merchant business is itself valuable and that LMs may wish to maintain their reputation for honesty and diligence in order to keep the business active.

The most obvious problem with this reputation-based account is that it seems to presume that a trader who is extorted by the Law Merchant can somehow make his injury widely known to the community of traders. It might be that the Law Merchant is a more sedentary merchant than the long-distance traders whom he serves, so that idea is perhaps not so far-fetched. Nevertheless, we shall argue that even if, in the spirit of our earlier analysis, there is no way for the trader to inform others about his injury, it may still be an equilibrium for the LM to behave honestly, due to the "client" incentives in the long-term relationship between the LM and each individual trader. More precisely, we will show that there is an equilibrium of the system in which every trader expects that if he pays a bribe he will be subjected to repeated attempts at extortion in the future; this dissuades the trader from paying any bribe. Then, a Law Merchant who commits to his threat to damage the reputation of a trader succeeds only in losing business, so he does not profit from making the threat.

To set the context for the formal extension, we modify the Law Merchant system stage game to regard the Law Merchant as a player. In the original version, the LM was allowed no choices, but let us nevertheless suppose that the LM earned a payoff of $2\epsilon > 0$ per contract, which is paid for as part of the $2Q$ that the parties spend to query the LM.

Next, we create a Modified Law Merchant System game in which our basic model is altered to allow the LM to solicit bribes. Initially, we consider only one kind of bribe – that extorted from a trader with no unpaid judgments by an LM who threatens to report falsely that there *are* unpaid judgments. Thus, we assume that before the traders make their queries, the LM may demand that one of the traders who has no unpaid judgment pay a bribe, $B \geq 0$. The amount B demanded is chosen by the LM. If the bribe is not paid and a query is made, the LM is committed to report falsely that the trader has an unpaid judgment.[8] The trader next decides whether to pay the bribe. The stage game then continues as previously described. When a bribe of B is paid, the LM's payoff is increased by B and the victim's payoff is reduced by an equal amount.[9]

Now consider the following variation of the Law Merchant System Strategy for the traders. If a player has no unpaid judgments and no bribe is solicited from him at the current stage, then he plays the LMSS as previously described. If the player has never before paid a bribe and a bribe is solicited, then he refuses to pay the bribe and does not query the LM in the current period. If the player has ever before paid a bribe, then he pays any bribe up to $\alpha - Q$ that is demanded of him. A player who has paid a bribe at the current round plays Cheat at that round and refuses to pay any judgment made against him. We call this specification the Extended Law Merchant System Strategy (ELMSS).

The Law Merchant's expected behavior is specified by the LM's Bribe Solicitation Strategy (BSS). If one of the present traders has no unpaid judgment but has previously paid a bribe, then the LM demands a payment of $\alpha - Q$. Otherwise, the LM does not demand any payment.

THEOREM 4   *If condition (6) holds and, in addition,*

$$\alpha \leq 1 + (1 - Q)(2\delta - 1)/(1 - \delta), \tag{12}$$

then there is a sequential equilibrium of the Modified Law Merchant System game in which each trader adopts the strategy ELMSS and the Law Merchant adopts the strategy BSS.

PROOF   Once again, we check that there is no contingency after which a one-time deviation by any player is profitable, when each player expects that the others have adhered to the strategy except where deviations have been explicitly observed, and each expects that all will adhere to it in the future. As before, we begin again from the last stage and work forward.

Consider a trader who has paid a bribe and cheated, and been assessed a judgment of $J > 0$. He expects a zero future payoff in each future period if he pays the judgment (because he will be extorted again and again). He expects the same zero payoff if he does not pay, since he will then have an unpaid judgment on his record. Since $-f(J) < 0$, he will find it most profitable to refuse to pay the judgment.

Having paid a bribe B, a trader expects to earn α this period and zero in the future if he cheats today, or 1 this period and zero in the future if he does not. Since $\alpha > 1$, cheating is most profitable.

Given that a player has paid a bribe before, if a bribe B is demanded today, then the profits from paying the bribe, querying, and cheating are expected to be $\alpha - Q - B$; not paying leads to profits of zero. Hence, it is at least as profitable to pay the bribe whenever $B \leq \alpha - Q$.

If a trader has paid a bribe before, the strategy specifies that he will pay any bribe up to $\alpha - Q$ in the current period. In this case, according to the strategies, no trader's play in future periods will depend on whether the LM demands a bribe or on the amount of the bribe, so his most profitable play is to demand $\alpha - Q$.

Suppose a trader has not paid a bribe before and a bribe, B, is demanded currently. If the trader pays the bribe then, according to the strategy, he will cheat and refuse to pay the judgment. The resulting payoff is $\alpha - B - Q$ in the current period and, as a trader with an unpaid judgment, zero in future periods. If the refuses to pay the bribe, then his expected payoff is zero in the current period and $1 - Q$ in subsequent periods. So, it is most profitable for him to refuse to pay if

$$(1 - \delta)(\alpha - B - Q) + \delta \cdot 0 \le (1 - \delta) \cdot 0 + \delta \cdot (1 - Q),$$

which is equivalent to condition (12).

Finally, when facing a trader who has never before paid a bribe, the LM expects that any demand for a bribe will be refused and that the trader will also not query in the current period, leading to a loss of revenues of ϵ, with no effect on play in future periods. Hence, it is most profitable for the LM not to demand any bribe in this case. □

Theorem 4 pertains to a model in which only one kind of dishonest behavior by the LM is possible. The problem of discouraging other kinds of dishonest behavior may require other strategies. From our preliminary analysis, it appears that the most difficult problem is to deter the LM from soliciting or accepting bribes from traders who have an unpaid judgment but wish to conceal that fact. By concealing the judgment, cheating, and refusing to pay the new judgment, the trader could "earn" $\alpha - Q$ and a portion of that might be offered as a bribe to the LM. As we add richness to the possibilities for cheating, it is natural to expect that the necessary institutions and strategies must respond in a correspondingly rich way.

6 Conclusion

We began our analysis by studying an environment in which private information about behavior in exchanges is a potential impediment to trade. Under complete information, even if meetings among particular pairs of traders are infrequent, informal norms of behavior are theoretically sufficient to police deviations. But when information is costly, the equilibrium may potentially break down and informal means may not be sufficient to police deviations.

The Law Merchant enforcement system that we have studied restores the equilibrium status of Honest behavior. It succeeds even though there is no state with police power and authority over a wide geographical realm to enforce contracts. Instead, the system works by making the reputation system of enforcement work better. The institutions we have studied provide people with the information they need to recognize those who have cheated, and it provides incentives for those who have been cheated to provide evidence of their injuries. Then, the reputation system itself provides the incentives for honest behavior and for payment by those who are found to have violated the code, and it encourages traders to boycott those who have flouted the system. Neither the reputation mechanism nor the institutions can be effective by themselves. They are complementary parts of a total system that works together to enforce honest behavior.

Our account of the Law Merchant system is, of course, incomplete. Once disputes came to be resolved in a centralized way, the merchants in Western Europe enhanced and refined their private legal code to serve the needs of the merchant trade – all prior to the rise of the nation-state. Without this code and the system for enforcement, trade among virtual strangers would have been much more cumbersome, or even impossible.[10] Remarkably, the Law Merchant institution appears to have been structured to support trade in a way that minimizes transaction costs, or at least incurs costs only in categories that are indispensable to any system that relies on boycotts as sanctions.

Our model is a stylization, not set in a particular locality at a particular date. Necessarily, then, it omits many important elements that some historians will argue are essential to understanding the institutions that are found there and then. However, our core contention that institutions sometimes arise to make reputation mechanisms more effective by communicating information seems almost beyond dispute. The Mishipora, described in the Hebrew Talmud, according to which those who failed to keep promises were punished by being publicly denounced; the use of the "hue and cry" to identify cheaters in medieval England; the famed "Scarlet Letter," described in Hawthorne's famous story; and the public stocks and pillories of seventeenth-century New England, which were sometimes used to punish errant local merchants, are all examples of institutions and practices in which a principal aim is to convey information to the community about who has violated its norms.

It is our contention that an enduring pattern of trade over a wide geographical area cannot be sustained if it is profitable for merchants to renege on promises or repudiate agreements. In the larger trading towns and cities of northern Europe in the tenth through thirteenth centuries, it was not possible for every merchant to know the reputations of all others, so extensive trade required the development of some system like the Law Merchant system to fill in the gap.

Many of the key characteristics of our model correspond to practices found at the Champagne Fairs. While merchants at the Fairs were not required to query prior to any contract, the institutions of the Fair provided this information in another manner. As noted above, the Fairs closely controlled entry and exit. A merchant could not enter the Fair without being in good standing with those who controlled entry, and any merchant caught cheating at the Fair would be incarcerated and brought to justice under the rules of the Fair. So anyone a merchant met at the Fair could be presumed to have a "good reputation" in precisely the sense of our model. It did not indicate that all free merchants had never cheated in the past; but it did indicate that anyone who had been convicted of cheating had made good on the judgment against him. Moreover, because merchants might disappear rather than pay their judgments, judges at the Fairs had to balance the size of their judgment so that the value of being able to attend future Fairs exceeded the award.

According to Verlinden (1963, p. 132): "At the end of the twelfth century and during the first half of the thirteenth, the Champagne Fairs were indeed the centre of international commercial activity of the western world." This is a long time for a single fair to maintain such dominance, but the Champagne Fair had two advantages over its potential competitors. First, it had an effective system for enforcing exchange contracts. Second, as we observed earlier, there are important economies of scope and scale in reputation mechanisms. Other, smaller fairs that tried to compete with the Champagne Fairs on an equal footing would have to contend with merchants who participated only long enough to make a profitable cheating transaction and then return to the Champagne Fairs where their participation rights were intact.

Despite this observation, it must be counted a weakness of the model that it does not fully account for trade outside of a single trading center. Even if the Law Merchant and related systems were effective underpinnings for local trade, how was information about a trader's dishonesty in one location transmitted to another? The model in this paper is too simple to handle this problem, but we hope to extend our approach to the institutions that developed during the middle ages to protect against the added problems raised by spatial separation. This includes the merchant guilds in northern Europe, the consulates of the Italian city states, and the organization of alien merchants into colonies (like the Steelyard in medieval London) with local privileges and duties. These institutions can also be understood from the perspective developed in this paper – they are designed to reinforce reputation mechanisms that alone are insufficient to support trade.

The Law Merchant system of judges and reputations was eventually replaced by a system of state enforcement, typically in the late middle ages or the early modern era in Western Europe. Enforcement of the private codes by the state added a new dimension to enforcement, especially in later periods when nation-states exercised extensive geographic control. Rather than depend for punishment upon the decentralized behavior of merchants, state enforcement could seize the property of individuals who resisted paying judgments, or put them into jail. If judgments could be enforced this way, then, in principle, the costs of keeping the merchants well informed about one another's past behavior could be saved. To the extent that the costs of running state adjudication and enforcement were roughly similar to the costs of running the private system and to the extent that taxes can be efficiently collected, a comprehensive state-run system would have the advantage that it eliminates the need for each individual to pay Q each period. As the volume of trade increased in the late middle ages, the cost saving from that source would have been substantial.[11] Thus our approach suggests that the importance of the role of the state enforcement of contracts was not that it provided a means of enforcing contracts where one previously did not exist. Rather, it was to reduce the transaction costs of policing exchange.[12]

In closing, we return to the broader implications of our work for the study of institutions. In complete information settings, institutions are frequently unnecessary because decentralized enforcement is sufficient to police deviations. However, this conclusion fails in environments where information is incomplete or costly. In the context of our model, the Adjusted Tit-for-Tat strategy requires that a trader know his current partner's previous history. When such information is difficult or costly to obtain, decentralized enforcement mechanisms break down. Institutions like those of the Law Merchant system resolve the fundamental problems of restoring the information that underpins an effective reputation system while both economizing on information and overcoming a whole array of incentive problems that obstruct the gathering and dissemination of that information.

Notes

*   Department of Economics, Stanford University; Department of Economics. Washington University; Hoover Institution, Stanford University. The authors thank Robert Aumann, Gary Becker,

Peter DeMarzo, Avner Greif, Michihiro Kandori, Bart Lipson, Uwe Schimack and the participants at numerous workshops for helpful conversations. Mr Milgrom and Mr Weingast thank the National Science Foundation for partial support.

1   Either by facilitating coordination (Banks and Calvert, 1989) or by preventing reneging on contracts.
2   Of course, considerable variation existed across locations, especially between northern and southern Europe. In the latter area, city-states arose, providing law and protection beyond the immediate area of the city. Further, over time, as the nature of governments changed, so too did their involvement in the legal and enforcement process.
3   This is also the premise of the game-theoretic analysis of Kandori (1989).
4   This matching rule is often called the "Townsend Turnpike," for Townsend suggested that one way to think of it is as two infinitely long sets of traders moving in opposite directions.
5   Kandori (1989) has shown that there exist other matching rules for which, despite the absence of sufficient bilateral trade and each player's ignorance about what has happened in trades among other players, there may nevertheless be a code of behavior that supports efficient exchange. However, as Kandori argues, the resulting system is "brittle" and leads to a breakdown of honest trade when there are even minor disturbances to the system. Both Kandori (1989) and Okuno-Fujiwara and Postlewaite (1989) consider other institutional solutions to this problem.
6   And, given that our model has a fixed starting date, there is really nothing to be learned from the initial query, so that could be eliminated with some small cost savings. However, this is just an artifact of our desire for modeling simplicity and not an inherent extra cost of the system.
7   Kandori (1989) shows that in the repeated Prisoners' Dilemma, players must know at least two periods of history for each partner to sustain an equilibrium with Honest behavior.
8   If the Law Merchant cannot commit to this action, then it is easy to show that there is an equilibrium in which the trader ignores the threat and the LM does not carry it out. It is no doubt true that some threats are disposed of in just this way – the victim simply calls the LM's bluff. We are interested in showing that the reputation mechanism can sometimes function even when the LM's threat must be taken at face value.
9   If we assumed that transfers are costly here, as in the case of judgments, then the victim would become more reluctant to pay and bribery would be less likely to succeed.
10 Of course, merchants could and did communicate extensively, writing letters, engaging in trial relations, and checking the credentials of their trading partners. Where possible, they also relied on family members and client relationships to provide reliable services. But with geographic specialization in production, these devices alone could not allow merchants to escape the need to rely on the promises of individuals with whom they were not well acquainted.
11 Historically, the successful state enforcement came in a series of stages. As suggested above, state enforcement began with the adoption of the legal codes by a wide range of cities and towns. Some of these evolved over time into large city-states (e.g., Venice or Genoa) or, later, became part of a larger nation-state (e.g., London). For a discussion of the evolution of legal codes underpinning merchant trade, see North (1987).
12 As we emphasized in section 4, however, a full evaluation of state enforcement must also assess the potential for corruption in the enforcement mechanisms of state enforcement.

References

Abreu, Dilip (1988) On the Theory of Infinitely Repeated Games with Discounting, *Econometrica*, 39: 383–96.

Aumann, Robert (1985) Repeated Games, in George Feiwel (ed.), *Issues in Contemporary Micro-economics and Welfare*. Macmillan Press, London, 209–42.

Axelrod, Robert (1984) *The Evolution of Cooperation*. Basic Books, New York.

Axelrod, Robert (1986) An Evolutionary Approach to Social Norms, *American Political Science Review*, 80: 1095–111.

Banks, Jeffrey and Randall Calvert (1989) Equilibria in Coordination Games. MS, University of Rochester.

Benson, Bruce (1989) The Spontaneous Evolution of Commercial Law, *Southern Economic Journal*, 644–61.

Berman, Harold (1983) *Law and Revolution: The Formation of Western Legal Tradition*, Harvard University Press.

Calvert, Randall (1986) Reciprocity Among Self-interested Actors, in Peter C. Ordeshook (ed.), *Models of Strategic Choice in Politics*, Michigan University Press.

Fudenberg, Drew and Eric Maskin (1986) The Folk Theorem in Repeated Games with Discounting or with Incomplete Information, *Econometrica*, 54: 533–54.

DeRoover, Raymond (1963) The Organization of Trade, *Cambridge Economic History of Europe*, vol. III.

Greif, Avner (1989) Reputation and Coalitions in Medieval Trade, *Journal of Economic History*, 49: 857–82.

Jones, William Catron (1961) The Settlement of Merchants' Disputes by Merchants: An Approach to the Study of the History of Commercial Law, PhD dissertation, University of Chicago.

Kandori, Michihiro (1989) Information and Coordination in Strategic Interaction over Time, PhD dissertation, Stanford University.

Klein, Benjamin and Keith Leffler (1981) The Role of Market Forces in Assuring Contractual Performance. *Journal of Political Economy*, 89: 615–41.

Lopez, Robert S. (1976) *Commercial Revolution of the Middle Ages, 950–1350*, Cambridge University Press, Cambridge.

Lopez, Robert S. and Irving W. Raymond (1955) *Medieval Trade in the Mediterranean World*, Columbia University Press, New York.

Mitchell, W. (1904) *Essay on the Early History of the Law Merchant*, Cambridge University Press, Cambridge.

North, Douglass (1987) Institutions, Transactions Costs, and the Rise of Merchant Empires, in James Tracey (ed.), *The Economics of the Rise of Merchant Empires*, vol. 2.

North, Douglass (1990) *Institutions, Institutional Change, and Economic Performance*, Cambridge University Press, Cambridge.

North, Douglass and Robert Thomas (1973) *Rise of the Western World*, Cambridge University Press, Cambridge.

Okuno-Fujiwara, M. and Andrew Postlewaite (1989) Social Norms in Random Matching Games, mimeo, University of Pennsylvania.

Pirenne, Henri (1925) *Medieval Cities: Their Origins and the Revival of Trade*, Princeton University Press.

Rorig, Fritz (1967) *The Medieval Town*, University of California Press, Berkeley.

Scutton, Thomas E. (1909) General Survey of the History of the Law Merchant, in *Select Essays in Anglo American Legal History*, compiled by the Association of American Law Schools.

Shapiro, Carl (1983) Premiums for High Quality Products as Returns to Reputations, *Quarterly Journal of Economics*, 98(4): 659–79.

Shapiro, Carl and Joseph Stiglitz (1984) Equilibrium Unemployment as a Worker Discipline Device, *American Economic Review*, 74(3), 433–44.

Thrupp, Silvia (1948) *The Merchant Class of Medieval London*, University of Chicago Press, Chicago.

Townsend, Robert M. (1981) Models of Money with Spatially Separated Agents, in J. H. Kareken and Neil Wallace (eds.), *Models of Monetary Economies*, Federal Reserve Bank, Minneapolis.

Trakman, L. (1983) *The Law Merchant*, Littleton, Rothman.

Verlinden, C. (1963) Markets and Fairs, *Cambridge Economic History of Europe*, vol. III.

Weingast, Barry R. and William Marshall (1988) The Industrial Organization of Congress; or Why Legislatures, like Firms, are not Organized as Markets, *Journal of Political Economy*, 96: 132–63.

SIX

Institutions and International Trade: Lessons from the Commercial Revolution

AVNER GREIF*

Source: From *American Economic Review* (1992), 82: 128–33.

International trade theory distances itself from an examination of the institutions that govern trade. To it, trade is determined by endowments, technology, preferences, and the nature of the competition in international markets. Historical institutional analysis indicates, however, that understanding the determination of actual, rather than potential, trade requires institutional analysis. Following the approach advanced by Oliver E. Williamson (1985), it views trade across political and economic entities as based on and composed of a series of political and economic exchange relations. Since institutions "determine . . . costs and hence the profitability and feasibility of . . . economic activity" (Douglass C. North, 1991 p. 97), the nature of the institutions that govern these exchange relations affect trade's magnitude and direction. At each point in time, the combined impact of institutions, endowments, technology, and preferences determines actual trade.

The relationship between institutions and trade is well reflected in the history of the Commercial Revolution (eleventh to fourteenth centuries), during which Mediterranean and European long-distance trade reemerged after a long period of decline (see, e.g., R. S. Lopez, 1976). This reemergence was not a response to changes in endowments or technology. Rather, institutional changes caused by political and social events provided the impetus required to initiate trade and a complementary process of institutional evolution and trade expansion. Before the emergence of appropriate institutions, the presence of gains from trade was insufficient either to initiate trade or to generate the required institutions.

While the emerging institutions reflected an attempt to gain from trade, they were a product of social and political processes. Social and political factors affected institutions by, for example, coordinating actions and expectations, determining the availability of information, the ability to initiate collective action, and the ability to use coercive power in the pursuit of economic ends. As a result of the interrelations between social and political factors and institutions that facilitated trade, these institutions were not even "second best." That is, they did not maximize gains from trade given the (navigation, information, and contract enforcement) technology of the period. This paper comes to substantiate these points by examining the origins, complexity, and implications of institutions that governed exchange relations that constituted or enabled trade during the Commercial Revolution.

I   Institutions that Governed the Relations between Rulers and Alien Merchants

Having monopoly over coercive power, a medieval ruler faced the temptation to abuse the rights of alien merchants who frequented his realm. Without an institution that enabled the ruler *ex ante* to commit to secure their rights, alien merchants were not likely to frequent that ruler's territory, thereby forgoing efficient trade. This point was clear to the English king Edward I, who in 1283 noted that "many merchants [fearing lack of protection] are put off from coming to this land with their merchandise to the detriment of merchants and of the whole kingdom" (*English Historical Documents*, 1975 p. 420).

Since trade relationships were expected to repeat, one may conjecture that a *bilateral reputation mechanism* in which a merchant whose rights were abused ceased trading, or an uncoordinated *multilateral reputation mechanism* in which a subgroup larger than the one that was abused ceased trading, could surmount this commitment problem. Under such mechanisms, conditioning future trade on past conduct may enable the ruler to commit. It is shown in Greif et al. (1991), however, that although each mechanism can support some level of trade, neither can support the *efficient level of trade*. The bilateral reputation mechanism fails because the value of the future trade of the "marginal" traders to the ruler is zero, and hence, the ruler is tempted to abuse these traders' rights. In a world characterized by information asymmetries, slow communication, and different plausible interpretations of facts, the multilateral reputation mechanism fails for a similar reason.

To overcome the ruler's commitment problem at the efficient level of trade, there is a need for an organization that coordinates traders' responses. When this need is fulfilled, there exists an equilibrium in which the threat of all the merchants to cease trading if any merchant's rights are abused enables the ruler to commit. This equilibrium, however, is not reasonable since it entails a complete boycott during which trade shrinks to below the point at which (for example) a bilateral reputation mechanism is effective, and hence some traders will renegotiate to resume trading. This impedes the organization's ability to surmount the commitment problem by reducing the penalty it can impose on the ruler. Thus, to support the efficient level of trade, a multilateral reputation mechanism must be supplemented by an organization with the ability to coordinate responses and to ensure traders' compliance to boycott decisions.

Historical evidence provided by Greif et al. (1991) indicates that during the Commercial Revolution an institution with the above attributes, the *merchant guild*, supported trade expansion. While a merchant guild was a precondition for trade expansion, its rise in various places was not caused by the appearance of new gains from trade. Rather, the timing of its rise and hence of trade expansion was determined by social and political factors.

Consider, for example, the differences between guilds in southern and northern Europe. The major Italian city-states grew large because of social and political events around the

Mediterranean. Italian trade expanded, since each city functioned as a merchant guild, and its size implied that its traders were not "marginal." Although the potential gains from trade in the Baltic Sea were substantial as well, that region's settlement process led to small towns which could not assure the safety of their traders abroad. Only after a long process of institutional evolution were these towns incorporated into an intercity merchant guild, the German Hansa, which enabled Baltic trade to prosper (Philippe Dollinger, 1970). As the emergence and evolution of these merchant guilds were determined by social and political factors, there is no reason to believe that they were second best. This claim is substantiated by the observation concerning the slow institutional evolution of the German Hansa. This evolution does not reflect technical changes, indicating that at each point in time the existing institution was not second best.

II Institutions that Governed the Relations between Merchants and Overseas Agents

During the Commercial Revolution trade expansion was facilitated by the employment of *overseas agents* who enabled merchants to reduce the cost of trade by saving the time and risk of traveling, diversifying sales, and so forth. To reduce cost, however, overseas agents had to have control over a merchant's capital abroad, enabling them to act opportunistically and expropriate that capital. Hence, in the absence of institutions limiting opportunism, merchants were not likely to hire agents. What were the institutions that governed agency relations and enabled trade expansion? Did their emergence reflect changes in technology or endowments? Did these institutions reduce the cost of trade to its lowest feasible level?

In previous work (Greif, 1989, 1990a), I have examined the institution that governed agency relations among Maghribi traders who operated in the Muslim Mediterranean during the eleventh century. The Maghribis were the descendants of Jewish traders who left the increasingly politically insecure surroundings of Baghdad and emigrated to North Africa during the tenth century. By coordinating expectations and providing a social network for information transmission, this emigration process enabled the Maghribis to organize agency relations within a coalition based on a multilateral reputation mechanism. The Maghribis employed each other as agents, and all retaliated against any agent who had cheated a coalition member. Their social and commercial network provided the information required to detect and announce cheating, and the multilateral punishment was self-enforcing, since the value of future relations with all the Maghribis kept an agent honest. An agent who was not expected to be hired by the Maghribis did not stand to lose the value of future relations with them if he were caught cheating. Therefore, a Maghribi merchant who nevertheless hired him had to pay more to keep that agent honest. Hence, each merchant was induced to hire only agents who were expected to be hired by others.

Furthermore, if an agent who had cheated employed other Maghribis as agents, these were free to cheat him without being punished. Hence, by serving as a bond, one's trade investment enhanced his ability to commit. Thus, merchants were motivated to hire other merchants who also invested in trade as agents, thereby determining the social identity of the Maghribis as a group of middle-class merchants. The operation of the coalition was supported by a set of cultural rules of behavior that obviated the need for comprehensive contracts and coordinated responses by indicating what constituted "cheating."

Multilateral punishment enabled the employment of agents even when the relations between a specific merchant and agent were not expected to repeat. The resulting additional gains from cooperation, the value of the information flows, and the expectations concerning future hiring ensured the "closeness" of the coalition. Maghribis were motivated to hire and to be hired only by other Maghribis, while non-Maghribis were discouraged from hiring Maghribis.

Institutions that governed agency relations also emerged among the Italian traders, although a different political and social history led to the emergence of institutions based on political control and bilateral reputation. I have argued (Greif, 1990b) that around the middle of the twelfth century, agency relations between Genoese merchants and their overseas agents were governed by a "political coalition." The political faction that controlled Genoa held a monopoly over the city's lucrative overseas trade. This monopoly was utilized to provide agents with the stream of rents required to keep them honest by conditioning agents' future trade investment on past conduct.

Political events in Genoa during the last decade of the twelfth century eliminated this political monopoly, opening the lucrative overseas trade to all Genoese. The city itself grew rapidly (despite a high mortality rate) with immigration. These social and political events led to unstable social networks and hindered the emergence of a coalition based on multilateral reputation. Instead, the *patron system*, based on a bilateral reputation mechanism, evolved to govern agency relations. Each merchant, by conditioning future employment on past actions and by paying a sufficiently high wage, motivated his agents to be honest.

The Maghribis' coalition, the political coalition, and the patron system were different institutions linked to specific historical, political, and social processes of which they were integral parts. These processes determined the nature of these institutions and the timing of their emergence and disappearance. By defining feasible agency relations, these institutions determined the cost of various agency relations and hence affected the magnitude and direction of trade.

Furthermore, the evolution of these institutions and the details of their operation suggest that they were not second best. Among the Maghribis, the volume of trade was limited by the coalition's size, which had been determined by an immigration process and not by the needs of trade. Although this deficiency could have been remedied by an appropriate coordinating organization, such an organization did not emerge. Further, the multilateral reputation mechanism led the Maghribis to forgo efficient relations with non-Maghribis in favor of more profitable but less efficient agency relations among themselves.

Neither the political coalition nor the patron system could support agency relations that were not expected to repeat. Under the former system, however, trade magnitude was politically determined, while under the latter system free entry enabled trade to expand further. On the other hand, the operation of the patron system required a wealth differential between merchants and agents that restricted agency relations. Although this deficiency could have been remedied by an appropriate organization, such an organization did not emerge until a century later (Greif, 1992).

The limitation on the size of a coalition implies that an economy in which agency relations are governed by coalitions will capture few new trade opportunities, compared to an economy based on the patron system. Indeed, the Italian traders did not have a technology superior to those of traders from the Muslim world. Nevertheless, they came to dominate the frontiers of trade in the Far East during this period, suggesting that their institutional structure made them the exporters of trade services.

The above institutions also influenced the process of institutional evolution by providing distinct inducements. For example, when agency relations are governed by the patron system, merchants are motivated to establish "family firms" which employ agents and whose essence is preserving wealth under common ownership. Indeed, the Genoese who used the patron system during the twelfth century organized agency relations during the thirteenth century within family firms. A family firm, whose life span is "infinite" and which is less likely to go bankrupt than an individual merchant, reduces the wage that has to be paid to keep agents honest. Within a coalition based on multilateral punishment, however, a family firm does not reduce wages, since the wage required to keep an agent honest is independent of the expected length of the relations with any particular merchant. The rise of the family firm in Italy led to the development of a market in family firms' shares and bonds which enabled an expansion of trade investment. Hence, different initial institutions led to the evolution of diverse institutions that further affected trade (Greif, 1992).

III   Institutions that Governed Relations among Merchants with Limited Information

During the twelfth and the thirteenth centuries much of the trade between northern and southern Europe was conducted at the Champagne fairs where merchants from different localities entered into contracts that required enforcement through time, such as contracts for future delivery. How could a merchant from one community commit to honor contractual obligations toward a member of another? What were the efficiency implications of the institution that governed this exchange?

Paul R. Milgrom et al. (1990; see Chapter 5 of this volume) suggest that in the large merchants' community that frequented the fairs, a reputation mechanism could not surmount this commitment problem. Large communities lack the social networks required to make past actions known to all. Milgrom et al. suggest that contract enforceability at the Champagne fairs was achieved by the *law merchant* system, in which the court was used to supplement a multilateral reputation mechanism.

Suppose that each pair of traders is matched only once and each trader knows only his own experience. Since the fairs' court lacked the ability to enforce judgment once a trader left the fairs, assume that the court is capable only of verifying past actions and keeping records of traders who cheated in the past. Acquiring information and appealing to the court is costly for each merchant. Despite these costs, there exists a (symmetric sequential) equilibrium in which cheating does not occur and merchants are induced to provide the court with the information required to support cooperation. It is the court's ability to activate a multilateral reputation mechanism by controlling information that provides the appropriate incentives.

This analysis suggests that the centrality of the Champagne fairs in European trade reflects economies of scale in the operation of a multilateral reputation mechanism supported by the court. If this is the case, the geographical distribution of much of the European trade of the period reflects the historical process that led to the emergence of that specific institution at that specific time and place. As theoretical studies of path dependence indicate, this process need not be optimal (see, e.g., A. Paul David, 1988).

IV Conclusions

This paper examines some institutions that surmounted commitment problems and thereby supported trade expansion during the Commercial Revolution. While these institutions facilitated trade, they were by-products of (and interwoven into) the social, political, economic, and technological fabric of the period. As such, there is no reason to believe that they were second best. Rather, the evidence suggests that they were self-enforcing stable systems that were not prone to respond to welfare-enhancing opportunities. This claim is supported by the micro-level examination of these institutions and by the macro-level phenomena, that is, the Commercial Revolution itself, 'as it was not a response to new gains from trade.

Institutions during the Commercial Revolution constrained decision-makers and determined the relations between profitability and efficiency in the exchange relations that constituted or enabled trade. Hence, they determined the efficiency, magnitude, and geographical distribution of trade flows and influenced the social, political, and institutional evolution that further affected trade. Current international trade is also influenced by institutions that govern, for example, commodity futures markets, the international accumulation and diffusion of knowledge, the relations between foreign investors and governments, and the relations between producers and overseas suppliers and distributors. A comprehensive understanding of the factors that determine actual, rather than potential, international trade in the past, present, and future requires a detailed analysis of the institutions that govern the exchange relations that constitute or enable international commerce.

*   Assistant Professor, Department of Economics, Stanford University, Stanford, CA 94305. This research was supported by the National Science Foundation grant 9009598-01. The remarks of Yossef Spiege greatly improved this paper. I thank Timothy Bresnahan, Paul David, Steven N. Durlauf, Harry Hizinga, Douglas A. Irwin, Paul R. Milgrom, Daniel M. G. Raff, and Gavin Wright for helpful comments. The usual caveat applies.

References

David, A. Paul (1988) The Future of Path-Dependent Equilibrium Economics. CEPR Working paper No. 155, Stanford University.
Dollinger, Philippe (1970) *The German Hansa*. Stanford, CA: Stanford University Press.
Greif, Avner (1989) Reputation and Coalitions in Medieval Trade: Evidence on the Maghribi Traders, *Journal of Economic History* December, 49: 857–82.
Greif, Avner (1990a) Contract Enforceability and Economic Institutions in Early Trade: the Maghribi Traders' Coalition. Working paper, Stanford University. *American Economic Review* (1993).
Greif, Avner (1990b) Reputation and Coalitions in Medieval Trade: Evidence on the Genoese Traders. Working paper. Stanford University.

Greif, Avner (1992) Cultural Beliefs as a Common Resource in an Integrating World: an Example from the Theory and History of Collectivist and Individualist Societies. In P. Dasgupta, K.-G. Mäler, and A. Vercelli (eds.), *The Economics of Transnational Commons*, unpublished collective volume.

Greif, Avner, Milgrom, Paul R. and Weingast, Barry R. (1991) The Merchant Gilds as a Nexus of Contracts. Working paper, Stanford University.

Lopez, R. S. (1976) *The Commercial Revolution of the Middle Ages, 950–1350*. Cambridge: Cambridge University Press.

Milgrom, Paul R., North, Douglass C., and Weingast, Barry R. (1990) The Role of Institutions in the Revival of Trade: the Law Merchant, Private Judges, and the Champagne Fairs, *Economics and Politics* (March) 2: 1–23.

North, Douglass C. (1991) Institutions, *Journal of Economic Perspectives*, 5: 97–112.

Williamson, Oliver E. (1985) *The Economic Institutions of Capitalism*. New York: Free Press.

English Historical Documents, 1189–1327, vol. 3, ed. Harry Rothwell, London: Eyre and Spottis-woode, 1975.

SEVEN

Implications from the Disequilibrium of Majority Rule for the Study of Institutions

WILLIAM H. RIKER

Source: From *American Political Science Review* (1980), 74: 432–46.

Social scientists are now, and probably always have been, of divided opinion about the degree to which institutions as well as personal values, opinions, and tastes affect the content of social decisions. (I use the words "values," "opinions," and "tastes" interchangeably, not because they mean exactly the same thing, but because the processes by which they can influence decisions are identical.) It is clear that the values of at least some members of society do ineradicably influence these decisions. Even when it is claimed that God, or the law of nature, or the sovereign people, or the working class, or some other abstract non-human entity determines outcomes, it is still true that some members of society, say, priests, judges, parliamentarians, dictators, etc., must interpret what the abstraction directs. In the most extreme cases, the voice the people hear and the words spoken come immediately from the Delphic priestess, not from the god who is said to inspire her. That being so, we can never leave out the influence of some person's values and tastes on social decisions. Even if the priestess is unintelligible, the priestly interpreter tells the supplicants what to do.

On the other hand, we cannot leave out the force of institutions. The people whose values and tastes are influential live in a world of conventions about both language and values themselves. These conventions are in turn condensed into institutions, which are simply rules about behavior, especially about making decisions. Even the priestess in her frenzy probably behaves according to rules and, for certain, her interpreter is constrained by specifiable conventions. So interpersonal rules, that is, institutions, must affect social outcomes just as much as personal values.

Ambiguity arises, however, when we attempt to assess the relative significance of these two kinds of forces. Very probably, both are necessary and neither is alone a sufficient condition for outcomes. If so, a full statement of social causation must include them both. But, nevertheless, it is often believed to be convenient and practically useful to assume that one force (either the personal or the impersonal) is constant, while the other is variable and thus in some sense marginal and "more significant" than the other. With this assumption, if the institutions are constant, then one can predict outcomes from tastes, or, if tastes are constant, then one can predict outcomes from institutions. It is of course true that this easy predictability is an illusion – but it is an illusion by which many scholars are hoodwinked because in quiet times the institutions are constant and only tastes are in dispute, while in turbulent times the institutions are in flux and only human greed seems constant. One fundamental and unsolved problem of social science is to penetrate the illusion and to learn to take both values and institutions into account. In the last generation we have made some small progress in this direction, if only to acquire a bit of sophistication about the problem, and the purpose of this article is to chronicle this progress.

Methodological Traditions in Political Science

Political science draws almost equally on traditions that overemphasize institutions and traditions that overemphasize tastes, which is perhaps why political scientists seem so eclectic as compared to, say, sociologists (whose tradition is almost exclusively Institutional) or to economists (whose recent tradition, at least, stresses tastes).

The emphasis on institutions is our classical heritage. Aristotle collected and described 150 constitutions because he believed that constitutions determined both social outcomes and individual character. Even Plato, who initially argued for the rule of men rather than the rule of law, nevertheless devoted most of the *Republic* to a description of the institutions necessary to produce the kind of people he wanted for rulers, thereby implying that the institutions were primary and the particular rulers merely intermediaries between the institutions and the outcome. The notion that the quality of men's character is controlled by the laws under which they live, a notion that comes to us from ancient Greece by way of Roman law and eighteenth-century philosophers like Montesquieu, is, consequently, very much a part of contemporary political science. For example, it is said, with astonishing variety, that both the welfare state and restraints on government make people free, productive, contented, and self-respecting; or, for another example, it is said that incompatible varieties of economic institutions such as capitalism and socialism make people better off both morally and economically. Doubtless, the most extreme and absurd of the modern versions of classical institutionalism is Marxism, a picture of society in which economic institutions determine not only individual character but also the whole course of human history.

The emphasis on taste and values, on the other hand, is our Christian heritage. Because Christianity based the social order on personal decisions about faith and love and because it rejected the Judaic system of rules and forms (which came close to classical institutionalism), Christian theologians – at least from the Middle Ages onward – insisted that the quality of social outcomes depended almost entirely on the moral quality of rulers: Christian kings make good decisions; pagan or irreligious kings do not. Even in this secular century, some writers directly in the Christian tradition have described society in exactly this way. For example, T. S. Eliot, responding to the Munich crisis with *The Idea of a Christian Society* (1940, p. 34), saw only a change in *beliefs* as a way out of the world crisis: a community of Christians in a Christian state governed by rulers who accept Christianity, "not simply as their own faith, ... but as the system under which they are to govern." It would be hard to find a more complete conviction that social outcomes (and personal character) are determined by what people believe.

Owing, however, to the lack of interest in theology among twentieth-century intellectuals, the contemporary force associating individual values and social outcomes is wholly secular, though probably derived (as is, for example, extreme methodological individualism) from Christian modes of thought. In the ideology of democracy, which may well be a kind of secularized Christian theology, that form of government is often, though I believe quite inaccurately, defined as the rule of the people – by which it is meant that the people's values solely determine public decisions. For reasons that I have discussed at length elsewhere, this picture of democracy is internally inconsistent and cannot be sustained (Riker, 1978, 1980). At most, democracy involves a popular veto on rulers, not a popular rule. Nevertheless inconsistencies and inaccuracies do not deter most ideologues, so that it is probably the case that nowadays the most widely accepted interpretation of democracy is that it is a device to combine individual values into decisions of government. Furthermore, this understanding, which went by the name of Benthamite "radicalism" in nineteenth-century England and of "popular sovereignty" in nineteenth-century America, is today believed by huge numbers of people (incorrectly, of course) to describe what actually happens in democratic governments.

While this supposed political description is mere ideology, it is nevertheless an important part of some contemporary political science and contributes greatly to the scientific emphasis on tastes and values, an emphasis expressed, for example, in the great amount of research on public opinion (which concerns the nature of tastes and values), political socialization (which concerns the creation of tastes and values), and representation (which concerns the incorporation of tastes and values in public decisions).

Great as is the contribution of democratic ideology to an emphasis on tastes and values, there is an even greater contribution, I believe, from the example of microeconomics. The theory of price in a competitive market – one of the few well-tested and verified theories in all of social science – is a theory in which institutions (i.e., the market) are held constant, while tastes determine outcomes. The theory takes this form: given an auction market for a continuously divisible commodity with several buyers and several sellers whose tastes are constant over the period of the auction, then the price of the commodity is jointly and completely determined in a particular, describable way by the sum of the buyers' desires to buy and the sum of the sellers' desires to sell. (These desires are, of course, tastes and values.) Furthermore, as long as tastes are constant the price so determined is a Pareto-optimal equilibrium in the sense that no *pair* of traders would agree to depart from it because any departure in favor of one trader would hurt another.

Since this theory admits prediction of an equilibrium and since the actual occurrences of numerous predicted equilibria have been verified, the prestige of this theory is higher, I believe, than that of any other theory in the social sciences. Indeed, it seems to me that this success alone (i.e., predictions from the theory of price) elevates the science of economics above all other social sciences in popular esteem among intellectuals, and renders economists believable even when they write of totally different subjects such as macroeconomics and social welfare, about both of which subjects their theories are as unverified as most others in social science. The scientific and intellectual success of price theorists in discovering equilibria has, of course, led many other social scientists to emulate them. We see, therefore, searches for equilibria of tastes in all branches of social science, not least of all political science.

The Search for General Equilibria

As I noted at the beginning of the previous section, political science draws eclectically both on traditions that overemphasize institutions and on traditions that overemphasize tastes. But, in the last 30 years or so, it seems to me that the traditions overemphasizing tastes have predominated. The study of constitutions, which characterized political science in the first half of the century, has latterly given way to the study of political culture, political behavior, and public opinion, all of which concern values and tastes. Simultaneously, with a kind of unspoken intellectual coordination, political theorists have analyzed the conditions for equilibria in abstract majority voting systems, which are in fact the conditions for an equilibrium of values. This development in political theory, which is described in this and subsequent sections, has by now revealed precisely what kind of equilibria can be expected, thereby allowing us to understand, with much more sophistication than was previously possible, the relation of values and institutions in structuring political outcomes.

The beginning of the search for conditions of equilibria is Duncan Black's rediscovery (in the mid-1940s) of the paradox of voting. Before that time scholars had indeed often discussed the equity and effect of voting systems, especially in disputes over proportional representation, methods of nomination, and forms of ballots. But, so far as I have been able to discover from a desultory survey, hardly anyone had recognized that the supposed defects might be based on individual tastes rather than structures of systems. If based on tastes, the defects are irremediable because, given an appropriate distribution of tastes, even a perfected system of voting might produce imperfect results. This is precisely the inference one draws from an analysis of the paradox and it is perhaps owing to an unspoken, even unrecognized, repugnance at this deduction that, when the paradox was initially discovered by Condorcet and rediscovered by Lewis Carroll, E. J. Nanson, and E. V. Huntington, it was nevertheless ignored (or perhaps repressed) by political scientists (see Black, 1958, pp. 156–238; Riker, 1961). Once Black brought the paradox irrepressibly to scholarly attention and showed that the disequilibria inherent in it depended not on the institutions of voting but on the distributions of taste, the search for conditions of equilibrium seemed an intellectual necessity.

To discuss this question, one needs an abstract society of these elements:

1. *Alternatives* $\{a_1, a_2, \ldots, a_n\}$. If $n = 2$, equilibrium is certain because a_1 beats or ties a_2 or vice versa. Problems of equilibrium arise, however, when $n \geq 3$.
2. *Voters* $\{1, 2, \ldots, m\}$. When $m = 1$, the problem is trivial, so it should be that $m \geq 2$.
3. *Preference* Assuming that voters can compare alternatives and value some of them more than others, there are binary relations of preference, P_i (where $i = 1, 2, \ldots, m$), of indifference, I_i, and of the two combined, R_i, expressing a voter's estimate of the relative value of any pair of alternatives. (One writes "$a_j R_i a_k$" to mean "voter i prefers a_j to a_k or is indifferent between them.") Conventionally, R is assumed to be reflexive ($a_j R_j a_j$), connected (either $a_i R_i a_k$ or $a_k R_i a_j$), and transitive (if $a_h R_i a_j$ and $a_j R_i a_k$, then $a_h R_i a_k$), so that by R (or P or I) a voter orders any triplet of alternatives from best to worst: $a_h R_i a_j R_i a_k$ or $a_h a_j a_k$. [Notationally, $a_h P_i a_j I_i a_k$ is written: $a_h(a_j a_k)$.] Perhaps

the attribution of the ability to order places unwarranted confidence in the fragile human ability to concentrate. By the assumption of the transitivity of R, however, we give voting on values a chance at equilibrium with the best of human participation. If, then, voting fails, it fails the easiest possible test.

4   *Outcomes from voting*   Given a society of m voters faced with n alternatives, there are $(n!)^m$ possible profiles of preference D, that is possible ways the members of the group can individually order the alternatives. (That is, there are $n!$ possible orders of n alternatives and each of the m voters can select one of those orders.) The operation on a profile, D, of majority voting on pairs of alternatives yields an outcome relation, M, where "a_h M a_k" means: "(the number of i such that a_h P_i a_k) $\geq$ (the number of i such that a_k P_i a_h)," assuming, of course, that no i such that a_h I_i a_k participates in the voting. M may be, but need not be, a transitive relation so that M may yield either some one of the $n!$ orders of alternatives or intransitive cycles like a_h M a_j M a_k M a_n.

To consider the problems involved in the summation of preferences, observe the profiles, $D^1 \rightarrow D^4$, where $n = m = 3$:

D^1	D^2
1. a_h a_j a_k	1. a_h a_j a_k
2. a_h a_k a_j	2. a_j a_h a_k
3. a_j a_k a_h	3. a_k a_h a_j

a_h M a_j M a_k a_h M a_j M a_k

D^3	D^3
1. a_h a_j a_k	1. a_h a_k a_j
2. a_j a_k a_h	2. a_j a_h a_k
3. a_k a_h a_j	3. a_k a_j a_h

a_h M a_j M a_k M a_h a_h M a_k M a_j M a_h
"forward cycle"   "backward cycle"

In profiles D^1 and D^2 there is a decisive winner by M in the sense that a_h beats each of $n - 1$ other alternatives. But in profiles D^3 and D^4, which are examples of the paradox of voting, there is no decisive winner because in, say, D^3, a_h will win if the sequence of voting is a_j versus a_k and then a_j versus a_h, a_j will win if the sequence is a_k versus a_h and then a_j versus a_k, etc., or no alternative will win if a round robin is conducted. The absence of a decisive winner is particularly disconcerting because, after assuming that each voter can order his or her values, it turns out that the group of voters cannot order them. Indeed, the people are coherent but the group is incoherent.

It is precisely the absence of a decisive winner that constitutes disequilibrium and the paradox of voting shows that disequilibrium can occur with majority voting, the relation M. Furthermore, the possibility of this kind of disequilibrium is present in *any* fair voting method, so it is not the institution of M, but the distribution of tastes, that is at fault (Arrow, 1963). One is consequently driven to ask what properties distinguish profiles with an equilibrium outcome (like D^1 and D^2) from profiles without one, like D^3 and D^4. (This question has usually been posed with respect to the relation M, so I will restrict my discussion to it. But, by reason of Arrow's theorem, we know that similar questions could be raised about any voting method, say, positional methods like plurality voting or approval voting.)

During the late 1960s, a systematic answer was developed, based on the observation that, for the 3! orders of a triplet of alternatives,

1. $a_h\ a_j\ a_k$
2. $a_h\ a_k\ a_j$
3. $a_j\ a_h\ a_k$
4. $a_j\ a_k\ a_h$
5. $a_k\ a_h\ a_j$
6. $a_k\ a_j\ a_h,$

numbers 1, 4, and 5 constitute D^3 and result in the forward cycle and numbers 2, 3, and 6 constitute D^4, and D^4 exhausts the ways in which intransitive triples can occur. Any conditions on orderings by individuals such that either $a_h\ a_j\ a_k\ a_h$ or $a_h\ a_k\ a_j\ a_h$ are rendered impossible by M is thus a guarantee of equilibrium. One such condition is, for example, that, for any number of voters, some alternative in a triple is never in first place in a voter's order (as a_k is not in D^1) or some is never in last place (as a_h is not in D^2) or never in the middle place (as a_h is not in D^1) — this is the condition of "value restriction" (Sen, 1966). Or another condition is "extremal restriction," which is that, for any number of voters and for some order $a_j\ a_h\ a_k$ in D, if another order has a_k first, then this other order must have a_j last (as in D^2, $a_j\ a_h\ a_k$ is voter 2's order and $a_k\ a_h\ a_j$ is voter 3's) (Sen and Pattanaik, 1969). An exhaustive list of similar conditions is set forth in Fishburn (1973).

In addition to their completeness, the merit of these conditions on profiles is their clear revelation that equilibrium depends entirely on the accident of a non-cyclical set of voters' preferences. The defect of these conditions is, on the other hand, their failure to indicate the likelihood that tastes might or might not be cyclical. Lacking that indication, they do not admit assessment of the practical significance of disequilibrium. Fortunately there exist less complete but intuitively more vivid geometric or topological conditions for equilibrium that do allow practical interpretation.

Historically, the first such condition, single-peakedness, was devised by Black even before Arrow's theorem was formulated (Black, 1948). If alternatives are arranged on a horizontal axis and the voters' ordinal valuation is measured on a vertical axis, then a voter's ordering may be represented as a curve on the positive quadrant connecting the voter's valuation of alternatives (see figure 7.1). Such a preference curve is single-peaked if, as it flows from left to right, it is always rising, always falling, or rising to a peak or a plateau and then falling. By an appropriate arrangement of alternatives on the horizontal axis, any ordering of alternatives may be expressed as a single-peaked curve. If, however, three or more preference curves are drawn above a particular arrangement of alternatives on the horizontal axis, it may happen that all curves cannot be single-peaked. (See figure 7.2, in which the reader may verify that, no matter how the three alternatives are ordered on the horizontal axis, at least one of the three curves from D^4 – a cyclical profile – must fail to be single-peaked. In the particular ordering of figure 7.2, voter 3's curve fails; but, were the ordering on the horizontal axis to be, say, $a_h\ a_k\ a_j$, then voter 2's curve would fail.)

Black's discovery was that, if any ordering on the horizontal axis exists such that all voters' preference curves are single-peaked, then an equilibrium exists in the sense that one

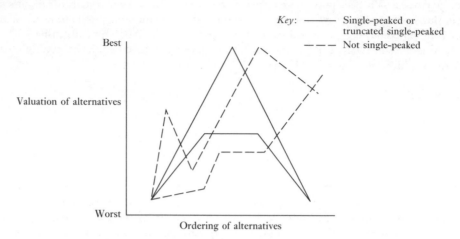

Figure 7.1 Preference curves

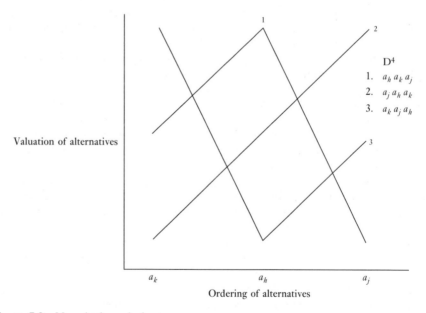

Figure 7.2 Non single-peakedness

alternative can beat or tie $(n - 1)$ others. Moreover the winning alternative(s) can be specified: identifying the alternative beneath the peak of voter i's curve as O_i (for "optimum for i") and numbering the optima so that O_1 is at the far left and O_m at the far right, then, if m is odd, $O_{(m+1)/2}$ wins and, if m is even, $O_{m/2}$ and $O_{(m+1)/2}$ tie. For proof, when m is odd, note that, if a curve is rising from a_h to a_j, then the voter prefers a_j to a_h

and, conversely, when the curve is falling, the voter prefers a_h to a_j. Placing some a_k to the left of $O_{(m+1)/2}$ against $O_{(m+1)/2}$ in a vote, note that $O_{(m+1)/2}$ wins because over half the curves are rising between a_k and $O_{(m+1)/2}$, specifically all those curves with optima numbered $O_{(m+1)/2}$ to O_m (which is a majority itself) and all curves with optima lying between a_k and $O_{(m+1)/2}$. Similarly, placing some $a_{k'}$ to the right of $O_{(m+1)/2}$ against it, note that $O_{(m+1)/2}$ wins because over half the curves are falling between $O_{(m+1)/2}$ and $a_{k'}$, specifically all those from O_1 to $O_{(m+1)/2}$ (a bare majority) and those with optima between $O_{(m+1)/2}$ and $a_{k'}$. A similar argument establishes that $O_{m/2}$ and $O_{(m+1)/2}$ tie when n is even.

It should be noted that this equilibrium at the median optimum is characterized by a balancing of opposites, a feature found in all other geometrically defined equilibria of voting. There are an equal number of voters on either side of the median, which is why it is the equilibrium. Suppose one subtracts (or adds) two voters whose optima are on opposite sides of the median, then the equality is unaffected and the equilibrium is characterized in some fundamental way by a pairing of opposites.

As a condition of equilibrium, single-peakedness (like the previously mentioned conditions, all of which were, however, discovered later) guarantees that neither a_h M a_j M a_k M a_h nor a_h M a_k M a_j M a_h occurs. It has the additional merit, moreover, of revealing a rationale for the existence of equilibria: that all curves are single-peaked means that all voters judge the alternatives consistently with respect to one issue, namely, that measured by the dimension on the horizontal axis. They may, of course, disagree about the best position on the issue, but they do agree that this single issue is the relevant basis for judgment.

This is why this condition has an intuitively obvious application to political campaigns, as in Downs' proposition that party platforms in a two-party system converge to the values of the median voter (1957, pp. 114–25). While Downs derived this argument from an economic model of the spatial location of firms, still his argument for equilibrium at the median voter's optimum assumes single-peakedness and is indeed invalid without it. This application suggests just how restrictive the condition is in practice because it seldom appears to be satisfied in the real world (Robertson, 1977). Despite the frequent journalistic use of dichotomies, e.g., "left–right," "Catholic–Protestant," "Fleming–Walloon," etc. – all of which are extremes on one issue dimension – still, scholarly efforts to describe real politics on one dimension seem always to break down. Indeed, once Downs set forth his model, it seemed so inadequate that other theorists soon developed an n-dimensional analogue (Davis and Hinich, 1966; Davis, Hinich, and Ordeshook, 1970).

Given the intuition that the one-dimensional model is inadequate for description, the appropriate next step is to search for equilibria in two-dimensional and ultimately in n-dimensional issue spaces. Black and Newing (1951) started the search with three voters in a two-dimensional model in which the peaks of figures 7.1, 7.2, and 7.3 have become the humps of figure 7.4. The vertical axis in that figure is, like the vertical axes in previous figures, for the ordinal measure of valuations. The two horizontal axes are issue dimensions or bases of judgment that define a plane (rather than a line) on which alternatives are located. Voter i's optimum (O_i) lies in that plane directly beneath the highest point of the hump. Curves e and f, which are reflections into the $x_1 x_2$-plane of two levels of preference, are indifference curves in the sense that voter i prefers all alternatives in the open space between e and f to any alternative on e but i is indifferent among all alternatives on, say, e.

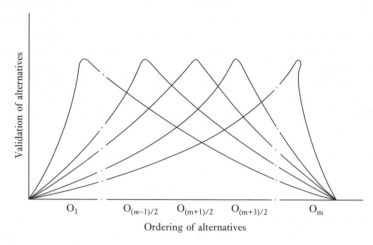

Figure 7.3   Voter's optima

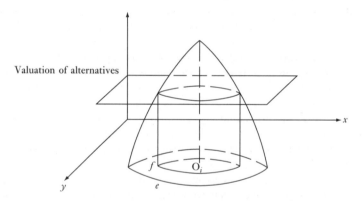

Figure 7.4   Single-humped valuation of alternatives in two dimensions (x,y)

To search for an equilibrium we need look only at the indifference curves in the x_1x_2-plane, as in figure 7.5. Between two voters, with optima at O_1 and O_2, is a "contract curve" which connects points of tangencies of the voters' indifference curves. All the points on which voters 1 and 2 might agree lie on the contract curve. To see why, consider point a_k which lies, for each voter, on the outer of the two sets of indifference curves displayed. By definition, all points in the open shaded space are preferred by *both* voters to a_k. By successive reduction of the shaded area, one arrives at some point on the contract curve. When there are three voters, however, agreement is less easy to arrive at. Observe in figure 7.6 that, while voters 1 and 2 might agree by majority vote on a_k, still a_j M a_k by voters 2 and 3. Nevertheless a_h M a_j (by 1 and 3) and a_k M a_h (by 1 and 2), so a cycle exists and there is no equilibrium.

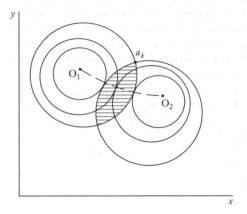

Figure 7.5 Indifference curves

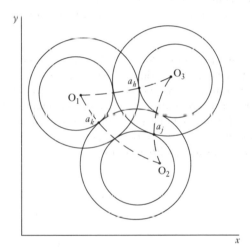

Figure 7.6 Contract curves for three voters

There is, however, some chance for equilibria in this situation: if O_3 were to lie on the contract curve between O_1 and O_2, say, at a_k, then $O_3 = a_k$ would be a median between O_1 and O_2 and hence preferred by some pair (either 1 and 3 or 2 and 3) to *any* other point in the plane. In general, if one voter's optima lies on a contract curve between two others, then there is an equilibrium outcome. Note that, as in the one-dimensional case, there is a balance between opposites, because a_k would remain the equilibrium if O_1 and O_2 were removed or if additional pairs of optima were added, one of each pair on the O_1 O_2 contract curve between a_k and O_1 and the other between a_k and O_2. This discovery was generalized by Charles Plott (1967). For the expanded situation we need some new notation. Since we now assume an infinite number of alternatives and continuously differentiable utility (as a measure on individual preference), we can no longer use n for the number of alternatives. Rather we use it to identify dimensions by which voters judge alternatives, $1, 2, \ldots,$ n-dimensions. Then $U^i = U^i(x_1, x_2, \ldots, x_n)$ is the utility to the ith voter of some point, a, in n-dimensional space. Let there be a status quo alternative, $\bar{a}$, that is, the alternative currently in force and let some a_j, which is a "small" distance, d, from $\bar{a}$, be placed against $\bar{a}$ in a majority vote. If $a_j \, P_i \, \bar{a}$, voter i obtains an increase in utility from a_j over $\bar{a}$. Let ΔU^i be the measure in utility of a vector in n-space from $\bar{a}$ toward some (unspecified) other point. Specifying the other point as a_j, one can say that, if $\Delta U^i \, a_j > 0$, then voter i prefers a_j, that, if $\Delta U^i a_j < 0$, voter i prefers $\bar{a}$, and if $\Delta U^i a_j = 0$, voter i is indifferent between a_j and $\bar{a}$. If there is some set of voters of size $\frac{m+1}{2}$ such that the gradient vectors, of utility for each voter, i, in the set are $\Delta U^i \, a_j \leq 0$, then a majority prefers $\bar{a}$ to a_j and $\bar{a}$ is a Condorcet winner or equilibrium.

A set of sufficient conditions for $\bar{a}$ to be in equilibrium are, for m odd:

1 that indifferent voters do not vote on a motion;
2 that there is at least one voter, i, for whom $\bar{a}$ provides the maximum utility;
3 that the $m - 1$ remaining voters – an even number – can be divided into pairs, i and i', the interests of voters i and i' are diametrically opposed in direction and amounts of utility.

It is intuitively evident (and proved in Plott [1967]) that for m voters for which conditions 1, 2, and 3 hold, the voters would not wish to move from $\bar{a}$. One voter prefers $\bar{a}$ to anything else and for any a_j different from $\bar{a}$ one voter in each pair would prefer a_j to $\bar{a}$ and the other in the pair would prefer $\bar{a}$ to a_j. In figure 7.7, where the maxima for voters 1, 2, 3, 4, 5 are at points numbered 1, 2, 3, 4, 5, $\bar{a}$ would beat a_j with a majority of 2, 3, and 5 or $\bar{a}$ would beat a' with a majority of 2, 4, and 5. Furthermore, any point $a' \neq \bar{a}$ can be beaten by some other point a_j, as in Figure 7.7 a_j beats a' with 2, 4, and 5.

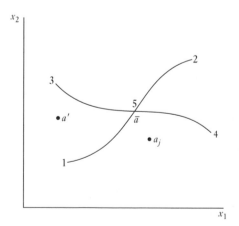

Figure 7.7   Equilibrium for $m = 5$ voters in $n = 2$ space

The interesting feature of Plott's conditions for equilibrium are that the likelihood of satisfying them in the real world is extremely remote. Even if they were, by some amazing chance, to be satisfied, it would still be true that even a slight change in *one* voter's preferences would disrupt the equilibrium, because it would upset the necessary pairing of opposites. For all practical purposes, therefore, we can say that, given $m > 2$ voters and $n \geq 2$ dimensions of judgment with continuous alternatives, equilibrium of tastes is non-existent.

This conclusion has been extended further by translating it into the language of game theory. When a majority prefers a_h to a_j, one says a_h *dominates* a_j and one defines a *core* as the set of undominated points, which is the same as the definition of Condorcet winners. Schloss (1973) has shown that the Plott equilibrium defines a core, given that the differentiability feature is removed; and Rubinstein (1979) has shown that, generically, cores of voting games, in which only continuous preferences are assumed, are empty.

Just how devastating is the absence of equilibria has been impressively demonstrated by Richard McKelvey, whose work has been aimed at showing that, when equilibrium breaks down, it breaks down completely (McKelvey, 1976, 1978). It has been frequently supposed that, although it is extremely unlikely that an alternative can beat $n - 1$ others, still all members of a relatively small set of k alternatives (themselves in cycle) can probably all beat the remaining $n \quad k$ others. If this were so, then some alternative in this "top cycle" might reasonably be regarded as a satisfactory winner and disequilibrium would simply mean the absence of a clear choice among several generally preferred outcomes. McKelvey has shown, however, that given continuous utilities, the top cycle can be expected to include all possible alternatives in an n-dimensional space. In a fashion similar to Plott's, McKelvey showed with an extremely general topological model, that the conditions for an equilibrium were:

1   that the indifference contour for some voter i (not restricted as to convexity or any of the usual economic assumptions) must coincide with the frontier of the set of points that can beat some point a_h;
2   that all other voters' indifference contours can be paired up in the sense that, if some points a_j and a_k are on voter i'''s indifference frontier, then they must also be on at least one other voter i'''s indifference frontier.

These are, of course, very general formulations of the same kind of symmetry conditions that have been required all along, by Black, by Black and Newing, and by Plott. And they tell us about the same thing, namely, that conditions for equilibria are so restrictive as to render equilibria virtually nonexistent. Furthermore, even in the unlikely event that they should be satisfied, any single individual who is paired with another to generate equilibrium, can break it up by dissembling about his or her true preferences. Hence, not only are equilibria rare, they are also extremely fragile.

An important feature of McKelvey's conditions is that, if they are not met, then the top cycle includes all points in the policy space. This fact means that there is some way by which *any* point can beat the status quo. Suppose $\bar{a}$ is the status quo; then, if it is desired to replace $\bar{a}$ with a', there is some sequence of majority rule decisions (and often many such sequences) such that a' beats a_n, a_n beats a_j, ..., a_k beats $\bar{a}$. Hence, any official or participant who can control the agenda can bring about the adoption of his or her desired alternative a'. But, of course, there is also a path by which $\bar{a}$ may then beat a'. So a second participant may foil the first.

A result similar to McKelvey's has been arrived at from a quite different topological model by Schofield (1978). His analysis begins with the observation that, for any point, x, in a multidimensional issue space, some indifference curve for each participant passes through x. Given these indifference curves, one can find the set of points, $P_C(x)$, which is the set of points in the neighborhood of x that are preferred to x by some winning coalition, C_k, $k = 1$, 2, $\ldots$. If, for the set, W, of all winning coalitions, $P_W(x)$ is such that there are some points, y, in the neighborhood of x that cannot be included in $P_W(x)$ by some path $(y \, M_{C_i} \, 2, \ldots, w M_{C_k} \, x$, when C_i and C_k are any specific-winning coalitions), that is, if there are some points y that x can defeat no matter what, then there may be an equilibrium at x. If, however, all points in some arbitrary neighborhood of x can by some sequence of majority coalitions defeat x, then equilibrium at x is impossible. Furthermore, if for any particular set of individual ideal points and indifference curves, there is even just one point x for which equilibrium is impossible, then the system as a whole is cyclical. Effectively, this means that unless the individual preferences are highly similar – so that *all* winning coalitions are similar – social choices are certain to be cyclical. While this condition does not in itself indicate the likelihood of cyclical outcomes, Schofield has also shown that, if the issue space has at least as many dimensions as one more than the number of persons necessary for a minimal winning coalition, then the system is, for certain, cyclical. In legislatures most members probably have on every decision a dimension concerning the effect of the several alternatives on their chances of re-election and in electorates on all political platforms containing issues of a distributive nature ("who gets what") each participant is concerned, *inter alia*, with what he or she gets. Hence for these types of voting situations, there are at least as many dimensions as voters and disequilibrium is, therefore, certain.

In comparison with McKelvey's statement of the condition for a global cycle from $\bar{a}$ to $\bar{a}$, Schofield's theorem is a condition for a local cycle in an open neighborhood of $\bar{a}$. Practically, the difference is that McKelvey's condition guarantees instability by admitting what may seem like farfetched alternatives. (For example, the free soil issue that broke up the great Jeffersonian–Jacksonian agrarian coalition seemed to Democratic politicians, southerner and dough-face alike, to be an absurd irrelevancy because it was an issue more or less proscribed by the constitutional settlement. Nevertheless it broke up a seemingly overwhelming and persistent majority. This is the kind of event that we are assured is possible by McKelvey's theorem.) Schofield's theorem, while not excluding global cycles, assures us that local cycles can occur based presumably on only "slight" changes in the alternatives. (This is the kind of change we see in ordinary American politics where parties that appear extremely close ideologically turn each other out of office.) Hence, for most practical politics disequilibrium is assured.

The Significance of Disequilibrium

I now return to the philosophical question I raised in the beginning by asking what is the relevance for politics of the rarity and fragility of majority rule equilibria. And I start off by observing that the discoveries about majority rule probably apply to all methods of summing individual preferences. We know from Arrow's theorem that cycles cannot be avoided by any fair system, but we do not know from that fact much about the likelihood or fragility of a cyclical outcome for other methods of summation. We do know, however, that other methods of voting (e.g., positional methods like plurality voting and approval voting and point counting or electoral methods like proportional representation which are intended to make minorities win) are subject to disequilibria, manipulation, agenda control, etc., in much the same way as majority rule. It seems fairly safe to conjecture, therefore, that equilibria in other voting systems are as rare and fragile as in majority rule. And this rarity and fragility are doubtless as much features of systems based upon co-opted committees as of those based on popular election. Turning to non-voting methods of summation (e.g., statements of the sense of the meeting by a speaker or the selection of alternatives by a dictator), we know that the single summarizer necessarily imposes his or her own order on the outcome. Inasmuch as equilibrium is thus achieved by suppressing alternatives that might beat the single summarizer's own choice, such an equilibrium is not the product of summation, but of force. The rebellious discontent of those whose preferred alternatives are suppressed is simply evidence that the equilibrium achieved by a dictator or single summarizer is spurious. It seems to me, therefore, that what we have learned about equilibria under majority rule applies equally well to any political society whether it uses the institutions of majority rule or some other kind of voting or merely dictatorship.

And what we have learned is simply this: disequilibrium, or the potential that the status quo be upset, is the characteristic feature of politics.

In the nineteenth century, economics was often called the "dismal science" largely because the equilibria predicted from price theory were not palatable to those who called it dismal. In what seems to me a deeper sense, however, politics is *the* dismal science because we have learned from it that there are no fundamental equilibria to predict. In the absence of such equilibria we cannot know much about the future at all, whether it is likely to be palatable or unpalatable, and in that sense our future is subject to the tricks and accidents of the way in which questions are posed and alternatives are offered and eliminated.

Yet there are some features of social decisions that we do understand and, in the short run at least, those do grant us some prevision. Although there are not likely to be equilibria based entirely on tastes, still there are outcomes of social decision processes, those outcomes do embody some people's values, and the outcomes themselves are not wholly random and unexpected. What prevents purely random embodiments of tastes is the fact that decisions are customarily made within the framework of known rules, which are what we commonly call institutions. Since institutions certainly affect the content of decisions, we can see something of the future by specifying just what these effects are and how they are produced. Thus, despite the recent enthusiasm for studying tastes (e.g., public opinion, political culture, and the like), what we learn from recent political theory is that the particular structure of an institution is at least as likely to be predictive of socially enforced values as are the preferences of the citizen body. So the sum of the recent discoveries is to re-emphasize some of the classical heritage of political science. It is important to study constitutions simply because, if there are repetitive equilibria in social decisions, these equilibria derive at least as much from institutions as from tastes and values.

The outcome, then, of the search for equilibria of tastes is the discovery that, failing such equilibria, there must be some institutional element in the regularities (or actual equilibria) we observe. We are forced back, therefore, to the eclectic stance that political scientists have typically taken. Outcomes are, of course, partially based on tastes because some person's (not necessarily a majority of people's) tastes are embodied in outcomes. But the ways the tastes and values are brought forward for consideration, eliminated, and finally selected are controlled by the institutions. And institutions may have systematic biases in them so that they regularly produce one kind of outcome rather than another. In this sense, therefore, both institutions and tastes contribute to outcomes. To offer an example, in electoral systems it not infrequently happens that the same party or coalition of parties wins election after election. Conceivably, this stability may be caused by the fact that tastes are constant, but more often it is caused by the fact that exactly those issues likely to upset the stability of tastes are kept out of the electoral process by structures like constitutions and political parties. (An excellent example of this process is the exclusion of the issues of slavery and free soil from American national politics from the 1780s to the 1840s. The hegemony during that period of the Jefferson–Jackson Democracy, which did provide a long-term equilibrium, could exist only by suppressing the slavery issue. Once it was raised, dividing rural slaveholders from rural yeomen, the Democracy and the nation were disrupted.) What results, therefore, is an outcome based both on tastes and on the way in which some tastes are admitted to and some not admitted to and some not admitted to the decision process.

Consequently, we cannot study simply tastes and values, but must study institutions as well. Nevertheless, as we return to the study of institutions after a generation of preoccupation with values and preferences, we do so with a deeper appreciation of the appropriate scientific program and of our opportunities and limitations as scientists. The scientific program is to explain by the application of covering laws to particular situations how institutions generate equilibrium by systematically excluding or including certain tastes or values. As for our opportunities and limitations, we have already learned from the developments chronicled here that we cannot expect to find equilibria of preferences, but we may be able to find equilibria generated from a given subset of preferences by particular institutions.

In the earlier tradition of studying constitutions, it was customary to look for the centers of power in a constitutional structure – to look, that is, for who could control which portions of the political process. This is, of course, an interesting practical question for the world, because it concerns the distribution of "power." But while such distributions are a fascinating subject for ideologues and inside dopesters, they are not of much scientific interest because the idea of power is itself an inexact and probably meaningless notion (Riker, 1965). What is instead scientifically interesting is the interaction among the several participants in a system to discover the particular kinds of outcomes that are both feasible and likely, given a particular institutional arrangement.

This is the kind of study of institutions that has developed more or less unconsciously among specialists on the US Congress, who are among the first political scientists to study a single institution in intensive detail. Having identified the several centers of authority in the conventional kind of constitutional analysis, they have gone on to generalize about how these centers interact in the selection of values to be incorporated into legislation. So sophisticated has this kind of inquiry become that Kenneth Shepsle, a scientist trained in both fields, has attempted to integrate it formally with the study of equilibria of preferences. Thereby he has managed to lay down an outline of what the new kind of study of institutions might typically look like (Shepsle, 1979). Shepsle distinguishes two ways in which rules and structures may impose conditions that affect the outcome of the decision-making process in a legislature, or indeed in many other kinds of decision-making bodies. One is decentralization: to divide the body into subsets which act on some issues for the whole body: e.g., committees or parties in legislatures, departments in colleges or firms or bureaucracies, etc. The other is the creation of jurisdictions: to divide up for separate consideration the dimensions of decision so that, in a policy space with m dimensions, it may be required that each dimension, $x_1, \ldots, x_m$, be considered by itself. Sometimes these two kinds of rules are combined, as when a congressional committee is given control over one feature, and only one feature, of a bill. Shepsle defines a structure-induced equilibrium as one in which, taking tastes as given, a particular arrangement of subsets of decision makers and particular assignment of jurisdictions allow for the passage of a motion that cannot be defeated by any other alternative. (Of course, an equilibrium of tastes, where, regardless of institutions, a motion can beat any other, implies an equilibrium of structure. But the converse does not hold: a structural equilibrium does not imply an equilibrium of preferences. In that sense, the notion of a structural equilibrium is narrower in meaning than an equilibrium of values or tastes.) Shepsle's main theorem is that structural equilibria exist in a committee system, provided the members' preferences can be represented by quasi-concave, continuous utility functions and the committee system operates in an m-dimensional space in such a way that each dimension is under the jurisdiction of a particular committee. (Particular assignments of jurisdiction are assumed to be protected by a germaneness rule that permits amendments in committee only on the appropriate dimension.)

The secret of this theorem is that, when social choices are made dimension by dimension, then, if an equilibrium condition (say, single-peakedness) is satisfied on one of the dimensions, some degree of stability is imposed on the whole system. Since equilibrium conditions often do exist when choice is on only one dimension, especially if the decision-making body shares cultural standards, it follows that structural equilibrium is much easier to obtain than a pure equilibrium of tastes.

But, asks Shepsle, how robust is a structural equilibrium? The answer is that, insofar as a constitutional system supplies an outcome that is not the same as outcomes that might have been obtained from simple majority rule in the system without committees, jurisdictions, etc., the losers are likely to want to change the committees and jurisdictions in the hope of winning on another day. In the end, therefore, institutions are no more than rules, and rules are themselves the product of social decisions. Consequently, the rules are also not in equilibrium. One can expect that losers on a series of decisions under a particular set of rules will attempt (often successfully) to change institutions and hence the kind of decisions produced under them. In that sense rules or institutions are just more alternatives in the policy space and the status quo of one set of rules can be supplanted with another set of rules. Thus the only difference between values and institutions is that the revelation of institutional disequilibria is probably a longer process than the revelation of disequilibria of taste.

Our new sophistication about institutions, induced by our long foray into the search for equilibria of tastes, is that institutions are probably best seen as congealed tastes. We ought, I think, to be thoroughly aware that the distinction between constitutional questions and policy questions is at most one of degree of longevity. If institutions are congealed tastes and if tastes lack equilibria, then so do institutions, except for short-run events.

It is true that we can get a lot of mileage out of relatively stable institutions. If elections are zero-sum or constant-sum, then all the restrictions embodied in game theory notions of solutions of zero-or constant-sum games and all the restrictions embodied in sociological laws like the size principle are more or less permanently imposed on outcomes. Only the abolition of zero-sum or constant-sum methods of election is likely to eliminate these restrictions. Similarly, while it is easy enough to change some prisoners' dilemmas to situations with Pareto-optimal outcomes (as for example the so-called "tragedy of the commons" was solved by the enclosure of common lands into private property), still there are other apparently intractable prisoners' dilemmas (such as arms races and the extinction of species of creatures like passenger pigeons and perhaps whales). In the former cases there are governmental organizations inclusive enough to change the institutions of the dilemma. But the latter sort of institutions are likely to last for a very long time.

Nevertheless, if the non-Pareto optimal feature of an institution is sufficiently distasteful to most participants, it is possible to reconstruct institutions. Private property in land was extended to the commons to prevent the destruction of soil, and it is not impossible to imagine private property in whales. If institutions do generate an outcome in which everyone loses, it is reasonable to expect some new and less distasteful institutions – which is to say that even the most fundamental institutions lack equilibria, although it may take generations to alter them.

The sum of our new sophistication is, therefore, that political outcomes truly are unpredictable in the long run. We may have a few pretty well-verified generalizations to guide us (for example, the size principle or Duverger's law), but for the most part we live in a world that is uncertain because it lacks equilibria.

Conclusion

And this conclusion sets the problem of political science: in the long run, outcomes are the consequence not only of institutions and tastes, but also of the political skill and artistry of those who manipulate agenda, formulate and reformulate questions, generate "false" issues, etc., in order to exploit the disequilibrium of tastes for their own advantage. And just what combination of institutions, tastes, and artistry will appear in any given political system is, it seems to me, as unpredictable as poetry. But given the short-term structural and cultural constants, there is some stability, some predictability of outcomes, and the function of the science of politics is to identify these "unstable constants."

Appendix

This paper was originally presented at the meeting of the International Political Science Association, Moscow, 1979. For that occasion the concluding remarks were as follows:

Given the location of the platform for the presentation of this paper, I should conclude with the observation that political science can exist only in an open society, that is, a society with unfettered freedom of speech. Insofar as the science involves a study of values and tastes, scientists can be accurate in their predictions only if they are able to ignore official doctrine (as for example in

Marxism) about the preferences and interests of groups and classes. Official doctrine may be right or wrong, but whether it is or is not right is a subject not for official decree but rather for empirical investigation, which is possible only an open society. Moreover, insofar as the science of politics involves the study of institutions, scientists must be able to examine critically the way governmental institutions operate at the highest as well as lowest levels of government. Only thus can they study the way institutions systematically bias the selection among preferences. Of course, this means that governmental secrecy, if it exists, prohibits scientific investigation of political structures.

Which of the two – official doctrine about preferences or governmental secrecy – is the more inhibiting for scientific inquiry probably varies from place to place. But I believe secrecy is more often a barrier. The scientist can often guess fairly well about tastes and preferences, but the way institutions work is extremely difficult to guess about. Consequently, if I am correct in believing that the study of tastes is not enough and that one must study institutions as well, then it follows that the new emphasis on institutions as a necessary part of the science of politics probably precludes this science in any society governed secretly.

Finally, there is another way in which the conclusions of this paper imply that political science can exist only in an open society. One important conclusion, indeed the most important conclusion, of the line of reasoning set forth in this paper is that, in the long run, nearly anything can happen in politics. Naturally this conclusion is a sharp contradiction of all philosophies of history (such as Marxism) that necessitate a belief in the existence of a determined course for the future. This belief is precisely what the discoveries recounted in this paper deny. So, if these discoveries are true – and mathematically they appear to be irrefutable – then a science of politics is incompatible with Marxism.

References

Arrow, Kenneth J. (1963) *Social Choice and Individual Values*, 2nd edn. New Haven: Yale University Press.

Black, Duncan (1948) On the Rationale of Group Decision Making, *Journal of Political Economy*, 56: 23–34.

Black, Duncan (1958) *The Theory of Committees and Elections*. Cambridge: Cambridge University Press.

Black, Duncan, and R. A. Newing (1951) *Committee Decision with Complementary Valuation*. Edinburgh: William Hodge.

Davis, Otto, and Melvin Hinich (1966) A Mathematical Model of Policy Formation in a Democratic Society. In J. Bernd (ed.), *Mathematical Applications in Political Science*. Dallas: Southern Methodist University Press.

Davis, Otto, Melvin Hinich, and Peter Ordeshook (1970) An Expository Development of a Mathematical Model of the Electoral Process, *American Political Science Review*, 64: 426–8.

Downs, Anthony (1957) *An Economic Theory of Democracy*. New York: Harper.

Eliot, T. S. (1940) *The Idea of a Christian Society*. New York: Harcourt Brace.

Fishburn, Peter (1973) *The Theory of Social Choice*. Princeton, NJ: Princeton University Press.

McKelvey, Richard D. (1976) Intransitivities in Multidimensional Voting Models and Some Implications for Agenda Control, *Journal of Economic Theory*, 12: 472–82.

McKelvey, Richard D. (1978) General Conditions for Global Intransitivities in Formal Voting Models. Unpublished, Carnegie Mellon University.

Plott, Charles R. (1967) A Notion of Equilibrium and its Possibility under Majority Rule, *American Economic Review*, 67: 787–806.

Riker, William H. (1961) Voting and the Summation of Preferences, *American Political Science Review*, 55: 900–11.

Riker, William H. (1965) Some Ambiguities in the Notion of Power, *American Political Science Review*, 57: 341–9.

Riker, William H. (1978) A Confrontation between the Theory of Democracy and the Theory of Social Choice. New York: American Political Science Association.

Riker, William H. (1980) *Liberalism against Populism*. San Francisco: W. H. Freeman.

Robertson, Dennis (1977) *A Theory of Party Competition*. New York: John Wiley.

Rubinstein, Ariel (1979) A Note about the 'Nowhere Denseness' of Societies Having an Equilibrium under Majority Rule, *Econometrica*, 47: 511–14.

Schofield, Norman (1978) Instability of Simple Dynamic Games, *The Review of Economic Studies*, 45: 575–94.

Sen, A. K. (1966) A Possibility Theorem on Majority Decisions, *Econometrica*, 34: 491–9.

Sen, A. K. and P. K. Pattanaik (1969) Necessary and Sufficient Conditions for Rational Choice and Majority Decision, *Journal of Economic Theory*, 1: 178–202.

Schloss, Judith (1973) Stable Outcomes in Majority Voting Games, *Public Choice*, 15: 19–48.

Shepsle, Kenneth (1979) Institutional Arrangements and Equilibrium in Multidimensional Voting Models, *American Journal of Political Science*, 23: 27–59.

PART III

Alternative Conceptions of the State

EIGHT

The Coase Theorem and the Theory of the State[*]

James M. Buchanan

Source: From *Natural Resources Journal* (1973), 13: 579–94.

Things were really quite simple in the post-Pigovian world of microeconomic policy, a world characterized by possible divergencies between private and social marginal cost (or product). The classically nefarious factory might be observed to spew its smoke on the neighboring housewife's laundry, and in so doing impose costs that were not reckoned in its presumed strict profit-maximizing calculus. The remedy seemed straightforward. The "government" should impose a corrective tax on the factory owner, related directly to the smoke-generating output (or, if required, a particular input) and measured by the marginal external or spillover cost. Through this device the firm would be forced to make its decisions on the basis of a "socially correct" comparison of costs and revenues. Its profit-maximizing objective should then lead it to results that would be "socially optimal."

Things have not seemed nearly so simple since R. H. Coase presented his analysis of social cost.[1] Coase's central insight lay in his recognition that there are two sides to any potential economic interdependence, two parties to any potential exchange, and that this ensures at least some pressure toward fully voluntary and freely negotiated agreements. Moreover, such agreements tend to insure the attainment of efficiency without the necessity of governmental intervention beyond the initial definition of rights and the enforcement of contracts. Applied to the example in hand, if the damage to the housewife's laundry exceeds in value the benefits that the firm derives from allowing its stacks to smoke, a range of mutual gain persists, and utility and profit-maximizing behavior on the part of the two parties involved will result in at least some reduction in the observed level of smoke damage, a reduction that can be taken to be efficient in terms of total product value. No governmental remedy may be called for at all, and indeed Coase argued that attempted correction by government might create inefficiency. Such intervention might forestall or distort the negotiations between the affected parties. As a further aspect of his analysis, Coase advanced the theorem on allocational neutrality that now bears his name. This states that under idealized conditions when transactions costs are absent and where income–effect feedbacks are not relevant, the allocational results of voluntarily negotiated agreements will be invariant over differing assignments of property rights among the parties to the interaction.

Much of the discussion since 1960 has involved the limitations of this theorem in the presence of positive transactions costs. In this setting, differing assignments of rights may affect allocative outcomes. Furthermore, the transactions costs barrier to voluntarily negotiated agreements that can be classified as tolerably efficient may be all but prohibitive in some situations, notably those that may require simultaneous agreement among many parties. The generalized transactions costs rubric may be used to array alternative institutional structures, with the implied objective being that of minimizing these costs.

My purpose in this paper is not to elaborate these extensions and/or limitations of the Coase analysis, many of which have become familiar even if an exhaustive taxonomy of cases has not been completed. My purpose is almost the opposite. I want to extend the Coase analysis, within his assumptions of zero transactions costs and insignificant income–effect feedbacks, to differing institutional settings than those that have normally been implicitly assumed in the discussions of the neutrality theorem. This approach leads to the question: Why did Coase suggest that the Pigovian prescriptions might produce inefficient results? Or, to put this somewhat differently, why does the theorem of allocational neutrality stop short at certain ill-defined institutional limits? Why can it not be extended to encompass all possible institutional variations, variations that may be broadly interpreted as differences in the assignments of property rights? What is there in the implied Pigovian institutional framework that might inhibit the voluntary negotiations among parties, always assuming zero transactions costs? If the neutrality theorem holds, why should the political economist be overly concerned about institutional reform, as such?

There is a paradox of sorts here between the theorem of allocational neutrality, interpreted in its most general sense, and Coase's basic policy position. One implication of the theorem, so interpreted, would be that the thrust of classical political economy may have been misdirected. Adam Smith's central message points toward institutional reform and reconstruction as means of guaranteeing overall efficiency in resource usage, and, as noted, we can always interpret institutions as embodying specific property rights. Governmental authorities were to be stripped of their traditionally established rights to interfere in the workings of the market economy; or, stated conversely, individual traders were to be granted rights to negotiate on their own terms. The central theorem of classical economics might be summarized as the demonstration of the differences in allocational results under divergent institutional structures. I do not think that Coase would disagree with my statements here, and I think that he shares with me an admiration for Adam Smith, and that Coase, too, places Smith's emphasis on institutional–structural reform above the modern policy emphasis on detailed and particularistic manipulation of observed results.

The apparent paradox may be resolved when we take account of the theory of the state or of government that is, perhaps surprisingly, shared by Adam Smith, Pigou, and Coase. My argument proceeds in several steps. First, it is necessary to distinguish carefully between property rights and liability rules. Secondly, I shall demonstrate that governmental or collective action, if conceived in the Wicksellian framework or model, does not modify the applicability of the neutrality theorem. Thirdly, I shall show that government, conceived in a non-Wicksellian model, need not modify the applicability of the theorem, but that, in such case, property rights are explicitly changed with the introduction of governmental action. Finally, I shall suggest that the theory of government decision-making implicit in both classical and neoclassical economics, and carried over in Coase's analysis, offers the source of the seemingly paradoxical limits on the neutrality theorem.

Property Rules and Liability Rules

In his basic paper, Coase did not carefully make a distinction between the assignment of rights to particular individuals and the rules determining the liability of particular individuals for damage that their behavior might impose on others. His example, the now-familiar one of the interaction between the rancher and the farmer, was discussed in terms of alternative rules for bearing liability for damages. Either the rancher, whose cattle strayed onto the neighboring croplands, was liable for damages that the farmer might suffer, or he was not liable. If both cattle and grain were marketed competitively, the neutrality theorem showed that the same allocative outcome would be generated, regardless of which set of liability rules should be in existence. In the former case, the rancher, knowing in advance that he would be liable for damages caused by his straying animals, would include these payments as an anticipated cost in making his size-of-herd decisions. In the latter case, the farmer, knowing that he can collect no damages from the rancher (and that he must respect the property rights of the rancher to cattle), will find it advantageous to initiate payments to the latter in exchange for agreements limiting the size of herd, if indeed the value of crop damage at the margin exceeds the value of the additional grazing to the rancher.

Coase overlooked the fact that the institutional structure was significantly different in the two cases. In the second case, the shift toward an efficient outcome takes place through an ordinary market or exchange process, in which none other than the two parties need get involved. In the first case, however, as presented by Coase, there must be third-party interference by a "judge" to assess charges for damage that has been done. In the context of his discussions, this institutional difference does not matter, since the third-party can, presumably, measure and assess damages with complete accuracy. The difference is nonetheless important in the more general setting. Consistency should have dictated that the first case be presented, not as one where the rancher was liable *ex post* for damages caused by his straying animals, but as one where the farmer held enforceable property rights in his croplands, rights that were inviolate except on his own agreement. In this framework, the rancher would have had to negotiate an agreement with the farmer in advance of any actual straying of cattle. This converts the institutional setting on this side into one that is parallel to the converse case. No third party, no judge, is required to intervene and to assess damage *ex post*.

We may define this setting as one in which property rules are established and enforced, as opposed to liability rules.[2] This setting calls direct attention to the motivation that both parties have to exploit the potentially realizable surplus by moving from the initial inefficient position. This setting also allows for an extension of the neutrality-efficiency theorem beyond those strictly objectifiable circumstances suggested to be present in the Coase example. If the precise degree of damage caused by external imposition is ambiguous, the third party must necessarily exercise his own best judgment in making a settlement. By contrast, if property rules are defined, with the necessity of prior agreement on the part of the potentially damaged party, the latter's own subjective assessment of potential damage becomes controlling in determining the range over which final outcomes may settle. This assessment is, of course, a better measure of actual value lost than the estimate made by any third party.

Wicksellian Unanimity

For my purposes in this paper, the specification that parties to an interaction are defined by property rather than liability rules facilitates relating the Coase theorem on allocational neutrality to the underlying conception or theory of government or of the State. In the simplest possible model, we may conceive of a polity that is limited in membership to the parties directly involved in the potential interaction. The interacting group can be made coincident in membership with the political unit. On this basis, we can interpret the "trades" among the parties as being analogous to collective or governmental decisions reached under the operation of a Wicksellian rule of unanimity.[3] Consider either the earlier factory–housewife example, or Coase's familiar rancher–farmer one. In either illustration, we can think of the two-party group as comprising the all-inclusive membership in the political community, in which case agreement between the two parties on any matter is equivalent to unanimous accord. Resort to third-party adjudication is impossible for the simple reason that no third party exists.

From this context, it becomes easier to conceive "the State" merely as the instrumental means or device through which individuals attempt to carry out activities aimed to securing jointly desired objectives. This is, of course, the traditional framework for all theories of social-contract origins of government. In this setting, all activities of the public sector are explained in exchange terms, even if it is recognized that the exchange process is significantly more complex than that which makes up the central subject matter of orthodox economic theory. There is at least no conceptual or logical necessity to think of "the State" as an entity that exists separate from and apart from citizens.

If we remain within the strict contractarian conception of collective action, where all decisions require unanimous consent by all members of the political community, and if we retain the assumption that transactions costs are absent, the Coase theorem on allocational neutrality may be applied beyond those limits within which it has normally been discussed. In this model, collective or governmental decision-making remains equivalent to freely negotiated voluntary exchange. Hence, there is little or no cause for concern about "governmental intervention" as such, because any action that might properly be classified as "governmental" would not emerge unless all parties agree on the contractual terms.

Differences in the assignment of rights might, as in the standard simple exchange cases, generate differences in distributional outcomes, but the contractual process would lead to allocational results that are both efficient and invariant. Consider a classic example, that introduces what we may appropriately call collective or public goods, David Hume's villagers whose utility would be increased by drainage of a meadow. The neutrality theorem, applied to this example, demonstrates that an efficient and unchanged allocational result will emerge from freely negotiated contract whether the postulated initial position should be one in which individuals own separate plots of land through which the swampy stream flows or whether the whole meadow is defined as communal property, accessible to all parties. With an effective unanimity rule, and with zero transactions costs, the complex exchange that is required for efficiency would be worked out under any initial structure of individual rights. The sharing of the gross gains-from-trade among separate persons would, of course, be influenced by the particular property assignment in being. If the sharing of such gains modifies individual demands for the common good, at the margin, that is, if income effects are present, differing assignments can produce slight differences in allocational results, but, under the assumptions here, those results produced will continue to be efficient.

Simple Majority Voting

When the unanimity requirement for collective decisions is abandoned, governmental action no longer represents a complex equivalent of a voluntary exchange process.[4] If decisions that are to be binding over the inclusive group can be made by a subset of this group, there is no guarantee that a particular individual holds against the imposition of net harm or damage. Once his own contractual agreement to the terms of governmental or collective action is dropped as a requirement, an individual can no longer be certain that he will share in the gross gains that governmental action will, presumably, generate. From this it seems to follow that collective action, motivated by improvement in the positions of members of a decisive coalition smaller than the totality of community membership, need not produce results that are efficient, even with zero transactions costs.[5] Any nonunanimity voting rule, for example, that of simple majority voting, would seem to produce results that may be, in the net, inefficient.

The neutrality theorem is, however, more powerful than might be suggested by cursory attention to this example. Efficient outcomes will tend to emerge from the contractual process, even under less-than-unanimity voting rules for collective action, if the modified structure of property rights consequent on the departure from unanimity is acknowledged, and if individuals are allowed freely to negotiate trades in these rights. Economists have not fully incorporated the property-rights structure of less-than-unanimity voting rules into their orthodoxy, and they tend to stop short of the extension of the neutrality theorem herein suggested.

Consider a situation in which individuals hold well-defined rights, which are acknowledged by all parties, and which are known to be enforceable without costs. If no collective action is undertaken, individuals trade such rights among themselves in simple exchanges, ensuring mutuality of gain. If collective action is undertaken, but only on the agreement of all parties, mutuality of gain (or, at the limit, absence of loss) is ensured. If this requirement is dropped, and individuals may be subjected to damage or harm through collective action, the value of their initial holdings is necessarily changed, again on the assumption of zero transactions costs. Individuals no longer hold claims that are inviolate against imposed reductions in value. A new and ambiguous set of rights is brought into being by the authorization of governmental action taken without the approval of all parties. Any potentially decisive decision-making coalition, a simple majority of voters in our example here, possesses rights to the nominal holdings of the minority. These rights are, in this instance, ambiguous because they emerge only upon the identification of the majority coalition that is to be decisive with respect to the issue under consideration for collective action. Once identified, however, members of the effective majority hold potentially marketable rights. These may be exchanged, directly or indirectly, and the contractual process will again ensure that the efficient allocative outcome will be achieved, and that this will be invariant, given the appropriate assumptions about transactions costs and income effects.

We may illustrate this in a highly-simplified three-person example. Consider a community that includes three men: A, B, and C. Collective decisions are to be made by simple majority voting. Initial holdings of units of an all-purpose and numberable consumption good are, let us say, 100 for A, 60 for B, and 30 for C. In this environment, let us suppose that a governmental project is proposed, one that promises to yield benefits of 30 units, distributed equally among the three persons. The gross costs of this project are, however, 40 units; clearly, the proposal is inefficient. Despite this, if B and C can succeed in organizing themselves into a majority coalition, and if they can impose the full tax costs of the proposal on A, they can make net gains. In this case, the results would appear as follows:

Person	Benefits	Costs	Net
A	10	40	−30
B	10	0	10
C	10	0	10

Once B and C are identified as the decisive members of the coalition, however, individual A can negotiate trades, or side payments, that will be mutually beneficial to all parties, and which will keep this inefficient outcome from being achieved. Individual A can, for example, offer either B or C a net gain of 15 units to join a different majority coalition that will disapprove the project. Or, if both B and C hold firm, they can exact from A a payment of 10 units for their agreement to withhold the project. The side payments, which must be allowed to take place under our assumption of zero transactions costs, will ensure that all inefficient projects are forestalled, and, similarly, that all efficient projects will be carried out.[6]

The values to individuals of the "property rights in franchise" embodied in a majority-voting regime depend critically on the constitutional limits within which majorities are allowed to take collective-political action. These values will also depend on the technological possibilities for potential coalition gains within the given set of constitutional constraints defined. Detailed exploration of these interesting and mostly unresolved issues would not be suitable in this paper. For present purposes, the points to be recognized are, firstly, that any departure from unanimity in collective decision processes modifies the structure of rights from that which is defined exclusively by private-sector claims and obligations, and, secondly, that even with this modified set of rights, the theorem on allocational neutrality remains valid within the required, and highly restricted, assumptions concerning transactions costs and income effects.[7]

Administrative Authority

In traditional economic-policy discussions, the arguments for and/or against governmental intervention in the private sector rarely take place under explicitly defined models for collective decision making. For the most part, those who propose "corrections" to the outcomes of voluntary exchange processes, like those who oppose them, are content to treat governmental decisions as exogenous to the valuations of the persons in the economy itself. If, however, these arguments are interpreted consistently within any collective decision-making framework, the structure that can most readily be inferred is neither that of unanimity nor simple majority voting. The model of government that accords most closely with economic policy discussions is one in which authority to take collective action is vested in an administrator, a bureaucrat, an expert, who chooses for the community, presumably on the basis of his own version of the "public interest," or, in technical economist's jargon, some "social welfare function."

It is useful, therefore, to extend our analysis of the theorem on allocational neutrality to this administrative-decision model of public choice. Probably because the model is essentially implicit rather than explicitly postulated, little or no attention has been paid to the alternative means through which the single decision-maker for the collectivity may be selected. Nor need this concern us here. Strictly speaking, the conclusions developed below follow whether the decision-maker be divinely ordained, democratically elected, arbitrarily appointed, selected in competitive examination, or hereditarily determined.[8] I want to examine a model in which a single person has been empowered to make decisions for a whole community. This defines a specific structure of rights, an assignment, and the problem is to determine the allocative results that will emerge in comparison with those predicted under alternative structures. The first point to be noted is the same as that made with respect to simple majority voting. The delegation of decision-making power to the single person modifies the set of rights in existence, even prior to the onset of any imposed governmental action. The designated chooser for the community holds potentially valued claims that were nonexistent before he is constitutionally authorized to act.

Consider again Hume's drainage of the village meadow. Instead of operating through a rule of unanimity, we now assume that the village has empowered a single person to act on behalf of all persons in the group and, furthermore, it is acknowledged that his decisions will be enforced. Formally, it does not matter whether the decision-maker is chosen from within or from outside the group. For expositional simplicity, however, we shall assume that he is selected from outside the village. We now assume that a drainage project, lumpy in nature, will yield symmetrically distributed benefits to villagers valued at 1000 units of the numeraire commodity. The project will cost a total of 800 units and the taxing institution requires symmetrical sharing. The project is clearly Pareto-efficient, and, as indicated earlier, under an operating rule of unanimity, the project will be undertaken, given our zero transactions costs assumption, and including all free-rider behavior under the transactions costs rubric. The question becomes: would this project necessarily be selected by the single decision-maker, the alternative structure of property rights under consideration?

It is illegitimate to assume that the single administrator knows the preferences of the citizens, or, even should these be estimated with accuracy, that he would necessarily embody individual values dollar-for-dollar in his own choice calculus. The administrator or bureaucrat will select the project if the costs that he bears are less than the benefits that he, personally, secures. But these costs and benefits are not, and cannot possibly be, those of the community of citizens. Apparently, there is nothing in this model to ensure correspondence between the bureaucrat's choices and those results that are to be classified as efficient by orthodox economists' criteria. This suggests that the theorem of allocational neutrality breaks down.

If, however, we move beyond this naive model of administrative behavior, the applicability of the neutrality theorem may be restored. By acting in accordance with his own subjective evaluation, the bureaucrat may be failing to maximize the value of the property right that has been assigned to him constitutionally. To show this, let us assume that, naively, the decision-taker decides against the project noted. In this decision, he deprives the citizenry of benefits valued at 1000 units and, at the same time, avoids the imposition of tax costs of 800 units on the community. In a setting with zero transactions costs, where large numbers can readily reach contractual agreements, the citizenry, as an inclusive group of taxpayer-beneficiaries, would be willing to offer side payments up to a total of 200 units to secure a change from negative to positive action on the project.[9] If the decision-maker, the administrator or bureaucrat, uses these side payments, either indicatively or actually, to determine his final choice, the drainage project will be carried out. The theorem of allocational neutrality is apparently validated in this more sophisticated model for bureaucratic behavior. So long as the decision-maker acts to maximize the potential rent on the property right delegated to him, the right to make the final decision for the whole community, the allocative result will be identical to that forthcoming under alternative rights structures, with, of course, the transactions-costs, income-effect assumptions postulated. As in all property-assignment shifts, the distributional results may be quite different under differing assignments. If the bureaucrat maximizes the potential rent on his right to choose for the group, and, furthermore, if he collects this in the form of a personal side payment, there is an income transfer from members of the original group to the "outsider" selected as decision-taker.[10]

Objection may be raised to rent-maximizing as the appropriate norm for bureaucratic behavior, even if we neglect ethical considerations (these will be introduced in later). To postulate that the designated decision-maker maximizes the potential side payments that he can receive from taxpayer-beneficiaries, as a group, implies that the decision-maker, himself, is indifferent as among the choice alternatives, that he places no personal evaluation on the differences among these opportunities available to him. If, in fact, the bureaucrat or administrator is external to the affected group of persons in the community, this assumption may seem plausibly realistic. If, however, he is chosen from within the community itself, his own evaluation must be taken into account. Whether the decision-taker is selected from within or without the original group of members, his own evaluation can be, and must be, included in any correct assessment of costs and benefits.

We may return to the numerical illustration introduced above. Suppose that the gross benefits of the proposed drainage project, to all persons other than the decision-taker, amount to 1000 units of a numeraire good (we may call these "dollars"), and that the gross costs, to all persons other than the decision-taker, amount to 800. Suppose, however, that the decision-maker, himself, places a monetary value of, say, $400 on the "natural beauty" of the swampy and undrained meadow. Even should he be required to pay no part of the tax costs of the project, this 400 units of value necessarily becomes a component in the total opportunity cost of the drainage scheme. Under these conditions, the bureaucrat will refuse the proffered side payment of 200 units. The project will not be undertaken.

Does this result suggest that the theorem of allocational neutrality breaks down? The question of whether the decision-taker is selected from within or without the initial membership of the group becomes critical at this point. If the selection is internal, the project is inefficient under the conditions suggested, and it will not be undertaken under any rights assignment. This is because the person's negative evaluation would be an input in any internal contractual negotiations that might produce an allocative outcome. In this case, the neutrality theorem remains valid. Suppose, however, that the bureaucrat is not in the initial group of members. In such case, his own personal evaluation of the project alternatives will not enter and will not affect allocative outcomes when the assignment of rights is limited to initial members. This decision-maker's evaluation will, however, enter as a determinant when he is assigned the rights to choose for the group. The neutrality theorem would not hold valid under these conditions unless the decision-maker should be, in fact, wholly indifferent as among the choice alternatives.

This result should not be at all surprising. The theorem on allocational neutrality, even under its restricted set of required assumptions, should hardly be expected to extend to rights assignments that embody differing memberships in the group. For fixed memberships, the theorem remains fully valid. Even when the decision-maker is selected from outside, the theorem suggests that any change in rights assignments, once the additional member is included, among this new membership will produce identical allocational results.

The Theory of the State

It is possible to interpret both the policy implications of Coase's theorem on allocational neutrality and Pigovian corrective policy prescriptions in terms of the underlying conceptions, models, or theories of government. As the analysis above has suggested, under certain conceptions of governmental process, neither Coase nor the Pigovians should have been greatly concerned about institutional change as means of generating allocative efficiency. If distributional considerations are neglected, and if decision-makers for the community are chosen from within the group, the structure of rights will modify allocative outcomes only because of differentials in levels of transactions costs, provided that the decision-takers are motivated by economic self-interest. The policy thrust of Coase's discussion is, however, to the effect that governmental or collective intrusion into the negotiation processes of the market economy tends to retard rather than to advance movement toward allocative efficiency. Conversely, the policy thrust of the whole Pigovian tradition is that governmental or collective intrusion into the market economy tends to be corrective of distortions and leads toward rather than away from those results that might satisfy agreed-on efficiency criteria.

The Pigovian model of the state may be examined first. The decision-taker, the person or group empowered to impose the corrective taxes and subsidies, is presumed to act in accordance with rules laid down for him by the welfare economist. His task is that of measuring social costs and social benefits from alternative courses of action, a task that he is presumed able to carry out effectively. On the basis of such measurements, the decision-taker is to follow the rules laid down, quite independently of the personal opportunity costs that he may face in refusing side payment offers. The Pigovian policy-maker must be an economic eunuch. The idealized allocative results are, of course, identical with those that would emerge under a regime where the decision-maker is wholly "corrupt" in the sense of strict maximization of the potential side payments or rents on his rights to make decisions. If he is expected to behave as a rent-maximizer, however, there would be no need for elaborated and detailed instruction in the form of rules or norms, as derived from the theorems of welfare economics. Within this Pigovian conception, the decision-maker for the group does not and/or should not maximize the rental value of the rights of decision that he is granted. This may be treated either as a positive prediction about bureaucratic behavior or as a normative proposition for bureaucratic behavior.

In the Coase conception,[11] an interpretation that is similar in certain respects seems to follow. If, in fact, governmental decision-makers act as strict rent-maximizers, the neutrality theorem suggests that there should be little or no concern about allocative results, *per se*. The evidence of such concern must, therefore, indicate some denial of the rent-maximizing behavioral hypothesis. Again, this may be taken as positive prediction or normative statement. The governmental decision-maker, the bureaucrat, empowered to act on behalf of the group, either does not maximize rents on the rights that he commands or he should not do so on moral–ethical grounds. In either case, the Coase concern for allocational efficiency returns since the negotiating pressure toward optimality is removed once the decision-making power is shifted from the market to the public sector.

It is perhaps surprising to find common elements in the basic conceptions of political process held by the proponents of essentially opposing policy positions. But in both the Pigovian framework and in that imputed here to Coase, the governmental decision-maker, either singly or as a member of a choosing group, is and/or should be "incorruptible." In this respect, the two conceptions of governmental process seem identical, despite the sharp differences in information possibilities attributed to the governmental authority in the two models. In the Pigovian tradition, the bureaucrat is both informed and incorruptible; in the Coase framework, he is ignorant and incorruptible.

Agreement on this "incorruptibility" characteristic of governmental decision-makers, and indeed the introduction of the term "corruptible" in this familiar usage, suggests that there exist widely shared ethical presuppositions concerning the inalienability of the delegated rights to make collective choices. That is to say, some shift away from the unanimity rule for collective decisions may be accepted as necessary, with the accompanying acknowledgment that new and previously nonexistent "rights of decision" are brought into being, rights that have economic value that is potentially capturable by the subset of the citizenry empowered to take decisions on behalf of all. Such rights may, however, be considered to be inalienable; that is, the holder is not entitled to sell them or to exploit his possession of them through collection of personal rewards, either directly or indirectly.[12] It would be inappropriate in this paper to examine in detail the validity of such ethical presuppositions, although this opens up many interesting and highly controversial topics for analysis.[13]

The existence of such presuppositions can scarcely be denied. The pejorative content of such terms as "vote-trading," "logrolling," "political favoritism," "spoils system," "pork-barrel legislation" attests to the pervasiveness of negative attitudes toward even minor attempts on the part of possessors of political decision-making rights to increase rental returns. If these attitudes are sufficiently widespread, prohibitions against bureaucratic and political rent-maximization may extend beyond the mere promulgation of ethical norms for behavior. The rewards and punishments that are consciously built into the governmental structure may be specifically aimed at making such rent-maximization unprofitable for any person empowered to take decisions on behalf of the whole group. The designated bureaucrat who is assigned authority over one specific aspect of public policy may not be morally or ethically inhibited from accepting side payments. But he may face harsh legal penalties should he accede to monetary temptations. To the extent that these constitutionally determined constraints ensure that the economic self-interests of governmental decision-makers dictate behavior unresponsive to proffered side-payments (direct or indirect) it may be argued, almost tautologically, that any outcomes chosen for the community by the "incorruptibles" must be, by definition, classified as "efficient." This would produce the paradoxical conclusion that the conditions for efficiency depend critically on the institutional structure and that, even with unchanged personal evaluations, solutions which are deemed efficient under one set of institutions may be inefficient under another.

The avoidance of this paradox becomes possible if we are content to define as allocationally efficient only that set of possible outcomes that could emerge from the contractual negotiation process among persons in the community, on the assumption that no rights are inalienable. In this case, the introduction of inalienability in the rights of governmental decision-takers clearly makes the theorem of allocational neutrality invalid. Under the highly restricted assumptions of zero transactions costs, any activity will be efficiently organized in the absence of governmental intervention, and, absent income effect feedbacks, the allocational outcome will be invariant over differing assignments of private and alienable rights. Under such conditions as these, it is the inalienability of rights that the shift to the public sector introduces which removes the guarantee that outcomes will be efficient, not the shift to governmental decision-taking *per se*. If we avoid the apparent paradox in this manner, however, the implication is left that the constitutional shift of activities to the public sector is an almost necessary source of inefficiency. When other considerations are accounted for, however, this implication need not follow. When transactions costs are recognized, and especially when distributional implications are considered, efficiency "in the large" may dictate the governmental organization of activities along with the inalienability of the rights delegated necessarily to bureaucratic decision-makers. There is no final escape from the requirements that each particular institutional change proposed must be examined on its own merits, on some case-by-case procedure, with the interdependence among separate organizational decisions firmly in mind.

Notes

*   I am indebted to my colleagues Winston Bush, Dennis Mueller, and Gordon Tullock for helpful suggestions.

1   R. H. Coase, *The Problem of Social Cost*, J. Law & Econ. 3: 1–44 (1960).

2   This terminology is adopted from the discussion by Calabresi and Melamed, whose paper clarifies the distinction between these two. As they state, a property rule "is the form of entitlement which gives rise to the least amount of state intervention." *See* Calabresi and Melamed, Property Rules, Liability Rules, and Inalienability: One View of the Cathedral, *Harv. L. Rev*, 85: 1089–146 (1972); *see also* Demsetz, Some Aspects of Property Rights, *J. Law & Econ*, 9: 64–5 (1966).

    In a paper to be published, I have also called attention to the distinction between these two institutional arrangements, noting in particular the necessary resort to third-party action under liability rules. See Buchanan, The Institutional Structure of Externality, *Pub. Choice* (forthcoming).

3   Collective decision-making under a rule of unanimity is associated with the name of Knut Wicksell in modern public-finance theory analysis because he proposed institutional reforms that embodied unanimity in the reaching of tax and expenditure decisions. See K. Wicksell, *Finanztheoretische Untersuchungen* (Jena: Gustav Fischer, 1896). The central portion of this work appears in English translation as *A New Principle of Just Taxation*, in Classics in the Theory of Public Finance, eds. R. Musgrave and A. Peacock (1959), 72–118.

4 It is possible to use the analogue to voluntary exchange at the level of constitutional, as opposed to day-to-day choice. That is to say, we might analyze the selection of a political constitution, the rules for the reaching of collective decisions, under a postulated unanimity rule. It is then possible to derive a logical basis for non-unanimity rules from unanimous agreement at the constitutional level. This is the approach taken in J. Buchanan and G. Tullock, *The Calculus of Consent* (1962).

5 With zero transactions costs, any departure from unanimity voting rules for collective action would hardly be acceptable at the constitutional level. But this modification is introduced here for purposes of developing the exposition of the argument, not for descriptive relevance.

6 It is often erroneously argued that individuals with the superior economic power, A in our example, can exercise more influence in the formation of dominant coalitions than individuals with inferior economic power, C in our example. If, however, C fully recognizes the exploitation potential available in the situation described, he can offer B precisely the same terms as those offered by A. In the basic arithmetic here, there is no more likelihood that the net gains from not undertaking the project, 10 units, will be shared by A rather than by B or C. In effect, the Von Neumann–Morgenstern solution set of imputations to the simple majority game becomes:

(5,5,0)   (5,0,5)   (0,5,5).

For an elaboration of this analysis, see Buchanan and Tullock, *The Calculus of Consent*, at chapters 11 and 12.

7 In another paper, I have developed somewhat more fully some of the possible implications of the modified rights structure that majority voting rules embody. See Buchanan, The Political Economy of the Welfare State. Center for the Study of Public Choice Research Paper No. 808231–1–8 (June 1972). This paper was prepared for the Conference on Capitalism and Freedom, in honor of Milton Friedman, in Charlottesville, Virginia, October 1972; it will be published in the volume of conference proceedings.

8 The method of selection may affect the motivation of the decision-maker and, in this way, modify the likelihood that the behavioral hypotheses implicit in the orthodox conceptions will be corroborated.

9 In the numerical examples, the potentially-capturable rent seems to be 200 units because of the assumptions that both benefits and costs of the drainage project are shared symmetrically among all of the villagers. If these assumptions are relaxed, the decision-maker can collect a larger sum in rent. His potential gain will, in all cases, be the sum of the *larger* of the *positive* or the *negative* differences between benefits and costs, the sum being taken over all members of the community.

10 This modifies the standard economist's treatment of the distinction between allocational and distributional results. The latter may, for certain purposes, be neglected if the zero-sum aspects are confined to a stable group of "members." If, however, a new rights assignment, such as that discussed, generates distributional transfers outside the original group, the effects, for this group, are negative-sum. Applied to the realistic setting in which transactions costs are present, this suggests that a community may, under certain conditions, find it advantageous to put up with allocative inefficiency rather than to secure its removal at the expense of distributional transfers to delegated decision-takers.

11 For an explicit statement of the Coase–Chicago position, *see* Demsetz, The Exchange and Enforcement of Property Rights, *J. Law & Econ.* 7: 21–2 (1964).

12 In the paper previously cited, Calabresi and Melamed discuss the inalienability of rights at some length, and particularly they draw attention to several examples where inalienability is accepted. See Calabresi and Melamed, *supra* note 2.

The precise location of "inalienability" in the situation discussed may be questioned. In delegating decision-making authority to an agent, citizens may not be considered to be transferring the economic value inherent in the "right to choose." In this framework, it is the rights of the citizenry which are "inalienable" in some fundamental sense, and the agent could scarcely transfer a "right" which he does not possess. In my discussion, I have equated the empirically observed delegation of decision-making authority with an effective transfer of a valuable "right" which is then supposed to be "inalienable."

13   The ethical bases for such widely shared attitudes may be challenged when the economic analysis is carefully developed. In the case of marketing rights to make decisions for the community, the relative undesirability of the distributional results provide a sufficient reason for inalienability. Conceptually, the decision-maker can capture *all* of the potential surplus from constitutionally-authorized action. In this limit, those who presumably make the constitutional delegation of authority, the citizenry, find themselves with zero net gains from collective action. So long as the delegation of decision rights along with inalienability is predicted to generate positive net gains, the citizenry's economic position is enhanced. The possible inefficiency in the standard allocative sense is more than offset by the distributional gains.

NINE

Dictatorship, Democracy, and Development

MANCUR OLSON

Source: From *American Political Science Review* (September 1993), 87: 567–76.

In my student days, in reading Edward Banfield's (1958) account of the beliefs of the people in a poor village in Southern Italy, I came upon a remarkable statement by a village monarchist. He said, "Monarchy is the best kind of government because the King is then owner of the country. Like the owner of a house, when the wiring is wrong, he fixes it" (p. 26). The villager's argument jarred against my democratic convictions. I could not deny that the owner of a country would have an incentive to make his property productive. Could the germ of truth in the monarchist's argument be reconciled with the case for democracy?

It is only in recent years that I have arrived at an answer to this question. It turns out that for a satisfactory answer one needs a new theory of dictatorship and democracy and of how each of these types of government affects economic development. Once this new theory is understood, one can begin to see how autocracies and democracies first emerge. I shall set out this conception in a brief and informal way and use it to explain some of the most conspicuous features of historical experience.

The starting point for the theory is that no society can work satisfactorily if it does not have a peaceful order and usually other public goods as well. Obviously, anarchic violence cannot be rational for a society: the victims of violence and theft lose not only what is taken from them but also the incentive to produce any goods that would be taken by others. There is accordingly little or no production in the absence of a peaceful order. Thus there are colossal gains from providing domestic tranquility and other basic public goods. These gains can be shared in ways that leave everyone in a society better off. Can we conclude that because everyone could gain from it, a peaceful order emerges by voluntary agreement?

From the logic of the matter, we should expect that in small groups a generally peaceful order will normally emerge by voluntary agreement but that in large populations it will not. The key to the matter is that each individual bears the full costs or risks of anything he or she does to help establish a peaceful order or to provide other public goods but receives only a share of the benefits. In a tiny group, such as a hunter–gatherer band, each person or family will obtain a significant share of the benefits of a peaceful order, and the net advantages of such an order are so great that even a single family's share of the gains can easily outweigh the sacrifices needed to obtain it. Moreover, when there are only a few, the welfare of each noticeably depends on whether each of the others acts in a group-oriented way. Thus each family, by making clear that cooperation by another will bring forth its cooperation but that noncooperation will not, can increase the likelihood that another will match its behavior, thereby increasing the incentive each has to act in the group interest. The theoretical prediction that sufficiently small groups can often organize for collective action is corroborated by countless observations (Olson 1965).

This prediction is also in accord with the anthropological observations of the most primitive societies. The simplest food-gathering and hunting societies are normally made up of bands that have, including the children, only about 50 or 100 people. In other words, such a band will normally contain only a few families that need to cooperate. Anthropologists find that primitive tribes normally maintain peace and order by voluntary agreement, and that is to some extent what Tacitus, Caesar, and other classical writers observed among the less advanced Germanic tribes. The most primitive tribes tend to make all important collective decisions by consensus, and many of them do not even have chiefs. When a band becomes too large or disagreement is intense, the band may split, but the new bands normally also make decisions by unanimous consent. If a tribe is in the hunting-and-gathering stage, there is also little or no incentive for anyone to subjugate another tribe or to keep slaves, since captives cannot generate enough surplus above subsistence to justify the costs of guarding them.[1] Thus within the most primitive tribes of pre-agricultural history, the logical presumption that the great gains from a peaceful order can be achieved by voluntary agreement appears to hold true.

Once peoples learned how to raise crops effectively, production increased, population grew, and large populations needed governments. When there is a large population, the same logic that shows why small groups can act consensually in their common interest, tells us that voluntary collective action *cannot* obtain the gains from a peaceful order or other public goods, even when the aggregate net gains from the provision of basic public goods are large.[2] The main reason is that the typical individual in a society with, say, a million people will get only about one-millionth of the gain from a collective good, but will bear the whole cost of whatever he or she does to help provide it, and therefore has little or no incentive to contribute to the provision of the collective good. There is by now a huge theoretical and empirical literature on this point, and the great preponderance of this literature agrees that, just as small groups can usually engage in spontaneous collective action, very large groups are not able to achieve collective goals through voluntary collective action.[3]

Thus we should not be surprised that while there have been lots of writings about the desirability of "social contracts" to obtain the benefits of law and order, no one has ever found a large society that obtained a peaceful order or other public goods through an agreement among the individuals in the society.

The First Blessing of the Invisible Hand

Why, then, have most populous societies throughout history normally avoided anarchy? An answer came to me by chance when reading about a Chinese warlord (see Sheridan 1966). In the 1920s, China was in large part under the control of various warlords. They were men who led some armed band with which they conquered some territory and who then appointed themselves lords of that territory. They taxed the population heavily and pocketed much of the proceeds. The warlord Feng Yu-hsiang was noted for the exceptional extent to which he used his army for suppressing bandits and for his defeat of the relatively substantial army of the *roving bandit*, White Wolf. Apparently most people in Feng's domain found him much preferable to the roving bandits.

At first, this seems puzzling: why should warlords, who were *stationary bandits* continuously stealing from a given group of victims, be preferred, by those victims, to roving bandits who soon departed? The warlords had no claim to legitimacy and their thefts were distinguished from those of roving bandits only because they took the form of continuing taxation rather than occasional plunder.

In fact, if a roving bandit rationally settles down and takes his theft in the form of regular taxation and at the same time maintains a monopoly on theft in his domain, then those from whom he exacts taxes will have an incentive to produce. The rational stationary bandit will take only a *part* of income in taxes, because he will be able to exact a larger total amount of income from his subjects if he leaves them with an incentive to generate income that he can tax.

If the stationary bandit successfully monopolizes the theft in his domain, then his victims do not need to worry about theft by others. If he steals only through regular taxation, then his subjects know that they can keep whatever proportion of their output is left after they have paid their taxes. Since all of the settled bandit's victims are for him a source of tax payments, he also has an incentive to prohibit the murder or maiming of his subjects. With the rational monopolization of theft – in contrast to uncoordinated competitive theft – the victims of the theft can expect to retain whatever capital they accumulate out of after-tax income and therefore also have an incentive to save and to invest, thereby increasing future income and tax receipts. The monopolization of theft and the protection of the tax-generating subjects thereby eliminates anarchy. Since the warlord takes a part of total production in the form of tax theft, it will also pay him to provide other public goods whenever the provision of these goods increases taxable income sufficiently.

In a world of roving banditry there is little or no incentive for anyone to produce or accumulate anything that may be stolen and, thus, little for bandits to steal. Bandit rationality, accordingly, induces the bandit leader to seize a given domain, to make himself the ruler of that domain, and to provide a peaceful order and other public goods for its inhabitants, thereby obtaining more in tax theft than he could have obtained from migratory plunder. Thus we have "the first blessing of the invisible hand": the rational, self-interested leader of a band of roving bandits is led, as though by an invisible hand, to settle down, wear a crown, and replace anarchy with government. The gigantic increase in output that normally arises from the provision of a peaceful order and other public goods gives the stationary bandit a far larger take than he could obtain without providing government.

Thus government for groups larger than tribes normally arises, not because of social contracts or voluntary transactions of any kind, but rather because of rational self-interest among those who can organize the greatest capacity for violence. These violent entrepreneurs naturally do not call themselves bandits but, on the contrary, give themselves and their descendants exalted titles. They sometimes even claim to rule by divine right. Since history is written by the winners, the origins of ruling dynasties are, of course, conventionally explained in terms of lofty motives rather than by self-interest. Autocrats of all kinds usually claim that their subjects want them to rule and thereby nourish the unhistorical assumption that government arose out of some kind of voluntary choice. (These claims have an echo in some literature in the "transactions costs" tradition that attempts to explain the emergence of various kinds of governments partly or wholly through voluntary contracts and the costs of the transactions associated with them. See Kiser and Barzel 1991; North 1981; North and Thomas 1973.)[4]

Any individual who has autocratic control over a country will provide public goods to that country because he has an "encompassing interest" in it.[5] The extent of the encompassing interest of an officeholder, political party, interest group, monarch, or any other partial or total "owner" of a society varies with the size of the stake in the society. The larger or more encompassing the stake an organization or individual has in a society, the greater the incentive the organization or individual has to take action to provide public goods for the society. If an autocrat received one-third of any increase in the income of his domain in increased tax collections, he would then get one-third of the benefits of the public goods he provided. He would then have an incentive to provide public goods up to the point where the national income rose by the reciprocal of one-third, or three, from his last unit of public good expenditure. Though the society's income and welfare would obviously be greater from a larger expenditure on public goods, the gain to society from the public goods that a rational self-interested autocrat provides are nonetheless often colossal. Consider, for example, the gains from replacing a violent anarchy with a minimal degree of public order.

From history, we know that the encompassing interest of the tax-collecting autocrat permits a considerable development of civilization. From not long after the first development of settled agriculture until, say, about the time of the French Revolution, the overwhelming majority of mankind was subject to autocracy and tax theft. History until relatively recent times has been mostly a story of the gradual progress of civilization under stationary bandits interrupted by occasional episodes of roving banditry. From about the time that Sargon's conquests created the empire of Akkad until, say, the time of Louis XVI and Voltaire, there was an impressive development of civilization that occurred in large part under stationary banditry.[6]

The Grasping Hand

We can now begin to reconcile the village monarchist's insight and the foregoing argument with the case for democracy. Though the village monarchist was right in saying that the absolute ruler has as much incentive to fix what needs repair as the owner of a house, his analogy is nonetheless profoundly misleading. The autocrat is not in a position analogous to the owner of a single house or even to the owner of all housing, but rather to the owner of *all* wealth, both tangible and human, in a country. The autocrat does indeed have an incentive to maintain and increase the productivity of everything and everyone in his domain, and his subjects will gain from this. But he also has an incentive to charge a *monopoly* rent and to levy this monopoly charge on *everything*, including human labor.

In other words, the autocratic ruler has an incentive to extract the maximum possible surplus from the whole society and to use it for his own purposes. Exactly the *same* rational self-interest that makes a roving bandit settle down and provide government for his subjects also makes him extract the maximum possible amount from the society for himself. He will use his monopoly of coercive power to obtain the maximum take in taxes and other exactions.

The consumption of an autocratic ruler is, moreover, not limited by his personal capacities to use food, shelter, or clothing. Though the pyramids, the palace of Versailles, the Taj Mahal, and even Imelda Marcos's 3000 pairs of shoes were expensive, the social costs of autocratic leaders arise mostly out of their appetites for military power, international prestige, and larger domains. It took a large proportion of the total output of the Soviet Union, for example, to satisfy the preferences of its dictators.[7]

Some writers use the metaphor of the "predatory state" but this is misleading, even for autocracies. As we saw earlier, a stationary bandit has an encompassing interest in the territory he controls and accordingly provides domestic order and other public goods. Thus he is not like the wolf that preys on the elk, but more like the rancher who makes sure that his cattle are protected and given water. The metaphor of predation obscures the great superiority of stationary banditry over anarchy and the advances of civilization that have resulted from it. No metaphor or model of even the autocratic state can therefore be correct unless it simultaneously takes account of the stationary bandit's incentive to provide public goods at the same time that he extracts the largest possible net surplus for himself.

Although the forms that stationary banditry has taken over the course of history are diverse, the essence of the matter can be seen by assuming that the autocrat gets all of his receipts in the form of explicit taxation. The rational autocrat will devote some of the resources he obtains through taxation to public goods but will impose far higher tax rates than are needed to pay for the public goods since he also uses tax collections to maximize his net surplus. The higher the level of provision of public goods, given the tax rate, the higher the society's income and the yield from this tax rate. At the same time, the higher the tax rate, given the level of public-good provision, the lower the income of society, since taxes distort incentives.

So what tax rate and what level of public good provision will the rational self-interested autocrat choose? Assume for the moment that the autocrat's level of public-good expenditure is given. As Joseph Schumpeter (1991) lucidly pointed out, and Ibn Kalduhn (1967) sensed much earlier,[8] tax receipts will (if we start with low taxation) increase as tax rates increase, but after the revenue-maximizing rate is reached, higher tax rates distort incentives and reduce income so much that tax collections fall. The rational self-interested autocrat chooses the revenue-maximizing tax rate.

Though the amount collected at any tax rate will vary with the level of public-good provision, the revenue-maximizing tax *rate* for the autocrat should not. This optimal tax rate determines exactly how encompassing the interest of the autocrat in the society is; that is, it determines what share of any increase in the national income he receives. He will then spend money on public goods up to the point where his last dollar of expenditure on public goods generates a dollar's increase in his *share* of the national income. At this point, the gain to society will, as we know, be the reciprocal of his share.

Though the subjects of the autocrat are better off than they would be under anarchy, they must endure taxes or other impositions so high that, if they were increased further, income would fall by so much that even the autocrat, who absorbs only a portion of the fall in income in the form of lower tax collections, would be worse off.

There is no lack of historical examples in which autocrats for their own political and military purposes collected as much revenue as they possibly could. Consider the largest autocratic jurisdictions in Western history. The Bourbon kings of France were (especially on the eve of the French Revolution) collecting all they could in taxes. The Hapsburg kings of Spain did the same. The Roman Empire ultimately pushed its tax rates at least to the revenue-maximizing level.

The Reach of Dictatorships and Democracies Compared

How would government by a rational self-interested autocrat compare with a democracy? Democracies vary so much that no one conclusion can cover all cases. Nonetheless, many practical insights can be obtained by thinking first about one of the simplest democratic situations. This is a situation in which there are two candidates for a presidency or two well-disciplined parties seeking to form the government. This simplifying assumption will be favorable to democratic performance, for it gives the democracy an "encompassing" interest rather like the one that motivates the stationary bandit to provide some public goods. I shall make the opposite assumption later. But throughout, I shall avoid giving democracy an unfair advantage by assuming better motivation. I shall impartially assume that the democratic political leaders are just as self-interested as the stationary bandit and will use any expedient to obtain majority support.

Observation of two-party democracies tells us that incumbents like to run on a "you-never-had-it-so-good" record. An incumbent obviously would not leave himself with such a record if, like the self-interested autocrat, he took for himself the largest possible net surplus from the society. But we are too favorable to democracy if we assume that the incumbent party or president will maximize his chances of reelection simply by making the electorate as a whole as well-off as possible.

A candidate needs only a majority to win, and he might be able to "buy" a majority by transferring income from the population at large to a prospective majority. The taxes needed for this transfer would impair incentives and reduce society's output just as an autocrat's redistribution to himself does. Would this competition to buy votes generate as much distortion of incentives through taxation as a rational autocracy does? That is, would a vote-buying democratic leader, like the rational autocrat, have an incentive to push tax rates to the revenue-maximizing level?

No. Though both the majority and the autocrat have an encompassing interest in the society because they control tax collections, the majority in addition earns a significant share of the market income of the society, and this gives it a more encompassing interest in the productivity of the society. The majority's interest in its market earnings induces it to redistribute less to itself than an autocrat redistributes to himself. This is evident from considering an option that a democratic majority would have if it were at the revenue-maximizing tax rate. At the revenue-maximizing tax rate, a minuscule change in the tax rates will not alter tax collections. A minuscule *increase* in the tax rate will reduce the national income by enough so that even though a larger percentage of income is taken in taxes, the amount collected remains unchanged, and a tiny *reduction* in the tax rate will increase the national income so much that even though a smaller percentage is taken in taxes, receipts are unchanged. This is the optimal tax rate for the autocrat because changes in the national income affect his income only by changing tax collections.

But a majority at the revenue-maximizing tax rate is bound to increase its income from a *reduction* in tax rates: when the national income goes up, it not only, like the autocrat, collects taxes on a larger national income but also earns more income in the market. So the optimal tax rate for it is bound to be lower than the autocrat's. The easiest arithmetic example comes from supposing that the revenue-maximizing tax rate is one-third and that the majority earns one-third of the national income in the marketplace. The rational autocrat will then find that the last dollar in taxes that he collects reduces the national income by three dollars. One-third of this loss is his loss, so he just breaks even on this last dollar of tax collection and is at his revenue-maximizing rate. But if a majority mistakenly chose this same tax rate, it would be hurting itself, for it would lose two dollars (the same dollar lost by the autocrat plus one dollar of market income) from the last dollar it collected in taxes. Thus a majority would maximize its total income with a lower tax rate and a smaller redistribution to itself than would be chosen by an autocrat.[9]

More generally, it pays a ruling interest (whether an autocrat, a majority, or any other) to stop redistributing income to itself when the national income falls by the reciprocal of the share of the national income it receives. If the revenue-maximizing tax rate were one-half, an autocrat would stop increasing taxes when the national income fell by two dollars from his last dollar of tax collection. A majority that, say, earned three-fifths of the national income in the market and found it optimal to take one-fifth of the national income to transfer to itself would necessarily be reducing the national income by five-fourths, or $1.25, from the last dollar that it redistributed to itself. Thus the more encompassing an interest – the larger the share of the national income it receives taking all sources together – the less the social losses from its redistributions to itself. Conversely, the narrower the interest, the less it will take account of the social costs of redistributions to itself.

This last consideration makes it clear why the assumption that the democracy is governed by an encompassing interest can lead to much-too-optimistic predictions about many real-world democracies. The small parties that often emerge under proportional representation, for example, may encompass only a tiny percentage of a society and therefore may have little or no incentive to consider the social cost of the steps they take on behalf of their narrow constituencies. The special interest groups that are the main determinant of what government policies prevail in the particular areas of interest to those interest groups have almost no incentive to consider the social costs of the redistributions they obtain. A typical lobby in the United States, for example, represents less than 1% of the income-earning capacity of the country. It follows from the reciprocal rule that such a group has an incentive to stop arranging further redistributions to its clients only when the social costs of the redistribution become at least a hundred times as great as the amount they win in redistributional struggle (Olson 1982).

It would therefore be wrong to conclude that democracies will necessarily redistribute less than dictatorships. Their redistributions will, however, be shared, often quite un-equally, by the citizenry. Democratic political competition, even when it works very badly, does not give the leader of the government the incentive that an autocrat has to extract the maximum attainable social surplus from the society to achieve his personal objectives.

Long Live the King

We know that an economy will generate its maximum income only if there is a high rate of investment and that much of the return on long-term investments is received long after the investment is made. This means that an autocrat who is taking a long view will try to convince his subjects that their assets will be permanently protected not only from theft by others but also from expropriation by the autocrat himself. If his subjects fear expropriation, they will invest less, and in the long run his tax collections will be reduced. To reach the maximum income attainable at a given tax rate, a society will also need to enforce contracts, such as contracts for long-term loans, impartially; but the full gains are again reaped only in the long run. To obtain the full advantage from long-run contracts a country also needs a stable currency. A stationary bandit will therefore reap the maximum harvest in taxes – and his subjects will get the largest gain from his encompassing interest in the productivity of his domain – only if he is taking an indefinitely long view and only if his subjects have total confidence that their "rights" to private property and to impartial contract enforcement will be permanently respected and that the coin or currency will retain its full value.

Now suppose that an autocrat is only concerned about getting through the next year. He will then gain by expropriating any convenient capital asset whose *tax yield* over the year is less than its *total* value. He will also gain from forgetting about the enforcement of long-term contracts, from repudiating his debts, and from coining or printing new money that he can spend even though this ultimately brings inflation. At the limit, when an autocrat has no reason to consider the future output of the society at all, his incentives are those of a roving bandit and that is what he becomes.[10]

To be sure, the rational autocrat will have an incentive, because of his interest in increasing the investment and trade of his subjects, to promise that he will never confiscate wealth or repudiate assets. But the promise of an autocrat is not enforceable by an independent judiciary or any other independent source of power, because autocratic power by definition implies that there cannot be any judges or other sources of power in the society that the autocrat cannot overrule. Because of this and the obvious possibility that any dictator could, because of an insecure hold on power or the absence of an heir, take a short-term view, the promises of an autocrat are never completely credible. Thus the model of the rational self-interested autocrat I have offered is, in fact, somewhat too sanguine about economic performance under such autocrats because it implicitly assumed that they have (and that their subjects believe that they have) an indefinitely long planning horizon.

Many autocrats, at least at times, have had short time horizons: the examples of confiscations, repudiated loans, debased coinages, and inflated currencies perpetrated by monarchs and dictators over the course of history are almost beyond counting.

Perhaps the most interesting evidence about the importance of a monarch's time horizon comes from the historical concern about the longevity of monarchs and from the once-widespread belief in the social desirability of dynasties. There are many ways to wish a king well; but the king's subjects, as the foregoing argument shows, have more reason to be sincere when they say "long live the king." If the king anticipates and values dynastic succession, that further lengthens the planning horizon and is good for his subjects.

The historical prevalence of dynastic succession, in spite of the near-zero probability that the son of a king is the most talented person for the job, probably also owes something to another neglected feature of absolutisms. Any ruler with absolute power cannot, by definition, also have an independent source of power within the society that will select the next ruler and impose its choice upon the society. An independent capacity to install a new ruler would imply that this capacity can be used to remove or constrain the present autocrat. Thus, as is evident from modern dictatorships in Africa and Latin America, most dictatorships are by their nature especially susceptible to succession crises and uncertainty about the future. These uncertainties add to the problem of short time horizons that has just been described. In these circumstances, it may be advantageous to a society if a consensus emerges about who the next ruler will probably be, since this reduces the social losses arising from the absence in an autocracy of any independent power that could ensure a smooth succession. Given autocracy, then, dynastic succession can be socially desirable, both because it may reduce the likelihood of succession crises and because it may give monarchs more concern for the long run and the productivity of their societies.

Democracy, Individual Rights, and Economic Development

We have seen that whenever a dictator has a sufficiently short time horizon, it is in his interest to confiscate the property of his subjects, to abrogate any contracts he has signed in borrowing money from them, and generally to ignore the long-run economic consequences of his choices. Even the ever-present possibility that an autocracy will come to be led by someone with a short time horizon always reduces confidence in investments and in the enforcement of long-run contracts. What do the individuals in an economy need if they are to have the maximum confidence that any property they accumulate will be respected and that any contracts they sign will be impartially enforced?

They need a secure government that respects individual rights. But individual rights are normally an artifact of a special set of governmental institutions. There is no private property without government! In a world of roving bandits some individuals may have possessions, but no one has a claim to private property that is enforced by the society. There is typically no reliable contract enforcement unless there is an impartial court system that can call upon the coercive power of the state to require individuals to honor the contracts they have made.

But individuals need their property and their contract rights protected from violation not only by other individuals in the private sector but also by the entity that has the greatest power in the society, namely, the government itself. An economy will be able to reap all potential gains from investment and from long-term transactions only if it has a government that is believed to be both strong enough to last and inhibited from violating individual rights to property and rights to contract enforcement. What does a society need in order to have a government that satisfies both of these conditions?

Interestingly, the conditions that are needed to have the individual rights needed for maximum economic development are exactly the same conditions that are needed to have a *lasting* democracy. Obviously, a democracy is not viable if individuals, including the leading rivals of the administration in power, lack the rights to free speech and to security for their property and contracts or if the rule of law is not followed even when it calls for the current administration to leave office. Thus the *same* court system, independent judiciary, and respect for law and individual rights that are needed for a lasting democracy are also required for security of property and contract rights.

As the foregoing reasoning suggests, the only societies where individual rights to property and contract are confidently expected to last across generations are the securely democratic societies. In an autocracy, the autocrat will often have a short time horizon, and the absence of any independent power to assure an orderly legal succession means that there is always substantial uncertainty about what will happen when the current autocrat is gone. History provides not even a single example of a long and uninterrupted sequence of absolute rulers who continuously respected the property and contract-enforcement rights of their subjects. Admittedly, the terms, tenures, and time horizons of democratic political leaders are perhaps even shorter than those of the typical autocrat, and democracies lose a good deal of efficiency because of this. But in the secure democracy with predictable succession of power under the rule of law, the adjudication and enforcement of individual rights is not similarly short-sighted. Many individuals in the secure democracies confidently make even very long-term contracts, establish trusts for great-grandchildren, and create foundations that they expect will last indefinitely and thereby reveal that they expect their legal rights to be secure for the indefinite future.

Not surprisingly, then, capital often flees from countries with continuing or episodic dictatorships (even when these countries have relatively little capital) to the stable democracies, even though the latter are already relatively well supplied with capital and thus offer only modest rates of return. Similarly, the gains from contract-intensive activities such as banking, insurance, and capital markets are also mainly reaped by stable democracies like the United States, the United Kingdom, and Switzerland. Though experience shows that relatively poor countries can grow extraordinarily rapidly when they have a strong dictator who happens to have unusually good economic policies, such growth lasts only for the ruling span of one or two dictators. It is no accident that the countries that have reached the highest level of economic development and have enjoyed good economic performance across generations are all stable democracies. Democracies have also been about twice as likely to win wars as have dictatorships (Lake 1992).

The Improbable Transition

How do democracies emerge out of autocracies? It is relatively easy to see how autocratic government emerges and why it has been the predominant form of government since the development of settled agriculture: there is never a shortage of strong men who enjoy getting a fortune from tax receipts. It is much harder to see how democratic government can emerge out of autocracy.

It is a logical mistake to suppose that because the subjects of an autocrat suffer from his exactions, they will overthrow him. The same logic of collective action that ensures the absence of social contracts in the historical record whereby large groups agreed to obtain the advantages of government also implies that the masses will not overthrow an autocrat simply because they would be better off if they did so. Historical evidence from at least the first pharaohs through Saddam Hussein indicates that resolute autocrats can survive even when they impose heinous amounts of suffering upon their peoples. When they are replaced, it is for other reasons (e.g. succession crises) and often by another stationary bandit.[11] What special circumstances explain the cases where a more or less democratic[12] or at least pluralistic government emerges out of an autocracy?

One obvious special circumstance is that, partly for the reasons just set out, the richest countries are democracies, and democracies have usually prevailed in the competitions with their major autocratic competitors, whether fascist or communist. The triumphant democracies have sometimes encouraged or subsidized transitions to democracy in other countries. In some cases, such as Germany, Japan, and Italy after World War II, the victorious democracies more or less demanded democratic institutions as a price for giving independence to the vanquished nations. The theoretical challenge is to explain not these transitions but rather those that are entirely internal and spontaneous.

Easy as it would be to argue that the initially or spontaneously democratic countries were blessed with democratic cultures or selfless leaders, this would be an *ad hoc* evasion. The obligation here is to explain the spontaneous transitions to democracy from the same parsimonious theory that has been used in the rest of this essay.

The theory suggests that the key to an explanation of the spontaneous emergence of democracy is the *absence* of the commonplace conditions that generate autocracy. The task is to explain why a leader who organized the overthrow of an autocrat would not make himself the next dictator or why any group of conspirators who overthrew an autocrat would not form a governing junta. We have seen that autocracy is a most profitable occupation and that the authors of most coups and upheavals have appointed themselves dictators. So the theory here predicts that democracy would be most likely to emerge spontaneously when the individual, individuals or group leaders who orchestrated the overthrow of an autocracy could not establish another autocracy, much as they would gain from doing so. We can deduce from the theory offered here that autocracy is prevented and democracy permitted by the accidents of history that leave a balance of power or stalemate – a dispersion of force and resources that makes it impossible for any one leader or group to overpower all of the others.

But this deduction does *not* give us any *original* conclusion: rather, it points directly toward one of the major inductive findings in some of the literature in history and in political science on the emergence of democracy. If the theory here is right, there must be a considerable element of truth in the famous "Whig interpretation" of British history and in the explanations of democracy offered by political scientists such as Robert Dahl and, especially, Tatu Vanhanen. If the theory offered here is right, the literature that argues that the emergence of democracy is due to historical conditions and dispersions of resources that make it impossible for any one leader or group to assume all power is also right.

Yet it is also necessary to go back again to the theory for a crucial detail. Even when there is a balance of power that keeps any one leader or group from assuming total control of a large area or jurisdiction, the leader of each group may be able to establish himself as an autocrat of a small domain. A dispersion of power and resources over a large area can result in a set of small-scale autocracies but no democracy. If, however, the different contending groups are scrambled together over a wide and well-delineated domain, then small autocracies are not feasible. They may not be feasible also if each of the leaders capable of forming a small-scale autocracy believes that a domain of that small scale would not be viable, whether because of aggression by other autocrats or for any reason.

If scrambled constituencies or any other reason rules out division of a domain into miniautocracies, then the best attainable option for the leader of each group when there is a balance of power is power sharing. If no one leader can subdue the others or segregate his followers into a separate domain, then the alternative is either to engage in fruitless fighting or to work out a truce with mutual toleration. The provision of a peaceful order and other public goods will, in these circumstances, be advantageous for all of the groups; thus, the leaders of the different groups have an incentive to work out mutually satisfactory arrangements for the provision of such goods. Given peaceful conditions, there are great gains to leaders and other individuals in each group from being able to make mutually advantageous contracts with others and thereby a common interest in establishing a disinterested and independent judiciary. With several groups, it is not certain in advance how elections will turn out, yet each group can, by allying with other groups, ensure that no one other group will continually dominate elections. Thus elections as well as consensual agreements among the leaders of the different groups can be consistent with the interest of the leaders and members of each group.

Though there are a fair number of democracies, there have not been many spontaneous and entirely autonomous transitions from autocracy to democracy. Most of the democracies in the English-speaking world owed a good deal to the pluralism and democracy that emerged in late seventeenth-century Britain and thus they usually do not offer a completely independent test of the argument about the transition to democracy offered here.

Happily, the initial emergence of democracy with the Glorious Revolution of 1689 in England (and its very gradual transition from a democracy with a highly restricted franchise to universal suffrage) nicely fits the logic of the democratic transition predicted by the present theory. There were no lasting winners in the English civil wars. The different tendencies in British Protestantism and the economic and social forces with which they were linked were more or less evenly matched. There had been a lot of costly fighting and, certainly after Cromwell, no one had the power to defeat all of the others. The restored Stuart kings might have been able to do this, but their many mistakes and the choices that ultimately united almost all of the normally conflicting Protestant and other political tendencies against them finally led to their total defeat.

None of the victorious leaders, groups, or tendencies was then strong enough to impose its will upon all of the others or to create a new autocracy. None had any incentive to give William and Mary the power to establish one either. The best option available to each of the leaders and groups with power was to agree upon the ascendancy of a Parliament that included them all and to take out some insurance against the power of the others through an independent judiciary and a Bill of Rights. (The spread of the franchise is too long a story to tell here. But it is not difficult to see how, once the society was definitely nonautocratic and safely pluralist, additional groups could parlay the profitable interactions that particular enfranchised interests had with them – and the costs of suppression that they could force the enfranchised to bear – into a wider suffrage.)

With a carefully constrained monarchy, an independent judiciary, and a Bill of Rights, people in England in due course came to have a relatively high degree of confidence that any contracts they entered into would be impartially enforced and that private property rights, even for critics of the government, were relatively secure. Individual rights to property and contract enforcement were probably more secure in Britain after 1689 than anywhere else, and it was in Britain, not very long after the Glorious Revolution, that the Industrial Revolution began.[13]

Though the emergence of a democratic national government in the United States (and in some other areas of British settlement, such as Australia and Canada) was partly due to the example or influence of Great Britain, it also was due in part to the absence of any one group or colonial government that was capable of suppressing the others. The 13 colonies were different from one another even on such important matters as slavery and religion, and none of them had the power to control the others. The separate colonies had, in general, experienced a considerable degree of internal democracy under British rule, and many of the colonies were, because of the different religious and economic groups they contained, also internally diverse. Many of the authors of the US Constitution were, of course, also profoundly aware of the importance of retaining a dispersion of power (checks and balances) that would prevent autocracy.

The Different Sources of Progress in Autocracies and Democracies

Since human nature is profoundly complex and individuals rarely act out of unmixed motives, the assumption of rational self-interest that I have been using to develop this theory is obviously much too simple to do justice to reality. But the caricature assumption that I have been using has not only simplified a forbiddingly complex reality but also introduced an element of impartiality: the same motivation was assumed in all regimes. The results are probably also robust enough to hold under richer and more realistic behavioral assumptions.

The use of the same motivational assumption and the same theory to treat both autocracy and democracy also illuminates the main difference in the sources of economic growth and the obstacles to progress under autocracy and under democracy. In an autocracy, the source of order and other public goods and likewise the source of the social progress that these public goods make possible is the encompassing interest of the autocrat. The main obstacle to long-run progress in autocracies is that individual rights even to such relatively unpolitical or economic matters as property and contracts can never be secure, at least over the long run.

Although democracies can also obtain great advantages from encompassing offices and political parties, this is by no means always understood (Olson 1982, 1986); nor are the awesome difficulties in keeping narrow special interests from dominating economic policy-making in the long-stable democracy. On the other hand, democracies have the great advantage of preventing significant extraction of social surplus by their leaders. They also have the extraordinary virtue that the same emphasis on individual rights that is necessary to lasting democracy is also necessary for secure rights to both property and the enforcement of contracts. The moral appeal of democracy is now almost universally appreciated, but its economic advantages are scarcely understood.

Notes

*   I am grateful to the US Agency for International Development for support of my research on this subject through my Center for Institutional Reform and the Informal Sector.

1   There is quantitative evidence from an exhaustive survey of ethnographic accounts showing that references to slaves are virtually absent in the accounts of the most primitive peoples but rather common in more advanced agricultural societies (Hobhouse, Wheeler, and Ginsberg 1965). Slavery is unprofitable in hunting–gathering societies (Olson 1967).

2   Small tribes can sometimes form federations and thereby increase the number who can obtain collective goods through voluntary action (Olson 1965, 62–3). Some of the very earliest agricultural societies may have been of this character. But when the number of small groups itself becomes very large, the large-number problem is evident again and voluntary collective action is infeasible.

3   For citations to much of the best literature extending and testing the argument in *The Logic of Collective Action*, as well as for valuable new analyses, see Hardin 1982 and Sandler 1992.

4   This literature is most constructive and interesting, but to the extend to which it tries to explain government in terms of voluntary transactions, it is not convincing. North, while emphasizing transactions costs and contracts, also uses the notion of the "predatory state" and the logic of collective action in his account of the state, so his approach must be distinguished from Barzel's.

5   For the definition of an encompassing interest and evidence of its importance, see Olson 1982. The logical structure of the theory that encompassing interests will be concerned with the outcome for society whereas narrow groups will not is identical with the logic that shows that small groups can engage in voluntary collective action when large groups cannot.

6   Many of the more remarkable advances in civilization even in historic times took place in somewhat democratic or nondictatorial societies such as ancient Athens, the Roman Republic, the North Italian city-states, the Netherlands in the seventeenth century, and (at least after 1689) Great Britain. The explanation for the disproportionate representation of nonautocratic jurisdictions in human progress is presented later in the article.

7   The theory offered here applies to communist autocracies as much as to other types, though the theory needs to be elaborated to take account of the "implicit tax–price discrimination" pioneered by Joseph Stalin. This innovation enabled Stalinist regimes to obtain a larger proportion of social output for their own purposes than any other regimes had been able to do. This explained Stalin's success in making the Soviet Union a superpower and the great military capacity of many communist regimes. It also generated a unique dependence of the system on its management cadre, which ultimately proved fatal. For how the offered theory applies to communist autocracies and the societies in transition, see Clague and Rausser 1992, pref., chapter 4; Murrell and Olson 1991; Olson 1993.

8   Schumpeter's analysis is in his "Crisis of the Tax State," written in the highly taxed Austria–Hungarian Empire late in World War I; Ibn Kalduhn's is in his classic *The Mugaddimah*.

9   A mathematical and a geometrical proof of this conclusion and an analysis of many other technical questions raised by the present theory is available on request.

10   When war erodes confidence about what the boundaries of an autocrat's domain will be, an autocrat's time horizon with respect to his possession of any given territory shortens – even if he believes that he will remain in control of some territory somewhere. In the limit, complete uncertainty about what territory an autocrat will control implies roving banditry. The advantages of stationary banditry over roving banditry are obviously greatest when there are natural and militarily defensible frontiers. Interestingly, the earliest states in history emerged mainly in what one anthropologist calls "environmentally circumscribed" areas, that is, areas of arable land surrounded by deserts, mountains, or coasts (see Carneiro 1970). The environmental circumscription not only provides militarily viable frontiers but also limits the opportunity for defeated tribes to flee to other areas in which they could support themselves (as Carneiro points out). This in turn means that the consensual democracy characteristic of the earliest stages of social evolution is, in these geographical conditions, replaced by autocratic states earlier than in other conditions.

11   For more examples of other types of reason, see Olson 1990.

12   In the interest of brevity, democracy is here defined as competitive elections, social pluralism, and the absence of autocracy, rather than in terms of universal suffrage. Although how a narrower suffrage turns into a wider suffrage can be explained by straightforward extensions of the logic of the theory offered here, developing these extensions and testing them against the historical evidence would not be a small undertaking.

13   For striking evidence on how the growth of cities was much greater in medieval and early modern Europe in democratic or less autocratic regimes, see DeLong and Shleifer 1992. In effect, the DeLong and Shleifer paper is a test of the advantages of democracy that I put forward.

References

Banfield, Edward (1958). *The Moral Basis of a Backward Society*. Glencoe, IL: Free Press.

Carneiro, Robert L. (1970). A Theory of the Origin of the State. *Science*, 169:733–8.

Clague, Christopher, and Gordon Rausser (eds.) (1992). *The Emergence of Market Economies in Eastern Europe*. Cambridge: Blackwell.

DeLong, J. Bradford, and Andrei Shleifer (1992). Princes and Merchants: European City Growth before the Industrial Revolution. Harvard University, mimeo.

Hardin, Russell (1982). *Collective Action*. Baltimore: Johns Hopkins University Press.

Hobhouse, L. T., G. C. Wheeler, and M. Ginsberg (1965). *The Material Culture and Social Institutions of the Simpler Peoples*. London: Routledge & Kegan Paul.

Kalduhn, Ibn (1967). *The Mugaddimah* trans. Franz Rosenthal. Princeton: Princeton University Press.

Kiser, Edgar, and Yoram Barzel (1991). Origins of Democracy in England. *Journal of Rationality and Society*, 3:396.

Lake, David A. (1992). Powerful Pacifists: Democratic States and War. *American Political Science Review*, 86:24–37.

Murrell, Peter, and Mancur Olson (1991). The Devolution of Centrally Planned Economies. *Journal of Comparative Economics*, 15:239–65.

North, Douglass (1981). *Growth and Structural Change*. New York, Norton.

North, Douglass, and Robert Thomas (1973). *The Rise of the West*. Cambridge: Cambridge University Press.

Olson, Mancur (1965). *The Logic of Collective Action*. Cambridge, MA: Harvard University Press.

Olson, Mancur (1967). Some Historic Variation in Property Institutions. Princeton University, mimeo.

Olson, Mancur (1982). *The Rise and Decline of Nations*. New Haven, CT: Yale University Press.

Olson, Mancur (1986). A Theory of the Incentives Facing Political Organizations: Neo-corporatism and the Hegemonic State. *International Political Science Review*, 7:165–89.

Olson, Mancur (1990). The Logic of Collective Action in Soviet-type Societies. *Journal of Soviet Nationalities*, 1(2): 8–33.

Olson, Mancur (1993). From Communism to a Market Democracy. Center for Institutional Reform and the Informal Sector, typescript.

Sandler, Todd (1992). *Collective Action: Theory and Applications*. Ann Arbor: University of Michigan Press.

Schumpeter, Joseph (1991). The Crisis of the Tax State. In *Joseph A. Schumpeter: The Economics and Sociology of Capitalism*, ed. Richard Swedberg, Princeton: Princeton University Press.

Sheridan, James E. (1966) *Chinese Warlord: The Career of Feng Yu-hsiang*. Stanford, CA: Stanford University Press.

TEN

Will Free Trade with Political Science Put Normative Economists out of Work?

Brendan O'Flaherty and Jagdish Bhagwati*

Source: From *Economics and Politics* (1997), 9(3): 207–19.

Will free trade with political science put normative economists out of work? Normative economics has traditionally given advice to a "puppet government" – a government "whose role is to echo the policy that the economist, presented with technocratic information on the economy and choosing an appropriate objective function, proposes as the optimal one from a set of policy instruments" (Bhagwati, 1990). Intellectual free trade with political science forces economists to realize that governments are not puppets – or, at least, not *their* puppets. Without puppets, is there any job for puppeteers?

Consider, for instance, Tabellini and Alesina's (1990) model of voting on the budget deficit. The current majority of voters is unsure whether it will be the majority in the future; perhaps another group with different tastes about the composition of government will be the majority then. This gives the current majority an incentive to finance its spending by issuing debt, because the burden of paying off the debt will fall on a government that might want to alter the composition of government spending from the one the current majority favors. *Ex ante*, before anyone knew what her tastes were, everyone would be better off with a balanced budget rule, but once the game has begun and people know who they are, the current majority always wants to run an excessive deficit.

What are the policy implications of the Tabellini–Alesina model? There aren't any. Tabellini and Alesina's goal is to explain public policies, not to rank them. Governments act the way they must; they are not waiting for Tabellini and Alesina to tell them what to do. One can engage in variational exercises, to be sure – asking, for instance, what the effect of a balanced budget amendment would be.[1] But variational exercises are not policy recommendations; they are counterfactual explorations like Fogel's (1964) reconstruction of American history without railroads.

Nothing is wrong, of course, with models that don't have policy implications. Neither the meteorite theory of dinosaur extinction, for instance, nor the big bang theory of cosmology has any policy implications that we can discern. No one would criticize them on this account. Like the Tabellini–Alesina model, they invite variational exercises – one can speculate, for instance, on whether dinosaurs would have developed opposable thumbs or differential calculus if the meteorite had missed. Such speculations, however, are not policy recommendations; indeed, they already have a name of their own – science fiction.

But especially for a teleological group like economists, models without policy implications may seem like trips without a destination or tennis games without a score. In Stigler's (1982) words, we like to preach. Many economists like to think of themselves as active participants in history, not as members of a contemplative order trying to understand a world they cannot influence, or even as science fiction writers. We write op-ed pieces and letters to the editor, sign advertisements, appear on television shows, testify before Congressional committees, and sometimes even try to take presidents and presidential candidates under our tutelage. The White House has a Council of Economic Advisers, but not a Council of Paleo-Archeological or Cosmological Advisers. For many economists, what makes economics more appealing than cosmology is the possibility of drawing policy implications and influencing the course of history.

Once models like Tabellini–Alesina, however, open up intellectual trade between economics and political science, these hopes seem to be empty and the actions they inspire futile. This is the "determinacy paradox" (Bhagwati, Brecher, and Srinivasan, 1984; Bhagwati, 1984, 1990).[2] The grand conditions of political–economic equilibrium (whatever they may be) have already determined what will happen. Telling the government to lower tariffs makes no more sense than telling a monopolist to lower prices or telling the dinosaurs to wear overcoats. Stigler (1976) and Basu (1992b) express similar thoughts.

The problem is serious.[3] It is a philosophical difficulty that strikes at the heart of economists' ability to think they are accomplishing anything. Practical economists may think these concerns are academic musings unrelated to the important business of health care costs or deficit reduction in which they are busily engaged, but they should realize that the logic of determinacy and self-interest that they consistently apply when discussing other people, if applied to themselves and the people they are talking to, leads to the conclusion that they are wasting their time.

So the unemployment of normative economists that this kind of free trade threatens is not a happy prospect. In this paper we will argue that such unemployment is not inevitable, although most popular re-employment schemes are doomed to failure. Free trade opens up opportunities, but these cannot be exploited if people continue to think and act in the old ways. We are presenting a way to think about retraining normative economists. The chief purpose of this paper will be to outline the new ways of thinking and acting that are appropriate in a free trade regime. The new ways, it turns out, are not really new at all: they are the methods that Smith, Marx and Keynes, among others, used to great effect.

Before we can do that, we will first try to persuade readers that the determinacy paradox cannot be dismissed without careful consideration. We will do this by showing the inadequacy of the four popular responses to free trade with political science – protectionism, constitutionalism, multiple equilibria, and modesty. There is no easy way out.

In section 3 we begin tackling the difficult problem that the determinacy paradox presents. We start with a fundamental philosophical question: in what sense can we think of our own actions as being freely chosen? The question is fundamental because if all of our own thoughts and deeds are also determined by the conditions of grand political-economic equilibrium, we can have no more hope of influencing the course of events than a rock can. The answer we give to this question will show why giving advice can, under proper circumstances, be a sensible activity.

With this background, section 4 turns to the question of how to give advice. Advice stands a chance of being taken only when it is given by certain people to certain other people at certain times; this section is about identifying those pairs and times. Section 5 concludes.

1   False Escapes from the Determinacy Paradox

1.1   Protectionism

Can unemployment of economic advisers be avoided simply by restricting the flow of ideas from political science to economics? Such an outcome is neither feasible nor desirable.

It is not feasible because economists don't have a government that can coerce them not to trade; there is no way to punish deviations. The genie is out of the bottle: increasing numbers of economists are now in the game of building models where policies are endogenous and governments matter.

Nor is it desirable: governments really are not economists' puppets, and to pretend that they are merely invites derision and wastes intellectual resources. Such ostrich-like behavior can carry a heavy price. In the field of transportation, for instance, economists have known since at least 1959 that peak-hour toll schemes on the Hudson River crossings could make people in the New York metropolitan area a lot better off, and yet we have little idea of why these schemes have not been implemented or what steps could be taken that would get them implemented.

1.2   Constitutionalism

Buchanan and Tullock (1962), and writers who have followed in the tradition they established, have looked at constitutional design as the key arena in which normative economists can make a contribution. Once a constitution is in place, political–economic equilibrium is determined and there is no longer any room for advice. So what economists (and political scientists) need to do is devise a constitution that will lead to a good equilibrium. To this task Buchanan, Tullock, and their followers have devoted considerable wisdom, ingenuity, and effort.

This approach is in fact only a slight modification of the traditional practice of advising puppets; the only difference is that it takes constitutional conventions to be the puppets instead of everyday governments. It takes the actions of constitutional conventions to be exogenous, rather than the actions of governments.

There is, however, no reason to believe that constitutional conventions are autonomous, unmoved movers, any more than everyday governments are, or that they are any more receptive to economists' advice than the San Andreas fault is.[4] Anyone who has read the section of the New Jersey constitution dealing with senior citizen bingo games (article IV, section VIII, paragraph 2.A) or the section of the Pennsylvania constitution dealing with police and fire collective bargaining (article III, section 31) would be hard pressed to think that these provisions emerged from any process qualitatively different from normal legislation.[5]

1.3   Multiple equilibria

Often, economists will give the impression that multiple equilibria can fortuitously provide the freedom that policy intervention requires. They will show that a certain model has multiple equilibria, and then (usually in the paper's conclusion) argue that this multiplicity gives the government or some other benevolent entity an opportunity to intervene and kick the system to one of the more desirable equilibria. A *deus ex machina* appears at the end of these stories, and the authors argue that its actions are plausible because nothing else in the story contradicts anything about it. Thus even though the equilibria might arise from solving an endogenous policy model, normatively the economist is still left with a function: she can rank order two or more equilibria, and resurrect the role of policy adviser.

Why aren't multiple equilibria a good way to escape the determinacy paradox? Because multiple equilibria are signs of incomplete modelling, not of actual freedom. In reality, only one thing happens. Multiple equilibria say something about the logical structure of a model; they say nothing about the reality that the model is trying to capture.

Consider a classical symmetrical battle-of-the-sexes game. Under any popular refinement, such a game has two pure-strategy equilibria – both players go to the ballet and both players go to the football game. By that statement is meant that both outcomes are fully compatible with everything stated in the model – the payoff functions, the temporal sequence, the rationality description, the information structure, and so on. (Battle-of-the-sexes also has a mixed strategy Nash equilibrium, but there exist solution concepts like evolutionary stability that exclude this equilibrium.) However, the couple will either go to the ballet or they will go to the football game; they will not go to both. Whatever it is that determines which they go to is something we have left out of the model – perhaps who is stronger or more persistent. All we know now is that the information the model uses is insufficient to answer the question, "Where will they go?" As a way of answering this question, the model is a failure.

But the fact that a particular model fails to answer this question doesn't mean that *no* model can answer this question or that the couple is waiting around for a benevolent economist to tell them what to do. Something left out of the model matters. This particular model's failure doesn't give us the freedom to impose any answer we want. Having a calculator that doesn't take square roots does not entitle you to assert that the square root of 7 is 5.

An example with a model not usually thought of as having multiple equilibria can make the point clearer. The theory of human capital is compatible with the president of General Motors wearing a red tie and also compatible with his wearing a blue tie; so there are (at least) two equilibria. We conclude from the existence of these multiple equilibria that the theory of human capital is not very useful if we are interested in tie color – but no one ever claimed it was. We do not conclude that the president's tie color is indeterminate or that we can tell him what color tie to wear. We conclude only that to answer tie color questions we need another model. The same conclusion should be reached whenever multiple equilibria are encountered.

1.4   Modesty

A final argument is that the determinacy paradox is the product of a degree of hubris that only a few economists are afflicted with. Most of us do not live our lives concerned with the grand conditions of political–economic equilibrium; instead we build and test little models that are at best fables about how pieces of the world work. Thinking that our models are in danger of explaining everything is taking them too seriously.

The Tabellini–Alesina example we used to begin this paper, however, shows that modesty is no escape from the determinacy paradox. The model there was not grand or elaborate; it was just the sort of fable that is typical of economic theory as it is now practiced. Yet because it included a polity whose actions were endogenous no policy implications could be drawn. Modest models are just as susceptible to the determinacy paradox as grand ones are.

2   Free to Advise?

Thus the determinacy paradox is a real problem. Better models endogenize more actors and explain more actions, and so a demand that some actor be considered exogenous or some action be unexplained seems to be a demand for poorer models. Normative economics seems to be simply bad economics. "*Tout comprendre, c'est tout pardonner,*" and so how can the drive to understand the world be reconciled with the urge to improve it?

We think there's a way to make this reconciliation. Normative economics can make a difference in the world, or, at least, we ought to act as if it could.

To understand how, we need to begin at a very rudimentary level. Consider the decisions we make about how to conduct our personal lives – what we will eat for breakfast, what order we will eat it in, how we will travel to work, what papers we will write, what we will say in those papers, what order we will say it in.

For a social scientist who had constructed a very good model of the Columbia economics department, our actions would be completely endogenous. Something caused us to drink orange juice before milk, and such a social scientist could explain what that something was. Private life seems to be prey to the same sort of determinacy paradox that bedevils public life.[6]

And yet when we think about whether to drink orange juice or what article to write, we believe we are making real decisions – decisions that are neither foreordained nor ineffective. We pause and scratch our heads and wonder, "What should I do?" We believe these decisions are effective in the sense that if we decide on a feasible action, then we will do it. Friedman wrote a book about decisions like these and called it *Free to Choose* (1980).

In what sense, then, are we really "free to choose" in private life? Answering this question will start us on the track to understanding normative economics.

In private life, we think to ourselves as free to choose because the hypothetical social scientist studying the Columbia economics department makes no difference to the actual conduct of our lives. Whether or not such a social scientist is around, we still have to think about what to eat for breakfast, what sentence to put next in this paper, what conclusion to come to in the next paper. Knowing that a book of our lives might exist makes no difference if we cannot read it and find out what we are going to do. Even if we could read the book of our lives we would have to decide whether to believe it – whence Newcomb's problem (Nozick, 1969).[7] As Levi (1991, chapter 4) argues, we cannot predict our own decisions before we make them; otherwise we would have already made them.[8] Thus worrying about what to eat for breakfast is compatible with having a scientific world view. We might as well act as if we were free to choose.

Giving and receiving advice, too, are compatible with a scientific world view. Since it makes sense to worry about what to eat for breakfast, it makes sense to learn about nutrition, cooking, and the prices in various supermarkets. Since it makes sense to worry what to write in a paper, it makes sense to read articles, analyze data, and talk to colleagues. Of course, to the social scientist studying the Columbia economics department, the nutritional and professional advice we get is just as endogenous as anything we ourselves do, and so is our reaction to it. Once again, however, this endogeneity does not concern either our adviser or us. Our adviser had to decide what advice to give without consulting the book of her life, and we didn't know what the advice would be until we got it.

In summary, we should treat ourselves as exogenous in everything we do, including giving and seeking advice. This conclusion applies to public as well as private life. We have met the degree of freedom, and it is us.

3   How to Give Advice

> The first rule of giving advice is you only give it when it's sought. It's rude to go around giving advice to people who haven't asked for it. And it's futile, too, because they won't take it. It's more than a rule of etiquette. It's a rule of practicality.
>
> Miss Manners (Judith Martin), quoted in Rosenbaum (1992)

The traditional activity of normative economics, giving advice, can thus be rescued from the determinacy paradox. We can, for instance, agree with Stigler (1976) that a future historian of the world could both tell us what advice we will give before we give it, and whether it will be taken – but still, because we have no access to any such historian, think seriously and give advice. But then we may ask: how should economists give advice? To whom should they give it?

Let us begin by considering two polar cases. Telling the San Andreas fault to be quiet is silly. But if a friend you are eager to see and who is eager to see you calls and asks for directions, you should obviously comply. What distinguishes these two cases?

On one level the answer is simple: whether it is possible to construct a good model with the content of your advice as exogenous (as it should always be), and in this model being able to rank the outcomes that follow different kinds of advice. By a "good model" we mean just a model that meets the usual criteria we use for judging models – predictive ability, generality, simplicity, and so forth. By "rank" we mean a nontrivial ranking where some outcomes are better than others. Advising the San Andreas fault is not sensible because there aren't any good geological models where that advice makes a difference. Giving directions to a friend is sensible because there is a good model where the friend follows the directions and the result is happy.

On the next level, the problem is more difficult: what sort of situations satisfy these criteria? Basu (1992a, 1992b) has investigated this game-theoretic question, and Srinivasan (1992a, 1992b) has properly pointed out that some of Basu's results lack robustness, while others retain applicability. Then again, political scientists have studied the strategic aspects of advice-giving by the subjects of their work; gains from trade are thus easy to find. Some political science work in this area can be found in Krebhiel (1991), Cameron and Jung (1993), and Austen-Smith and Wright (1992).

Two conditions for making advising sensible typically emerge from this literature, both agreeing with common sense.

The first condition is asymmetric information. An adviser has to know something the advisee doesn't know. Otherwise the adviser couldn't give advice. Here we are using "know" in the colloquial sense that the implications of known propositions are not necessarily known (you can know the rules of arithmetic without knowing the 10,000-th digit of pi, even though it follows from the rules of arithmetic). This condition is fairly easy to meet.

The second condition is coincidence of interests. Players in zero-sum two-person games don't exchange information. Coincidence doesn't have to be exact (perhaps you want to see your friend but not until after the ball game is over), and, at any rate, one of the things about which an advisee is most likely to be unsure is an adviser's true motivation. Still, people don't take advice from their antagonists – Saddam Hussein is unlikely to revise the Iraqi agricultural price system just because some American economists tell him that doing so would be nice. As Basu points out, some asymmetry is involved here: you can get a friend to do what you want by telling him what you want, but you generally can't get an enemy to do what you want by telling him what you don't want. If American economists tell Saddam to raise the price of wheat, he won't lower it; he'll ignore the advice. Unless the would-be advisee is truly dim-witted, an adviser's cleverness is not a good substitute for a true coincidence of interests.[9]

Here we see another reason why free trade with political science raises the specter of unemployment for normative economists. If the "government" that our would-be adviser wants to influence is something other than a puppet, its interests could well be substantially different from those of economists, and giving advice to the government will likely be a waste of time. Short of engaging in an extraordinarily elaborate swindle, an economist in a country ruled by a vicious autocrat whose aims she does not approve of should thus see no value-added in advising the government; an elitist economist in a democratic, populist country may find herself in a similar position. So there is no reason to think that any particular economist in any particular situation will always be able to give useful advice. (Thus, for instance, the Tabellini–Alesina paper is probably advice to no one.)

Even if a particular economist cannot advise a particular president or minister at a particular time, however, all is not lost. Sometimes the economist will find her goals are close to the goals of some government officials, or to the goals of some members of another branch of government like Congress. Then advice about what the government should do can be freely given and happily received. More often, though, things will not work out so well, as political science constantly reminds us. Sometimes there may be no one to listen to a particular economist's advice. At other times, especially in developed countries, other opportunities for advising can easily be found – but only if economists look to citizens rather than governments as advisees.

The advantages of advising citizens rather than governments are several. First is information asymmetry: citizens are more likely to differ from economists in their knowledge than government officials do, and so can gain more from hearing what economists have to say.

The second advantage is a closer coincidence of interests. Many economists judge a policy proposal not by what it does for them but by what it does for a lot of the people in society; criteria like Pareto optimality and distributional equity are basically "public-regarding." One doesn't win an argument for free trade in a university seminar by saying, "I like Japanese cameras," and to a large extent economists have internalized the public-regarding values that win arguments at university seminars. To this extent, then, there is some coincidence between what economists say is good for the public and what really is good for the public; and this coincidence forms the base for effective advising. If economists do in fact seek the goals they profess to be seeking when they devise policies, then those policies should serve the interests of the public better than they serve the interests of government officials.

Advice that a great deal of the public accepts can make a difference. Public opinion matters in many good models of politics – in the Western democracies at least. If most of the public believed that AIDS victims were immoral scum who deserved to suffer, government policies towards AIDS would be different from what they would be if most of the public believed AIDS victims were unlucky losers of life's lottery. Economists who influence public opinion can change government policies.

Political scientists have been aware of this relationship for a long time. In this tradition, for instance, Zaller (1992) is a study of how policy elites completely changed their position on the Vietnam War between the early 1960s and the early 1970s. Elites' changed attitudes affected how the media reported on the war, and the media's changed reporting swung mass attitudes. Zaller concludes that changes in the way elites look at the world can have significant effects on public policies.

Advice to citizens is not necessarily advice to *all* citizens. Often (as with Zaller's elites early in the Vietnam War) only a portion of the public is in a position to understand or accept what an economist is saying. More importantly, often only a portion of the public will find its interests aligned with those of the economist. Not all policies that economists advocate result in Pareto improvements.

The idea that the role of normative economists is to advise citizens rather than governments has had a distinguished history; it is not original with us. Marx and Keynes both saw their job as advising citizens, and it is difficult to think of more influential economists.

Marx clearly was not advising the governments of his day – the coincidence of interests are conspicuously missing. Instead he was advising the working class – a portion of the public. Keynes, too, was advising a portion of the public. Even though he sometimes worked for one government or another, he states in his famous conclusion to *The General Theory* (1936) that his goal is to influence future generations of citizens (and perhaps also madmen who hear voices in the air). We are advocating a return to the tradition of Marx and Keynes.

4   Conclusion

Whether it is sensible to give advice – the question we addressed in this paper – is not the only question that free trade with political science poses for normative economics. When we look at the government as something other than a puppet oozing inchoate benevolence, whatever ethical significance could be ascribed to its objective function – the social welfare function – vanishes. For if, as Srinivasan puts it, "the level of a policy instrument is determined along with the price of chapatis in one grand politico-economic general equilibrium" (1992, p. 5), the objective function of policy makers can have no more ethical significance than the objective function of chapati makers. On what, then, can normative economists base their policy recommendations?

This is a large question that needs to be answered in further work. The implications of endogenous policy making are varied and deep. In this paper we have examined only one set of implications, but in that set our conclusions are not surprising: as usual, free trade is better.

Notes

* We have benefited from helpful comments by Charles Cameron, Andrew Caplin, Isaac Levi, and Aaron Tornell. The errors are our own responsibility.
1 The uses of these variational exercises are discussed at greater length in Bhagwati, Brecher and Srinivasan (1984) and Bhagwati (1989).
2 The determinacy paradox is quite distinct from the Lucas (1976) critique of monetary policy. The Lucas critique is about why, if the government accepted certain kinds of advice from economists, that advice would turn out to be wrong. The determinacy paradox is about advice that would never be accepted anyway, since the government is going to do what it is going to do.
3 The problem is serious enough, in fact, to cause George Stigler to criticize Adam Smith. Stigler (1971) contrasts Smith's usual "ability to examine the most pompous and ceremonial of institutions and conduct with the jaundiced eye of a master economist – and the evident delight he took in such amusement" (pp. 143–44), with his attitude toward political behavior – "not dissimilar to that of a parent toward a child: the child was often mistaken and sometimes perverse, but normally it would improve in conduct if properly instructed" (p. 142). Stigler wonders, for instance, why Smith sets forth maxims and makes recommendations for good systems of taxation, when in fact taxes will be adopted by ministers and Parliaments acting for their own interests: "Why tell the French sovereign to abandon the *taille* and capitations and increase the *vingtiemes*, when only a revolution could dislodge the tax-favored classes?" (p. 143). Of course, the genius of Adam Smith lay, not in analyzing the question as to how one could politically get to the (markets-based) institutional structure that would ensure a socially productive harnessing of private greed to public good, but in demonstrating that such a structure could in principle be devised in the first place.
4 Occasionally, of course, constitution writers for, say, a newly independent society, may find themselves behind a truly thick veil of ignorance about what their roles in the new society will be. See, for instance, Bhagwati (1989) for a discussion of some of the possibilities. But the rarity and the artificiality of these exceptions shows that they can form no basis for normative economics.
5 Tabellini and Alesina (1990) make a similar point about balanced budget amendments.
6 Similarly, positive economics is just as susceptible to the determinacy paradox in this form as normative economics is. To the hypothetical social scientist studying us, the content of all the positive articles Columbia economists will write is also endogenous, and so positive economists are at best plagiarists. Endogeneity is no reason to elevate the positive over the normative. In this we differ from Stigler (1981).
7 Newcomb's problem is the following: A marvelous being has appeared on Earth and claimed to be able to predict what people will do. This claim has been put to the test a fabulously large number of times in all manner of circumstances and has always been confirmed. The predictor has even predicted your own actions faultlessly on an incredibly large number of occasions.

   One day while you are out the predictor comes to your house and leaves two boxes and a note. One box has a clear plastic lid and in it you can see $100. The other box is sealed and you can't see what's in it. The note says: "You may take either both boxes or the sealed box alone. If I predicted you would take both boxes, I put nothing in the sealed box. If I predicted you would take only the sealed box, I put $1 million in it. Choose wisely."

The argument for taking both boxes is the sure-thing principle: no matter what the predictor put in the sealed box, you're always going to be $100 better off if you take both boxes. The argument for taking one box is the principle of maximizing expected utility: if you take only one box you're almost certain to end up with $1 million while if you take both boxes you're almost certain to end up with $100. The philosophical interest in Newcomb's problem comes from the conflict between the sure-thing principle and the expected utility principle.

In our context, Newcomb's problem shows that relations with a being who can almost certainly read the book of your life are very far from trivial.

8   Levi goes on to argue that the only reason we could fail to predict our decisions is that we are not sure we will choose rationally. It follows that we should not be able to invoke rationality to predict the actions of other people either. In other words, Levi holds that the (correct, to Levi) belief in our inability to predict our own decisions is incompatible with the (incorrect, to Levi) belief in our ability to use rationality to predict what other people will do. Our tentative reconciliation of the two beliefs (if the two beliefs were not reconciled one would have to believe either that one could predict one's own decisions or the economics is impossible) is to reject Levi's explanation for why we are unable to predict our own decisions. Should it not be possible to be confident that we will act for the best, all things considered, before considering all things?

9   Another way, of course, to bring about the desired concordance between the would-be adviser's goals and those of the government is for the adviser to forsake whatever her own goals are and adopt the government's as her own. In this case, the adviser becomes the puppet of the advisee. Klein (1994) provides an interesting account of how this "reverse-puppetry" might occur. Stigler (1976) argues that in fact whenever governments appear to be economists' puppets, in fact it is the reverse that is occurring.

References

Austen-Smith, D. and J. Wright (1992) Competitive Lobbying for a Legislator's Vote. *Social Choice and Welfare*, 9: 229–57.

Basu, K. (1992a) Modelling Government and Endogenizing Policy. In S. Jha and K. Parikh (eds.), *Methods of Planning and Policy Analysis for a Mixed Economy* (Allied Publishers, Bombay).

Basu, K. (1992b) Bad Advice. *Economic and Political Weekly*, March 7, 525–30.

Buchanan, J. and G. Tullock (1962) *The Calculus of Consent: Logical Foundations of Constitutional Democracy* (University of Michigan Press, Ann Arbor).

Bhagwati, J. (1989) Is Free Trade Passé After All? *Weltwirtshaftliches Archiv*, 125: 17–44.

Bhagwati, J. (1990) The Theory of Political Economy, Economic Policy, and Foreign Investment. In M. Scott and D. Lal (eds.), *Public Policy and Economic Development* (Clarendon Press, Oxford).

Bhagwati, J., R. Brecher, and T. N. Srinivasan (1984) DUP Activities and Economic Theory. In D. Colander (ed.), *Neoclassical Political Economy* (Ballinger, Cambridge, MA).

Bhagwati, J. (1984) Comment on Raul Prebisch's Paper. In G. M. Meier and D. Seers (eds.), *Pioneers in Development* (Oxford University Press, New York).

Cameron, C. and J. P. Jung (1993) Strategic Endorsements, mimeo, Columbia University Department of Political Science.

Fogel, R. (1964) *Railroads and American Economic Growth: Essays in Econometric History* (Johns Hopkins Press, Baltimore).

Friedman, M. (1980) *Free to Choose: A Personal Statement* (Harcourt Brace Jovanovich, New York).

Klein, D. B. (1994) If the Government is so Villainous, How Come Government Officials Don't Seem Like Villains? *Economics and Philosophy*, 10: 91–106.

Krebhiel, K. (1991) *Information and Legislative Organization* (University of Michigan Press, Ann Arbor).

Kydland, F. and E. Prescott (1977) Rules Rather than Discretion: the Inconsistency of Optimal Plans. *Journal of Political Economy*, 85: 473–91.

Levi, I. (1991) *Hard Choices: Decision Making under Unresolved Conflict* (Cambridge University Press, New York).

Lucas, R. E., Jr. (1976) Econometric Policy Evaluation: A Critique. In K. Brunner and A. Meltzer (eds.), *The Phillips Curve and the Labor Market* (North-Holland, Amsterdam).

Nozick, R. (1969) Newcomb's Problem and Two Principles of Choice. In N. Rescher (ed.), *Essays in Honor of Carl Hempel* (Reidel, Boston).

Rosenbaum, D. (1992) Long Bottled Up, Advice from Democrats Flows. *New York Times*, November 15, 36.

Srinivasan, T. N. (1992a) Comment on "Modelling Government and Endogenizing Policy," In S. Jha and K. Parikh (eds.), *Methods of Planning and Policy Analysis for a Mixed Economy* (Allied Publishers, Bombay).

Srinivasan, T. N. (1992b) Bad Advice: A Comment, mimeo, Yale University Department of Economics.

Stigler, G. J. (1971) Smith's Travels on the Ship of State. *History of Political Economy* (1971); reprinted in Stigler (1982), 136–45.

Stigler, G. J. (1976) Do Economists Matter? *Southern Economic Journal*, 42, January; reprinted in Stigler (1982), 57–67.

Stigler, G. J. (1981) The Economist as Preacher. *The Tanner Lectures on Human Values*, vol. 2 (University of Utah Press, Salt Lake City; Cambridge University Press, Cambridge).

Stigler, G. J. (1982) *The Economist as Preacher and Other Essays* (University of Chicago Press, Chicago).

Tabellini, G. and A. Alesina (1990) Voting on the Budget Deficit. *American Economic Review*, 80: 37–49.

Zaller, J. (1992) *The Nature and Origins of Mass Opinion* (Cambridge University Press, New York).

ELEVEN

On Misunderstanding Government: an Analysis of the Art of Policy Advice

KAUSHIK BASU

Source: From *Economics and Politics* (1997), 9: 231–50.

1 On Misunderstanding Government

There are situations in life where individuals, left to themselves, create inefficiency and anarchy. This was the concern that drove Hobbes to philosophize about the Leviathan that can bring order into chaos; and this is a concern that has provoked much contemporary writing. The Prisoner's Dilemma is the classic description of this predicament (see Taylor, 1976). It codifies how in some situations individuals, left to pursue their individual interests, can harm themselves. The Prisoner's Dilemma is an illustration of extreme externality between individuals. Smaller externalities are pervasive in life. They form the basis of our contemporary environmental concerns. If individuals work in their atomistic interest, then each individual may ignore the pollutants their actions inject into the atmosphere or the little damage that their factories may do to the ozone layer. However, the totality of these actions can leave all individuals worse off with severe environmental damage.

What should be done about this problem? To many the answer is obvious. The above discussion shows how individual rationality may fail to be an adequate organizing force in society and so what we need is government intervention to bring *individual* actions into alignment with *social* interests. Thus what the two prisoners in the Prisoner's Dilemma need is a third party to help them maximize their own welfare (by, for instance, punishing the person who defects and confesses).

This advice for government intervention is flawed for a non-obvious reason. If the advice were followed it would bring about the kind of world being recommended. So in *that* sense there is nothing wrong with the advice. What is wrong is that it is unlikely to be followed, because it takes an excessively simplistic view of government. Government is treated as a benevolent agent, exogenous to the economy, whose intervention can be invoked at will. It ignores the fact that government is itself a collection of individuals with their own motivations and aspirations.

Likewise, as we just saw, dismayed by the outcome of the Prisoner's Dilemma, economists and political scientists often recommend that what is needed is a "third party" to induce individuals to behave in their group interest. The problem with this remedy is that if there is such a third party around then we had no right to model the game as a two–person Prisoner's Dilemma in the first place. The agent who is willed out of thin air should have been a part of the game to start with. If the presence of the third person means that we do not have a Prisoner's Dilemma then we never had a Prisoner's Dilemma; and if even with the third person included we still have a Prisoner's Dilemma then that *is* our plight – there is no escape from it.

In this same spirit the persons who comprise government should, strictly, be thought of as players in the "economy game". In his recent monograph on the political process, Dixit (1996, p. 2) takes a similar line: "Most important, I will argue that the political process should be viewed as a game. What follows from these observations is orthogonal to, and perhaps destructive of, the whole 'markets versus governments' debate."

If prices are high very few economists today would say that their advice is that the producers should lower the price. They do not give this advice because the advice is wrong but because they feel it is a futile advice since producers have their own objectives and will not heed such advice. Hence, the profusion of advice that economists target at government reflects, more than anything else, how little they understand government.

Our poor understanding of government has showed up in other places too. Some economists argue that individuals should be entirely free to pursue their own interest, free from government intervention. This misses the point that government is itself an assemblage of individuals.

Similarly some economists believe that institutions that have emerged out of individual actions are optimal; they are there because their benefits outweigh the costs (Anderson and Hill, 1975; Posner, 1981). Government, according to this view, is an organization that distorts these natural civic institutions. Such a view is made possible only by not asking ourselves where government itself has come from. Government did not create government; so we cannot castigate it as one more manifestation of the evils of government. Indeed government is a fairly modern institution (Strayer, 1970). It has evolved through the ages, through a multitude of individual actions. (We return to some of these issues in section 6.) Hence, if we maintain that individuals, left to themselves, bring about desirable institutions, then we cannot say that such institutions need to be protected from government because government is such an institution.

Moreover, to take the view that it is all right for individuals to bring about institutions which help them cooperate and enhance their well-being but that they should not create the Leviathan amounts to placing an exogenous constraint on *individual* effort. It is the fallacy that Newt Gingrich commits when he says that government should get out of charitable and welfare work and leave these to community efforts. What this misses out on is that government itself is one such community effort.

To see the intricacy of this argument and the ease with which we can err in our conception of government, let us consider Taylor's celebrated critique of Hobbes's (1651) justification for strong government. As Taylor observes in his *Preface*, in the West the most popular justification of the state is that "without the state, people would not act so as to realize their common interests; more specifically, they would not voluntarily cooperate to provide themselves with certain public goods". The roots of this view, he argues, go back principally to Hobbes (and also to Hume). Taylor's book is meant to be a critique of this view. He is right in challenging this view, which is based on the "third party" (or exogenous or "puppet") view of government which we have already taken to task. However, one does not have to be a careful reader to see that his criticism is very different from the one made earlier in this section. Taylor shows how individuals can voluntarily cooperate, for instance, through repeated play of the Prisoner's Dilemma. This then becomes the basis of his rejection of the Hobbesian recommendation whereby individuals create the Sovereign who then ensures order and cooperation among the citizens by "creating appropriate laws and punishing transgressors" (Taylor, 1976, p. 104).

The error in this viewpoint is to characterize the government-led path to order as a "coercive one" and the repeated Prisoner's Dilemma path as the "voluntary one". Hence, Taylor's critique also commits the fallacy of the exogenous conception of government. Since in reality government is itself a creation of the individuals and is run by the individuals, the government-led path to social order is nothing but a self-enforcing equilibrium among the individuals – a point that is made with great ingenuity by David Friedman (1994). After all, even in the repeated Prisoner's Dilemma cooperation arises from the threat of punishment to deviators from the cooperative path. Just because in the Hobbesian route the "punishers" are *called* members of government this does not make the Hobbesian path any more coercive than the one sustained by a trigger strategy in a repeated game.

In brief, we cannot maintain that (a) individuals are always rational, (b) institutions that emerge from the actions and choices of individual are desirable, and (c) big governments are undesirable.

Much of the popular debate concerning "big" and "small" governments is of such intellectually poor quality precisely because it is rooted in this fallacy. We can argue that governments are often too big and too oppressive but we have to construct such an argument on the negation of (a) or (b).

The endogenization of government is a large research agenda. The works of Buchanan (1968), Taylor (1976), Bhagwati, Brecher and Srinivasan (1984), Dixit (1996) and other contemporary writers have contributed building blocks to this project. In the next four sections, I also focus on a small part of this big agenda. The question that is addressed is this: once we take an endogenous, game-theoretic view of government, how do we, as economists or political scientists, advise such a government? This question belongs to the genre of problems raised in O'Flaherty and Bhagwati (1996; see chapter 10 of this book). I will argue that the conventional view on *how* we should give advice is simplistic and inadequate, being predicated on a flawed conception of government. Once this is corrected, advising governments turns out to be a subject of considerable intellectual challenge, which has the potential of bridging the gap between research and actual policy.

2   A Science of Advising?

Viewed through Machiavellian lenses, the economist's faulty conception of government is not so much an act of folly as a ruse or an act of strategem. It is the existence of such a "puppet government" (Bhagwati, 1990; Srinivasan, 1992) or what Milton Friedman (1986) called a "public interest" conception of government that justifies the existence of the traditional policy adviser. And economists like to give advice. As O'Flaherty and Bhagwati (1996) observe, "Many economists like to think of themselves as active participants in history, not as members of a contemplative order trying to understand a world they cannot influence."

But a strategy constructed over such severe fault lines, as discussed in the previous section, cannot work too well. And indeed economists, and, more generally, social scientists have faltered when it has come to the "how" of giving advice.

It is a pity that there does not exist a science of advising. The accumulated expertise and knowledge of the social sciences have failed to translate adequately into action because we have neglected the study of the *process* of transmission of information from the expert (the adviser) to the minister, senator or politician (more generically, the advisee) who is responsible for putting plans into action.

Our traditional conception of government is not only empirically flawed, as argued above, but it also has problems of internal consistency with the standard model of economics.

Consider the Arrow–Debreu model of general equilibrium. In it individuals choose points from their budget sets, buy and sell goods; and out of this emerges what are called equilibrium prices. In this economy what person i *says* does not affect what person j *does*. In brief, it is an economy that works in silence. This is not to deny that in the Arrow–Debreu world people may be chatting, laughing and singing, but it is simply that that aspect of their lives does not impinge on what happens in the domain of economics and in the market-place.

Having studied such a model in which i's speech has no effect on what j does, the policy economist has gone on to give advice. But what is advice but a set of spoken or written words? If the advice is based on a model in which such words cannot have any affect, then it is surely inconsistent to believe that the advice can have an effect.

This, in essence, is closely related to the "determinacy paradox" of Bhagwati, Brecher and Srinivasan (1984). Once we endogenize all agents the system we are studying may become fully determined leaving no scope for the policy adviser. While the mainstream of economics has overlooked this paradox, there is a small body of writing that has tried to contend with this deep problem.[1]

There are two broad ways in which a piece of advice can be considered defective. First, advice can be "wrong advice" in the sense of it being based on an erroneous view of the world so that *if* it were followed, it would not bring about the kind of world it was intended to bring about. Second, advice can be "futile advice" in the sense that it either urges the advisee to do something that is beyond the advisee's control or against the advisee's interest.[2]

It is ironical but should come as no surprise in the light of the above discussion that the pervasive error of the advising economist has been that of futile advising.

In the *Economic Times* of July 12, 1991, Abhijit Sen presents, with his usual clarity, a set of detailed instructions about what the Indian government should do about India's foreign exchange problem. But having done so, and just as the reader begins to warm to the idea that here at last is the solution to a stubborn problem, Sen goes on to observe, "But for this [that is, for his advice to be followed] the existing culture in government must be turned upside down". But what is the value of advice the prerequisite for which is that government be turned upside down? This is virtually tantamount to saying that the advice cannot be followed. So whatever else be the value of such an essay, as advice it belongs to the category of "futile".

In the *National Review* of September 30, 1996, we find Deal Hudson advising America on how to recover its "intellect and its freedom". "Our best bet", he argues, is the "church-related university, illumined by the light of faith, confident in its curriculum, rooted in history, concerned for the student as a whole person". In such a university, he goes on to urge, the primary concern should be "the development of character, the discernment of true values, and the preparation for heaven". The trouble with this advice is that it seems compellingly beyond the reach of anybody.

Without questioning the content of the advice, one can multiply the examples, given above, of advice that is futile – for which there is no hope of even the most diligent advisee being able to carry it out.

A very different set of problems arise once we move away from traditional models of the economy to ones where one person's utterances can influence another's action. Such a world raises not only issues of analytical interest to the economist or the game-theorist[3] but also moral dilemmas for the adviser. And if we are to ever have a science of advising we will need to contend with these issues and dilemmas.

3   Advising Endogenous Government

To make room for advice that will not fall on deaf ears a *necessary* step is to move away from the Walrasian world to one in which information is imperfect and asymmetric. In particular, we shall assume that government consists of individuals (the politicians) with their own aims and objectives but who have inadequate information about the projects or plans from which they have to choose and implement one. On the other hand, there are the advisers who, through training, research or, for that matter, clairvoyance, have information about the effects of each project or plan. But they are not allowed to choose; they can only advise the politicians about what to choose. In brief, we are taking a small step towards a more realistic model of government by recognizing that (1) government is not an exogenous agent, but a collection of individuals with their own motivations, and (2) information in society is incomplete and asymmetric. It is interesting to note that Green's model (Green, 1993), while addressing very different issues, nevertheless uses an argument concerning asymmetric information and communication to explain the emergence of parliamentary democracy.

These assumptions make it possible for one agent to influence another through advice. But (1) and (2) are by no means *sufficient* for this to be so. The aim of this section is to demonstrate this by constructing some simple game-theoretic examples.

If the adviser and the advisee have the same objective functions then all is well. There is scope for "cheap talk" and advice takes place in the usual way, that is, by saying that x should be done when the adviser believes that x should be done (Farrell and Rabin, 1996).[4] Trouble arises if the adviser and the politician have different aims.

Let me assume that the adviser works entirely in the interest of the people,[5] while the politician is self-interested; and the people's (and, therefore, the adviser's) interest is not the same as that of the politician.[6] The simplest illustrative example of this (see Basu, 1992) is where there are two projects: N (a nuclear power plant) and T (a thermal one), from which the politician has to choose one. Like all such projects the impact of each project on society is very complicated, and the politician does not know what effect the projects will have on his and other people's welfare.

We can formalize this information structure by supposing that there are two states of the world, w_1 and w_2, which occur with probability $\frac{1}{2}$ each. In the language of game theory, "nature" makes an equi-probable choice between w_1 and w_2. In w_1, the payoffs from N to the adviser and the politician are 1 and 0 and from T the adviser gets 0 and the politician gets 1. In w_2 the payoffs from N and T are reversed. The adviser knows which state of the world has occurred and makes the first move. He has to choose between saying "Do N" and "Do T". These two actions are denoted by N and T in state w_1, and by N' and T' in state w_2. The politician hears the advice but does not know whether w_1 or w_2 has occurred, and has to choose between the nuclear and thermal power plants. The politician's choice is implemented and the players reap payoffs as already explained. This game is described using the standard device of a game tree in figure 11.1, and is called the *orthogonal game*. Note that nodes x and y belong to the same information set, which captures the idea that the politician cannot tell whether he is at x or y, when he is at one of them. In both these nodes he has just heard his rather taciturn adviser say "Do N". And, since he does not know whether w_1 or w_2 had occurred, for him x and y are indistinguishable. His choice of the nuclear and thermal plants at these nodes is denoted by n and t.

What will be the outcome of this game? Will the adviser be able to influence the choice of the politician?

Let us first check intuitively how they will play this game. Suppose w_1 occurs. The adviser will of course want the politician to choose the nuclear project. Let us suppose that he is naive, and so says exactly that: "Sir, I advise you to go for the nuclear project", or, equivalently, "Do N". The politician, knowing about her adviser's "strange" political

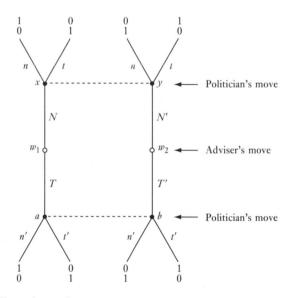

Figure 11.1   The orthogonal game

leanings, would, it seems, promptly choose the thermal plant. This happens in the same way that a child told by the mother not to watch channel 29 that evening because there will be "a boring film" called *The Last Tango in Paris* knows that that is one evening when the child should not watch *Mr. Rogers' Neighborhood* and instead turn to channel 29.

If the adviser were rational and knew that the politician would do the opposite, then the above outcome would not occur. The adviser may then give the false advice "Go Thermal" and hope that the politician will go nuclear. Indeed there are not too many mothers who would instruct their child as in the above paragraph.

But, of course, if the politician knows that the adviser is rational and that the adviser knows that the politician is rational, then this simple trick of the adviser will not work.

It is actually easy to check that the only Nash equilibrium is one in which the adviser's advice is completely uncorrelated to which state of the world actually occurs and the politician's choice is completely uninfluenced by the adviser's advice.

What the above example points to is not just the difficulty of advising but to some deep problems of communication in general. As Glenn Loury (1994, p. 432) points out in his engaging essay on self-censorship and political correctness: "There is always some uncertainty when ideas and information are exchanged between parties who may not have the same objectives. Each message bears interpretation." He goes on to point out how he himself (as a prominent commentator on racial issues in the USA) has to be cautious (p. 435):

> I must tread carefully as I try to express my particular "truth". If you will "read between the lines" for my true meaning . . . , then I am determined to write between the lines – avoiding (or embracing) certain "code words", choosing carefully my illustrative examples, concealing some of my thinking while exaggerating other sentiments – so as to control the impression I make on my audience.

It may appear that the problem that the orthogonal game highlights is the difficulty of advising when preferences are *diametrically opposite* between the adviser and the advisee. As O'Flaherty and Bhagwati (1996) observe: "Saddam Hussein is unlikely to revise the Iraqi agricultural price system just because some American economists tell him that doing so would be nice."[7]

This naturally leads to the suggestion that for an adviser to play a positive role there must be a reasonable affinity of interests between the adviser and the politician and, more generally, the speaker and the listener. Thus O'Flaherty and Bhagwati speak about the importance of the "coincidence of interests," and to stress that this need not be a non-generic special case, add that "coincidence does not have to be exact". In the same spirit, Loury (p. 436) remarks, "If we know a speaker shares our values, we more readily accept observations from him"; and "when we believe the speaker has goals similar to our own, we are confident that any effort on his part to manipulate us is undertaken to advance ends similar to those we would pursue ourselves".

What I want to illustrate, however, is that the prognosis is gloomier than these observations suggest. Similarity of objectives is not enough. Anything short of an exact coincidence of preference may result in a complete breakdown in communication. This paradoxical result is driven by a familiar "infection" argument where a small anomaly or some informational event far away becomes pervasive and has real effects (see Morris and Shin, 1995). This is proved in the next section by constructing a game which I call the *cheater's roulette*.

4 The Cheater's Roulette

To illustrate the result mentioned in the last paragraph of the previous section consider a continuum of projects $\Omega = [0, 1]$. What effect each project has on the adviser and the politician is known by the adviser but not by the politician. The adviser gives an advice to the politician which takes the form of saying "Do x," where $x \in \Omega$ and the politician then chooses some $y \in \Omega$. We shall describe a way of measuring the nearness of the preferences of the politician and her adviser, and show that unless the preferences are identical the politician will not pay any heed to the adviser's advice.

Some abstraction makes it easier to describe this game, which I call the Cheater's Roulette. It consists of a roulette board, the circumference of which is a unit circle. Let us call the northern-most point 0 and the same point also 1 (in the same way that in a clock 0 and 12 refer to the same point). This is illustrated in figure 11.2. The circumference then is our set of projects $\Omega = [0, 1]$.

The board has a "hand" which is pivoted to the center of the roulette board. The hand can be made to spin. The line with the arrow in figure 11.2 denotes the hand. The game is played as follows. The politician sits where she cannot see the board. The hand is given a spin (by "Nature" let us say) and after it comes to rest the politician is asked to choose a point from Ω. If the hand comes to rest at point m, as shown in the figure, then the politician is paid as follows. She gets 100 dollars if she chooses m; 0 dollars if she chooses the point diametrically opposite to m (i.e. point m' in figure 11.2) and the payoff drops off linearly (though monotonically would do) as she chooses points further and further away from m.

This may be stated formally as follows. For any two points, x, $y \in \Omega$, the distance between them, denoted by $d(x, y)$, is the shortest distance between x and y along the circumference. It follows that

$$d(x, y) = \min\{|x - y|, 1 - |x - y|\}.$$

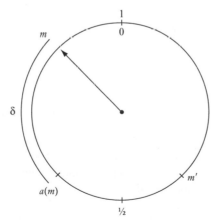

Figure 11.2 The cheater's roulette

If Nature selects $m \in \Omega$ and the politician $x \in \Omega$, then the politician's payoff is

$$100 - d(x, m)200.$$

Note that $d(x, m)$ can vary between 0 and $\frac{1}{2}$. Hence the payoff varies between 100 and 0.

The adviser in this game is actually an accomplice who watches Nature's selection and whispers a piece of advice to the politician about what she should choose.

The adviser also gets a payoff which depends on what Nature and the politician choose. This may be described as follows. Note that whatever Nature chooses is the politician's ideal point. Let us suppose that the adviser is to the "left" of the politician and define the "adviser's ideal point", $a(m)$, to be a point which is at a distance of δ ($\leq \frac{1}{2}$) to the left of m. An illustration of $a(m)$, where δ is $\frac{1}{4}$ is shown in figure 11.2. To remind ourselves that $a(m)$ depends on δ we could write it as a $a_\delta(m)$ but I am not doing so for reasons of notational simplicity.

If Nature selects m and the politician chooses x, the adviser is paid 100 dollars if $x = a(m)$ (that is, if the politician chooses the adviser's ideal point), 0 dollars if x is diametrically opposite $a(m)$ and the payoff falls off linearly as x moves away from $a(m)$. Formally, the adviser's payoff is

$$100 - d(x, a(m))200.$$

If $\delta = 0$, then the adviser's preference is exactly the same as the politician's and his every advice will be taken by the latter. The paradoxical result is this: if $\delta > 0$, then no matter how small δ is, communication will break down totally between the adviser and the politician. The only Nash equilibrium is one in which the politician ignores her adviser's whisper in making her choice.[8] Attention is throughout restricted to pure strategies.

In order to sketch a proof of this, I need to introduce some new terminology. Let the adviser's strategy be denoted by ϕ where

$$\phi: \Omega \to \Omega.$$

For every selection $x \in \Omega$ by Nature, $\phi(x)$ is what the adviser asks the politician to choose.

The politician's strategy is c, where

$$c: \Omega \to \Omega.$$

For every advice $x \in \Omega$ given by the adviser, $c(x)$ is the element of Ω that the politician chooses.

Hence, if Nature selects $m \in \Omega$, the politician chooses $c(\phi(m))$ and her payoff is $100 - d(c(\phi(m)), m)200$. And the adviser's payoff is $100 - d(c(\phi(m)), a(m))200$. Since Nature selects by spinning the hand, it selects from a uniform density function on Ω. Hence, given ϕ and c, we can compute the expected payoff of each player. Let (ϕ^*, c^*) be a Nash equilibrium of this game. What we need to show is that $c^*(x)$ is independent of x (i.e. the politician's choice is independent of the advice she receives). That is, there exists $y \in \Omega$, such that $c^*(x) = y$, for all $x \in \Omega$.

First note that if $y \in c^*(\Omega)$ then there exists points z and x strictly to the right and left of y, respectively such that[9] $y \in [x, z]$ and no other point (i.e. other than y) in $[x, z]$ is in $c^*(\Omega)$. If this were not true, we could find $x, z \in \Omega$ such that $c^*(\Omega)$ is dense in the interval $[x, z]$. Then c^* cannot be an optimum strategy for the politician. Let y be in the interior of $[x, z]$, such that for some $r \in \Omega, c^*(r) = y$. Then if Nature selects m such that $a(m) = r, \phi^*(r)$ must be such that $c^*(\phi^*(r)) = a(m)$. Clearly then the politician would be better off deviating from her choice $c^*(\phi^*(r))$. This establishes the first sentence of this paragraph and thereby proves that $\#c^*(\Omega) < \infty$.

Denote $c^*(\Omega) \equiv \{x_1, \ldots, x_n\}$ where x_1 is the first point in $c^*(\Omega)$ at or to the right of 0; and $x_2, x_3, \ldots$, follow clockwise as shown in figure 11.3. Suppose $n \geq 2$.

It is now easy to check that c^* cannot be optimal for the politicians unless the length of x_i to x_{i-1} exceeds the length of x_{i+1} to x_i (lengths being measured along the anti-clockwise arc). If this is not the case it is possible to check that the politician can do better by choosing slightly clockwise away from x_i when the advice y is such that $c^*(y) = x_i$. Since the projects belong to a modular number system, it is not possible for the gaps between adjacent x_is to increase throughout as we move in one direction. Hence, $n = 1$. *This completes the proof of the paradoxical result.*

What we have proved is this. There exists $x \in \Omega$, such that for all $y \in \Omega, c^*(y) = x$. In equilibrium the adviser's advice has no effect on the politician's choice. The politician just arbitrarily picks a point $x \in \Omega$. It follows that in equilibrium the adviser just babbles – he gives advice which conveys no information about the state that has occurred (that is, Nature's choice).

Before proceeding further it may be useful to explain my use of a unit circle, as opposed to the more conventional unit interval. The immediate reason for doing this is the mathematical convenience of being able to describe one person at being a distance δ to the left of another, irrespective of the latter's location. Second, this description can describe some very real problems. Some years ago, the Ministry of Finance in New Delhi was considering changing the time of the annual budget of the Government of India (the budget year started April 1). There were many real issues involved. A budget in October, for instance, would mean that we would know how the monsoons have been and therefore

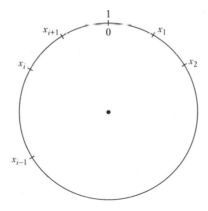

Figure 11.3

be better placed to plan ahead. There were in fact so many variables involved that expert advice was sought about when the budget year should start. If we now think of the unit circle as representing the calendar year from January 1 to December 31, then this problem has the same algebra as our model.

Can advice then have no role unless there is a total coincidence of preference? Despite the above result the answer to this question is in the negative. First, there is now a small body of literature that shows that even when precise advising can be shown to have no role, ambiguity in speech or vagueness of expression can be used to convey *some* information from the speaker to the listener (see the seminal work of Crawford and Sobel, 1982; also Stein, 1989). This in itself is a very interesting result because it shows how moving away from precision to ambiguity may help us to actually convey more.[10]

Second, we could appeal precisely to the fact that the outcome of the Cheater's Roulette is *paradoxical* and urge the reader to reject the game-theoretic solution. In this respect the Cheater's Roulette is akin to the Traveler's Dilemma (Basu, 1994) because in that game (in a sense) it is rational to reject playing the game rationally because it seems reasonable to expect that the other player will do the same. Now put yourself in the shoes of the adviser in the Cheater's Roulette and suppose that δ is very small, that is, the adviser and the advisee have almost identical objectives. If the roulette hand stops at m, one reasonable way of thinking is this: "A Nash equilibrium play could make both of us lose a lot. So why don't I advise something in the vicinity of m. Surely the politician will also realize that the Nash equilibrium play does us no good and so choose something in the vicinity of m." This is not watertight reasoning but nevertheless not one to be dismissed. Note also that "the vicinity of m" is an imprecise expression. But, as I had argued in Basu (1994), meta-rational behavior depends on the use of imprecise (and hence realistic) categories of thinking.

No matter how we seek to resolve the problem one thing is evident. Barring the non-generic special case in which there is a complete coincidence of wants, it does not pay to give the advice that one believes in. That is, the same morality that leads you to think that "X should be done" prompts you not to *say* "X should be done." This creates a moral dilemma which may have no easy solution and this is the subject matter of the next section. But before moving on to it I want to dwell on two caveats of the present analysis and a related observation.

First, we have in this paper, for reasons of tractability, taken "advice" to be simple normative statements or, more generally, any message which can influence behavior by *informing* the advisee. However, in reality advice often takes the form of persuasion, which involves attempts to influence the advisee's *preference*. What complicates this is the fact that people often voluntarily go for this kind of advice. This is true not just of the alcoholic seeking counselling, but in politics and in government there is the continuous play of forces jockeying and buffeting to influence preferences and of individuals voluntarily leaving themselves vulnerable to preference shifts.

Second, once we move away from the assumption of preferences being mutually known, communication (and, for that matter, certain kinds of actions) may acquire some new strategic element whereby the communicator seeks to influence the belief of the listener about the communicator's preference. Preferences of political actors are often important to others because they indicate what the politician might do in contingencies which arise in the future (some of which may not even currently be conceivable). Thus it is arguable that President Clinton supported the Helms–Burton act aiming to punish companies outside the USA that do business with Cuba not because he believes in it (there is actually some evidence suggesting that he does not) but because he wanted to *appear* more conservative before the presidential election and thereby create the expectation that in future decision-making he will pick the more conservative alternative.

By assuming that preferences are exogenously given and common knowledge among the agents, the present essay stays clear of these two complications. But they are important in reality and deserve to be on the agenda for future research.

Finally, the related observation. I have posed the problem of communication in the asymmetric context involving an adviser and an advisee. The same problem can however also arise when the agents involved are symmetrically placed, for example, the members of parliament taking a vote or the members of a jury deciding by majority. An interesting paper by Austen-Smith and Banks (1996) illustrates how the dilemma of not revealing one's information sincerely can arise in the context of problems such as the celebrated Condorcet jury theorem. In their model this can happen even when all members have the same preference.

5   A Moral Conundrum

An act of speaking or writing usually has consequences for the world. The *Communist Manifesto* was nothing but some words on paper. So were the *Bible*, the *Koran* and even *The Satanic Verses*. But these "words" have had consequences for the world of action, creating or destroying wealth, stirring human beings into acts of bravery or cowardice. Hence, anyone who writes or speaks has to take into account the consequences of the writing and the speech. This is especially so for those who write for and speak to large audiences. Nevertheless, the scientist writing *positive* science can at least claim no *inconsistency* if he chooses to write whatever is the truth with no thought to the consequence of his writing.

On the other hand, a scientist, or, for that matter, anybody, making a normative statement may face a deeper moral conundrum, a problem which is virtually one of consistency. The politician beseeching the public to act, the economist advising the politician and the journalist urging the economist to say something, all face this problem. Unlike the positive scientist, these people cannot disclaim having a normative purpose because their very act of speaking reveals it.

As we have already seen, when an expert or an informed person utters something, people try (or should try) to elicit information from that utterance, in the same way that the politician in the Cheater's Roulette tries to deduce the outcome on the roulette board from his adviser's whisper. Similarly when you read or hear Mr Stephen R. Covey, the author of popular improve-yourself books such as *The Seven Habits of Highly Effective People*, tell you to be goal-oriented or to keep "the end in mind" you have reason to believe that *he* believes in being goal-oriented. Given that it seems unlikely that Mr Covey's goal is to make *you* goal-oriented, and his much more likely goal is to maximize the sales of his books, you have reason to suspect that some of the things he advises people are the advice people *like* to hear. And you could decide, not totally unreasonably, that, given the great success of his books, following not his advice but him is the more profitable strategy. Of course, you may be wrong in attributing the best-seller motive to Mr Covey; he perhaps has a missionary purpose. But the fact remains that people do look for meanings other than the one explicitly stated,[11] which is the subject matter of Kuran's (1995) persuasive book.

Now suppose you want to tell government: "Government should do x." This will make people try to guess what you know and they do not, make them act in certain ways and, let us suppose, bring about the kind of world that you do not morally approve of. And suppose your giving the opposite advice will bring about a desirable world (in terms of your own morals). Then you face a moral conundrum because what is in conflict is not your self-interest with your moral judgement but your morals with your morals. Should you say what you believe in or should you say the reverse and bring about the kind of world that you believe in? Note that a person making a normative statement cannot even use the alibi of being normatively disinterested. He has to confront the dilemma.

In brief, this is a conundrum that one has to confront if one wishes to advise and pronounce publicly on policy. It may be possible to construct models of repeated advice which brings the two moral options discussed in the above paragraph into alignment. That is, it may be morally best to say what you actually believe in because otherwise your "strategic" behavior will get revealed in the long run. But at this stage we have no option but to leave this problem as an open-ended issue since even if there are repeated-game stories which can resolve it, these are not transparent. Till this is resolved we will be right in trying to read between the lines of not only what politicians and other government officials say, but also what the economic adviser and the economist in public life says.

6   Remarks on Endogenizing Government

It is natural for the modern person to take government for granted. Government is a necessary concomitant of state and, for certain discourses, it is state. Yet in the history of human beings, state and government are relatively modern institutions. People belonged to tribes and had chiefs rather than governments and heads of states. This is true even in some contemporary cases. Many tribals, for instance those living in the Andaman and Nicobar Islands, are not aware that they are Indians. To them the agents of the state – the police, the civil servants – are not representatives of the "law" but, on the contrary, illegal trespassers on whom the use of poison arrows is considered well worth the poison. Barring some such small exceptions, all people treat government and its agencies as part of life.

As Strayer's (1970) elegant little book reminds us this was not always so. Up to as late as the eleventh century there were no states as we know now. There were some small city states and there were empires. According to Strayer, state as a moral authority, as an agent with a "monopoly of the legitimate use of physical force" – to steal a description from Max Weber, and as an institution for providing public goods is a phenomenon of the last millennium.

Why did the state emerge in the twelfth and thirteenth centuries? This is a subject matter for history and one that may well require the longevity of an historian's professional life for successful investigation, but one suggestion in Strayer's essay is particularly interesting. The twelfth and thirteenth centuries saw a steep rise in learning and literacy. It therefore allowed the codification of law and the signing of contracts in a way that may not have been possible earlier. This gave rise to the need for an enforcer of contracts, and government soon became that ubiquitous "third party", the enforcer of contracts. Modern society, it is arguable, would be unsustainable without an institution for supporting contracts and covenants. The prosperity of contemporary economies owes as much to the slow evolution of this institution as it does to the many sudden scientific breakthroughs.[12]

It is now increasingly recognised that the "market" cannot function efficiently unless it is "embedded" in suitable institutions (Granovetter, 1985; Platteau, 1994).[13] For reasons of *analytical* convenience economists often ignore this embedding feature. What is troubling is that, having made this assumption of treating the market as functioning in a vacuum, many economists forget that this was an *assumption*. This can be costly.

Let me illustrate this with an example. One of the two celebrated "fundamental theorems" of welfare economics may be stated, taking the liberty of colloquialism, as follows:

> *If individuals maximize their own selfish utility, then (given that certain technical conditions are satisfied) the competitive equilibrium that arises is always Pareto optimal.*

In itself, this is a mathematical theorem which tells us nothing about the real world. Its application to the real world depends on how we interpret it, *beyond* what it actually tells us. One popular interpretation of this theorem is that it shows that if individuals are left free to choose whatever they want to, then society attains optimality. And, conversely, taxes and other government interventions which limit the feasible sets of individuals tend to result in suboptimality. In defense of this position one would typically point out that in the standard competitive model in which the theorem is established, it is assumed that individual consumers are free to choose any point (or basket of goods) from within their budget sets (or what their incomes permit).

Let us now think for a moment what are the kinds of choices a person can in reality make. It is true that a person can choose from a variety of alternative baskets of goods which lie within his budget; but a person can also choose to rob, steal and plunder; he can try to take away the endowment of another individual, invoking the age-old principle of more being better than less; he can commit blackmail, larceny and arson. Hence, when we allow an individual to choose any point within his budget set, there are two ways of viewing this. We could view this as giving him great freedom: he can choose *any* point; or view this as very restrictive: he is not allowed to choose anything (from the large menu of options he has in life) apart from choosing a point from his budget set. If we follow the latter, then here is a view of the fundamental theorem which is a "dual" to the popular interpretation: the fundamental theorem shows that society attains optimality if individual choice is severely restricted and in particular confined to choosing points from within the budget set.

One may argue that the restriction of not allowing theft of other people's endowment, larceny and blackmail is not a restriction at all but is in the self-interest of the individual. If that is so then we need to formally show this by starting with a model where all these "extra-economic" activities are allowed. And once we start from such a large domain, to get to the case where the pure general equilibrium model works, we need the institution of government or some other related institution[14] to prevent individuals from finding some of these "extra-economic" activities worthwhile. Since this exercise of embedding the market model has not been done thus far, we do not really know whether the model of the market, abstracted from its social and political moorings, can ever be realised. This would be an easy agenda, if government was conceived of as an exogenous body that makes it costly for individuals to steal and rob. But as argued through this essay, this is not a permissible strategy. We have to allow for the fact that government is run by individuals, who respond to incentives, and explain the survival of government and government's power from a model of individual decision-making.

In order to model the survival of government and the people's respect of authority, we need to make room for "triadic" arrangements (Basu, 1986) in our economic models. We need to allow for the fact that i respects government authority for fear of what j will do to i (for instance ostracize i) if i shows open disrespect towards governmental authority. In Friedman's (1994, p. 10) words "I will accept one [the tax collector] and fight the other [the robber] because of my beliefs about other people's behavior – what they will or will not fight for.... We are bound together by a set of mutually reinforcing strategic expectations."

Once we have modeled government as an endogenous part of the economy, we can no longer will government into action whenever we wish and however we wish, nor can we treat it as the repository of exogenous variables for our macromodels; but we shall have a description of an economy that reflects reality much better, and, though the policy advisors will probably have to practice greater reticence than they currently do, they will know better *how* to give policy advice.

Notes

*   I have benefited from conversations with Joe Halpern, Peter Katzenstein, Andrew Rutten, Eduardo Saavedra, Nirvikar Singh, Jorgen Weibull and Eduardo Zambrano.
1   Magee and Brock (1983), Barro (1984), M. Friedman (1986), Basu (1992), Srinivasan (1992), Austen-Smith (1990). The subject of endogenizing government policy and policy change in order to gain a better understanding of development is addressed in Ranis and Fei (1988).
2   A more detailed taxonomy of "bad advice" is developed in Basu (1992).
3   The rapidly growing literature on cheap talk is testimony to this (see Crawford and Sobel, 1982; Stein, 1989; and, for a recent survey, Farrell and Rabin, 1996).
4   Even here there can be trouble if there is coordination of action needed between the adviser and the advisee and there is a non-zero probability of an advice failing to be common knowledge after it is announced (Rubinstein, 1989; Halpern and Moses, 1990).
5   Nothing formal hinges on this assumption but it prepares the ground for some moral dilemmas that are discussed in the next section.
6   It is important to understand that the fact that one may try to delude one's listeners does not in itself suggest a selfish motivation. As Goffman (1959, p. 18) points out: "It is not assumed, of course, that all cynical performers are interested in deluding their audiences for purposes of what is called "self-interest" or private gain. A cynical individual may delude his audience for what he considers to be their own good, or for the good of the community."
7   And, as the orthogonal game shows, neither should Saddam Hussein not revise it *because* he has been asked to revise. Such a response would also make him vulnerable to manipulation.
8   Some readers may wish to skip the proof of this claim which stretches over the next few paragraphs up to the point where it says "*This completes the proof of the paradoxical result*".
9   For $x, y \in \Omega$, $[x,y]$ denotes the shorter arc between x and y, the tie being broken arbitrarily for x and y diametrically opposite to each other.
10 There is a related (though analytically distinct) result which shows how an incumbent politician confronting an ill-informed electorate may gain most by being ambiguous about his preference (Alesina and Cukierman, 1991).

11 And, while on the topic of popular writing one may quote the celebrated Agony Aunt, Ann Landers, warning people not to be too literal: "Resist the temptation to tell your friends about your indigestion. 'How are you?' is a greeting, not a question" (*The Ithaca Journal*, October 5, 1996).

12 In understanding the state, an alternative to studying its origins is to examine the conditions for its existence. "Functional theories of the state", as these are called in the political science literature (Tilly, 1975), study the concomitants of the national state. Like the market, the state also is in reality embedded in other institutions. An understanding of the latter can give us insights into the very meaning of the national state.

13 Bowles and Gintis (1992) try to show that the Walrasian model instead of capturing the consequences of perfectly-rational, self-interested behavior by individuals, describes a situation where individual rationality is restricted to certain domains of decisionmaking.

14 A range of alternative institutions that can emerge out of individual initiative to help cooperation is discussed in Ostrom (1990). The position that I am taking is that government is also one such institution.

References

Alesina, A. and A. Cukierman (1991) The Politics of Ambiguity. *Quarterly Journal of Economics*, 105: 829–50.

Anderson, T. J. and P. J. Hill (1975) The Evolution of Property Rights: a Study of the American West. *Journal of Law and Economics*, 18: 163–79.

Austen-Smith, D. (1990) Information Transmission in Debate. *American Journal of Political Science*, 34: 124–52.

Austen-Smith, D. and J. Banks (1996) Information Aggregation, Rationality, and the Condorcet Jury Theorem. *American Political Science Review*, 90: 34–45.

Barro, R. J. (1984) Discussion [of Sargent's paper]. *American Economic Review*, May, 74: 179–87.

Basu, K. (1986) One Kind of Power. *Oxford Economic Papers*, 38: 259–82.

Basu, K. (1992) Bad Advice. *Economic and Political Weekly*, 27: 525–30.

Basu, K. (1994) The Traveler's Dilemma: Paradoxes of Rationality in Game Theory. *American Economic Review*, May, 48: 391–5.

Bhagwati, J. (1990) The Theory of Political Economy, Economic Policy, and Foreign Investment; in: M. Scott and D. Lal (eds.), *Public Policy and Economic Development* (Clarendon Press, Oxford).

Bhagwati, J., R. Brecher, and T. N. Srinivasan (1984) DUP Activities and Economic Theory, in: D. Colander (ed.), *Neoclassical Political Economy* (Ballinger, Cambridge, MA).

Bowles, S. and H. Gintis (1992) Power and Wealth in a Competitive Capitalist Economy. *Philosophy and Public Affairs*, 21: 324–53.

Buchanan, J. M. (1968) An Economist's Approach to "Scientific Politics", in: M. Parsons (ed.), *Perspectives in the Study of Politics* (Chicago, Rand McNally).

Crawford, V. and J. Sobel (1982) Strategic Information Transmission. *Econometrica*, 50: 1431–51.

Dixit, A. (1996) *The Making of Economic Policy* (MIT Press, Cambridge, MA).

Farrell, J. and M. Rabin (1996) Cheap Talk. *Journal of Economic Perspectives*, 10: 103–18.

Friedman, D. (1994) A Positive Account of Property Rights, in: E. F. Paul, F. D. Miller and J. Paul (eds.) *Property Rights* (Cambridge University Press, Cambridge).

Friedman, M. (1986) Economists and Economic Policy. *Economic Inquiry*, 1–10.

Goffman, E. (1959) *The Presentation of Self in Everyday Life* (Doubleday, New York).

Granovetter, M. (1985) Economic Action and Social Structure: The Problem of Embeddedness. *American Journal of Sociology*, 91: 481–510.

Green, E. J. (1993) On the Emergence of Parliamentary Government: The Role of Private Information. *Federal Reserve Bank of Minneapolis Quarterly Review*, 2–16.

Halpern, J. Y. and Y. Moses (1990) Knowledge and Common Knowledge in a Distributed Environment. *Journal of the ACM*, 3: 549–587.

Hobbes, T. (1651) *Leviathan*, ed. R. Tuck (Cambridge University Press, Cambridge, 1991).

Kuran, T. (1995) *Private Truths, Public Lies: The Social Consequences of Preference Falsification* (Harvard University Press, Cambridge, MA).

Loury, G. (1994) Self-Censorship in Public Discourse: A Theory of "Political Correctness" and Related Phenomena. *Rationality and Society*, 6: 428–61.

Magee, S. P. and W. A. Brock (1983) A Model of Politics, Tariffs and Rent-seeking in General Equilibrium, in: B. Weisbrod and H. Hughes (eds.), *Human Resources, Employment and Development*, vol. 3 (Macmillan, London).

Morris, S. and H. S. Shin (1995) Informational Events which Trigger Currency Attacks. Mimeo, University of Pennsylvania.

O'Flaherty, B. and J. Bhagwati (1996) Will Free Trade with Political Science put Normative Economists Out of Work? Mimeo, Columbia University.

Ostrom, E. (1990) *Governing the Commons: The Evolution of Institutions for Collective Action* (Cambridge University Press, Cambridge).

Platteau, J. P. (1994) Behind the market Stage where Real Societies Exist: The Role of Public and Private Order Institutions. *Journal of Development Studies*, 30: 533–77.

Posner, R. A. (1981) *The Economics of Justice* (Harvard University Press, Cambridge, MA).

Ranis, G. and J. C. H. Fei (1988) Development Economics: What Next? in: G. Ranis and T. P. Schultz (eds.), *The State of Development Economics: Progress and Perspectives* (Blackwell Publishers, Oxford).

Rubinstein, A. (1989) The Electronic Mail Game: Strategic Behavior under Complete Uncertainty. *American Economic Review*, 79: 385–91.

Stein, J. C. (1989) Cheap Talk and the Fed: a Theory of Imprecise Policy Announcements. *American Economic Review*, 79: 32–42.

Srinivasan, T. N. (1992) Bad Advice: A Comment. *Economic and Political Weekly*, 27: 1507–08.

Strayer, J. R. (1970) *The Medieval Origins of the Modern State* (Princeton University Press, Princeton).

Taylor, M. (1976) *Anarchy and Cooperation* (John Wiley, London).

Tilly, C. (1975) Western State-Making and Theories of Political Transformation, in: C. Tilly (eds.), *The Formation of National States in Western Europe* (Princeton University Press, Princeton).

PART IV

Government and Agency

Multitask Principal–Agent Analyses: Incentive Contracts, Asset Ownership, and Job Design

Bengt Holmstrom and Paul R. Milgrom*

Source: From *Journal of Law, Economics and Organization* (1991), 7: 24–52.

1 Introduction

In the standard economic treatment of the principal–agent problem, compensation systems serve the dual function of allocating risks and rewarding productive work. A tension between these two functions arises when the agent is risk averse, for providing the agent with effective work incentives often forces him to bear unwanted risk. Existing formal models that have analyzed this tension, however, have produced only limited results.[1] It remains a puzzle for this theory that employment contracts so often specify fixed wages and more generally that incentives within firms appear to be so muted, especially compared to those of the market. Also, the models have remained too intractable to effectively address broader organizational issues such as asset ownership, job design, and allocation of authority.

In this article, we will analyze a principal–agent model that (i) can account for paying fixed wages even when good, objective output measures are available and agents are highly responsive to incentive pay; (ii) can make recommendations and predictions about ownership patterns even when contracts can take full account of all observable variables and court enforcement is perfect; (iii) can explain why employment is sometimes superior to independent contracting even when there are no productive advantages to specific physical or human capital and no financial market imperfections to limit the agent's borrowings; (iv) can explain bureaucratic constraints; and (v) can shed light on how tasks get allocated to different jobs.

The distinguishing mark of our model is that the principal either has several different tasks for the agent or agents to perform, or the agent's single task has several dimensions to it. Some of the issues raised by this modeling are well illustrated by the current controversy over the use of incentive pay for teachers based on their students' test scores.[2] Proponents of the system, guided by a conception very like the standard one-dimensional incentive model, argue that these incentives will lead teachers to work harder at teaching and to take greater interest in their students' success. Opponents counter that the principal effect of the proposed reform would be that teachers would sacrifice such activities as promoting curiosity and creative thinking and refining students' oral and written communication skills in order to teach the narrowly defined basic skills that are tested on standardized exams. *It would be better, these critics argue, to pay a fixed wage without any incentive scheme than to base teachers' compensation only on the limited dimensions of student achievement that can be effectively measured.*[3]

Multidimensional tasks are ubiquitous in the world of business. As simple examples, production workers may be responsible for producing a *high volume* of *good quality* output, or they may be required both to produce output and to care for the machines they use. In the first case, if volume of output is easy to measure but the quality is not, then a system of piece rates for output may lead agents to increase the volume of output at the expense of quality. Or, if quality can be assured by a system of monitoring or by a robust product design, then piece rates may lead agents to abuse shared equipment or to take inadequate care of it. In general, when there are multiple tasks, incentive pay serves not only to allocate risks and to motivate hard work, it also serves to direct the allocation of the agents' attention *among* their various duties. This represents the first fundamental difference between the multidimensional theory and the more common one-dimensional principal–agent models.

There is a second fundamental difference as well, and it, too, can be illustrated by reference to the problem of teaching basic skills: If the task of teaching basic skills could be separated from that of teaching higher-level thinking, then these tasks could be carried out by different teachers at different times during the day. Similarly, in the example of the production worker, when the care and maintenance of a productive asset can be separated from the use of that asset in producing output, the problem that a piece rate system would lead to inadequate care can be mitigated or even eliminated. In general, in multitask principal–agent problems, *job design is an important instrument for the control of incentives*. In the standard model, when each agent can engage in only one task, the grouping of tasks into jobs is not a relevant issue.[4]

Our formal modeling of these issues utilizes our linear principal–agent model (Holmstrom and Milgrom, 1987), mainly specialized to the case where the agent's costs depend only on the *total* effort or attention the agent devotes to all of his tasks. This modeling assures that an increase in an agent's compensation in any one task will cause some reallocation of attention away from other tasks. First, we show that an optimal incentive contract can be to pay a fixed wage independent of measured performance, just as the opponents of incentives based on educational testing have argued. More generally, the desirability of providing incentives for any one activity decreases with the difficulty of measuring performance in any other activities that make competing demands on the agent's time and attention. This result may explain a substantial part of the puzzle of why incentive clauses are so much less common than one-dimensional theories would predict.

Second, we specialize our model to the case where the unmeasurable aspect of performance is how the value of a productive asset changes over time. The difficulties of valuing assets are well recognized, and the vast majority of accounting systems value assets using fixed depreciation schedules based on historical costs, deviating from this procedure only in exceptional circumstances. Under these conditions, when the principal owns the returns from the asset, the optimal incentive contract will provide only muted incentives for the agent to produce output, in order to mitigate any abuse of the asset or any substitution of effort away from asset maintenance. However, when the agent owns the asset returns, the optimal incentive contract will provide more intensive incentives to engage in production, in order to alleviate the reverse problem that the agent may use the asset too cautiously or devote too much attention to its care and improvement. This analysis supports Williamson's observation that "high-powered" incentives are more common in market arrangements than within firms, without relying on any assumptions about specific investments. Moreover, it provides a rudimentary theory of ownership, according to which the conditions that favor the agent owning the assets are (i) that the agent is not too risk averse, (ii) that the variance of asset returns is low, and (iii) that the variance of measurement error in other aspects of the agent's performance is low. Thus, it emphasizes measurement cost as an important determinant of integration in contrast to the leading approaches, which stress asset specificity.[5]

Our prediction fits well with the empirical evidence reported by Anderson (1985) and Anderson and Schmittlein (1984). They found that firms in the electronics industry tend to employ their own sales forces rather than independent manufacturer's representatives when some aspects of the representative's performance are hard to measure. Our result can also help explain why franchisees face steep performance incentives, while managers of identical company-owned stores receive no incentive pay at all (Krueger, 1991; Brickley and Dark, 1987), and why a freelance writer might be paid for articles by the word, while a staff reporter for the same publication receives a fixed wage.

Third, we explore how a firm might optimally set policies limiting personal business activities on company time. Again, it is not just the characteristics of the "outside activities" themselves that determine whether these activities should be permitted. We find that outside activities should be most severely restricted when performance in the tasks that benefit the firm – the "inside activities" – are hard to measure and reward. Thus, a salesperson whose pay is mostly in the form of commissions will optimally be permitted to engage in more personal activities during business hours than a bureaucrat who is paid a fixed wage, because the commissions direct the salesperson toward inside activities in a way that cannot be duplicated for the bureaucrat. Our theory also predicts that home office work should be accompanied by a stronger reliance on performance-based pay incentives, a prediction that seems to fit casual observation.

Our analysis of restrictions on outside activities underscores the fact that incentives for a task can be provided in two ways: either the task itself can be rewarded or the marginal opportunity cost for the task can be lowered by removing or reducing the incentives on competing tasks. Constraints are substitutes for performance incentives and are extensively used when it is hard to assess the performance of the agent. We believe this opens a new avenue for understanding large-scale organization. It also offers an alternative interpretation of the Anderson–Schmittlein evidence. It is inefficient to let a salesperson, whose performance is poorly measured, divert his time into commission selling of competing products. If the employer has an advantage in restricting the employees' other activities, as both Simon and Coase have argued, then problems with measuring sales performance will lead to employing an in-house sales force.

Finally, we obtain a series of results in the theory of job design, using a model in which the employer can divide responsibility for many small tasks between two agents and can determine how performance in each task will be compensated. The resulting optimization problem is a fundamentally non-convex one, and we have had to make some extra assumptions to keep the analysis tractable. Nevertheless, the results we obtain seem intriguing and suggestive. First, we find that each task should be made the responsibility of just one agent. To our knowledge, this is the first formal derivation in the incentive literature of the principle of unity of responsibility, which underlies the theory of hierarchy. Second, we find that tasks should be grouped into jobs in such a way that the tasks in which performance is most easily measured are assigned to one worker and the remaining tasks are assigned to the other worker. This conclusion squares nicely with the intuition that it is the *differences* between the measurability of quantity and quality in production, or of the so-called "basic skills" and "higher-order thinking skills" in education, that make those incentive problems difficult. The theory indicates that even when the agents have identical *ex ante* characteristics, the principal should still design their jobs to have measurement characteristics that differ as widely as possible. The principal should then provide more intensive incentives and require more work effort from the jobholder whose performance is more easily measured.

Our results are variations on the general theme of second best, which stresses that when prices cannot allocate inputs efficiently, then optimal incentives will typically be provided by subsidizing or taxing all inputs. For instance, Greenwald and Stiglitz (1986), in a vivid metaphor, point out the value of a government subsidy for home fire extinguishers, since homeowners with fire insurance have too little incentive to invest in all forms of fire prevention and to fight fires once they have started. This mechanism has been most extensively analyzed in the theory of optimal taxation and in welfare theory.

However, the study of interdependencies among incentives and the use of instruments other than compensation to alleviate incentive problems have entered agency analyses more recently. Lazear (1989) argues that where cooperation among workers is important, we should expect to see less wage differentiation, that is, "lower-powered" incentives. Holmstrom and Ricart i Costa (1986) have observed how a firm's capital budgeting policy, including the hurdle rate and the way the firm assesses idiosyncratic risks, can affect the willingness of risk-averse managers to propose risky investment projects. Milgrom (1988) and Milgrom and Roberts (1988) have studied how organizational decision processes affect the allocation of effort between politicking and directly productive work. Farrell and Shapiro (1989) show that a price clause may be worse than no contract at all, because it reduces incentives to supply quality; this is similar to our result that it may be optimal to provide no quantity incentives when quality is poorly measured.

Some articles containing related ideas have been developed contemporaneously. Itoh (1991), in an analysis complementary to ours, studies conditions under which an employer might induce workers to work separately on their tasks, and those in which it is best for them to spend some effort helping one another. Laffont and Tirole (1989) show that concerns for quality help explain the use of cost-plus contracting in procurement. Baker (1989) investigates a model in which observable proxies of marginal product are imperfect in a way that causes the agent to misallocate effort across contingencies and therefore leads to incentives that are not as powerful as standard theory would suggest. Minahan (1988) reports a result on task separation that suggests a job design similar to ours but based on a different argument, as we will later explain.

The remainder of this article is organized as follows. In section 2, we recapitulate our basic principal–agent theory, upon which the entire analysis is based. In section 3, we specialize the analysis to the case where the agent's costs depend only on the total attention supplied and prove the various propositions about the optimality of fixed wages, the factors determining the assignment of ownership, and the optimal limits on outside business activities. In section 4, we consider restrictions on private tasks. In section 5, we offer a summary and suggest directions in which this line of research can be taken.

2   The Linear Principal–Agent Model

2.1   Description of the model

Consider a principal–agent relationship in which the agent makes a one-time choice of a vector of efforts $t = (t_1, \ldots, t_n)$ at personal cost $C(t)$. The efforts t lead to expected gross benefits of $B(t)$, which accrue directly to the principal. We assume that the function C is strictly convex and that the function B is strictly concave. The agent's efforts also generate a vector of information signals.

$$x = \mu(t) + \varepsilon,$$

where we assume that $\mu: \Re^n_+ \to \Re^k$ is concave and ε is normally distributed with mean vector zero and covariance matrix Σ. If the compensation contract specifies a wage of $w(x)$, then the agent's expected utility is assumed to take the form

$$u(CE) = E\{u[w(\mu(t) + \varepsilon) - C(t)]\},$$

where $u(w) = -e^{-rw}$ and CE denotes the agent's "certainty equivalent" money payoff. The coefficient r measures the agent's risk aversion. The principal is risk neutral.

If the compensation rule were linear of the form $w(x) = \alpha^T x + \beta$, then one could utilize the exponential form to deduce that the agent's certainty equivalent is

$$CE = \alpha^T \mu(t) + \beta - C(t) - \tfrac{1}{2} r \alpha^T \Sigma \alpha.$$

That is, the agent's certainty equivalent consists of the expected wage minus the private cost of action and minus a risk premium. The term $\alpha^T \Sigma \alpha$ is the variance of the agent's income under this linear compensation scheme.

The principal's expected profit is $B(t) - E\{w[\mu(t) + \varepsilon]\}$ which, under the linear compensation scheme, is $B(t) - \alpha^T \mu(t) - \beta$. Consequently, the total certainty equivalent of the principal and the agent (their joint surplus) under the linear compensation plan is $B(t) - C(t) - \tfrac{1}{2} r \alpha^T \Sigma \alpha$. Notice that this expression is independent of the intercept term β; this intercept serves only to allocate the total certainty equivalent between the two parties. This last observation simplifies the principal–agent problem drastically. It implies that, given any technological and incentive constraints on the set of feasible (α, t) pairs, the utility possibility frontier, expressed in certainty equivalent terms, is a line in $\Re^2$ with slope -1. Hence, the incentive-efficient linear contracts are precisely those that maximize the total certainty equivalent subject to the constraints. If (t, α, β) is such a contract, then (t, α) must be a solution to

$$\text{Maximize } B(t) - C(t) - \tfrac{1}{2}r\alpha'\Sigma\alpha, \qquad\qquad\qquad\qquad (1)$$
$$\scriptstyle t,\,\alpha$$

subject to

$$t \text{ maximizes } \alpha^T\mu(t') - C(t'). \qquad\qquad\qquad\qquad (2)$$

If the agent's certainty equivalent is CE, then it follows that the intercept is $\beta = CE - \alpha^T\mu(t) + C(t) + \tfrac{1}{2}r\alpha^T\Sigma\alpha$. This intercept is equal to the agent's certainty equivalent income, minus the expected compensation from the incentive term, plus compensation for the cost that the agent incurs, plus a compensation for risk.

A central feature of our model is the general way in which we may allow observables to enter. We can study situations in which different activities can be measured with varying degrees of precision, including the important special case in which certain activities cannot be measured at all.[6] We can study cases in which performance measures can be influenced by activities other than those the principal desires the agent to undertake – for instance, the manipulation of accounting figures. We can study cases in which the number of observables is much smaller than the number of activities in t, forcing the contract to be based on aggregate information about the agent's activities. A special case of this, discussed in Holmstrom and Milgrom (1987), occurs when the agent acts on private information (to avoid adverse selection, one assumes that the information is observed after contracting). We can bring in contingent actions explicitly by specializing the model as follows. Let $\lambda^T = (\lambda_1, \ldots , \lambda_m)$ be a vector of probabilities of m possible states. Let t_i be the agent's contingent action in state i and let $B_i(t_i), C_i(t_i), \mu_i(t_i)$, and ε_i represent state-contingent profits, costs, signal functions, and memory errors, respectively. The analysis of that contingent-action model is equivalent to the analysis of our model with the specifications:

$$B(t) = \Sigma\lambda_i B_i(t_i), \quad C(t) = \Sigma\lambda_i C_i(t_i),$$
$$\mu(t) = \Sigma\lambda_i \mu_i(t_i), \quad \varepsilon = \Sigma\lambda_i \varepsilon_i.$$

Another important feature of the model is that B need not be part of x (i.e., the returns to the principal may not be observed). This puts B and C in a symmetric role. Indeed, if $B = -C$, the principal and the agent share the same objective and first best can be achieved in (1) and (2) by setting $\alpha = 0$. On the other hand, if B is different from $-C$, (1) and (2) may lead to a nontrivial agency problem even without the agent being risk averse. This occurs when the standard solution of making the agent a residual claimant is rendered infeasible because B is insufficiently well observed – a point made in Baker (1989) using a model with state-contingent actions of the type described above. Thus, risk aversion is not essential for the analysis to follow. The cost of measurement error, as expressed in (1), could alternatively arise out of a risk-neutral formulation.[7]

2.2   Optimality of linear performance incentives

The model described above involves two seemingly ad hoc assumptions. The more obvious one is that the contract that the parties sign specifies a wage payment that is a linear function of measured performance. The second assumption is more conventional and therefore less likely to be noticed, but it is no less troubling. It is the assumption that the agent is required to make a single, once-and-for-all choice of how he will allocate his efforts during the relationship without regard to the arrival of performance information over time. A remarkable fact, which we established in Holmstrom and Milgrom (1987), is that *these two simplifying assumptions are exactly offsetting in this model*. That is, the solution to the program (1) and (2) coincides with the solution to a principal–agent problem in which (i) the agent chooses efforts continuously over the time interval [0, 1] to control the drift vector of a stationary stochastic process (Brownian motion) $\{X(\tau); 0 \leq \tau \leq 1\}$, and (ii) the agent can observe his accumulated performance before acting. We show that in this continuous time model an efficient contract specifies that the agent will choose $t(\tau)$ to be constant over time, regardless of the history at time τ, and that the agent's wage will be of the form $w = \alpha^T x + \beta$, that is, it is a linear function of the final outcome x alone, without regard to any intermediate outcomes. The constant t and the slope vector α are the solution to problem (1) and (2).

In view of its underlying assumptions, the model seems especially well suited for representing compensation paid over a short period, like a month, a quarter, or perhaps a year, in environments where profits are the cumulative result of persistent efforts over time. As such, the model seems most appropriate for analyzing the use of piece rates or commission systems; however, because the model is so tractable, we shall not avoid the temptation to stretch its use somewhat further in this article.

2.3 Simple interactions among tasks

To explore some of the properties of our model, let us now work with the special case in which $\mu(t) = t$,[8] Then, when t is strictly positive in all components ($t \gg 0$), the incentive constraint (2) becomes

$$\alpha_i = C_i(t) \quad \text{for all } i, \tag{3}$$

where subscripts on C denote partial derivatives. Differentiating (3), we may write

$$\frac{\partial \alpha}{\partial t} = [C_{ij}] \quad \text{and} \quad \frac{\partial t}{\partial \alpha} = [C_{ij}]^{-1} \tag{4}$$

by the inverse function theorem. The second equation in (4) characterizes how changes in the "prices" α affect the level of effort that will be supplied.

Using equations (3) and (4), one can compute first-order necessary conditions for an optimum in (1) and (2) when $t \gg 0$:

$$\alpha = (l + r[C_{ij}]\Sigma)^{-1} B', \tag{5}$$

where $B' = (B_1, \ldots, B_n)$ is the vector of first derivatives of B. Condition (5) is also sufficient when the expression $C'(t)^T \Sigma C'(t)$ is convex in t.

As a benchmark case, note that when the error terms are stochastically independent (Σ is a diagonal matrix) and the activities are technologically independent (all cross-partials of the cost function are zero), the solution in (5) simplifies to $\alpha_i = B_i(1 + rC_{ii}\sigma_i^2)^{-1}$, for all i. In this case, commissions are set independently of each other since the cost of inducing the agent to perform any given task is independent of the other tasks. As expected, α_i is decreasing in risk aversion (r) and risk (σ_i^2). It is also decreasing in C_{ii}. To interpret this, note from (4) that $\partial t_i / \partial \alpha_i = 1/C_{ii}$. Thus, the above formula says that α_i should be higher, the more responsive the agent is to incentives.

In the general case, notice that the cross-partials of C but not those of B enter into (5). Complementarities in the agent's private cost of generating signals can have an important role in determining optimal incentive pay. To illustrate, consider again the case of motivating teachers to teach both basic skills and higher-order thinking skills, but assuming that higher-order thinking skills cannot be measured. We model this by supposing that there are two activities so that the agent chooses the pair (t_1, t_2), but that only one activity (teaching basic skills) is observable:

$$x = t_1 + \varepsilon. \tag{6}$$

We can apply (5) assuming that σ_2^2 is infinite and σ_{12} is zero. Then, if the optimal solution entails $t \gg 0$, it must satisfy

$$\alpha_1 = (B_1 - B_2 C_{12}/C_{22})/[1 + r\sigma_1^2(C_{11} - C_{12}^2/C_{22})].^9 \tag{7}$$

When C_{12} is negative, making it more negative leads to a larger optimal value of α_1. That is, when the activities of teaching basic skills and higher-thinking skills are complementary in the agent-teacher's private cost function, the desirability of rewarding achievement in teaching basic skills is enhanced. If the two dimensions of teaching are substitutes in the agent's cost function ($C_{12} > 0$), then α_1 is correspondingly reduced, because high values of α_1 cause the teacher to substitute effort away from teaching higher-thinking skills.

In general, when inputs are substitutes, incentives for any given activity t_i can be provided either by rewarding that activity or by reducing its opportunity cost (by reducing the incentives for the other activities). Here, t_2 cannot be measured at all, so the only way to provide incentives for t_2 is to reduce α_1 as (7) shows.

Notice that (7) allows the possibility that it may be optimal to set α_1 negative even if B_1 is positive, provided $B_1 < B_2 C_{12}/C_{22}$. If the agent can always reduce measured performance at no cost to himself, then this observation can be used to produce robust examples in which it is optimal to provide zero incentives for a desirable activity even when perfectly reliable performance measures ($\sigma_1^2 = 0$) may exist. A second case in which zero incentives can arise in this example is when effort in the two activities are perfect substitutes in the agent's cost function and the second activity is unobservable – that is, when $C(t_1, t_2) = c(t_1 + t_2)$ and $\sigma_2^2 = +\infty$. Then, if $t \gg 0$, the incentive constraint in (3) implies that $\alpha_1 = \alpha_2$ (intuitively, the agent must equate the marginal return to effort in various tasks). If, as in our teaching example, $\sigma_2^2 = \infty$, it then follows that $0 = \alpha_2 = \alpha_1$. This idea resurfaces in several of the applications in section 3.

Another important possibility is that (5) does not apply because it is not optimal to set $t \gg 0$. Even in the model where t is one dimensional, the cost of providing positive incentives for a small amount of effort is discontinuously higher than the cost of providing no incentive for effort if $C'(0) > 0$. If no effort is required and no incentive is provided, then the risk premium incurred by the agent is zero. If a small amount of effort t is required, then $\alpha = C'(t) > C'(0) > 0$ and the risk premium is therefore at least $\frac{1}{2}r[C'(0)]^2\sigma^2$. Providing incentives for an activity involves an inherent fixed cost, and the size of that cost can be affected by the selection and levels of the agent's other activities. These observations will prove to be important when we apply our theory to issues of employment and job design.

3 Allocation Incentives for Effort and Attention

3.1 The effort and attention allocation model

We now move to a group of models in which the agent's effort or attention is a homogeneous input that can be allocated among tasks however the agent likes. We shall suppose that effort in the various tasks is perfectly substitutable in the agent's cost function. More formally, we suppose that the agent chooses a vector $t = (t_1, \ldots, t_m)$ at a personal (strictly convex) cost $C(t_1 + \cdots + t_m)$, leading to expected profits $B(t)$ and generating signals $x(t) = \mu(t) + \varepsilon$. Then, if the agent increases the amount of time or attention devoted to one activity, the marginal cost of attention to the other activities will grow larger.

Contrary to most earlier principal–agent models, we shall not suppose that all work is unpleasant (see note 9). A worker on the job may take pleasure in working up to some limit; incentives are only required to encourage work beyond that limit. Formally, we assume that there is some number $\bar{t} > 0$ such that $C'(t) \leq 0$ for $t \leq \bar{t}$ and $C(\bar{t}) = 0$. This is important, because it means that contracts that provide for fixed wages may still elicit some effort, though more may be elicited by providing positive incentives. It also means that there is a range of effort allocations among which the agent is indifferent and willing to follow the principal's preference.

3.2 Missing incentive clauses in contracts

One of the most puzzling and troubling failures of incentive models has been their inability to account for the paucity of explicit incentive provisions in actual contracts. For example, it is surprisingly uncommon in contracts for home remodeling to incorporate explicit incentives for timely completion of construction, even though construction delays arise frequently and can be profoundly disruptive to the homeowner. There can be little doubt that such clauses could be written into the contracts; similar clauses are common in commercial construction contracts. We shall argue that these facts can best be understood as a result of the greater standardization of commercial construction and the consequent ability of commercial buyers to specify and monitor quality standards. The innovation in our analysis is that our explanation of the presence or absence of the timely completion clause lies in an examination of the principal's ability to monitor *other aspects* of the agent's performance.[10]

Thus, suppose that some desirable attributes of the contractor's performance (such as courtesy, attention to detail, or helpful advice) are unmeasurable but are enhanced by attention t_1 spent on that activity, while other aspects of quality (such as timely completion) are measurable (perhaps imperfectly) and enhanced by attention t_2 devoted to this second

activity. Supposing that the measured quality is one dimensional, we may write
$\mu(t_1, t_2) = \mu(t_2), x = \mu + \varepsilon$. As we have seen, the agent's efficient compensation contract
pays an amount $S = \alpha x + \beta$.

Suppose that the overall value of the job to the homeowner is determined by the function
$B(t_1, t_2)$. To model the idea that the first activity is "very important" and that both
activities are valuable, we assume that B is increasing and that $B(0, t_2) = 0$, for all $t_2 \geq 0$.

Proposition 1

For the home contractor model specified in the last paragraph, the efficient linear compensation rule pays a fixed wage and contains no incentive component ($\alpha = 0$), even if the
contractor is risk neutral.[11]

Proof

If $\alpha = 0$, then the agent can be instructed to spend total time $\tilde{t}$ where $C'(\tilde{t}) = 0$ and to choose
$\tilde{t}_1 \in [0, \tilde{t}]$ to maximize $B(\tilde{t}_1, \tilde{t} - \tilde{t}_1)$, which is strictly positive because $\tilde{t} > 0$. In this case, the
cost of risk-bearing by the agent is zero, so the total wealth will be $B(\tilde{t}_1, \tilde{t} - \tilde{t}_1) - C(\tilde{t})$.
If $\alpha > 0$, then t_1 will be set to zero and the total wealth will be $0 - C(\hat{t}) - r\alpha^2 \sigma_\varepsilon^2 / 2$
$\leq -C(\hat{t}) < B(\tilde{t}_1, \tilde{t} - \tilde{t}_1) - C(\tilde{t})$ because $\tilde{t}$ is cost minimizing for the agent. If $\alpha < 0$, then
$t_2 = 0$ and $t_1 < \tilde{t}$ [because $C'(t_1) < 0 = C'(\tilde{t})$] so the total profits are

$$B(t_1, 0) - C(t_1) - r\alpha^2 \sigma_\varepsilon^2 < B(\tilde{t}, 0) - C(\tilde{t}) < B(\tilde{t}_1, \tilde{t} - \tilde{t}_1) - C(\tilde{t}). \qquad \qquad Q.E.D.$$

The ideas that underlie this analysis have many applications. For example, piece rates are
relatively rare in manufacturing and, where they are used, they are frequently accompanied
by careful attention to monitoring the quality of the work. Our analysis indicates that if
quality were poorly measured, it would be expensive or impossible to maintain good quality
while using a piece-rate scheme. Similarly, where individuals spend part of their efforts on
individual projects and part on team production, and assuming that individual contributions to the team effort are difficult to assess, it would be dangerous to provide incentives
for good performance on the individual projects. The problem, of course, is that individuals
may shift their attention from the team activity where their individual contributions are
poorly measured to the better measured and well-compensated individual activity. For this
reason, piece-rate schemes may be especially dysfunctional in large hierarchies.

3.3   *"Low-powered incentives" in firms*

A similar model can be used to explain Williamson's observation that the incentives offered to
employees in firms are generally "low-powered" compared to the "high-powered" incentives offered to independent contractors (1985). Like Williamson, we distinguish employees
from independent contractors by the condition of asset ownership: employees use and
develop assets that are owned by others while contractors use and develop their own assets.

Once again, the heart of our modeling is our assumption that there are multiple activities
to be undertaken and that the allocation of time and attention between them is crucial.
Thus, let the expected gross profit from the enterprise be the sum of two parts,
$B(t_1) + V(t_2)$, where B represents the expected net receipts and V the expected change
in the net asset value. We assume that B and V are increasing, concave, and twice

continuously differentiable and that $B(0) = V(0) = 0$. The actual change in asset value, $V + \varepsilon_v$, accrues to whoever owns the asset. Assets are notoriously hard to value (that is why accountants generally use historical cost as a valuation basis), so we assume that there is no performance indicator for the asset enhancement activity t_2. The primary activity t_1 is to produce output for sale in the current period: its indicator is $x = \mu(t_1) + \varepsilon_x$, where μ is increasing and concave. We assume that ε_x and ε_v are independent.

We consider two alternative organizational modes – *contracting*, in which the change in asset value accrues to the agent, and *employment*, in which the change in asset value accrues to the firm or principal. The crucial difference between these lies in the incentives for the agent to engage in the two kinds of activities. To focus on the most interesting case, we will assume that it is highly desirable to induce the agent to devote a positive amount of effort to both activities. Let

$$\pi^1 = \underset{t_1}{\text{Max}}\ B(t_1) - C(t_1),$$

$$\pi^2 = \underset{t_2}{\text{Max}}\ V(t_2) - C(t_2),$$

$$\pi^{12} = \underset{t_1}{\text{Max}}\ B(t_1) + V(\tilde{t} - t_1) - C(\tilde{t}).$$

Proposition 2

Assume that $\pi^{12} \geq (\pi^1, \pi^2)$. Then, the optimal employment contract always entails paying a fixed wage ($\alpha = 0$). Whenever the independent contracting relation is optimal, it involves "high-powered incentives" ($\alpha > 0$). Furthermore, there exist values of the parameters r, σ_v^2, and σ_x^2 for which employment contracts are optimal and others for which independent contracting is optimal. If employment contracting is optimal for some fixed parameters $(r, \sigma_v^2, \sigma_x^2)$, then it is also optimal for higher values of these parameters. Similarly, if independent contracting is optimal, then it is also optimal for lower values of these parameters.[12]

Proof

First, consider the case of the employment contract, where the returns $V(t_2)$ accrue to the firm. If the principal sets $\alpha > 0$, the agent will respond by setting t_1 so that $\alpha = C'(t_1)$ and setting $t_2 = 0$. The total certainty equivalent wealth is equal to $B(t_1) - C(t_1) - \frac{1}{2}r\sigma^2\alpha^2 < \pi^1 \leq \pi^{12}$. However, if $\alpha = 0$, the agent is willing to spend time $\tilde{t}$ in any proportions and so a total certainty equivalent wealth of π^{12} is obtained. Therefore, it is optimal for the principal to set $\alpha = 0$ in an employment contract.

For the independent contractor, the maximum total certainty equivalent wealth is computed as follows. Let $(\hat{t}_1(\alpha), \hat{t}_2(\alpha))$ maximize $\alpha\mu(t_1) + V(t_2) - C(t_1 + t_2) - r\sigma_v^2/2$; this represents the agent's optimal response to α. The total certainty equivalent wealth for any fixed α is

$$B(\hat{t}_1(\alpha)) + V(\hat{t}_2(\alpha)) - C(\hat{t}_1(\alpha) + \hat{t}_2(\alpha)) - \frac{1}{2}r\{\sigma_x^2[C'(\hat{t}_1(\alpha) + \hat{t}_2(\alpha))]^2 + \sigma_v^2\}$$

and the maximum surplus is the maximum of this expression over α. If we fix $\alpha = 0$, then this expression is lower for the independent contractor than for the employment regime.

Hence, whenever the independent contractor regime is optimal, it must be optimal to set $\alpha > 0$.

Note that if $\sigma_x^2 = \sigma_v^2 = 0$, first best is achieved by setting $\alpha = 1$ in the independent contractor regime. Since first best never can be achieved in the employment regime, the independent contractor regime is better in this case. Letting $r\sigma_v^2$, grow large makes the payoff to the independent contract regime fall without limit, so there are also some parameters for which the employment regime is better.

The last two sentences of Proposition 2 follow from the observation that the expression for the total certainty equivalent in the independent contractor regime is decreasing in $r\sigma_v^2$ and $r\sigma_x^2$, but these two terms do not affect the total certainty equivalent in the employment regime.   *Q.E.D*

Proposition 2 is consistent with the evidence reported by Anderson (1985) and Anderson and Schmittlein (1984). They attempted to identify the reasons why firms in the electronic components industry have an employed sales force in some districts and independent sales representatives in other districts. (Many, but not all firms, used both forms of sales organization, suggesting that economies of scale play a lesser role.) They found that the perceived difficulty of measuring sales of individual salespeople (due to team selling or costly record keeping) was the best empirical predictor of the use of an in-house sales force. Transaction cost variables – such as specific training, with the exception of confidential information – were not significant either alone or in conjunction with performance measurement. If we suppose that one function of the sales force is to build an asset that is impossible to measure, such as "goodwill" (how satisfied and loyal are the customers?), then our model suggests that the difficulty of measuring sales would lead to the pattern of sales organization that Anderson and Schmittlein observed, and that commission rates would be lower for company-run sales forces.[13]

Anderson also finds that the importance of nonselling activities, such as promoting new products or products with a long selling cycle, is positively related to the use of an in-house sales force. We can analyze this finding by introducing a third activity t_3, which benefits the principal, but not the agent. Since an independent contractor will spend no time on nonselling activities (just as practitioners claim), it is easy to see that an increase in the value of this activity will work in favor of an owner-run sales force in our model.

Another piece of evidence consistent with our model comes from the fast-food industry. Firms such as McDonald's and Burger King own about 30% of their stores and franchise the rest. The difference in incentives between franchisees and owner-managed firms is striking. Franchisees pay royalties that are at most 10% of sales, corresponding to at least a 90% commission, whereas managers of company-owned stores typically receive no explicit incentives either on profit or sales (Krueger, 1991; Brickley and Dark, 1987). The difference in incentives is all the more remarkable, considering how similar the two types of stores are in all other aspects. According to our theory, the discontinuous shift in residual returns $[V(t_2)]$ associated with franchising and the attendant shift in attention toward long-term asset values and cost containment, forces the franchise contract to increase short-term incentives sharply. Or, looked upon the other way, short-term incentives for employed managers must be muted to prevent them from allocating their attention away from important, but hard to measure, asset values.

4 Limits on Outside Activities

Our previous analysis emphasizes the importance of studying the full range of the agent's activities for analyzing incentives. If activities interact in the agent's cost function, incentive strength can be predicted only once the agent's whole portfolio of tasks is known. An equally important implication is that the principal can influence the agent's incentives by choosing the agent's portfolio of tasks. In the next section, we will study the optimal allocation of tasks between two agents. In this section, we consider how the principal might try to manage the agent's access to outside (private) activities.

Even casual observation makes it clear that the rules governing outside activities depend on the job. It is a commonplace observation that employees in "responsible positions" are allowed more freedom of action than other employees, and that they use that freedom in part to pursue personally beneficial activities. To analyze the issues that this observation raises, we begin with the assumption that it is easier for an employer to exclude an activity entirely than to monitor it and limit its extent. For example, a rule against personal telephone calls during business hours is found in many offices and seems to be motivated in part by its ease of enforcement compared, say, to a rule that limits the percentage of business hours devoted to personal calls to 2%. Although generalizations about employment all seem to have exceptions, a common feature of employment contracts is that the employer has authority to restrict the employee's outside activities during business hours, and sometimes after hours as well.

Assume then that the agent has a finite pool $K = \{1, \ldots, N\}$ of potential activities, which the principal can control only by exclusion. The returns to these tasks, which we will refer to as the *agent's personal business* for short, are assumed nonstochastic and to benefit the agent alone (in principle, these tasks could benefit the principal, too, but the analytics would be more complicated). The principal controls the agent's personal business by allowing the agent to engage only in a subset of tasks $A \subset K$. Within the *set of allowable tasks*, A, the agent can engage in as much or as little personal business as he pleases, but none outside A. To focus on the interactions between the agent's workplace activities and personal business, we represent workplace activities simply as a single task in which performance is imperfectly measured.

Let t denote the attention the agent devotes to the principal's task and t_k the time he devotes to personal business k. We model the personal benefits that the agent derives as an offset against, or deduction from, his personal cost of effort, as follows:

$$c(t, t_1, \ldots, t_N) = C(t + \Sigma_K t_k) - \Sigma_K v_k(t_k) \qquad (8)$$

The notation Σ_K stands for summation over k in K. Here C is the agent's private cost of the total attention he devotes to all his (permitted) personal activities. The return from personal activity k is measured by the function $v_k(t_k)$; these functions are assumed to be strictly concave with $v_k(0) = 0$. If $k \notin A$, then $t_k = 0$, so we could replace Σ_k with Σ_A in (8).

We make the simplifying assumptions that there are constant returns to time both in generating profits and in improving measured performance:

$$B(t, t_1, \ldots, t_N) = pt, \qquad x(t, t_1, \ldots, t_N) = t + \varepsilon. \tag{9}$$

The variance of ε is σ^2.

The principal's control instruments are the commission rate α and the allowed set of personal business tasks $A \subset K$. We will study the principal's problem in two stages. First, we fix α and consider the optimal choice of A, denoted $A(\alpha)$, and then we determine the optimal α.

Given the parameters α and A, the agent chooses t and t_k to maximize

$$\alpha t + \Sigma_A v_k(t_k) - C(t + \Sigma_A t_k).$$

Assume for the moment that this problem has an interior solution. Then the first-order conditions that characterize the agent's optimum are

$$\alpha = C'(t + \Sigma_A t_k), \tag{10}$$

$$\alpha = v_k'(t_k). \tag{11}$$

We note from (11) that the amount of time the agent chooses to spend on task k, denoted $t_k(\alpha)$, only depends on α and not on A. Also, the total time spent working, $t + \Sigma_A t_k$, is independent of A. Consequently, if the agent is allowed more personal tasks, without a change in α, all the time for those tasks will be reallocated away from the principal's task; this is the convenience of assuming (9) together with a cost function that only depends on total time. It makes it very simple to determine which personal tasks the agent should be allowed for a given α. The benefit of allowing the agent to spend time on task k is $v_k(t_k(\alpha))$, while the (opportunity) cost is $pt_k(\alpha)$. Therefore, the optimal set of allowable personal tasks is

$$A(\alpha) = \{\in K | v_k(t_k(\alpha)) > pt_k(\alpha)\}. \tag{12}$$

Figure 12.1 shows the determination of $A(\alpha)$. The pt line represents the returns from spending time on the principal's task. The v_1 and v_2 curves represent the returns from two private tasks. Both private tasks are socially valuable in that the v_k curves rise above the pt line on a positive interval $t_k \in [0, \hat{t}_k]$, where $\hat{t}_k$ is defined by the intersection $v_k(\hat{t}_k) = p\hat{t}_k$. However, for the chosen α, only task 1 is worth keeping; it is optimal to exclude task 2 since $t_2(\alpha) > \hat{t}_2$ – that is, time $t_2(\alpha)$ yields more in the principal's task than it yields in task 2.

The geometry of figure 12.1 makes it evident that $A(\alpha)$ expands as α is increased. This follows because $t_k(\alpha)$ is decreasing as v_k is strictly concave. As α is raised, the agent will spend less time on private business. This brings more projects into the efficient region $t_k(\alpha) \leq \hat{t}_k$, which is characterized by the condition that time $t_k(\alpha)$ in the private task yields more than the same amount of time spent in the principal's task. Furthermore, we see that the critical value of α at which private task k will be excluded is entirely determined by the slope of v_k at the point where v_k intersects the pt line. This follows since $t_k(\alpha) \leq \hat{t}_k$ if and only if $v_k'(\hat{t}_k) \leq \alpha$.

We record these observations in the following proposition.

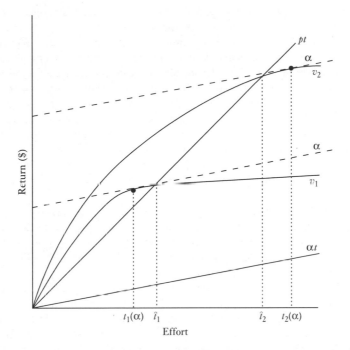

Figure 12.1   It is optimal to allow task 1 but to exclude task 2, because $t_1(\alpha) < \hat{\imath}_1$ but $\hat{\imath}_2 < t_2(\alpha)$. Note that this is true even though the social returns to task 2 are everywhere higher than those to task 1.

Proposition 3
Assume that α is such that $t(\alpha) > 0$. Then the following statements hold.

(i)   It is optimal to let the agent pursue exactly those private business opportunities that belong to $A(\alpha)$ defined in (12); that is, those tasks k for which the resulting *average product* $v_k(t_k(\alpha))/t_k(\alpha)$ exceeds the *marginal product* p in the principal's task.

(ii)   The higher is the agent's marginal reward for performance in the main job, the greater is his freedom to pursue personal business. Formally, if $\alpha \leq \alpha'$, then $A(\alpha) \supset A(\alpha')$.

(iii)   If it is optimal to exclude task k, then it is also optimal to exclude all tasks m, for which $v'_m(\hat{\imath}_m) > v'_k(\hat{\imath}_k)$, where $\hat{\imath}_j$ is defined by $v_j(\hat{\imath}_j) = p\hat{\imath}_j$.

It is possible that for small enough α it will be optimal to set $t(\alpha) = 0$ and hence $A(\alpha) = K$. In that case, there are no gains from trade and the principal will not employ the agent. Such a solution may be optimal if the cost of bearing risk becomes sufficiently large. One could exclude that case by assuming that the agent's private businesses are less productive than working for the principal with zero incentive (as we saw earlier, zero incentive does not preclude productive work), but there is no need to make such a restriction. Obviously, if $t(\alpha) = 0$, then $t(\alpha') = 0$, for all $\alpha' < \alpha$. Therefore, job separation will occur, if at all, below a critical cutoff value for α.

Part (ii) of Proposition 3 articulates a familiar and fundamental principle: responsibility and authority should go hand in hand. It is optimal to give the agent more freedom to pursue personal business when he is financially more responsible for his performance. In the extreme case, when performance can be measured without error and it is optimal to make the agent a residual claimant ($\alpha = p$), the agent will be free to engage in whatever private business he deems desirable. The responsibility principle again underscores that the agent's incentives can be influenced indirectly by altering the opportunity cost for supplying desired inputs. It is readily seen that the agent's marginal cost (but not total cost) of spending a given amount of time t in the principal's task is reduced by excluding private tasks. Exclusion will be more extensively used the more costly it is to provide financial rewards.[14]

Part (iii) of the Proposition shows that the social value of a personal activity, and the likelihood that it will be excluded, need bear little relationship to each other. For instance, in figure 12.1 the social value of task 2 is higher than that of task 1 for any given amount of time spent on either, yet it is task 2 rather than task 1 that is excluded. The reason is that task 2 more easily invites excess attention.

Before turning to the choice of α, there is a point that deserves to be emphasized. The amount of personal business A that the principal will allow for a fixed α, as characterized in (12), does not depend directly on r or σ^2, nor on the cost function C. These factors affect A only through α. Therefore, given data about r, σ^2, α, C, and A, it is econometrically correct to regress A against the endogenous variable α. Proposition 3 predicts that the extent of agent freedom will be positively related to α, irrespective of which of the model parameters (other than v_k) are viewed as exogenous. The parameters r and σ^2 are a natural source of cross-sectional variation in α as indicated by the following.

Proposition 4

Assume that the optimal solution features $t(\alpha) > 0$. Then the following statements hold.

(i)   The optimal value of α is given by

$$\alpha = p/[1 + r\sigma^2/(dt/d\alpha)],$$

where $dt/d\alpha = 1/C'' + \Sigma_{A(\alpha)}(1/v_k'')$.

(ii)   If it becomes easier to measure the agent's performance (σ^2 decreases), or the agent becomes less risk averse (r decreases), then the agent's marginal reward α will be raised and his personal business activities will be less curtailed.

(iii)   Any personal task that would be excluded in a first-best arrangement [$v_k'(0) \leq p$] will also be excluded in a second-best arrangement. For sufficiently high values of $r\sigma^2$, some tasks that would be included at the first best will be excluded at the second best.

Proof

The equation in (i) is a special case of (5); the expression for $dt/d\alpha$ follows from the agent's first-order conditions. Revealed preference paired with Proposition 3 implies (ii).

Part (i) implies that $\alpha \leq p$ and that α goes to zero when $r\sigma^2$ goes to infinity; this proves (iii). $Q.E.D.$

If we assume that the agent's cost and benefit functions are quadratic, we see from (i) that the agent's responsiveness to incentives, $dt/d\alpha$, increases as the set of allowable tasks, $A(\alpha)$, expands. Consequently, viewing $A(\alpha)$ as exogenous, it is optimal to raise α in response to an increase in the agent's degree of freedom. Of course, $A(\alpha)$ is not exogenous; it expands with an increase in α. We see then that α and $A(\alpha)$ are complementary instruments: increasing either leads to an increase in the other.[15]

Part (ii) is the most interesting one. It predicts that there will be more constraints on an agent's activities in situations where performance rewards are weak because of measurement problems. The rigid rules and limits that characterize bureaucracy, in this view, constitute an optimal response to difficulties in measuring and rewarding performance. Among the "personal business" activities that bureaucracies try to limit are collusion (Tirole, 1986; Holmstrom and Milgrom, 1990; Itoh, 1989) and influence activities (Milgrom, 1988; Milgrom and Roberts, 1988). The restrictions on trade between employees that Holmstrom and Milgrom (1990) recommend and the restrictions on communications that Milgrom and Roberts propose are examples of optimal exclusion of activities that would be permitted or perhaps even encouraged in a first-best world.

The desire to exclude activities provides a second possible explanation of the empirical results of Anderson and Schmittlein. Here, rather than distinguishing the roles of employee and independent contractor on the basis of ownership of productive assets, the focus is on the discretionary authority of the employer to prevent salespeople from outside activities, such as selling the products of other manufacturers during business hours. As the difficulty of monitoring performance (measured by σ^2) rises, Proposition 4 asserts that there is an increasing degree of exclusivity in efficient contracts. If exclusivity is easier to enforce within firms than across firms, then poor sales measurement and employment are positively related.

Our two explanations of the Anderson–Schmittlein evidence are distinct but closely related. In the first, the extra incentive from employment comes from transferring to the firm the return stream associated with the goodwill created by customer satisfaction. In the second, the extra incentive comes from eliminating (rather than transferring) a return stream – that associated with personal business. In each case, eliminating the agent's direct profits from an activity reduces the opportunity cost of work to the employee and lowers the cost of providing incentives.

5 Allocating Tasks between Two Agents

In the single-agent model, the commission rates α_i serve three purposes: they allocate risk, motivate work, and direct the agent's efforts among his various activities. A trade-off arises when these objectives are in conflict with each other: Optimal risk-sharing may be inconsistent with motivating work, and motivating hard work may distort the agent's allocation of efforts across tasks. Among the instruments available to the principal to alleviate these problems are job restructuring and relative performance evaluation: the former allows the principal to reduce the distortions in how attention is allocated among activities, while the latter enables the principal to lower the cost of incentives by using a more sensitive measure of actual performance.

5.1   Optimal groupings of tasks into jobs

Here we initiate the study of how incentive considerations might affect the grouping of tasks into jobs. We use a model that eliminates other important effects, such as differences among the agents and complementarities among task assignments. There are two identical agents, indexed $i = 1, 2$, who allocate their attention across a continuum of tasks indexed by $k \in [0, 1]$. Let $t_i(k)$ denote the attention agent i devotes to task k. We assume that the two agents can share a task and that their labor inputs are perfect substitutes. Thus, profit $B(t)$ is a function of the total time vector $t \equiv \{t(k): k \in [0, 1]\}$, where $t(k) = t_1(k) + t_2(k)$. Likewise, the performance signal from task k, $\mu(t(k), k)$, only depends on the total attention $t(k)$ devoted to it. The error variance of task k is $\sigma^2(k) > 0$ and the errors are assumed independent.

Agent i's total labor input is given by

$$\tilde{t}_i = \int t_i(k)dk. \tag{13}$$

His private cost is $C(\tilde{t}_i)$; the cost function is assumed differentiable and strictly convex.

Since the *ex ante* specification of the model is symmetric in the roles of the two agents, if the problem entailed a concave objective and convex constraints, we would expect the optimal solution to be symmetric. However, as we shall see, the optimal solution is not symmetric, so we must be careful to deal correctly with the inherent nonconvexities of the problem.

We begin by studying the problem of implementing, at minimum cost, a given vector $t = \{t(k)\}$ of total attention to be devoted to the various tasks, given the constraint that the total attention devoted by agent i is $\tilde{t}_i$. Denoting the commission paid to agent i for task k by $\alpha_i(k)$, this problem is described by

$$\underset{\substack{t_1(.),t_2(.) \\ \alpha_1(.),\alpha_2(.)}}{\text{Minimize}} \; C(\tilde{t}_1) + C(\tilde{t}_2) + \frac{r}{2} \int [\alpha_1^2(k) + \alpha_1^2(k)]\sigma^2(k)dk, \tag{14}$$

subject to (12), (13), and the incentive constraints

$$\begin{aligned} \alpha_i(k)\mu'(t(k), k) &\leq C'(\tilde{t}_i), \quad \text{if } t_i(k) = 0, \\ \alpha_i(k)\mu'(t(k), k) &= C'(t_i), \quad \text{if } t_i(k) > 0, i = 1, 2, k \in [0, 1]. \end{aligned} \tag{15}$$

The incentive constraints can be correctly described by first-order conditions, because the agent's choice problem is a concave maximization problem. As usual, the implementation cost reflects both the direct cost of work as well as the cost of risk–bearing, since both costs are deducted when determining the total certainty equivalent of the parties.

We shall say that the principal makes the two agents *jointly responsible for task* k if $\alpha_1(k) > 0$ and $\alpha_2(k) > 0$. Similarly, agent i is *solely responsible for task* k if $\alpha_i(k) > 0$ and $\alpha_j(k) = 0$, $i \neq j$.

Proposition 5

In the model described above, it is never optimal for the two agents to be jointly responsible for any task k.

Proof

Let k be a set of tasks for which there is joint responsibility – that is, $\alpha_1(k)\alpha_2(k) > 0$, for $k \in K$ – and suppose K has positive measure. Let $t_i(K) \equiv \int_k t_i(k)dk$ and choose $K' \subset K$ such that $\int_{K'} t(k)dk = t_1(K)$. Define a new set of attention allocations and commission rates $\{\hat{t}_i(k), \hat{\alpha}_i(k)\}$ so that these coincide with the original specification for $k \notin K$. For $k \in K'$, set $\hat{t}_1(k) = t(k)$, $\hat{\alpha}_1(k) = \alpha_1(k)$, and $\hat{t}_2(k) = \hat{\alpha}_2(k) = 0$; for $k \in K \backslash K'$, set $\hat{t}_1(k) = \hat{\alpha}_1(k) = 0$, $\hat{t}_2(k) = t(k)$, and $\hat{\alpha}_2(k) = \alpha_2(k)$.

The total attention devoted to each task as well as the total attention of each of the two agents is unaltered in the new scheme. By construction, therefore, the first-order conditions (15) hold and the new scheme is feasible. The new scheme strictly improves the objective function as some of the commission rates are lowered to zero for a set of tasks of nonzero measure. $\qquad Q.E.D.$

This proposition reflects our earlier observation that providing incentives for an agent in any task incurs a fixed cost as the agent assumes some nontrivial fraction of the risk associated with that task (or its measurement). Since we have assumed that the tasks are small relative to the agent's capabilities, assigning joint responsibility for any task would incur two fixed costs unnecessarily. As the proof demonstrates, if one begins with an arrangement in which some tasks are shared, it is possible to split the same tasks among the agents without affecting either the total effort required of either agent or the total effort allocated to any task. This rearrangement makes it possible to eliminate some of each agent's responsibilities [setting $\alpha_i(k) = 0$], thereby reducing the risk that the agent must bear and so increasing the total surplus of the three parties.

Having established that each task will be assigned to just one employee, we next turn to the issue of how the tasks will be grouped. With this in mind, it is convenient to redefine our variables. We reinterpret $\alpha_i(k)$ to be the *hypothetical* commission rate that the principal would need to pay in order to elicit the desired level of effort $t(k)$ from agent i if he were assigned task k [see (17) below]. We also define a task assignment variable $I_i(k)$, which is set equal to unity if agent i is assigned task k and is set equal to zero otherwise. Then, the *actual* commission rate paid to agent i for task k is $\alpha_i(k)I_i(k)$; that is, it is $\alpha_i(k)$ if i is assigned the task and it is zero otherwise. Proposition 3 implies that at the optimum, $t_i(k) = I_i(k)t(k)$. We can now state the principal's task assignment problem as follows:

$$\underset{I_1(k),\, I_2(k)}{\text{Minimize}} \; C(t_1) + C(t_2) + \frac{r}{2}\int_0^1 [I_1(k)\alpha_1^2(k) + I_2(k)\alpha_2^2(k)]\sigma^2(K)dk, \qquad (16)$$

subject to

$$\alpha_i(k)\mu'(t(k), k) = C'(\bar{t}_i), \qquad i = 1, 2, k \in [0, 1], \tag{17}$$

$$\int I_i(k)t(k) = \bar{t}_i, \qquad i = 1, 2. \tag{18}$$

$$I_1(k) + I_2(k) = 1, \qquad k \in [0, 1], \tag{19}$$

$$I_i(k) = 0 \text{ or } 1, \qquad i = 1, 2 \text{ and } k \in [0, 1]. \tag{20}$$

Constraint (17) merely defines $\alpha_i(k)$, since $t(k)$ and $\bar{t}_i$ are fixed. If $\tilde{t}_1 = \tilde{t}_2$, then it is clear from (17) that $\alpha_1(k) = \alpha_2(k)$, and hence that the objective (16) is independent of the task assignment. All feasible assignments then yield the same total certainty equivalent wealth. As we will see below, the important case is the asymmetric one, so let us assume that $\tilde{t}_1 < \tilde{t}_2$.

To solve program (16)–(20), we first solve the relaxed program in which (20) is replaced by the less restrictive constraint

$$I_i(k) \geq 0, \qquad i = 1, 2 \text{ and } k \in [0, 1]. \tag{21}$$

In the relaxed problem the objective and constraints are all linear (hence, convex) in the choice variables $I_i(k)$, so first-order conditions fully characterize the optimum. Let γ_i be the Lagrange multiplier associated with constraint (18). Then, optimizing in the usual way, we find that

$$I_1(k) = 0, \qquad \text{if } (r/2)[\alpha_1^2(k) - \alpha_2^2(k)]\sigma^2(k) + (\gamma_1 - \gamma_2)t(k) > 0$$

and $\tag{22}$

$$I_1(k) = 1, \qquad \text{if } (r/2)[\alpha_1^2(k) - \alpha_2^2(k)]\sigma^2(k) + (\gamma_1 - \gamma_2)t(k) < 0.$$

By (17), $\alpha_1 < \alpha_2$ as $\tilde{t}_1 < \tilde{t}_2$; therefore, (22) implies that $\gamma_1 > \gamma_2$. Since $I_i(k)$ takes values 0 and 1 at the optimum of the relaxed program with constraint (21) in place of (20), equations (22) also characterize the solution to the original problem and identify the marginal tasks. A marginal task is one where the advantage of assigning the task to agent 1, in terms of the lower risk premium required, is just offset by the higher marginal value of agent 1's time. The first of these costs varies with the measurement error attached to the task and the second varies with the amount of time the task requires. These observations suggest an alternative characterization of the optimum assignment policy.

Define the *noise-to-signal ratio* of task k by $n(k) = \sigma^2(k)/\mu'(t(k), k)^2$ and the *information coefficient* by $\varrho(k) = n(k)/t(k)$. Let

$$\varrho \equiv (2/r)(\gamma_1 - \gamma_2)[C'(\bar{t}_2)^2 - C'(\bar{t}_1)^2]^{-1}. \tag{23}$$

We can then restate (22) as follows.

Proposition 6

Suppose that the two agents devote different amounts of total attention to their tasks (i.e., $\tilde{t}_1 < \tilde{t}_2$). Then, tasks are optimally assigned in this model so that all the hardest-to-monitor tasks are undertaken by agent 1 and all the easiest-to-monitor tasks are undertaken by agent 2. That is, agent 1 is assigned all the tasks k for which $\varrho(k) \geq \varrho$, and agent 2 is assigned all those with $\varrho(k) < \varrho$, where ϱ is defined in (23).

Corollary

Suppose that $\tilde{t}_1 < \tilde{t}_2$, the required allocation of attention is uniform [i.e., $t(k) = 1$ for all k] and the signal functions are identical [i.e., $\mu(t, k) = \mu(t)$]. Then there exists a χ such that agent 1 will optimally be given all the tasks k for which $\sigma^2(k) \geq \sigma^2(\chi)$, and agent 2 all the tasks for which $\sigma^2(k) < \sigma^2(\chi)$.

These results provide, in purely incentive-theoretic terms, an account of how activities might be grouped, with some employees specializing in activities that are hard to monitor and others in activities that are easily monitored.[16] Separating tasks according to their measurability characteristics [$\varrho(k)$] allows the principal to give strong incentives for tasks that are easy to measure without fearing that the agent will substitute efforts away from other, harder-to-measure tasks. The present model oversimplifies these issues by assuming that there are no restrictions on how the principal may group tasks. In the case of piece rates discussed in section 3, it might not be possible to separate the tasks of providing high output from those of providing high quality: the worker might always be able to substitute speed for attention to details. Nevertheless, the results of Proposition 6 are suggestive.[17]

The appearance of $\varrho(k)$ in these results is unfamiliar, and seems worth reviewing in detail. Let realized performance in task k be measured by

$$x_k(t) = \mu(t, k) + \varepsilon_k,$$

where ε_k is distributed normally with zero mean and variance $\sigma^2(k)$. The *normalized performance measure*,

$$\hat{x}_k(t) = [\mu(t, k) + \varepsilon_k]/\mu'(t(k), k),$$

provides the same information and has error variance equal to the noise-to-signal ratio $n(k)$. If we let $\hat{\alpha}_i(k)$ denote the commission paid based on normalized performance, it follows from (17) that

$$\hat{\alpha}_i(k) = C'(\tilde{t}_i) \equiv \hat{\alpha}_i, \quad \text{for all } k. \tag{24}$$

Thus, normalized commissions $\hat{\alpha}_i(k)$ must all be equal for an agent. This is an implication of the assumption that attention to various tasks are perfect substitutes in the cost function. Since all commissions are equal, the risk cost from allocating task k to agent i is $(r/2)\hat{\alpha}_i^2 n(k)$. Task k requiring attention $t(k)$ will be optimally assigned to the agent with the lowest price per unit effort. The risk cost for agent i per unit effort is $(r/2)\hat{\alpha}_i^2 \varrho(k)$ and the value of the agent's attention in its best alternative use is γ_i. Therefore, task k is optimally assigned to agent i if i's total cost of $\gamma_i + (r/2)\hat{\alpha}_i^2 \varrho(k)$ per unit effort is less than j's corresponding cost. From this observation and (24), it is evidently optimal to assign the higher $\varrho(k)$ tasks to the agent with the lower $\tilde{t}_i$ and to pay that agent a lower "normalized commission rate." This observation is incorporated into the next proposition, but the proposition's main purpose is different: it verifies that even though the two agents in our model are identical *ex ante*, an optimal solution necessarily treats them asymmetrically, requiring them to specialize in different tasks.

Proposition 7

Suppose that the information coefficients $\varrho(k)$ are not all identical and consider the variant of program (16)–(20) in which the variables $\tilde{t}_i$ ($i = 1, 2$) are added to the list of choice variables. This program has no symmetric optimal solution ($\tilde{t}_1 \neq \tilde{t}_2$). There is an optimum at which agent 1 is assigned less strenuous work ($\tilde{t}_1 < \tilde{t}_2$), takes responsibility for the hard-to-measure tasks [those with $\varrho(k) > \varrho$], and receives lower "normalized commissions" [$\hat{\alpha}_1(k) < \hat{\alpha}_2(k)$].

Proof

First, we show that there is no optimum with $\tilde{t}_1 = \tilde{t}_2 = \tilde{t}$. If there were, then – in view of (16), (17), and (19) – every feasible allocation of tasks to agents leads to the same total payoff. In particular, there is an optimal solution in which agent 1 is assigned the high $\varrho(k)$ tasks; that is, all tasks for which $\varrho(k) > \varrho$, where ϱ is set to just exhaust the attention $\tilde{t}_1$. Agent 2 is then assigned the remaining [low $\varrho(k)$] tasks.

Now consider the family of feasible solutions, parameterized by ε, in which $\tilde{t}_1(\varepsilon) = \tilde{t} - \varepsilon, \tilde{t}_2(\varepsilon) = \tilde{t} + \varepsilon$, and all the highest $\varrho(k)$ tasks are assigned to agent 1 until the total attention required is $\tilde{t}_1(\varepsilon)$. In order for the symmetric solution to be optimal, it is necessary that the derivative of the objective with respect to ε be zero. The following calculation shows that the derivative is negative – that is, that it would be better to specify that the agent who is assigned the hard-to-measure tasks work a bit less than his counterpart. Indeed, the derivative of the objective with respect to ε at $\varepsilon = 0$ is equal to

$$2C'' \frac{\tilde{t}}{2} C' \frac{\tilde{t}}{2} \frac{r}{2} \int_0^1 (l_2(k) - l_1(k)) \frac{\sigma^2(k)}{\mu'^2(t(k), k)} dk$$

$$= rC'' \frac{\tilde{t}}{2} C' \frac{\tilde{t}}{2} \int_0^1 l_2(k) \varrho(k) t(k) dk - \int_0^1 l_1(k) \varrho(k) t(k) dk$$

$$< rC'' \frac{\tilde{t}}{2} C' \frac{\tilde{t}}{2} \varrho(\tilde{t}_2 - \tilde{t}_1) = 0$$

The last step uses (18) and the facts that $\varrho(k) \geq \varrho$ when $I_1(k) = 1$ and $\varrho(k) \leq \varrho$ when $I_2(k) = 1$ [and that $\varrho(k)$ is not constant so that the inequality is strict].

The remainder of the proposition is verified in the paragraphs preceding the proposition.

Q.E.D.

5.2   Caveats

The model presented in the previous subsection represents merely a first pass at studying the optimal grouping of tasks into jobs. Although it provides some interesting insights, we have omitted so many key elements of the problem and made so many special assumptions to simplify an already complex analysis that it is as well to make a preliminary list of these features and omissions and to speculate about how they may have affected our analysis.

First, we had assumed that all tasks are "small" and that the principal has perfect freedom to group them in any way to form a job. Neither of these assumptions is particularly attractive. The assumption that all tasks are small could be replaced by the assumption that there are a finite number of tasks that all required the same amount of time [$t(k)$ constant]; this, however, introduces the possibility that $\tilde{t}_1 = \tilde{t}_2$, in which case all task assignments are equally good. When tasks require non-negligible amounts of time and vary in size, then the need to minimize costs borne by the agents by equalizing workloads may reverse some of our conclusions. Moreover, tasks like maintaining quality and producing output cannot always be separated. In short, our model exaggerates the principal's ability to group tasks into homogeneous measurement classes and in so doing caricatures the problem of how jobs are constructed. The main virtue of our model is that it is structured so that incentive considerations alone determine the optimal solution, so that it lends some new insights into the very limited question of how incentive concerns may affect job design.

Second, we had assumed that the errors of measurement in the agent's various tasks are all independent. We know from previous analyses, such as Holmstrom (1982), that when errors are positively correlated, separating the tasks among the two agents allows the use of comparative performance evaluation, which can help to reduce the risk premium incurred in providing incentives. It is not hard to see that even without comparative performance evaluation, separating tasks with positively correlated measurement errors creates a better diversified portfolio of tasks that reduces the risk that the agent must bear. Similarly, grouping tasks in which performance is negatively correlated reduces the agent's risk premium. So, even in the incentive domain, our present model is highly incomplete.

Third, the attention allocation model that we have used throughout is itself a simplification, which forces all activities to be equal substitutes in the agent's cost function and excludes the possibility that some activities may be complementary. In our discussion in section 2 of the issue of how teachers should be compensated, we found that complementarities in the agent's private cost of attention can have an important effect both on how jobs should be designed and how agents should be compensated, but that complementarities among the same variables in the production function have no similar effect. These are subtle distinctions that our theory, in its attention allocation version, cannot address.

Fourth, the models we have studied assume that the agents focus their attention on the same tasks for all time. As discussed in section 2, the model we are using is explicitly temporal, and issues of job rotation are an important aspect of real job design. Our preliminary analysis shows that these issues may be susceptible to analysis using an extension of the section 2 model, in which the players are uncertain about the difficulty of production and use the past performance to learn about it. We hope to be able to discuss these issues more fully in follow-up work.

Conclusion

The problem of providing incentives to agents and employees is far more intricate than is represented in standard principal–agent models. The performance measures upon which rewards are based may aggregate highly disparate aspects of performance into a single number and omit other aspects of performance that are essential if the firm is to achieve its goals. Commonly, the principal–agent problem boils down to this: given a highly incomplete set of performance measures and a highly complex set of potential responses from the agent, how can the agent be motivated to act in the social interest?

Our approach emphasizes that incentive problems must be analyzed in totality; one cannot make correct inferences about the proper incentives for an activity by studying the attributes of that activity alone. Moreover, the range of instruments that can be used to control an agent's performance in one activity is much wider than just deciding how to pay for performance. One can also shift ownership of related assets, vary restrictions on the ways a job can be done, vary limits and incentives for competing activities, group related tasks into a single job, and so on.

In a related article (Holmstrom and Milgrom, 1991), we study the simultaneous use of various instruments for controlling agents to derive new, testable results from the theory of organization. Our emphasis there is on how cross-sectional variations in the parameters that determine the optimal design of jobs, the optimal intensity of incentives, and the optimal allocation of ownership lead to covariations among endogenous variables that are similar to the patterns we find in actual firms.

Most past models of organization focus only on one instrument at a time for determining incentives and a single activity to be motivated. Newer theories, such as ours, that explicitly recognize connections between instruments and activities, offer new promise to explain the richer patterns of actual practice.

Notes

*   We are grateful to the National Science Foundation for financial support and to Gary Becker, James Brickley, Murray Brown, Joel Demski, Joseph Farrell, Oliver Hart, David Kreps, Kevin Murphy, Eric Rasmussen, Steve Ross, Steve Stern, and especially Avner Greif, Jane Hannaway, and Hal Varian for their many insightful comments, examples, and suggestions. We also wish to thank Froystein Gjesdal for pointing out two errors in an earlier draft.

1   Some of the predictive weaknesses of standard agency models are discussed in the surveys by MacDonald (1984), Hart and Holmstrom (1987), and Baker, Jensen, and Murphy (1988).

2   See Hannaway (1991) for a discussion of these issues.

3   As a concrete illustration of the distortions that testing can cause, in 1989 a ninth-grade teacher in Greenville, South Carolina, was caught having passed answers to questions on the statewide tests of basic skills to students in her geography classes in order to improve her performance rating (*Wall Street Journal*, November 2, 1989).

4   Riordan and Sappington (1987) also analyze an incentive model in which job assignment is central, but for a very different reason. They ask when the principal should do one of two sequential production stages herself in order to reduce the agent's information advantage. In our model, job assignments do not affect the principal's information.

5 Alchian and Demsetz (1972) argued that monitoring difficulties account for the formation of firms, but their theory was subsequently rejected in favor of the view that asset specificity and expost bargaining problems drive integration (Grossman and Hart (1986), and Williamson (1985)). We are reintroducing measurement cost as a key factor, but in a way that differs from the original Alchian–Demsetz theory. In particular, we do not argue that owners can better monitor the work force. Our approach is more closely related to Barzel's work (1982).

6 Note that if an activity can be measured without error, then a linear scheme allows the principal to set this activity at any desired level costlessly, assuming that the cost function is convex.

7 It is of interest to note that instead of a measurement error the incentive problem could be driven by a nonstochastic measurement bias. Suppose the agent can manipulate the performance measure. If this activity wastes resources, then incentives will optimally be set to balance this loss against genuine work incentives. One can specify the cost of manipulation so that optimal incentives come out exactly the same as in the stochastic model we are studying.

8 This is really not a special case, since we can always reformulate the model by redefining the agent's choice variables so that $\mu(t) > t$.

9 We are assuming that teachers are motivated to teach some higher-thinking skills even without explicit financial incentives to do so. In one-dimensional agency models, it is typically assumed that the agent will not work without incentive pay. The reason for this is not that the agent dislikes even small amounts of work, but rather that the level of work the agent would provide without explicit incentives does not affect the optimal solution. In multitask models, however, the fact that agents supply inputs even without incentive pay can be quite consequential as the teacher example and the example in section 3.2 show.

10 Another plausible explanation is that home construction contracts are frequently changed to reflect design modifications, and timely completion clauses would be nullified by these changes.

11 A related conclusion – that incorrect weightings of profit contributions in an accounting system lead the optimizing employer to weaken effort incentives – is derived by Baker (1989). Baker's analysis can be conducted within our model by recognizing that a state-contingent strategy for the agent – that is, making different decisions in different states – is equivalent to a vector effort strategy. Baker's assumption that the principal cannot distinguish the state in which an action is taken is then the same as assuming that the principal cannot distinguish performance along the several dimensions of the vector strategy. The formal mapping from these "hidden information" models to our "hidden action" model is discussed in Holmstrom and Milgrom (1987).

12 One can derive a similar result with a general quadratic cost function $C(t_1, t_2)$. The only difference is that the commission rate would not necessarily be zero for an employed agent, though it would always be smaller than for an independent contractor.

13 It may be argued that risk aversion cannot be a very relevant factor if the independent sales representative is itself a large firm. Recall, however, that the cost of risk can equivalently be derived from imperfect observability of B, paired with a convex cost C, in a risk-neutral model (see Baker, 1989). We can rely on work aversion instead of risk aversion. In this case, to make sure that it is not optimal to transfer B to the independent sales firm (i.e., make the manufacturer a subcontractor), one has to add an imperfectly observed input by the manufacturer. With two equally important, equally costly, and imperfectly observed inputs, the residual return B will be allocated to the party whose input is more difficult to measure.

14 One can also show that by excluding private tasks the agent becomes less responsive to increases in the commission. A less flexible job design is associated with weaker incentives as we mentioned earlier.

15 Nonlinearities in the principal's task would not alter the conclusion that α is reduced when r or σ^2 is increased; this part is just a revealed preference argument. However, the set $A(\alpha)$ would be harder to characterize as the exclusion of tasks would interact with each other as a result of integer problems. One could even find that a personal task is included when α is reduced.

16   Minahan (1988) derives a result that is related. In his model there are four tasks: two easy to measure and two hard to measure. He shows that it is better not to mix the tasks. The main difference between his model and ours is that in his model the principal cannot provide incentives on individual tasks, just on the sum of the tasks. This would greatly simplify our analysis. On the other hand, Minahan's analysis deals with nonlinear incentives and general utility functions, which adds to the complexity.

17   One manifestation of the task allocation principle may be found in the organization of R & D activities in firms [see Holmstrom (1989)].

References

Alchian, Armen, and Harold Demsetz (1972) Production, Information Costs and Economic Organization. *American Economic Review*, 62: 777–95.

Anderson, Erin (1985) The Salesperson as Outside Agent or Employee: A Transaction Cost Analysis. *Management Science*, 4: 234–54.

Anderson, Erin, and David Schmittlein (1984) Integration of the Sales Force: An Empirical Examination. *Rand Journal of Economics*, 15: 385–95.

Baker, George (1989) Piece Rate Contracts and Performance Measurement Error. Manuscript Graduate School of Business, Harvard University.

Baker, George, Michael Jensen, and Kevin Murphy (1988) Competition and Incentives: Practice vs Theory, 43: *Journal of Finance*, 43: 593–616.

Barzel, Yoram (1982) Measurement Costs and the Organization of Markets. *Journal of Law and Economics*, 25: 27–48.

Brickley, James, and Frederick Dark (1987) The Choice of Organizational Form: The Case of Franchising. *Journal of Financial Economics*, 18: 401–20.

Coase, Ronald (1937) The Nature of the Firm. *Economica*, 4: 386–405.

Farrell, Joseph, and Carl Shapiro (1989) Optimal Contracts with Lock-in. *American Economic Review*, 79: 51–68.

Greenwald, Bruce, and Joseph Stiglitz (1986) Externalities in Economies with Imperfect Information and Incomplete Markets. *Quarterly Journal of Economics*, 101: 229–64.

Grossman, Sanford, and Oliver Hart (1986) The Costs and Benefits of Ownership: A Theory of Vertical and Lateral Integration. *Journal of Political Economy*, 94: 691–719.

Hannaway, Jane (1991) Higher Order Thinking, Job Design and Incentives: An Analysis and Proposal. *American Education Research Journal* (forthcoming).

Hart, Oliver, and Bengt Holmstrom (1987) The Theory of Contracts. In T. Bewley (ed.), *Advances in Economic Theory, Fifth World Congress*. Cambridge: Cambridge University Press.

Holmstrom, Bengt (1982) Moral Hazard in Teams. *Bell Journal of Economics*, 13: 324–40.

Holmstrom, Bengt (1989) Agency Costs and Innovation. *Journal of Economic Behavior and Organization*, 12: 305–27.

Holmstrom, Bengt, and Paul Milgrom (1987) Aggregation and Linearity in the Provision of Intertemporal Incentives. *Econometrica*, 55: 303–28.

Holmstrom, Bengt, and Paul Milgrom (1990) Regulating Trade Among Agents. *Journal of Institutional and Theoretical Economics*, 146: 85–105.

Holmstrom, Bengt, and Paul Milgrom (1991) Measurement Cost and Organization Theory. Working paper, Stanford University.

Holmstrom, Bengt, and Joan Ricart i Costa (1986) Managerial Incentives and Capital Management. *Quarterly Journal of Economics*, 101: 835–60.

Itoh, Hideshi (1989) Coalitions, Incentives and Risk Sharing. Mimeograph, Kyoto University, Japan.

Itoh, Hideshi (1991) Incentives to Help in Multi-Agent Situations. *Econometrica*, 59: 611–37.

Krueger, Alan (1991). "Ownership, Agency and Wages: An Examination of Franchising in the Fast Food Industry". *Quarterly Journal of Economics*, 106: 75–101.

Laffont, Jean-Jacques, and Jean Tirole (1989) Provision of Quality and Power of Incentive Schemes in Regulated Industries. In W. Barnett, B. Cornet, C. d'Aspremont, J. Gabsewicz, and A. Mas Colell (eds.), *Equilibrium Theory and Applications*. Cambridge: Cambridge University Press.

Lazear, Edward (1989) Pay Equality and Industrial Politics. *Journal of Political Economy*, 97: 561–80.

MacDonald, Glenn (1984) New Directions in the Economic Theory of Agency. *Canadian Journal of Economics*, 17: 415–40.

Milgrom, Paul (1988) Employment Contracts, Influence Activities and Efficient Organization Design. *Journal of Political Economy*, 96: 42–60.

Milgrom, Paul, and John Roberts (1988) An Economic Approach to Influence Activities and Organizational Responses. *American Journal of Sociology*, 94: S154–79.

Minahan, John (1988) Managerial Incentive Schemes and the Divisional Structure of Firms. Mimeograph, University of Massachusetts.

Riordan, Michael, and David Sappington (1987) Information, Incentives and Organizational Mode. *Quarterly Journal of Economics*, 102: 243–64.

Simon, Herbert (1951) A Formal Theory of the Employment Relationship. *Econometrica*, 19: 293–305.

Tirole, Jean (1986) Hierarchies and Bureaucracies: On the Role of Collusion in Organizations. *Journal of Law, Economics & Organization*, 2: 181–214.

Williamson, Oliver (1985) *The Economic Institutions of Capitalism*. New York: Free Press.

THIRTEEN

The Internal Organization of Government

JEAN TIROLE

Source: From *Oxford Economic Papers* (1994), 46: 1–29.

1 Introduction

One of the accomplishments of economic theory has been the development of a theory of organizations. Three paradigms – adverse selection, moral hazard, and incomplete contracting – have been used to analyze how workers, managers, directors or investors respond to various incentives. Self-interested economic agents can be motivated in roughly three ways. Formal incentives such as piece rate wages, bonuses, stock options and relative performance evaluation are based on verifiable measures of performance. Work inputs are monitored by foremen, fellow employees, bosses or boards of directors. Last, career concerns inside and outside the firm may encourage a forward-looking employee to work hard.

So far, incentive theory has been mainly motivated by and applied to private organizations. Yet, in view of the important role played by civil servants and politicians in our economies, one may wonder why limited attention has been devoted in this field to the internal organization of government. An answer to this question might be that there is little conceptual difference between governments and firms. Any distinction would be quantitative and left to empirical analysis. While this point of view has some appeal, there still seems to be some scope for a separate theoretical appraisal of the organization of government. The purpose of this paper is not to supply such an appraisal. Rather, its goal is to suggest some of the building blocks and some directions for research. I apologize to the reader for the lightness of the analysis, and just hope that this chapter's only ambition, namely to encourage interest in the topic, will be fulfilled.

The general thrust of the paper is that the new methodology of incentive theory ought to enable economists to participate in and enrich a debate that has by and large been confined to other social sciences, in particular political science and sociology.

The first part of the paper (section 2) discusses some specificities of the design of incentives in the public sector. While private enterprises are in a first approximation instructed to maximize profits, government agencies generally pursue multiple goals. Many of these goals are hard to measure. Furthermore, incentives based on measurable goals must be limited to not completely jeopardize the nonmeasurable dimensions of social welfare. Lack of comparison and heterogeneity of tastes of principals are identified as further factors leading to low powered incentives.

The second part of the paper discusses some implications of low powered individual incentives in government. First, career concerns, associated with the prospect of re-election, promotion or employment in the private sector, are at least as pervasive as in the private sector (section 3). Career concerns are articulated around some mission that is followed by the government official. The mission can be simple – pursue goal 1 – or composite – achieve a balance between goals 1 and 2. Neither the choice of the mission nor the intensity with which it is pursued need be socially optimal. Indeed, there is a potential multiplicity of missions that can be followed by rational officials. Also, several missions can be pursued by different officials of the same agency. Last, composite missions that reflect the several goals of social optimization may not fit with the officials' self-interest. Our economic analysis here complements recent work in political science on government agencies.

Another topic that is particularly relevant under low powered incentives is the issue of regulatory capture and collusion (section 4). It is argued that viewing intermediate layers of a hierarchy (such as government agencies) as being better informed than their principals lays the foundations for a theory of regulatory capture. The officials can manipulate information to favor specific interest groups. The civil service and the regulatory structure are then partly designed to limit such manipulations. The paper discusses a few implications of this view, concerning the stakes of the interest groups, the determinants of the influence of an interest group and the design of institutions.

While the second part of the paper analyzes individual incentives, the third part studies the division of labor within government. Section 5 points out that legal restrictions on commitment by government agencies can be viewed as a division of control rights between successive administrations. Balancing their well-known limitations, short-term commitments by the government have the benefit of allowing correction of wrongful policies (possibly due to capture of the current administration) by future administrations. Section 6 discusses a few elements of the division of labor between government and the private sector in the context of privatization.

Sections 7 and 8 investigate the following puzzle: why isn't government designed to behave as a coherent entity? Government agencies as well as politicians are not expected (individually) to maximize social welfare, but rather to pursue antinomic missions. Section 7 argues that the control of economic agents such as a public enterprise may be best performed by creating multiple principals with dissonant objectives. For instance, public enterprises are often subject to two masters with substantially different goals: a 'spending ministry' represents the 'technical point of view' and behaves rather softly with regard to the firm. When the firm runs a large deficit, this ministry must relinquish control to a more rigorous ministry of finance that is primarily concerned with the budget deficit. The basic idea of the section is that this division of labor within government promotes better behavior by the public enterprise through the threat of a shift of control to a tough ministry in case of financial hardship.

Section 8 arrives at a similar conclusion on the optimality of a division of labor in government from a quite distinct perspective. Its premise is that competition in government among advocates of specific interests or causes may give rise to good policy setting. Using enfranchised advocates generates precious information on the pros and cons of alternative policies, and creates a system of checks and balances. The idea can be applied to justify the existence and behavior of specialized ministries, biased representatives, multi-partism or our democratic legal system.

2   Specificities of Incentives in Government

Why do the incentives of a high official in a foreign ministry differ from those of a top executive at IBM? What distinguishes the task of a correctional officer from that of an AT&T sales representative? Such questions may seem trivial or irrelevant. Yet they condition much of what we perceive as a good organization of government. If differences exist between the public and private sectors, they must be traced either to differences in the measurement system (sections 2.1 and 2.2 below) or to differences in the governance structure (sections 2.3 and 2.4). Before proceeding, it is important to stress that the differences are differences in degree, not fundamental nature.[1]

2.1   Multiplicity of goals

The owners of a private corporation set the goal of 'maximizing profit' for the organization.[2] Some measurable variables, such as earnings or stock prices, are clearly related to this goal and can be used to build managerial incentive schemes. In contrast, the mandate of many government agencies is multidimensional. Indeed, the very intervention of government is often motivated by the idea that profit incentives by themselves would not yield socially optimal allocations. Other criteria such as consumer net surplus, pollution, development, or redistribution must also be taken into account.

The multidimensionality of goals *per se* does not hinder the construction of powerful incentive schemes. Such schemes can in principle carefully balance the use of measures of the various dimensions of performance. A clearly specified social welfare function with explicit weights on all dimensions of performance would be as implementable as profit. But the multidimensionality of goals often goes hand in hand with two difficulties.

First, several dimensions of performance are, unlike profit or cost, hard to measure. A regulator of a natural monopoly is supposed to ensure 'reasonable' prices, but even an econometrician may have a hard time measuring the regulator's contribution to the net consumer surplus. And who will put reliable numbers on the US Department of State's performance in 'promoting the long-range security and well-being of the United States' and on the US Department of Labor's success in 'fostering, promoting, and developing the welfare of the wage earners of the United States'?

Second, and relatedly, the multiplicity of goals raises the issue of their weights. The Environmental Protection Agency (EPA) is instructed to curb pollution at a reasonable cost for the industries. Suppose, perhaps heroically, that the levels of pollution and the costs imposed on the industries are measurable. Setting up a formal incentive scheme for the EPA requires putting weights on these two measures. Yet, it is difficult to define what is reasonable and what is not. 'Optimal' pollution levels depend on available technologies, on the shadow cost of unemployment, on atmospheric conditions and so forth. The very contingencies that are supposed to condition the formal incentive schemes are hard to include in an incentive scheme.[3] It should also be noted, and we will come back to this point, that what is meant to be 'optimal' depends on what the EPA perceives to be its constituency.

2.2   Lack of comparison

A noisy observation of managerial performance reduces the efficacy of formal incentive schemes. One way of alleviating the imperfection of measurement of a manager's performance is to separate idiosyncratic risk from aggregate risk, that is the risk faced by only the manager from that faced by other managers in a similar situation. More prosaically, the performance of GM's managers ought to be compared to that of Ford's or more generally to that of the car industry before drawing conclusions on their efficiency. The feasibility of such 'yardstick competition' or 'relative performance evaluation' enhances the desirability and the strength of performance related incentives. In contrast, as Hicks (1935) pointed out, 'the best of all monopoly profits is a quiet life'. A modern version of this would be that the absence of yardstick is conducive to low-powered incentive schemes, where a low-powered scheme is one in which the agent bears only a small fraction of his performance.

That many government agencies have a monopoly position in their activity therefore suggests that their performance is hard to assess. True, elements of relative performance evaluation can be found at several levels of government. First, the performance of employees in an agency, for instance tax collectors with similar tasks, can be compared. But, at a higher level, the activity of the IRS as a whole can only be compared with that of its counterparts in foreign countries. Second, some government institutions such as hospitals or schools may face competition from the private sector. Third, there may be explicit competition among government organizations, as is the case among cities or states, or among agencies to gather intelligence or to catch drug dealers.

While this paper will discuss some aspects of competition in government, it will ignore some of the central issues in this regard.[4] The next two distinctions relate to qualitative differences in 'corporate governance' (the role of the organization's outsiders).

2.3   Heterogeneity of owners' tastes

A corporation's ownership in principle aims at maximizing total firm value. This goal is shared among investors and is stable over time. True, managerial incentives among other things require creating several constituencies, such as equityholders and debtholders, with somewhat conflicting goals. But the corporation issues heterogeneous securities in a controlled way. Contrast this with government agencies. The tastes of their principals, namely the people, are quite diverse and furthermore changing. While a corporation's goal is well defined[5] and time consistent, and preference heterogeneity among claimholders is a deliberate construction, the goals of an agency are defined by a political process. And, because this 'aggregate goal' (if such a thing exists) changes over time in a noncontractible manner, incentives governing long-term choices by agency management that are deemed legitimate today may no longer be considered so tomorrow. This lack of time consistency of agencies' objective functions suggests that commitment possibilities in the public sector will be more limited than in the private sector. (Section 5 will study another reason why commitment is limited in government.)

2.4   Dispersed ownership

Corporations often face dispersed shareholders and creditors. Agencies are in this situation with a vengeance. Big shareholders, bank debt, and boards of directors, which alleviate the representation problem in corporations, have imperfect counterparts in government. Political parties and interest groups do coordinate subgroups of voters, but their incentives need not be perfectly aligned with the preferences of their constituents.[6] Agencies, like corporations, have their own boards of directors (e.g., congressional oversight committees), but the boards' incentives are different. Last, political takeovers also differ from private takeovers. Two limitations of political takeovers are, first, that they are a somewhat cumbersome way to replace management (the government),[7] and, second (and this is related to section 2.3 above) that they may be motivated by changing tastes of the electorate rather than by a poor managerial performance, which may not be ideal for incentives purposes.

Overall, we have little to say on the issue of diversity of ownership and monitoring in government, although this is a potentially important distinction between government and corporations. Differences seem to be quantitative rather than qualitative. Also, for reasons we will discuss later, formal institutions for monitoring agencies are often more developed than for monitoring corporations. Thus, even if one can build a case that monitoring by owners is less effective in government, it may also be the case that monitoring plays as big a role in government as in corporations.

3   The Incentives of Politicians and Civil Servants

3.1   Formal incentives

Let us begin with monetary incentives. Such incentives do exist in the civil service, but we would expect, and do observe, low powered incentives[8] to prevail in government, for two reasons.

The first factor for low powered incentives was mentioned in the introduction and relates to the difficulty in measuring precisely the performance of officials. The second factor is the tension that exists between measurable and nonmeasurable objectives. Very often, the latter conflict with the former. For instance, keeping a regulated firm's cost down conflicts with the provision of quality. Collecting high levels of taxes (a measurable dimension) may mean that the tax collector annoys the taxpayers. Lowering the cost of delivering mail while keeping delivery time constant implies a larger number of mistakes. The incentives literature has insisted on such conflicts among goals. Among recent entries in this literature, Laffont and Tirole (1991) argue that, when the goods or services provided by a regulated firm are experience goods, a concern for quality calls for low powered incentives. The reasoning is straightforward. While for search goods (whose quality is by definition observed before consumption) incentives for quality can be based on the level of sales, the provision of quality for experience goods (whose quality is revealed only by consuming) relies on the reputation concern of the firm. Reimbursing a high fraction of the firm's cost amounts to reducing the firm's cost of investing in reputation and thus raises the incentive to provide quality. In a similar spirit, Holmström and Milgrom (1991) analyze a general multi-task model of moral hazard. They show how incentives on one activity must take into account their effect on substitute or complementary activities (see chapter 12 of this volume for other references and related ideas).

The trade off between high powered schemes and quality exists in the private sector as well as in government. I would conjecture, though, that the quality concern is stronger in government than in the private sector. First, the government is mandated to internalize the effect of quality on consumer's surplus while the managers of a private corporation are not. Second, there is no such thing as the stock price of a government agency that would somewhat reflect the value of the agency's investment in reputation for high quality. At this stage, all this is very informal. In particular, non-monetary incentives (to be considered shortly) differ in the two sectors and only a global analysis of the packages of incentives can drive the point home.

The other two incentives are monitoring and career concerns. We will be particularly interested in career concerns here. Because formal incentives are weaker, career concerns may play an even bigger role in government that in the private sector.[9]

3.2   Career concerns and missions

Perhaps the main drive for civil servants and politicians is career concerns. They are concerned by the effect of their current performance not so much on their monetary reward, but rather on their reputation or image in view of future promotions, job prospects in the private and public sectors, and re-elections. This concern induces them to work to 'mislead' the internal or external labor markets about their ability.

A decade ago (1982), Bengt Holmström provided us with a tractable model of career concerns. A bare-bones version of his model goes as follows. There are two periods: today and tomorrow. A manager's performance today (output, profit, . . .), denoted by x, depends on his talent θ and on his current effort e:

$$x = \theta + e \tag{1}$$

The manager's ability $\theta \in (-\infty, \infty)$ has mean $\bar{\theta}$ and is unknown to everybody. The manager's effort $e \geq 0$ involves disutility $g(e)$ with $g(0) = 0$, $g' > 0$, $g'' > 0$, and is known to the manager only. The performance x is observable by everyone. Yet it is not verifiable in the sense that it cannot be described *ex ante* in a formal compensation contract. The manager is thus paid a fixed wage w_1 today. The model is a good approximation of situations in which formal incentive schemes play a minor role.

Tomorrow the manager will be employed in the same firm or an identical firm. For simplicity, his productivity for the employer will be.[10] The manager will be free to choose among potential employees, and his wage tomorrow will equal the expectation of his ability given today's performance:[11]

$$w_2(x) = E(\theta|x).$$

Letting δ denote the discount factor between the two periods, the intertemporal utility of a risk neutral manager is:

$$w_1 - g(e) + \delta w_2(\theta + e).$$

Let us look for a pure strategy equilibrium, with effort level e^*. Then

$$E(\theta|x) = x - e^* = \theta + e - e^*.$$

The manager chooses e^* such that

$$g'(e^*) = \delta.$$

The socially optimal level of effort is obtained only when the manager weighs the present and the future equally ($\delta = 1$).

Holmström's model points at four conditions for career concerns in government to be effective. First, the performance on the task should be visible by those who grant promotions and wage increases, are potential employers or will vote for or against the official. Second, the current performance should be informative about the official's ability in future tasks. Third, the official should be forward looking and not discount the future too much. And, fourth, signalling should not be too costly to the official.

I now build on Holmström's insight using ongoing research with Mathias Dewatripont. An aspect of career concerns that has seemingly gone unnoticed is the scope for multiple interpretations of performance. With the additive form presumed in (1), there is a unique pure strategy equilibrium. Yet, in most situations, this additive form may not be the most appropriate one. For, outcomes often reveal talent only if the manager devotes his attention to the task. Suppose that a Department of Justice lawyer sets himself the goal of maximizing the number of successful cases rather than that of ensuring the conformity of case selection and treatment to economic principles. Then an economic analysis of the cases prosecuted under his supervision reveals little about his talent. And if his superiors or the private sector understand this, future promotions and wages will hardly reflect performance in this direction. Therefore, the DOJ lawyer is right not to pay much attention to economic consistency. Similarly, a defense program officer whose talent is assessed on whether his programs are started and are kept going has little incentive to pay attention to costs and should focus on getting the programs done; and conversely the superiors and the labor market won't pay much attention to his cost performance. As a last example, suppose students have the choice among focusing on mathematics, focusing on Latin and working on both. Suppose further that both tasks are equally difficult and socially desirable. Yet, it may be the case that universities select the students on the basis of math grades and students neglect Latin because it is endogenously less informative than math.

To formalize the idea of multiple interpretations of performance in an example (a fuller treatment is out of the scope of this paper), suppose that (1) is replaced by a multiplicative form:

$$x = \theta e \qquad\qquad\qquad\qquad\qquad\qquad\qquad\qquad (2)$$

and (from now on) that the support of the distribution of θ is $[0, \infty)$, and keep the other assumptions unchanged. In particular we assume that the second-period wage is $w_2(x) = E(\theta|x)$. (What is needed for the theory more generally is that a better performance shifts beliefs about talent in the sense of first-order stochastic dominance and thus raises the second-period wage.) Again, we look for pure strategy equilibria.

If no attention is devoted to the task ($e = 0$), then the performance is uninformative about ability, and w_2 is not affected by the observation of performance: $w_2(x) = \bar{\theta}$ for all x.[12] And, hence the manager rationally does not exert any effort. We will call this equilibrium the unfocused equilibrium.

There exists a second pure strategy equilibrium or focused equilibrium, in which the manager takes the task seriously and chooses effort $\hat{e} > 0$, and the labor market pays attention to his performance. By choosing e, the manager is perceived as having ability $\hat{\theta}$ while having real ability θ, where

$$\hat{\theta}\hat{e} = \theta e.$$

The expected second-period wage is therefore $\bar{\theta}e/\hat{e}$, and the manager chooses e so as to maximize

$$w_1 - g(e) + \delta \frac{\bar{\theta}}{\hat{e}} e$$

yielding

$$g'(\hat{e})\hat{e} - \delta\bar{\theta}$$

which has a unique solution. The manager's utility in the focused equilibrium is

$$U_1 = w_1 - g(\hat{e}) + \delta\bar{\theta} \tag{3}$$

as opposed to

$$U_0 = w_1 + \delta\bar{\theta} \tag{4}$$

in the unfocused equilibrium.[13]

Basically the same point can be made in the context of multiple tasks, or goals, which is particularly relevant in government. A goal can be 'simple' or 'clear', or 'single' (pursue task 1 or pursue task 2) or 'composite' (pursue some combination of task 1 and task 2). Again, there is scope for a multiplicity of equilibria. A government official will pursue mission 1 if the government or private labor markets, or else voters, pay attention mainly to his performance on task 1. Accordingly, he will neglect task 2. Conversely, mission 1 may be ignored because attention is focused on mission 2.

Because social welfare is generally an aggregation of multiple goals, the existence of equilibria in which the government official pursues a composite mission, for instance splits his effort between the two tasks, is of much interest. Or, to put it another way, single-mission equilibria of the type discussed above do not fulfill the whole array of social goals. As Wilson (1989) notes:

> These advantages of infusing an agency with a sense of mission are purchased at a price. An agency with a strong mission will give perfunctory attention, if any at all, to tasks that are not

central to that mission. Diplomats in the State Department will have little interest in
embassy security; intelligence officers in the CIA will not worry as much as they should about
counter-intelligence; narcotics agents in the DEA will minimize the importance of improper
prescriptions written by physicians; power engineers in the TVA will not think as hard about
environmental protection or conservation as about maximizing the efficiency of generating
units; fighter pilots in the USAF will look at air transport as a homely stepchild; and navy
admirals who earned their flag serving on aircraft carriers will not press zealously to expand the
role of minesweepers.

Composite mission equilibria may or may not exist. For example, suppose that the
official may have high or low ability. The official has two tasks, 1 and 2, and may reach a
poor or a good performance in either task. Assume further that an official with a low ability
obtains a poor outcome in tasks 1 and 2 regardless of his allocation of effort. What then
matters to the official is to demonstrate high ability when this is indeed the case. It is then
optimal for the official to 'put all his eggs in the same basket', that is to allocate all his
attention to a single task; for there is no extra gain having a high performance in both tasks;
it is far more important to make sure that at least one task is successful.[14] In contrast, if high
ability were demonstrated primarily by being successful in both tasks, then composite
mission equilibria would exist.

Last, we should point at an interesting third possible type of equilibrium, the 'fuzzy
mission equilibrium'. In such equilibria, the official pursues a single mission (unlike in the
composite mission equilibria), but the market does not know which (unlike in the single
mission equilibrium). For instance, he chooses to focus on goal 1 with probability 1/2, and
on goal 2 with probability 1/2. Equivalently, in the organization, half the officials pursue
mission 1 and half pursue mission 2.

While the labor market does not observe the choice of the mission, it makes some *ex post*
inference about which was chosen. To come back to the student example, one will put
probability greater than 1/2, but lower than 1, that the student focused on Latin when
passing Latin and failing mathematics. The reason why fuzzy mission equilibria may exist
is that the market puts more weight on the best performance, and therefore it is important
for the official to excel in his best performance. It is worth noting that, in the examples
Mathias Dewatripont and I have developed so far, work incentives are stronger in the single
mission equilibria than in the fuzzy mission ones even though the official focuses all his
attention on a single task in both. The point is that the market is uncertain about the
official's objective in a fuzzy mission equilibrium, and does not give full credit for a good
performance, and full stigma for a poor one.

3.3   Mission setting

The multiplicity of equilibria when career concerns determine incentives suggests a
possible lack of focus of managers. Some factors may help ensure that the mission will be
followed. First, following Schelling (1960), one may posit that some apparently irrelevant
factors can help select a 'focal' equilibrium. In our context, the setting of a mission by a
constitution, a law or a charismatic boss may create a common understanding between the
sender and receiver of the performance signals. Wilson (1989) finds that clearly defined
goals, such as 'pay benefits on time and accurately' for the US Social Security Administration and the associated client-serving ethic, work well. In contrast, multiple goals raise

the issue of what weights should be put by the manager on the different goals, and therefore lead to a possible multiplicity of interpretations. Second, a mission forcefully articulated by a strong leader such as Pinchot at the US Bureau of Forestry or Hoover at the FBI may be more likely to be adopted.

Another factor facilitating the accomplishment of a mission is its alignment with professional norms. The Federal Trade Commission staff will emphasize legal or economic aspects of a case depending on whether the case is handled by lawyers or economists. This may be because lawyers want to signal their legal skills to law firms while economists are keen on proving their talents as economists to fellow economists in academia and consulting firms.

Yet another factor influencing the success of a mission is immediate self-interest. If 'producing power at the lowest cost' (as made explicit in the statutes of the Tennessee Valley Authority) gives rise to immediate rewards such as lack of Congressional hassle, the mandate is more likely to be followed. In other words, small formal incentives added to career concerns may help tilt the balance toward one equilibrium. Relatedly, career concerns must swamp short term incentives to escape the mission. As Wilson (1989, p. 38) notes, the focus of a correctional officer's energy is not his mission, be it rehabilitation or deterrence, but the control of inmates.

This brings us to the issue of where missions come from. They may be either externally determined or self-imposed. We have reasoned as if missions were imposed on (or, rather, suggested to) officials, and examined some factors that may affect the success of the mission. In practice, officials sometimes pick a clear mission when their overall mission is vague. We mentioned the case of Pinchot who, from 1898 on, through personnel training and tight managing imposed the mission of managing forests to the US Forest Service, rather than just studying them and educating people as to their uses.

Do officials gain from having a mission? Consider the two equilibria $e = 0$ and $e = \hat{e}$ for the activity given by (2). While the employer prefers that $e = \hat{e}$, the official prefers $e = 0$. Because in equilibrium the official fools no one by working, he would prefer not to have to live up to expectations.[15]

We feel the argument for the officials' aversion towards missions is less strong where they know their ability before choosing effort. Our intuition is that high ability officials prefer having a mission in order to be able to demonstrate this ability. Supposing that the announcement of a mission is credible (we haven't specified why), high ability officials want to make such an announcement. Lower ability officials are then forced to do the same in order not to reveal they are low ability, while they still have a chance of being perceived as having high ability if they are lucky in the mission.[16] A complete justification of this intuition seems difficult to obtain given the multiplicity of equilibria created by the interpretation of signals such as announcing a mission.

Whatever the difficulties in uniquely pinning down equilibrium behavior, we think that the fact that the officials may gain from the existence of a mission when informed about their ability while they don't when they are uninformed may have some bearing on mission setting. While we are in the realm of conjectures, we would expect officials to be more prone to refuse new tasks for which they have little information about their ability. This may shed some light on the many instances of agencies that refuse to take on new assignments (see Wilson, 1989, chapter 10), behavior that flies in the face of Niskanen's and Tullock's postulate that bureaucrats try to maximize their agency's size. It remains however to be assessed whether other factors such as fear of increased oversight, clashes of culture, and competition for resources, would not be better explanations for these non-imperialistic agency behaviors.

4   Rules *vs* Discretion

The difficulty in giving formal incentive schemes to civil servants and elected politicians suggests that capture of decision making by interest groups is of greater concern in government than in private corporations. Indeed political scientists and constitution designers (Montesquieu, the American Federalists, Marx, Bernstein, ...) as well as political economists of the Chicago and Virginia Schools have long insisted on the possibility of corruption of government decision making.

Jean-Jacques Laffont and I[17] have attempted to unveil the implications of the potential for capture for the organization of government and regulation. Our starting point is that the scope for capture stems from the government officials' discretionary power, which in turn results from the superiority of their information relative to that of their political principals, e.g. Congress for agencies or voters for politicians. We endow the government official with superior information about desirable policy choices, presumably because he has more time or because he is more competent. The policy choices may concern procurement prices, consumer charges, rate structures, entry rules, subsidies to the industry and so forth. The official's use of his information affects the welfare of interest groups: incumbent firms, entrants, customers, taxpayers, or environmentalists. Each group has therefore an incentive to influence the government official to release only the information that favors it. The theory then traces the design of the civil service and regulation to the prevention of such behavior.

The formal analysis emphasizes a few main themes.

4.1   Reduction of stakes

To reduce the government officials' temptation to be captured, one may reduce the stakes interest groups have in the regulatory decision. This means relying less on the information held by the government officials and regulating instead by the rule-book. In our view, the central feature of a bureaucracy is that its members are not trusted to make use of information that affects members other than themselves, and that decisions are therefore based on rigid rules.

Let us illustrate the reduction of stakes with a few examples. Consider first the issue of what fraction of their cost government contractors or public utilities should bear. A low-powered incentive scheme is one in which the firm bears a small fraction of its cost; for instance a cost-plus contract reimburses all the firm's cost. In contrast, the firm bears a high fraction of its cost in a high-powered scheme, such as a fixed-price contract in which the firm is residual claimant for its cost savings. Suppose that society has two goals: induce government contractors and utilities to produce at a low cost, and (because of a shadow cost of public funds or for redistributive reasons) prevent them from making profits. It turns out that these two objectives are in conflict if the firm knows more than the regulator about its technology. A high-powered scheme gives good incentives for cost-reduction, while a low-powered scheme is efficient at preventing rents (the firm does not benefit from being luckily endowed with low costs if its cost is fully reimbursed).

Let us now posit that the regulator's role is to bring information to bear on the contract to be offered to the firm. And let us introduce the possibility of capture by the firm of the regulator. That is, the firm may influence the regulator to manipulate his report of information about desirable contracts. A low-powered incentive scheme fares better under a threat of 'producer protection', because it leaves low rents to the firm and those rents are fairly insensitive to the official's information: there is little freedom in designing a cost-plus contract, while the regulator has substantial discretion in the choice of a price in a fixed-price contract![18]

A second example is given by government competition policies. Suppose that the government has better information than voters about the desirability of opening a regulated market to competition. Competition promotes product diversity, and, by providing yardsticks, improves incentives. But there are costs to competition such as the duplication of fixed costs. Whether the market should be opened to competition depends on the relative assessment of these costs and benefits. It is intuitive that the threat of capture of the government officials by incumbents, potential entrants or customer groups, and the concomitant threat of excessively anti- or pro-competition policies, will tend to remove the officials' discretion in choosing the level of competition and favor mechanistic rules for determining industry structures.

A similar idea can be applied to government auctions. While ordinary goods (under some assumptions) can be efficiently auctioned off by simple, non-discretionary mechanisms such as first- and second-bid auctions, most government contracts have multidimensional characteristics. Price is one of them; various components of quality are others: reliability, speed, reputation for honesty, financial stability of the contractor, and so forth. The procurement officer's discretion resides in the assessment of these quality attributes as well as, possibly, in the weighing of these attributes and price. Again, it comes as no surprise that a concern about potential favoritism by the procurement officer leads to auctions that give tangible variables such as price precedence over non-tangible ones such as quality assessments. And, when such precedence is not imposed, government procurement rules often require a detailed and convincing description of the motivations for selecting a high-cost bidder.

4.2   Determinants of the influence of an interest group

Olson (1965) and others have argued that the influence of an interest group depends on the group's organization. Producers and their large customers are usually well organized pressure groups (Stigler, 1971). Taxpayers in contrast are widely dispersed, and, in the absence of a taxpayer representative, extreme free riding prevents them from intervening in any specific regulatory issue. Small consumers and environmentalists traditionally suffered from the same problem, but have become better organized recently. A second, and trivial determinant of the influence of an interest group is the existence of a stake; one would not expect IBM to have much influence on agricultural policies.

An informational approach to capture economics, besides explaining why capture can occur, also unveils a third determinant of the influence of interest groups: the nature of the informational asymmetries. Consider an example in which Congress relies on an agency to obtain information about the desirability of an industrial project. This project, if undertaken, pollutes. It will pass muster if the agency demonstrates that the project is sufficiently profitable. Let the agency, but not its political principal, have such information. The agency and environmentalists can collude to suppress this information and jeopardize the project. In this context, environmentalists have potential power. In contrast, consider a similar situation except that the project is a pollution-abatement one. When the agency has information favorable to the project (low implementation cost, say), environmentalists have no incentives to induce the agency to conceal this information. More generally, an interest group has more potential influence when its members gain from the government officials' restricting information flow than when they lose.

4.3   *Incentive schemes* vs *institutions*

Formal studies of corporate organizations have used two paradigms. One has been well established since the early seventies and presumes that complete contracts are designed to address incentive problems. The adverse selection model assigns private information to some parties about exogenous parameters. The moral hazard model assumes that some parties' endogenous choices remain private information. In both cases, incentive contracts are based on current and future commonly verifiable variables. The second, and conceptually more difficult paradigm is that of incomplete contracting. When contingencies cannot be costlessly included in contracts, the allocation of control rights, that is of rights to decide what to do in unforeseen or unspecified contingencies, starts playing a role (Grossman and Hart, 1986).

One can also approach government organization from these two angles. First, one can envision the government as a group of agents motivated by formal and complete incentive schemes. The agents are induced to choose discretionary actions and to reveal their information appropriately. Second, and maybe more realistically, one can view the government as a distribution of control rights over various kinds of decisions. This division is determined by constitutions, laws and tradition. Because control rights are only rough substitutes for optimal complete contracts, the exercise of control rights conferred on a single group of government officials may lead to substantial abuse such as self-serving actions and capture. This suggests, first, why control rights are often divided among several branches of government (for instance, executive and bicameral legislature); and, second, why a well-functioning democracy ought to make use of private watchdogs (media), independent judges, and advocates for underrepresented groups (such as consumer advocates within government).

In our view, part of the reason the economics of organization haven't had more impact on political science is that many of the interesting normative questions in that field (how should government be organized?) relate to the allocation of control rights and therefore rely on a yet unsettled incomplete contract methodology.

5   Division of Labor within Government: Intertemporal Aspects

The rest of the chapter focuses on the division of labor in government (or, in section 6, between the government and the private sector). This section analyzes how capture issues affect the intertemporal allocation of control rights in government. A recurrent argument in economics is that social welfare is optimized when a benevolent government can commit intertemporally. For instance, noncommitment by the central bank to a future path of the money supply creates an excessive incentive for the government to collect seignorage and induces suboptimal holdings of money by consumers. Similarly noncommitment to future tax rates on capital reduces the accumulation of private investment. In regulation, non-commitment to future schemes creates scope for the expropriation of a public utility's investment; it also makes the firm wary of demonstrating efficiency and gives rise to the ratchet effect. Very generally, it is clear that a benevolent government maximizes social welfare when committing to a long-term, complete contract, because it can always duplicate what would obtain under noncommitment and in general do better.

It is also clear that contracting costs put limits on commitment. Yet contracting costs cannot account for the many legal restrictions on commitment faced by governments. For instance, in many industries, the regulators are forced to sign short-term regulatory contracts.

Such restrictions can easily be rationalized by dropping the assumption of benevolence. If there is a chance that any given government favors specific interest groups, long-term commitment may be socially detrimental. In contrast, short-term commitments together with the rotation of governments (through elections, say) provide some check against inappropriate decisions.

The following simple example[19] illustrates the costs and benefits of commitment. A firm supplies one unit of a good or service to the government in each of two periods. The firm's production cost may be low or high. The firm can also turn a high first-period production cost into a low second-period cost by sinking some private investment in period 1. Suppose, in a first step, that there are two consecutive and separate administrations or governments G_1 and G_2 in the two periods, and that administration G_t observes the firm's date-t cost at the beginning of date t. Assume that administration G_1 is allowed to sign a two-period (that is, long-term) procurement contract. In particular, it can commit to a fixed second-period price. The firm therefore invests when having high first-period cost as long as the reduction in the production cost exceeds the private investment cost. The benefit of a long-term contract is thus to allow efficient investment by the firm. In contrast, under short-term contracting, the firm knows that, once its investment is sunk, the date-2 administration will have the possibility to ratchet down the second-period price to the low cost level. Therefore, it anticipates no private gain from investment, and is better off not investing.

The cost of allowing long-term contracting arises when administration G_1 colludes with the contractor. A high price can then be sustained even when the firm starts with a low cost. In contrast, a short-term contract allows administration G_2 not to keep with administration G_1's lenient contracting practices. (Our discussion is couched in terms of a choice between two institutions, allowing long-term contracting or not. But the same points can be made under complete contracting. Indeed, under some assumptions, the optimal complete contract can be implemented by one of these two simple institutions.)

The model can be extended to let administration G_1 be re-elected with some probability. Suppose that the probability of re-election increases with the voters' posterior beliefs that administration G_1 is 'honest' (that is, is averse to protecting the firm). Then administration G_1 has less incentives to collude with the firm, as a high procurement price conveys (imperfect) information that G_1 might be prone to protect the industry. An election with rational voters may thus make the government more accountable and may raise the desirability of commitment.

6   Division of Labor between the Government and the Private Sector

To what extent should the state intervene in the economy? This topic has wide ramifications, but its problematic nature is nicely epitomized by the issue of privatization. When should a firm be a public enterprise, a regulated private corporation or an unregulated firm? What should be the allocation of production between government and the private sector?

Schmidt (1991), Shapiro and Willig (1991), and Laffont and Tirole (1993, chapter 17) have offered preliminary analyses of the choice between a public enterprise and a private regulated firm. The starting point follows Grossman and Hart (1986) by noting that the ownership structure matters only to the extent that contracts are incomplete. The premise is thus that the government cannot commit to a detailed incentive contract when nationalizing or privatizing the firm.

In Laffont and Tirole (1993), the cost of public ownership is a suboptimal investment by the firm's managers in those assets that can be redeployed to serve social goals pursued by the public owners. The idea is related to section 2.1. Social welfare maximization requires taking into account non-verifiable variables such as the effect of a policy on employment, regional development, level of imports, and other externalities. In contrast, the objective of the private owners of a corporation (maximization of profit) is aligned with verifiable performance measures (earnings, stock price). So private owners have no incentive to exert their control rights to redeploy investments to serve social goals, thereby perturbing formal managerial incentive schemes that necessarily do not incorporate those nonverifiable social goals. In other words, in a private firm there is coherence between owners' incentives and variables underlying the managerial incentive scheme. In contrast, in a public enterprise, the managers' pursuit of performance in the verifiable dimension (profit) is hampered by interference that may divert investments from their original goal.

The cost of private ownership in Laffont and Tirole is that the firm's managers must respond to two masters – the regulator and the shareholders. As is well understood from the theory of common agency (see Bernheim and Whinston, 1986, for moral hazard, and Stole, 1990, and Martimort, 1991, for adverse selection), two parties contracting with the same agent exert externalities on each other unless the agent carries full responsibility for social welfare. In the case of a private regulated firm, the regulator in his choice of regulatory scheme and the shareholders in their choice of managerial incentive contract compete to extract managerial informational rent. Each provides incentives that are deemed too low powered by the other, a problem sometimes mentioned in regulation. This conflict about the power of managerial incentive schemes is but one instance of the inefficiencies created by the divergence of objectives between principals.

It should be emphasized that our distinction between a regulated private firm as having two principals and a public enterprise as having a single is simple minded. Indeed we argue in the next section that dividing tasks within government may be an efficient way of controlling public enterprises. But the main point – that for a given organization of government, privatization introduces a new principal with divergent incentives – is robust, and the fact that we would not expect the government's organization to be the same when handling public enterprises and private regulated firms does not invalidate this cost of privatization.

In Schmidt (1991) and Shapiro and Willig (1991), the cost and benefit of public ownership differ from those described above. The basic postulate in both articles is that public ownership, by giving the government residual rights over the accounting structure, allows the government to have more precise information about the firm's cost than it would have in a regulatory context. The benefit of public ownership is thus that the government is better able to extract the firm's informational rent. The cost of public ownership differs between the two articles. Shapiro and Willig allow the government to be malevolent sometimes; one may prefer malevolent governments to be hampered by informational limitations, and thus one may prefer regulation to a public enterprise. Schmidt presumes a benevolent regulator who cannot commit intertemporally. The lack of information associated with private ownership in a sense commits the regulator not to expropriate too much the firm's investment.

7   Division of Labor within Government: Multiministry Oversight

The last two sections are based on preliminary work with Mathias Dewatripont, and investigate the following puzzle: why isn't government designed to behave as a coherent entity? Examples of dissonant objectives and tight systems of checks and balances abound. Contractors and public enterprises are often subject to control by several government officials with substantially different goals. Public enterprises must respond to at least two masters: a 'spending ministry' with the mission of developing the industry and a finance ministry instructed to reduce the budget deficit. In France, the 'responsible minister' (*ministre de tutelle*) is meant to defend the 'technical point of view' and is *a priori* in charge of the public enterprise. But, many times, this minister is less powerful than the finance minister,[20] whose control becomes pervasive when the firm runs a large deficit. Financial control and the control right over new debt issues by the public enterprise give the minister of finance substantial power to impose his rigorous views on the firm. Even in Italy, where the Ministry for State Holdings is powerful, the required consent of the Treasury for major financial operations gives it nonnegligible influence. Overall, as Friedmann (1970) notes, 'he who pays the piper calls the tune'.

Similarly, the fate of US defense contractors depends on the relative powers of two principals, the Department of Defense and Congress, with substantially different object-ives. Another example is provided by the division of labor between the executive and the legislature. The objective of the president, with a national constituency, necessarily di-verges from that of a parliament where each member by design is meant to defend a limited constituency. Furthermore, voters have the possibility to elect executive and legislative bodies with politically conflicting objectives.

Now, the puzzle is not the existence of multiple parties in government. After all, agency theory has taught us that employing several parties to monitor each other or to create yardsticks may reduce agency costs. The puzzle is rather that government officials are given missions that differ from social welfare maximization and furthermore are at odds with each other. This section argues that multiheaded government may be an efficient institution to deal with external bodies such as public enterprises (or the private sector). The next section develops the idea that multiheaded government may help create a system of checks and balances within the government.

As we just mentioned, this section views multiheaded government as an instrument to control public enterprises. The starting point is quite simple and leads to a formalization of Kornai's celebrated 'soft budget constraint'. Suppose a public enterprise wishes to undertake a new investment such as going nuclear (electricity monopoly) or developing a space shuttle (space agency). Investment costs are incurred at two points of time. The size of the first installment depends on the firm's efficiency in developing, purchasing or installing the new technology, and is learned later on. Then the government must decide whether to pay a completion cost. Consider a welfare maximizing government's decision of whether to incur the second installment and thus complete the project. If the total investment cost is high, the government regrets having started the project in the first place, but given that the first installment is a sunk cost, it may well decide to complete the project anyway. Ideally, the government would like at the start of the project to commit not to finance the second installment if costs run over, in order to provide the firm with incentives to keep the investment cost down. Yet such a commitment lacks credibility. This time consistency problem weakens the firm's incentives. To restore the government's credibility, one can threaten the public enterprise with a shift of control to a cost-conscious ministry when further investment requires substantial borrowing. This is done by subjecting borrowing to approval by a ministry of finance, and by giving this ministry a mission (budget balance, say) that does not internalize nonmonetary benefits of continuing the project.[21]

To formalize this idea, we use a variation of the endogenous multiprincipal model in Dewatripont and Tirole (1992). The public enterprise undertakes a new project. The project's initial investment cost $I \in \{I_0, I_1\}$, with $I_0 < I_1$, is random and depends on the firm's effort $e \in \{\underline{e}, \bar{e}\}$. The firm's manager incurs disutility K (respectively, 0) from exerting effort $\bar{e}$ (respectively, $\underline{e}$). The completion of the project costs $\mathcal{J} > 0$, and yields a random benefit $\Delta \in [\Delta^{\min}, \Delta^{\max}]$, that for simplicity we decompose into a monetary benefit $\alpha\Delta$ and a nonmonetary benefit $(1 - \alpha)\Delta$, where $0 < \alpha < 1$ (see below for a discussion of this division in terms of cost reduction and increase in the net consumer surplus). We assume that I is verifiable while the action of stopping or completing the project is noncontractible; one interpretation may be that the level of new debt contracted by the firm is verifiable while other decisions are not. We also assume that Δ cannot be extracted from accounting data; for simplicity Δ is considered to be noncontractible. The effort determines the density of the benefit Δ of completing the project: $\bar{f}(\Delta)$ for effort $\bar{e}$ and $\underline{f}(\Delta)$ for effort $\underline{e}$. Let $\bar{F}(\cdot)$ and $\underline{F}(\cdot)$ denote the associated cumulative distributions, and $\bar{x}$ and $\underline{x}$ the probabilities that $I = I_0$. The variables I and Δ are independent conditionally on effort. We assume the monotone likelihood ratio property: $\bar{f}(\Delta)/\underline{f}(\Delta)$ is increasing in Δ and $\bar{x} > \underline{x}$.

The firm's manager does not respond to monetary incentives and receives a fixed wage; that is, he has no utility for money as long as he receives some minimum wage level (the theory can be extended to monetary incentives as discussed below). The manager derives private benefit B if the project is completed, and 0 if it is not. This benefit may stem from perks attached to playing with the new technology, from an associated increase in human capital, or else (in an extension of the model with imperfect information about the manager's ability) from the signal sent to the labor market when the project is completed. The manager has reservation utility equal to 0.

Let us summarize the timing: the control rights within government are allocated (see below); the manager then chooses his effort; the uncertainty about I and Δ is resolved; the ministry in control for vertifiable variable I decides whether to stop or complete the project. Note that we do not allow for renegotiation after the uncertainty is resolved and before the completion decision is chosen. It is easy to see that the same qualitative results would obtain if renegotiation were allowed, as long as the manager makes some concession of private benefits in order to induce completion when the ministry in control has a preference for stopping.

We now derive the optimal managerial incentive scheme (which is here confined to the state contingent decision of project completion, since formal incentive schemes are ruled out) by maximizing the expected benefit of completion subject to the constraint that the manager prefers $\bar{e}$. [We ignore the manager's welfare for simplicity.] Let $\Delta_k, k \in \{0, 1\}$, denote the cutoff benefit when $I = I_k$. That is, the project is completed if and only if $\Delta \geq \Delta_k$. We have

$$\max_{\{\Delta_0, \Delta_1\}} \left\{ \bar{x} \int_{\Delta_0}^{\Delta^{\max}} (\Delta - \mathcal{J}) \bar{f}(\Delta) d\Delta + (1 - \bar{x}) \int_{\Delta_1}^{\Delta^{\max}} (\Delta - \mathcal{J}) \bar{f}(\Delta) d\Delta \right\},$$

subject to the incentive compatibility constraint:

$$B[\bar{x}(1 - \bar{F}(\Delta_0)) + (1 - \bar{x})(1 - \bar{F}(\Delta_1))] \geq B[\underline{x}(1 - \underline{F}(\Delta_0)) + (1 - \underline{x})(1 - \underline{F}(\Delta_1))] + K.$$

The solution is straightforward. The cutoff rule satisfies $\Delta_0 < \mathcal{J} < \Delta_1$. That is, optimal incentives require the government to be tougher when costs run over.

Now a single headed government maximizing social welfare would not create appropriate incentives. This government would complete the project if and only if $\Delta \geq \mathcal{J}$, regardless of the realisation of I! The soft budget constraint phenomenon occurs when

$$B(\underline{F}(\mathcal{J}) - \bar{F}(\mathcal{J})) < K,$$

that is when the incentive constraint is not satisfied for a completion rule that is insensitive to cost overruns.

Let us now turn to the implementation of the optimal completion rule. We start with the special case where $\Delta_0 = \Delta^{\min}$, and $\alpha \Delta_1 = \mathcal{J}$. Then, the optimal completion rule can be implemented by the following institution: when investment costs remain reasonable ($I = I_0$), control remains with a spending ministry, whose mission is to complete projects, or indifferently, maximize output, technical progress or minimize consumer prices in some interpretations. This will implement $\Delta_0 = \Delta^{\min}$. When investment costs run over ($I = I_1$), control shifts to the finance ministry, which is instructed to strive for budget balance for the state. The finance ministry then compares the monetary return $\alpha \Delta$ and and completion cost $\mathcal{J}$ and implements $\Delta_1 = \mathcal{J}/\alpha$. This example contains the gist of our idea. Of course, those particular values of Δ_0 and Δ_1 can arise only by a fluke, and less simple-minded missions must be given to our two ministries. We will come back after the next two remarks to missions for the finance ministry when $\mathcal{J} > \alpha\Delta_1$ (purely monetary concerns makes this ministry too tough) or $\mathcal{J} < \alpha\Delta_1$ (purely monetary concerns do not make it tough enough).

REMARK 1   The model above is one of moral hazard. Alternatively, one could endow the managers with private information about the likely costs and benefits of the project before it is started. The logic of the model is then hardly changed. The shift of control to a tough principal in case of large financial needs then serves to reduce the firm's incentive to push a worthless project.

REMARK 2   The intuition about why the theory can be extended to managerial monetary benefits (as in Dewatripont and Tirole, 1992) is the following: suppose that the project reduces the firm's cost and leads to lower consumer prices and higher demand. If managerial rents associated with production increase with the level of activity of the firm (as in Laffont and Tirole, 1993), project completion is then a reward for the manager.

To return to some of the open questions mentioned before, let us specialize the model by assuming project completion brings about a reduction in the firm's marginal cost. The price charged to consumers therefore depends on whether the process innovation takes place. There are many pricing rules that can be followed: for instance, marginal cost pricing, monopoly pricing, and Ramsey pricing (where the Ramsey price maximizes the sum of the consumer net surplus plus the firm's revenue evaluated at one plus the shadow cost of public funds). For concreteness, let us assume that the price is set optimally given that taxation is socially costly, that is that the price is equal to the Ramsey price. The monetary benefit alluded to before ($\alpha\Delta$) is then equal to (one plus the shadow cost times) the firm's increase in profit associated with the reduction in marginal cost. The nonmonetary benefit ($(1 - \alpha)\Delta$) is equal to the increase in consumer net surplus.

When $\alpha\Delta_1 < \mathcal{J}$, a ministry of finance with purely monetary objectives is too tough, that is completes too little. To soften its behavior, it suffices to build as its objective a weighted average of the budget surplus and (minus) the consumer price index. Because the completion of the project reduces marginal cost and thus price, the ministry of finance becomes softer, and picks Δ_1 as its cutoff benefit if the weights are chosen appropriately. It is interesting in this respect to note that the French ministry of finance is in charge of keeping consumer prices low as well as obtaining financial balance.

When $\alpha\Delta_1 > \mathcal{J}$, a ministry of finance with purely monetary objectives is too soft. It does not seem reasonable to reward it for high consumer prices, though, even if this would make it more prone to stop the project. A costly way to fine tune the ministry of finance's objective function is to give it the control rights not only on the amount of borrowing, but also on pricing. Indeed, a ministry of finance with purely monetary objectives would charge the monopoly price. Because a process innovation raises profit less when prices are monopoly, rather than Ramsey prices (the marginal cost reductions apply to a lower number of units), the ministry of finance has fewer incentives to complete the project if it has control rights over prices than when it does not. Giving full control rights when $I = I_1$ to the ministry of finance thus makes it tougher. Such a policy, however, makes sense only if the deadweight loss associated with high prices is not too large.

8   Division of Labor within Government: Checks and Balances

Section 7 argued that goal setting in government may reflect a desire to control the behavior of other economic agents. It suggested why social welfare maximization perhaps should not be pursued by ministries with control rights. This section (also based on ideas developed with Mathias Dewatripont) arrives at a similar conclusion from a quite distinct perspective. Its idea is that competition in government among advocates of specific interests or causes may give rise to good policy setting.

The use of competition among enfranchized advocates has wider scope than government. The archetypal example of this can be found in courts. The defense attorney is expected to stand for the defendant, to the point that he is not meant to reveal information that would be useful for the jury in reaching a decision but would hurt the defendant's case. Similarly, the prosecutor's job is to be as tough with the defendant as possible. No social welfare maximization or impartiality is expected from them. This system of conflict and partiality has prevailed for centuries and is deemed to be an integral piece of a democratic system. Another non-government example is that of a union or management in a firm that are not meant to represent the same interests.

Similar situations abound in government. No ministry's mandate is to maximize social welfare. The ministry of labor is there to defend wage earners, the ministry of industry to promote the industry, the ministry of the environment to protect the environment, and so forth. A second example is provided by the legislature. A representative is expected to make a case for his constituency, and not for the others. A third example is the division of labor between a nationally elected president and the legislature representing local interests against the center. Similarly, the US Senate, with its two senators per state, defends the interests of underpopulated states better than the House of Representatives with its roughly proportional representation. Last, multipartism is often a system of advocates with parties representing distinct political constituencies.

Several interpretations can be given to the notion of 'checks and balances'. We here take the view that for government to exhibit checks and balances, the cases for alternative policies or causes must be defended properly. Information must be created and clearly exposited, that bears on the pros and cons of those alternatives. Of course, this is only a necessary condition for good government, as political decision making must act on this information appropriately. This section ignores the second issue by assuming that, somehow, the decision, that maximizes 'social welfare' conditional on the information created and diffused, is picked. This of course is a strong assumption, but its implications seem somewhat tangential to the main points we want to make here.

We thus study the creation of information for decision making. We first argue that a single information collector faces conflicting tasks when asked to gather information concerning opposing causes. Consider for instance a redistribution issue in which money can be given to A, or to B, or shared between the two. It is no easy task to structure incentives for an information collector that makes the case for both A and B by searching for grounds to favor one or the other. For a decision to share money between the two may be motivated either by a complete lack of information or by the discovery of two opposing effects. Now, it would be straightforward to structure incentives if one could give direct incentives based on the information collected, as is assumed in the literature. The information collector would be rewarded more for collecting pieces of evidence favoring both even if those cancel out in decision making, than for collecting evidence in favor of one, than in turn for collecting no evidence. In contrast, if rewards for information collection are indirect and based only on the final decision, the reward is constrained to be the same when two conflicting pieces of evidence are created and when none is created. The information collector's task is not focused enough if he must make the case for both. We will see that competition between open advocates of the two causes may generate better decision making, and we will analyze the costs and benefits of such competition.

We find the idea of indirect reward appealing in many problems. For information is often a difficult object to describe *ex ante* in an incentive scheme. A lawyer is paid by the plaintiff as a function of whether the case is won and of the level of damages awarded, but not of the information brought to bear or of the quality of the case made by the lawyer. Similarly, politicians and parties are often rewarded by voters on the basis of which decision was made rather than on how the decision was reached. Representatives are often judged on what they obtained for their constituencies. A minister's tenure is often assessed by how well he fulfilled the mission of his ministry, rather than by the quality of the arguments he gave to defend his cause. To be certain, I am here overstating the case for indirect rewards. Direct rewards for information collection and diffusion also exist in the form of career concerns. Some close to the decision making process will recall not only whether the bureaucrat or politician succeeded in pushing his point of view, but also whether a good case was made. So, in general, we have a mixture of direct and indirect rewards for information collection. The purpose of this section is to investigate the consequences of indirect rewards by ignoring direct ones.

Consider the following simple example. There are three possible policies: A, B and status quo (indexed by a zero). For instance, A and B might be more nuclear or coal oriented policies. Or A and B might be two constituencies to distribute money between, the status quo corresponding to equal sharing. There are two potential pieces of information: one that favors A and the other that favors B. The decision chosen is to favor a cause (A or B) if there is a piece of information favoring it, but none favoring the other. In the absence of information or in the presence of conflicting information, the status quo is chosen. Let us assume for the moment that a single information collector, or agent is used. This agent is risk neutral and has reservation utility equal to zero. To collect information favorable to cause i ($i = A, B$), he must incur private cost K; with probability x, he then finds a piece of evidence favoring cause i, and with probability $(1 - x)$, he finds no evidence. He finds no evidence if he does not spend K. For the moment, we assume that the evidence is disclosed once discovered and is therefore used for decision making. We also assume that the stakes are sufficiently important that one would want the collector to spend $2K$ to search for the two possible pieces of information. We will take a complete contract perspective in which the agent's (indirect) reward is based on the decision. Let w_A, w_B, and w_0 denote wages when A is favored, when B is favored and when the status quo is chosen. The complete contract perspective is more appropriate in the case of a lawyer than for a politician, but the same points can be made in an incomplete contracting set up.

Let us look at the agent's incentive constraint. He obtains w_0 when exerting no effort. He gets

$$xw_i + (1 - x)w_0 - K$$

when he looks for information favorable to cause i and

$$x(1 - x)(w_A + w_B) + (1 - 2x(1 - x))w_0 - 2K$$

when he looks for the two kinds of information. Suppose, without loss of generality, that $w_A \geq w_B$. If the agent exerts any effort, necessarily $w_A \geq w_0$. It is easy to show that for $x \geq 1/2$, the agent never chooses to look for evidence in both directions. Thus, having two agents, each looking in one direction, is the only way to obtain the maximum information. To obtain effort in the two directions, it suffices to pay $w_0 = w_j = 0$ $(j \neq i)$ and $w_i = K/x(1 - x)$ to agent i who is in charge of collecting information favorable to cause i.

Competition between the two agents thus allows society to obtain more information. Note that having one or two agents would be equivalent if direct rewards could be specified. It would then suffice to promise a single agent K/x per piece of evidence.

In this example, the single agent is reluctant to exert a second effort to find evidence favorable to cause B because he is afraid that this new evidence might annihilate the benefit he will derive if he finds evidence favorable to cause A. One may object that, if the agent can conceal evidence, he will do so if he finds evidence favorable to the two conflicting causes. He will keep one piece of evidence and throw away the other. It is interesting in this respect to note that, with a single agent and when $x \geq 1/2$, society obtains more effort by letting the agent have property rights on his information and letting him dispose of information as he wishes.[22]

This brings us to a more general discussion of the costs and benefits of competition in information creation.[23] In the example above, competition always dominates monopoly. To introduce a cost to competition, assume that an agent can destroy evidence and that in the process of searching for evidence favorable to cause i, advocate i has some probability of finding evidence favorable to cause j: the ministry of the environment may find that pollution is costly to curb, the ministry of energy may find that nuclear power will be expensive, and so forth. The advocate has no incentive to release this sort of information, while a more impartial agent would have some such incentive.

It is outside the scope of this paper to develop the analysis when agents can find favorable and unfavorable information. Here is some flavor of the results: competition may lead to a 'lack of decisiveness' or 'immobility' or 'excessive balancing', in the sense that the status quo may be chosen because one camp is concealing information unfavorable to its cause while the other has not found any information at all. In contrast, monopoly may excessively favor decisions favoring a specific cause; as we saw earlier, a single agent has an incentive to conceal one of two pieces of information that cancel out in order to show that he has been busy and gotten things to move.

9 Concluding Remark

The overdue interaction between the economics of organization and political science will most likely be very fruitful. Classical agency models of moral hazard and adverse selection can be used to explain low powered formal incentives, and to study the specificities of career concerns, capture, and monitoring in government. The newer, and less settled paradigm of incomplete contracting and property rights will be invoked to understand the size and involvement of government, its division in branches, the ministerial organization, the constitution and other institutions, and so forth. After all, much of the realm of normative political science is about the allocation of control rights!

In the introduction to his fascinating book on bureaucracy, J. Q. Wilson (1989) writes:

> When I was a young and giddy scholar, I had hopes that [a theory of bureaucratic behavior] could be created (ideally, by me). I even tried my hand at a few versions. What resulted was not a theory of bureaucracy, but rather a few modest additions to the long list of theories about some aspect of bureaucracy. Over thirty years ago, James G. March and Herbert A. Simon wrote that not a great deal [of theoretical interest] has been said about organizations, but it has been said over and over in a variety of languages. That is still pretty much the case, as is evident from how often people still cite studies by March and Simon as support for one point or another. After all these decades of wrestling with the subject, I have come to have grave doubts that anything worth calling 'organization theory' will ever exist.

In view of the recent tremendous progress in incentive theory, I am more optimistic than this. While economists have a lot to learn from political scientists and sociologists, they also have a powerful language and powerful tools that in the future may yield a better understanding of government.

Acknowledgments

This paper is the written version of the Hicks lecture given at Oxford by the author on April 29, 1992. Financial support from the Institute for Policy Reform (IPR) and the Agency for International Development (AID) under cooperative agreement PDC-0095-A-00-1126-00 is gratefully acknowledged. Views expressed in this paper are those of the author and not necessarily those of IPR and AID. The author is grateful to Jacques Crémer, Mathias Dewatripont, Bengt Holmström, Jean-Jacques Laffont, John Vickers and an anonymous referee for helpful comments. This chapter makes substantial use of joint work with Mathias Dewatripont and Jean-Jacques Laffont.

Notes

1   This section has met with very opposite reactions. Some argued to me that the public sector cannot be compared with the private sector since government employees first face low powered incentives and, second, are on average more socially motivated. On the other hand, some thought I was overstressing the distinction between public and private sectors. I concur with the first group's assessment of the specificities of government, but also believe that these specificities cannot just be presumed but should be derived from the same first principles that govern the organization of the private sector.

2   This of course is not quite correct. Because asset markets are incomplete in practice, the firm's objective (whatever it is, given that claimholders in general will not agree on this objective) may differ from profit maximization. We here take the view that such spanning issues can be ignored in a first approximation and that claimholders want the maximization of total firm value.

3   A second example is provided by a procurement officer who is instructed to minimize costs while leaving reasonable profits to the contractor. What 'reasonable' means depends on hard-to-describe contingencies such as the effect of a bankruptcy on employment, the degree of competition in the industry, and so forth.

4   Yet, some of these issues are amenable to a modern industrial organization treatment. Take
    federalism *vs* centralism. The costs of federalism resemble those falling under the heading of
    'wasteful competition' in industries: non-exploitation of returns to scale, imperfect taxation,
    excessive screening or segmentation (see Benabou, 1991), and so forth. The benefit of federalism
    is that competition keeps a lid on potential abuses of central decision making, namely incompe-
    tence or capture of decision makers, by offering the possibility of comparison. Competition may
    also promote product diversity in cases where central decision making fails to do so. A systematic
    analysis of the costs and benefits of federalism in terms of the new economics of organization
    would be welcome.

5   Heterogeneity of goals in the private sector is important in family-run firms, partnerships and
    cooperatives (see, e.g., Hansmann, 1988).

6   We must admit, though, that big shareholders or debtholders, the monetary preferences of which
    are aligned with those of small holders of similar claims, may collude with other parties, or else
    enjoy non-monetary gains of following particular policies.

7   Also, such a takeover replaces the overall government, rather than a minister or the top officials
    in an agency (although good officials or ministers are sometimes kept when the government
    changes).

8   Low powered incentives mean that the agent receives a small fraction of his or her marginal
    product.

9   It should be noted that, for the same reason, monitoring often is more pervasive in government
    as well. As Wilson (1989) observes: 'government executives spend much more of their time and
    energy on handling, face to face, external constituencies than do business executives' (pp. 31–2;
    Wilson, for instance, notes that the director of the FBI meets with his board of directors (the
    congressional committees) more than 18 times a year). And Fox (1988) estimates that a US
    weapons program manager must spend 30–50 percent of his time defending his project inside the
    Department of Defense and Congress.

10 A justification may be that the manager has no career concern tomorrow and therefore does not
    exert any effort. Alternatively, one could generate effort by subsequent career concerns, as in
    Holmström (1982).

11 We assume for simplicity that the manager is always paid a wage equal to his expected ability,
    and ignore problems associated with negative wages (which are negligible if the distribution puts
    little weight on negative values).

12 What if the manager chooses a positive level of effort, so that $x > 0$? To sustain our no-effort
    equilibrium, we assume that the off-the-equilibrium-path observation $x > 0$ is interpreted as
    stemming from a type $\theta < \tilde{\theta}$.

    A possibly more satisfactory approach is to introduce noise in the observation of perform-
    ance:

$$x = \theta e + \varepsilon \tag{2'}$$

    where distributed on support $(-\infty, \infty)$. Then the issue of inferences off the equilibrium path
    does not arise. Note also that the specification in (2') is more satisfactory than that in (2) for
    another reason. The no-effort equilibrium is robust to small perturbations in the technology
    (such as $x\theta(e + \alpha) + \varepsilon$, with α close to 0) if $g'(0) > 0$, for specification (2'), but not for
    specification (2).

13 See note 15 below for a discussion of whether w_1 should take the same value in (3) and (4).

14 To illustrate these ideas with a continuous example such as the one developed above, let a
    manager allocate his effort $\bar{e}$ between tasks 1 and 2:

$$e_1 + e_2 = \bar{e} \quad \text{and} \quad e_k \geq 0 \text{ for } k \in \{1,\ 2\}.$$

(For instance, one might assume $g(e) = 0$ for $e \leq \bar{e}$, and $= \infty$ for $e > \bar{e}$. The results can be extended to the case where total effort is not fixed.)

And let performance be two-dimensional:

$$x_k = \theta_{e_k} + \varepsilon_k \quad k \in \{1, 2\}$$

where the ability θ and the noise terms ε_1 and ε_2 are normal and independent, and ε_1 and ε_2 have mean zero and the same variance. Then, $\{e_1 = \bar{e}, e_2 = 0\}$ and $\{e_1 = 0, e_2 = \bar{e}\}$ are both equilibria. In these equilibria, there is a wrong allocation of effort if the optimum is to spread effort more evenly between the two tasks. Such inefficiencies could here trivially be solved, were a formal contract feasible (see Holmström and Milgrom, 1991).

In this example, there also exists a composite mission equilibrium, in which the official splits his attention between the two tasks. The market's posterior expectation of the official's ability is then of the form

$$\alpha\theta + \beta(x_1 + x_2)$$

where α and β depend on the precisions of the prior and of the noises. The official therefore maximizes $E(x_1 + x_2) = \bar{\theta}(e_1 + e_2)$ and is indifferent as to his allocation of effort (assuming of course $\theta > 0$). Two remarks are in order here.

First, the composite equilibrium is unique in its class. An equilibrium allocation (e_1^*, e_2^*) would yield posterior expectation

$$\alpha'\theta + \beta'(e_1^* x_1 + e_2^* x_2)$$

The official would then maximize $E(e_1^* x_1 + e_2^* x_2) = \bar{\theta}(e_1^* e_1 + e_2^* e_2)$. The equilibrium is therefore either a single mission one or the composite mission one described above.

Second, the composite mission equilibrium is here quite unstable. Suppose that the official has some small intrinsic preference for one task over the other, which can be expressed by a private information variable with continuous distribution on a support including 0. Then, given the market's updating rule, the official (with probability 1) chooses either $e_1 = \bar{e}$ or $e_2 = \bar{e}$. Hence the updating rule is no longer appropriate and the composite mission equilibrium disappears.

15   The assumption that w_1 is unresponsive to which equilibrium one is in seems a good approximation in the case of a civil servant. If the first-period wage reflected expected marginal productivity ($w_1 = 0$ in the first equilibrium and $w_1 = \bar{\theta}\hat{e}$ in the second), the official might prefer the second equilibrium because it creates a commitment to work in the first period.

16   Assume that w_1 is fixed and consider the following two-stage game: First, the official announces a mission or not (this is 'cheap talk'). Second, the official chooses and effort. A first equilibrium of this game exists with 'no mission, and $e = 0$'. A second equilibrium, assuming $g(e) = e$, exists with 'mission, $w_2(x) = \sqrt{2x/\delta}, \hat{e}(\theta) = \delta\theta/2$ and $U(\theta) = w_1 + (\delta\theta/2)$.' There exist other equilibria as well. The officials with ability θ such that $(\delta\theta/2) > \delta\bar{\theta}$ prefer having a mission while the others would prefer no mission but are trapped in trying to prove their ability.

17   1993, chapters 11–16.

18   On the other hand, low-powered schemes may be particularly prone to the corruption of the government auditors because of the importance they give to cost measurement.

19   Building on Laffont and Tirole (1993, chapter 16) and Tai (1990).

20   See, e.g., Levy (1970).

21   This reasoning assumes some independence of the ministry of finance from intervention by the prime minister. A prime minister who would aggregate goals and systematically take over the ministerial tasks would recreate the single principal situation.

    Similarly, having two principals would not improve on a single one if the two principals renegotiated only between themselves and required no concession from the firm (that is, if the firm obtained its best feasible outcome in the three-way renegotiation game). In such a case, only asymmetric information between the principals (created, say, by separate information collection) or other bargaining costs would yield a role for multiple principals, by limiting the efficiency of renegotation.

22   If $w_A \geq w_B$ and $(x - x^2)(W_B - w_0) \geq K$, the agent will want to exert the second effort if he has the property rights.

23   Holmström and Milgrom (1990) identify another factor affecting the choice between one and two agents, namely the correlation of tasks. High correlation between tasks generates high benefits from relative performance evaluation and therefore favors competition between agents. (Formally, their model always has two agents. The issue is whether to prohibit side trading between them, or to allow it. In the latter case, the two agents behave much like a single one.)

References

Benabou, R. (1991) Workings of a City: Location, Education, and Production. Working paper no. 582, MIT, Cambridge, MA.

Bernheim, D. and Whinston, M. (1986) Common Agency. *Econometrica*, 54: 923–43.

Dewatripont, M. and Tirole, J. (1992) A Theory of Debt and Equity: Diversity of Securities and Manager-Shareholder Congruence. Mimeo, Université Libre, Bruxells, and IDEI, Toulouse.

Fox, R. (with J. Field) (1988) *The Defense Management Challenge: Weapons Acquisition*. Harvard Business School Press, Boston.

Friedmann, W. (1970) Government Enterprise: a Comparative Analysis In W. Friedmann and J. Garner (eds), *Government Enterprise: A Comparative Study*. Columbia University Press, New York, Chapter 16.

Grossman, S. and Hart, O. (1986) The Costs and Benefits of Ownership: a Theory of Lateral and Vertical Integration. *Journal of Political Economy*, 94: 691–719.

Hansmann, H. (1988) The Ownership of the Firm. *Journal of Law, Economics and Organization*, 4: 267–304.

Hicks, J. (1935) Annual Survey of Economic Theory: the Theory of Monopoly. *Econometrica*, 3: 1–20.

Holmström, B. (1982) Managerial Incentive Problems: a Dynamic Perspective. In *Essays in Economics and Management in Honor of Lars Wahlbeck*, Swedish School of Economics, Helsinki.

Holmström, B. and Milgrom, P. (1990) Regulating Trade Among Agents. *Journal of Institutional and Theoretical Economics*, 146: 85–105.

Holmström, B. and Milgrom, P. (1991) Multitask Principal–Agent Analyses: Incentive Contracts, Asset Ownership, and Job Design. *Journal of Law, Economics and Organization*, 7: 24–52.

Laffont, J.-J. and Tirole, J. (1991) Provision of Quality and Power of Incentive Schemes in Regulated Industries. In W. Barnett, B. Cornet, C. d'Aspremont, J. Gabszewicz and A. Mas-Colell (eds), *Equilibrium Theory and Applications* (*Proceedings of the Sixth International Symposium in Economic Theory and Econometrics*). Cambridge University Press. Cambridge, MA, 161–96.

Laffont, J.-J. and Tirole, J. (1993) *A Theory of Incentives in Regulation and Procurement*. MIT Press, Cambridge, MA.

Levy, D. (1970) Control of Public Enterprises in France. In W. Friedmann and J. Garner (eds), *Government Enterprise: A Comparative Study*, Columbia University Press, New York, chapter 7.

Martimort, D. (1991) Multiple Principals and Asymmetric Information. Mimeo, Université de Toulouse.

Olson, M. (1965) *The Logic of Collective Action*. Harvard University Press, Cambridge, MA.

Schelling, T. (1960) *The Strategy of Conflict*, Harvard University Press, Cambridge, MA.

Schmidt, K. (1991) The Costs and Benefits of Privatization. Mimeo, University of Bonn.

Shapiro, C. and Willig, R. (1991) Economic Rationales for the Scope of Privatization. Mimeo, Princeton University.

Stigler, J. (1971) The Economic Theory of Regulation. *Bell Journal of Economics*, 2: 3–21.

Stole, I. (1990) Mechanism Design under Common Agency. Mimeo, MIT, Cambridge, MA.

Tai, A. J. (1990) Commitment in Repeated Hierarchical Relationships. Mimeo, MIT, Cambridge, MA.

Wilson, J. Q. (1989) *Bureaucracy: What Government Agencies Do and Why They Do It*. Basic Books, New York.

FOURTEEN

Power of Incentives in Private versus Public Organizations

AVINASH DIXIT*

Source: From *American Economic Review* (1997), 87(2): 378–82.

Government agencies and public enterprises are generally thought to perform poorly because their managers and workers lack the high-powered incentives that are believed to prevail in private firms. This belief motivates many attempts to privatize public services and reform government bureaucracies. In the report of the recent US initiative to reinvent government, Al Gore (1995, pp. 12, 62–6) emphasized the importance of measuring and rewarding "results, not red tape."

Considerable research on the design of incentives in government agencies also exists (see Susan Rose-Ackerman, 1986; Jean Tirole, 1994). This draws upon the general theory of incentives, whose main application concerns the organization and regulation of private firms. Government firms and agencies are in some ways like large, complex, private firms but differ in other important respects.

Some differences are matters of degree. Government agencies' outputs are often harder to quantify and measure. The goods and services they supply usually have few close substitutes, making it difficult to use market-based or yardstick competition for incentives. Sometimes this can be done; the Gore report (1995, pp. 95–8, 130–1) stresses the concept and gives examples.

Some government agencies have one advantage over private firms: they provide services to poor, old, or disabled people, and the managers' or workers' own compassion or social concern can motivate their performance without the need for incentives. In fact, the workers may go so far in helping their clientele as to clash with the agency's other objectives; James Heckman et al. (1996) provide an example of this.

In this paper I focus on another very important, almost defining, distinct feature of public organizations: they are answerable to several different constituencies with different objectives. In technical terms they are "common agencies" with several "principals." In the United States the system of open government has this effect. An agency may be formally answerable only to the executive (say), but in practice Congress, courts, media, and organized lobbies, all have a say. In the European Union the sovereign member countries are principals to the bureaucracy in Brussels.

Thus government agencies are not merely managerial or administrative organizations; they must operate in a framework of *politics*. James Wilson (1989) has identified this as the reason they have weak incentives. This finds support in my formal analysis (Dixit, 1996), which I discuss and generalize below.

The incentives in such public organizations need not be financial; more often they are complex quid pro quos in a larger, multidimensional bargaining game. I develop the theory in the familiar mode of transfers and utilities, but these should be interpreted metaphorically or in a generalized sense.

I   Why Large Organizations have Low-Powered Incentives

In reality, incentives are low-powered even within private firms. The main reason was identified by Oliver Williamson (1985, chapter 6). The organization performs several tasks, the outputs of which are observable with different degrees of accuracy. Considering each task in isolation, one with a more accurately observed outcome would have a higher-powered incentive because the outcome is a better indicator of the effort one wants to motivate. But considering them together, giving a more powerful incentive to one task draws effort away from other tasks; therefore the existence of some inaccurately observed (or unobservable) dimensions of outcome pulls down the power of incentives for all tasks. For example, the manager of a supply division who is paid by net receipts may use his fixed equipment too intensively or may fail to maintain it adequately. Then the firm must use weak material incentives (salaries) plus costly monitoring to ensure adequate attention to all tasks.

This idea was further developed, formalized, and applied by others, including Bengt Holmström (1989), Holmström and Paul Milgrom (1991), and Tirole (1994). Holmström argues that larger firms perform more tasks and, therefore, they have weaker incentives and suffer a relative disadvantage in activities like innovation that are hard to measure. Larger firms with more market power are also less able to use yardstick competition.

II   How Multiple Principals Influence Public Organizations

I argue that a distinct feature of government bureaucracies is that they must answer to multiple principals. I now develop a model of a common agency to show how the interaction among many principals results in a loss of the power of incentives. I treat the case of moral hazard, where the agent's action is not observable to the principals but all outcomes can be observed by all. The case where the agent has private information (adverse selection) is treated by David Martimort (1995) and yields some similar results.

The model generalizes that presented in the appendix of Dixit (1996), which in turn builds upon the multitask model of Holmström and Milgrom (1991). I shall omit all details of derivation to save space.[1]

The agent makes a k-dimensional unobservable (or unverifiable) effort denoted by the vector $\mathbf{x}$. The result is $\mathbf{y}$, an observable and verifiable m-dimensional output vector.[2] The two are linked by

$$\mathbf{y} = \mathbf{F}\mathbf{x} + \varepsilon \tag{1}$$

where F is an $m \times k$ matrix, and ε is an m-dimensional error vector, distributed normally with mean 0 and variance–covariance matrix Ω.

There are n principals indexed by $i = 1, 2, \ldots n$. If the ith principal pays the agent z_i, that principal's expected utility is

$$E[- \exp\{ - r_i(\mathbf{b}'_i\mathbf{y} - z_i)\}]$$

and the agent's expected utility is

$$E\left[- \exp\left\{ -r_a(\mathbf{b}'_a\mathbf{y} + \sum_i z_i - \tfrac{1}{2}\mathbf{x}'\mathbf{C}\mathbf{x}) \right\} \right].$$

Thus all players have constant absolute risk aversion, r_i for principal i and r_a for the agent. The ith principal values outputs linearly, and the components of the vector $\mathbf{b}_i$ are his unit valuations of the corresponding components of output. Some principals can actually dislike some types of outputs, so some components of each $\mathbf{b}_i$ can be negative, but I assume the sum of these vectors, denoted by $\mathbf{b}_0$, is strictly positive. I also allow the agent to have some concern for output for its own sake, and the components of the vector $\mathbf{b}_a$ are his unit valuations. The quadratic form $\tfrac{1}{2}\mathbf{x}'\mathbf{C}\mathbf{x}$ is the agent's disutility of effort, and $\mathbf{C}$ is a $k \times k$ positive definite matrix.

I assume that the principals use linear payment schemes:

$$z_i = \boldsymbol{\alpha}'_i\mathbf{y} + \beta_i. \tag{2}$$

This makes the analysis tractable and yields clear intuitions; for a discussion see Holmström and Milgrom (1991) and Dixit (1996, appendix). The β_i merely serve to split the surplus between the parties and ensure that the agent's participation constraint is met; the interest focuses on the coefficient vectors $\boldsymbol{\alpha}_i$, which are the marginal rewards promised by the principals to the agent for producing more output.

First, suppose the principals act collusively: they set a linear scheme $z = \boldsymbol{\alpha}'\mathbf{y} + \beta$ and optimally split the joint surplus among themselves. Define r_0 by

$$1/r_0 = \sum_i (1/r_i). \tag{3}$$

This r_0 acts as the joint risk-aversion of the principals when they collude and pool risks; it should normally be quite small. Finally, define

$$\mathbf{G} = \mathbf{F}\mathbf{C}^{-1}\mathbf{F}'$$

where $\mathbf{F}$ and $\mathbf{C}$ are as defined above.

With this notation, the agent's choice of effort is given by

$$\mathbf{x} = \mathbf{C}^{-1}\mathbf{F}'(\boldsymbol{\alpha} + \mathbf{b}_a).$$

Substituting in the principals' objective, it can be shown that the marginal incentive vector $\boldsymbol{\alpha}^j$ of the principals' jointly optimal scheme satisfies

$$[\mathbf{G} + (r_0 + r_a)\Omega](\boldsymbol{\alpha}^j + \mathbf{b}_a) = [\mathbf{G} + r_0\Omega](\mathbf{b}_0 + \mathbf{b}_a). \tag{4}$$

This shows how risk-sharing weakens incentives. If the agent were risk-neutral ($r_a = 0$), then (4) would collapse to $\boldsymbol{\alpha}^j = \mathbf{b}_0$. The agent's receipt for marginal output would equal the principals' combined valuation; the incentives would have 100 percent power. When the agent is risk-averse ($r_a > 0$), it becomes optimal to share some risk with him, and this leads to weaker incentives. As $r_a \to \infty$ in (4), $\boldsymbol{\alpha}^j + \mathbf{b}_a \to 0$. If the principals are so risk-averse as to make r_0 significant, then the agent bears more risk, and the optimal incentives are more powerful.

Holmström and Milgrom (1991) show how the multidimensional efforts and outputs interact to weaken incentives. I shall take this for granted and focus on the extra effect that arises when the principals cannot collude. Now the situation is a two-stage game; in the first stage the principals choose their (linear) incentive schemes, and in the second stage the agent chooses his optimal action (effort) given the aggregate of the incentives offered. I look for a subgame-perfect equilibrium.

Let $\boldsymbol{\alpha}^s$ denote the sum of the principals' $\boldsymbol{\alpha}_i$ in this equilibrium, that is, the aggregate marginal incentives received by the agent when the principals act separately. Suppose that all principals have equal risk-aversion R, so $r_0 = R/n$. Then it can be shown that:[3]

$$[\mathbf{G} + n(r_0 + r_a)\Omega](\boldsymbol{\alpha}^s + \mathbf{b}_a) = [\mathbf{G} + nr_0\Omega](\mathbf{b}_0 + \mathbf{b}_a). \tag{5}$$

Compare this with the jointly optimal incentives $\boldsymbol{\alpha}^j$ defined by (4). The two formulas are identical except that all the risk-aversion parameters in (5) are multiplied by n, the number of principals.

The magnification of the agent's risk-aversion is what leads to weak incentives in a common agency. In fact if the principals are risk-neutral, as is often supposed in agency models, this is the only new effect, and it magnifies n-fold any problems with incentives that might exist even with unified principals. The point is not merely that when some principals dislike some objectives there are cancellations when their valuation vectors $\mathbf{b}_i$ are added to get $\mathbf{b}_0$; that effect if any was already present in (4) where the principals acted jointly. Rather, there is now an externality among the principals. Each principal can strike a mutually beneficial deal with the agent by offering some insurance (negative marginal payment) for outcomes of tasks that are primarily of interest to other principals. The cost of this, namely, lower effort in those dimensions, is borne by those others. This negative externality is over-provided in Nash equilibrium. The same applies to all principals; therefore incentives are weak all round.

If the competing political principals are risk-averse, they are not able to pool their risk-aversion as in (3). The effect of the principals' risk-aversion in (5) is also multiplied n-fold as compared to (4); this may restore some power to incentives.

But suppose the number of principals n is very large. In (5), nr_0 stays constant at R, the risk-aversion of each principal, while nr_a goes to infinity. Then (5) becomes $\boldsymbol{\alpha}^s + \mathbf{b}_a = \mathbf{0}$, and the agent's action is $x = 0$. The principals do not merely provide no extra incentive, leaving the agent to follow his own motivation. If that were the case, a constitutional rule or procedure that endows each government agency with a clear mission, and relies on self-selection to recruit agents dedicated to this mission, would obviate the need for incentives. Rather, in equilibrium the incentives exactly offset the chosen agent's motives, leading to inaction.

Better solutions may be possible at a prior stage where the constitution is written, or rules of the political game are fixed. First, one may restrict the principals' incentive schemes so that each one is allowed to observe and reward only the dimension of output that concerns him. If different kinds of efforts are substitutes in the agent's utility, this makes each principal offer strong incentives in an attempt to attract the agent's effort to his own concerns (see Dixit, 1996, pp. 170–1). Second, it may be possible to group together principals whose interests are better aligned, who can then collude within each group. Devolution of political power to states or localities can achieve this. Third, agencies can be so designed that each performs fewer tasks, thus reducing the externalities among the principals affected by its actions.

III   Politicization of Private Firms

Private firms are supposed to have just one principal, namely, the shareholders. These may be a diverse group, but capital markets with a sufficiently rich menu of assets align their interests. The executive officers and the board of directors have almost total control over the incentives of the managers and the workers. This creates its own agency problems, but they are not of the political multi-principal kind.

Recently in the United States and the United Kingdom a concept of a "stakeholder economy" has evolved, according to which firms are supposed to be responsible not merely to their shareholders, but to a more varied collection of "stakeholders": workers, creditors, the local community, and so forth. If this comes to be accepted and built into the legal and organizational structure of corporations, all these groups will become principals, with firms as their common agents. Such "politicization" of firms will further lower the power of incentives, which is often already low for other reasons.

We have multi-principal politics for a reason, namely, to provide checks and balances against biased or arbitrary exercise of power. This was emphasized in the *Federalist Papers*, especially Numbers 10 and 51; Tirole (1994, section 8) develops some formal analysis. But one should recognize that this benefit comes with an attendant cost, namely, weak incentives, which can lead to indecision or gridlock. In politics, as in economics, the first-best is elusive, and we must accept many unsatisfactory compromises.

Notes

*   Department of Economics, Princeton University, Princeton, NJ 08544-1021. I thank participants in a seminar at the London School of Economics and my discussant, Edward Lazear, for perceptive comments, and the National Science Foundation for financial support.
1   The algebra is messy but not difficult to reconstruct; the derivations are in an unpublished appendix available upon request from the author.

2   If any components of x are observable, they can simply be included as components of y, so the formal model is actually more general.

3   The unpublished appendix (which is available from the author upon request) considers the more general case of unequal risk-aversions and derives a similar but more messy formula.

References

Dixit, Avinash (1996) *The Making of Economic Policy*. Cambridge, MA: MIT Press.

Gore, Al (1995) *Common Sense Government*. New York: Random House.

Heckman, James, Smith, Jeffrey, and Taber, Christopher (1996) What Do Bureaucrats Do? In *Advances in the Study of Entrepreneurship, Innovation, and Growth*, vol. 7. Greenwich, CT: JAI Press. pp. 197–217.

Holmström, Bengt (1989) Agency Costs and Innovation. *Journal of Economic Behavior and Organization* (December) 12(3): 305–27.

Holmström, Bengt and Milgrom, Paul (1991) Multitask Principal–Agent Analysis. *Journal of Law, Economics, and Organization*, Special Issue, 7: 24–51.

Martimort, David (1995) The Multiprincipal Nature of Government. Mimeo, IDEI, Toulouse, France.

Rose-Ackerman, Susan (1986) Reforming Public Bureaucracy through Economic Incentives? *Journal of Law, Economics, and Organization* (Spring) 2(1): 131–61.

Tirole, Jean (1994) The Internal Organization of Government. *Oxford Economic Papers* (January) 46(1): pp. 1–29.

Williamson, Oliver (1985) *The Economic Institution of Capitalism*. New York: Free Press.

Wilson, James (1989) *Bureaucracy*. New York: Basic Books.

Extracts from Avinash Dixit, *The Making of Economic Policy: A Transaction Cost*. Cambridge, MA: MIT Press, 1996, pp. 94–102.

The Low Power of Incentives in Policymaking

... The brief review above dealt with incentive schemes that can be implemented by a benevolent dictator to elicit some information or effort from private firms and consumers in an attempt to implement a better economic outcome. Incentive schemes can influence the information and actions of the political or administrative institutions themselves. These differ from corresponding schemes that we see in private economic transactions in some important ways: the rewards or penalties are often nonmonetary, and the incentives are often low-powered.

Even in economic contexts, rewards or penalties may be financial or nonmonetary. The former category must be interpreted broadly to include career concerns, that is, future material rewards as well as the immediate payoff; similarly, a broad interpretation of nonmonetary incentives includes status, power, and job satisfaction. In political contexts the nonfinancial aspects are likely to be more important than in economics. Even with this understanding, however, it is commonly observed that incentives for policymakers are quite low-powered; the marginal rewards for producing an outcome of greater value to society, or the marginal penalties for doing worse, are generally a very low percentage of the value added or lost. A bureaucrat in the Office of Management and Budget, or an international trade negotiator, can take actions that benefit or hurt the economy to the tune of billions of dollars, but the effect on his own compensation, monetary or otherwise, is at most a very tiny fraction of this. Much of the commonly held belief that political processes and institutions cope poorly with agency problems can be attributed to the low power of their incentives. Previous analysts have offered several reasons for this; I will now review them and add another that seems to me to be of even greater importance.

The discussion can be organized by reference to Wilson's (1989) excellent observations about agency relationships in government bureaucracies. He identifies two key features: (1) government bureaucracies typically have several dimensions of effort (input) and result (output), and each of these is only imperfectly observable or verifiable (pp. 129–31); (2) each agency deals with several "principals" who are simultaneously trying to influence its decisions – the executive and legislative branches of government, the courts, interest groups, media, and so on (pp. 236–7, 300). Wilson argues that, as a result, the principals impose a variety of constraints on the agency, instead of the kind of powerful incentive schemes that are more commonly suggested in economic agency problems (pp. 115, 125, 133, 332). The outcome, according to Wilson, is that government agencies can stop things from happening but find it difficult to get anything positive done (p. 317). Wilson's argument is informal, but sufficiently intriguing to be worth formal exploration using the modern theories of multitask and common agencies.

Multitask agencies

Holmström and Milgrom (1991) have developed a model of multitask agencies that helps us understand some of the features of government agencies stressed by Wilson. The agent has to perform several tasks, which are at least partly competing for the agent's attention and effort. The agency's priorities over these tasks do not coincide with those of the principal, perhaps because they require different qualities of effort, or because new tasks have less value to the agency in terms of its original mission. In any case, the principal must devise an incentive scheme to alter the effort allocation of the agent. The choice will depend on the degree of observability of different inputs and outputs, as well as on the differences in values between the two parties.

Holmström and Milgrom (1991) find two important results. First, if the result of one task is very poorly observable, then the incentive scheme for a competing task must have lower power in order to avoid excessive diversion of effort away from this task to more observable ones. Second, if some tasks are primarily of value to the agent, and can be controlled in an all-or-nothing fashion, then it may be desirable for the principal to simply prohibit these, rather than try to give extra incentives for others. This point is especially important if the incentives for other tasks must be low-powered in conformity with the first result.

An example close to home will make the point clear. University professors have two tasks, teaching and research. The output of research is relatively easily measurable in terms of prestigious publication and citations; that of teaching is more nebulous because the real effects are long term, and the students' evaluations have their own biases. If the university considered each task and its incentives in isolation, it would recognize the different precisions of information and set up a high-powered reward scheme for research and a low-powered one for teaching; but that would induce professors to divert effort away from teaching and into research. Therefore, considering the two together, the university is forced to reduce the power of its scheme for rewarding research, too.[1]

Now introduce a third activity, outside consulting, that is primarily of value to the professor rather than to the university. If the reward schemes for teaching *and* research are low-powered for the reasons explained above, then teachers will divert their effort into consulting. The university could cope with this by increasing the power of the incentives for teaching and research together, but that is a costly alternative because teaching effort is not easily observable. (The reward must be based on observables such as students' performance or their evaluations of the teaching; therefore teachers may get rewarded for their luck in having better students, or for gimmicks that appeal to students and raise the evaluations without really improving the quality of the education.) The university therefore instead prohibits consulting, or at least restricts the time allowed for it. Some consulting will be allowed if that makes it easier to ensure that the professor gets enough utility from the whole bundle of activities to be willing to work for the university, that is, to satisfy the professor's individual rationality (participation) constraint. But this calculation will involve comparing the average product of consulting time and the marginal reward for teaching and research. A full social optimum would equate the marginal products of the two. This departure from the ideal is the unavoidable cost of the information asymmetry in this case.

Laffont and Tirole (1993, pp. 225–6) and Tirole (1994, pp. 6–7) develop this idea further. When the output of the agent's effort is an "experience good" whose quality will be revealed only with a delay, then the immediate incentive scheme must be low-powered so as not to destroy the incentive to maintain quality.

Multiprincipal agencies

Let us turn to the second important feature of government bureaucracies that was pointed out by Wilson, namely, the existence of multiple principals, all of whom have some power to influence the actions of the agency. Their interests in the outputs of the agency are at least partly in conflict, and the agent's actions taken on behalf of different principals are substitutes. How do incentive schemes fare in such a situation? The general conclusion is that the power of incentives in the equilibrium among several such principals is weakened, sometimes dramatically.

Let us begin by asking why common agency is so prevalent. The various principals clearly stand to gain by getting together: the scheme that results from their noncooperative actions remains feasible, so a cooperative scheme cannot do worse and in general will do better. At least two problems may preclude such collusion. First, they may not share the same information, most naturally so in the case of adverse selection. Although this seems to force noncooperative behavior, I will argue later that the compartmentalization of information may actually be beneficial. Second, the multiple principals may find it difficult to agree on the split of the total gain from cooperation, or be unable to make the internal transfers necessary to implement an agreed-upon split. This is particularly important in the political context, where the benefits of the principals are often nonmonetary and are measured in noncomparable, nontransferable units, whereas monetary compensations are often illegal.

Later I construct a simple model of common agency with moral hazard to show that the multiplicity of conflicting principals is a powerful additional reason for the incentive schemes to be low-powered. The intuition is that each principal tries to free ride on the incentives provided by the others.

To illustrate the mathematics in simple terms, suppose two principals A and B are trying to influence the agent, who controls two tasks a and b. Principal A is primarily interested in the outcome of a, and principal B in that of b. The amount of effort the agent devotes to the tasks is not observable, but the outcomes are commonly observable to all.

Since the agent's time or effort is scarce, more spent on a will necessarily mean less spent on b and vice versa. Therefore principal A will offer an incentive scheme that responds positively to a-output and negatively to b-output, that is, one that gives the agent a marginal reward for producing more a and a marginal fine or penalty for producing more b. The scheme also has a constant term, or a sure payment, whose level can be adjusted to make sure that the agent is willing to work, that is, to satisfy the agent's participation constraint. Similarly, principal B offers a scheme that rewards the agent for producing more of b and penalizes him for producing more of a.

Now suppose principal A offers a high-powered scheme, that is, one with larger marginal reward for producing an extra unit of a. When the agent responds by making more effort on task a, he gets more money from principal A; but because principal B employs a negative marginal payment for this task, the agent pays more to principal B. In other words, some of A's money simply passes to B via the agent. Recognizing this, principal A will not find it desirable to offer such a high-powered scheme. The leakage of one principal's money to the other is less than one-for-one, so each principal continues to find it desirable to offer some incentives to the agent; but in the final outcome of the whole calculation, that is, the Nash equilibrium of the game of strategy between the principals, the overall power of the incentives received by the agent is quite low.

In the mathematical model, the outcome is very simple: the equilibrium with n principals is exactly as if there is just one hypothetical principal with an objective function that is the sum of all the separate principals' objectives, but the agent's risk aversion is multiplied n-fold. Remember that the more risk averse the agent, the lower the power of the incentive scheme. Thus, the Nash equilibrium incentive scheme with n principals has, roughly speaking, only $(1/n)$-th the power of the second-best scheme that would be offered by one truly unified principal.

The low power of the incentives in turn makes the second result of Holmström and Milgrom even more important. The agent's actions may often be influenced better by prohibiting some activities than by rewarding others with conventional marginal incentives.

One must distinguish different levels of efficiency in the outcomes. The hypothetical ideal with observable efforts and Coasean bargaining between all principals and the agent would be the first-best. Respecting the information asymmetry but allowing all principals to get together and offer a combined incentive scheme would give the second-best. If the principals cannot be so united, their Nash equilibrium is in general a third-best (see Bernheim and Whinston 1986 for the exact relationships among these). In these formal terms, the result above says that the third-best outcome that is achieved has very low-powered incentives.

To do better than the Nash equilibrium, one would have to allow some explicit cooperation among the multiple principals. This may not be feasible in the context of their day-today interaction or in the course of what I have called policy acts; but at a prior stage, closer to that of Buchanan's constitution design, we may be able to think of some improvements. One such device would restrict each principal to basing his incentive scheme only on the dimension of the agent's action that is of primary concern to that principal, and would prohibit any attempts to penalize the agent for actions in other dimensions. In the example above, this means that principal A cannot condition his payment to the agent on the output of task b, nor principal B on that of task a. This could be done by preventing each from observing the other's outcome, or forbidding each to act on any such observation. Now each principal, in order to attempt to induce the agent to put more effort into the task that concerns him (principal), offers a higher-powered incentive scheme. In the resulting equilibrium, the overall incentive scheme is actually higher powered than the one that would be offered by a single unified principal who aggregates the interests of A and B. It is shown later that in the limiting case where the agent's efforts on behalf of the different principals become perfect substitutes, the equilibrium where the principals are so restricted in their schemes is actually first-best! Thus a constitutional restriction on the actions of principals can improve the power of incentives and can lead to a socially preferable outcome.[2] Of course, as usual, the enforcement of such a constitutional restriction is problematic, given the desire of politically powerful principals in their policy acts to influence every dimension of the agent's activity.

Note that even if each of A and B can observe the outputs of both tasks a and b, it may be beneficial to forbid each to take the other into account in setting his own incentive scheme, just as if he could not observe the outcome of the other task. Thus an improvement can result from making the information asymmetry apparently worse. This is like the Lipsey–Lancaster general theory of the second-best: if some market failure precludes the attainment of an ideal first-best, then it is no longer necessarily desirable to let the rest of the markets function without any interference.

Tirole (1994, section 8) suggests that compartmentalization of responsibilities across different ministries or agencies of the government can perform a useful function by placing the onus to create, disclose, and defend each item of information necessary for decision-making on the party who is particularly interested in that dimension of policy. This argument for "checks and balances" is similar to that behind the adversarial mode of judicial procedures in common law. This idea is formally modeled and further developed by Dewatripont and Tirole (1995). My argument above is different, but it supports the same conclusion.

A similar phenomenon arises in common agencies with adverse selection; these are studied by Martimort (1992, 1995) and Stole (1990). They assume (as seems appropriate in the context of adverse selection) that each principal can observe only that dimension of the outcome which concerns his payoffs. Each offers a rent-sharing schedule that makes his payment to the agent a function of that dimension of output. If the two principals collaborate, they will offer a second-best joint schedule that reduces their loss of rent by distorting the agent's actions below their first-best level. When they cannot cooperate, for example, when each cannot observe or act upon the other's outcome, there arises an externality between them. When one principal increases the distortion of his dimension, the agent shifts his action at the margin to the other dimension, to the benefit of the other principal. This is a positive externality, so in the noncooperative equilibrium each principal carries out too little of it. In other words, the noncooperative equilibrium has less distortion than the cooperative one, and so the former is closer to the full-information first-best than the latter. As in the case of moral hazard, the compartmentalization of information increases the power of the incentives toward the first-best.[3]

A very different kind of effect of multiple principals is found in the argument of James Madison in his famous tenth Federalist Paper. He says that when several special interest groups – "factions" in his terminology – are trying to influence the decisions of the government, none of them is likely to prevail over the others, and the result will be the pursuit of general or aggregate national interest. This finds partial support in the formal models of Becker (1983), and most particularly, of Grossman and Helpman (1994). They consider competition among organized special-interest groups to influence tariff policy. They find that if the entire population belongs to one organized group or another, the equilibrium policy is one of free trade. But this is a kind of Prisoners' Dilemma: in the process every group gives a contribution in its attempt to influence the decision, so the distribution of the output is not the same as it would be if there were no lobbying at all.

Epstein and O'Halloran (1994) model a common agency with adverse selection in a more directly political setting. Consider two interest groups offering contributions to a legislator in exchange for policies. They find if the strengths of the two groups are very unequal, the resulting policy is the same as it would be if only the stronger group were present, but the rent given to the agent is larger in order to meet the potential competition of the other group. But if the groups attain a minimum strength, which they call a "representation floor," then the agent is no longer captured by one of them, and the resulting policy is efficient. This qualifies Madison's argument from the other side. He feared the emergence of a faction so large that it would constitute a majority and impose its will on others; this result shows that a mere multiplicity of opposing interests is not a guarantee of efficiency unless the smaller factions have a certain minimum size.[4]

Lack of competition

Tirole (1994, p. 4) offers yet another explanation for the low-powered incentives in policymaking. If there are several agents performing similar tasks and subject to common risks, then each agent's performance can be compared with that of the others to get a better estimate of his effort or skills that were not directly observable. Therefore an incentive scheme based on comparative performance, or "yardstick competition," can be effective and high-powered. In politics and bureaucracy, such competition is often limited or even nonexistent; therefore incentives must have lower power. In some cases, for example provision of some urban services, competition can exist or even be created for the specific purpose of allowing better incentive schemes. We increasingly observe examples of this in garbage collection, mail delivery, and even in policing and prison management; Britain has recently set up an internal market mechanism in its National Health Service. However, the multitask nature of these activities often precludes the use of such devices to their full extent; there exist other "principals" who are more interested in other dimensions of these agencies such as equity and accountability, and their influence limits the use of competition to promote efficiency (see Wilson 1989, chapter 19).

Lack of transparency

Spiller (1990) offers a different perspective on the common agency aspect. He considers the Congress and special interests as principals, with the regulators as agents. But these are in a vertical relationship: Congress creates the agency and appoints regulators, who then can convey benefits – economic rents – to the special interests. These interests can reward the regulators by offering them post-government jobs. Congress can use its appointment power to extract these rents in the form of direct or indirect contributions from potential regulators. For example, many regulators are appointed from the ranks of Congressional staff.

This model seems to confirm the worst fears of those who regard government as the pessimum form of economic management; but so long as the agency relationship is necessitated by an underlying information problem (a transaction cost), the system may have found the least-cost way of coping with that problem. If an ethics bill is passed prohibiting a public servant from going on to work or lobby for the industry that he formerly regulated, then the special interests and politicians may find an even costlier way of arranging their relationships. When rents exist, there will be competition for them, and the only question for design of feasible policy is to minimize the costs of that competition.

Transparency is generally regarded as a good thing in policymaking (see Krueger 1990 for a good statement of arguments in its favor). Greater transparency often makes information more accurate and more symmetric; therefore it reduces or even eliminates some transaction costs. To this extent the argument is clearly valid, but the Spiller model suggests that transparency may sometimes make matters worse. Some mechanisms, such as employment links between the public sector and business, may be relatively good ways of coping with transaction costs, but making them more transparent may simply lead to a prohibition on their use, either on moral grounds or because it is a visible symptom of the underlying inefficiency. So long as that basic problem persists, these mechanisms will merely be substituted by other, even less efficient ones.

If it is desirable to preserve some opaqueness for such strategic reasons, the observations of outcomes will not be as informative as they could be, and incentive schemes based on these observables will have to be lower-powered. We saw earlier that diversion of effort into a nonobservable activity lowers the power of incentives based on observable outcomes of other activities; here some other considerations make it desirable to keep some activities unobservable, thus reinforcing that phenomenon.

To sum up, the formal analysis gives some support to Wilson's assertion that government bureaucracies often have low-powered incentives and are subjected to constraints on their behavior. The analysis also casts some new light on the phenomenon. The lack of incentives, and the proliferation of the constraints, are often claimed to be proof of inefficiency of government. Agencies often have to say no. Nothing gets done, or at least requires long delays to ensure that all the constraints have been met. In the model, however, the weak incentives, and the prohibitions or constraints, can emerge as a part of the Nash equilibrium. In other words, they may be a reasonable way for the system to cope with the transaction costs. I would not claim that what one finds in reality is always a constrained optimum, but at least the result suggests that we should not jump to the opposite conclusion either.

Notes

1 A better solution may be greater specialization among universities. Some can place more emphasis and reward on research, while others concentrate on teaching; then, each will attract the type of students who value its favored activity relatively more highly. In the context of politics, such specialization is not be feasible for national governments, although it may be for localities within a country.
2 Holmström and Milgrom (1990) have a similar result concerning the desirability of restricting side trading among multiple agents of one principal.
3 The argument will go the other way if the agent's actions for the two principals are complements; in this case there are further complications including nonuniqueness of equilibrium.
4 Cassing and Hillman (1986) have a "catastrophe-theory" model where the political power of a special-interest group collapses suddenly when its size falls below a minimum threshold.

References

Becker, Gary W. (1983) "A Theory of Competition among Pressure Groups for Political Influence." *Quarterly Journal of Economics*, 98, no. 3: 371–400.

Bernheim, B. Douglas, and Michael Whinston (1986) "Common Agency." *Econometrica*, 54, no. 4: 911–30.

Cassing, James H., and Arye L. Hillman (1986) "Shifting Comparative Advantage and Senescent Industry Collapse." *American Economic Review*, 76, no. 3: 516–23.

Dewatripont, Mathias, and Jean Tirole (1995) "Advocates." Working paper, ECARE, Institut d'Etudes Européennes, Brussell, April.

Epstein, David, and Sharyn O'Halloran (1994) "Common Agency and Representation." Working paper, Columbia University, April.

Grossman, Gene M., and Elhanan Helpman (1994) "Protection for Sale." *American Economic Review*, 84, no. 4: 833–50.

Holmström, Bengt, and Paul Milgrom (1990) "Regulating Trade Among Agents." *Journal of Institutional and Theoretical Economics*, 146, no. 1: 85–105.

Holmström, Bengt, and Paul Milgrom (1991) "Multitask Principal–Agent Analysis: Incentive Contracts, Asset Ownership, and Job Design." *Journal of Law, Economics, and Organization*, 7, Special Issue: 24–51.

Krueger, Anne O. (1990) "The Political Economy of Controls: American Sugar." In *Public Policy and Economic Development*, eds. Maurice Scott and Deepak Lal. Oxford: Clarendon Press.

Laffont, Jean-Jacques, and Jean Tirole (1993) *A Theory of Incentives in Procurement and Regulation* (Cambridge, MA: MIT Press).

Martimort, David (1992) "Multi-Principaux avec Anti-Selection." *Annales D'Économie et de Statistique*, no. 28, pp. 1–37.

Martimort, David (1995) "Exclusive Dealing, Common Agency, and Multiprincipals Incentive Theory." Working paper, IDEI, Université des Sciences Sociales, Toulouse.

Spiller, Pablo T. (1990) "Politicians, Interest Groups, and Regulators." *Journal of Law and Economics*, 23, no. 1: 65–101.

Stole, Lars (1990) "Mechanism Design under Common Agency." Working paper, MIT, Cambridge, MA.

Tirole, Jean (1994) "The Internal Organization of Government." *Oxford Economic Papers*, 46, no. 1: 1–29.

Wilson, James Q. (1989) *Bureaucracy: What Government Agencies Do and Why They Do It*. New York: Basic Books.

PART V

The Political Process, Voting, and Public Choice

FIFTEEN

The Statics and Dynamics of Party Ideologies

ANTHONY DOWNS

Source: From Anthony Downs, *An Economic Theory of Democracy*. New York: Harper & Row, 1957, pp. 114–41.

Introduction

If political ideologies are truly means to the end of obtaining votes, and if we know something about the distribution of voters' preferences, we can make specific predictions about how ideologies change in content as parties maneuver to gain power. Or, conversely, we can state the conditions under which ideologies come to resemble each other, diverge from each other, or remain in some fixed relationship.

Objectives

In this chapter we attempt to prove the following propositions:

1 A two-party democracy cannot provide stable and effective government unless there is a large measure of ideological consensus among its citizens.
2 Parties in a two-party system deliberately change their platforms so that they resemble one another; whereas parties in a multi-party system try to remain as ideologically distinct from each other as possible.
3 If the distribution of ideologies in a society's citizenry remains constant, its political system will move toward a position of equilibrium in which the number of parties and their ideological positions are stable over time.
4 New parties can be most successfully launched immediately after some significant change in the distribution of ideological views among eligible voters.
5 In a two-party system, it is rational for each party to encourage voters to be irrational by making its platform vague and ambiguous.

I   The Spatial Analogy and its Early Use

To carry out this analysis, we borrow and elaborate upon an apparatus invented by Harold Hotelling. It first appeared in a famous article on spatial competition published in

1929, and was later refined by Arthur Smithies.[1] Our version of Hotelling's spatial market consists of a linear scale running from zero to 100 in the usual left-to-right fashion. To make this politically meaningful, we assume that political preferences can be ordered from left to right in a manner agreed upon by all voters. They need not agree on which point they personally prefer, only on the ordering of parties from one extreme to the other.

In addition, we assume that every voter's preferences are single-peaked and slope downward monotonically on either side of the peak (unless his peak lies at one extreme on the scale). For example, if a voter likes position 35 best, we can immediately deduce that he prefers 30 to 25 and 40 to 45. He always prefers some point X to another point Y if X is closer to 35 than Y and both are on the same side of 35. The slope downward from the apex need not be identical on both sides, but we do presume no sharp asymmetry exists.

These assumptions can perhaps be made more plausible if we reduce all political questions to their bearing upon one crucial issue: how much government intervention in the economy should there be? If we assume that the left end of the scale represents full government control, and the right end means a completely free market, we can rank parties by their views on this issue in a way that might be nearly universally recognized as accurate. In order to coordinate this left–right orientation with our numerical scale, we will arbitrarily assume that the number denoting any party's position indicates the percentage of the economy it wants left in private hands (excluding those minimal state operations which even the most Hayekian economists favor). Thus the extreme left position is zero, and the extreme right is 100. Admittedly, this apparatus is unrealistic for the following two reasons: (1) actually each party is leftish on some issues and rightish on others, and (2) the parties designated as right-wing extremists in the real world are for fascist control of the economy rather than free markets. However, we will ignore these limitations temporarily and see what conclusions of interest we can draw from this spatial analogy.

Both Hotelling and Smithies have already applied their versions of this model to politics. Hotelling assumed that people were evenly spaced along the straight-line scale, and reasoned that competition in a two-party system would cause each party to move towards its opponent ideologically. Such convergence would occur because each party knows that extremists at its end of the scale prefer it to the opposition, since it is necessarily closer to them than the opposition party is. Therefore the best way for it to gain more support is to move toward the other extreme, so as to get more voters outside of it – i.e., to come between them and its opponent. As the two parties move closer together, they become more moderate and less extreme in policy in an effort to win the crucial middle-of-the-road voters, i.e., those whose views place them between the two parties. This center area becomes smaller and smaller as both parties strive to capture moderate votes; finally the two parties become nearly identical in platforms and actions. For example, if there is one voter at every point on the scale, and parties A and B start at points 25 and 75 respectively, they will move towards each other and meet at 50, assuming they move at the same speed (figure 15.1). Like the two grocery stores in Hotelling's famous example, they will converge on the same location until practically all voters are indifferent between them.

Smithies improved this model by introducing elastic demand at each point on the scale. Thus as the grocery stores moved away from the extremes, they lost customers there because of the increased cost of transportation; this checked them from coming together at the center. In our model, this is analogous to political extremists becoming disgusted at the

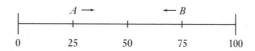

Figure 15.1

Note for figures 15.1–15.9: Horizontal scale represents political orientation; vertical scale represents number of citizens.

identity of the parties, and refusing to vote for either if they become too much alike. At exactly what point this leakage checks the convergence of *A* and *B* depends upon how many extremists each loses by moving towards the center compared with how many moderates it gains thereby.

II The Effects of Various Distributions of Voters

In two-party systems

An important addition we can make to this model is a variable distribution of voters along the scale. Instead of assuming there is one voter at each point on the scale, let us assume there are 100,000 voters whose preferences cause them to be normally distributed with a mean of 50 (figure 15.2). Again, if we place parties *A* and *B* initially at 25 and 75, they will converge rapidly upon the center. The possible loss of extremists will not deter their movement toward each other, because there are so few voters to be lost at the margins compared with the number to be gained in the middle. However, if we alter the distribution to that shown in figure 15.3, the two parties will not move away from their initial positions at 25 and 75 at all; if they did, they would lose far more voters at the extremes than they could possibly gain in the center. Therefore a two-party system need not lead to the convergence on moderation that Hotelling and Smithies predicted. If voters' preferences are distributed so that voters are massed bimodally near the extremes, the parties will remain poles apart in ideology.

The possibility that parties will be kept from converging ideologically in a two-party system depends upon the refusal of extremist voters to support either party if both become

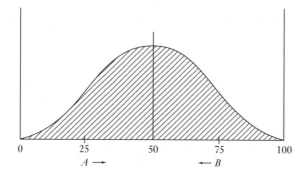

Figure 15.2

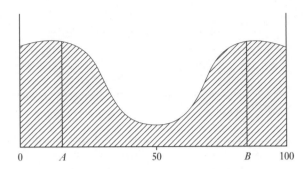

Figure 15.3

alike – not identical, but merely similar. In a certain world – where information is complete and costless, there is no future-oriented voting, and the act of voting uses up no scarce resources – such abstention by extremists would be irrational. As long as there is even the most infinitesimal difference between *A* and *B*, extremist voters would be forced to vote for the one closest to them, no matter how distasteful its policies seemed in comparison with those of their ideal government. It is always rational *ex definitione* to select a greater good before a lesser, or a lesser evil before a greater; consequently, abstention would be irrational because it increases the chances of the worse party for victory.

Even in a certain world, however, abstention is rational for extremist voters who are future oriented. They are willing to let the worse party win today in order to keep the better party from moving towards the center, so that in future elections it will be closer to them. Then when it does win, its victory is more valuable in their eyes. Abstention thus becomes a threat to use against the party nearest one's own extreme position so as to keep it away from the center.[2]

Uncertainty increases the possibility that rational extremist voters will abstain if the party nearest them moves toward its opponent, even if it does not become ideologically identical with the latter. When information is limited and costly, it is difficult to detect infinitesimal differences between parties. Perhaps even relatively significant differences will pass un-noticed by the radical whose own views are so immoderate that all moderates look alike. This means that the differential threshold of such extremists is likely to be very high – they will regard all small differences between moderate parties as irrelevant to their voting decision, i.e., as unreal distinctions.

Having established the rationality of abstention by extremist voters, let us again consider a bimodal distribution of voters with modes near each extreme (figure 15.3). In a two-party system, whichever party wins will attempt to implement policies radically opposed to the other party's ideology, since the two are at opposite extremes. This means that government policy will be highly unstable, and that democracy is likely to produce chaos. Unfortunately, the growth of balancing center parties is unlikely. Any party which forms in the center will eventually move toward one extreme or the other to increase its votes, since there are so few moderate voters. Furthermore, any center party could govern only in coalition with one of the extremist parties, which would alienate the other, and thus not eliminate the basic problem. In such a situation, unless voters can somehow be moved to the center of the scale to eliminate their polar split, democratic government is not going to function at all well. In fact, no government can operate so as to please most of the people; hence this situation may lead to revolution.

The political cycle typical of revolutions can be viewed as a series of movements of men along the political scale.[3] Preliminary to the upheaval, the once centralized distribution begins to polarize into two extremes as the incumbents increasingly antagonize those who feel themselves oppressed. When the distribution has become so split that one extreme is imposing by force policies abhorred by the other extreme, open warfare breaks out, and a clique of underdogs seizes power. This radical switch from one extreme to the other is partly responsible for the reign of terror which marks most revolutions; the new governors want to eliminate their predecessors, who have bitterly opposed them. Finally violence exhausts itself, a new concensus is reached on the principles of the revolution, and the distribution becomes centralized again – often under a new dictatorship as rigid as the old, but not faced with a polarized distribution of opinions.[4]

Under more normal circumstances, in countries where there are two opposite social classes and no sizeable middle class, the numerical distribution is more likely to be skewed to the left, with a small mode at the right extreme (figure 15.4). The large mode at the left represents the lower or working class; on the right is the upper class. Here democracy, if effective, will bring about the installation of a leftish government because of the numerical preponderance of the lower classes. Fear of this result is precisely what caused many European aristocrats to fight the introduction of universal suffrage. Of course, our schema oversimplifies the situation considerably. On our political scale, every voter has equal weight with every other, whereas in fact the unequal distribution of income allows a numerically small group to control political power quite disproportionate to its size.

In spite of this oversimplification, it is clear that the numerical distribution of voters along the political scale determines to a great extent what kind of democracy will develop. For example, a distribution like that of figure 15.2 encourages a two-party system with both parties located near the center in relatively moderate positions. This type of government is likely to have stable policies, and whichever party is in power, its policies will not be far from the views of the vast majority of people. On the other hand, if a nation's voters are distributed as shown in figure 15.5, a multiparty system will almost inevitably result.

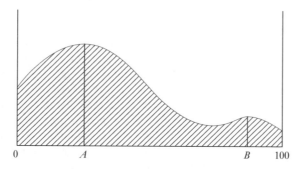

Figure 15.4

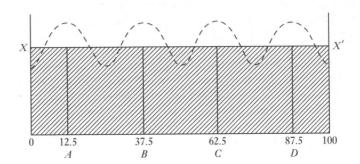

Figure 15.5

The number of parties in equilibrium

Before examining the dynamics of multiparty systems, we should point out that our political version of Hotelling's model does not suffer from the outstanding limitation of the economic version he used. In Hotelling's spatial market, it was impossible to reach stable equilibrium with more than two grocery stores. The ones in the middle would always become the target of convergence from either side; consequently they would leap to the outside to keep from being squeezed. There was no device to restrict the perfect mobility that caused this disequilibrium.

But political parties cannot move ideologically past each other. Integrity and responsibility create relative immobility, which prevents a party from making ideological leaps over the heads of its neighbors. Thus ideological movement is restricted to horizontal progress at most up to – and never beyond – the nearest party on either side. Coupled with our device of variable distribution, this attribute of the model nearly always ensures stable equilibrium.

It is true that new parties can be introduced between two formerly adjacent ones or outside one of them. Nevertheless, this possibility cannot upset stable equilibrium in the long run for two reasons. First, once a party has come into being, it cannot leap over the heads of its neighbors, as explained. Second, there is a limit to the number of parties which can be supported by any one distribution. When that limit is reached, no more new parties can be successfully introduced. The parties extant at that point arrange themselves through competition so that no party can gain more votes by moving to the right than it loses on the left by doing so, and vice versa. The political system thus reaches a state of long-run equilibrium in so far as the number and positions of its parties are concerned, assuming no change in the distribution of voters along the scale.

Whether the political system contains two or many parties in this state of equilibrium depends upon (1) the nature of the limit upon the introduction of new parties, and (2) the shape of the distribution of voters. We will examine these factors in order.

In our model, every party is a team of men who seek to attain office – a party cannot survive in the long run if none of its members get elected.[5] But in order to get at least some of its members elected, the party must gain the support of a certain minimum number of voters. The size of this minimum depends upon the type of electoral system in operation.

To get any of its members in office at all, a party in our model must win more votes than any other party running. This arrangement encourages parties which repeatedly lose to merge with each other so as to capture a combined total of votes larger than the total received by the party which repeatedly wins. Such amalgamation continues until each of the survivors has a reasonable chance of winning a majority of the votes cast, which is the only way it can be sure of gaining office. Thus the winner-take-all outcome of a plurality electoral structure tends to narrow the field to two competing parties.[6]

Where proportional representation exists, a party which wins only a small percentage of the total vote may place some of its members in the government, since coalition governments often rule.[7] Thus the minimum amount of support necessary to keep a party going is much smaller than in a plurality system; so a multiparty system is encouraged. Nevertheless, each party must still obtain a certain minimum number of votes in order to elect members of the legislature who might possibly enter a coalition. For this reason, a given distribution of voters can support only a limited number of parties even under proportional representation.[8] Therefore the conditions for equilibrium exist in both two- and multiparty systems.

The type of electoral structure extant in a political system may be either a cause or a result of the original distribution of voters along the scale. Thus if the distribution has a single mode around which nearly all voters are clustered, the framers of the electoral structure may believe that plurality rule will not cause any large group to be ignored politically. Or if the distribution has many small modes, the law-makers may choose proportional representation in order to allow sizeable extremist groups to have a voice in government.

Causality can also be reversed because the number of parties in existence molds the political views of rising generations, thereby influencing their positions on the scale. In a plurality structure, since a two-party system is encouraged and the two parties usually converge, voters' tastes may become relatively homogeneous in the long run; whereas the opposite effect may occur in a proportional representation structure.

From this analysis it is clear that both the electoral structure and the distribution of voters are important in determining how many parties a given democracy will contain when it reaches equilibrium. Each factor influences the other indirectly, but it also has some impact independent of the other. For example, if a proportional representation system is established in a society where the distribution of voters has a single mode and a small variance, it is possible that only two parties will exist in equilibrium because there is not enough political room on the scale for more than two significantly different positions to gain measurable support.[9]

Having explored the impact of the two major types of electoral structure upon the number of parties in a political system, we will concentrate our attention from now on upon the impact of the distribution of voters along the scale. In order to do so, we assume that this distribution is the only factor in determining how many parties there are.[10]

In multiparty systems

Multiparty systems – those with three or more major parties – are likely to occur whenever the distribution of voters is polymodal. The existence of two or more outstanding modes creates conditions favorable to one party at each mode, and perhaps balancing parties between them. Figure 15.5 represents an extreme example of this structure, since voters are equally distributed along the scale (on XX′); i.e., each point on the scale is a mode (or the distribution can be seen as having no modes). However, not every point can support a party if we assume that the electoral structure allows only a certain number of parties to compete for power with reasonable chances of success. Therefore a definite number of parties will spring up along the scale and maneuver until the distance between each party and its immediately adjacent neighbors is the same for all parties. In figure 15.5 we have assumed that the total number of parties is limited to four; hence in equilibrium they will space themselves as shown (assuming extremists abstain if parties A and D move toward the center).[11]

An important difference between a distribution like that in figure 15.5 and one like that in figure 15.2 is that the former provides no incentive for parties to move toward each other ideologically. Party B in figure 15.5, for example, cannot gain more votes by moving toward A or towards C. If it started toward C, it would win votes away from C, but it would lose just as many to A; the reverse happens if it moves toward A. Therefore it will stay at 37.5 and maintain its ideological purity – unlike party B in figure 15.2.[12] The latter party is pulled toward the center because, by moving toward A, it wins more votes among the moderates than it loses among the extremists, as mentioned before.

Thus it is likely that in multiparty systems, parties will strive to distinguish themselves ideologically from each other and maintain the purity of their positions; whereas in two-party systems, each party will try to resemble its opponent as closely as possible.[13]

This phenomenon helps to explain certain peculiarities of the two political systems. If our reasoning is correct, voters in multiparty systems are much more likely to be swayed by doctrinal considerations – matters of ideology and policy – than are voters in two-party systems. The latter voters are massed in the moderate range where both ideologies lie; hence they are likely to view personality or technical competence, or some other non-ideological factor as decisive. Because they are not really offered much choice between policies, they may need other factors to discriminate between parties.

Voters in multiparty systems, however, are given a wide range of ideological choice, with parties emphasizing rather than soft-pedalling their doctrinal differences. Hence regarding ideologies as a decisive factor in one's voting decision is usually more rational in a multi-party system than in a two-party system. In spite of this fact, the ideology of the government in a multiparty system (as opposed to the parties) is often less cohesive than its counterpart in a two–party system.

III   The Origin of New Parties

In analyzing the birth of new parties, we must distinguish between two types of new parties. The first is designed *to win elections*. Its originators feel that it can locate itself so as to represent a large number of voters whose views are not being expressed by any extant party. The second type is designed *to influence already existent parties* to change their policies, or not to change them; it is not primarily aimed at winning elections.

Of course, no party is ever begun by people who think it will never get any votes, or win any offices, especially if our hypothesis about party motivation is true. Nevertheless, some parties – founded by perfectly rational men – are meant to be threats to other parties and not means of gaining immediate power or prestige. An example is the States' Rights Party of 1948, intended to threaten the Democrats because of their policy on civil rights. Such blackmail parties are future oriented, since their purpose is to alter the choices offered to voters by the extant parties at some future date.

To distinguish between these two kinds of parties is often difficult, because many parties founded primarily to gain office actually perform the function of influencing the policies of previously existing parties. This impact has been typical of third parties in United States history, none of which ever won a national election, though many had great influence upon the platforms of parties that did win. Thus if we classify new parties by intention, nearly all of them are of the "real" type; whereas if we classify them by results, most of them, at least in American history, are of the "influence" type. However, we will assume that the new parties we discuss are designed to win elections, unless otherwise specified.

No party, new or old, can survive without gaining the support of a sizeable fraction of the electorate – a support active enough to be expressed by votes in elections. This does not mean that a party must locate right in the midst of a big lump of voters on our political scale; rather it must be nearer a large number of voters than any other parties are. Its location is as dependent upon where other parties are as it is upon where voters are.

New parties are most likely to appear and survive when there is an opportunity for them to cut off a large part of the support of an older party by sprouting up between it and its former voters. An outstanding case in point is the birth of the Labour Party in England, which can be illustrated very roughly by figure 15.6. Before 1900, there were two major British parties, the Liberals (A) and the Tories (B). They were under the usual two–party pressure to converge. However, the enfranchisement of the working class in the late nineteenth century had shifted the center of voter distribution far to the left of its old position. And the Liberal Party, even after it moved to the left, was to the right of the new center of gravity, although it was the more left of the two parties. The founders of the Labour Party correctly guessed that they could out-flank the Liberals by forming a new party (C) to the left of the latter, which they did. This trapped the Liberals between the two modes of the electorate, and their support rapidly diminished to insignificant size.[14]

The crucial factor in this case was the shift of the electorate's distribution along the political scale as a result of the extension of suffrage to a vast number of new voters, many of whom were near the extreme left. Whenever such a radical change in the distribution of

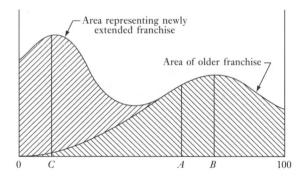

Figure 15.6

voters occurs, existent parties will probably be unable to adjust rapidly because they are ideologically immobile. New parties, however, are not weighed down by this impediment. Unencumbered by ideological commitments, they can select the most opportune point on the scale at which to locate, and structure their ideologies accordingly. Opportunities to do so will be especially tempting if the old parties have converged toward the previous center of gravity as a result of the normal two–party process, and the new distribution is heavily skewed to one or both extremes. This is roughly what happened in the case of the Labour Party.

Another situation which may be productive of new parties is a social stalemate caused by a voter distribution like that in figure 15.3. Where voters are massed bimodally at opposite ends of the scale, peaceful democratic government is difficult, as mentioned previously. A faction desirous of compromise may grow up, thus altering the distribution so it resembles the one shown in figure 15.7. Here an opportunity exists for a new party to be formed at C. If this party grows as a result of continuous shifts of voters to the center, eventually a new situation like that in figure 15.8 may appear. The center has become preponderant, but has split into three parts because new parties have arisen to exploit the large moderate voting mass.

It is clear that a major prerequisite for the appearance of new parties is a change in the distribution of voters along the political scale. A shift in the universality of franchise, a

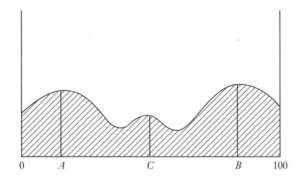

Figure 15.7

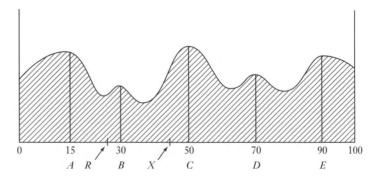

Figure 15.8

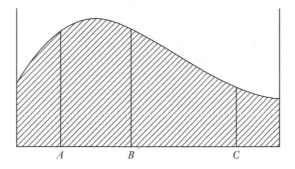

Figure 15.9

weakening of traditional views by some cataclysmic event like World War II, a social revolution like that following upon industrialization – any such disturbing occurrence may move the modes on the political scale. A change in the number of voters *per se* is irrelevant; it is the distribution which counts. Hence women's suffrage does not create any new parties, although it raises the total vote enormously.

There is one situation in which a new party is likely to appear without any change in voter distribution, but this will be the influence type of party, not the kind that aims at getting itself elected. When one of the parties in a two-party system has drifted away from the extreme nearest it toward the moderate center, its extremist supporters may form a new party to pull the policies of the old one back toward them. In figure 15.9, party *B* has moved away to the left of its right-wing members because it wants to gain votes from the large mass of voters near the leftish mode. In order to threaten party *B* with defeat unless it moves back toward the right, the right-wing extremists found party *C*. This party cannot possibly win itself, but it can throw the election to *A* by diverting extremist votes from *B*.

To get rid of this menace, party *B* must adopt some of *C*'s policies, thus moving back to the right and taking the wind out of *C*'s sails. This will cause party *C* to collapse, but it will have accomplished its purpose of improving the platform of one of the real contenders, *B*, in the eyes of its extremist supporters. As mentioned previously, the States' Rights Party formed in 1948 had just such an aim.

In situations like this, it is a movement of party ideology, not of voter distribution, which gives rise to a new party. Party ideologies are relatively immobile in multiparty systems; so this type of new party will appear almost exclusively in two-party systems. Fear of these blackmail parties may strongly counteract the centripetal pull normal to such systems.

IV   Ideological Coherence and Integration

Alteration of our model to include multipolicy parties

Elsewhere, we showed that each party's ideology will be coherent but not integrated. That is, it will not contain internal contradictions, but neither will it be too closely tied to any one philosophic *Weltanschauung*. This outcome results from the conflicting desires each party feels when forming its ideology. On the one hand, it wishes to appeal to as many voters as possible; on the other hand, it wishes to have a strong appeal for each individual voter. The first desire implies a platform containing a wide range of policies representing many different ideological outlooks. The second desire implies a close integration of policies around the philosophic viewpoint of whichever voter is being wooed. Obviously, the more either desire is achieved, the less will the other be satisfied.

This dualism can be depicted on our graph of political space. First we must remove the assumption that each party's platform contains only its stand on the proper degree of government intervention in the economy. Let us assume instead that each party takes stands on many issues, and that each stand can be assigned a position on our left–right scale.[15] Then the party's net position on this scale is a weighted average of the positions of all the particular policies it upholds.

Furthermore, each citizen may apply different weights to the individual policies, since each policy affects some citizens more than others. Therefore the party has no unique, universally recognized net position. Some voters may feel it is more right-wing than others, and no one view can be proved correct. However, there will be some consensus as to the range in which the party's net position lies; so we can still distinguish right-wing parties from center and left-wing ones.

Under these conditions, the rational party strategy is to adopt a spread of policies which covers a whole range of the left–right scale. The wider this spread is, the more viewpoints the party's ideology and platform will appeal to. But a wider spread also weakens the strength of the appeal to any one viewpoint, because each citizen sees the party upholding policies he does not approve of.

Thus a voter's judgment of each party becomes two-dimensional: he must balance its net position (the mean of its policies) against its spread (their variance) in deciding whether he wants to support it. If some party has a mean identical with his own position (which we assume single-valued) but an enormous variance, he may reject it in favor of another party with a mean not as close to him but with a much smaller variance. In short, voters choose policy vectors rather than policy scalars, and each vector is really a weighted frequency distribution of policies on the left–right scale.

Integration strategies in two-party and multiparty systems

If we assume that each point on the political scale represents a definite *Weltanschauung*, the width of the spread formed by a party's policies varies inversely with their integration around a single such *Weltanschauung*. Therefore, the degree of integration in a party's ideology depends upon what fraction of the scale it is trying to cover with its policy spread. We have already seen that this fraction will be smaller in a multiparty system than in a two-party system, simply because dividing a constant in half yields larger parts than dividing it into any greater number of equal pieces. If we rule out any overlapping of policy spreads, we may conclude that ideologies will be more integrated in multiparty systems than in two-party systems. Each party's platform will more clearly reflect some one philosophic viewpoint, around which its policies will be more closely grouped. This accords with our previous conclusion that each party in a multiparty system will try to differentiate its product sharply from the products of all other parties, whereas each party in a two-party system will try to resemble its rival.

To illustrate this conclusion, let us compare figure 15.2 with figure 15.5. In figure 15.2, after parties A and B have approached each other near the center of the scale, each is drawing votes from half the scale. Its supporters range in viewpoint from those at one extreme to those at dead center; hence it must design a policy spread which includes all of them. But there are more voters in the middle than at the extremes. Therefore each party structures its policies so that its net position is moderate, even though it makes a few concessions to the extremists. In this way, it hopes to keep the extremists from abstaining and yet woo the middle-of-the-roaders massed around 50.

In contrast to the parties in figure 15.2, those in figure 15.5 do not have to appeal to a wide range of viewpoints. The policy span of each is much narrower, and any attempt to widen it soon causes a collision with another party. This restricts each party's spread even if we allow overlapping to occur.

For example, party B in figure 15.5 cannot gain by trying to spread its policies so as to please voters at positions 10 and 60. If it wishes to retain its net position at 35, it can only cast a few policies out as far as 10 and 60. But parties A and C are massing most of their policies so as to please voters at 10 and 60 respectively; hence B cannot hope to compete with A and C in these locations. In fact, B is much better off concentrating its policies around 35, since this keeps it from spreading itself too thin and losing votes to A and C from its own bailiwick. Thus no party in a multiparty system has much incentive to spread out or to overlap another ideologically, and each will closely integrate its policies around some definite philosophic outlook.

Overlapping and ambiguity in two-party systems

If we allow overlapping in a two-party system, the results are radically different from those just described. Each party casts some policies into the other's territory in order to convince voters there that its net position is near them. In such maneuvering, there is much room for skill because different voters assign different weights to the same policies. For example, assume that there are two social groups, farmers and workers, whose positions are respectively right and left of 50. They have exactly opposite views on two laws, one on farm price supports and the other on labor practices. However, the farmers weigh the farm law heavily in their voting decisions and consider the labor law much less significant; whereas the workers' emphasis is just the reverse. Each group thus views any party's net position differently from the way the other views it. Realizing this, a clever party will take a stand favoring farmers on the farm law and workers on the labor law. By doing so, it can establish a net position simultaneously close to both groups, even though they are far apart from each other!

This possibility of having a net position in many different places at once makes overlapping policies a rational strategy in a two-party system. Therefore, in the middle of the scale where most voters are massed, each party scatters its policies on both sides of the mid point. It attempts to make each voter in this area feel that it is centered right at his position. Naturally, this causes an enormous overlapping of moderate policies.

However, each party will sprinkle these moderate policies with a few extreme stands in order to please its far-out voters. Obviously, each party is trying to please an extreme opposite to that being pleased by the other party. Therefore it is possible to detect on which side of the mid point each party is actually located by looking at the extremist policies it espouses. In fact, this may be the only way to tell the two parties apart ideologically, since most of their policies are conglomerated in an overlapping mass in the middle of the scale.

Clearly, both parties are trying to be as ambiguous as possible about their actual net position. Therefore why should they not accomplish the same end by being equally ambiguous about each policy? Then every policy stand can cover a spread of voters, too. Not only can voters differently weight individual policies, they can also interpret the meaning of each policy differently – each seeing it in a light which brings it as close as possible to his own position. This vastly widens the band on the political scale into which various interpretations of a party's net position may fall.

Ambiguity thus increases the number of voters to whom a party may appeal. This fact encourages parties in a two-party system to be as equivocal as possible about their stands on each controversial issue. And since both parties find it rational to be ambiguous, neither is forced by the other's clarity to take a more precise stand.

Thus political rationality leads parties in a two-party system to becloud their policies in a fog of ambiguity. True, their tendency towards obscurity is limited by their desire to attract voters to the polls, since citizens abstain if all parties seem identical or no party makes testable promises. Nevertheless, competition forces both parties to be much less than perfectly clear about what they stand for. Naturally, this makes it more difficult for each citizen to vote rationally; he has a hard time finding out what his ballot supports when cast for either party. As a result, voters are encouraged to make decisions on some basis other than the issues, i.e., on the personalities of candidates, traditional family voting patterns, loyalty to past party heroes, etc. But only the parties' decisions on issues are relevant to voters' utility incomes from government, so making decisions on any other basis is irrational. We are forced to conclude that rational behavior by political parties tends to discourage rational behavior by voters.

This conclusion may seem startling, since it implies that there is a conflict between party rationality and voter rationality in a two-party system. But in fact this conflict has also been observed by students of political behavior, as the following quotation shows:

> The tendency toward agreement between parties under a bipartisan system flows from the fact that party leaders must seek to build a majority of the electorate. In the nation as a whole a majority cannot be built upon the support of organized labor alone; the farmers cannot muster enough votes to form a majority; businessmen are decidedly in a minority. Given the traditional attachment to one party or another of large blocs of voters in all these classes, about the only way in which a party can form a majority is to draw further support from voters of all classes and interests. To succeed in this endeavor party leaders cannot afford to antagonize any major segment of the population. A convenient way to antagonize an element in the population is to take at an inopportune moment an unequivocal stand on an issue of importance. Similarities of composition, hence, contribute to two features of American parties: their similarity of view and their addiction to equivocation and ambiguity.[16]

Our model of "political space" has led us to exactly the same conclusion: parties will try to be similar and to equivocate. And the more they succeed, the more difficult it is for voters to behave rationally.

Does this mean that our assumption of rationality leads to a contradiction in a two-party system? Apparently the more rational political parties are, the less rational voters must be, and vice versa. How does this affect our model?

A fundamental tension in our model

To answer these questions, we must review briefly the basic structure of our mythical political system. In it are two sets of agents: voters and parties. Each set uses the other to achieve its own goal. Voters have as their goal the attainment of a government responsive to their wants; they make use of parties to run this government. Parties have as their goal the rewards of being in office; they make use of voters to get elected. Thus the interlocking of two different goal-pursuing processes forms the political system.

The only end common to both sets of agents is the continuance of the system. Otherwise, neither set cares whether the other's goals are achieved unless that achievement is beneficial to itself. Therefore if a member of one set can gain by impairing the ability of all the members of the other set to attain their goals, he will do so. This follows from our axiom that each man seeks his own good and to get it will sacrifice the good of others, if necessary.

To put it more concretely, if any party believes it can increase its chances of gaining office by discouraging voters from being rational, its own rational course is to do so. The only exception to this rule occurs when voter irrationality is likely to destroy the political system. Since parties have a stake in this system, they are irrational if they encourage anything which might wreck it.

However, it is not obvious that ambiguous policies and similar ideologies are likely to destroy democracy. What they might do is make voting less than perfectly rational as a mechanism for selecting governments. But rationality as we define it is not a dichotomous concept; i.e., the possible states of rationality are not limited to 100 percent and 0 percent. Therefore making voting less than perfectly rational does not render it absolutely useless but merely reduces its efficiency as a government-selection process. Knowing this, parties will not be deterred by fear of the end of democracy when they increase ambiguity and match each other's platforms.

Voters have two defenses against being forced into irrationality. The first is to limit the operations of parties by law. In the United States, parties have been forced to make financial reports, refrain from fraudulent statements, submit their primaries to public control, accept only limited contributions from any one source, and otherwise act in ways not likely to exploit the citizenry. Since it would be irrational for citizens to allow parties to exploit them, these laws indirectly protect voters from being forced into irrationality. But voters can hardly expect to induce government to pass laws against platform ambiguity and similarity, so this defense is not much help.

The second defense is to change the political system from a two-party one to a multi-party one. This will cause parties to narrow the spread of their policies, differentiate their platforms more sharply, and reduce ambiguity. However, such a conversion will also give rise to tremendous problems not present in two-party systems. Therefore it is doubtful whether the change would improve prospects for rational voting; they might get worse.

After weighing all these considerations, we may conclude that our model is not necessarily contradictory. However, it does contain two sets of agents in tension with each other. If either of these is allowed to dominate the other fully, the model may become contradictory; i.e., one of the two sets of agents may cease to behave rationally. Thus if parties succeed in obscuring their policy decisions in a mist of generalities, and voters are unable to discover what their votes really mean, a *rationality crisis* develops. Since such a crisis is even more likely to occur in a multiparty system, we will defer our analysis of it until later.

V   A Basic Determinant of a Nation's Politics

From everything we have said, it is clear that a basic determinant of how a nation's political life develops is the distribution of voters along the political scale, assuming our oversimplified model has some application in the real world. In the first place, the number of modes in the distribution helps determine whether the political system will be two-party or multiparty in character. This in turn determines whether party ideologies will be similar and ambiguous or different and definite; hence it influences the difficulties voters face in behaving rationally. Second, whether democracy can lead to stable government depends upon whether the mass of voters is centrally conglomerated, or lumped at the extremes with low density in the center; only in the former case will democracy really work. Third, the distribution's stability determines whether new parties will constantly be replacing the old, or the old will dominate and new ones merely influence their policy.

Of course, the distribution of voters is not the only factor basic to a nation's policies. For example, some theorists argue that the use of single-member districts instead of proportional representation is the main cause of a two-party political system.[17] Nevertheless, whether it is seen as a cause in itself or as a result of more fundamental factors, the distribution is a crucial political parameter.

What forces shape this important parameter? At the beginning of our study, we assumed that voters' tastes were fixed, which means that the voter distribution is given. Thus we dodged the question just posed, and have been evading it ever since. Even now we cannot answer, because the determinants are historic, cultural, and psychological, as well as economic; to attempt to analyze them would be to undertake a study vast beyond our scope.

All we can say is the following: (1) the distribution of voters is a crucial determinant molding a nation's political life, (2) major changes in it are among the most important political events possible, and (3) though parties will move ideologically to adjust to the distribution under some circumstances, they will also attempt to move voters toward their own locations, thus altering it.

VI   Summary

We can turn Harold Hotelling's famous spatial market into a useful device for analyzing political ideologies by adding to it: (1) variable distribution of population, (2) an unequivocal left-to-right ordering of parties, (3) relative ideological immobility, and (4) peaked political preferences for all voters.

This model confirms Hotelling's conclusion that the parties in a two-party system converge ideologically upon the center, and Smithies' addendum that fear of losing extremist voters keeps them from becoming identical. But we discover that such convergence depends upon a unimodal distribution of voters which has a low variance and most of its mass clustered around the mode.

If the distribution of voters along the scale remains constant in a society, its political system tends to move towards an equilibrium in which the number of parties and their ideological positions are fixed. Whether it will then have two or many parties depends upon (1) the shape of the distribution and (2) whether the electoral structure is based upon plurality or proportional representation.

No tendency toward imitation exists in a multiparty system; in fact, parties strive to accentuate ideological "product differentiation" by maintaining purity of doctrine. This difference between the two systems helps explain why certain practices are peculiar to each.

New parties are usually intended to win elections, but they are often more important as means of influencing the policies of previously existent parties. Since old parties are ideologically immobile, they cannot adjust rapidly to changes in voter distribution, but new parties can enter wherever it is most advantageous. Influence parties may crop up in two-party systems whenever convergence has pulled one of the major parties away from the extreme, and its extremist supporters want to move it back towards them.

If we assume a party's position on the scale is a weighted average of the positions occupied by each of its policy decisions, we can account for the tendency of parties to spread their policies: they wish to appeal to many different viewpoints at once. Parties in a two-party system have a much wider spread of policies – hence a looser integration of them – than those in a multiparty system. In fact, in two-party systems there is a large area of overlapping policies near the middle of the scale, so that parties closely resemble each other.

This tendency towards similarity is reinforced by deliberate equivocation about each particular issue. Party policies may become so vague, and parties so alike, that voters find it difficult to make rational decisions. Nevertheless, fostering ambiguity is the rational course for each party in a two-party system.

A basic determinant of a nation's political development is the distribution of its voters along the political scale. Upon this factor, to a great extent, depend whether the nation will have two or many major parties, whether democracy will lead to stable or unstable government, and whether new parties will continually replace old or play only a minor role.

Notes

1   Harold Hotelling, "Stability in Competition," *The Economic Journal*, XXXIX (1929), 41–57, and Arthur Smithies, "Optimum Location in Spatial Competition," *The Journal of Political Economy*, XLIX (1941), 423–39. For other aspects of the spatial-competition problem, see F. Zeuthen, "Theoretical Remarks on Price Policy: Hotelling's Case with Variations," *Quarterly Journal of Economics*, XLVII (1933), 231–53; Erich Schneider, "Bemerkungen zu Einer Theorie der Raum-wirtschaft," *Econometrica*, III (1935), 79–105; A. P. Lerner and H. W. Singer, "Some Notes on Duopoly and Spatial Competition," *Journal of Political Economy*, XLV (1937), 145–86; and August Lösch, *The Economics of Location* (New Haven: Yale University Press, 1954).

2   In reality, since so many ballots are cast, each individual voter has so little influence upon the election that his acts cannot be realistically appraised as a threat to any party, assuming the actions of all other citizens are given. Since we deal with this atomistic problem fully elsewhere, we evade it here by assuming each man behaves as though his vote has a high probability of being decisive.

3   The following description should not be construed as a causal explanation of revolutions; it is rather a translation of the events that occur in them into movements along the scale we have developed. Hence we make no attempt to discuss why revolutions follow the cycle portrayed. For

an analysis of this problem, see Lyford P. Edwards, *The Natural History of Revolution* (Chicago: University of Chicago Press, 1927).

4   The application of this model to revolutions was suggested by Robert A. Dahl and Kenneth Arrow. Professor Dahl develops a similar model in *A Preface to Democratic Theory* (Chicago: University of Chicago Press, 1956), pp. 90–102.

5   This definition of party does not cover many actual parties that continue to exist even though their chances for election are practically zero; e.g., the Vegetarians and Socialists in the United States. These parties are politically irrational from the point of view of our hypothesis; i.e., the motives we posit as politically rational are not the ones impelling their members. Even future-oriented rationality does not cover them, since past experience demonstrates that their future chances of election are also nearly nonexistent unless some highly unlikely catastrophe occurs.

6   For a more extensive discussion of this assertion, see V. O. Key Jr., *Politics, Parties, and Pressure Groups* (New York: Thomas Y. Crowell, 1953), pp. 224–31.

7   A detailed analysis of the problems raised by coalition governments is presented later in the book.

8   Another reason why new parties cannot form *ad infinitum* is that political parties are specialized agencies in the division of labor. Therefore not everyone can be in a political party; in fact, in a given society, there is probably a definite limit imposed by efficiency on the number of persons who can specialize in being party members. The size of this limit depends upon such factors as the importance of government action in that society, the need for differing representation (i.e., the scattering of voters on the scale), the social prestige and economic income attached to being in politics, and the general standard of living produced by the division of labor.

9   This example ignores the possibility of a tiny third party occupying a crucial balancing position between two other large parties. Actually such an outcome is also possible in a plurality system if the government is chosen by a series of district elections rather than a single national election. As in Great Britain, a small party may gain only a few seats in the legislature, but if the two large parties are equally powerful, its decisive role in the balance of power may keep it alive even though it never gains office in the government directly. Our plurality model precludes this outcome because we posit election on a strictly national basis.

10   Of course there are many factors influencing the number of parties in a given system, but most of them can be subsumed under the electoral structure (which we just discussed) or the distribution of voters (which we are about to discuss).

11   As new voters appear on the scene, they may cluster around the four locations where parties exist and thus form a tetramodal distribution like that shown by the dotted line in figure 15.5. In other words, a perfectly even distribution is probably not stable over time but tends to become a distribution with definite modes and less populated areas between them. Such a development further restricts the manner in which new parties may enter the system, since it makes some locations much more desirable than others but also concentrates extant parties at the most favorable spots.

12   At this point we are ignoring the possibility of *B*'s gaining power by forming a coalition with either *A* or *C* or both. The forces influencing *B*'s movement when it is in such a coalition are described later in this book.

13   A two–party system like that shown in figure 15.3 will not exhibit ideological convergence. However, as we have pointed out, it is doubtful whether such a distribution can function as a democracy, since internal conflict will be intense no matter which party wins.

14   Interestingly enough, now that the Liberal Party has dwindled in support, the British electoral system has reverted to its former two–party pattern. Since the new center of gravity is far left of the old, the Conservative Party has moved farther leftward than the Labour Party has moved rightward. Nevertheless, a tendency toward convergence clearly exists.

15   We can state this assumption formally as follows: all citizens agree on a left–right ordering of the stands taken by the various parties on any given issue. Thus it is not necessary for every citizen to

have the same cardinal ordering of stands on the left–right scale as every other; i.e., citizen *A* may feel that party *X*'s stand on some issue is at point 35, while citizen *B* may believe the same stand is at point 30, but both must agree it is on the same side of party *Y*'s stand on that issue and bears the same ordinal relation to the stands of parties *W*, *Y* and *Z*. Although in the text we implicitly assume agreement on the exact location of each party stand in order to simplify the argument, our conclusions also follow from purely ordinal premises.

16 V. O. Key Jr., *Politics, Parties and Pressure Groups*, pp. 231–2.
17 We have already discussed this point in section II of this chapter.

SIXTEEN

Rationality and Social Choice

AMARTYA SEN*

Source: From *American Economic Review* (1995), 85: 1–24.

While Aristotle agreed with Agathon that even God could not change the past, he did think that the future was ours to make – by basing our choices on reasoning. The idea of using reason to identify and promote better – or more acceptable – societies, and to eliminate intolerable deprivations of different kinds, has powerfully moved people in the past and continues to do so now. In this lecture I would like to discuss some aspects of this question which have received attention in the recent literature in social-choice and public-choice theories. The contemporary world suffers from many new as well as old economic problems, including, among others, the persistence of poverty and deprivation despite general economic progress, the occurrence of famines and more widespread hunger, and threats to our environment and to the sustainability of the world in which we live. Rational use of the opportunities offered by modern science and technology, in line with our values and ends, is a powerful challenge today.

I Problems and Difficulties

How are we to view the demands of rationality in social decisions? How much guidance do we get from Aristotle's general recommendation that choice should be governed by "desire and reasoning directed to some end"? There are several deep-seated difficulties here.

The first problem relates to the question: *whose* desires, *whose* ends? Different persons have disparate objects and interests, and as Horace put it, "there are as many preferences as there are people." Kenneth Arrow (1951) has shown, through his famous "General Possibility Theorem" (an oddly optimistic name for what is more commonly – and more revealingly – called Arrow's "impossibility theorem"), that in trying to obtain an integrated social preference from diverse individual preferences, it is not in general possible to satisfy even some mild-looking conditions that would seem to reflect elementary demands of reasonableness.[1] Other impossibility results have also emerged, even without using some of Arrow's conditions, but involving other elementary criteria, such as the priority of individual liberty.[2] We have to discuss why these difficulties arise, and how we can deal with them. Are the pessimistic conclusions that some have drawn from them justified? Can we sensibly make aggregative social-welfare judgments? Do procedures for social decision-making exist that reasonably respect individual values and preferences?

Second, another set of problems relates to questions raised by James Buchanan (1954a,b), which were partly a response to Arrow's results, but they are momentous in their own right.[3] Pointing to "the fundamental philosophical issues" involved in "the idea of social rationality," Buchanan (1954a) argued that "rationality or irrationality as an attribute of the social group implies the imputation to that group of an organic existence apart from that of its individual components" (p. 116). Buchanan was perhaps "the first commentator to interpret Arrow's impossibility theorem as the result of a mistaken attempt to impose the logic of welfare maximization on the procedures of collective choice" (Robert Sugden, 1993, p. 1948). But in addition, he was arguing that there was a deep "confusion surrounding the Arrow analysis" (not just the impossibility theorem but the entire framework used by Arrow and his followers) which ensued from the mistaken idea of "social or collective rationality in terms of producing results indicated by a social ordering" (Buchanan, 1960, pp. 88–9). We certainly have to examine whether Buchanan's critique negates the impossibility results, but we must also investigate the more general issues raised by Buchanan.[4]

Third, Buchanan's reasoned questioning of the idea of "social preference" suggests, at the very least, a need for caution in imposing strong "consistency properties" in social choice, but his emphasis on procedural judgments may be taken to suggest, much more ambitiously, that we should abandon altogether consequence-based evaluation of social happenings, opting instead for a procedural approach. In its pure form, such an approach would look for "right" institutions rather than "good" outcomes and would demand the priority of appropriate procedures (including the acceptance of what follows from these procedures). This approach, which is the polar opposite of the welfare–economic tradition based on classical utilitarianism of founding every decision on an ordering of different states of affairs (treating procedures just as instruments to generate good states), has not been fully endorsed by Buchanan himself, but significant work in that direction has occurred in public choice theory and in other writings influenced by Buchanan's work (most notably in the important contributions of Sugden [1981, 1986]).

This contrast is particularly important in characterizing rights in general and liberties in particular. In the social choice literature, these characterizations have typically been in terms of states of affairs, concentrating on what happens vis-à-vis what the person wanted or chose to do. In contrast, in the libertarian literature, inspired by the pioneering work of Robert Nozick (1974), and in related contributions using "game-form" formulations (most notably, by Wulf Gaertner, Pattanaik, and Suzumura [1992]), rights have been characterized in procedural terms, without referring to states of affairs. We have to examine how deep the differences between the disparate formulations are, and we must also scrutinize their respective adequacies.

Fourth, the prospects of rationality in social decisions must be fundamentally conditional on the nature of *individual* rationality. There are many different conceptions of rational behavior of the individual. There is, for example, the view of rationality as canny maximization of self-interest (the presumption of human beings as "*homo economicus*," used in public choice theory, fits into this framework). Arrow's (1951) formulation is more permissive; it allows social considerations to influence the choices people make. Individual preferences, in this interpretation reflect "values" in general, rather than being based only on what Arrow calls "tastes" (p. 23). How adequate are the respective characterizations of individual rationality, and through the presumption of rational behavior (shared by most economic models), the depiction of actual conduct and choices?

Another issue, related to individual behavior and rationality, concerns the role of social interactions in the development of values, and also the connection between value formation and the decision-making processes. Social choice theory has tended to avoid this issue, following Arrow's own abstinence: "we will also assume in the present study that individual values are taken as data and are not capable of being altered by the nature of the decision process itself" (Arrow, 1951, p. 7).[5] On this subject, Buchanan has taken a more permissive position – indeed emphatically so: "The definition of democracy as 'government by discussion' implies that individual values can and do change in the process of decision-making" (Buchanan, 1954a, p. 120).[6] We have to scrutinize the importance of this difference as well.

This is a long and somewhat exacting list, but the different issues relate to each other, and I shall try to examine them briefly and also comment on some of their practical implications.

II   Social Welfare Judgments and Arrow's Impossibility Theorem

The subject of welfare economics was dominated for a long time by the utilitarian tradition, which performs interpersonal aggregation through the device of looking at the sum-total of the utilities of all the people involved. By the 1930s, however, economists came to be persuaded by arguments presented by Lionel Robbins (1938) and others (influenced by the philosophy of "logical positivism") that interpersonal comparisons of utility had no scientific basis.[7] Thus, the epistemic foundations of utilitarian welfare economics were seen as incurably defective.

Because of the eschewal of interpersonal comparability of individual utilities, the "new welfare economics" that emerged tried to rely only on one basic criterion of social improvement, the Pareto criterion. Since this confines the recognition of a social improvement only to the case in which everyone's utility goes up (or someone's goes up and no one's goes down), it does not require any interpersonal comparison nor, for that matter, any cardinality of individual utilities. However, Pareto efficiency can scarcely be an adequate condition for a good society. It is quite insensitive to the *distribution* of utilities (including inequalities of happiness and miseries), and it takes no direct note of anything *other than* utilities (such as rights or freedoms) beyond their indirect role in generating utilities. There is a need, certainly, for *further* criteria for social welfare judgments.

The demands of orderly, overall judgments of "social welfare" (or the general goodness of states of affairs) were clarified by Abram Bergson (1938, 1966) and extensively explored by Paul Samuelson (1947). The concentration was on the need for a real-valued function W of "social welfare" defined over all the alternative social states, or at least an aggregate ordering R over them, the so-called "social preference." In the re-examination that followed the Bergson–Samuelson initiative (including the development of social choice theory as a discipline), the search for principles underlying a social welfare function played a prominent part.

Arrow (1951) defined a "social welfare function" as a functional relation that specifies a social ordering R over all the social states for every set of individual preference orderings. In addition to assuming – not especially controversially – that there are at least three distinct social states and at least two (but not infinitely many) individuals, Arrow also wanted a social welfare function to yield a social ordering for every possible combination of individual preferences; that is, it must have a *universal domain*. A second condition is called *the independence of irrelevant alternatives*. This can be defined in different ways, and I shall choose an extremely simple form. The way a society ranks a pair of alternative social states x and y should depend on the individual preferences only over *that* pair – in particular, *not* on how the other ("irrelevant") alternatives are ranked.

Now consider the idea of some people being "decisive": a set G of people – I shall call them a group G – having their way no matter what others prefer. In ranking a pair x and y, if it turns out that x gets socially ranked above y *whenever* everyone in group G prefers x to y (no matter what preferences those not in G have), then G is decisive over that ordered pair (x, y). When a group G is decisive over all ordered pairs, it is simply "decisive."

Arrow required that no individual (formally, no single-member group) should be decisive (*nondictatorship*), but – following the Paretian tradition – also demanded that the group of all individuals taken together should be decisive (the *Pareto principle*). The "impossibility theorem," in this version (presented in Arrow [1963]), shows that it is impossible to have a social welfare function with *universal domain*, satisfying *independence*, the *Pareto principle*, and *nondictatorship*.

The theorem can be proved in three simple steps.[8] The first two steps are the following (with the second lemma drawing on the first).

FIELD-EXPANSION LEMMA   If a group is decisive over any pair of states, it is decisive.[9]

GROUP-CONTRACTION LEMMA   If a group (of more than one person) is decisive, then so is some smaller group contained in it.[10]

The final step uses the Group-Contraction Lemma to prove the theorem. By the Pareto principle, the group of all individuals is decisive. Since it is finite, by successive partitioning (and each time picking the decisive part), we arrive at a decisive individual, who must, thus, be a dictator. Hence the impossibility.

III   Social Preference, Social Choice, and Impossibility

The preceding discussion makes abundant use of the idea of "social preference." Should it be dropped, as suggested by Buchanan? And if so, what would remain of Arrow's impossibility theorem?

We have to distinguish between two quite different uses of the notion of "social preference," related respectively to (i) the operation of *decision mechanisms*, and (ii) the making of *social welfare judgments*. The first notion of "social preference" is something like the "underlying preference" on which *choices* actually made for the society by prevailing mechanisms are implicitly based – a kind of "revealed preference" of the society.[11] This "derivative" view of social preference would be, formally, a binary representation of the choices emerging from decision mechanisms.

The second idea of "social preference" – as social welfare judgments – reflects a view of the social good: some ranking of what would be better or worse for the society. Such judgments would be typically made by a given person or agency. Here too an aggregation is involved, since an individual who is making judgments about social welfare, or about the relative goodness of distinct social states, must somehow combine the diverse interests and preferences of different people.

Buchanan's objection is quite persuasive for the first interpretation (involving decision mechanisms), especially since there is no a priori presumption that the mechanisms used *must* – or even *should* – necessarily lead to choices that satisfy the requirements of binary representation (not to mention the more exacting demands of an ordering representation).[12] On the other hand, the second interpretation does not involve this problem, and even an individual when expressing a view about social welfare needs a concept of this kind.[13] When applied to the making of social welfare judgments by an individual or an agency, Arrow's impossibility theorem thus cannot be disputed on the ground that some organic existence is being imputed to the society. The amelioration of impossibility must be sought elsewhere (see section IV). However, Buchanan's critique of Arrow's theorem would apply to *mechanisms* of social decision (such as voting procedures).

Would the dropping of the requirement that social choices be based on a binary relation – in particular a transitive ordering – negate the result in the case of social decision mechanisms? A large literature has already established that the arbitrariness of power, of which Arrow's case of dictatorship is an extreme example, lingers in one form or another even when transitivity is dropped, so long as *some* regularity is demanded (such as the absence of cycles).[14] There is, however, cause for going further, precisely for the reasons identified by Buchanan, and to eschew not just the transitivity of social preference, but the idea of social preference itself. All that is needed from the point of view of choice is that the decision mechanisms determine a "choice function" for the society, which identifies what is picked from each alternative "menu" (or opportunity set).[15]

However, provided some conditions are imposed on the "internal consistency" of the choice function (relating decisions over one menu in a "consistent" way to decisions over other – related – menus), it can be shown that some arbitrariness of power would still survive.[16] But the methodological critique of James Buchanan would still apply forcefully, as reformulated in the following way: why should *any* restriction whatever be placed a priori on the choice function for the society? Why should not the decisions emerging from agreed social mechanisms be acceptable without having to check them against some preconceived idea of how choices made in different situations should relate to each other?

What happens, then, to Arrow's impossibility problem if no restrictions whatever are placed on the so-called "internal consistency" of the choice function for the society? Would the conditions relating individual preferences to social choice (i.e., the Pareto principle, nondictatorship, and independence) then be consistent with each other? The answer, in fact, is no, not so. If the Pareto principle and the conditions of nondictatorship and independence are redefined to take full note of the fact that they must relate to social *choices*, not to any prior notion of social *preference*, then a very similar impossibility re-emerges (see Theorem 3 in Sen [1993]).

How does this "general choice-functional impossibility theorem" work? The underlying intuition is this. Each of the conditions relating individual preferences to social decisions eliminates – either on its own or in the presence of the other conditions – the possibility of choosing *some* alternatives. And the conjunction of these conditions can lead to an empty choice set, making it "impossible" to choose anything.

For example, the Pareto principle is just such a condition, and the object of this condition in a choice context, surely, is to avoid the selection of a Pareto-inferior alternative. Therefore this condition can be sensibly redefined to demand that if everyone prefers x to y, then the social decision mechanism should be such that y should not get chosen if x is available.[17] Indeed, to eliminate any possibility that we are implicitly or indirectly using any intermenu consistency condition for social choice, we can define all the conditions for only *one given menu* (or opportunity set) S; that is, we can consider the choice problem exclusively over a given set of alternative states. The Pareto principle for that set S then only demands that if everyone prefers some x to some y in that set, then y must not be chosen from that set.

Similarly, nondictatorship would demand that there be no person such that whenever she prefers any x to any y in that set S, then y cannot be chosen from that set. What about independence? We have to modify the idea of decisiveness of a group in this choice context, related to choices over this given set S. A group would be decisive for x against y if and only if, whenever all members of this group prefer any x to any y in this set S, then y is not to be chosen from S. Independence would now demand that any group's power of decisiveness over a pair (x, y) be completely independent of individual preferences over pairs other than (x, y). It can be shown that there is no way of going from individual preferences to social choice satisfying these choice-oriented conditions of independence, the Pareto principle, nondictatorship, and unrestricted domain, even without invoking any "social preference," and without imposing any demand of "collective rationality," or any intermenu consistency condition on social choice.[18]

The morals to be drawn from all this for Buchanan's questioning of "social preference" would appear to be the following. The "impossibility" result identified in a particular form by Arrow can be extended and shown to hold even when the idea of "social preference" is totally dropped and even when no conditions are imposed on "internal consistency" of social choice. This does not, however, annul the importance of Buchanan's criticism of the idea of social preference (in the context of choices emerging from *decision mechanisms* for the society), since it is a valid criticism on its own right. But the "impossibility" problem identified by Arrow cannot be escaped by this move.

IV On Reasoned Social Welfare Judgments

How might we then avoid that impossibility? It is important to distinguish the bearing of the problem in the making of aggregative social welfare judgments, as opposed to the operation of social decision mechanisms. I start with the former.

It may be recalled that the Bergson–Samuelson analysis and Arrow's impossibility theorem followed a turn in welfare economics that had involved the dropping of interpersonal comparisons of utility. As it happens, because of its utilitarian form, traditional welfare economics had informational exclusions of its own, and it had been opposed to any basic use of nonutility information, since everything had to be judged ultimately by utility sum-totals in consequent states of affairs. To this was now added the exclusion of interpersonal comparisons of utilities, without removing the exclusion of nonutility information. This barren informational landscape makes it hard to arrive at systematic judgments of social welfare. Arrow's theorem can be interpreted, in this context, as a demonstration that even some very weak conditions relating individual preferences to social welfare judgments cannot be simultaneously satisfied given this informational privation.[19]

The problem is not just one of impossibility. Consider the Field-Expansion Lemma: decisiveness over *any* pair of alternatives entails decisiveness over *every* pair of alternatives, *irrespective of the nature of the states involved*. Consider three divisions of a given cake between two persons: (99,1), (50,50), and (1,99). Let us begin with the assumption that each person – as *homo economicus* – prefers a larger personal share of the cake. So they happen to have opposite preferences. Consider now the ranking of (99,1) and (50,50). If it is decided that (50,50) is better for the society than (99,1), then in terms of preference-based information, person 2's preference is getting priority over person 1's.

A variant of the Field-Expansion Lemma would then claim that person 2's preference must get priority over all other pairs as well, so that even (1,99) must be preferred to (50,50).[20] Indeed, it is not possible, given the assumptions, to regard (50,50) as best of the three; we could either have (99,1), giving priority to person 1's preference, or (1,99), giving priority to 2's preference. But *not* (50,50). I am not arguing here that (50,50) must necessarily be taken to be the best, but it is absurd that we are not even permitted to consider (50,50) as a claimant to being the best element in this cake-division problem.

It is useful to consider what arguments there might be for considering (50,50) as a good possibility, and why we cannot use any of these arguments in the information framework resulting from Arrow's conditions. First, it might seem good to divide the cake equally on some general *non-welfarist* ground, without even going into preferences or utilities. This is not permitted because of the exclusion of evaluative use of nonutility information, and this is what the Field-Expansion Lemma is formalizing. Second, presuming that everyone has the same strictly concave utility function, we might think that the sum-total of utilities would be maximized by an equal division of the cake. But this utilitarian argument involves comparability of cardinal utilities, which is ruled out. Third, we might think that equal division of the cake will equate utilities, and there are arguments for utility-centered egalitarianism (see James Meade, 1976). But that involves interpersonal comparison of ordinal utilities, which too is ruled out. None of the standard ways of discriminating between the alternative states is viable in this informational framework, and the only way to choose between them is to go by the preference of one person or another (since they have opposite preferences).

To try to make social welfare judgments *without* using any interpersonal comparison of utilities, and *without* using any nonutility information, is not a fruitful enterprise. We do care about the size and distribution of the overall achievements; we have reasons to want to reduce deprivation, poverty, and inequality; and all these call for interpersonal comparisons – either of utilities or of other indicators of individual advantages, such as real incomes, opportunities, primary goods, or capabilities.[21] Once interpersonal comparisons are introduced, the impossibility problem, in the appropriately redefined framework, vanishes.[22] The comparisons may have to be rough and ready and often open to disputation, but such comparisons are staple elements of systematic social welfare judgments. Even without any cardinality, ordinal interpersonal comparisons permit the use of such rules of social judgment as maximin, or lexicographic maximin.[23] This satisfies all of Arrow's conditions (and many others), though the class of permissible social welfare rules that do this is quite limited, unless cardinality is also admitted, along with interpersonal comparisons (see Louis Gevers, 1979; Kevin Roberts, 1980a). With the possibility of using interpersonal comparisons, other classes of possible rules for social welfare judgments (including *inter alia*, utilitarianism) become usable.[24]

While the axiomatic derivations of different social-welfare rules in this literature are based on applying interpersonal comparisons to utilities only, the analytical problems are, in many respects, rather similar when people are compared in terms of some other feature, such as real income, holdings of primary goods, or capabilities to function. There are, thus, whole varieties of ways in which social welfare judgments can be made using richer information than in the Arrow framework.

This applies also to *procedures* specifically aimed at making social welfare judgments and other aggregative evaluations, based on institutionally accepted ways of making interpersonal comparisons: for example, in using indexes of income inequality (see Serge Kolm's [1969] and Anthony Atkinson's [1970] pioneering work on this), or in aggregate measures of distribution-corrected real national income (Sen, 1976a), or of aggregate poverty (Sen, 1976b).[25] This links the theory of social choice to some of the most intensely practical debates on economic policy.[26] While Arrow's impossibility theorem is a negative result, the challenge it provided has led, dialectically, to a great many constructive developments.

V   On Social Decision Mechanisms

Moving from the exercise of making social judgments to that of choosing social decision mechanisms, there are other difficulties to be faced. While systematic interpersonal comparisons of utilities (and other ways of seeing individual advantage) can be used by a person making social welfare judgment, or in agreed *procedures* for social judgments (based on interpreting available statistics to arrive at, say, orderings of aggregate poverty or inequality or distribution-corrected real national income), this is not an easy thing to do in social-decision mechanisms which must rely on some standard expressions of individual preference (such as voting), which do not readily lend themselves to interpersonal comparisons.

The impossibility problem, thus, has greater resilience here. While it is also the case that the critique of James Buchanan (and others) of the idea of "social rationality" and the concept of "social preference" applies particularly in this case (that of judging social *decision mechanisms*), the impossibility problem does indeed survive, as we have seen, even when the concept of social preference is eschewed and the idea of social rationality in the Arrovian form is dropped altogether (section III). How, then, can we respond to the challenge in this case?

We may begin by noting that the conditions formulated and used by Arrow, while appealing enough, are not beyond criticism. First, not every conceivable combination of individual preferences need be considered in devising a social decision procedure, since only some would come up in practice. As Arrow had himself noted, if the condition of unrestricted domain is relaxed, we can find decision rules that satisfy all the other conditions (and many other demands) over substantial domains of individual preference profiles. Arrow (1951), along with Duncan Black, had particularly explored the case of "single-peaked preferences," but it can be shown (Sen, 1966) that this condition can be far extended and generalized to a much less demanding restriction called "value restriction."[27]

The plausibility of different profiles of individual preferences depends on the nature of the problem and on the characteristics of individual motivations. It is readily checked that with three or more people, if everyone acts as *homo economicus* in a cake-division problem (always preferring more cake for oneself over all else), then value restriction and the related conditions would all be violated, and majority rule would standardly lead to intransitivities. It is also easy to show that in the commodity space, with each concentrating on her own commodity basket, the Arrow conditions could not be all satisfied by any decision mechanism over that domain. Majority rule and other voting procedures of this kind do cause cycles in general in what is called "the economic domain" (of interpersonal commodity space), if everyone votes in a narrowly self-interested way.

However, majority rule would be a terrible decision procedure in this case, and its intransitivity is hardly the main problem here. For example, taking the most deprived person in a community and passing on half her share of the cake divided between two richer persons would be a majority improvement, but scarcely a great welfare-economic triumph. In view of this, it is perhaps just as well that the majority rule is not only nasty and brutish, but also short in consistency.[28] The tension between social welfare judgments (of different kinds explored, for example, by Meade [1976], Arrow [1977], Mirrlees (1982), William J. Baumol [1986], or John Broome [1991]) and mechanical decision rules (like majority decision) with inward-looking, self-centered individuals is most obvious here. Also, as Buchanan (1994a,b) has argued, the acceptability of majority rule is, in fact, related to its tendency to generate cycles, and the endemic cyclicity of majority decisions is inescapable, given the endogeneity of alternative proposals that can be presented for consideration.

In practice, in facing political decisions, the choices may not come in these stark forms (there are many issues that are mixed together in political programs and proposals), and also individuals do not necessarily only look at their "own share of the cake" in taking up political positions and attitudes.[29] The "public choice" school has tended to emphasize the role of logrolling in political compromises and social decisions. While that school has also been rather wedded to the presumption of each person being *homo economicus* even in these exercises (see Buchanan and Tullock, 1962), there is a more general social process here (involving a variety of motivations) that can be fruitfully considered in examining decision mechanisms. Central to this is the role of public discussion in the formation of preferences and values, which has been emphasized by Buchanan (1954a, b).

The condition of independence of irrelevant alternatives is also not beyond disputation and, indeed, has led to debates – explicitly or by implication – for a very long time. It was one of the issues that divided J. C. Borda (1781) and Marquis de Condorcet (1785), the two French mathematicians, who had pioneered the systematic theory of voting and group decision procedures in the eighteenth century. One version of the rule proposed by Borda, based on adding the rank-order numbers of candidates in each voter's preference list, violates the independence condition rather robustly, but it is not devoid of other merits (and is frequently used in practice).[30] Other types of voting rules have also been shown to have different desirable properties.[31]

In examining social decision mechanisms, we have to take the Arrow conditions seriously, but not as inescapable commandments. Our intuitions vary on these matters, and Arrow's own theorem shows that not everything that appeals to us initially would really be simultaneously sustainable. There is a need for some de-escalation in the grim "fight for basic principles." The issue is not the likely absence of rationally defendable procedures for social decisions, but the relative importance of disparate considerations that pull us in different directions in evaluating diverse procedures. We are not at the edge of a precipice, trying to determine whether it is at all "possible" for us to hang on.

VI Procedures and Consequences

I turn now to the general issue, identified earlier, of the contrast between relying respectively on (i) the "rightness" of procedures, and (ii) the "goodness" of outcomes. Social choice theory, in its traditional form, would seem to belong to the latter part of the dichotomy, with the states of affairs judged first (the subject matter of "social preference" or "social welfare judgements"), followed by identification of procedures that generate the "best" or "maximal" or "satisficing" states. There are two issues here. First, can consequences really be judged adequately without any notion of the process through which they are brought about? I shall also presently question whether this presumption of *process-independence* is the right way of seeing the claims of social choice theory. Second, can we do the converse of this, and judge procedures adequately in a *consequence-independent* way? This issue I take up first.

Sugden (1981, 1986), who has extensively analyzed this dichotomy (between procedural and consequence-based views), explains that in the public choice approach, which he supports, "the primary role of the government is not to maximize the social good, but rather to maintain a framework of rules within which individuals are left free to pursue their own ends" (Sugden, 1993, p. 1948). This is indeed so, but even in judging a "framework of rules" in this way, we do need some consequential analysis, dealing with the *effectiveness* of these frameworks in letting individuals be *actually* "free to pursue their own ends." In an interdependent world, examples of permissive rules that fail to generate the freedom to pursue the respective individual ends are not hard to find (see Sen, 1982b).

Indeed, it is not easy to believe that the public-choice approach is — or can be — really consequence-independent. For example, Buchanan's support of market systems is based on a reading of the consequences that the market mechanism tends to produce, and consequences certainly do enter substantially in Buchanan's evaluation of procedures: "To the extent that voluntary exchange among persons is valued positively while coercion is valued negatively, there emerges the implication that substitution of the former for the latter is desired, on the presumption, of course, that such substitution is technologically feasible and is not prohibitively costly in resources" (Buchanan, 1986, p. 22). While this is not in serious conflict with Buchanan's rejection of any "transcendental" evaluation of the outcomes (p. 22), nevertheless the assessment of outcomes must, in *some* form, enter this evaluative exercise.[32]

There are, however, other — more purely procedural — systems to be found in this literature. If the utilitarian tradition of judging everything by the consequent utilities is one extreme in the contrast (focusing only on a limited class of consequences), Nozick's (1974) elegant exploration of libertarian "entitlement theory" comes close to the other end (focusing on the right rules that cover personal liberties as well as rights of holding, using, exchanging, and bequeathing legitimately owned property). But the possibility of having unacceptable consequences has to be addressed by any such procedural system. What if the results are dreadful for many, or even all?

Indeed, it can be shown that even gigantic famines can actually take place in an economy that fulfills all the libertarian rights and entitlements specified in the Nozick system.[33] It is, thus, particularly appropriate that Nozick (1974) makes exceptions to consequence-independence in cases where the exercise of these rights would lead to "catastrophic moral horrors."[34] Because of this qualification, consequences are made to matter after all, and underlying this concession is Nozick's good sense (similar to Buchanan's) that a procedural system of entitlements that happens to yield catastrophic moral horrors (we have to have some consensus on what these are) would be – and should be – ethically unacceptable. However, once consequences are brought into the story, not only is the purity of a consequence-independent system lost, but also the issue of deciding on the relative importance of "right rules" and "good consequences" is forcefully re-established.

I turn now to the other side of the dichotomy: can we have sensible outcome judgments in a totally procedure-independent way? Classical utilitarianism does indeed propose such a system, but it is hard to be convinced that we can plausibly judge any given utility distribution ignoring *altogether* the process that led to that distribution (attaching, for example, no intrinsic importance whatever to whether a particular utility redistribution is caused by charity, or taxation, or torture).[35]

This recognition of the role of processes is not, in fact, hostile to social choice theory, since there is nothing to prevent us from seeing the description of processes as a part of the consequent states generated by them.[36] If action A is performed, then "action A has been done" must be one – indeed, the most elementary – consequence of that event. If Mr. John Major were to wish not merely that he should be re-elected as Prime Minister, but that he should be "re-elected fairly" (I am not, of course, insinuating that any such preference has been expressed by Mr. Major), the consequence that he would be seeking would have procedural requirements incorporated within it.

This is not to claim that every process can be comfortably placed within the description of states of affairs without changing anything in social choice theory. Parts of the literature that deal with comparisons of decision mechanisms in arriving at *given* states would need modification. If, in general, processes leading to the emergence of a social state were standardly included in the characterization of that state, then we have to construct "equivalence classes" to *ignore* some differences (in this case, between some antecedent processes) to be able to discuss cogently the "same state" being brought about by different decision mechanisms. To make sense of such ideas as, say, "path independence" (on which see Plott [1973]), so that they are not rendered vacuous, equivalence classes of this type would certainly have to be constructed (on the concepts of equivalence classes and invariance conditions, see Sen [1986b]).

The contrast between the procedural and consequential approaches is, thus, somewhat overdrawn, and it may be possible to combine them, to a considerable extent, in an adequately rich characterization of states of affairs. The dichotomy is far from pure, and it is mainly a question of relative concentration.

VII   Liberties, Rights, and Preferences

The need to integrate procedural considerations in consequential analysis is especially important in the field of rights and liberties. The violation or fulfillment of basic liberties or rights tends to be ignored in traditional utilitarian welfare economics not just because of its consequentialist focus, but particularly because of its "welfarism," whereby consequent states of affairs are judged exclusively by the utilities generated in the respective states.[37] While processes may end up getting some *indirect* attention insofar as they influence people's utilities, nevertheless no direct and basic importance is attached in the utilitarian framework to rights and liberties in the evaluation of states of affairs.

The initial formulation of social choice did not depart in this respect from the utilitarian heritage, but it is possible to change this within a broadly Arrovian framework (see Sen, 1970, 1982a), and a good deal of work has been done in later social choice theory to accommodate the basic relevance of rights and liberties in assessing states of affairs, and thus to evaluate economic, political, and social arrangements. If a person is prevented from doing some preferred thing even though that choice is sensibly seen to be in her "personal domain," then the state of affairs can be seen to have been worsened by this failure. The extent of worsening is not to be judged only by the magnitude of the utility loss resulting from this (to be compared with utility gains of others, if any), since something more is also at stake. As John Stuart Mill (1859, p. 140) noted, "there is no parity between the feeling of a person for his own opinion, and the feeling of another who is offended at his holding it."[38] The need to guarantee some "minimal liberties" on a priority basis can be incorporated in social choice formulations.

It turns out, however, that such unconditional priority being given even to minimal liberty can conflict with other principles of social choice, including the redoubtable Pareto principle. The "impossibility of the Paretian liberal" captures the conflict between (i) the special importance of a person's preferences over her own personal sphere, and (ii) the general importance of people's preferences over any choice, irrespective of field. This impossibility theorem has led to a large literature extending, explaining, disputing, and ameliorating the result.[39] The "ways out" that have been sought have varied between (i) weakening the priority of liberties (thereby qualifying the minimal liberty condition), (ii) constraining the field-independent general force of preferences (thereby qualifying the Pareto principle), and (iii) restricting the domain of permissible individual-preference profiles. As in the case of the Arrow impossibility problem, the different ways of resolving this conflict have variable relevance depending on the exact nature of the social choice exercise involved.

There have also been attempts to redefine liberty in purely *procedural* terms. The last is an important subject on its own (quite independently of any use it might have as an attempt to resolve the impossibility), and I shall presently consider it. But as has been noted by Gaertner, Pattanaik, and Suzumura (1992), who have recently provided the most extensive recharacterization of liberty (in terms of "game forms"), the impossibility problem "persists under virtually every plausible concept of individual rights" (p. 161).[40]

The decisive move in the direction of a purely procedural view of liberty was made by Nozick (1974), responding to my social choice formulation and to the impossibility of the Paretian liberal (Sen, 1970). This has been followed by important constructive contributions by Gärdenfors (1981) and Sugden (1981), and the approach has been extended and developed into game-form formulations by Gaertner et al. (1992). In the game-form view, each of the players has a set of permissible strategies, and the outcome is a function of the combination of strategies chosen by each of the players (perhaps qualified by an additional "move" by "nature"). The liberties and rights of the different persons are defined by specifying a permissible subset from the product of the strategy sets of the different individuals. A person can exercise his rights as he likes, subject to the strategy combination belonging to the permissible set.

In defining what rights a person has, or in checking whether his rights were respected, there is, on this account, no need to examine or evaluate the resulting state of affairs, and no necessity to examine what states the individuals involved prefer. In contrasting this characterization of preference-independent, consequence-detached rights with the social choice approach to rights, perhaps the central question that is raised is the plausibility of making people's putative rights, in general, so dissociated from the effects of exercising them. This is a general issue that was already discussed at a broader level (section VI).

In some contexts, the idea of seeing rights in the form of permission to act can be quite inadequate, particularly because of "choice inhibition" that might arise from a variety of causes. The long British discussion on the failure of millions of potential welfare recipients from making legitimate claims (apparently due to the shame and stigma of having one's penury publicized and recorded) illustrates a kind of nonrealization of rights in which permission is not the main issue at all.[41] Similarly, the inability of women in traditionally sexist societies to use even those rights that have not been formally denied to them also illustrates a type of rights failure that is not helpfully seen in terms of game forms (see Sen, 1992b, pp. 148–50). Even the questions that standardly come up in this country in determining whether a rape has occurred have to go well beyond checking whether the victim in question was "free" to defy.

Leaving out such cases, it might well be plausible to argue that rights can be nicely characterized by game forms in many situations. However, even when that is the case, in deciding on what rights to protect and codify, and in determining how the underlying purpose might be most effectively achieved, there is a need to look at the likely consequences of different game-form specifications and to relate them to what people value and desire. If, for example, it appears that not banning smoking in certain gatherings (leaving the matter to the discretion of the people involved) would actually lead to unwilling victims having to inhale other people's smoke, then there would be a case for considering that the game-form be so modified that smoking is simply banned in those gatherings. Whether or not to make this move must depend crucially on consequential analysis. The object, in this case, is the prevention of the state of affairs in which nonsmokers have to inhale unwillingly other people's smoke: a situation they resent and which – it is assumed – they have a right to avoid. We proceed from there, through consequential analysis (in an "inverse" form: from consequences to antecedents), to the particular game-form formulation that would not achieve an acceptable result. The fact that the *articulation* of the game-form would be consequence-independent and preference-independent is not a terribly profound assertion and is quite consistent with the fundamental relevance of consequences and preferences.

The contrast between game-form formulations and social-choice conceptions of rights is, thus, less deep than it might first appear (see Sen, 1992b).[42] As in other fields considered earlier (section VI), in this area too, the need to combine procedural concerns with those of actual events and outcomes is quite strong.

VIII Values and Individual Choices

I have so far postponed discussing individual behavior and rationality, though the issue has indirectly figured in the preceding discussions (for example, in dealing with norms for social choice, individual interest in social welfare judgments, and determination of voting behavior). The public choice tradition has tended to rely a good deal on the presumption that people behave in a rather narrowly self-centered way – as *homo economicus* in particular, even though Buchanan (1986, p. 26) himself notes some "tension" on this issue (see also Geoffrey Brennan and Loren Lomarsky, 1993). Public servants *inter alia* are to be seen as working for their own well-being and success.

Adam Smith is sometimes described as the original proponent of the ubiquity and ethical adequacy of "the economic man," but that would be fairly sloppy history. In fact, Smith (1776, 1790) had examined the distinct disciplines of "self-love," "prudence," "sympathy," "generosity," and "public spirit," among others, and had discussed not only their intrinsic importance, but also their instrumental roles in the success of a society, and also their practical influence on actual behavior. The demands of rationality need not be geared entirely to the use of only one of these motivations (such as self-love), and there is plenty of empirical evidence to indicate that the presumption of uncompromising pursuit of narrowly defined self-interest is as mistaken today as it was in Smith's time.[43] Just as it is necessary to avoid the high-minded sentimentalism of assuming that all human beings (and public servants, in particular) try constantly to promote some selfless "social good," it is also important to escape what may be called the "low-minded sentimentalism" of assuming that everyone is constantly motivated entirely by personal self-interest.[44]

This does not, however, negate an important implication of the question raised by Buchanan and others that public servants would tend to have their own objective functions; I would dissociate that point from the further claim, with which it has come mixed, that these objective functions are narrowly confined to the officials' own self-interest. The important issue to emerge is that there is something missing in a large part of the resource-allocation literature (for example, in proposals of algorithms for decentralized resource allocation, from Oscar Lange and Abba Lerner onward) which make do without any independent objective function of the agents of public action. The additional assumption of *homo economicus* is not needed to point to this general lacuna.

While this has been a somewhat neglected question in social choice theory (though partially dealt with in the related literature on implementation), there is no particular reason why such plurality of motivations cannot be accommodated within a social choice framework with more richly described social states and more articulated characterization of individual choices and behavior. In the formulation of individual preference used by Arrow (1951) and in traditional social choice theory, the nature of the objective function of each individual is left unspecified. While there is need for supplementary work here, this is a helpfully permissive framework – not tied either to ceaseless do-gooding, or to uncompromising self-centeredness.

Even with this extended framework, taking us well beyond the *homo economicus*, there remain some difficulties with the notion of individual rationality used here. There is a problem of "insufficiency" shared by this approach to rationality with other "instrumental" approaches to rationality, since it does not have any condition of critical scrutiny of the objectives themselves. Socrates might have overstated matters a bit when he proclaimed that "the unexamined life is not worth living," but an examination of what kind of life one should sensibly choose cannot really be completely irrelevant to rational choice.[45] An "instrumental rationalist" is a decision expert whose response to seeing a man engaged in slicing his toes with a blunt knife is to rush to advise him that he should use a sharper knife to better serve his evident objective.

This is perhaps more of a limitation in the normative context than in using the presumption of rationality as a device for predicting behavior, since such critical scrutiny might not be very widely practiced. However, the last is not altogether clear, since discussions and exchange, and even political arguments, contribute to the formation and revision of values. As Frank Knight (1947, p. 280) noted, "Values are established or validated and recognized through *discussion*, an activity which is at once social, intellectual, and creative." There is, in fact, much force in Buchanan's (1954a, p. 120) assertion that this is a central component of democracy ("government by discussion") and that "individual values can and do change in the process of decision-making."

This issue has some real practical importance. To illustrate, in studying the fact that famines occur in some countries but not in others, I have tried to point to the phenomenon that no major famine has ever taken place in any country with a multiparty democracy with regular elections and with a reasonably free press (Sen, 1984).[46] This applies as much to the poorer democratic countries (such as India, Zimbabwe, or Botswana) as to the richer ones.[47] This is largely because famines, while killing millions, do not much affect the direct well-being of the ruling classes and dictators, who have little political incentive to prevent famines unless their rule is threatened by them. The economic analysis of famines across the world indicates that only a small proportion of the population tends to be stricken – rarely more than 5 percent or so. Since the shares of income and food of these poor groups tend normally to be no more than 3 percent of the total for the nation, it is not hard to rebuild their lost share of income and food, even in very poor countries, if a serious effort is made in that direction (see Sen, 1981; Drèze and Sen, 1989). Famines are thus easily preventable, and the need to face public criticism and to encounter the electorate provides the government with the political incentive to take preventive action with some urgency.

The question that remains is this. Since only a very small proportion of the population is struck by a famine (typically 5 percent or less), how does it become such a potent force in elections and in public criticism? This is in some tension with the assumption of universal self-centeredness, and presumably we do have the capacity – and often the inclination – to understand and respond to the predicament of others.[48] There is a particular need in this context to examine value formation that results from public discussion of miserable events, in generating sympathy and commitment on the part of citizens to do something to prevent their occurrence.

Even the idea of "basic needs," fruitfully used in the development literature, has to be related to the fact that what is taken as a "need" is not determined only by biological and uninfluencible factors. For example, in those parts of the so-called Third World in which there has been increased and extensive public discussion of the consequences of frequent childbearing on the well-being and freedom of mothers, the perception that a smaller family is a "basic need" of women (and men too) has grown, and in this value formation a combination of democracy, free public media, and basic education (especially female education) has been very potent. The implications of this finding are particularly important for rational consideration of the so-called "world population problem."[49]

Similar issues arise in dealing with environmental problems. The threats that we face call for organized international action as well as changes in national policies, particularly for better reflecting social costs in prices and incentives. But they are also dependent on value formation, related to public discussions, both for their influence on individual behavior and for bringing about policy changes through the political process. There are plenty of "social choice problems" in all this, but in analyzing them, we have to go beyond looking only for the best reflection of *given* individual preferences, or the most acceptable procedures for choices based on those preferences. We need to depart both from the assumption of given preferences (as in traditional social choice theory) and from the presumption that people are narrowly self-interested *homo economicus* (as in traditional public choice theory).

IX Concluding Remarks

Perhaps I could end by briefly returning to the questions with which I began. Arrow's impossibility theorem does indeed identify a profound difficulty in combining individual preference orderings into aggregative social welfare judgments (section II). But the result must not be seen as mainly a negative one, since it directly leads on to questions about how to overcome these problems. In the context of social welfare judgments, the natural resolution of these problems lies in enriching the informational base, and there are several distinct ways of doing this (section IV). These approaches are used in practice for aggregative judgments made by individuals, but they can also be used for organized procedures for arriving at social measures of poverty, inequality, distribution-adjusted real national incomes, and other such aggregative indicators.

Second, Buchanan's questioning of the concept of social preference (and of its use as an ordering to make – or explain – social choices) is indeed appropriate in the case of social decision *mechanisms*, though less so for social welfare *judgments* (section III). The Arrow theorem, in its original form, does not apply once social decision-making is characterized in terms of choice functions *without* any imposed requirement of intermenu consistency. However, when the natural implications of taking a choice-functional view of social decisions are worked out, Arrow's conditions have to be correspondingly restated, and then the impossibility result returns in its entirety once again (section III). The idea of social preference or internal consistency of social choice is basically redundant for this impossibility result. So Buchanan's move does not negate Arrow's impossibility. On the other hand, it is an important departure in its own right.

Coming to terms with the impossibility problem in the case of social decision mechanisms is largely a matter of give and take between different principles with respective appeals. This calls for a less rigid interpretation of the role of axiomatic demands on permissible social decision rules (section V).

Third, Buchanan's argument for a more procedural view of social decisions has much merit. Nevertheless, there are good reasons to doubt the adequacy of a purely procedural view (independent of consequences), just as there are serious defects in narrowly consequentialist views (independent of procedures). Procedural concerns can, however, be amalgamated with consequential ones by recharacterizing states of affairs appropriately, and the evaluation of states can then take note of the two aspects together (section VI). This combination is especially important in accommodating liberty and rights in social judgments as well as social decision mechanisms (section VII).

Finally, there is room for paying more attention to the rationality of individual behavior as an integral component of rational social decisions. In particular, the practical reach of social choice theory, in its traditional form, is considerably reduced by its tendency to ignore value formation through social interactions. Buchanan is right to emphasize the role of public discussion in the development of preferences (as an important part of democracy). However, traditional public choice theory is made unduly narrow by the insistence that individuals invariably behave as *homo economicus* (a subject on which social choice theory is much more permissive). This uncompromising restriction can significantly misrepresent the nature of social concerns and values. But aside from this descriptive limitation, there is also an important issue of "practical reason" here. Many of the more exacting problems of the contemporary world – varying from famine prevention to environmental preservation – actually call for value formation through public discussion (section VIII).

On the rationality of social decisions, many important lessons have emerged from the discipline of social choice theory as well as the public choice approach. In fact, we can get quite a bit more by *combining* these lessons. As a social choice theorist, I had not, in fact, planned to be particularly even-handed in this paper, but need not, I suppose, apologize for ending up with rather even hands.

Notes

*   Department of Economics, Littauer Center. Harvard University, Cambridge, MA 02138. For helpful discussions I am most grateful to Eric Maskin and to Sudhir Anand, Kenneth Arrow, Nick Baigent. Kaushik Basu, Anthony de Jasay, Frank Hahn, Pia Malaney, Dennis Mueller, Robert Nozick, Mancur Olson, Ben Polak, Louis Putterman, Emma Rothschild, Kotaro Suzumura, Vivian Walsh, and Stefano Zamagni.

1   For discussions of the axioms involved and alternative formulations and proofs, see Arrow (1951, 1963), Sen (1970, 1986b), Peter C. Fishburn (1973), Robert Wilson (1975), Bengt Hansson (1976), Jerry S. Kelly (1978), Graciela Chichilnisky (1982), Chichilnisky and Geoffrey Heal (1983), Prasanta Pattanaik and Maurice Salles (1983), Kotaro Suzumura (1983), Charles Blackorby et al. (1984), and Ken Binmore (1994), among others.

2   On "the impossibility of the Paretian liberal," see Sen (1970, 1983), Kelly (1978), Suzumura (1983). John Wriglesworth (1985), and Jonathan Riley (1987), among other contributions. Other results related to Arrow's theorem include the demonstration by Allan F. Gibbard (1973) and Mark A. Satterthwaite (1975) that "manipulability" is a ubiquitous characteristic of voting schemes: on related issues see Pattanaik (1978), Jean-Jacques Laffont (1979), Hervé Moulin (1983), Bazalel Peleg (1984), and Salvador Barberá and Bhaskar Dutta (1986), among others.

3   Dennis C. Mueller (1989) provides an excellent introduction to public choice theory and its relation to social choice theory. See also Atkinson (1987) and Sandmo (1990) on Buchanan's contributions.

4 The canonical treatise on the "public choice" approach is Buchanan and Tullock (1962), but it is important to note the differences in emphases between the appendix by Buchanan and that by Tullock.

5 Arrow (1951) himself points out "the unreality of this assumption" (p. 8).

6 The importance of politics as discussion has also been stressed in the Habermasian tradition; on this see Jon Elster and Aanund Hylland (1986) and Jürgen Habermas (1994). See also Albert Hirschman (1970) and the works inspired by his writings.

7 Robbins (1938) himself was opposed not so much to making interpersonal comparisons, but to claiming them to be "scientific."

8 The strategy of proof employed here (as in Sen [1986b]) is more direct and simpler than the versions used in Arrow (1963) and Sen (1970) and does not require defining additional concepts (such as "almost decisiveness").

9 For proof, take two pairs of alternative states (x, y) and (a, b), all distinct (the proof when they are not all distinct is quite similar). Group G is decisive over (x, y); we have to show that it is decisive over (a, b) as well. By unrestricted domain, let everyone in G prefer a to x to y to b, while all others prefer a to x, and y to b, but rank the other pairs in any way whatever. By the decisiveness of G over (x, y), x is socially preferred to y. By the Pareto principle, a is socially preferred to x, and y to b. Therefore, by transitivity, a is socially preferred to b. If this result is influenced by individual preferences over any pair other than (a, b), then the condition of independence would be violated. Thus, a must be ranked above b simply by virtue of everyone in G preferring a to b (since others can have any preference whatever over this pair). So G is indeed decisive over (a, b).

10 For proof, take a decisive group G and partition it into G_1 and G_2. Let everyone in G_1 prefer x to y and x to z, with any possible ranking of (y, z), and let everyone in group G_2 prefer x to y and z to y, with any possible ranking of (x, z). It does not matter what those not in G prefer. If, now, x is socially preferred to z then the members of group G_1 would be decisive over this pair, since they alone definitely prefer x to z (the others can rank this pair in any way). If G_1 is not to be decisive, we must have z at least as good as x for some individual preferences over (x, z) of nonmembers of G_1. Take that case, and combine this social ranking (that z is at least as good as x) with the social preference for x over y (a consequence of the decisiveness of G and the fact that everyone in G prefers x to y). By transitivity, z is socially preferred to y. But only G_2 members definitely prefer z to y. Thus G_2 is decisive over this pair (z, y). Thus, from the Field-Expansion Lemma, G_2 is decisive. So either G_1 or G_2 must be decisive – proving the lemma.

11 On some analytical problems involved in deriving "the revealed preference of a government" by observing its choices, see Kaushik Basu (1980).

12 Binariness requires a combination of two types of choice consistency: basic "contraction consistency" (α) and basic "expansion consistency" (γ). These conditions are quite exacting, and they have to be further strengthened to get transitivity and other additional properties (on this, see Sen [1971, 1977a], Rajat Deb [1983], and Isaac Levi [1986]).

13 On this, see Harsanyi (1955 p. 310): "Of course when I speak of preferences 'from a social standpoint,' often abbreviated to 'social' preferences and the like, I always mean preferences based on a given individual's value judgments concerning 'social welfare.'"

14 This has been established in a sequence of results, presented by Gibbard, Hansson, Andreu Mas-Colell, Hugo Sonnenschein, Donald Brown, Georges Bordes, Kelly, Suzumura, Douglas Blair, Robert Pollak, Julian Blau, Deb. David Kelsey, and others; for critical overviews, see Blair and Pollak (1982), Suzumura (1983), and Sen (1986a).

15 The pioneering work on choice-functional formulations came from Hansson (1968, 1969), Thomas Schwartz (1972, 1985), Fishburn (1973), and Plott (1973). Mark Aizerman and his colleagues at the Institute of Control Sciences in Moscow provided a series of penetrating investigations of the general choice-functional features of moving from individual-choice

functions to social-choice functions (see Aizerman, 1985; Aizerman and Fuad Aleskerov, 1986). On related matters see also Aizerman and A. V. Malishevski (1981).

16   A sequence of contributions on this and related issues has come from Plott, Fishburn, Hansson, Donald Campbell, Bordes, Blair, Kelly, Suzumura, Deb, R. R. Parks, John Ferejohn, D. M. Grether, Kelsey, V. Denicolo, and Yasumi Matsumoto, among others. For general overviews and critiques, see Blair et al. (1976), Suzumura (1983), and Sen (1986a).

17   See also Buchanan and Tullock (1962).

18   For exact statements of the conditions and a proof of the theorem, see Sen (1993).

19   On this issue, see Sen (1977b, 1982a).

20   Formally, person 2 is "almost decisive" over the first pair (in the sense of winning against opposition by all others – in this case, person 1), and an alternative version of the Field-Expansion Lemma shows that he will be almost decisive (indeed fully decisive) over all other pairs as well (see Lemma 3a in Sen [1970 pp. 43–4]). Note that "field expansion" is based inter alia on the use of the condition of "unrestricted domain," allowing the possibility that the individuals involved *could have* had other preferences as well.

21   On different types of interpersonal comparisons, and the relevance of distinct "spaces" in making efficiency and equity judgments, see Sen (1982a, 1992a), John Roemer (1986), Martha Nussbaum (1988), Richard Arneson (1989), G. A. Cohen (1989), Arrow (1991), Elster and Roemer (1991), and Nussbaum and Sen (1993).

22   On the other hand, Arrow's impossibility theorem can be generalized to accommodate cardinality of utilities without interpersonal comparisons; see Theorem 8.2 in Sen (1970).

23   Maximin gives complete priority to the interest of the worst off. It was proposed by John Rawls (1963), as a part of his "difference principle" (though the comparisons that he uses are not of utilities, but of holdings of primary goods). Lexicographic maximin, sometimes called "leximin," was proposed in Sen (1970) to make the Rawlsian approach consistent with the strong Pareto principle, and it has been endorsed and used in his *Theory of Justice* by Rawls (1971). Axiomatic derivations of leximin were pioneered by Peter J. Hammond (1976), and Claude d'Aspremont and Gevers (1977), among others. See also Edmund Phelps (1973).

24   See Harsanyi (1955), Patrick Suppes (1966), Sen (1970, 1977b), Phelps (1973), Hammond (1976, 1985), Arrow (1977), d'Aspremont and Gevers (1977), Gevers (1979), Eric Maskin (1978, 1979), Roberts (1980a, b), Roger B. Myerson (1981), James Mirrlees (1982), Suzumura (1983), Blackorby et al. (1984), d'Aspremont (1985), and Kelsey (1987), among others.

25   The literature on such measures is now quite large. Different types of exercises are illustrated by Sen (1973), Frank Cowell (1977), Blackorby and Donaldson (1978, 1980). Siddiq Osmani (1982), Sudhir Anand (1983), Atkinson (1983, 1989), S. R. Chakravarty (1983), Anthony Shorrocks (1983), Suzumura (1983), James E. Foster (1984, 1985), Ravi Kanbur (1984), Michel Le Breton and Alain Trannoy (1987), W. Eichhorn (1988), Peter J. Lambert (1989), and Martin Ravallion (1994), among many other contributions.

26   The policy discussions include those surrounding the influential *Human Development Reports*, produced by the United Nations Development Programme. Another strong force in that direction has been the sequence of UNICEF reports on *The State of the World's Children*. Policy issues related to such social judgments have been discussed by Paul Streeten et al. (1981), Nanak Kakwani (1986), Jean Drèze and Sen (1989), Alan Hamlin and Philip Pettit (1989), Keith Griffin and John Knight (1990), Anand and Ravallion (1993), Partha Dasgupta (1993), and Meghnad Desai (1995).

27   "Value restriction" turns out to be necessary and sufficient for this class of domain conditions for consistent majority rule when individual preferences are linear orderings, though the conditions are more complex in the general case of weak orderings (see Sen and Prasanta Pattanaik, 1969; see also Ken-ichi Inada, 1969, 1970). These relations can be generalized to all Arrovian social welfare functions and for nonmanipulable voting procedures (on which see Maskin [1976]

and E. Kalai and E. Muller [1977]). Other types of conditions have been proposed by Tullock (1967) (with a somewhat exaggerated title: "The General Irrelevance of the General Possibility Theorem") and in a definitive paper by Jean-Michel Grandmont (1978). Fine discussions of the issues involved in the different types of domain conditions can be found in Gaertner (1979) and Arrow and Hervé Raynaud (1986).

28 The ubiquitous presence of voting cycles in majority rule has been extensively studied by R. D. McKelvey (1979) and Norman Schofield (1983).

29 Even individual social welfare judgments (and more generally, individual views of social appropriateness) presumably have some influence on political preferences.

30 Positional rules of other kinds have been studied extensively by Peter Gärdenfors (1973) and Ben Fine and Kit Fine (1974a,b). On different versions of the Borda rule, see Sen (1977a, 1982a, pp. 186–7).

31 For example, Andrew Caplin and Barry Nalebuff (1988) provide a case for 64-percent majority rule. Also see the symposium on voting procedures led by Jonathan Levin and Nalebuff (1995).

32 Buchanan (1986) expresses some basic sympathy for "libertarian socialists" (as opposed to *antilibertarian* socialists) but attributes what he sees as their well-intentioned but mistaken opposition to markets to their not having "the foggiest notion of the way the market works" and to their being "blissfully ignorant of economic theory" (pp. 4–5). *Consequential* analysis incorporated in economic theory is precisely what Buchanan is invoking here to dispute the libertarian socialist position.

33 On this see Sen (1981), linking starvation to unequal entitlements, with actual case studies of four famines. See also Ravallion (1987), Drèze and Sen (1989), and Desai (1995).

34 See also Nozick's (1974) discussion of "Locke's proviso."

35 On this question, see Sen (1982a,b).

36 On this question, see Sen (1982b), Hammond (1986), and Levi (1986).

37 Utilities can be defined in terms of choices made, desires entertained, or satisfactions received, but the point at issue applies to each of these interpretations. Utilitarian welfare economics has tended traditionally to focus on satisfactions, partly because individual choices do not immediately yield any basis for interpersonal comparisons unless some elaborately hypothetical choices are considered, on which see Harsanyi [1955]), but also because "satisfaction" had appeared to utilitarian economists as providing a more solid basis for judging individual welfare. For example, this was the reason given by A. C. Pigou (1951, pp. 288–9):

> Some economists . . . have employed the term "utility" indifferently for satisfactions and for desiredness. I shall employ it here to mean satisfactions, so that we may say that a man's economic welfare is made up of his utilities.

38 The idea of "personal domains" and "protected spheres" goes back to Mill (see Riley, 1987), and more recently has found strong and eloquent expression in the writings of Friedrich Hayek (1960).

39 For general accounts of the literature, see Kelly (1978), Suzumura (1983, 1991), Wriglesworth (1985), Paul Seabright (1989), and Pattanaik and Suzumura (1994a,b). For public-choice critiques, see Sugden (1981, 1993) and Rowley (1993).

40 The belief that the problem can be resolved through Pareto-improving contracts, which has been suggested by some authors, overlooks the incentive-incompatibility of the touted solution and, perhaps more importantly, confounds the nature of the conflict itself, since the conflict in values keeps open the question as to what contracts would be offered or accepted by the persons involved. For example, in the (rather overdiscussed) case of whether the prude or the lewd should read *Lady Chatterley's Lover*, it is not at all clear that the prude, if he has any libertarian inclinations, would actually offer a contract by which he agrees to read a book that he hates to

make the lewd refrain from reading a book he loves. In fact, while the prude may prefer that the lewd does not read that book, consistent with that he may not want to bring this about through an enforceable contract, and the "dilemma of the Paretian liberal" could be his dilemma too. The lewd too faces a decision problem about whether to try to alter the prude's personal life rather than minding his own business. On these issues, see Sen (1983, 1992b), Basu (1984), and Elster and Hylland (1986).

41   Stig Kanger (1985) has illuminatingly discussed "nonrealization" of rights, and the variety of ways this can occur.

42   On related matters, see also Pattanaik and Suzumura (1994a, b).

43   A set of studies on this and related issues is presented in Jane Mansbridge (1990).

44   Efforts to explain every socially motivated action as some kind of a cunning attempt at maximization of purely private gain are frequent in part of modern economics. There is an interesting question as to whether the presumption of exclusive self-interestedness is a more common general belief in America than in Europe, without being a general characteristic of *actual* behavior. Alexis de Tocqueville thought so:

> The Americans...are fond of explaining almost all the actions of their lives by the principle of self-interest rightly understood; they show with complacency how an enlightened regard for themselves constantly prompts them to assist one another and inclines them willingly to sacrifice a portion of their time and property to the welfare of the state. In this respect, they frequently fail to do themselves justice: for in the United States as well as elsewhere people are sometimes seen to give way to those disinterested and spontaneous impulses that are natural to man; but the Americans seldom admit that they yield to emotions of this kind; they are more anxious to do honor to their philosophy than to themselves.

(Tocqueville, 1840 [Book II, Chapter VIII; in the 1945 edition, p. 122]).

45   On this subject, see Nozick (1989).

46   See also Drèze and Sen (1989) and *World Disasters Report* (1994, pp. 33–7).

47   In contrast, China – despite its fine record of public health and education even before the reforms – managed to have perhaps the largest famine in recorded history, during 1959–62, in which 23–30 million people died, while the mistaken public policies were not revised for three years through the famine. In India, on the other hand, despite its bungling ways, large famines stopped abruptly with independence in 1947 and the installing of a multiparty democracy (the last such famine, "the great Bengal famine," had occurred in 1943).

48   On this general question, see Rawls (1971) and Thomas Scanlon (1982). See also Daniel Hausman and Michael McPherson (1993).

49   See the discussion and the literature cited in Sen (1994, pp. 62–71), particularly Dasgupta (1993). See also Adam Przeworski and Fernando Limongi's (1994) international comparisons, which indicate a fairly strong association between democracy and fertility reduction. In the rapid reduction of the total fertility rate in the Indian state of Kerala from 4.4 in the 1950s to the present figure of 1.8 (a level similar to that in Britain and France and lower than in the United States), value formation related to education, democracy, and public discussion has played a major part. While the fertility rate has also come down in China (though not as much as in Kerala), China's use of compulsion rather than consensual progress has resulted in relatively high infant-mortality rates (28 per thousand for boys and 33 per thousand for girls, compared with Kerala's 17 per thousand for boys and 16 per thousand for girls in 1991). Such public dialogues are, however, hard to achieve in many other parts of India, despite democracy, because of the low level of elementary education, especially for women. These and related issues are discussed in Drèze and Sen (1995).

References

Aizerman, M. A. (1985) "New Problems in the General Choice Theory." *Social Choice and Welfare*, December, *2*(4), pp. 235–82.

Aizerman, Mark A. and Aleskerov, Fuad (1986) "Voting Operators in the Space of Choice Functions." *Mathematical Social Sciences*, June, *11*(3), pp. 201–42; corrigendum, June 1988, *13*(3), p. 305.

Aizerman, Mark A. and Malishevski, A. V. (1981) "General Theory of Best Variants Choice: Some Aspects." *IEEE Transactions on Automatic Control*, AC-26, pp. 1031–41.

Anand, Sudhir (1983) *Inequality and Poverty in Malaysia: Measurement and Decomposition.* New York: Oxford University Press.

Anand, Sudhir and Ravallion, Martin (1993) "Human Development in Poor Countries: On the Role of Private Incomes and Public Services." *Journal of Economic Perspectives*, *7*(1), pp. 133–50.

Arneson, Richard J. (1989) "Equality and Equal Opportunity for Welfare." *Philosophical Studies*, May *56*(1), pp. 77–93.

Arrow, Kenneth J. (1951/1963) *Social Choice and Individual Values.* New York: Wiley; 2nd ed., 1963.

Arrow, Kenneth J. (1977) "Extended Sympathy and the Possibility of Social Choice." *American Economic Review (Papers and Proceedings)*, *67*(1), pp. 219–25.

Arrow, Kenneth J. (ed.) (1991) *Markets and Welfare.* London: Macmillan.

Arrow, Kenneth J. and Raynaud, Hervé (1986) *Social Choice and Multicriterion Decision-making.* Cambridge, MA: MIT Press.

Atkinson, Anthony B. (1970) "On the Measurement of Inequality." *Journal of Economic Theory*, *2*(3), pp. 244–63.

Atkinson, Anthony B. (1983) *Social Justice and Public Policy.* Cambridge, MA: MIT Press.

Atkinson, Anthony B. (1987) "James M. Buchanan's Contributions to Economics." *Scandinavian Journal of Economics*, *89*(1), pp. 5–15.

Atkinson, Anthony B. (1989) *Poverty and Social Security.* New York: Harvester Wheatsheaf.

Barberá, Salvador and Dutta, Bhaskar (1986) "General, Direct and Self Implementation of Social Choice Functions via Protective Equilibria." *Mathematical Social Sciences*, *11*(2), pp. 109–27.

Basu, Kaushik (1980) *Revealed Preference of Government.* Cambridge: Cambridge University Press.

——(1984) "The Right to Give up Rights." *Economica*, *51*(204), pp. 413–22.

Baumol, William J. (1986) *Superfairness.* Cambridge, MA: MIT Press.

Bergson, Abram (1938) "A Reformulation of Certain Aspects of Welfare Economics." *Quarterly Journal of Economics*, *52*(1), pp. 310–34.

Bergson, Abram (1966) *Essays in Normative Economics.* Cambridge, MA: Harvard University Press.

Binmore, Ken (1994) *Playing Fair: Game Theory and the Social Contract*, vol. I. London: MIT Press.

Blackorby, Charles and Donaldson, David (1978) "Measures of Relative Equality and Their Meaning in Terms of Social Welfare." *Journal of Economic Theory*, *18*(1), pp. 59–80.

——(1980) "Ethical Indices for the Measurement of Poverty." *Econometrica*, *48*(4), pp. 1053–60.

Blackorby, Charles; Donaldson, David and Weymark, John (1984) "Social Choice with Interpersonal Utility Comparisons: A Diagrammatic Introduction." *International Economic Review*, *25*(2), pp. 325–56.

Blair, Douglas H.; Bordes, Georges A.; Kelly, Jerry S. and Suzumura, Kotaro (1976) "Impossibility Theorems without Collective Rationality." *Journal of Economic Theory*, *13*(3), pp. 361–79.

Blair, Douglas H. and Pollak, Robert A. (1982) "Acyclic Collective Choice Rules." *Econometrica*, *50*(4), pp. 931–44.

Borda, J. C. (1781) "Mémoire sur les Élections au Scrutin." *Mémoires de l'Académie Royale des Sciences* (Paris).

Brennan, Geoffrey and Lomasky, Loren (1993) *Democracy and Decision: The Pure Theory of Electoral Preference.* Cambridge: Cambridge University Press.

Broome, John (1991) *Weighing Goods*. Oxford: Blackwell.

Buchanan, James M. (1954a) "Social Choice, Democracy, and Free Markets." *Journal of Political Economy*, April *62*(2), pp. 114–23.

Buchanan, James (1954b) "Individual Choice in Voting and the Market." *Journal of Political Economy*, August, *62*(3), pp. 334–43.

Buchanan, James (1960) *Fiscal Theory and Political Economy*. Chapel Hill, NC: University of North Carolina Press.

Buchanan, James (1986) *Liberty, Market and the State*. Brighton: Wheatsheaf.

Buchanan, James (1994a) "Foundational Concerns: A Criticism of Public Choice Theory." Unpublished manuscript presented at the European Public Choice Meeting, Valencia, Spain.

Buchanan, James (1994b) "Dimensionality, Rights and Choices among Relevant Alternatives." Unpublished manuscript presented at a meeting honoring Peter Bernholz, Basel, Switzerland.

Buchanan, James M. and Tullock, Gordon (1962) *The Calculus of Consent*. Ann Arbor: University of Michigan Press.

Caplin, Andrew and Nalebuff, Barry (1988) "On 64% Majority Rule." *Econometrica*, *56*(4), pp. 787–814.

Chakravarty, S. R. (1983) "Ethically Flexible Measures of Poverty." *Canadian Journal of Economics*, *16*(1), pp. 74–85.

Chichilnisky, Graciela (1982) "Social Aggregation Rules and Continuity." *Quarterly Journal of Economics*, *97*(2), pp. 337–52.

Chichilnisky, Graciela and Heal, Geoffrey M. (1983) "Necessary and Sufficient Conditions for a Resolution of the Social Choice Paradox." *Journal of Economic Theory*, *31*(1), pp. 68–87.

Cohen, G. A. (1989) "On the Currency of Egalitarian Justice." *Ethics*, *99*(4), pp. 906–44.

Condorcet, Marquis de (1785) *Essai sur l'application de l'analyse à la probabilité des décisions rendues à la pluralité des voix*. Paris: L'Imprimerie Royale.

Cowell, Frank A. (1977) *Measuring Inequality*. New York: Wiley.

Dasgupta, Partha (1993) *An Inquiry into Well-being and Destitution*. Oxford: Oxford University Press.

d'Aspremont, Claude (1985) "Axioms for Social Welfare Ordering," in Leonid Hurwicz, David Schmeidler, and Hugo Sonnenschein (eds.), *Social Goals and Social Organization*. Cambridge: Cambridge University Press, pp. 19–76.

d'Aspremont, Claude and Gevers, Louis (1977) "Equity and the Informational Basis of Collective Choice." *Review of Economic Studies*, *44*(2), pp. 199–209.

Deb, Rajat (1983) "Binariness and Rational Choice." *Mathematical Social Sciences*, *5*(1), pp. 97–106.

Desai, Meghnad (1995) *Poverty, Famine and Economic Development*. Aldershot: Elgar.

Drèze, Jean and Sen, Amartya (1989) *Hunger and Public Action*. Oxford: Oxford University Press.

Drèze, Jean (1995) *India: Economic Development and Social Opportunity*. Oxford: Oxford University Press.

Eichhorn, W. (1988) *Measurement in Economics*. New York: Physica-Verlag.

Elster, Jon and Hylland, Aanund (eds.) (1986) *Foundations of Social Choice Theory*. Cambridge: Cambridge University Press.

Elster, Jon and Roemer, John (eds.) (1991) *Interpersonal Comparisons of Well-being*. Cambridge: Cambridge University Press.

Fine, Ben and Fine, Kit (1974a) "Social Choice and Individual Ranking I." *Review of Economic Studies*, *41*(3), pp. 303–22.

Fine, Ben, (1974b) "Social Choice and Individual Rankings II." *Review of Economic Studies 41*(4), pp. 459–75.

Fishburn, Peter C. (1973) *The Theory of Social Choice*. Princeton, NJ: Princeton University Press.

Foster, James E. (1984) "On Economic Poverty: A Survey of Aggregate Measures." *Advances in Econometrics*, *3*, pp. 215–51.

Foster, James E. (1985) "Inequality Measurement," in H. Peyton Young (ed.), *Fair Allocation*. Providence, RI: American Mathematical Society, pp. 31–68.

Gaertner, Wulf (1979) "An Analysis and Comparison of Several Necessary and Sufficient Conditions for Transitivity of Majority Decision Rule," in Jean-Jacques Laffont (ed.), *Aggregation and Revelation of Preferences*. Amsterdam: North-Holland, pp. 91–112.

Gaertner, Wulf; Pattanaik, Prasanta K. and Suzumura, Kotaro (1992) "Individual Rights Revisited." *Economica*, 59(234), pp. 161–78.

Gärdenfors, Peter (1973) "Positional Voting Functions." *Theory and Decision*, 4(1), pp. 1–24.

Gärdenfors, Peter (1981) "Rights, Games and Social Choice." *Nous*, 15(3), pp. 341–56.

Gevers, Louis (1979) "On Interpersonal Comparability and Social Welfare Orderings." *Econometrica*, 47(1), pp. 75–89.

Gibbard, Allan F. (1973) "Manipulation of Voting Schemes: A General Result." *Econometrica*, 41(4), pp. 587–601.

Grandmont, Jean-Michel (1978) "Intermediate Preferences and the Majority Rule." *Econometrica*, 46(2), pp. 317–30.

Griffin, Keith and Knight, John (eds.) (1990) *Human Development and the International Development Strategy for the 1990s*. London: Macmillan.

Habermas, J. (1994) "Three Models of Democracy." *Constellations*, 1(1), pp. 1–10.

Hamlin, Alan and Pettit, Philip (eds.) (1989) *The Good Polity*. Oxford: Blackwell.

Hammond, Peter J. (1976) "Equity, Arrow's Conditions, and Rawls' Difference Principle." *Econometrica*, 44(4), pp. 793–804.

Hammond, Peter J. (1985) "Welfare Economics," in G. Feiwel (ed.), *Issues in Contemporary Microeconomics and Welfare*. Albany: State University of New York Press, pp. 405–34.

Hammond, Peter J. (1986) "Consequentialist Social Norms for Public Decisions," in Walter P. Heller, Ross M. Starr, and David A. Starrett, (eds.), *Social Choice and Public Decision-making, vol. 1: Essays in Honor of Kenneth J. Arrow*. Cambridge: Cambridge University Press, pp. 3–27.

Hansson, Bengt (1968) "Choice Structures and Preference Relations." *Synthese*, 18(4), pp. 443–58.

Hansson, Bengt (1969) "Voting and Group Decision Functions." *Synthese*, 20(4), pp. 526–37.

Hansson, Bengt (1976) "The Existence of Group Preference." *Public Choice*, 28, pp. 89–98.

Harsanyi, John C. (1955) "Cardinal Welfare, Individualistic Ethics, and Interpersonal Comparisons of Utility." *Journal of Political Economy*, 63(3), pp. 309–21.

Hausman, Daniel M. and McPherson, Michael S. (1993) "Taking Ethics Seriously: Economics and Contemporary Moral Philosophy." *Journal of Economic Literature*, 31(2), pp. 671–731.

Hayek, Friedrich A. (1960) *The Constitution of Liberty*. London: Routledge and Kegan Paul.

Heller, Walter P.; Starr, Ross M. and Starrett, David A. (eds.) (1986) *Social Choice and Public Decision-making, vol. 1: Essays in Honor of Kenneth J. Arrow*, Cambridge: Cambridge University Press.

Hirschman, Albert (1970) *Exit, Voice and Loyalty*. Cambridge, MA: Harvard University Press.

Inada, Ken-ichi (1969) "On the Simple Majority Decision Rule." *Econometrica*, 37(3), pp. 490–506.

Inada, Ken-ichi (1970) "Majority Rule and Rationality." *Journal of Economic Theory*, 2(1), pp. 27–40.

Kakwani, Nanak (1986) *Analyzing Redistribution Policies*. Cambridge: Cambridge University Press.

Kalai, E. and Muller, E. (1977) "Characterization of Domains Admitting Nondictatorial Social Welfare Functions and Nonmanipulable Voting Procedures." *Journal of Economic Theory*, 16(2), pp. 457–69.

Kanbur, S. M. (Ravi) (1954) "The Measurement and Decomposition of Inequality and Poverty," in F. van der Ploeg (ed.), *Mathematical Methods in Economics*. New York: Wiley, pp. 403–32.

Kanger, Stig (1985) "On Realization of Human Rights." *Acta Philosophica Fennica*, 38, pp. 71–78.

Kelly, Jerry S. (1978) *Arrow Impossibility Theorems*. New York: Academic Press.

Kelsey, David (1987) "The Role of Information in Social Welfare Judgments." *Oxford Economic Papers*, 39(2), pp. 301–17.

Knight, Frank (1947) *Freedom and Reform: Essays in Economic and Social Philosophy*. New York: Harper; republished, Indianapolis: Liberty, 1982.

Kolm, Serge Ch. (1969) "The Optimal Production of Social Justice," in J. Margolis and H. Guitton (eds.), *Public Economics*. London: Macmillan, pp. 145–200.

Laffont, Jean-Jacques (ed.) (1979) *Aggregation and Revelation of Preferences*. Amsterdam: North-Holland.

Lambert, Peter J. (1989) *The Distribution and Redistribution of Income: A Mathematical Analysis*. Oxford: Blackwell.

Le Breton, Michel and Trannoy, Alain (1987) "Measures of Inequalities as an Aggregation of Individual Preferences about Income Distribution: The Arrovian Case." *Journal of Economic Theory*, *41*(2), pp. 248–69.

Levi, Isaac (1986) *Hard Choices*. Cambridge: Cambridge University Press.

Levin, Jonathan and Nalebuff, Barry (1995) "An Introduction to Vote-Counting Schemes." *Journal of Economic Perspectives*, forthcoming.

Mansbridge, Jane J. (ed.) (1990) *Beyond Self-interest*. Chicago: University of Chicago Press.

Maskin, Eric (1976) "Social Welfare Functions on Restricted Domain." Mimeo, Harvard University.

Maskin, Eric (1978) "A Theorem on Utilitarianism." *Review of Economic Studies*, *45*(1), pp. 93–96.

Maskin, Eric (1979) "Decision-making under Ignorance with Implications for Social Choice." *Theory and Decision*, *11*(3), pp. 319–37.

McKelvey, R. D. (1979) "General Conditions for Global Intransitivities in Formal Voting Models." *Econometrica*, *47*(5), pp. 1085–1112.

Meade, James E. (1976) *The Just Economy*. London: Allen and Unwin.

Mill, John Stuart (1859) *On Liberty*. London: Parker; republished in *Utilitarianism; On Liberty; Representative Government*. London: Everyman's Library, 1910.

Mirrlees, James A. (1982) "The Economic Uses of Utilitarianism," in Amartya Sen and Bernard Williams (eds.), *Utilitarianism and Beyond*. Cambridge: Cambridge University Press, pp. 63–84.

Moulin, Hervé (1983) *The Strategy of Social Choice*. Amsterdam: North-Holland.

Mueller, Dennis C. (1989) *Public Choice II*. Cambridge: Cambridge University Press.

Myerson, Roger B. (1981) "Utilitarianism, Egalitarianism, and the Timing Effect in Social Choice Problems." *Econometrica*, *49*(4), pp. 883–97.

Nozick, Robert (1974) *Anarchy, State, and Utopia*. New York: Basic Books.

Nozick, Robert (1989) *The Examined Life*. New York: Simon and Schuster.

Nussbaum, Martha (1988) "Nature, Function and Capability: Aristotle on Political Distribution." *Oxford Studies in Ancient Philosophy*, Supplementary volume, pp. 145–84.

Nussbaum, Martha and Sen, Amartya (eds.) (1993) *The Quality of Life*. Oxford: Oxford University Press.

Osmani, Siddiq R. (1982) *Economic Inequality and Group Welfare*. Oxford: Oxford University Press.

Pattanaik, Prasanta K. (1978) *Strategy and Group Choice*. Amsterdam: North-Holland.

Pattanaik, Prasanta K. and Salles, Maurice (eds.) (1983) *Social Choice and Welfare*. Amsterdam: North-Holland.

Pattanaik, Prasanta K. and Suzumura, Kotaro (1994a) "Rights, Welfarism and Social Choice." *American Economic Review (Papers and Proceedings)*, *84*(2), pp. 435–39.

Pattanaik, Prasanta K. (1994b) "Individual Rights and Social Evaluation: A Conceptual Framework." Mimeo, University of California, Riverside.

Peleg, Bazalel (1984) *Game Theoretic Analysis of Voting in Committees*. Cambridge: Cambridge University Press.

Phelps, Edmund S. (ed.) (1973) *Economic Justice*. Harmondsworth: Penguin.

Pigou, Arthur C. (1951) "Some Aspects of Welfare Economics." *American Economic Review*, *41*(3), pp. 287–302.

Plott, Charles (1973) "Path Independence, Rationality and Social Choice." *Econometrica*, *41*(6), pp. 1075–91.

Przeworski, Adam and Limongi, Fernando (1994) "Democracy and Development." Mimeo, University of Chicago.

Ravallion, Martin (1987) *Markets and Famines*. Oxford: Oxford University Press.

Ravallion, Martin (1994) *Poverty Comparisons*. Chur, Switzerland: Harwood.

Rawls, John (1963) "The Sense of Justice." *Philosophical Review*, *72*(3), pp. 281–305.

Rawls, John (1971) *A Theory of Justice*. Cambridge, MA: Harvard University Press.

Riley, Jonathan (1987) *Liberal Utilitarianism: Social Choice Theory and J. S. Mill's Philosophy*. Cambridge: Cambridge University Press.

Robbins, Lionel (1938) "Interpersonal Comparisons of Utility: A Comment." *Economic Journal*, *48*(192), pp. 635–41.

Roberts, Kevin W. S. (1980a) "Possibility Theorems with Interpersonally Comparable Welfare Levels." *Review of Economic Studies*, *47*(2), pp. 409–20.

Roberts, Kevin W. S. (1980b) "Interpersonal Comparability and Social Choice Theory." *Review of Economic Studies*, *47*(2), pp. 421–39.

Roemer, John (1986) "An Historical Materialist Alternative to Welfarism," in Jon Elster and Aanund Hylland (eds.), *Foundations of Social Choice Theory*. Cambridge: Cambridge University Press, pp. 133–64.

Rowley, Charles K. (1993) *Liberty and the State*. Aldershot: Elgar.

Samuelson, Paul A. (1947) *Foundations of Economic Analysis*. Cambridge, MA: Harvard University Press.

Sandmo, Agnar (1990) "Buchanan on Political Economy: A Review Article." *Journal of Economic Literature*, *28*(1), pp. 50–65.

Satterthwaite, Mark A. (1975) "Strategy-proofness and Arrow's Conditions: Existence and Correspondence Theorems for Voting Procedures and Social Welfare Functions." *Journal of Economic Theory*, *10*(2), pp. 187–217.

Scanlon, Thomas M. (1982) "Contractualism and Utilitarianism," in Amartya Sen and Bernard Williams (eds.), *Utilitarianism and Beyond*. Cambridge: Cambridge University Press, pp. 103–28.

Schofield, Norman, J. (1983) "Generic Instability of Majority Rule." *Review of Economic Studies*, *50*(4), pp. 695–705.

Schwartz, Thomas (1972) "Rationality and the Myth of the Maximum." *Nous*, *6*(2), pp. 97–117.

Schwartz, Thomas (1985) *The Logic of Collective Choice*. New York: Columbia University Press.

Seabright, Paul (1989) "Social Choice and Social Theories." *Philosophy and Public Affairs*, *18*(4), pp. 365–87.

Sen, Amartya K. (1966) "A Possibility Theorem on Majority Decisions." *Econometrica*, *34*(2), pp. 491–99.

Sen, Amartya K. (1970) *Collective Choice and Social Welfare*. San Francisco: Holden-Day; reprinted, Amsterdam: North-Holland, 1979.

Sen, Amartya K. (1971) "Choice Functions and Revealed Preference." *Review of Economic Studies*, *38*(3), pp. 307–17; reprinted in Sen (1982a).

Sen, Amartya K. (1973) *On Economic Inequality*. Oxford: Oxford University Press.

Sen, Amartya K. (1976a) "Real National Income." *Review of Economic Studies*, *43*(1), pp. 19–39; reprinted in Sen (1982a).

Sen, Amartya K. (1976b) "Poverty: An Ordinal Approach to Measurement." *Econometrica*, *44*(2), pp. 219–31; reprinted in Sen (1982a).

Sen, Amartya K. (1977a) "Social Choice Theory: A Reexamination." *Econometrica*, *45*(1), pp. 53–89; reprinted in Sen (1982a).

Sen, Amartya K. (1977b) "On Weights and Measures: Informational Constraints in Social Welfare Analysis." *Econometrica*, *45*(7), pp. 1539–72; reprinted in Sen (1982a).

Sen, Amartya K. (1981) *Poverty and Famines: An Essay on Entitlement and Deprivation*. Oxford: Oxford University Press.

Sen, Amartya K. (1982a) *Choice, Welfare and Measurement*. Oxford: Blackwell.

Sen, Amartya K. (1982b) "Rights and Agency." *Philosophy and Public Affairs*, *11*(2), pp. 113–32.

Sen, Amartya K. (1983) "Liberty and Social Choice." *Journal of Philosophy*, *80*(1), pp. 5–28.

Sen, Amartya K. (1984) *Resources, Values and Development*. Oxford: Blackwell.

Sen, Amartya K. (1986a) "Social Choice Theory," in Kenneth J. Arrow and Michael Intriligator (eds.), *Handbook of Mathematical Economics*, vol. III. Amsterdam: North-Holland, pp. 1073–1181.

Sen, Amartya K. (1986b) "Information and Invariance in Normative Choice," in Walter P. Heller, Ross M. Starr, and David A. Starrett (eds.), *Social Choice and Public Decision-making*, vol. 1: *Essays in Honor of Kenneth J. Arrow*. Cambridge: Cambridge University Press, pp. 29–55.

Sen, Amartya K. (1992a) *Inequality Reexamined*. Oxford: Oxford University Press.

Sen, Amartya K. (1992b) "Minimal Liberty." *Economica*, *59*(234), pp. 139–60.

Sen, Amartya K. (1993) "Internal Consistency of Choice." *Econometrica*, *61*(3), pp. 495–521.

Sen, Amartya K. (1994) "Population: Delusion and Reality." *New York Review of Books*, 22 September, *41*(15), pp. 62–71.

Sen, Amartya K. and Pattanaik, Prasanta K. (1969) "Necessary and Sufficient Conditions for Rational Choice under Majority Decision." *Journal of Economic Theory*, *1*(2), pp. 178–202.

Shorrocks, Anthony F. (1983) "Ranking Income Distributions." *Economica*, *50*(197), pp. 3–17.

Smith, Adam (1776) *An Inquiry into the Nature and Causes of the Wealth of Nations*. London: W. Strahan and T. Cadell; republished, Oxford: Oxford University Press, 1976.

Smith, Adam (1790) *The Theory of Moral Sentiments*, revised edition. London: T. Cadell; republished Oxford: Oxford University Press, 1975.

Streeten, Paul; Burki, S. J.; Haq, Mahbub ul; Hicks, Norman and Stewart, Frances (1981) *First Things First: Meeting Basic Human Needs in Developing Countries*. London: Oxford University Press.

Sugden, Robert (1981) *The Political Economy of Public Choice*. Oxford: Martin Robertson.

Sugden, Robert (1986) *The Economics of Rights, Co-operation and Welfare*. Oxford: Blackwell.

Sugden, Robert (1993) "Welfare, Resources, and Capabilities: A Review of *Inequality Reexamined* by Amartya Sen." *Journal of Economic Literature*, *31*(4), pp. 1947–62.

Suppes, Patrick (1966) "Some Formal Models of Grading Principles." *Synthese*, *16*(3/4), pp. 284–306.

Suzumura, Kotaro (1983) *Rational Choice, Collective Decisions and Social Welfare*. Cambridge: Cambridge University Press.

Suzumura, Kotaro (1991) "Alternative Approaches to Libertarian Rights," in Kenneth J. Arrow (ed.), *Markets and Welfare*. London: Macmillan, pp. 215–42.

Tocqueville, Alexis de (1840) *Democracy in America*. New York: Langley; republished New York: Knopf, 1945.

Tullock, Gordon (1967) "The General Irrelevance of the General Possibility Theorem." *Quarterly Journal of Economics*, *81*(2), pp. 256–70.

Wilson, Robert (1975) "On the Theory of Aggregation." *Journal of Economic Theory*, *10*(1), pp. 89–99.

World Disasters Report (1994). Geneva: International Federation of Red Cross and Red Crescent Societies.

Wriglesworth, John (1985) *Libertarian Conflicts in Social Choice*. Cambridge: Cambridge University Press.

Young, H. Peyton (ed.) (1985) *Fair Allocation*. Providence, RI: American Mathematical Society.

SEVENTEEN

An Economic Model of Representative Democracy[*]

Timothy Besley and Stephen Coate

Source: *Quarterly Journal of Economics* (1997), 112: 85–114.

> In the real world, individuals, as such, do not seem to make fiscal choices. They seem limited to choosing 'leaders,' who will, in turn, make fiscal decisions
>
> Buchanan (1967) p. v

I Introduction

The principal role of political economy is to yield insights into the formation of policy. To this end, the model put forward by Downs (1957) has played a central role in studies of democratic settings. This paper develops an alternative theory of policy choice in representative democracies. The primitives of the approach are the citizens of a polity, their policy alternatives, and a constitution that specifies the rules of the political process. The theory builds from these to provide an account of citizens' decisions to participate as candidates for public office, their voting decisions, and the policy choices of elected representatives. No pre-existing political actors are assumed, and no restrictions are made on the number of type of policy issues to be decided. Political outcomes are thus derived directly from the underlying tastes and policy technology.

The paper tackles the standard case where a community elects a single representative to choose policy for one period.[1] Citizens care about policy outcomes, and may also have intrinsic preferences about the identity of the representative. Citizens can also differ in their policy-making abilities. The political process is modeled as a three-stage game. Stage 1 sees each citizen deciding whether or not to become a candidate for public office. Each citizen is allowed to run, although doing so is costly. At the second stage, voting takes place over the declared candidates, with all citizens having the right to vote. At stage 3 the candidate with the most votes chooses policy.

This game-theoretic structure implies that candidates who win implement their preferred policies; they cannot credibly commit to do otherwise. Understanding this, citizens will vote for candidates on the basis of their policy preferences and policy-making abilities. A voting equilibrium is then a set of voting decisions such that each citizen's vote is a (weakly undominated) best response to others. Citizens contemplating standing for office must anticipate who else will enter the race and the resulting voting equilibrium. An equilibrium at the entry stage is therefore a set of entry decisions such that each citizen's decision is optimal given the decisions of others and the anticipated voting behavior.

We investigate the positive and normative implications of this theory. The key positive issues concern the number and policy preferences of candidates who choose to run. In addition, we study the possibility of "spoiler" candidates who run simply to prevent others from winning. The principal normative concern is with efficiency. The social choice problem faced by the polity has two components: selecting a policy-maker and a policy alternative. Representative democracy provides a particular method of generating such selections, and we ask whether these selections are Pareto efficient.

The same basic model of democratic policy-making to be studied here was suggested, independently, by Osborne and Slivinski (1996), who coined the term "citizen-candidates" to describe the approach. There are, however, some important differences between our setup and theirs. First, they focus exclusively on a one-dimensional model with Euclidean preferences, and second, they work with a continuum of citizens who are assumed to vote sincerely. The sincerity assumption produces very different implications from the model, which we discuss below. In terms of scope, the analyses are complementary. We develop a more general version of the model and explore the normative issues discussed above. They use their one-dimensional version to derive some interesting implications of different electoral systems (plurality rule and majority rule with runoffs) for the number and type of candidates.

The remainder of the paper is organized as follows. Section II lays out the model and shows that an equilibrium exists, in either pure or mixed strategies. Section III provides a fairly complete characterization of pure strategy equilibria. Section IV develops the implications of our theory for the standard one-dimensional policy model with Euclidean preferences and compares the findings with those of Osborne and Slivinski (1996). Section V develops the normative analysis, and section VI concludes.

II   The Model

A community made up of N citizens, labeled $i \in \mathcal{N} = \{1, \ldots, N\}$, must choose a representative to select and implement a policy alternative, denoted by x. In many applications, these are conventional policy instruments, such as taxes and public expenditures. The set of policy alternatives available if individual i is the policy-maker is denoted by $\mathcal{A}^i$. This set takes account of both technological and constitutional constraints on policy choices. Differences in $\mathcal{A}^i$ across citizens reflect varying levels of policy-making competence. Let $\mathcal{A} = \cup_{i=1}^{N} \mathcal{A}^i$ be the set of all possible policy alternatives.

Each citizen's utility depends upon the policy outcome and the identity of the representative. The latter captures the possibility of idiosyncratic utility from holding office oneself ("ego rent") or from having another making policy (for example, liking a "good-looking" representative). We denote the utility of individual i when the policy choice is $x \in \mathcal{A}$ and the representative is $j \in \mathcal{N} \cup \{0\}$ by $V^i(x, j)$. The notation $j = 0$ refers to the case in which the community has no representative.

The polity selects its representative in an election. All citizens can run for office, but face a (possibly small) utility cost δ, if they do so. The constitution governing elections specifies that all citizens have one vote that, if used, must be cast for one of the self-declared candidates. The candidate who receives the most votes is elected, and in the event of ties, the winning candidate is chosen with equal probability from among the tying candidates. If only one candidate runs, then he is automatically selected to choose policy, and if no one runs, a default policy $x_0 (\in \cap_i \mathscr{A}^i)$ is implemented.

The political process has three stages. At stage 1 candidates declare themselves. At stage 2 citizens choose for whom to vote from among the declared candidates. At the final stage the elected candidate makes a policy choice. These stages are analyzed in reverse order.

Policy choice

The citizen who wins the election implements his preferred policy – promising anything else is not credible.[2] Citizen i's preferred policy is given by

$$x_i^* = \underset{x}{\arg\max} \{ V^i(x, \ i) | x \in \mathscr{A}^i \}. \tag{1}$$

We assume that the solution to (1) is unique. Associated with each citizen's election, therefore, is a utility imputation $(v_{1i}, \ \ldots, \ v_{Ni})$, where $v_{ji} = V^j(x_i^*, \ i)$ is individual j's utility if i is elected. If no citizen stands for office, the default policy x_0 is selected, with the utility imputation in this case being $(v_{10}, \ \ldots, \ v_{N0})$, where $v_{j0} = V^j(x_0, \ 0)$.

Voting

Given a candidate set $\mathscr{C} \subseteq \mathscr{N}$, each citizen may decide to vote for any candidate in $\mathscr{C}$ or abstain. Let $\alpha_j \in \mathscr{C} \cup \{0\}$ denote citizen j's decision. If $\alpha_j = i$, then j casts his vote for candidate i; while if $\alpha_j = 0$, he abstains. A vector of voting decisions is denoted by $\alpha = (\alpha_1, \ \ldots, \ \alpha_N)$.

The set of winning candidates (i.e., those who receive the most votes) when voting decisions are α is denoted by $W(\mathscr{C}, \ \alpha)$. Since if only one candidate runs he is automatically elected, we adopt the convention that $W(\mathscr{C}, \ \alpha) = \mathscr{C}$ (for all α) when $\#\mathscr{C} = 1$. Given our assumptions, the probability that candidate i wins, denoted $P^i(\mathscr{C}, \ \alpha)$, is then $1/\#W(\mathscr{C}, \ \alpha)$ if i is in the winning set and 0 otherwise.

Citizens correctly anticipate the policies that would be chosen by each candidate and vote strategically. A *voting equilibrium* is thus a vector of voting decisions α^* such that, for each citizen $j \in \mathscr{N}(i), \alpha_j^*$ is a best response to α_{-j}^*, i.e.,

$$\alpha_j^* \in \arg\max \left\{ \sum_{j \in \ell} P^i \left(\mathscr{C}, \ \left(\alpha_j, \ \alpha_{-j}^* \right) \right) v_{ji} | \alpha_j \in \mathscr{C} \cup \{0\} \right\}, \tag{2}$$

and (ii) α_j^* is not a weakly dominated voting strategy.[3] Ruling out the use of weakly dominated voting strategies implies sincere voting in two-candidate elections. It is straightforward to show that a voting equilibrium exists for any nonempty candidate set. Indeed, in elections with three or more candidates, there will typically be multiple voting equilibria.

Entry

Each citizen must decide whether or not to run for office. The potential benefit from running is either directly from winning or indirectly by affecting who else is victorious. Since an individual's benefit from running depends on the entire candidate set, the entry decision is strategic.

Citizen i's pure strategy is $s^i \in \{0, 1\}$, where $s^i = 1$ denotes entry, and a pure strategy profile is $s = (s^1, \ldots, s^N)$. Given s, the set of candidates is $\mathscr{C}(s) = \{i \mid s^i = 1\}$. Each citizen's expected payoff from this strategy profile depends on voting behavior. Let $\alpha(\mathscr{C})$ denote the commonly anticipated voting decisions when the candidate set is $\mathscr{C}$.

Given $\alpha(\cdot)$, the expected payoff to a citizen i from the pure strategy profile s is

$$U^i(s;\alpha(\cdot)) = \sum_{j \in \mathscr{C}(s)} P^j(\mathscr{C}(s), \ \alpha(\mathscr{C}(s)))v_{ij} + P^0(\mathscr{C}(s))v_{i0} - \delta s^i. \tag{3}$$

The notation $P^0(\mathscr{C})$ denotes the probability that the default outcome is selected. Thus, $P^0(\mathscr{C}(s))$ equals 1 if $\mathscr{C}(s) = \emptyset$ and 0 otherwise. Citizen i's payoff represents the probability that each candidate j wins multiplied by i's payoff from j's preferred policy, less the entry cost if i is a candidate.

To ensure the existence of an equilibrium at the entry stage, we need to allow for mixed strategies. Let γ^i be a mixed strategy for citizen i, giving the probability that i runs for office. The set of mixed strategies for each citizen is then the unit interval [0,1]. A mixed strategy profile is denoted by $\gamma = (\gamma^1, \ldots, \gamma^N)$, and citizen i's expected payoff from γ is denoted by $u^i(\gamma; \alpha(\cdot))$.[4] An *equilibrium of the entry game* given $\alpha(\cdot)$ is a mixed strategy profile γ such that for each citizen i, γ^i is a best response to γ_{-i} given $\alpha(\cdot)$. The entry game is *finite* since each citizen has only two alternatives: enter or not enter. We may therefore apply the standard existence result due to Nash (1950) to conclude that an equilibrium of the entry game exists.

Combining the analysis of the three stages, we define a *political equilibrium* to be a vector of entry decisions γ and a function describing voting behavior $\alpha(\cdot)$ such that (i) γ is an equilibrium of the entry game given $\alpha(\cdot)$ and (ii) for all nonempty candidate sets $\mathscr{C}$, $\alpha(\mathscr{C})$ is a voting equilibrium. Given that a voting equilibrium exists for any nonempty candidate set and that an equilibrium of the entry game exists for any specification of voting behavior, we have

PROPOSITION 1   A political equilibrium exists.

A political equilibrium $\{\gamma, \alpha(\cdot)\}$ is a *pure strategy* equilibrium if citizens employ pure strategies at the entry stage (i.e., $\gamma = s$ for some $s \in \{0, 1\}^N$) and a *mixed strategy* equilibrium otherwise. Since pure strategy equilibria exist quite broadly, they are the main focus of our attention.[5]

III   Characterization of Pure Strategy Political Equilibria

This section characterizes pure strategy political equilibria with one, two, and three or more candidates. Our characterization exploits the fact that s is a pure strategy equilibrium of the entry game given the voting function $\alpha(\cdot)$ if and only if the following two conditions are satisfied. First, for all $i \in \mathscr{C}(s)$,

$$\sum_{j \in \mathscr{C}(s)} P^j(\mathscr{C}(s), \alpha(\mathscr{C}(s)))v_{ij} - \delta$$

$$\geq \sum_{j \in \mathscr{C}(s)/\{i\}} P^j(\mathscr{C}(s)/\{i\}, \alpha(\mathscr{C}(s)/\{i\}))v_{ij} + P^0(\mathscr{C}(s)/\{i\})v_{i0}, \tag{4}$$

where $\mathscr{C}/\{i\}$ is the candidate set with individual i removed. This says that each candidate must be willing to run given who else is in the race. Second, for all $i \notin \mathscr{C}(s)$,

$$\sum_{j \in \mathscr{C}(s)} P^j(\mathscr{C}(s), \alpha(\mathscr{C}(s)))v_{ij} + P^0(\mathscr{C}(s))v_{i0}$$

$$\geq \sum_{j \in \mathscr{C}(s) \cup \{i\}} P^j(\mathscr{C}(s) \cup \{i\}, \alpha(\mathscr{C}(s) \cup \{i\}))v_{ij} - \delta. \tag{5}$$

This says that the equilibrium is *entry proof*; i.e., there is no individual not in the race who would like to enter. The analytical work largely involves a more detailed appreciation of what conditions (4) and (5) imply.

The results employ the notion of a *sincere partition*. Given a candidate set $\mathscr{C}$, a partition[6] of the electorate $(N_i)_{i \in \mathscr{C} \cup \{0\}}$ is said to be *sincere* if and only if (i) $l \in N_i$ implies that $v_{li} \geq v_{lj}$ for all $j \in \mathscr{C}$ and (ii) $l \in N_0$ implies that $v_{li} = v_{lj}$ for all $i, j \in \mathscr{C}$. Intuitively, a sincere partition divides the electorate among the candidates so that every citizen is associated with his/her preferred candidate. There are many such partitions if some voters are indifferent between candidates.

One-candidate equilibria

In some situations there is an equilibrium in which a single citizen runs and is elected unopposed. The following proposition develops the necessary and sufficient conditions for this to arise.[7]

PROPOSITION 2   A political equilibrium in which citizen i runs unopposed exists if and only if
(i) $v_{ii} - v_{i0} \geq \delta$, and
(ii) for all $k \in \mathscr{N}/\{i\}$ such that $\#N_k \geq \#N_i$ for all sincere partitions (N_i, N_k, N_0), then $1/2(v_{kk} - v_{ki}) \leq \delta$ if there exists a sincere partition such that $\#N_i = \#N_k$ and $v_{kk} - v_{ki} \leq \delta$ otherwise.

Condition (i) guarantees that the hypothesized candidate's gain from running is sufficient to compensate him for the entry cost. Condition (ii) guarantees that no other citizen has an incentive to enter the race. Since citizens vote sincerely in two-candidate races, any entrant who is preferred by a majority could win and hence must have no incentive to enter.

Finding an individual for whom condition (i) is satisfied is not a problem if the default option is poor enough and the costs of running are small. Condition (ii) is much more difficult to satisfy. It requires that citizen i's policy alternative be preferred by a majority to the policy alternative of any other citizen with significantly different policy preferences. If entry costs are small, this condition is satisfied if and only if citizen i's policy choice is a Condorcet winner in the set of preferred policy alternatives of the N citizens.[8] Formally, we have

COROLLARY 1   Suppose that for all $j \in \mathcal{N}$, $\mathscr{A} = \mathscr{A}$ and $V^j(x, h) = V^j(x)$ for all $h \in \mathcal{N}$ and $x \in \mathscr{A}$. Then
   (i) if for sufficiently small δ a political equilibrium exists in which citizen i runs unopposed, then x_i^* must be a Condorcet winner in the set of alternatives $\{x_j^*: j \in \mathcal{N}\}$, and
   (ii) if x_i^* is a strict Condorcet winner in the set of alternatives $\{x_j^*: j \in \mathcal{N}\}$ and if $x_i^* \neq x_0$, then a political equilibrium exists in which citizen i runs unopposed for sufficiently small δ.

The conditions for the existence of a Condorcet winner are well known to be extremely restrictive, making it unlikely that one-candidate pure strategy equilibria exist in most environments. Nonetheless, since the standard model of political competition, introduced in Downs (1957), only produces a prediction in such cases, such equilibria will exist in most cases where that model is used (see section IV for an example).[9]

Two-candidate equilibria

The majority of formal models in political science begin with the assumption of two competing political actors.[10] This makes two-candidate pure strategy equilibria of our model especially interesting. As the following result demonstrates, they exist in our model under fairly weak conditions.

PROPOSITION 3   Suppose that a political equilibrium exists in which citizens i and j run against each other. Then
   (i)   there exists a sincere partition (N_i, N_j, N_0) such that $\#N_i = \#N_j$, and
   (ii) $1/2(v_{ii} - v_{ij}) \geq \delta$ and $1/2(v_{jj} - v_{ji}) \geq \delta$.
         Furthermore, if $N_0 = \{l \in N | v_{li} = v_{lj}\}$ and $\#N_0 + 1 < \#N_i = \#N_j$, then these conditions are sufficient for a political equilibrium to exist in which i and j run against each other.

To find two candidates who are willing to run against each other, both must believe that they stand some chance of winning. Since citizens vote sincerely in two-candidate races, this implies that condition (i) must be satisfied. In addition, the expected utility gain from being elected and implementing one's preferred policy must be sufficient to compensate both candidates for incurring the entry costs. This is the content of condition (ii). It requires either that the two candidates' preferred policies be sufficiently different or that there is an intrinsic benefit from holding office.

The remainder of the proposition states that if N_i and N_j consist solely of citizens who have a strict preference for one candidate over the other and if strictly less than one-third of the electorate is indifferent between the two candidates, conditions (i) and (ii) are sufficient for i and j running against each other to be an equilibrium. The voting behavior which justifies this is that supporters of i and j continue to vote for their candidates even if a third candidate enters, so that an entrant can pick up at most all of the voters who are currently abstaining. Intuitively, this captures the idea that, even though they may prefer the entrant, supporters of i (j) will be reluctant to switch their votes for fear that they will cause j (i) to win. Entry is therefore deterred.

The Proposition provides a fairly weak condition for the existence of a pure strategy equilibrium with two candidates if δ is small. Basically, *any* pair of candidates who split the voters evenly can be an equilibrium of this form, provided that they are not "too close" together. In many environments, even those with multiple policy dimensions, it will be possible to find such pairs of candidates.

Equilibria with three or more candidates

Equilibria with three or more candidates are perfectly possible in our framework. Our first result develops some conditions that must be satisfied by the set of winning candidates in any multicandidate equilibrium.

PROPOSITION 4 Let $\{s, \alpha(\cdot)\}$ be a political equilibrium with $\#\mathscr{C}(s) \geq 3$, and let $\hat{W}(s) = W(\mathscr{C}(s), \alpha(\mathscr{C}(s)))$ denote the set of winning candidates. If $\#\hat{W}(s) \geq 2$, there must exist a sincere partition $(N_i)_{i \in \hat{W}(s) \cup \{0\}}$ for the candidate set $\hat{W}(s)$ such that

(i) $\#N_i = \#N_j$ for all $i, j \in \hat{W}(s)$, and

(ii) for all $i \in \hat{W}(s)$

$$\sum_{j \in \hat{W}(s)} \left(\frac{1}{\#\hat{W}(s)}\right) v_{lj} \geq \max \ \{v_{lj} | j \in \hat{W}(s)/\{i\}\} \text{ for all } \ell \in N_i.$$

To understand this result, observe that, in a multi-candidate election where two or more candidates are tying, each voter is decisive. This implies that each citizen is either voting for his most preferred candidate among the set of winners or is indifferent between all the winning candidates. If this were not the case, the citizen could switch his vote to his most preferred candidate in the set of winners and cause his election (see also Lemma 1 of Feddersen, Sened, and Wright [1990]). Thus, there must exist a sincere partition for the set of winning candidates where (i) is satisfied. The inequality condition in (ii) should also hold; each citizen must prefer the lottery over all the winning candidates to the certain victory of his next most preferred winning candidate.

In many applications, Proposition 4 can be used to rule out multi-candidate equilibria with three or more (nonidentical) tying candidates. In a large community with continuous variation in citizens' preferences, then for any set of three or more candidates, there will be some set of citizens nearly indifferent between two candidates.[11] The inequality in condition (ii) then fails. In the next section we use Proposition 4 to rule out equilibria with three or more winning candidates in the one-dimensional model.[12]

Proposition 4 provides us with conditions that the set of winning candidates must satisfy. The next Proposition deals with the losing candidates.

PROPOSITION 5　Let $\{s, \alpha(\cdot)\}$ be a political equilibrium with $\#\mathscr{C}(s) \geq 3$, and let $\hat{W}(s)$ $= W(\mathscr{C}(s), \alpha(\mathscr{C}(s)))$ denote the set of winning candidates. Then, for each losing candidate $j \in \mathscr{C}(s)/\hat{W}(s)$,

　(i)　$W(\mathscr{C}(s)/\{j\}, \alpha(\mathscr{C}(s)/\{j\})) \neq \hat{W}(s)$, and
　(ii)　there exists $k \in \mathscr{C}(s)$ such that

$$\sum_{i \in \hat{W}(s)} \left(\frac{1}{\#\hat{W}(s)}\right) v_{ji} - \delta > v_{jk}.$$

These conditions follow directly from considering the incentives for losing candidates to run. If a losing candidate is in the race, he must affect the outcome, which implies condition (i). In addition, he must prefer the lottery over the current winners' policies to what would happen if he dropped out, which implies condition (ii).

　Proposition 5 provides some useful necessary conditions for political equilibria with losing candidates. However, it does not tell us about their plausibility. The following example studies a model, due to Stiglitz (1974), where the policy-maker can choose to publicly provide a private good at different quality levels and citizens can choose whether to opt for market or public sector consumption of the good. We show that it can support a three-candidate equilibrium where only one candidate has a chance of winning.

EXAMPLE:　Public provision of a private good with opt-out
The community chooses the level of a publicly provided private good, such as education or health care. Citizens consume at most one unit of the good, but may do so at different quality levels. Each citizen may buy the good in the market, opting out of the public sector in this instance. The quality level provided in the public sector can be "low," q_L, or "high," q_H. The set of policy alternatives is therefore $\{0, q_L, q_H\}$ with 0 denoting no provision. Higher quality public provision leads to larger tax bills for the citizens.[13]

　Citizens are assumed to be indifferent to the identity of their representative (for all citizens i, $V^i(x, j) = V^i(x)$ for all $j \in \mathcal{N}$ and all $x \in \mathcal{A}$). We suppose that there are five groups of policy preferences, indexed by $\tau \in \{a, b, c, d, e\}$. Type a citizens do not consume the good in question and therefore dislike any public expenditures on it. They have preference ordering $V^a(0) > V^a(q_L) > V^a(q_H)$. Type b citizens prefer to use the private sector, but will use the public sector if quality is high. Thus, since they get no benefit from low-quality public provision, their preferences are $V^b(0) > V^b(q_H) > V^b(q_L)$. Type c citizens prefer to consume in the public sector if quality is high, with preference ordering $V^c(q_H) > V^c(0) > V^c(q_L)$. Type d citizens always choose the public sector, but prefer high to low quality so that $V^d(q_H) > V^d(q_L) > V^d(0)$. Finally, type e citizens always choose the public sector but, since they have low incomes, prefer low quality to high quality so that $V^e(q_L) > V^e(q_H) > V^e(0)$.

　Let T^τ be the number of citizens of type τ. Assume that (i) $T^a + T^b + T^c > T^d + T^e$; (ii) $T^b + T^c + T^d > T^a + T^e$, and (iii) $T^e > \max\{T^a + T^b, T^c + T^d\} + 1$. Part (i) says that a majority of the population prefers no public provision to low quality public provision, and part (ii) says that a majority prefers high quality public provision to low quality provision. Part (iii) says that, in a threeway race, low quality public provision would receive a plurality. Under these assumptions there is a three-candidate equilibrium in which a citizen from groups a, d, and e contest the election. In this equilibrium citizens from group e vote for the type e candidate; citizens from groups a and b vote for the type a candidate; and the remaining citizens vote for the type d candidate. Thus, by (iii) the type e candidate wins, and the policy choice is low quality provision. The type a citizen stays in the race because he knows that if he exited, then by (ii) the type d candidate would defeat the type e candidate resulting in high quality public provision. Similarly, the type d citizen stays in the race because he knows that if he exited, then by (i) the type a candidate would win resulting in no public provision. Voting behavior is such that new entrants receive no votes. Thus, additional citizens have no incentive to enter.

In this example, preferences are not single-peaked, and each spoiler candidate stays in the race to prevent the other from winning. There are many interesting environments where this logic can be applied. Constructing political equilibria with four or more candidates is even more straightforward – it is even possible in a one-dimensional policy model with single peaked preferences. This takes advantage of multiple voting equilibria that permit flexibility in constructing voting outcomes to support losing candidates' fears about what would happen if they withdrew from the race.

The results of this section provide a fairly complete account of pure strategy equilibria. Since one-candidate equilibria parallel the existence of a Condorcet winner, we expect them to be rare in practice. Thus, our model reinforces the idea that building theories of political equilibrium resting on the existence of a Condorcet winner is unlikely to be fruitful. This mirrors the fact that we so rarely find uncontested elections.

Two-candidate equilibria are more promising as far as existence goes, with any pair of sufficiently antagonistic candidates who split the space being an equilibrium. The theory suggests that two-candidate competition can become a self-fulfilling prophecy, with citizens' beliefs in the inevitability of two-candidate competition guaranteeing that the system survives by deterring costly political entry. In many environments, including that studied in the next section, there will be many two-candidate equilibria, and some will involve candidates who are "far apart." Hence, our model does not yield any central tendency for political outcomes. On the other hand, extremism does require a counter-weight; if a very right-wing individual is running, then a very left-wing one must be opposing him.

While two-candidate competition is considered the norm under plurality rule, our model does not rule out equilibria with more than two candidates. It is true that races in which the outcome is a close run between three or more candidates are unlikely to exist in most environments. However, multi-candidate races with one or two winning candidates and one or more losers are a possibility. These equilibria make sense of the commonly held notion that candidates sometimes run as spoilers, preventing another candidate from winning.

For those who would like a clean empirical prediction, our multiple equilibria will raise a sense of dissatisfaction. However, this finding squares with the more familiar problem of game-theoretic models: that rationality alone does not typically pin down equilibrium play with complete precision (a message that echoes Myerson and Weber's (1993) discussion of voting behavior). This suggests the need to understand better the role of political institutions as coordinating devices, giving some greater determinacy to equilibrium outcomes.

IV　A One-Dimensional Model with Euclidean Preferences

The standard one-dimensional issue space model from formal political science is ideal to illustrate the model at work. It also highlights some differences between our approach and that of Osborne and Slivinski (1996). The set of policy alternatives is the unit interval [0,1]. Each citizen i has Euclidean preferences over these alternatives with distinct ideal point ω_i and cares only about policy outcomes, not the identity of their representative. Thus, for all $i \in \mathcal{N}$, $V^i(x, j) = -|\omega_i - x|$.[14] The default policy alternative is $x_0 = 0$. For simplicity, we assume that the number of citizens in the community is odd, with m denoting the median ideal point.

Using Proposition 2, we obtain the following result.

PROPOSITION 6　A political equilibrium exists in which citizen i runs unopposed if and only if
(i)　$\omega_i \geq \delta$, and
(ii)　there is no citizen k such that $2m - \omega_i < \omega_k < \omega_i - \delta$ or $\omega_i + \delta < \omega_k < 2m - \omega_i$.

The first condition guarantees that citizen i wishes to run against the default outcome. The second condition guarantees that citizen i's ideal point is not too far away from the median. Corollary 1 may be verified by noting that (given that there exists a citizen k such that $\omega_k = m$) condition (ii) is satisfied for sufficiently small δ if and only if $\omega_i = m$. Thus, for sufficiently small entry costs, the policy choice in a one-candidate equilibrium is the ideal point of the median voter – the same as that emerging from the Downsian model.

Turning to two-candidate equilibria, we apply Proposition 3 to obtain

PROPOSITION 7　There exists a political equilibrium in which citizens i and j run against each other if and only if
(i)　$(\omega_i + \omega_j)/2 = m$, and
(ii)　$|\omega_j - \omega_i| \geq 2\delta$.

The first condition says that the ideal points of the two candidates must be on opposite sides and equidistant from the median, ensuring that the two candidates split the electorate and the race is tied. The second condition says that the candidates must be far enough apart so that each finds it worthwhile to compete against the other. This prevents policy convergence. These two-candidate equilibria are at variance with the predictions of the standard Downsian model. Our model predicts a seesaw across the political spectrum by candidates whose ideologies counterbalance each other. Osborne and Slivinski (1996) show that the two candidates cannot be too far apart if citizens vote sincerely. With sufficient distance between them, a third candidate could enter in the middle and attract sufficient support to win the race. However, if citizens vote strategically, such "consensus" candidates are not guaranteed support.

Finally, we turn to races with more than two candidates. We first show how Proposition 4 rules out equilibria where three or more candidates tie provided that citizens' preferences are not clumped together. Our "nonclumping" assumption is extremely mild:

ASSUMPTION 1   Let I be any interval of the policy space $[0,1]$. Then, if there exists an interval $I' \subset [0, 1]$ of smaller length that contains the ideal points of at least one-third of the citizens, the interval I must contain the ideal point of at least one citizen.

We can then establish:

PROPOSITION 8   Suppose that Assumption 1 is satisfied. Then, there are no pure strategy political equilibria in which three or more candidates tie.

The proof of this result draws on Proposition 4. By considering the implications of condition (ii) of that proposition for those citizens who are running, we first establish that there can be only three winning candidates in such an equilibrium. We then show that, if condition (ii) is satisfied for all citizens in the polity, Assumption 1 must be violated.

It remains to examine the possibility of multicandidate equilibria in which one or two candidates win. Our next result shows that there are no three-candidate equilibria of this form provided that voting behavior satisfies a mild restriction. The restriction, which we call *Abstinence of Indifferent Voters* (AIV), is that citizens will abstain whenever they are indifferent between *all* candidates.[15]

PROPOSITION 9   Suppose that Assumption 1 is satisfied. Then, there are no pure strategy political equilibria involving three candidates in which voting behavior satisfies AIV.

If there was an equilibrium with three candidates, only one of whom was winning, then the winner would be the candidate whose ideal point is in-between those of the other two. The logic of the example developed in the previous section suggests that each losing "extremist" must then anticipate that the centrist candidate would lose to the other candidate in a two-way race. However, this is inconsistent with voting equilibrium. In an equilibrium with three candidates involving two candidates winning, the median citizen must be indifferent between the two winners and be voting for the losing candidate. If voting behavior satisfies AIV, the median citizen would abstain if the losing candidate dropped out, and thus his presence can have no effect on the outcome, violating condition (ii) of Proposition 5.

Proposition 9 contrasts with Osborne and Slivinski (1996) whose model yields two kinds of three-candidate equilibria. In the first there are three tying candidates, while the second has two tying candidates and a losing spoiler candidate. Both of these rest on sincere voting and independent benefits to holding office. Without such benefits, at least one candidate would be better off withdrawing and transferring his supporters to a contiguous candidate.[16] As noted earlier, Proposition 9 notwithstanding, pure strategy equilibria of the entry game involving four or more candidates in which only one or two candidates winning are possible. We leave to the interested reader the task of constructing examples.[17]

V   Normative Analysis of Representative Democracy

A long-standing concern in political economy is whether outcomes in political equilibrium are efficient. Writers in the Chicago tradition, such as Stigler (1982) and Becker (1985), have argued that political competition should ensure efficient policy choices. However, the legitimacy of this view remains unresolved. We now study this issue in the current model.

Representative democracy produces *a selection* $(x, i) \in \mathcal{A} \times \mathcal{N} \cup \{0\}$ consisting of a policy-maker i and a policy alternative x. A selection (x, i) with $i \in \mathcal{N}$ is *feasible* if the policy selected can be implemented by citizen i ($x \in \mathcal{A}^i$). (The case of $i = 0$ requires that the policy is the default outcome, $x = x_0$.) A selection (x, i) is *efficient* if it is feasible and there exists no alternative feasible selection (x', j) such that $V^h(x', j) > V^h(x, i)$ for all $h \in \mathcal{N}$. Thus, it must not be possible to find a citizen to govern and a policy choice that makes everyone better off.[18]

Any political equilibrium *generates* a set of possible selections for the community. If $\{s, \alpha(\cdot)\}$ is a pure strategy political equilibrium, it generates the set of selections $\{(x_i^*, i): i \in W(\mathcal{C}(s), \alpha(\mathcal{C}(s)))\}$ if $s \neq 0$ and $\{(x_0, 0)\}$ if $s = 0$. If $\{\gamma, \alpha(\cdot)\}$ is a mixed strategy political equilibrium, the set of selections it generates is simply those associated with all the vectors of entry decisions that may arise with positive probability in equilibrium. We now investigate whether the selections generated by representative democracy are efficient.[19]

Identical policy-making abilities

We begin with the case in which all citizens have identical policy-making abilities; i.e., for all $i \in \mathcal{N}$, $\mathcal{A}^i = \mathcal{A}$. In this case, given that holding office is desirable, it is clearly not possible to give citizen i any higher level of utility than $V^i(x_i^*, i)$. But if (x, i) is a selection generated by a political equilibrium and $(x, i) \neq (x_0, 0)$, then $x = x_i^*$. Thus, it is clearly not possible to make citizen i better off. (Indeed, since each citizen has a unique optimal policy, any change must make him worse off.) This yields

PROPOSITION 10   Suppose that citizens have identical policy-making abilities and that for all $i \in \mathcal{N}$ and $x \in \mathcal{A}$, $V^i(x, i) \geq V^i(x, j)$ for all $j \in \mathcal{N}$. Let $\{\gamma, \alpha(\cdot)\}$ be a political equilibrium in which $\gamma^i = 1$, for some $i \in \mathcal{N}$. Then, the selections generated by $\{\gamma, \alpha(\cdot)\}$ are efficient.

This is a powerful (if obvious) result.[20] Consistent with the Chicago view, it implies that policy choices made in representative democracy will be efficient when citizens have identical policy-making abilities. The result holds because representative democracy vests policy authority in a particular citizen who makes an optimal policy choice.[21]

A common reaction is to suggest that the preferences of policy-makers should not count. This is understandable given the tradition of modeling policy choices by planners or political parties whose political action is not rooted in citizens' preferences. However, policies *are* chosen and implemented by citizens, and Pareto efficiency properly demands that the policy-maker's preferences be counted. To do otherwise would be to make an implicit distributional judgment about the social value of different individuals' utilities.

This efficiency result does require that at least one citizen enter with probability one. If $\gamma^i < 1$ for all $i \in \mathcal{N}$, the selection $(x_0, 0)$ is in the set of those generated by γ, and there is no guarantee that this is efficient. Equilibria in which no citizens enter the race with probability one may arise when the preferences of the electorate are similar or the entry cost is high. In such cases, citizens might decide to subsidize others' entry costs, establish public funding of candidates, or set an attractive salary for the community's representative, or some combination of the three.

Heterogeneous policy-making abilities

The idea that candidates differ in their policy-making abilities appears to be a presumption of political campaigns and has figured in previous theoretical literature (for example, Rogoff, 1990). In this model such differences can be captured by supposing that feasible policy sets $\mathscr{A}^i$ differ. The following example demonstrates that in such circumstances representative democracy can yield inefficient selections.

EXAMPLE: Public goods provision with differing competence levels
There are two kinds of citizens, labeled α and β, with the latter in the majority. There are two goods: a private good and a public good g. Each citizen is endowed with y units of the private good. The task of the representative is to choose a level of the public good for the community that must be financed with a head tax T. The default outcome is that no public good is provided.

Citizens of type $\gamma \in \{\alpha, \beta\}$ have Cobb–Douglas preferences $g^\gamma(y - T)^{1-\gamma}$. Is it assumed that $\alpha < \beta$, so that type β citizens have a stronger taste for public goods than type α citizens. When in office, citizens of type γ are assumed able to provide g units of the public good at cost $\theta_\gamma g$. The feasible set of policy alternatives for a type γ citizen is therefore

$$\mathscr{A}^\gamma = \{(T, \, g) \in [0, \, y] \times \mathfrak{N}_+ : \theta_\gamma g \leq NT\}.$$

We assume that type α citizens are more competent policy-makers than type β citizens, so that $\theta_\alpha < \theta_\beta$. This implies that $\mathscr{A}^\beta \subset \mathscr{A}^\alpha$.

If a type γ citizen is selected to govern, he will choose the policy alternative $(T_\gamma^*, \, g_\gamma^*) = (\gamma y, \, \gamma y / \theta_\gamma)$. It is easy to show that if $[(1 - \alpha)/(1 - \beta)]^{((1-\beta)/\beta)}$ $\alpha/\beta < \theta_\alpha/\theta_\beta$, type β citizens prefer not to have a type α citizen in power. Since the latter are a majority, Proposition 2 implies the existence (for sufficiently small δ) of a political equilibrium in which a type β citizen runs unopposed. However, all citizens would be better off with a type α citizen as policy-maker, selecting the alternative $(\beta y, \, \beta y / \theta_\alpha)$.

Here, citizens who are better at policy-making (type α) cannot be trusted to serve the interests of the majority (type β). Hence to actually generate a Pareto improvement would require some way of forcing a type α citizen to act faithfully on behalf of the majority. If there were some citizens who shared type β citizens' preferences but had the policy-making abilities of type α citizens, then this problem ought not to arise. This is like saying that the space of types is sufficiently rich to encompass a broad array of tastes and policy-making abilities. An assumption along these lines is

ASSUMPTION 2 For every citizen $i \in \mathcal{N}$, if there exists some citizen j and policy choice $x \in A^j$ such that $V^h(x, \, j) > v_{hi}$ for all $h \in \mathcal{N}$, then there exists a citizen k such that $v_{hk} > v_{hi}$ for all $h \in \mathcal{N}$.

This says that, if there is a citizen who could in principle Pareto dominate another by virtue of his superior policy-making abilities, then there must be a citizen who would actually deliver a Pareto superior policy choice if elected. This failed in the example because there was no citizen who shared the type β citizens' preferences and who could produce public goods at low cost. The assumption permits some positive results.

PROPOSITION 11   Suppose that Assumption 2 holds, and let $\{s,\ \alpha(\cdot)\}$ be a political equilibrium in which a single citizen runs unopposed. Then, if δ is sufficiently small, the selection generated by $\{s,\ \alpha(\cdot)\}$ is efficient.

An appealing logic underlies this result. Suppose that the single candidate running is inefficient in the sense that $(x_i^*,\ i)$ is an inefficient selection. Then, under Assumption 2 there would exist another citizen who, if elected, would produce a Pareto superior outcome. Since voting sincerely is the only weakly undominated strategy in two-candidate races, if this citizen entered, he would win. Thus, he will enter if the entry cost is small enough. Political competition therefore ensures the selection of citizens with superior policy-making abilities.

Unfortunately, this logic does not generalize to political equilibria in which two candidates run against each other. Suppose that one of the candidates is inefficient. If a Pareto superior candidate entered, there is no guarantee that the supporters of the inefficient candidate would switch their votes. They may fear that switching their votes would result in the opposing candidate winning.[22] As a consequence, the more efficient citizen is deterred from entering.

An efficiency result can be obtained by further restricting voting behavior. One could, for example, assume that Pareto-dominated candidates will attract no votes, which we call *Irrelevance of Inefficient Candidates* (IIC). Thus, whenever there are two candidates i and j such that $(x_i^*,\ i)$ Pareto dominates $(x_j^*,\ j)$, then $\alpha_k \neq j$ for all citizens $k \in \mathcal{N}$. Under this assumption, we obtain:

PROPOSITION 12   Suppose that Assumption 2 holds, and let $\{s,\ \alpha(\cdot)\}$ be a political equilibrium in which two candidates run against each other and voting behavior satisfies IIC. Then, if δ is sufficiently small, the selections generated by $\{s,\ \alpha(\cdot)\}$ are efficient.

However, even the assumption of IIC is not sufficient to guarantee that political equilibria involving three or more candidates produce efficient selections. Consider, for example, a three-candidate race in which all candidates are in the winning set, but one would produce an inefficient selection. There is no guarantee that a Pareto-dominant candidate would be in the winning set if he entered, even if the inefficient candidate received no votes. If the entrant is preferred by all the supporters of the inefficient candidate (say, candidate 1) together with a small number of another candidate's (say, candidate 2), the remaining supporters of candidate 2 may switch their votes to candidate 3 causing the entrant to lose! Thus, there seems to be little hope of obtaining a general efficiency result for multi-candidate elections.

To summarize, our analysis identifies three reasons why representative democracy may not produce efficient selections when citizens differ in their policy-making abilities. First, if policy-making talent is concentrated among groups with certain policy preferences, then individuals may opt for a less able citizen who better represents their views. Second, even if the space of types is rich in the sense of Assumption 2, a problem can arise in elections with two (or more) winning candidates if voters are reluctant to switch their votes from an inefficient to an efficient candidate because they fear that transferring their support will simply result in another less preferred candidate winning. Finally, in races with three or more candidates, entry by Pareto superior candidates might simply produce a higher probability of winning for a candidate whom they like less than the inferior candidate whom they displace.

VI Concluding Remarks

This paper has developed a rudimentary understanding of an alternative model of representative democracy. The theory introduces the indisputable fact that representative democracy is about the participation of citizens in the political process. In addition, it has the merit that all decisions by citizens as voters, candidates, and policy-makers are derived from optimizing behavior. The model facilitates a rigorous normative analysis of political outcomes, which suggests an interesting agenda for future work linking normative public economics and political economy.

Nonetheless, the theoretical framework studied here is stark. A single elected official makes policy choices in an atemporal world without political parties or interest groups. Moreover, voters have complete information about the policy preferences and policy-making abilities of candidates. It is clear, therefore, that much remains to be done to develop the approach. Extensions that incorporate the election of representatives to a legislature and repeated elections are of interest. It will also be important to bring in uncertainty about candidates' preferences and abilities and to understand how campaigns convey information. With respect to political parties the model will hopefully facilitate the modeling of the formation of parties endogenously, rather than assuming them *deus ex machina*.

Appendix: Proofs of Results

Proof of Proposition 2

Sufficiency

Let $\hat{s}$ be the vector of entry decisions such that $\hat{s}^i = 1$ and $\hat{s}^j = 0$ for all citizens $j \neq i$. We will show that if (i) and (ii) are satisfied, there exists a voting function $\hat{\alpha}(\cdot)$ such that $\{\hat{s}, \hat{\alpha}(\cdot)\}$ is a political equilibrium. We construct the voting function $\hat{\alpha}(\cdot)$ as follows. For all candidate sets $\{i, k\}$ with $k \neq i$, let $(\hat{N}_i, \hat{N}_k, \hat{N}_0)$ denote the sincere partition in which $\#N_i - \#N_k$ is maximized. Then, let $\hat{\alpha}(\{i, k\})$ be the vector of voting decisions generated by $(\hat{N}_i, \hat{N}_k, \hat{N}_0)$; that is, $\hat{\alpha}_j(\{i, k\}) = i$ if $j \in \hat{N}_i$, $\hat{\alpha}_j(\{i, k\}) = k$ if $j \in \hat{N}_k$, and $\hat{\alpha}_j(\{i, k\}) = 0$ if $j \in \hat{N}_0$. Clearly, $\hat{\alpha}(\{i, k\})$ is a voting equilibrium. For all other candidate sets $\mathscr{C}$, let $\hat{\alpha}(\mathscr{C})$ be any voting equilibrium.

We now claim that $\hat{s}$ is an equilibrium of the entry game given $\hat{\alpha}(\cdot)$. Condition (i) guarantees that citizen i's entry decision is optimal. With anticipated voting behavior $\hat{\alpha}(\{i, k\})$, no citizen $k \neq i$ for whom there is a sincere partition (N_i, N_k, N_0) with $\#N_i > \#N_k$ will enter, since he will anticipate losing. No citizen $k \neq i$ for whom $(\hat{N}_i, \hat{N}_k, \hat{N}_0)$ is such that $\#\hat{N}_i = \#\hat{N}_k$ will enter since he will anticipate tying with citizen i, and the first part of condition (ii) says that, under these circumstances, entry will not be worthwhile. The second part of condition (ii) implies that the remaining citizens $k \neq i$ have no incentive to enter.

Necessity

Suppose now that either (i) or (ii) is not satisfied. We must show that there exists no voting function $\alpha(\cdot)$ such that $\{\hat{s}, \alpha(\cdot)\}$ is a political equilibrium. When (i) fails, citizen i is unwilling to run against the default option and hence will not be willing to enter if nobody else is running. Suppose that (ii) fails for some citizen k. Since voting sincerely is the only weakly undominated strategy in two-candidate races, we know that if α is a voting equilibrium when the candidate set is $\{i, k\}$ there must exist a sincere partition (N_i, N_k, N_0) which generates α. It follows that any voting equilibrium $\alpha(\{i, k\})$ has individual k winning if $\#N_i < \#N_k$ for all sincere partitions and at least tying if $\#N_i = \#N_k$ for some sincere partition. Thus, whatever voting equilibrium $\alpha(\{i, k\})$ is anticipated, k will enter if citizen i is running unopposed.

Proof of Corollary 1

This is a straightforward consequence of Proposition 2, which we leave to the reader.

Proof of Proposition 3

Necessity

If i and j wish to run against each other, then it must be the case that $W(\{i, j\}, \alpha(\{i, j\})) = \{i, j\}$. Since any voting equilibrium with two candidates involves sincere voting, it follows that there must exist a sincere partition (N_i, N_j, N_0) such that $\#N_i = \#N_j$ which gives condition (i). Furthermore, since each candidate wins with probability $1/2$, condition (ii) must hold if both candidates are willing to run against each other.

Sufficiency

The proof is completed by showing that conditions (i) and (ii) are sufficient for the existence of a political equilibrium in which i and j run against each other if $N_0 = \{l \in N | v_{li} = v_{lj}\}$ and $\#N_0 + 1 < \#N_i = \#N_j$. Let $\hat{s}$ be the vector of entry decisions such that $\hat{s}^i = \hat{s}^j = 1$ and $\hat{s}^k = 0$ for all citizens $k \notin \{i, j\}$. Now construct the voting function $\hat{\alpha}(\cdot)$ as follows: first, let $\hat{\alpha}(\{i, j\})$ be the voting decisions generated by the sincere partition (N_i, N_j, N_0); that is, $\hat{\alpha}_l(\{i, j\}) = i$ if $l \in N_i$, $\hat{\alpha}_l(\{i, j\}) = j$ if $l \in N_j$, and $\hat{\alpha}_l(\{i, j\}) = 0$ if $l \in N_0$. Clearly, $\hat{\alpha}(\{i, j\})$ is a voting equilibrium. Second, for all citizens $k \in \mathscr{N}/\{i, j\}$, let $\bar{N}_k = \{l \in \mathscr{N} | v_{lk} > v_{li} = v_{lj}\}$ and $\underline{N}_k = \{l \in \mathscr{N} | v_{lk} < v_{li} = v_{lj}\}$. For any citizen in $\bar{N}_k$, voting for any candidate other than k is weakly dominated. Similarly, for any citizen in $\underline{N}_k$ voting for candidate k is weakly dominated. Notice that both $\bar{N}_k$ and N_k are subsets of N_0, under our assumptions. Now if $v_{ki} \geq v_{kj}$, let $\hat{\alpha}(\{i, j, k\})$ be the vector of voting decisions generated by the partition $(N_i, N_j \cup N_k, \bar{N}_k, N_0/(\bar{N}_k \cup \underline{N}_k))$. On the other hand, if $v_{ki} < v_{kj}$, let $\hat{\alpha}(\{i, j, k\})$ be the vector of voting decisions generated by the partition $(N_i \cup \underline{N}_k, N_j, \bar{N}_k, N_0/(\bar{N}_k \cup \underline{N}_k))$. Since $\#\bar{N}_k < \#N_0 + 1 < \#N_i = \#N_j$, then it is clear that $\hat{\alpha}(\{i, j, k\})$ is a voting equilibrium for all citizens $k \in \mathscr{N}/\{i, j\}$ and that candidate k must lose. Finally, for all remaining candidate sets $\mathscr{C}$, let $\hat{\alpha}(\mathscr{C})$ be any voting equilibrium.

We now claim that $\hat{s}$ is an equilibrium of the entry game given $\hat{\alpha}(\cdot)$. Under the assumed voting behavior, if citizens i and j run against each other, they will both win with probability $1/2$ and hence condition (ii) implies that their voting decisions are optimal. All other citizens have no incentive to enter, since, given the assumed voting behavior, they will either not change the outcome (if $\underline{N}_k = \phi$) or will cause their preferred candidate of i and j to lose (if $\underline{N}_k \neq \phi$).

Proof of Proposition 4

For all $i \in \hat{W}(s)$ let $N_i = \{l \in \mathscr{N} | \alpha_l(\mathscr{C}(s)) = i\}$, and let $N_0 = \{l \in \mathscr{N} | \alpha_l(\mathscr{C}(s)) \notin \hat{W}(s)\}$. Then we know that $\#N_i = \#N_j$ for all $i, j \in \hat{W}(s)$, since all the candidates in $\hat{W}(s)$ are receiving an equal number of votes. It is also clear that $(N_i)_{i \in \hat{W}(s) \cup \{0\}}$ is a sincere partition for the candidate set $\hat{W}(s)$. If some citizen $l \in N_i$ did not prefer candidate i to another candidate $j \in \hat{W}(s)$, then by switching his vote to j, he could cause j to win, thereby improving his utility. Similarly, if some citizen $l \in N_0$ was not indifferent between all candidates in $\hat{W}(s)$, he would switch his vote to his preferred candidate in $\hat{W}(s)$ causing him to win. The inequality in condition (ii) of the proposition follows immediately from the observation that by simply switching his vote to any other candidate in $\hat{W}(s)$, citizen $l \in N_i$ could cause that candidate to win.

Proof of Proposition 5

This follows immediately from considering citizen j's incentive to enter the race. By hypothesis, candidate j has no chance of winning. Thus, the only reason he has for being in the race is to prevent some other candidate from winning. This means that the winning set must be affected by his exit (condition (i)) and that there must exist a candidate $k \in \mathscr{C}(s)$ such that $\sum_{i \in \hat{W}(s)} (1/\#\hat{W}(s))$ $v_{ji} - v_{jk} \geq \delta$ (condition (ii)).

Proof of Proposition 6

It is clear that condition (i) of this proposition is equivalent to condition (i) of Proposition 2, and thus to prove the result, we need to show that condition (ii) of this proposition is equivalent to condition (ii) of Proposition 2. This is a straightforward exercise that we leave to the reader.

Proof of Proposition 7

Necessity
Suppose that there exists a political equilibrium in which citizens i and j run against each other. Then conditions (i) and (ii) of Proposition 3 must be satisfied. Since

$$v_{ii} - v_{ij} = v_{jj} - v_{ji} = |\omega_i - \omega_j|,$$

condition (ii) of Proposition 3 immediately implies condition (ii) of the proposition. Condition (i) of Proposition 3, together with the fact that $\omega_i \neq \omega_j$ implies that $(\omega_i + \omega_j)/2 = m$, which is condition (i) of the proposition. To see this, note that if $(\omega_i + \omega_j)/2 < m$, then assuming $\omega_i < \omega_j$, the median citizen must prefer candidate j to candidate i. This means that all those citizens with ideal points greater than or equal to m prefer candidate j to candidate i. Thus, every sincere partition would involve $\#N_i < \#N_j$. Similarly, if $(\omega_i + \omega_j)/2 > m$, every sincere partition would involve $\#N_i > \#N_j$.

Sufficiency
Now suppose that conditions (i) and (ii) of the proposition are satisfied. Then it is immediate that condition (ii) of Proposition 3 is satisfied. In addition, since there is a single citizen with ideal point m, there exists a sincere partition (N_i, N_j, N_0), such that $\#N_i = \#N_j$, $N_0 = \{l \in \mathscr{N} | v_{li} = v_{lj}\}$, and $\#N_0 = 1$. Proposition 3 then implies that there exists a political equilibrium in which citizens i and j run against each other.

Proof of Proposition 8

Let $\{s, \alpha(\cdot)\}$ be a pure strategy equilibrium of the entry game, and let $\hat{W}(s) = W(\mathscr{C}(s), \alpha(\mathscr{C}(s)))$ be the set of winning candidates. Suppose that $r = \#\hat{W}(s) \geq 3$, and label the ideal points of the r winning candidates as $\{\beta_1, \ldots, \beta_r\}$. Relabeling as necessary, we may assume that $\beta_1 < \ldots < \beta_r$. We will prove the proposition by showing that the necessary conditions stated in Proposition 4 cannot be satisfied.

Proposition 4 tells us that there must exist a sincere partition $(N_i)_{i \in \hat{W}(s) \cup \{0\}}$ for the candidate set $\hat{W}(s)$ such that $\#N_i = \#N_j$ for all $i, j \in W(s)$, and for all $i \in \hat{W}(s)$, condition (ii) holds for all $l \in N_i$. To be sincere, the partition must satisfy

$$\left\{ \ell : \omega_\ell \in \left[0, \frac{\beta_1 + \beta_2}{2}\right) \right\} \subset N_1 \subset \left\{ \ell : \omega_\ell \in \left[0, \frac{\beta_1 + \beta_2}{2}\right] \right\},$$

$$\left\{ \ell : \omega_\ell \in \left(\frac{\beta_{i-1} + \beta_i}{2}, \frac{\beta_i + \beta_{i+1}}{2}\right) \right\} \subset N_i,$$

and

$$N_i \subset \left\{ \ell : \omega_\ell \in \left[\frac{\beta_{i-1} + \beta_i}{2}, \frac{\beta_i + \beta_{i+1}}{2}\right] \right\} \text{ for all } i \in \{2, \ldots, r-1\},$$

$$\left\{ \ell : \omega_\ell \in \left(\frac{\beta_{r-1} + \beta_r}{2}, 1\right] \right\} \subset N_r \subset \left\{ \ell : \omega_\ell \in \left[\frac{\beta_{r-1} + \beta_r}{2}, 1\right] \right\},$$

and

$$N_0 = \varnothing.$$

It is clear that candidate 1 is in N_1 and candidate r is in N_r. Condition (ii) of Proposition 4 therefore implies that

$$\frac{1}{r}[\|\beta_2 - \beta_1\| + \ldots + \|\beta_r - \beta_1\|] \leq \|\beta_2 - \beta_1\| \tag{6}$$

and

$$\frac{1}{r}[\|\beta_r - \beta_1\| + \ldots + \|\beta_r - \beta_{r-1}\|] \leq \|\beta_r - \beta_{r-1}\|. \tag{7}$$

Noting that for all $j = 2, \ldots, r$, $\|\beta_j - \beta_1\| = \|\beta_j - \beta_{j-1}\| + \ldots + \|\beta_2 - \beta_1\|$ and for all $j = 1, \ldots, r-1$, $\|\beta_r - \beta_j\| = \|\beta_r - \beta_{r-1}\| + \ldots + \|\beta_{j+1} - \beta_j\|$, we see that (6) and (7) can be written as

$$\|\beta_2 - \beta_1\| \geq (r-2)\|\beta_3 - \beta_2\| + \ldots + \|\beta_r - \beta_{r-1}\| \tag{8}$$

and

$$\|\beta_r - \beta_{r-1}\| \geq \|\beta_2 - \beta_1\| + \ldots + (r-2)\|\beta_{r-1} - \beta_{r-2}\|. \tag{9}$$

For both (8) and (9) to hold, it is necessary that $r = 3$ and that

$$\beta_3 - \beta_2 = \beta_2 - \beta_1. \tag{10}$$

Assume, therefore, that $r = 3$ and that (10) holds. It is clear that condition (ii) of Proposition 4 cannot be satisfied if there exists any citizen l such that $\omega_l = (\beta_1 + \beta_2)/2$ or $\omega_l = (\beta_2 + \beta_3)/2$.

Thus,

$$N_1 = \{\ell: \omega_\ell \in [0, \ (\beta_1 + \beta_2)/2)\},$$
$$N_2 = \{\ell: \omega_\ell \in ((\beta_1 + \beta_2)/2, \ (\beta_2 + \beta_3)/2)\},$$

and

$$N_3 = \{\ell: \omega_\ell \in ((\beta_2 + \beta_3)/2, \ 1]\}.$$

Moreover, each of these sets must contain exactly one-third of the citizens.

It is straightforward to show that condition (ii) of Proposition 4 does not hold for all those citizens in N_1 for whom $\omega_l \in (\beta_1, \ (\beta_1 + \beta_2)/2)$; all those citizens in N_2 for whom $\omega_\ell \in ((\beta_1 + \beta_2)/2, \ (3\beta_2 + \beta_1)/4)$ or $\omega_l \in ((3\beta_2 + \beta_3)/4, \ (\beta_2 + \beta_3)/2)$; and all those citizens in N_3 for whom $\omega_\ell \in ((\beta_2 + \beta_3)/2, \ \beta_3]$. It follows that these intervals cannot contain the ideal point of any citizen. Consequently, the interval $((3\beta_2 + \beta_1)/4, \ (3\beta_2 + \beta_3)/4) \subset N_2$ must contain the ideal points of exactly one-third of the citizens, while the interval $(\beta_1, \ (3\beta_2 + \beta_1)/4)$ contains the ideal points of none of the citizens. But this violates Assumption 1 because the latter interval is longer than the former.

Proof of Proposition 9

Proposition 8 tells us that there exist no three-candidate equilibria in which all candidates win. It remains to rule out the possibility of a three-candidate equilibrium in which one or two candidates are winning.

We begin with the one-candidate winning scenario. Let $\{s, \ \alpha(\cdot)\}$ be a pure strategy equilibrium such that $\#\mathscr{C}(s) = 3$, and suppose that $\#W(\mathscr{C}(s), \ \alpha(\mathscr{C}(s))) = 1$. Label the ideal points of the three candidates as $\{\beta_1, \ \beta_2, \ \beta_3\}$ and do so in such a way that $\beta_1 < \beta_2 < \beta_3$. Condition (ii) of Proposition 5 implies that candidate 2 must be the winning candidate. Thus, for candidate 1 to wish to remain in the race, equilibrium voting behavior must be such that $3 \in W(\{2, \ 3\}, \ \alpha(\{2, \ 3\}))$, while for candidate 3 to remain in the race, voting behavior must be such that $1 \in W(\{1, \ 2\}, \ \alpha(\{1, \ 2\}))$. Since citizens vote sincerely in two-candidate races, if $3 \in W(\{2, \ 3\}, \ \alpha(\{2, \ 3\}))$, then it must be the case that

$$(\beta_2 + \beta_3)/2 \leq m,$$

while if $1 \in W(\{1, \ 2\}, \ \alpha(\{1, \ 2\}))$, it must be the case that

$$(\beta_1 + \beta_2)/2 \geq m.$$

But the former inequality implies that $\beta_2 < m$, and the latter inequality implies that $\beta_2 > m$. Hence, we have a contradiction.

We now turn to the scenario in which two candidates are winning. Again, let $\{s, \ \alpha(\cdot)\}$ be a pure strategy equilibrium such that $\#\mathscr{C}(s) = 3$, and suppose that $\#W(\mathscr{C}(s), \ \alpha(\mathscr{C}(s))) = 2$. Label the ideal points of the three candidates as $\{\beta_1, \ \beta_2, \ \beta_3\}$, and do so in such a way that $\beta_1 < \beta_2 < \beta_3$.

We show first $W(\mathscr{C}(s), \ \alpha(\mathscr{C}(s))) \neq \{1, \ 2\}$. Suppose, to the contrary, that the winning set did consist of candidates 1 and 2. Then Proposition 4 implies that there must exist a sincere partition $(N_1, \ N_2, \ N_0)$ such that $\#N_1 = \#N_2$. This, in turn, implies that $(\beta_1 + \beta_2)/2 = m$. It follows that all those citizens with ideal points smaller than m will be voting for candidate 1, while all those with ideal points larger than m will be voting for candidate 2. But since $m < \beta_2 < \beta_3$, the citizen with the median ideal point prefers candidates 1 and 2 to candidate 3. Weak dominance therefore implies that the median citizen will vote for either candidate 1 or candidate 2. It follows that candidates 1 and 2 cannot have the same number of votes – a contradiction.

In a similar manner, it can be shown that $W(\mathscr{C}(s), \alpha(\mathscr{C}(s))) \neq \{2, 3\}$. The remaining possibility is that $W(\mathscr{C}(s), \alpha(\mathscr{C}(s))) = \{1, 3\}$. In this case, Proposition 4 implies that $(\beta_1 + \beta_3)/2 = m$, which means that all those citizens with ideal points smaller than m will be voting for candidate 1 and all those with ideal points larger than m will be voting for candidate 3. Since β_2 is closer to m than β_1 or β_3, the citizen with the median ideal point prefers candidate 2 to candidates 1 and 3. Weak dominance therefore implies that the median citizen will vote for candidate 2. Candidate 2 thus receives one vote, and the remaining voters are divided equally between candidates 1 and 3. Now suppose that candidate 2 were to drop out of the race. Voters vote sincerely in two-candidate races, so that those citizens supporting candidates 1 and 3 would continue to do so. Since voting behavior satisfies AIV, the median citizen will abstain. Thus, $W(\mathscr{C}(s)/\{2\}, \alpha(\mathscr{C}(s)/\{2\})) = \{1, 3\}$ which violates condition (i) of Proposition 5.

We have now ruled out the possibility of a three-candidate equilibrium in which two candidates win.   □

Proof of Proposition 11

Let i be the citizen who is running (i.e., $s^i = 1$). Then the selection generated by $\{s, \alpha(\cdot)\}$ is (x_i^*, i). If (x_i^*, i) were inefficient, there would exist an alternative selection (x, j) such that $V^h(x, j) > v_{hi}$ for all $h \in \mathscr{N}$. By Assumption 2, therefore, there would exist some citizen k such that $v_{hk} > v_{hi}$ for all $h \in \mathscr{N}$. It follows that $\#N_k > \#N_i$, for all sincere partitions (N_k, N_i, N_0). For sufficiently small δ, therefore, condition (ii) of Proposition 2 would be violated. Thus, for sufficiently small δ, (x_i^*, i) must be efficient.

Proof of Proposition 12

Let i and j be the citizens who are running (i.e., $s^i = s^j = 1$). Then the selections generated by $\{s, \alpha(\cdot)\}$ are (x_i^*, i) and (x_j^*, j). Suppose that, say, (x_i^*, i) were inefficient. Then there would exist an alternative selection (x, j) such that $V^h(x, j) > v_{hi}$ for all $h \in \mathscr{N}$. By Assumption 2, therefore, there would exist some citizen k such that $v_{hk} > v_{hi}$ for all $h \in \mathscr{N}$. Suppose that citizen k were to enter the race. Proposition 3 implies the existence of a sincere partition (N_i, N_j, N_0) such that $\#N_i = \#N_j$. We know that if $h \in N_i \cup N_0$ it must be the case that $v_{hk} > v_{hi} \geq v_{hj}$, which implies that voting for j and abstaining are weakly dominated voting strategies. Moreover, since voting behavior satisfies IIC, no citizen in $N_i \cup N_0$ would vote for candidate i. It follows that all citizens in $N_i \cup N_0$ would vote for citizen k. Since this group constitutes at least half the population, citizen k must win with a probability of at least one-half. For sufficiently small δ, therefore, citizen k would prefer to enter the race, contradicting the fact that i and j running against each other is an equilibrium.

Notes

*   We thank an anonymous referee, Abhijit Banerjee, Gene Grossman, Robert Inman, John Lott, Jr., Gillian Paull, Stephen Morris, Martin Osborne, Andrei Shleifer, Alex Tabarrok, Sharon Tennyson, a number of seminar participants, and, especially, Howard Rosenthal for comments and encouragement. The authors are grateful to the Institute for Policy Reform and the University of Pennsylvania Research Foundation for their respective support.
1   Osborne (1995) surveys the large literature that adopts this perspective on representative democracy.
2   Standard models assume that candidates can credibly commit to implement any policy promise. While legitimate in models where candidates have no policy preferences, one has otherwise to explain why winning candidates keep their promises (Alesina, 1988).

3 A voting decision α_j is weakly dominated for citizen j if there exists $\hat{\alpha}j \in \mathscr{C} \cup \{0\}$ such that

$$\sum_{i \in \mathscr{C}} P^i\left(\mathscr{C}, \; (\hat{\alpha}_j, \; \alpha_{-j})\right) v_{ji} \geq \sum_{i \in \mathscr{C}} P^i\left(\mathscr{C}, \; (\alpha_j, \; \alpha_{-j})\right) v_{ji}$$

for all α_{-j} with the inequality holding strictly for some α_{-j}.

4 This is given by

$$u^i(\gamma; \alpha(\cdot)) = \prod_{j=1}^{N} \gamma^j U^i(1, \; \ldots, \; 1; \alpha(\cdot)) + \prod_{j=2}^{N} \gamma^j (1 - \gamma^1) U^i(0, \; 1, \; \ldots, \; 1; \alpha(\ldots))$$

$$+ \ldots \prod_{j=1}^{N} (1 - \gamma^j) U^i(0, \; \ldots, \; 0; \alpha(\cdot)).$$

5 Nonetheless, there are reasonable environments where pure strategy political equilibria do not exist. Following Harsanyi (1973), mixed strategy equilibria can be interpreted as the limit of pure strategy equilibria of a perturbed game of incomplete information, where each citizen i has a slightly different entry cost given by $\delta_i = \delta + \epsilon \cdot \theta_i$, with $\epsilon \in (0, \; 1)$ and θ_i is the realization of a random variable with range $(-\delta, \; \delta)$ and distribution function $G(\theta)$. In this game, θ_i, and hence citizen i's entry cost, is private information. A pure strategy for citizen i is then a mapping $\sigma^i : (-\delta, \; \delta) \to \{0, \; 1\}$, where $\sigma^i(\theta_i)$ denotes citizen i's entry decision when his "type" is θ_i. The relevant limit for our mixed strategy equilibria is as ϵ goes to zero.

6 A *partition* is a collection of disjoint, nonempty subsets of $\mathcal{N}$, $(N_j)_{j \in J}$, such that $\cup_{j \in J} N_j = \mathcal{N}$.

7 The proof of this and all subsequent results can be found in the Appendix.

8 Suppose that for all $j \in \mathcal{N}$, $V^j(x, \; h) = V^j(x)$ for all $h \in \mathcal{N}$. Then an alternative $x \in \mathscr{G} \subset \mathscr{A}$ is a *Condorcet winner* in $\mathscr{G}$ if for all $z \in \mathscr{G}/\{x\}$,

$$\#\{j | V^j(x) \geq V^j(z)\} \geq \#\{j | V^j(x) < V^j(z)\}.$$

It is a *strict Condorcet winner* if the inequality is strict.

9 In Downs's model, two candidates, who care only about winning, compete by offering the electorate different platforms. There is an equilibrium in pure strategies only if a Condorcet winner exists in the set of feasible policies. One-candidate pure strategy equilibria are more likely in our setup, since we only require a Condorcet winner to exist in the set of policies that would be chosen by *some* citizen, rather than in the set of *all* feasible policies.

10 Notable exceptions are Palfrey (1984) and Feddersen, Sened, and Wright (1990). Palfrey analyzes a one-dimensional model with three vote-maximizing parties. The two "dominant" parties are assumed to announce their platforms before the "new" third party. The main result is that the two dominant parties offer divergent platforms and the entrant party loses. Feddersen et al. consider a one-dimensional model in which a fixed number of parties must decide whether to enter the race and what platform to adopt. Parties are assumed to care only about winning, and entry is costly. In contrast to Palfrey, voters are assumed to vote strategically. Their main result is that all entering parties adopt the median position, with the number of entering parties depending upon the entry costs and the benefits of holding office.

11 Feddersen (1992) exploits this fact in a related model. In his setup, voters may cast their votes for one of an infinite number of policy alternatives. The alternative that gets the most votes is implemented. Voting is costly, and voters vote strategically. His main result, which exploits an inequality similar to that in Proposition 4, is that only two alternatives receive support in equilibrium.

12   While multicandidate equilibria in which three or more candidates are in the winning set may be unusual, they are not entirely ruled out by our framework. An earlier version of the paper developed a set of sufficient conditions for an equilibrium with three or more candidates in which all candidates tie.

13   To save space, we work with citizens' "reduced-form" preferences over $\{0, q_L, q_H\}$ with the taxes used to finance public provision being implicit.

14   Osborne and Slivinski (1996) assume a continuum of citizens who receive some independent benefit from holding office $- V^i(x, i) = b - |\omega_i - x|$.

15   Formally, voting behavior satisfies AIV if for all citizens $k \in \mathcal{N}$ and candidate sets $\mathcal{C}$, if $v_{ki} = v_{kj}$ for all $i, j \in \mathcal{C}$ then $\alpha_k(\mathcal{C}) = 0$.

16   Introducing independent benefits from office into our model would not, however, restore the possibility of three-candidate equilibria in which all candidates tie. If Assumption 1 is satisfied, there will exist at least one voter for whom the inequality in Proposition 4 fails.

17   One such example is available from the authors.

18   We use this more permissive notion of efficiency to avoid some odd special cases that arise in the heterogeneous policy-making abilities case.

19   We neglect two other possible costs of democratic selection. First, the randomness in the selection if the winning set contains more than one candidate of individuals use mixed strategies may reduce citizens' *ex ante* expected utilities. Second, resources are used up in the process of generating the selection; a candidate set $\mathcal{C}$ results in aggregate utility costs $\#\mathcal{C} \cdot \delta$. Even if representative democracy produces an efficient selection, there may be a method of selecting policy that is both *ex post* efficient and uses fewer "campaign" resources.

20   Our model of representative democracy relates to the study of implementation in Nash equilibrium by Hurwicz and Schmeidler (1978). They investigate the existence of a nondictatorial mechanism for selecting a social outcome such that (i) for every preference profile there exists a Nash equilibrium and (ii) such equilibria are efficient. They prove by construction that there exists such a mechanism which they call the *kingmaker outcome function*. This involves one individual, or a group of individuals, selecting another to make social decisions. Our model of representative democracy can be thought of as a particular kingmaker outcome function. Propositions 1 and 10 confirm its desirable properties. Bergson (1976) discusses the social choice properties of "representative democracy," interpreted as selecting a citizen to decide. He observes that it satisfies all of the axioms of Arrow (1963), except Independence of Irrelevant Alternatives.

21   Besley and Coate (1996) consider the conflict between economic efficiency and payoff maximization by the incumbent that arises in a dynamic model.

22   A similar problem arises in Myerson's (1993) study of the effectiveness of different electoral systems in reducing government corruption. Under plurality rule, voters may be unwilling to switch their votes to less corrupt parties who represent their policy preferences, for fear that this will simply result in the victory of parties with opposing policy preferences.

References

Alesina, Alberto, "Credibility and Policy Convergence in a Two-Party System with Rational Voters," *American Economic Review*, LXXVIII (1988), 796–806.

Arrow, Kenneth, *Social Choice and Individual Values*, 2nd edn (New York: John Wiley, 1963).

Becker, Gary, "Public Policies, Pressure Groups and Dead Weight Costs," *Journal of Public Economics*, XXVIII (1985), 329–47.

Bergson, Abram, "Social Choice and Welfare Economics under Representative Government," *Journal of Public Economics*, VI (1976), 171–90.

Besley, Timothy, and Stephen Coate, "Sources of Inefficiency in a Representative Democracy: A Dynamic Analysis," typescript, 1996.

Buchanan, James M., *Public Finance in Democratic Process* (Chapel Hill: University of North Carolina Press, 1967).

Downs, Anthony, *An Economic Theory of Democracy* (New York: HarperCollins, 1957).

Feddersen, Timothy J., "A Voting Model Implying Duverger's Law and Positive Turnout," *American Journal of Political Science*, XXXVI (1992), 938–62.

Feddersen, Timothy J., Itai Sened, and Stephen G. Wright, "Rational Voting and Candidate Entry under Plurality Rule," *American Journal of Political Science*, XXXIV (1990), 1005–16.

Harsanyi, John, "Games with Randomly Disturbed Payoffs: A New Rationale for Mixed-Strategy Equilibrium Points," *International Journal of Game Theory*, II (1973), 1–23.

Hurwicz, Leonid, and David Schmeidler, "Construction of Outcome Functions Guaranteeing Existence and Pareto Optimality of Nash Equilibria," *Econometrica*, XLVI (1978), 1447–74.

Myerson, Roger B., "Effectiveness of Electoral Systems for Reducing Government Corruption," *Games and Economic Behavior*, V (1993), 118–32.

Myerson, Roger B., and Robert J. Weber, "A Theory of Voting Equilibria," *American Political Science Review*, LXXVII (1993), 102–14.

Nash, John, "Equilibrium Points in *n*-Person Games," *Proceedings of the National Academy of Sciences*, XXXVI (1950), 48–9.

Osborne, Martin J., "Spatial Models of Political Competition under Plurality Rule: A Survey of Some Explanations of the Number of Candidates and the Positions They Take," *Canadian Journal of Economics*, XXVIII (1995), 261–301.

Osborne, Martin J., and Al Slivinski, "A Model of Political Competition with Citizen Candidates," *Quarterly Journal of Economics*, CXI (1996), 65–96.

Palfrey, Thomas R., "Spatial Equilibrium with Entry," *Review of Economic Studies*, LI (1984), 139–56.

Rogoff, Kenneth, "Equilibrium Political Budget Cycles," *American Economic Review*, LXXX (1990), 21–36.

Stigler, George, "Economists and Public Policy," *Regulation* (May/June 1982), 7–13.

Stiglitz, Joseph E., "The Demand for Education in Public and Private Schools," *Journal of Public Economics*, III (1974), 349–85.

EIGHTEEN

Distributive Politics and Economic Growth

Alberto Alesina and Dani Rodrik*

Source: From *Quarterly Journal of Economics* (1994), 109: 465–90.

A crude distinction between economics and politics would be that economics is concerned with expanding the pie while politics is about distributing it. In this paper we analyze the relationship between the two. We focus on how an economy's initial configuration of resources shapes the political struggle for income and wealth distribution, and how that, in turn, affects long-run growth. Our main conclusion is that inequality is conducive to the adoption of growth-retarding policies. We derive this result from a simple political-economy model of growth, and present cross-country evidence consistent with it.

The key feature of our model is that individuals differ in their relative factor endowments. We distinguish between two types of factors: an accumulated factor (called "capital") and a nonaccumulated factor (called "labor"). Growth is driven by the expansion of the capital stock, which is in turn determined by individual saving decisions. Long-run growth is endogenous, as the aggregate production function is taken to be linearly homogeneous in capital and (productive) government services taken together. The provision of government services is financed by a tax on capital.

Because government services are productive, a "small" tax on capital benefits everyone. However, heterogeneity in the ownership of factors implies that individuals differ in their ideal rate of taxation. Since the tax on capital affects accumulation and growth, this difference also carries over to individuals' preferences over the ideal growth rate. An individual whose income derives entirely from capital prefers the tax rate that maximizes the economy's growth rate. Anyone else would prefer a higher tax, with a correspondingly lower growth rate. The lower an individual's share of capital income (relative to his labor income), the higher is his ideal tax, and the lower his ideal growth rate.

How is the actual choice of policy determined by individual preferences? The median voter theorem, according to which the tax rate selected by the government is the one preferred by the median voter, provides a useful benchmark. Using this theorem, we establish our main result on the relationship between income distribution and growth. The more equitable is distribution in the economy, the better endowed is the median voter with capital. Consequently, the lower is the equilibrium level of capital taxation, and the higher is the economy's growth. Furthermore, in our model the distribution of income is monotonically related to the distribution of capital. Thus, the central theoretical result that we shall test is that income and wealth inequality are inversely related to subsequent economic growth.

While an explicit analytical model is indispensable to lay out the logic of our story, the specific formalization we have chosen should be viewed as an illustration of a more general idea. When we use the term capital, for example, what we have in mind are all growth-producing assets, including physical capital, human capital, and proprietary technology. Labor, in turn, stands for *unskilled* labor. More importantly, our tax on capital must be interpreted as a metaphor for any kind of redistributive policy that transfers income to unskilled labor while reducing the incentive to accumulate. Governments have a wide variety of such policies at their disposal, and we shall mention some of them below.

Similarly, our use of the median-voter theorem should not be taken as a literal description of the political process we have in mind. We appeal to this theorem simply to capture the basic idea that any government is likely to be responsive to the wishes of the majority when key distributional issues are at stake. Even a dictator cannot completely ignore social demands, for fear of being overthrown. Thus, even in a dictatorship, distributional issues affecting the majority of the population will influence policy decisions. With these nuances kept in mind, our central idea becomes a simple and intuitive one: distributive struggles harmful to growth are more likely to take place when resources are distributed unevenly.

We present some empirical results consistent with our model at the end of the paper. Our model implies an inverse relationship between growth and the prior levels of both income and wealth equality. Measures of wealth distribution are hard to find, except for a measure of distribution of land ownership. Therefore, we focus on this measure of land distribution and on measures of income distribution. Controlling for initial levels of income and human capital, we find a statistically significant negative correlation between inequality in land distribution (measured around 1960) and economic growth over the subsequent two and a half decades. We obtain the same kind of results for income distribution as well: initial inequality in income is negatively correlated with subsequent growth.

Our work is related to four distinct strands in the economics literature. First, our model fits in with the tradition of the new literature on endogenous growth (Romer 1986; Lucas 1988; Barro 1990; Barro and Sala-i-Martin 1990) and extends it by showing how distributional considerations affect the choice of growth in a political equilibrium. Second, our basic ideas are related to the political-economy literature on majority voting on tax rates (Romer 1975; Roberts 1977; Meltzer and Richard 1981; Mayer 1984) and build a bridge between this literature and the new growth models. While the literature on voting on tax rates is static, our model is dynamic. Third, the questions we examine are reminiscent of some perennial issues in the development literature (Kuznets 1955; Fields 1980). This body of work has traditionally been concerned with the distributional implications of growth. Here we reverse the question and ask how distribution affects growth. Finally, a recent literature has emphasized links between income distribution and growth that operate through nonpolitical channels. In particular, Murphy, Shleifer, and Vishny (1989) were the first to argue that income distribution influences the size of home demand, and hence the potential for industrialization. This paper has empirical implications on the relationship between income distribution and growth which are similar to ours. Also, Galor and Zeira (1993) show that in models with liquidity constraints income distribution determines the share of the population that can invest in education: the relationship between inequality and growth is positive at low levels of income, but negative otherwise.

Several papers have recently explored political models linking income distribution and growth. The two papers most closely related to ours are Bertola (1993) and Persson and Tabellini (1991), both of which were written independently of ours. Bertola presents a model focusing on the distinction between accumulated and nonaccumulated factors of production and points to the conflict of interest regarding growth that exists among individuals with differing sources of income. Persson and Tabellini develop a model that, although it has empirical implications similar to ours, is quite different. They consider a simplified overlapping-generations framework, where agents live for two periods: income is taxed purely for redistributive purposes, and taxation influences investment in human capital. In our model agents have an infinite horizon, and taxes are not used only for redistributive purposes Tax revenues provide a public good necessary for private production. Thus, our model (unlike that of Persson and Tabellini) is consistent with the inverted U-curve relationship between taxes and growth as in Barro (1990). Persson and Tabellini also present empirical evidence consistent with ours, but using somewhat different data sets. Thus, our empirical results and theirs should be viewed as mutually reinforcing.

Finally, Perotti (1993), Saint-Paul and Verdier (1992), and Fernandez and Rogerson (1992) also develop various politico-economic models where income distribution affects the equilibrium level of investment in human capital and hence ultimately determines growth. Benhabib and Rustichini (1991) present a game-theoretic model in which individuals can appropriate society's resources to their own benefit (at the cost of future retaliation by others) and analyze the relationship between the level of wealth, income distribution, and growth.[1]

The plan of the paper is as follows. Section I lays out the basic theoretical framework and discusses the links among factor ownership, redistributive policy, and economic growth. Section II presents our empirical evidence. Section III concludes.

I   The Theory

We use a simple endogenous growth model with labor and capital as the primary factors of production. In addition, we assume that private production requires the provision of public services, which for concreteness we can think of as "law and order" services. Endogenous growth requires nondiminishing returns to the economy's reproducible resources. We obtain this feature by assuming that output is linear in capital and public services taken together. This yields our aggregate production function:

$$y = Ak^{\alpha}g^{1-\alpha}l^{1-\alpha}, \qquad 0 < \alpha < 1, \tag{1}$$

which is adapted from Barro (1990) and Barro and Sala-i-Martin (1990), with slight modification. A is a technological parameter, k and l are the aggregate stocks of capital and labor, respectively, and g is the aggregate level of government spending on productive services. The single good produced in this economy can be used for either consumption or investment, and we fix its price at unity. To save on notation, we shall not show the time dependence of each variable, unless doing so is required to avoid confusion. The appeal of this model for our purposes is that it attributes a constructive role for government.

Therefore, redistributive policies will interact with growth-enhancing policies. This feature is realistic: fiscal redistribution often takes place through various spending programs above and beyond direct cash transfers.

To finance spending on public services, the government has access to a tax on capital income, τ. The budget is balanced every instant, so that

$$g = \tau k. \tag{2}$$

The policy options are restricted in two important respects. First, we rule out expropriation of capital. Since capital taxation is distortionary, the government could improve welfare by expropriating the capital stock and then publicly operating it and distributing the profits. Alternatively, the government could expropriate the capital stock and rent it. These policies would achieve the command optimum and maximize welfare even from the point of view of a government that cares only about capital owners. We leave out considerations of expropriation, to avoid dealing with time-inconsistency problems in capital taxation, which are not our focus.[2] The reason why expropriation is not more common in the real world is clearly outside the scope of the model. Second, we allow only a *linear* tax on capital and hence rule out progressivity of tax rates on capital. In this type of model the median voter has an incentive to impose progressive taxation, which falls primarily (or exclusively) on income recipients richer than the median. Note, however, that even with a linear tax rate on capital, as long as wage income is relatively evenly distributed, our model will effectively yield a form of progressive taxation, with richer individuals (with higher capital income) being taxed more heavily than poorer ones.

Capital is to be interpreted in the broad sense indicated in the Introduction, namely, as including physical capital, human capital, and all proprietary technology. The tax on capital, therefore, should be viewed as a tax on all resources that are accumulated, including human capital. The (unskilled) labor force, which we take to be constant, is not subject to taxation. This assumption is built into the model to allow the government to discriminate between these two types of factors of production and to undertake redistributive policies. We could, in principle, allow taxes on labor income as well, without greatly altering our qualitative conclusions, but the analytics would get considerably more complicated.[3] We shall provide further justification for this asymmetry below.

We assume perfect competition in factor markets so that wages and rates of return on capital are determined by the usual marginal productivity conditions. Taking the appropriate partial derivatives of (1) and substituting from (2), we obtain

$$r = \frac{\partial y}{\partial k} = \alpha A \tau^{1-\alpha} \equiv r(\overset{+}{\tau}) \tag{3}$$

$$\omega = \frac{\partial y}{\partial l} = (1-\alpha)A\tau^{1-\alpha}k \equiv \omega(\overset{+}{\tau})k. \tag{4}$$

We assume that labor is supplied inelastically, which allows us to set the economy's aggregate labor endowment (l) equal to unity. Note that the marginal productivity of capital (r) is independent of the capital stock, once the tax on capital that finances government spending is taken into account. This prevents diminishing returns from setting in. Furthermore, the marginal productivities of labor and capital are both increasing in the tax rate on capital, as higher taxes allow more government spending on productive services for any given level of k. The wage rate is also increasing in the capital stock. Net of taxes, capital and labor income are given by

$$y^k = [r(\tau) - \tau]k \tag{5}$$

$$y^l = \omega(\tau)k. \tag{6}$$

For the national income identity to be satisfied, it is necessary that $y^k + y^l + g = y$, which is indeed the case here.

At this point we note that the tax on capital plays two critical roles in this model. First, and most directly, it affects the net return to owners of capital, and hence will alter the incentive to accumulate. Second, it increases the instantaneous *level* of wage income (while reducing its rate of growth insofar as it also induces a lower rate of capital accumulation). Wage income is increasing in τ because a higher rate of taxation allows the government to increase its spending on services that increase productivity.

Although we have modeled here a particular policy instrument (a tax on capital income) and a particular channel through which this instrument enhances labor income (government spending on productive services), our framework is meant to capture a much broader set of redistributive policies. Indeed, the type of redistributive policies we have in mind takes many different guises in practice and can be modeled in many different ways. Consider some examples:

(1)   In an economy where wage income is relatively evenly distributed, a progressive income tax yields a higher effective tax rate on capital income than on labor income. This shifts the tax burden from labor to capital. Furthermore, if capital includes human capital, a progressive tax on labor income redistributes from owners of human capital to owners of unskilled labor.

(2)   In an open economy import tariffs redistribute income from the economy's abundant factor of production to its scarce factor of production (Stolper and Samuelson, 1944). Therefore, in an economy like that of the United States which is rich in capital, import restrictions are effectively a tax on capital and a subsidy on (unskilled) labor.

(3)   In economies where labor relations are organized along corporatist lines (e.g., in some Western European countries), direct state intervention in collective bargaining can alter contract terms (for wages, benefits, and the like) to the advantage of workers, depressing the return to capital.

No single model can capture these and other ways in which redistribution takes place in practice. What should be clear, however, is that the policies listed above will all work in pretty much the same manner as a direct tax on capital.[4]

So our model is not meant to suggest that governments do not have other taxes besides capital taxes. Nor do we want to imply that capital taxes are the only policies that can redistribute. We are simply saying that in practice most policies that redistribute from capital to labor will have qualitatively the same impact as our capital tax.

Determinants of growth

We assume that individuals are alike in all respects except for their initial ownership shares in the economy's aggregate stocks of capital and labor. Each individual is indexed by his relative factor endowment σ^i:

$$\sigma^i = \frac{l^i}{k^i/k}, \quad \sigma^i \in [0, \infty). \tag{7}$$

(Remember that the aggregate labor endowment of the economy is normalized to unity.) An individual with a high σ is capital-poor, while one with low σ is capital-rich. In principle, σ^i may change over time; however, it will turn out, in our case, that σ^i will remain constant. Each individual can earn income from both capital and labor. Therefore, using (5) and (6),

$$y^i = \omega(\tau)kl^i + [r(\tau) - \tau]k^i = \omega(\tau)k^i\sigma^i + [r(\tau) - \tau]k^i. \tag{8}$$

Note that income depends both on individual ownership of capital and on the aggregate stock of capital.

We assume that all individuals have the same logarithmic utility function. The consumption-saving decisions of the ith individual are determined by solving the following problem:

$$\max U^i = \int \log c^i e^{-\rho t} dt \tag{9}$$

such that

$$\frac{dk^i}{dt} = \omega(\tau)k^i\sigma^i + [r(\tau) - \tau]k^i - c^i,$$

where c^i denotes consumption and ρ is the discount rate. The individual consumer takes the paths of r, k, and τ as given. The solution to this problem is given by the following equation:

$$\hat{c}^i = (r(\tau) - \tau) - \rho, \quad \text{for all } i, \tag{10}$$

where a circumflex denotes proportional changes (i.e., $\hat{x} = (dx/x)/dt$).

Now assume that τ remains unchanged over time. (We shall show in the next subsection that this will be the case in equilibrium.) Each individual then accumulates along a steady-state path given by

$$\hat{k}^i = \hat{c}^i = r(\tau) - \tau - \rho \equiv \gamma(\tau). \tag{11}$$

This has the helpful implication that all individuals accumulate at the same rate. Therefore, there is a common economywide growth rate $\gamma(\tau)$, which is independent of the initial distribution of factor endowments. Moreover, the relative factor endowments σ^i remain constant over time, and the distribution of factor ownership is time-invariant.

These results generalize to any time-separable, isoelastic utility function. Suppose that instantaneous utility took the more general form $(c^{1-\eta} - 1)/(1 - \eta)$, instead of $\log(c)$. The corresponding accumulation rate (under constant τ) would have become $\hat{k}^i = \hat{c}^i = \eta^{-1}(r - \tau - \rho)$, which is also independent of initial factor ownership shares. The crucial implication of this utility function which makes our model tractable is that wealth (and income) distribution is constant over time. If it were not, the voting process would become much more complicated, since the identity of the median voter would change over time, leading to strategic intertemporal voting (as will become clear below).

As shown in (11), growth is linear in the difference between the after-tax return to capital and the discount rate. It has the following properties:

$$\gamma_\tau \equiv \frac{\partial \gamma}{\partial \tau} = \frac{\partial r}{\partial \tau} - 1 \gtreqless 0 \quad \text{as} \quad \tau \lesseqgtr [\alpha(1 - \alpha)A]^{1/\alpha}.$$

The higher is the after-tax return to capital, the higher the economy's growth rate. The tax on capital has a nonlinear effect on growth. For small tax rates the productivity-enhancing effect of public spending dominates, and the after-tax return to capital *increases* in τ. For large tax rates, the after-tax return to capital falls as τ is raised further. Therefore, the relationship between the economy's growth rate and the tax on capital is represented by an inverse U-curve: the growth rate first increases, and then decreases, as τ is progressively raised. The growth-maximizing tax rate is given by

$$\tau^* = [\alpha(1 - \alpha)A]^{1/\alpha}, \tag{12}$$

where τ^* is determined by technological parameters and is time-invariant.

Policy preferences with heterogeneity in factor ownership

What is individual i's preferred policy, and how does it depend on σ^i? To answer this question, we look at the problem that would be solved by a government that selects τ in order to maximize i's well-being. We note first that, along the optimal path, the instantaneous level of consumption is given by

$$c^i = [\omega(\tau)\sigma^i + \rho]k^i \tag{13}$$

(from [9] and [10]). Hence individual i consumes his entire labor income ($\omega(\tau)\sigma^i k^i$) plus a fraction of his capital stock (ρk^i). The relevant maximization problem for the government then becomes

$$\max_\tau U^i = \int \log c^i e^{-\rho t} dt \tag{14}$$

such that

$$c^i = [\omega(\tau)\sigma^i + \rho]k^i$$

$$\hat{k}^i = \gamma(\tau)$$

$$\hat{k} = \gamma(\tau).$$

The constraints make clear that the choice of policy affects both the level of consumption and its growth rate. The economywide growth equation $\hat{k} = \gamma(\tau)$ belongs here as a constraint because k enters the definition of σ^i.

This exercise yields the following implicit characterization of individual i's most preferred tax, τ^i:

$$\tau^i\left\{1 - \alpha A(1 - \alpha)(\tau^i)^{-\alpha}\right\} = \rho(1 - \alpha)\theta^i(\tau^i), \tag{15}$$

where

$$\theta^i(\tau^i) = \omega(\tau^i)\sigma^i / [\omega(\tau^i)\sigma^i + \rho]. \tag{16}$$

$\theta^i(.)$ is the share of the labor-income component in consumption expenditures of individual i, and it is increasing in σ^i.[5] Since time does not enter these expressions, the government's optimal policy involves a constant tax rate over time. Hence individual behavior based on a fixed τ is fully consistent with the actual equilibrium outcome.

It can be verified that (15) and (16) yield a unique τ^i which increases with σ^i. In other words, the more capital-poor is an individual, the higher is his ideal tax on capital. One interesting benchmark case is provided by a pure capitalist, who has no labor income. In this case $\sigma^k = 0$, where the superscript k identifies this type of individual. Equation (15) yields the pure capitalist's ideal tax to be

$$\tau^k = [\alpha(1 - \alpha)A]^{1/\alpha} = \tau^*. \tag{17}$$

In view of the role played by public services in the aggregate production function, it is not surprising that the capitalist desires a positive rate of taxation. But as this expression makes clear, his ideal tax is precisely the one that maximizes the economy's growth, τ^*.

Since τ^i is increasing in σ^i, an immediate implication is that an individual with some labor income (i.e., with $\sigma^i > 0$), no matter how small this income is, prefers a tax rate that exceeds τ^* and a growth rate that falls short of the maximum, $\gamma(\tau^*)$. In particular, if wealth were evenly distributed in the economy, the representative individual (with $\sigma^i = 1$) would pick $\tau^i > \tau^*$. Consequently, a government that maximized the welfare of the representative individual would not want to maximize the economy's growth rate. This indicates that growth and welfare are not the same in our context.

The intuition behind these results is best seen by distinguishing between *level* and *growth* effects of tax policy. Along the optimal consumption path a pure capitalist (with $\sigma^i = 0$) consumes a constant fraction of his capital stock (given by ρk^i, see [13]) and the instantaneous level of his consumption is therefore independent of τ. The value of his consumption stream is maximized by simply selecting the level of τ that maximizes the rate of capital accumulation. For anyone else the instantaneous level of consumption has a labor-income component also, which depends on τ (see [13]). Whenever $\tau > \tau^*$, an increase in taxation has two distinct effects. First, it raises the level of consumption of any individual who receives labor income, and second, it reduces the rate of growth of aggregate income (including real wages) and consumption.

Now consider an initial situation with τ set at the growth-maximizing τ^*. A slight increase in τ would have only a second-order effect on accumulation (since growth is at its maximum), and hence only a second-order effect on the growth rate of consumption. But it would have a positive first-order effect on the instantaneous consumption level of any individual who receives labor income. On net, this increase in τ must therefore be beneficial, for anyone except a pure capitalist. This explains why the trade-off will always result in a level of taxation that exceeds the growth-maximizing one, except in the limiting case of a pure capitalist. Further, the larger is the share of labor income for an individual, the more significant is the level effect, and the higher the ideal tax.

Policy choice under majority voting

Suppose now that the decision over the tax rate is reached by pairwise comparison under simple majority rule. The median-voter theorem can be applied to this case because voting takes place over a single issue, preferences are single peaked, and there exists a monotonic relationship between ideal policies and voters' factor endowments. In addition, since the ideal policies are constant over time and the distribution of factor endowments is also time invariant, it does not matter whether voting takes place only once at time zero or is repeated every period.[6] We can conclude that the tax rate chosen by majority rule, τ^m, is defined implicitly by the following equation, where σ^m denotes the relative factor-endowment share of the median voter:

$$\tau^m \{1 - \alpha A(1 - \alpha)(\tau^m)^{-\alpha}\} = \rho(1 - \alpha)\theta^m(\tau^m), \tag{18}$$

where

$$\theta^m(\tau^m) = \omega(\tau^m)\sigma^m / [\omega(\tau^m)\sigma^m + \rho]$$

(compared with [15] and [16]). Under majority voting, the political equilibrium yields a tax rate that is the ideal tax rate of the median voter – the latter identified by his relative factor endowment σ^m.

Equation (18) establishes a relationship between the distribution of factor ownership and growth. In a perfectly egalitarian society everyone has the same labor/capital share, that is, $\sigma^m = \sigma^i = 1$ for all i. In actual, real-world distributions, the labor/capital share of the median voter is above the average share; that is, $\sigma^m - 1 > 0$. Furthermore, the greater the inequality, the larger is the difference between median and average likely to be. Hence, we can treat $(\sigma^m - 1)$ as the relevant indicator of inequality in the context of our model. This measure captures how much below the average share lies the median share of capital ownership. For example, a very high σ^m implies that 50 percent of the voters own a very low share of the economy's capital stock.

As mentioned before, factor ownership is directly related to income in this model. In fact, our results can be easily restated in terms of income inequality. To see this, note that by rearranging (8) we can express individual i's income as

$$y^i = \left[\omega + (r - \tau)(1/\sigma^i)\right] l^i k.$$

Since labor in our model refers to unskilled labor, it would seem natural that all individuals would have more or less a common value for l^i (that is, 24 hours). A direct implication is that y^i will be inversely related to σ^i. Consequently, the larger the gap between σ^m and unity, the larger the gap that will exist between median and average incomes. Equation (18) therefore leads to the following important result.

The higher is σ^m above unity, the lower is the rate of growth of the economy. Or, in more practical terms, *the more unequal is the distribution of income and wealth, the lower is the rate of growth.*

In the context of our model, "inequality" is given by how poor is the median relative to the average voter. It is of course possible to imagine distributions with different degrees of inequality which have the property that the difference between median and average voter remains identical. The crucial role played in our model by the median–average gap stems from the application of the median–voter theorem. As emphasized in the introduction, we view this theorem as a convenient and elegant way of capturing a more general point. The specific index of inequality ($\sigma^m - 1$) resulting from this theorem has to be viewed in the same light.

For growth to be as high as possible, we need the median voter to own as much capital as possible, and to have as high an income (relative to the average) as possible. When a large segment of the electorate is cut off from the expanding and income-generating assets of the economy, it is more likely to be willing to tax income from these assets and to undercut growth.[7] Note that it is practically impossible for majority voting to yield the economy's maximum growth rate. Maximum growth is attained only if the median voter has no labor endowment whatsoever, which is not a realistic possibility. But, as discussed above, this result has little normative significance, since maximizing growth does not maximize the "representative" individual's welfare in this context.

Finally, a word on dictatorships versus democracies. In principle, our model should be more directly applicable to democracies, where voting plays a significant role in policy making. Thus, the relationship between income distribution and growth should be stronger in democracies than in dictatorships. However, dictators' policy decisions are also influenced by social demands and social conflicts. For instance, a large group of impoverished workers or landless peasants may threaten the stability of the regime and force the leadership to implement growth-retarding redistributions.

Our model does not imply any type of correlation between regime type (democracy versus dictatorship) and growth for two reasons. First, as argued above, redistributive pressures may find a political outlet not only in democracies but also in dictatorships. Second, the weight placed on growth in a dictatorship would depend on the nature of the regime and its preferences. A pro-capital (or technocratic) regime would minimize redistribution and maximize growth, while a populist regime would do the opposite.[8] Thus, the model does *not* predict a systematic difference in the average rates of growth of democracies and nondemocracies.

II   Empirical Evidence

The basic implication of our model is that the more unequal is the distribution of resources in society, the lower is the rate of economic growth. The link between distribution and growth is given by redistributive policies. In less equal societies more redistribution is sought by a majority of the population. However, redistributive policies, in turn, reduce growth by introducing economic distortions.

The most direct way of testing the theory would be to relate measures of income (or wealth) inequality to measures of redistributive policies. The problem in pursuing this line of attack is that in different countries and time periods redistributive policies are pursued by different means. In our model we focus on capital taxation because this is the simplest way of formalizing redistributive policy. But as emphasized above, redistribution could be achieved by many other means: by a progressive income tax system, by minimum wage laws, by imposing trade and capital restrictions, and by the composition of government expenditures, just to name a few examples. It would be an almost impossible task to construct a meaningful cross-country index for the totality of such measures. For our purposes it does not matter which policy instruments are used to achieve redistribution. The only relevant point is that redistributive policies introduce distortions, and thereby reduce growth. Hence we focus our examination directly on the relationship between distribution of resources and growth. We attempt to determine whether initial inequality is a statistically significant predictor of long-term growth across countries.

Comparable data on wealth distribution for a large enough sample of countries do not exist. What we do have are distributional indicators on *income* and *on land*. With respect to income there exist several compilations of Gini coefficients and other indices drawn from national surveys (Jain 1975; Lecallion et al. 1984; Fields 1989). Some countries have distributional indicators available for different time periods, but the intertemporal and cross-country comparability of these data is quite weak. Fields (1989) has recently reviewed the sources of income distribution estimates for 70 *developing* countries and has found that only 35 of them have data that satisfy minimum criteria of quality and comparability.[9] The problem of data quality is less acute for developed countries. Therefore, we define and use a "high quality sample" that includes all the OECD countries for which we have data (from Jain 1975) and the developing countries chosen by Fields (1989).[10] In addition, we present results for a larger sample, which includes *all* countries for which we have distributional data. For a list of countries with sources, see the Appendices.

With respect to land distribution we are aware of only one compendium (Taylor and Hudson 1972), and this source provides the Gini coefficient of land distribution for 54 countries around 1960.[11] Land is only one component of wealth, and thus the Gini coefficient of land ownership is only a very imperfect proxy of a true measure of wealth distribution. Moreover, land does not exactly fit our model's notion of capital as an accumulating asset. But inequality in land ownership is likely to be highly correlated with inequality in the distribution of accumulating assets also. Since only Gini coefficients are available for land, we restrict the presentation of results to Gini coefficients for income as well. (However, we have also done work with quantile measures of income distribution and have reached very similar results; these additional results are available upon request.)

The correlation coefficient between the land and income Gini's is 0.35 in the sample of 41 countries for which both indicators are available.

To avoid reverse causation from growth to distribution, we tried to limit the sample to countries for which we had Gini coefficients measured not too far beyond the beginning of the time horizon for growth. In the case of Gini coefficients for land, this did not prove to be a problem because the most recent data point comes from 1964 and the majority of Gini's date from before 1960. However, many of the earliest income Gini coefficients are measured in the 1960s, and some in the 1970s (see the Appendices for details). Throwing out all of these cases would have reduced our sample size significantly. We have dealt with the simultaneity problem in two ways: first, by running two-stage least squares regressions and instrumenting for the Gini coefficients,[12] and second, by running regressions for the 1970–85 period as well as for the 1960–85 period.

In addition to the Gini coefficients, we have included in our regressions two additional explanatory variables emphasized in the recent growth literature (Barro 1991): (i) the initial level of per capita income and (ii) the primary school enrollment ratio. The first variable is entered to account for the possibility of convergence, and the second is a measure of the initial level of human capital. We do not include investment in our regressions, as this is an endogenous variable in our model. Except for the Gini coefficients, all data are from Heston and Summers (1988) and Barro and Wolf (1989).

Table 18.1 shows our results for the 1960–85 period. Columns (1) and (2) restrict the sample to countries for which income distribution data are more reliable: this is the high-quality sample described above. Columns (3) and (4) are the regressions for the larger sample of countries, where the previous sample is augmented by 24 additional developing countries. Columns (5)–(8) are the regressions that include the Gini coefficient for land, either alone or jointly with the income Gini (columns (6)–(8).

The results indicate that income inequality is negatively correlated with subsequent growth. When either one of the two Gini's is entered on its own, the relevant coefficient is almost uniformly statistically significant at the 5 percent level or better and has the expected (negative) sign. The only exception is the OLS regression for the large sample (column (3)), where the income Gini is statistically significant only at the 10 percent level. We also note that the t-statistics for the land Gini are remarkably high (above 4), as are the R^2's for the regressions that include the land Gini's. When the land and income Gini's are entered together, the former remains significant at the 1 percent level, while the latter is significant only at the 10 percent level (the sample size shrinks to 41 countries in this case, since many countries have only one of the two indicators). The estimated coefficients imply that an increase in, say, the land Gini coefficient by one standard deviation (an increase of 0.16 in the Gini index) would lead to a reduction in growth of 0.8 percentage points per year.

Column (7) reports the results obtained including a dummy variable for democracies interacted with the land Gini. The coefficient is not statistically significant, rejecting the hypothesis that the relationship between inequality and growth is different in democracies and nondemocracies. We have included this interactive democracy dummy in all other versions of our regressions; the results were uniformly insignificant. By contrast, Persson and Tabellini (1991) report that while the inverse relationship holds for democracies, it does not for nondemocracies. The difference in the results arises mostly because of different data sets on inequality, and to a lesser extent from some differences in specification

Table 18.1 Growth Regressions for 1960–85

	High-quality sample (N = 46)		Largest possible sample (N = 70)		Largest possible sample (N = 49)		(N = 41)	
	OLS (1)	TSLS (2)	OLS (3)	TSLS (4)	OLS (5)	OLS (6)	OLS (7)	OLS (8)
Const.	3.60	8.66	1.76	6.48	3.71	6.22	6.24	6.21
	(2.66)	(3.33)	(1.50)	(2.93)	(3.86)	(4.69)	(4.63)	(4.61)
GDP60	−0.44	−0.52	−0.48	−0.58	−0.38	−0.38	−0.39	−0.38
	(−3.28)	(−3.17)	(−3.37)	(−3.47)	(−3.61)	(−3.25)	(−3.06)	(−2.95)
PRIM60	3.26	2.85	−3.98	3.70	3.85	2.66	2.62	2.65
	(3.38)	(2.43)	(4.66)	(3.72)	(4.88)	(2.66)	(2.53)	(2.56)
GINI60	−5.70	−15.98	−3.58	−12.93		−3.47	−3.45	−3.47
	(−2.46)	(−3.21)	(−1.81)	(−3.12)		(−1.82)	(−1.79)	(−1.80)
GINILND					5.50	−5.23	−5.24	−5.21
					(−5.24)	(−4.38)	(−4.32)	(−4.19)
DEMOC GINILND							0.12	
							(0.12)	
DEMOC								0.02
								(0.05)
$\bar{R}^2$	0.28	0.27	0.25	0.26	0.53	0.53	0.51	0.51

The dependent variable is average per capita growth rate over 1960–85. t-statistics are in parentheses. Independent variables are defined as follows:

GDP60   per capita GDP level in 1960
PRIM60   primary school enrollment ratio in 1960
GINI60   Gini coefficient of income inequality, measured close to 1960 (see Appendix for dates)
GINILND Gini coefficient of land distribution inequality, measured close to 1960 (see Appendix for dates)
DEMOC   democracy dummy.

Two-stage least squares regressions use GDP60, PRIM60, literacy rate in 1960, infant mortality in 1965, secondary enrollment in 1960, fertility in 1965, and an Africa dummy as instruments.

and definition of democracies.[13] Finally, column (8) indicates that democracies do not grow faster than or more slowly than dictatorships.

The negative result in column (7) can be interpreted in two ways. One is that, as argued above, the pressure for redistribution coming from the majority is felt not only in democracies but also in other regimes. According to this view, some dictators are subject to political influences similar to those experienced by elected representatives. The alternative view is that income inequality influences growth through channels other than the political one. For instance, Murphy, Shleifer, and Vishny (1989) stress the role of home demand as shaped by income distribution.

Table 18.2 repeats these regressions for the 1970–85 period (except for the two-stage least squares regressions). As mentioned above, this may be a more relevant time period to try our story out as many of our income Gini's are measured during the 1960s (and some in

Table 18.2   Growth Regressions for 1970–85

	High-quality sample (N = 46)	Largest possible sample (N = 70)	Largest possible sample (N = 49)			(N = 41)
	OLS (9)	OLS (10)	OLS (11)	OLS (12)	OLS (13)	OLS (14)
Const.	4.56 (2.67)	2.80 (2.00)	4.88 (3.16)	7.22 (3.79)	7.18 (3.69)	7.22 (3.74)
GDP70	−0.29 (−2.60)	−0.27 (−2.33)	−0.21 (−2.09)	−0.28 (−2.58)	−0.28 (−2.23)	−0.27 (−2.15)
PRIM70	3.28 (2.46)	3.79 (3.52)	3.45 (2.65)	2.77 (1.83)	2.81 (1.79)	2.81 (1.80)
GINI70	−9.71 (−3.62)	−7.95 (−3.49)		−5.71 (−2.33)	−5.74 (−2.30)	−5.73 (−2.30)
GINILND			−8.14 (−5.49)	−6.41 (−3.79)	−6.39 (−3.69)	−6.46 (−3.71)
DEMOC GINILND					−0.11 (−0.13)	
DEMOC						−0.09 (−0.15)
$\bar{R}^2$	0.28	0.23	0.43	0.46	0.45	0.45

The dependent variable is average per capita growth rate over 1970–85. *t*-statistics are in parentheses. Independent variables are defined as follows:

GDP70   per capita GDP level in 1970
PRIM70   primary school enrollment ratio in 1970
GINI70   Gini coefficient of income inequality, measured close to 1970 (see Appendix for dates)
GINILND   Gini coefficient of land distribution inequality, measured close to 1960 (see Appendix for dates)
DEMOC   democracy dummy.

the 1970s). The results are indeed even stronger: the coefficient on the Gini is consistently significant at the 5 percent level or better. Moreover, both the land and income Gini's remain statistically significant (at the 1 percent and 5 percent levels, respectively) when they are entered jointly. The magnitude of the coefficients is commensurate with those in table 18.2.

Our results imply that countries that experienced a land reform in the aftermath of World War II and hence reduced the inequality in land ownership should have had higher growth than countries with no land reform. This argument is often mentioned in the literature on economic development as one explanation for the successful experience of several Asian countries, such as Japan, South Korea, or Taiwan, compared with the less stellar performance of most Latin American countries (see, for example, Ranis 1990, and Wade 1990, chapter 8). Asian countries had land reforms; Latin American countries did not.

Since our paper was first written and circulated in working paper form, more empirical work has been done on the relationship between income inequality and growth. Clarke

(1993), in particular, has analyzed the robustness of the negative relationship between inequality and growth. He finds that the result is robust across different income inequality measures (Gini, quintile measures, Theil's index, etc.) and different specifications of the growth regression. Under most of his specifications, the hypothesis that democracies and nondemocracies differ in the relationship between inequality and growth is rejected. His findings, together with ours, raise some questions about the generalizability of Persson and Tabellini's (1991) results on this front.

III   Concluding Remarks

The basic message of our model is that there will be a strong demand for redistribution in societies where a large section of the population does not have access to the productive resources of the economy. Such conflict over distribution will generally harm growth. Our empirical results are supportive of these hypotheses: they indicate that inequality in income and land distribution is negatively associated with subsequent growth.

An important extension of our model would be to examine more closely the dynamic interconnection between distribution and growth. In our model the distribution of assets is predetermined and remains constant. In reality growth itself affects income distribution. The serious technical problem introduced in this case is that when income distribution varies over time, as a function of growth, one cannot look at each voting decision in isolation. Voting decisions in any period affect growth in subsequent periods, which in turn affects distribution and future voting decisions. Thus, the outcome of future social choices depends on the voting decisions taken today. Therefore, when voting today, rational voters have to internalize this dynamic problem of social choice.

Appendix 1   List of Countries and Dates for Gini Coefficient for Income (High-Quality Sample: $N = 46$)

	Date measured		
Country*	1960–85 Sample	1970–85 Sample	Source
Australia (D)	67–8	67–8	J
Bangladesh	68–9	68–9	F
Brazil	60	70	F
Canada (D)	61	65	J
Chile (D)	68	68	F
Colombia (D)	71	71	F
Costa Rica (D)	61	71	F
Denmark (D)	63	66	J
Egypt	58–9	64–5	F
El Salvador	76–7	76–7	F

Continued

| Country* | Date measured | | Source |
	1960–85 Sample	1970–85 Sample	
Fiji	77	77	F
Finland (D)	62	62	J
France (D)	62	62	J
Germany (D)	68	70	J
Greece (D)	57–8	57–8	J
Honduras	67–8	67–8	F
Hong Kong	66	71	F
India (D)	75–6	75–6	F
Indonesia	64	70	F
Iran	73–4	73–4	F
Israel (D)	57–8	69	J
Jamaica (D)	68	68	F
Japan (D)	62	71	J
Korea	65	70	F
Malaysia (D)	57–8	70	F
Mexico	58	69	F
Nepal	76–7	76–7	F
Netherlands (D)	62	67	J
New Zealand (D)	66	70	J
Norway (D)	57	63	J
Pakistan	63–4	69–0	F
Panama	70	70	F
Philippines	57	71	F
Sierra Leone	67–8	67–8	F
Singapore	72–3	72–3	F
South Africa	65	65	J
Spain (D)	64	64	J
Sri Lanka (D)	53	73	F
Sweden (D)	63	70	J
Taiwan	64	72	F
Thailand	62–3	68–9	F
Trinidad & Tobago	71–2	71–2	F
Tunisia	74–5	74–5	F
Turkey (D)	68	68	F
UK (D)	60	68	J
USA (D)	60	70	J

* D = democracies; all the others are nondemocracies.
Sources: F = Fields and Jakubson (1993); J = Jain (1975).

Appendix 2   List of Countries and Dates for Gini Coefficient for Income Larger Sample ($N = 70$ in total): Includes the Previous Countries, Plus

Country*	Date measured	
	1960–85 Sample	1970–85 Sample
Argentina	61	61
Barbados	69–70	69–70
Botswana	71	71
Burma	58	58
Chad	58	58
Côte d'Ivoire	59	70
Cyprus	66	66
Dominican Rep.	69	69
Ecuador	65	70
Gabon	60	68
Guatemala	66	66
Guyana	55–6	55–6
Iraq	56	56
Kenya	69	69
Malawi	69	69
Peru	70	70
Senegal	60	60
Sudan	63	63
Surinam	62	62
Tanzania	67	69
Uruguay	67	67
Venezuela	62	71
Zambia	59	59
Zimbabwe	68	68

* All these countries are nondemocracies.
Source: Jain (1975).

Appendix 3   List of Countries and Dates for Gini Coefficients for Land ($N = 49$)

Country	Date measured
Argentina	1960
Australia	1960
Austria	1960
Belgium	1960
Brazil	1960

Continued

Country	Date measured
Colombia	1960
Costa Rica	1963
Dominican Republic	1960
Denmark	1959
Ecuador	1954
El Salvador	1961
Finland	1959
Guatemala	1950
Honduras	1952
India	1955
Iran	1959
Iraq	1958
Ireland	1963
Italy	1960
Jamaica	1960
Japan	1960
Kenya	1960
Luxembourg	1960
Malaysia	1960
Mali	1960
Malta	1960
Mexico	1960
Netherlands	1959
New Zealand	1960
Nicaragua	1963
Norway	1959
Pakistan	1960
Panama	1961
Peru	1961
Philippines	1960
South Africa	1960
South Korea	1961
Spain	1960
Sweden	1961
Taiwan	1960
Thailand	1963
Trinidad and Tobago	1963
Turkey	1960
United Arab Republic	1964
United Kingdom	1960
United States	1959
Uruguay	1961
Venezuela	1956
West Germany	1960

Source: Taylor and Hudson (1972).

Notes

1   See Perotti (1992) for a succinct survey of this rapidly growing literature.

2   On time-inconsistency of this kind see Fischer (1980) and the discussion in Rodrik (1993) regarding a government that has a redistributive motive.

3   Two analytical complications in particular would arise. First, we would have to allow for a labor supply decision (i.e., labor-leisure choice) to make sure that labor taxation induces resource costs. Second, we would not be able to appeal directly to the median-voter theorem, as voting would have to take place over *two* separate tax rates. Restrictions on preferences are needed for the median-voter theorem to hold in multidimensional voting problems. Our main point, that different individuals have different preferences over the taxation of capital, survives this generalization. Therefore, we think that setting the labor tax to zero is an acceptable shortcut.

4   Note also that we could model the transfer mechanism very differently, without relying on the provision of government services. Suppose, for example, that g stands for a productivity parameter (external to individual firms). Assume further that productivity g increases linearly in k. These assumptions then ensure that the model will exhibit endogenous growth. To model the transfer from capital to labor, we could then simply assume that the proceeds of the tax on capital are spent in the form of a wage subsidy. With these changes we would have a model that is very similar to the one that is described in the text.

5   For more detail on the derivations of these results, the reader is referred to the working paper version of this paper (Alesina and Rodrik 1991).

6   The importance of our restrictions on the utility function that lead to a time-invariant distribution of wealth is now clear.

7   This is related to the work by Romer (1975), Roberts (1977), and Meltzer and Richard (1981) on voting over linear tax rates on labor income. These authors analyze a static model in which an income tax has to be chosen, and show that the more unequal is the distribution of productivities (thus pretax income) the higher is the tax rate (and the transfer level) desired by the median voter. In a similar vein Mayer (1984) links factor ownership to desired trade interventions. Our discussion extends these results to a dynamic framework with endogenous growth.

8   In the working paper version of this paper (Alesina and Rodrik 1991), we develop this point in more detail.

9   His four criteria are (i) the estimates must be based on an actual household survey or census; (ii) the survey or census must be national in coverage; (iii) the data must be tabulated in enough categories that a meaningful index can be calculated if one is not already published; and (iv) for more than one year to be included, the surveys must have been comparable. See Fields and Jakubson (1993, pp. 3–4).

10   Of the 35 countries in the Fields sample, we could use only 29 because 4 of them were not in the Barro–Wolf (1989) data set (Bahamas, Puerto Rico, Réunion, and Seychelles) and 2 had data only for the 1980s (Cote d'Ivoire and Peru). The high-quality sample is made up of these 29 plus 17 developed countries from Jain (1975). See the Appendix for a complete listing of countries and sources. Turkey, an OECD member, is included in the Fields sample of developing countries.

11   In our regressions, we actually use only 49 of these countries as the rest (Puerto Rico, Libya, Vietnam, Poland, and Yugoslavia) are not included in the Barro–Wolf (1989) 118-country data set from which our other data are drawn.

12   The instruments we use are listed in the notes to table 18.1. We have experimented with alternative sets of instruments, and found that the results are generally robust.

13   In a previous version of this paper, we reported weak support for the difference between democracies and nondemocracies using a data set closer to that of Persson and Tabellini

(1991). The present work employs a revised and improved data set, based on recent research by Fields and Jakubson (1993).

References

Alesina, Alberto, and Dani Rodrik (1991) "Distributive Politics and Economic Growth," NBER Working Paper No. 3668.

Barro, Robert (1990) "Government Spending in a Simple Model of Economic Growth," *Journal of Political Economy*, 98: 103–25.

Barro, Robert (1991) "Economic Growth in a Cross Section of Countries," *Quarterly Journal of Economics*, CVI: 407–4.

Barro, Robert, and Holger Wolf (1989) "Data Appendix for Economic Growth in a Cross-Section of Countries," unpublished manuscript.

Barro, Robert, and Xavier Sala-i-Martin (1990) "Public Finance in the Theory of Economic Growth," unpublished manuscript.

Benhabib, Jess, and Aldo Rustichini (1991) "Social Conflict, Growth and Income Distribution," unpublished manuscript.

Bertola, Giuseppe (1993) "Factor Shares, Saving Propensities, and Endogenous Growth," *American Economic Review*, 83: 1184–98.

Clarke, George R. G. (1993) "More Evidence on Income Distribution and Growth," University of Rochester, unpublished paper.

Fernandez, Raquel, and Richard Rogerson (1992) "Human Capital Accumulation and Income Distribution," NBER Working Paper No. 3994.

Fields, Gary (1980) *Poverty, Inequality and Development* (Cambridge, MA: Harvard University Press).

Fields, Gary (1989) "A Compendium of Data on Inequality and Poverty for the Developing World," Cornell University, unpublished manuscript.

Fields, Gary, and George Jakubson (1993) "New Evidence on the Kuznets Curve," Cornell University, unpublished manuscript.

Fischer, Stanley (1980) "Dynamic Inconsistency, Cooperation and the Benevolent Dissembling Government," *Journal of Economic Dynamics and Control*, 2: 93–107.

Galor, Oded, and Joseph Zeira (1993) "Income Distribution and Macroeconomics," *Review of Economic Studies*, 60: 35–52.

Heston, Alan, and Robert Summers (1988) "A New Set of International Comparisons of Real Product and Price Levels: Estimates for 130 Countries," *The Review of Income and Wealth*, 34: 1–25.

Jain, S. (1975) "Size Distribution of Income: A Comparison of Data," The World Bank, unpublished manuscript.

Lecallion, Jack, Felix Paukert, Christian Morrison, and Dimitri Gemiolis (1984) "Income Distribution and Economic Development: Analytical Survey" (Geneva: International Labor Office).

Kuznets, Simon (1955) "Economic Growth and Income Inequality," *American Economic Review*, 45: 1–28.

Lucas, Robert E., Jr. (1988) "On the Mechanics of Economic Development," *Journal of Monetary Economics*, 22: 3–42.

Mayer, Wolfgang (1984) "Endogenous Tariff Formation," *American Economic Review*, 74: 970–85.

Meltzer, Allan H., and Scott F. Richard (1981) "A Rational Theory of the Size of the Government," *Journal of Political Economy*, 89: 914–27.

Murphy, Kevin M., Andrei Shleifer, and Robert Vishny (1989) "Income Distribution, Market Size, and Industrialization," *Quarterly Journal of Economics*, 104: 537–64.

Perotti, Roberto (1992) "Income Distribution, Politics, and Growth," *American Economic Review Papers and Proceedings*, 82: 311–16.

Perotti, Roberto (1993) "Political Equilibrium Income Distribution and Growth," *Review of Economic Studies*, 60: 755–76.

Persson, Torsten, and Guido Tabellini (1991) "Is Inequality Harmful for Growth? Theory and Evidence," unpublished paper.

Ranis, Gustav (1990) "Contrasts in the Political Economy of Development Policy Change," in Gary Gereffi and Donald L. Wyman (eds.), *Manufacturing Miracles: Paths of Industrialization in Latin America and East Asia* (Princeton, NJ: Princeton University Press).

Roberts, Kevin W. S. (1977) "Voting over Income Tax Schedules," *Journal of Public Economics*, 8: 329–40.

Rodrik, Dani (1993) "Redistributive Taxation without Excess Burden," *Economics & Politics*, V: 53–60.

Romer, Paul M. (1986) "Increasing Returns and Long-Run Growth," *Journal of Political Economy*, 94: 1002–37.

Romer, Thomas (1975) "Individual Welfare, Majority Voting, and the Properties of a Linear Income Tax," *Journal of Public Economics*, 14: 163–85.

Saint-Paul, Gilles, and Thierry Verdier (1992) "Education, Democracy and Growth," CEPR Discussion Paper No. 613.

Stolper, Wolfgang, and Paul Samuelson (1944) "Protection and Real Wages," *Review of Economic Studies*, 9: 58–73.

Taylor, C. L., and M. C. Hudson (1972) *World Handbook of Political and Social Indicators*, 2nd edn (New Haven, CT: Yale University Press).

Wade, Robert (1990) *Governing the Market: Economic Theory and the Role of Government in East Asian Industrialization* (Princeton, NJ: Princeton University Press).

World Bank (1990) *World Development Report, 1990* (Washington, DC: The World Bank).

NINETEEN

Is Inequality Harmful for Growth?

Torsten Persson and Guido Tabellini[*]

Source: From *American Economic Review* (1994), 84: 600–21.

Why do different countries – or the same country in different periods – grow at such different rates? And what is the role of income distribution in the growth process? To answer these old questions, we believe one should explain why growth-promoting policies are or are not adopted. In this paper we try to do just that by combining insights from two recent strands of literature, namely, the theory of endogenous growth and the theory of endogenous policy. We can summarize our tentative conclusion in a simple aphorism: inequality is harmful for growth.

The arguments that lead us to this conclusion run as follows. Economic growth is largely determined by the accumulation of capital, human capital, and knowledge usable in production. The incentives for such productive accumulation hinge on the ability of individuals to appropriate privately the fruits of their efforts, which in turn crucially hinges on what tax policies and regulatory policies are adopted. In a society where distributional conflict is more important, political decisions are likely to result in policies that allow less private appropriation and therefore less accumulation and less growth. But the growth rate also depends on political institutions, for it is through the political process that conflicting interests ultimately are aggregated into public-policy decisions.

In the paper we first formulate a simple general-equilibrium model that formally captures this idea. It is an overlapping-generations model in which heterogeneous individuals are born in every period and act as economic agents and voters. The model's politico-economic equilibrium determines a sequence of growth rates as a function of parameters and initial conditions. The greater is income inequality, the lower is equilibrium growth.

Next, we confront the model's empirical implications with two sets of data. The first is an historical panel of nine currently developed countries: the United States and eight European countries. The second sample contains postwar evidence from a broad cross-section of countries, both developed and less developed. The predictions of the model hold up in both samples. In particular, a strong negative relation between income inequality at the start of the period and growth in the subsequent period is present in both samples. To the best of our knowledge, this result is a genuinely new finding.[1] The evidence concerning political institutions is more mixed. In the historical sample, relevant data are available but exhibit little variation. In the postwar sample, relevant data are not available. However, the results in subsamples of democratic and nondemocratic countries are strikingly different, providing indirect support for our theory.

As we already mentioned, our work in this paper is related to both the theory of endogenous growth and the theory of endogenous policy. The work on endogenous growth has made clear the importance of policy for growth; but it has not yet made the link connecting distribution, politics, and policy.[2] Analogously, the literature on endogenous policy has made clear the importance of distribution for policy; but it has not yet made the link between policy and growth.[3] In complementary and independent work, Alberto Alesina and Dani Rodrik (1991) and Roberto Perotti (1993) have studied the determination of tax policy in the political equilibrium of an endogenous-growth model. Alesina and Rodrik also find a negative empirical link between inequality and growth.[4]

Obviously, our work is also related to the vast literature in economic history and economic development about the relation between development and income distribution. This work largely revolves around the so-called *Kuznets curve*: the hypothesis that income inequality first increases and then decreases with development.[5] The Kuznets curve remains a controversial concept both theoretically and empirically. The work on the Kuznets curve, however, deals with the question of how the *level* of income affects income distribution, while our work instead addresses the question of how income distribution affects the *change* in income. Our theory, as well as our empirical tests, remain valid both in the presence and in the absence of a Kuznets curve.

In section I of the paper we formulate our theoretical model of politico-economic equilibrium growth. We use the model to derive an equilibrium sequence of growth rates and spell out its empirical implications. In section II we describe our empirical results from the historical panel of countries. Section III presents our empirical work based on postwar evidence from a broad cross-section of countries. Section IV discusses the interpretation of our results. Final remarks are contained in Section V.

I   Theory

The model

We study an overlapping-generations model with constant population, where non-altruistic individuals live for two periods.[6] Every individual has the same *preferences*. Let the utility of the ith individual born in period $t - 1$, but indexed by t, be:

$$v_t^i = U\left(c_{t-1}^i, d_t^i\right). \tag{1}$$

In (1), c denotes the consumption when young, and d denotes the consumption when old. The utility function $U(\cdot)$ is concave, well behaved, and homothetic or (without loss of generality) linearly homogeneous.

Different individuals have different incomes. The *budget constraints* of the ith individual are

$$c_{t-1}^i + k_t^i = y_{t-1}^i \tag{2a}$$

$$d_t^i = r[(1 - \theta_t)k_t^i + \theta_t k_t],\tag{2b}$$

where y^i is the ith individual's income when young (to be defined below), k^i and k are the individual and average accumulation, respectively, of an asset, r is the exogenous rate of return on that asset, and θ is a policy variable (throughout the paper we use superscripts to denote individual-specific variables and no superscripts to denote average variables). Thus policy is purely redistributive: it takes from those who have invested more than the average and gives to those who have invested less than the average.

The income when young is defined as

$$y_{t-1}^i = (w + e^i)k_{t-1},\tag{3}$$

where w is an exogenous average endowment of "basic skills" and e^i is an exogenous individual-specific endowment of such skills with zero mean and nonpositive median. Thus the stock of k accumulated on average by the previous generation has a positive externality on the income of the newborn generation.

The most straightforward interpretation of this externality is to think of k as physical or human capital that has a "knowledge spillover" on the basic skills of the young, as in Kenneth Arrow (1962) or Paul Romer (1986). With this interpretation, θ would be interpreted as a proportional capital income tax, the proceeds of which are used to finance equal lump-sum transfers to every old citizen.[7] But it may be more relevant to think of k as a measure of knowledge that is useful in promoting technical progress. In this case, the owners of k earn monopoly rents from their previous investment in the accumulation of knowledge. The policy variable θ would then represent regulatory policy such as "patent legislation" or "protection of property rights," so that θ becomes an index of how well an individual can privately appropriate the returns on his investment.[8] Since technical progress is largely embodied in new capital, the two interpretations are not mutually exclusive.

Summarizing, average national income is a linear function of the asset already accumulated, $(w + r)k$, where wk and rk represent the average wage to the young and profit to the old, respectively. The distribution of income between wages and profits is determined exogenously by the extent of the externality. The model focuses only on redistributive taxation across profits, and it rules out any intergenerational redistribution.[9]

Events unfold according to the following timing. At the start of period $t - 1$ the eligible voters choose θ_t. Then investors choose k_t^i. Thus, we abstract from credibility problems and just assume that there is one-period-ahead commitment of policy. Since the old generation in period $t - 1$ is not affected by the policy enacted in period t, we assume without loss of generality that only the young generation participates in the vote. We start by assuming that the distribution of e^i in the population is stationary. This assumption is relaxed later on.

A politico-economic equilibrium is defined as a policy and a set of private economic decisions such that:

(i)   the economic decisions of all citizens are optimal, given the policy, and markets clear;

(ii)   the policy cannot be defeated by any alternative in a majority vote among the citizens in the enfranchised section of the population.

(Below we analyze the effects of constitutional limits on political participation.)

Economic equilibrium

With homothetic preferences, the ratio of consumption in the two periods is a function only of intertemporal prices and is independent of wealth: that is, for all i, $d_t^i/c_{t-1}^i = D(r, \theta_t)$, with $D_r > 0$ and $D_\theta < 0$. Equivalently, every individual has the same "savings rate" so that individuals with more skills accumulate more k. Using this fact and the budget constraints (2), we can write the amounts consumed by the ith individual as

$$d_t^i = \frac{rD(r, \theta_t)\left[(1 - \theta_t)y_{t-1}^i + \theta_t k_t\right]}{D(r, \theta_t) + r(1 - \theta_t)} \tag{4}$$

$$c_{t-1}^i = \frac{r\left[(1 - \theta_t)y_{t-1}^i + \theta_t k_t\right]}{D(r, \theta_t) + r(1 - \theta_t)}. \tag{5}$$

For the average individual, $k_t = y_{t-1} - c_{t-1}$. By repeated substitution and use of (2) and (3) we can therefore solve for the *growth rate* of k (and of national income, under our assumptions):

$$\begin{aligned} g_t &= G(w, r, \theta_t) = k_t/k_{t-1} - 1 \\ &= wD(r, \theta_t)/[r + D(r, \theta_t)] - 1. \end{aligned} \tag{6}$$

In (6) $G_w > 0$, $G_r \lessgtr 0$, and $G_\theta < 0$ (since $D_\theta < 0$). Thus, the higher are the average skills w, the higher is the growth rate of k. A higher gross of return may increase or decrease growth, depending on the usual balancing of substitution and income effects, but the more an individual can appropriate the fruits of his investment (i.e., the lower is θ), the higher is the growth rate (on average a change in θ has only a substitution effect, since the average individual receives a lump-sum transfer equal to the tax he pays).

Political Equilibrium

To characterize the political equilibrium we first study the ith individual's policy preferences. Simply differentiate his utility function $v_t^i = U(c_{t-1}^i, d_t^i)$ with respect to θ_t, subject to the budget constraints (2). Applying the envelope theorem and using (2b), we have

$$\frac{\partial v_t^i}{\partial \theta_t} = U_d(\cdot)\left[(k_t - k_t^i) + \theta_t \frac{\partial k_t}{\partial \theta_t}\right]r. \tag{7}$$

This expression reflects the trade-off facing the voters. On the one hand, an increase in θ redistributes income and welfare from individuals with $k^i > k$ to individuals with $k^i < k$.

On the other hand, an increase in θ is costly in that it diminishes investment and the base for redistribution. The optimal policy from the point of view of the ith voter exactly balances these two effects, which happens when the right-hand side of (7) is equal to zero (provided the second-order conditions are satisfied).

By (2a), (3), and (5),

$$k_t - k_t^i = \frac{-D(\cdot)k_{t-1}}{D(\cdot) + r(1 - \theta_t)}e_{t-1}^i \tag{8}$$

which says, very intuitively, that individuals born poorer ($e_{t-1}^i < 0$) or richer ($e_{t-1}^i > 0$) than average have respectively less or more capital than the average. Hence individual preferences for redistribution can be ranked by their idiosyncratic endowment, e^i. The political equilibrium policy is thus the value of θ preferred by the median voter, that is, the individual with median endowment, e^m (see Jean-Michel Grandmont, 1978). Combining (7) and (8) and computing the expression for $\partial k_t / \partial \theta_t$, the equilibrium policy θ^* is a function $\theta^*(w, r, e^m)$, defined implicitly by

$$-\frac{D(r, \theta)e^m}{D(r, \theta) + r(1 - \theta)} + \theta D_\theta(r, \theta)\frac{wr}{r + D(r, \theta)} = 0 \tag{9}$$

where the first term captures the marginal benefit of redistribution for the median voter and where the second term is the marginal cost of the tax distortions.

It is easy to verify from (9) that $\theta^* \gtrless 0$ as $e^m \lessgtr 0$, $\theta_e^* < 0$, $\theta_w^* \lessgtr 0$ as $e^m \lessgtr 0$, and $\theta_r^* \lessgtr 0$. Intuitively, if the median voter coincides with the average investor ($e^m = 0$), he prefers a nonredistributive policy ($\theta^* = 0$) whereas he prefers a tax (a subsidy) on investment if he is poorer (richer) than the average. More generally, a median voter with higher individual skills e^m and therefore a higher k^m prefers more private appropriability (a lower θ). A higher average skill level w gives higher average accumulation and hence increases the cost of redistribution, so that the voter prefers a less interventionist policy (a lower tax or a smaller subsidy). A higher rate of return r may either increase or decrease the preferred level of θ.

Combining (9) and (6), the growth rate in politico-economic equilibrium is

$$g^* - G(w, r, \theta^*(w, r, e^m)). \tag{10}$$

From (10) and the properties of the $G(\cdot)$ and $\theta^*(\cdot)$ functions derived above, we obtain some clear-cut and testable *ceteris paribus* implications:

$$dg^*/de^m = G_\theta \theta_e > 0 \tag{11}$$

(i.e., a more equal distribution of income increases growth); and

$$dg^*/dw = G_w + G_\theta \theta_w > 0, \qquad \text{if } e^m < 0 \tag{12}$$

(i.e., a higher average level of basic skills increases growth). The predictions regarding the effects on growth of the rate of return r are inconclusive. However, that may not be such a loss, since r in the model measures the gross (pretax or inclusive-of-externalities) return on accumulating productive knowledge, a variable that is notoriously difficult to observe empirically.

Dynamics of growth

So far we have assumed that the distribution of income and all relevant parameters were stationary. As a result, the equilibrium growth rate was also stationary. However, the model can easily be extended to allow for exogenous laws of motion of both income distribution and the key parameters. In this case, equilibrium growth can exhibit some interesting dynamics. A previous version of the paper, Persson and Tabellini (1991), discussed these extensions in detail. Here we only provide a brief sketch.

Consider first the distribution of income. Suppose that the idiosyncratic income of individual i born in period $t-1$, e_{t-1}^i, is distributed according to a given family of distribution functions, $F(e^i, k_{t-1})$. Suppose further that different levels of k_{t-1} induce a mean-preserving spread on $F(\cdot)$. Then, even though the model does not endogenously derive the properties of $F(\cdot)$, it may nevertheless be consistent with the dynamics of the Kuznets curve. Moreover, additional implications are obtained about the dynamics of equilibrium growth, depending on the specific assumptions about the function $F(\cdot)$.

Suppose, for instance, that the hypothesis underlying the Kuznets curve is valid, so that inequality increases with development at low levels of income but decreases at higher levels of income. In terms of the model, this means that median income e^m is now a function of k, first decreasing up to some point $\tilde{k}$ and then increasing. If initial capital, k_0, is below $\tilde{k}$, then by (10) the time path of equilibrium growth is nonmonotonic: it first falls until k reaches $\tilde{k}$ and then accelerates again at a higher level of development.

This nonmonotonicity implies that the equilibrium dynamics can exhibit path-dependence. If at the point of minimum growth and maximum inequality, $\tilde{k}$, equilibrium growth is nonpositive, then any country with $k_0 < \tilde{k}$ eventually falls in a "growth trap": income inequality is or becomes so pronounced that it discourages further accumulation and growth. In the growth trap, the only way the economy could take off again would be if the equilibrium growth path somehow were shifted upward, so that minimum growth is always positive.

Next, consider the parameters w and r. Since the economic model is recursive, the expressions for equilibrium growth are unchanged even if w and r are allowed to vary over time. When going from the model to our empirical tests, however, relaxing this assumption matters. If w and r vary over time, the growth rate of k no longer coincides with the growth rate of GDP, which is what we ultimately observe. A previous version of this paper (Persson and Tabellini, 1991) spelled out the specific assumptions that are needed to derive from the model a linear expression for per capita GDP growth that can be estimated.

Taking the model to the data

The remainder of the paper tests the two implications of (10) spelled out above, namely, that a more equal distribution of income and a higher average level of basic skills both increase growth. The theory also has predictions about the effect of inequality on economic policy, θ_t, and in turn about the link between policy and growth. The policy θ, however, can be interpreted in several ways: as a tax on human or physical capital, patent legislation, regulatory policy, or even more broadly as legal enforcement and general protection of property rights. These various policies are very difficult to measure, and focusing on only one of them could be misleading. For this reason, in the empirical analysis we consider mainly the reduced form of the equilibrium solution, focusing on the predictions (11) and (12) stated above. (See, however, the discussion in section IV below.)

The model is formulated in terms of per capita growth and abstracts from population growth and from short-run fluctuations. Given that the time unit of the model is a generation, equation (10) is relevant only for growth rates over relatively long periods of time. Further, it applies to a given country with particular economic and political institutions. Because usable data on relevant variables do not go back further than to the mid-nineteenth century, we cannot test these implications for a single country. In section II we therefore pool historical data from a cross-section of nine currently developed countries with similar economic and political histories. In section III, we then look at postwar data from a broad cross section of countries, developed as well as developing.

II Historical Evidence

Data

Our historical data cover nine countries: Austria, Denmark, Finland, Germany, the Netherlands, Norway, Sweden, the United Kingdom, and the United States. We divide the time period back to 1830 into subperiods of 20 years each, so that the first possible observation for each country comprises the years 1830–50 and the last observation comprises the years 1970–85 (the last observation is the only one that has 15 years rather than 20). For each country and variable, we go as far back as the data permit. Our rule for selecting the countries was that we could find data for all the variables below at least back to 1930. The data are put together from a variety of sources, which are detailed in the Appendix.

Per capita growth
The dependent variable in all our regressions is the annual average growth rate of GDP per capita (continuously compounded and expressed as a percentage) for each country and each 20-year episode. We have a total of 57 observations for this variable, which we call GROWTH. The mean value in the sample is 1.88, and the range goes from 0.17 (Austria, 1910–30) to 5.05 (Germany, 1950–70). Summary statistics for this and other variables appear in table 19.1.

For the independent variables, we try to find data that match our model as closely as possible. In each case, we also follow the model in trying to find an observation as close to the beginning of the time period as possible. Unless otherwise noted, the explanatory variables described below are measured at the *start* of each of the 20-year periods.

Income distribution
The best available data are based on personal income before tax. In the model, e^m is the distance between mean per capita national income and the median income of the eligible

Table 19.1   Summary Statistics for Historical Sample

	Number of observations	Mean	SD	Minimum	Maximum
GROWTH	57	1.875	1.026	0.17	5.05
GDPGAP	57	0.684	0.188	0.362	1.00
INCSH	38	0.504	0.068	0.38	0.67
SCHOOL	52	0.140	0.081	0.017	0.362
NOFRAN	59	0.278	0.312	−0.01	0.89

Correlation matrix

	Variable			
Variable	GROWTH	GDPGAP	INCSH	SCHOOL
GDPGAP	−0.354			
INCSH	−0.445	−0.056		
SCHOOL	0.401	0.120	−0.713	
NOFRAN	−0.367	0.078	0.574	−0.620

voters; but the data from the earlier part of the period at best only comprise the uppermost deciles in the distribution.[10] The variable we use in our regressions, INCSH, is therefore the share in personal income of the top 20 percent of the population. We have 38 observations for this variable. The mean value is 0.50, and the observations range from 0.38 (Sweden in 1970) to 0.67 (Finland in 1930). The expected sign of the coefficient of this variable in the regression is negative, since a higher value of INCSH means more inequality.

Political participation

The variable INCSH refers to the population at large. In the early part of the sample, however, only some citizens could vote in most countries. For this reason, we would also like to control for the effect of a limited franchise on the identity of the median voter. We do that by adding to the regressions the share of the enfranchised age and sex group in the population that is *not* in the electorate. This measure corrects for political discrimination of women and for different age limits for voting across countries, factors that do not seem directly relevant in our context. For this variable, NOFRAN, we have 59 observations, with a mean of 0.28 and a range from 0 (virtually all countries in the postwar period) to 0.89 (the United Kingdom in 1830 and the Netherlands in 1850 and 1870). Its expected sign is positive, since a more restrictive franchise (a higher value of NOFRAN) implies a richer median voter, given the distribution of income in the population at large.

Average skills

In the model, w measures the average basic skills of the young generation. The empirical counterpart of this variable clearly has to do with the general education level. To correct for possible differences in the classification of schools across countries and time and to take the quality of education into account, we constructed an index of schooling, SCHOOL. For each country and time period, we took a weighted average of the shares of the relevant age groups enrolled in primary school, lower secondary school, higher secondary school, and tertiary school, at the start of each period. The weights are increasing in the level of schooling. We have 52 observations for the index. Its mean is 0.14, and it ranges from 0.017 (England in 1850) to 0.362 (Finland in 1970). The expected sign of this variable is positive.

The level of development
Our simple model does not predict any convergence, so that poor countries grow faster than rich countries, once we control for other factors. However, this implication is not likely to survive slight variations in the model. Moreover, the question of whether or not there is convergence, once we control for other variables identified by our model, is interesting in its own right. We therefore include as an explanatory variable the ratio between GDP per capita and the highest level of GDP per capita in our sample at the same point in time. We call this variable GDPGAP. We also use the level of GDP per capita when constructing fitted values to replace missing observations (see below). To make real GDP levels comparable across countries, we use Robert Summers and Alan Heston's (1988) measures of GDP at international prices in 1950 and 1970. For earlier periods, we use the 1950 observations as a benchmark and splice them with the real GDP series for each country. (This procedure effectively assumes constant international relative prices for earlier periods.) For this variable, we have 57 observations, which range from 0.362 (Sweden in 1870) to 1 (the United Kingdom up to 1890 and the United States from then on). Its expected sign in the regression is negative if there is convergence.

Results

Table 19.2 reports the parameter estimates from the first set of regressions for our historical sample, all estimated by ordinary least squares (OLS). Columns (i)–(ii) in the table are based on the sample of those 38 growth episodes, for which we have observations on all our variables. Columns (iii)–(iv) are based on a larger sample, in which we replaced missing values for INCSH (18 observations) and SCHOOL (three observations) by the fitted values obtained by regressions on the independent variables and on GDP per capita (see G. S. Maddala, 1977).

The most striking result is the effect of inequality on growth. The coefficient on INCSH is of the expected negative sign and almost always statistically significant. The exceptions are tied to multicollinearity: INCSH is relatively strongly correlated with both SCHOOL and NOFRAN. The coefficient is also economically significant: an increase of 0.07 (one standard deviation in the sample) in the income share of the top 20 percent lowers the average annual growth rate just below half a percentage point. Differences in distribution alone explain about a fifth of the variance in growth rates across countries and time. None of the other variables alone explains more than a tenth of the variance.

NOFRAN, our measure of political participation, is insignificant and has the wrong sign.[11] However, that may just reflect the lack of variation in this variable in a large part of the sample: all observations for 1930 and later are close to zero for all countries. To study the effect of a limited franchise, it is preferable to look at column (iii) where there are 18 more observations from earlier periods. In this equation, the coefficient on NOFRAN indeed drops considerably to around zero. This (weakly) suggests that with more observations from the nineteenth century, we could possibly find stronger evidence for the model (see also the discussion at the end of section II).

Table 19.2   Regressions for GROWTH

Independent variable	Regression			
	(i)	(ii)	(iii)	(iv)
Constant	5.263	7.206	6.256	6.465
	(2.659)	(5.723)	(4.066)	(6.899)
INCSH	−3.481	−6.911	−6.107	−6.409
	(−1.017)	(−3.074)	(−2.234)	(−3.963)
NOFRAN	−0.782		−0.011	
	(−0.670)		(−0.018)	
SCHOOL	2.931		0.316	
	(0.913)		(0.204)	
GDPGAP	−2.591	−2.695	−1.720	−1.728
	(−2.739)	(−2.696)	(−2.708)	(−2.778)
Number of observations	38	38	56	56
$\bar{R}^2$	0.294	0.298	0.269	0.296
SEE	0.931	0.929	0.882	0.866

Notes: The table reports ordinary least-squares regressions; t values are shown in parentheses. SEE = standard error of the estimate.

SCHOOL, our index for average skills, has the expected sign, but is never statistically significant.[12] GDPGAP, the measure of income relative to the leading country, always has the correct (negative) sign and is significant. Its negative coefficient is likely to pick up specific effects tied to the two world wars.[13] But it also indicates some convergence in GDP levels over time. This finding is similar to the results found by Barro (1991), Gregory Mankiw et al. (1992), and others for postwar growth across a broad section of countries.

All these results hold almost identically for other specifications, reported in Persson and Tabellini (1991).

Sensitivity analysis

In this subsection we discuss three possible problems with the regressions reported above. First, one may ask whether our results are distorted by *reverse causation* leading to simultaneity bias. In particular, would not a systematic relation between income inequality and development (such as the Kuznets curve) give rise to a simultaneity problem? Let us first note that direct reverse causation is ruled out, because INCSH is measured at the beginning of each 20-year period and so is statistically predetermined relative to GROWTH. However, a systematic relation between inequality and development would make our inequality measure correlated with lagged growth. Indeed, the theoretical discussion about growth dynamics in section I relied precisely on such a relation. Hence, if the residual of the regression is serially correlated, then INCSH and GDPGAP are correlated with the error term, which could bias the estimated coefficients.

In Persson and Tabellini (1991), we found no direct evidence of serial correlation in the estimated residuals, nor did we find evidence of a systematic relation between lagged growth and inequality. However, the unbalanced panel with a small number of observations for each country and time period makes it difficult to conduct powerful tests. Further evidence is presented in table 19.3. Columns (i) and (ii) show results from two-stage least-squares regressions. The instruments include a constant plus observations of GDP per capita, SCHOOL, GDPGAP, and NOFRAN, all lagged 20 years. (That is, we use observations dated in 1910, say, to instrument for the 1930 variables explaining growth between 1930 and 1950.) The parameter estimates suggest that our results on the negative effect of inequality on growth are not due to reverse causation. If anything, the results are stronger than in the previous OLS regressions.

The second possible econometric problem is *measurement error*, given that the data go back to the mid-nineteenth century. In Persson and Tabellini (1991) we discussed this problem at some length, following the "reverse regression" approach of Stephen Klepper and Edward Leamer (1984) (see also section III, below). We found the results to be robust to measurement error in INCSH and GDP. In particular, the coefficients on INCSH seem to coincide with the lower bound (in absolute value) for the true maximum-likelihood estimates. Hence, if anything, measurement error would seem to bias the coefficients of interest against our hypothesis. The instrumental-variables estimates reported in table 19.3 provide additional evidence of the robustness to measurement error.

Finally, the third possible problem is *omitted variables* correlated with INCSH or other regressors. To investigate this problem, we ask whether the residuals show a particular pattern across countries or time. Consider first the variation across countries. When we add

Table 19.3 Sensitivity analysis

Independent variable	Regression			
	(i)	(ii)	(iii)	(iv)
Constant	8.331	8.267	4.151	4.277
	(2.564)	(2.443)	(1.761)	(1.797)
INCSH	11.859	11.606	−3.737	−5.427
	(−2.766)	(−2.098)	(−0.831)	(−1.206)
NOFRAN		−0.171	0.422	0.617
		(−0.073)	(0.648)	(0.942)
SCHOOL			−0.502	
			(−0.389)	
GDPGAP	−0.391	−0.458	−1.039	
	(−0.142)	(−0.156)	(−1.833)	
Number of observations	35	35	29	29
$\bar{R}^2$	0.089	0.078	0.032	−0.019
SEE	1.083	1.090	0.576	0.591

Notes: Columns (i) and (ii) report two-stage least-squares regressions; columns (iii) and (iv) report OLS regressions up to 1930 only. Numbers in parentheses are *t* values.

a set of country dummies to the regressions in table 19.2, the coefficient on INCSH typically becomes more negative and stays significant. Also, the country dummies add little explanatory power. Here, there is clearly no indication of a potential omitted-variable problem.

Consider next the variation across time. When we add a set of period dummies to the same regressions, all coefficients in the regression turn insignificant, except the coefficient on GDPGAP. Furthermore, the time dummies add considerable explanatory power. The dummy for 1950–70 is strongly significant and positive, and the dummy for 1970–85 is marginally significant and positive. Thus, the significant coefficients on INCSH seem predominantly to pick up the time variation in the data. Put differently, our model ascribes the higher average growth rates in the postwar period to a more equal distribution of income. It is possible, however, that income inequality is negatively correlated with some other growth-promoting variable which is omitted in our model and in our regressions. For instance, World War II brought about a more equal distribution of income as well as a set of important technological innovations. Our finding that growth is higher in the 1950s than in the 1930s, and that income inequality is lower in 1950 than in 1930, could thus simply reflect the effect of the war, rather than a causal link from inequality to growth.

To shed further light on the importance of the observations after and immediately before World War II, we re-estimated the model excluding all observations from the periods 1930–50, 1950–70, and 1970–85. Results from these regressions are displayed in columns (iii) and (iv) of table 19.3. Comparing the results for this early sample to the results in table 19.2, the overall fit is clearly worse. The coefficients on INCSH stay negative and have the same order of magnitude as before, but they are not significantly different from zero. The coefficient on GDPGAP is still marginally significant. Finally, the coefficients on NOFRAN are now positive (in accordance with our model) but do not reach statistical significance. Nevertheless, the latter result gives mild support to our speculation in section II that the effects of a restricted franchise on equilibrium policy may only be visible in nineteenth-century data.

All in all we conclude from this sensitivity analysis that the negative effect of inequality on growth is not due to reverse causation and is robust to measurement error. The possibility of an omitted-variable problem remains.

III Postwar Evidence

Data

Our sample consists of 56 countries for which we could find reliable data on income distribution. Each observation corresponds to a country.

Per capita growth
As in section II above, our dependent variable is the annual average growth rate of GDP per capita, which we again call GROWTH. The time period covered is 1960–85, and the source is Summers and Heston (1988). The mean value of GROWTH is 2.10 and it ranges from −2.83 (for Chad) to 5.95 (for Korea). Summary statistics for this variable, as well as the other variables in the data set, appear in table 19.4.

Table 19.4 Summary statistics for postwar sample

Variable	Number of observations	Mean	SD	Minimum	Maximum
GROWTH	53	2.10	1.827	−2.827	5.953
GDP	53	2,155	1,832	208	7,380
MIDDLE	56	13.305	3.099	7	18.8
PSCHOOL	49	78.326	31.959	5	144

Correlation matrix:

Variable	Variable		
	GROWTH	GDP	MIDDLE
GDP	0.076		
MIDDLE	0.203	0.532	
PSCHOOL	0.459	0.689	0.350

Income distribution

The source is Felix Paukert (1973), who in turn elaborated and aggregated data originally compiled by Irma Adelman and Cynthia Morris (1971). These data refer to pretax income of families or households and are probably among the most reliable data for international comparison of a broad sample of countries. The sampling data varies by country, and it ranges from 1956–7 for India to 1971 for Tunisia. For most countries it is around 1965, close to the start of the sample period for GROWTH.

Alternative measures of income inequality can be constructed from these data. In line with our model, we use the measure that best approximates the relative position of the median income recipient. This is the income share accruing to the third quintile (the 41st to the 60th percentile of households), which includes the median. Since this variable measures the relative position of the middle quintile, we call it MIDDLE. Obviously, income equality is greater the greater is MIDDLE, so its expected sign in the regressions is positive. The variable MIDDLE is measured in percentage points. It has a mean of 13.31 and ranges from 7.0 (for Gabon) to 18.8 (for Denmark).[14]

Average skills

As for the historical data set, we proxy this variable with a measure of education: the share (percentage) of the relevant age group attending primary school, PSCHOOL. All observations are from 1960. This measure is available for 49 countries. It has a mean of 78.3 and ranges from 5 (for Niger) to 144 (for France).[15] Previous versions of the paper also used other measures, such as the share attending secondary school and a weighted education index, and obtained similar results. The expected sign is positive.

Political participation

Unlike in the historical sample, we have not been able to construct any measure of restricted franchise. Nevertheless, our model captures policy-making in a democracy.

Therefore, what we do below is first to run our regressions for the whole cross-section. Then we control for whether a country is democratic or not, to see if the nature of the regime makes a difference.

Initial GDP

As for the historical sample, we also include the level of GDP per capita in 1960, to allow for differences in the stage of development and for the possibility of convergence.

A previous version of this paper also controlled for other observable differences in the economic structure (such as the percentage of national income originating in the industrial sector or the percentage of the population living in urban areas). The results were essentially the same. To summarize, the regressions we estimate look pretty much like those in section II, with the exception of a variable (like NOFRAN) that captures political participation.

Results

The results of estimating the model on the whole sample by OLS are reported in column (i) of table 19.5. They are surprisingly good, given the large variety of countries in the sample. All the variables have the expected sign, they are significant most of the time, and they explain about a third of the variance in growth.[16] In particular, MIDDLE always has a positive and highly significant coefficient, as predicted by our model. The effects of equality on growth are also quantitatively significant. A one-standard-deviation increase in equality increases growth by about half a percentage point. This is about the same number that we obtained in the historical sample of section II. In Persson and Tabellini (1991), we estimated additional specifications and obtained very similar results.

As we already mentioned, many countries in this sample have nondemocratic political institutions. In these countries there may be little relationship between income inequality in the population *at large* and the redistributive preferences of the government. Our theory predicts that growth should be inversely related to inequality in a democracy, but not necessarily in a dictatorship. The nature of the political regime, on the other hand, should not matter too much for how growth relates to the other variables, which mainly control for the features of the economy.

To test this implication, we first split the sample into two groups of countries: those that were democracies for at least 75 percent of the time between 1960 and 1985, and all the others. Our definition of democracy is based on the form of the constitution in place between 1960 and 1985, as detailed in Arthur Banks (1987). Thus, our sample of democracies consists of a large variety of political regimes, some more democratic than others, whereas the sample of nondemocracies is more homogeneous. (Reallocating borderline cases to one group or the other does not affect the results.) Democracies on average grow faster and have a higher initial level of per capita income, even though there are some very poor countries in this group. But the most striking difference between these two groups concerns the (partial) correlation coefficient of the variables GROWTH and MIDDLE. It is 0.401 for democracies and −0.309 for nondemocracies! Clearly, the association between inequality and growth is very different in the two samples. Except for this coefficient, the correlation matrix for democratic countries is remarkably similar to the correlation matrix for the whole sample in table 19.4.

Table 19.5 Regressions for GROWTH

	(i) Whole sample	(ii) Democracies	(iii) Nondemocracies	(iv) Whole sample
Constant	−2.589	−5.159	0.949	0.949
	(2.359)	(−3.363)	(0.526)	(0.572)
MIDDLE	0.189	0.326	−0.072	−0.072
	(2.350)	(3.235)	(−0.559)	(−0.608)
GDP	-5.3×10^{-4}	-5.8×10^{-4}	-1.7×10^{-3}	-1.7×10^{-3}
	(−3.070)	(−3.579)	(−2.967)	(−3.229)
PSCHOOL	0.041	0.049	0.057	0.057
	(4.432)	(3.627)	(3.119)	(3.396)
DEMOCRACY				−6.108
				(−2.624)
MIDDLEDM				0.398
				(2.489)
GDPDM				0.001
				(2.028)
PSCHOOLDM				−0.008
				(−0.377)
Number of observations	49	29	20	49
$\bar{R}^2$	0.32	0.46	0.31	0.44
SEE	1.483	1.265	1.466	1.347

Notes: The table reports ordinary least-squares regressions; *t* values are shown in parentheses; SEE = standard error of the estimate.

The results from re-estimating the model separately for the two samples of countries are shown in columns (ii) and (iii) of table 19.5. As predicted, the estimated coefficient on MIDDLE is positive and significant only for the democratic countries. The *t* statistics for the other (economic) variables are instead similar in the two samples.

Finally, we turn to a test of an even stricter hypothesis, namely, that *the only* difference between the two samples of countries is the effect of income inequality on growth. To test this, we re-estimate the model on the whole sample of countries but add a dummy variable (called DEMOCRACY) which takes a value of 1 if the country is a democracy (as defined above), and 0 otherwise. This dummy variable is entered separately, and it is interacted with all the explanatory variables in the regression.

Ordinary least-squares estimates are shown in column (iv) of table 19.5. The suffix-DM at the end of a variable indicates that it is interacted with the DEMOCRACY dummy. A previous version of this paper reported similar results for other, less parsimonious, specifications. The reported estimates, as well as those reported in the previous version, reject the strict hypothesis, though not overwhelmingly. The coefficient on income inequality is not the only difference between the two sample of countries; but it is almost the only difference. Specifically, as predicted by the theory, the coefficient on the variable

MIDDLE is significantly different from zero and of the correct sign only when interacted with DEMOCRACY. The coefficients of the remaining variables always have the expected sign and are significantly different from zero when they are entered in isolation. When interacted with DEMOCRACY, these other coefficients are generally insignificant, except for GDPDM which is significant (and with a sign opposite to that of GDP). Thus, even though the differences between the two samples are not exclusively due to the effect of inequality on growth, there are few other systematic differences.

We can summarize our findings in this section as follows. First, income equality at the start of the period has a positive effect on subsequent growth. Second, this positive correlation is present only in democratic countries, irrespective of whether or not we control for other economic variables. Third, the nature of the political regime does not seem to be very important for how the other (economic) variables relate to growth. These last two findings are particularly important, because they suggest that the effect of equality on growth may indeed operate through a political mechanism. We will say more on this in the next subsection.

Discussion

We now analyze the robustness of these results.

(i)   As in section II, it is likely that several regressors, and particularly MIDDLE, are measured with error. We deal with this problem in two ways. First, we re-estimate the model with instrumental variables. Our instruments for MIDDLE are the percentage of the labor force in the agricultural sector in 1960, the male life-expectancy ratio in 1960, secondary-school enrollments in 1960, and the independent variables GDP and PSCHOOL. We believe these are pretty good instruments. They capture different aspects of the economic and social structure of a country and are likely to be correlated with income inequality. Since they are all measured in 1960 and some of them belong to the regressors in the GROWTH equation, they are unlikely to be correlated with the error term of that equation or with the measurement error in MIDDLE.

Table 19.6 reports the two-stage least-squares (2SLS) estimates, for the whole sample and for democratic and nondemocratic countries. The results are very similar to those reported in table 19.5. In particular, MIDDLE is significant and has the right sign in the whole sample and in the sample of democratic countries, but not in the sample of dictatorships. The coefficients on the other variables, on the other hand, are quite stable across the three samples.

Second, we apply the techniques of Klepper and Leamer (1984) based on reverse regressions. Consider the whole sample and the sample of democratic countries: columns (i) and (ii), respectively, in table 19.5. When we regress these equations in all directions, all the variables retain their signs. Thus, the true maximum-likelihood estimates lie in the convex hull of the estimates so obtained. In particular, the coefficients of MIDDLE lie in the following intervals: whole sample, [0.189, 1.727]; democracies, [0.242, 1.104].

Compared to the least-squares estimates, we see that, if anything, measurement error tends to bias MIDDLE toward zero and thus against our theory. We obtain similar results for the other specifications in table 19.5.[17]

(ii)   The residuals reveal a few outlying observations (Venezuela, Chad, and Morocco). Removing them makes no difference for the results, neither for the whole sample nor for

Table 19.6 Sensitivity analysis

Independent variable	(i) Whole sample	(ii) Democracies	(iii) Nondemocracies
Constant	−5.527	−9.923	−3.607
	(−2.806)	(−2.726)	(−0.774)
MIDDLE	0.513	0.771	0.349
	(2.843)	(2.473)	(0.848)
GDP	-8×10^{-4}	-9×10^{-4}	-1.6×10^{-3}
	(−3.372)	(−3.020)	(2.216)
PSCHOOL	0.032	0.042	0.054
	(2.786)	(2.246)	(2.150)
Number of observations	46	29	17
$\bar{R}^2$	0.28	0.31	0.18
SEE	1.670	1.690	1.709

Notes: The table reports two-stage least-squares regressions; t values are shown in parentheses; SEE − standard error of the estimate.

the two samples of democratic and nondemocratic countries. However, the estimated residuals tend to be larger in absolute value for the countries with lower per capita income in 1960, indicating a potential heteroscedasticity problem. We therefore re-estimated the model weighting each observation with GDP. The results, reported in a previous version of this paper (Persson and Tabellini, 1991) remain supportive of the theoretical model, as do alternative specifications controlling for heteroscedasticity.

(iii) Despite our attempts to control for institutional differences, our measures of income inequality may pick up the effect of some *omitted variable*. To check for this possibility, we added three continental dummies (for Asia, Africa, and Latin America) to the previous regressions. In the most basic specifications (which include only MIDDLE, GDP, and PSCHOOL) estimated on the whole sample, the continental dummies are jointly (though not individually) significant and the estimated coefficient on MIDDLE becomes insignificant. However, when we estimate the equation on the two separate samples, or when we add the DEMOCRACY dummy, MIDDLE remains significant only when interacted with DEMOCRACY, or in the sample of democratic countries. Moreover, the continental dummies now become insignificant.

(iv) Generally (and in our sample) democratic countries have a much higher average GDP per capita than nondemocratic countries. Can we be sure that our results do not reflect genuinely different behavior in rich and poor countries, rather than in democracies and dictatorships? To check this, we split the sample into two halves according to 1960 GDP per capita, one made of rich countries, the other of poor countries. We then re-estimated column (iv) in table 19.5, with democracy dummies and interaction terms, in each subsample. The estimated coefficients on MIDDLE and MIDDLEDM are virtually identical to those in table 19.5 in both samples; but the standard errors on MIDDLEDM are higher, such that we can no longer reject the hypothesis that this coefficient is zero at conventional significance levels: the p value is 0.176 in the rich sample and 0.178 in the poor sample. Still, these results suggest that there are considerable differences between democracies and dictatorships *within* the groups of rich and poor countries.

All this sensitivity analysis strongly indicates that our results are not due to measurement error, to particular features of our samples, to reverse causation, or to omitted variables.

IV Discussion

Even though we believe that the empirical findings in sections II and III are statistically robust, the possibility remains that these findings reflect mechanisms other than the political theory outlined in section I. After all, these regressions only estimate the reduced form of the model, and not the two specific channels identified by the theory: from more equality to less policy-induced redistribution; and from less redistribution to more investment and faster growth. In this section we discuss the evidence concerning these separate channels of causation.

Consider first the link between investment and growth. According to the theory, inequality exerts its effect on growth by discouraging investment. The first two columns of table 19.7 provide evidence on this link for the whole sample of countries. We estimate a growth regression by two-stage least squares, where MIDDLE is replaced by the share of investment over GDP on average between 1960 and 1985 (INVESTMENT), and the latter is regressed on the remaining independent variables including MIDDLE. As expected, MIDDLE has a positive and almost significant estimated coefficient on INVESTMENT

Table 19.7 Investment and growth

Dependent variable	Whole sample		Democracies	Nondemocracies
	(i) GROWTH	(ii) INVESTMENT	(iii) INVESTMENT	(iv) INVESTMENT
Constant	−2.772 (−1.607)	0.962 (0.232)	−7.988 (−1.150)	2.637 (0.371)
INVESTMENT	0.312 (1.578)			
MIDDLE		0.581 (1.904)	1.024 (2.210)	0.481 (0.948)
GDP	-4.6×10^{-4} (−1.913)	-2×10^{-5} (−0.034)	-4.2×10^{-4} (−0.623)	0.002 (0.673)
PSCHOOL	−0.005 (−0.156)	0.143 (4.232)	0.173 (3.204)	0.117 (1.630)
Number of observations	43	43	23	20
$\bar{R}^2$	0.192	0.511	0.507	0.330
SEE	1.992	5.291	5.006	5.770

Notes: Column (i) is estimated by 2SLS; the remaining columns are estimated by OLS. Numbers in parentheses are *t* values; SEE = standard error of the estimate.

(its p value is 0.06), while INVESTMENT has a positive (but not quite significant) effect on GROWTH. The remaining coefficients have the expected sign in the INVESTMENT equation, even though the schooling variable loses significance and has the wrong sign in the GROWTH equation.

According to the theory, the variable MIDDLE should have a positive effect on INVESTMENT only in democracies. This proposition is tested in columns (iii) and (iv) of table 19.7, which split the sample into democracies and nondemocracies. The result is exactly as predicted. MIDDLE only affects INVESTMENT in the democratic countries.

Overall, thus, this decomposition further supports the theory. Equality affects growth by promoting investment, and this effect is present only in the democracies.

Next, let us turn to the other channel identified by the theory: from more equality to less redistribution, and from less redistribution to more growth and investment. As discussed in section I, the reason for emphasizing the reduced-form implications of the theory, rather than the "structural" implications, is the difficulty in observing the relevant redistributive policies. A government can redistribute through explicit transfers, but also more implicitly through regulation, lax law enforcement, patent protection, and so on. Reliable measures of these redistributive policies are not readily available.

Nevertheless, two recent studies of the OECD countries provide evidence in favor of the two separate theoretical hypotheses. Lorenzo Kristov et al. (1992) find that various measures of inequality explain the size of current transfers by OECD countries in the period 1960–81;[18] and Håkan Nordström (1992) finds evidence that greater government transfers in proportion to GDP are negatively associated with average growth in the OECD countries between 1970 and 1985.

Postwar data on the OECD countries are particularly reliable compared with those on other countries or earlier time periods, both because transfers in these countries are an important form of government redistribution and because OECD data on transfers are comparable across countries. For this reason, we focus exclusively on OECD postwar data below and run separate regressions for the two channels identified by our model. Matching the available OECD data on government transfers with our data on income distribution, we are left with a sample of 13 countries. Column (i) of Table 19.8 re-estimates our typical reduced-form equation for this smaller sample. The results are almost identical to those found in section III for the larger sample of democracies. In particular, the estimated coefficient on MIDDLE is remarkably stable: the coefficient in column (i) of Table 19.8 is very similar to that of the same variable in column (ii) of Table 19.5. This provides further evidence of the robustness of the reduced-form estimates.

Columns (ii)–(iv) of Table 19.8 estimate equations that correspond to the two separate theoretical hypotheses. We measure government-induced redistribution by current transfers as a fraction of GDP, on average between 1960 and 1981 (TRANSF).[19] In column (ii) this variable replaces MIDDLE, our measure of equality, in the GROWTH regression. Its estimated coefficient is negative, as expected, but it is not statistically significant.

Column (ii) is estimated by OLS. It is possible, though, that some unobservable determinant of TRANSF is correlated with the residuals of the GROWTH regression. For this reason, column (iii) reports an instrumental-variables estimation of the same equation. The instruments for TRANSF are MIDDLE, PSCHOOL, GDP, and transfers as a fraction of GDP, also in 1960. Now the t statistic of TRANSF rises in absolute value to -1.246. Even though it is still insignificant at conventional significance levels, this

Table 19.8   Growth and transfers

Dependent variable	(i) GROWTH	(ii) GROWTH	(iii) GROWTH	(iv) TRANSF
Constant	−1.763 (−0.473)	4.874 (3.414)	4.786 (3.314)	0.203 (1.790)
MIDDLE	0.337 (1.951)			−0.011 (−1.286)
GDP	-8.5×10^{-4} (−4.527)	-5.2×10^{-4} (−3.873)	-5.0×10^{-4} (−3.687)	1.8×10^{-5} (1.756)
PSCHOOL	0.031 (1.786)	0.011 (0.763)	0.013 (0.900)	
TRANSF		−4.742 (−0.970)	−6.723 (−1.246)	
Number of observations	13	13	13	13
$\bar{R}^2$	0.679	0.657	0.663	0.089
SEE	0.578	0.587	0.591	0.043

Notes: Columns (i), (ii), and (iv) report OLS regressions; column (iii) reports a 2SLS regression; numbers in parentheses are *t* values.

coefficient provides some weak evidence of a negative effect from TRANSF on GROWTH.

Finally, the last column of table 19.8 investigates the link between equality and redistribution. The variable MIDDLE has the expected negative coefficient, but its *t* statistic is again of the order of −1.2. Here too there is some (weak) evidence consistent with the theoretical hypothesis.

To summarize, OECD postwar data do not seem to be at odds with the two building blocks of our theory. Naturally, the degrees of freedom are so few that the results in table 19.8 are very tentative. They do suggest, however, that it may be worthwhile to explore these issues further with better data and a larger sample.

V   Final Remarks

Drawing on the theories of endogenous economic growth and endogenous economic policy, we formulated a model that relates equilibrium growth to income inequality and political institutions. The main theoretical result is that income inequality is harmful for growth, because it leads to policies that do not protect property rights and do not allow full private appropriation of returns from investment. This implication is strongly supported by the historical evidence of a narrow cross-section of countries and by the postwar evidence from a broad cross-section of countries.

The paper may serve as a stepping stone for further theoretical and empirical work along similar lines. On the theoretical side, the most important issue for future research is perhaps to endogenize growth and income distribution in a dynamic political equilibrium.

The model of this paper is recursive and takes the distribution of income as given or following a given law of motion. There is also a literature, surveyed by Philippe Aghion and Patrick Bolton (1992), which studies the endogenous evolution of income distribution in a growth model, abstracting from policy interventions. But, to date, how income distribution and economic growth are jointly determined in political equilibrium is not very well understood.

On the empirical side, the most important extension is to discriminate better between alternative explanations of our central finding, namely, that inequality is negatively correlated with subsequent growth.[20] We have provided two bits of evidence suggesting that this correlation is induced by government policies and by political forces. First, the correlation is only present under democratic institutions. Second, OECD postwar data weakly suport the two-way links identified by our theory: from inequality to government redistributive policies, and from these policies to economic growth. This transmission channel remains to be more extensively investigated, however, by paying more attention to the exact nature of government intervention.

Appendix

Sources for historical data

GROWTH: Average rate of growth of real GDP over 20-year periods, continuously compounded. Sources: Angus Maddison (1982) for the period 1830–1950, and Summers and Heston (1988) for the period 1950–85.

GDP: Level of GDP per capita in the first year of each 20-year period. Sources: Maddison (1982) for the period 1830–1950 and Summers and Heston (1988) for the period 1950–85. The 1950 indexes computed from Maddison were spliced with the 1950 values from Summers and Heston to get compatible series.

INCSH: Share of pretax income received by the top 20 percent of the population, computed from tax statistics and sometimes adjusted for incomplete coverage on the basis of census data. We only used sources with a wide original coverage, however. The income units and income concepts may vary across countries due to different tax laws. All observations except a few are close (within five years) to the beginning of the relevant 20 year period. Sources: for the United Kingdom 1870, 1890, and 1910, Lindert and Williamson (1985); for the Netherlands 1910, 1930, 1950, and 1970, Joop Hartog and J. G. Veenbergen (1978); for the United States 1930 and 1950, US Department of Commerce (1975); for the United States 1970, Shail Jain (1975); for all other observations, Peter Flora et al. (1987, ch. 6).

NOFRAN: Share of the enfranchised sex and age group not in the electorate at the year of the election closest to the beginning of the relevant time period, computed from data on electoral rules and from censuses. Sources: for the United States (presidential elections), Thomas Mackie and Robert Rose (1982) and US Department of Commerce (1975); for all other countries (parliamentary elections), Flora (1983, ch. 3).

SCHOOL: Index of Education computed as:

$$0.1(\text{PSCHOOL}) + 0.2(\text{LSSCHOOL}) + 0.3(\text{HSSCHOOL}) + 0.4(\text{UNIV})$$

where each component of the index and the sources are described below.

PSCHOOL: Share of the 5–14 age group enrolled in primary school, computed from detailed data on different types of schools and population data from censuses. Sources: for the United States, US Department of Commerce (1975); for all other countries, Flora (1983, ch. 10).

LSSCHOOL: Share of 10–14 age group enrolled in post-primary school and lower secondary school, computed from detailed data on different types of schools and population data from censuses. Sources: for the United States, US Department of Commerce (1975); for all other countries, Flora (1983, ch. 10).

HSSCHOOL: Share of 15–19 age group enrolled in higher secondary school, computed from detailed data on different types of schools and population data from censuses. Sources: for the United States, US Department of Commerce (1975); for all other countries, Flora (1983, ch. 10).

UNIV: Share of 20–4 age group in universities and institutes for higher education, computed from detailed data on different types of schools and population data from censuses. Sources: for the United States, US Department of Commerce (1975); for all other countries, Flora (1983, ch. 10).

Sources for postwar data

GROWTH: Average rate of growth in real GDP per capita over 1960–85, continuously compounded. Source: Summers and Heston (1988).

GDP: Real GDP per capita in 1960, expressed in "international $." Source: Summers and Heston (1988).

PSCHOOL: Percentage enrolled in primary school out of relevant age group in 1960. Source: World Bank (1984).

URB: Urban population as a percentage of total population in 1965. Source: World Bank (1984).

IND: Percentage of GDP originating in the industrial sector in 1960. Source: World Bank (1984).

DEMOCRACY: Dummy variable taking a value of 1 for a country that was a democracy for at least 75 percent of the time and 0 otherwise. Source: Banks (1987) and Charles Taylor and David Jodice (1983).

MIDDLE: Share of pretax income received by the 41st–60th percentile of the population. Source: Paukert (1973).

TRANSF: Pensions, unemployment compensations, and other social expenditures (other than health and education), scaled to GDP. Source: Organization for Economic Cooperation and Development (1985, 1992).

In the instrumental-variables regressions we also used the following variables taken from World Bank (1984): male life expectancy ratio in 1960, percentage of labor force in the agricultural sector in 1960, and percentage enrolled in secondary school out of the relevant age group in 1960.

Notes

* This paper was earlier circulating under the title "Politico-Economic Equilibrium Growth: Theory and Evidence." Torsten Persson acknowledges support from the Central Bank of Sweden Tercentenary Foundation and from the Fulbright Commission; Guido Tabellini had support from NSF grant no. SES-8909263, from the UCC Center for Pacific Rim Studies, and from Fondazione Mattei, Milan. We are grateful for many helpful comments by three anonymous referees, for helpful conversations with Irma Adelman, Robert Barro, Allan Drazen, Barry Eichengreen, Gene Grossman, Bronwyn Hall, Ken Judd, Peter Lindert, John Londregan, Christina Romer, David Romer, Paul Romer, and Robert Solow and for comments from participants in many seminars and conferences. We thank David Domeij for research assistance and Kerstin Blomquist, Cindy Miller, and Mercedes Ortiz for editorial and secretarial assistance.

1 Some preliminary evidence that growth is inversely related to inequality in a small cross-section of countries is also found by Andrew Berg and Jeffrey Sachs (1988).

2 Paul Romer (1989) surveys the literature on endogenous growth. Sergio Rebelo (1991) and Robert Barro and Xavier Sala-i-Martin (1992) discuss the growth consequences of alternative (exogenous) policies. Romer (1990) spells out the income-distribution consequences of trade policies in an endogenous-growth model of a small open economy and discusses informally how these distribution consequences may block growth-promoting policies from being pursued. Marco Terrones (1990) models redistributive policy and growth endogenously, but in a representative-agent model that does not address issues of distribution and politics. Giuseppe Bertola (1991) studies the relationship between growth and the *functional* (rather than the size) distribution of income.

3 In Persson and Tabellini (1990), we survey the literature on endogenous policy. The classic papers on how income distribution affects the choice of tax policy in a static voting model are Thomas Romer (1975), Kevin Roberts (1977), and Alan Meltzer and Scott Richard (1981).

4 Subsequently, quite a few papers have been written on the interaction among income distribution, politics, and accumulation. In Persson and Tabellini (1992), we briefly survey this growing literature.

5 As suggested by the name, the hypothesis is intimately associated with the writings of Simon Kuznets, notably Kuznets (1966). Peter Lindert and Jeffrey Williamson (1985) provide a recent evaluation of the theoretical as well as the empirical work on the Kuznets curve, while François Bourguignon and Christian Morrisson (1990) provide new cross-country evidence on the effects of economic development on income distribution.

6 The overlapping-generations structure enables us to disregard the effect of individual savings decisions on the wealth distribution of future generations, which considerably simplifies the analysis.

7 In principle, one could think of more sophisticated, nonlinear, redistribution schemes. However, we could rule out such schemes as infeasible because of tax arbitrage, if we extended the model so as to make individual skills unobservable.

8 Following the approach of Paul Romer (1987), a previous version of the paper (Persson and Tabellini, 1991), showed that the second interpretation is formally consistent with our model.

9 The linearity of the production function in k and the presence of a (linear) externality of k on wages is what allows unbounded growth in this model. See Larry Jones and Rodolfo Manuelli (1991) for a more general discussion of endogenous growth in overlapping-generations economies. Finally, note that r here denotes the return on capital net of depreciation. Hence, given r, the depreciation rate of capital (or knowledge) does not enter the model.

10 The reason for the incomplete coverage is that the data are based on income tax records, and only people at the top of the income distribution paid income taxes.

11   We also tried to interact the measure of political participation with the income-inequality measure without much success.

12   Running the regressions replacing the index with its separate components produces little difference in the results.

13   For instance, the three countries in our sample on the losing side of World War II (Austria, Finland, and Germany) have the three highest growth rates in 1950–1970 (and in the sample, 4.62, 4.04 and 5.05) as well as the three lowest GDP levels in 1950 of all the nine countries.

14   A previous version of the paper (Persson and Tabellini, 1991) also used other measures of income distribution: the Gini coefficient and the income share accruing to the top 5 percent of households. The empirical results were similar to those reported here.

15   The measure can exceed 100 percent because actual school age – as well as the classification of different levels of schooling – varies across countries, whereas our World Bank source assumes that "primary-school age" is everywhere the same.

16   Except for the results for the effects on growth of income inequality, these results are similar to those in Barro (1991), who does not include income inequality in his empirical study.

17   In a previous version of this paper (Persson and Tabellini, 1991) we also estimated the same regressions with data on income inequality obtained from other sources (primarily the United Nations) and for a slightly different sample of countries, and with other definitions of inequality. Even though these other data were less reliable and were generally dated in the mid-1970s, we obtained similar results.

18   This paper argues, however, that the evidence is more consistent with a "pressure group" explanation than with the hypothesis of Meltzer and Richard (1981) about the size of transfers.

19   This variable is taken from the Organization for Economic Cooperation and Development (1985) and is the same one used by Kristov et al. (1992). It consists of social expenditures on pensions, unemployment compensation, and other social expenditures (other than health and education). It is only available up to 1981.

20   Alternative, purely economic, reasons for why inequality might be harmful for growth have been analyzed by Kevin Murphy et al. (1989), who look at the composition of demand, and by Oded Galor and Joseph Zeira (1993), who look at imperfect credit markets. In the ambitious model of Jeremy Greenwood and Boyan Jovanovic (1990) income distribution and growth become correlated over time due to financial development.

References

Adelman, Irma and Morris, Cynthia (1971) "An Anatomy of Patterns of Income Distribution in Developing Nations." Part III of the *Final Report* (Grant AID/csd-2236), Northwestern University.

Aghion, Philippe and Bolton, Patrick (1992) "Distribution and Growth in Models of Imperfect Capital Markets." *European Economic Review*, *36*(2–3): pp. 603–11.

Alesina, Alberto and Rodrik, Dani (1991) "Redistributive Politics and Economic Growth." Mimeo, Harvard University.

Arrow, Kenneth J. (1962) "The Economic Implications of Learning by Doing." *Review of Economic Studies*, *29*(3): pp. 155–73.

Banks, Arthur (1987) *A Political Handbook of the World*. Binghamton, NY: CSA Publications, SUNY-Binghamton.

Barro, Robert J. (1991) "Economic Growth in a Cross Section of Countries." *Quarterly Journal of Economics*, *106*(2): pp. 407–43.

Barro, Robert J. and Sala-i-Martin, Xavier (1992) "Public Finance in Models of Economic Growth." *Review of Economic Studies*, *59*(4): pp. 645–61.

Berg, Andrew and Sachs, Jeffrey (1988) "The Debt Crisis: Structural Explanations of Country Performance." National Bureau of Economic Research (Cambridge, MA) Working Paper No. 2607.

Bertola, Giuseppe (1991) "Market Structure and Income Distribution in Endogenous Growth Models." Mimeo, Princeton University.

Bourguignon, François and Morrisson, Christian (1990) "Income Distribution, Development and Foreign Trade: a Cross-Sectional Analysis." *European Economic Review*, *34*(6): pp. 1113–32.

Flora, Peter (1983) *State, Economy and Society in Western Europe, 1815–1975: A Data Handbook*, vol. 1. Frankfurt: Campus Verlag.

Flora, Peter, Kraus, Franz, and Pfennig, Winfried (1987) *State, Economy and Society in Western Europe, 1815–1975: A Data Handbook*, vol. 2. Frankfurt: Campus Verlag.

Galor, Oded and Zeira, Joseph (1993) "Income Distribution and Macroeconomics." *Review of Economic Studies*, *60*(1): pp. 35–52.

Grandmont, Jean-Michel (1978) "Intermediate Preferences and the Majority Rule." *Econometrica*, *46*(2): pp. 317–30.

Greenwood, Jeremy and Jovanovic, Boyan (1990) "Financial Development, Growth, and the Distribution of Income." *Journal of Political Economy*, *98*(5): pp. 1076–107.

Hartog, Joop and Veenbergen, Jan G. (1978) "Dutch Treat: Long-Run Changes in Personal Income Distribution." *De Economist*, *126*(4): pp. 521–49.

Jain, Shail (1975) *The Size Distribution of Income: A Compilation of Data*. Washington, DC: World Bank.

Jones, Larry and Manuelli, Rodolfo (1991) "Finite Lifetimes and Growth." Mimeo, Northwestern University.

Klepper, Stephen and Leamer, Edward E. (1984) "Consistent Sets of Estimates for Regressions with Errors in All Variables." *Econometrica*, *52*(1): pp. 163–83.

Kristov, Lorenzo, Lindert, Peter and McClelland, Robert (1992) "Pressure Groups and Redistribution." *Journal of Public Economics*, *48*(2): pp. 135–63.

Kuznets, Simon (1966) *Modern Economic Growth*. New Haven, CT: Yale University Press

Lindert, Peter H. and Williamson, Jeffrey G. (1985) "Growth, Equality, and History." *Explorations in Economic History*, *22*(4): pp. 341–77.

Maddala, G. S. (1977) *Econometrics*. Tokyo: McGraw-Hill.

Mackie, Thomas and Rose, Robert (1982) *The International Almanac of Electoral History*. London: Macmillan.

Maddison, Angus (1982) *Phases of Capitalist Development*. Oxford: Oxford University Press.

Mankiw, Gregory N., Romer, David and Weil, David N. (1992) "A Contribution to the Empirics of Economic Growth." *Quarterly Journal of Economics*, *107*(2): pp. 407–37.

Meltzer, Allan H. and Richard, Scott F. (1981) "A Rational Theory of the Size of Government." *Journal of Political Economy*, *89*(5): pp. 914–27.

Murphy, Kevin M., Shleifer, Andrei and Vishny, Robert W. (1989) "Income Distribution, Market Size, and Industrialization." *Quarterly Journal of Economics*, *104*(3): pp. 537–64.

Nordström, Håkan (1992) *Studies in Trade Policy and Economic Growth*, Monograph No. 20, Stockholm: Institute for International Economic Studies.

Organization for Economic Cooperation and Development (1985) *Social Expenditure 1960–90: Problems of Growth and Control*. Paris: Organization for Economic Cooperation and Development.

Organization for Economic Cooperation and Development (1992) *Economic Outlook*, No. 51. Paris: Organization for Economic Cooperation and Development.

Paukert, Felix (1973) "Income Distribution at Different Levels of Development: A Survey of the Evidence." *International Labour Review*, *108*(2–3): pp. 97–125.

Perotti, Roberto (1993) "Political Equilibrium, Income Distribution and Growth." *Review of Economic Studies*, *60*(4): pp. 755–76.

Persson, Torsten and Tabellini, Guido (1990) *Macroeconomic Policy, Credibility and Politics*. London: Harwood.

Persson, Torsten and Tabellini, Guido (1991) "Is Inequality Harmful for Growth: Theory and Evidence." Center for Economic Policy Research (London) Discussion Paper No. 581.

Persson, Torsten and Tabellini, Guido (1992) "Growth, Distribution and Politics." *European Economic Review*, *36*(2–3): pp. 593–602.

Rebelo, Sergio (1991) "Long-Run Policy Analysis and Long-Run Growth." *Journal of Political Economy*, *99*(3): pp. 500–21.

Roberts, Kevin (1977) "Voting over Income Tax Schedules." *Journal of Public Economics*, *8*(3): pp. 329–40.

Romer, Paul M. (1986) "Increasing Returns and Long-Run Growth." *Journal of Political Economy*, *94*(5): pp. 1002–37.

Romer, Paul M. (1987) "Growth Based on Increasing Returns Due to Specialization." *American Economic Review (Papers and Proceedings)*, *77*(2): pp. 56–62.

Romer, Paul M. (1989) "Capital Accumulation in the Theory of Long-Run Growth," in R. Barro (ed.), *Modern Business Cycle Theory*. Cambridge, MA: Harvard University Press, pp. 51–127.

Romer, Paul M. (1990) "Trade, Politics, and Growth in a Small Less Developed Economy." Mimeo, Stanford University.

Romer, Thomas (1975) "Individual Welfare, Majority Voting and the Properties of a Linear Income Tax." *Journal of Public Economics*, *4*(2): pp. 163–85.

Summers, Robert and Heston, Alan (1988) "A New Set of International Comparisons of Real Product and Price Levels: Estimates for 130 Countries, 1950–1985." *Review of Income and Wealth*, *34*(1): pp. 1–25.

Taylor, Charles and Jodice, David (1983) *World Handbook of Political and Social Indicators*. New Haven, CT: Yale University Press.

Terrones, Marco (1990) "Influence Activities and Economic Growth." Mimeo, University of Western Ontario.

US Department of Commerce (1975) *Historical Statistics of the United States*. Washington, DC: US Government Printing Office.

World Bank (1984) *World Development Report*. Washington, DC: World Bank.

TWENTY

Social Norms and Economic Incentives in the Welfare State

Assar Lindbeck, Sten Nyberg, and Jörgen W. Weibull*

Source: From The Quarterly Journal of Economics (February 1999), 114: 1–35.

I Introduction

Both economic incentives and social norms influence individual behavior. While sociologists have emphasized social norms, economists have focused on economic incentives.[1] Most likely, the different approaches reflect the different subject matter dealt with in the two disciplines. Social norms are likely to play a major role in certain decisions that people make, while other decisions seem to be driven primarily by economic incentives. For some decisions, however, both social norms and economic incentives appear to be involved. This paper is an attempt to bring together social norms and economic incentives on an equal footing in a model of individual choice.[2] More precisely, we extend the traditional economic model of individual preferences to encompass social norms in a tractable way that enables an analysis of both economic and political decisions.

We have chosen to develop this point in a specific context, namely concerning decisions about work and benefits in the modern welfare state. The relevance of this topic is evident from the fact that such benefits have increased dramatically in recent decades and now constitute a sizable portion of national income in most OECD countries, particularly, in western Europe. Examples of such benefit systems are social assistance ("welfare" in US terminology), early retirement, sickness benefits, paid parental leave, and unemployment benefits. About 40 percent of the adult Swedish population, including old-age pensioners, and about 25 percent excluding this group, is at present largely financed in this way.[3] These figures do not include individuals who are only partially financed by social benefits such as child allowances, day-care subsidies, and housing allowances. Similar, though somewhat lower, figures are found in some other Western European countries such as Belgium and Denmark. In most countries the number of welfare state beneficiaries has risen dramatically in recent decades.[4]

Individual decisions concerning work seem to belong to the class of decisions where both economic incentives and social norms play a role. To quote Elster (1989, p. 121), "The work place is a hotbed of norm-guided action. . . . There is a social norm against living off other people and a corresponding normative pressure to earn one's income from work."

Such a social norm may in part explain why far from all who are eligible for welfare programs participate in the programs. For example, this participation rate has been estimated to be only 40–70 percent in certain US welfare programs in the 1970s. Moffitt (1983) finds econometric support for a model of "welfare stigma," where the stigma is modeled as a fixed utility loss to recipients.[5] In principle, one may distinguish between social norms in favor of work and social norms against living off specific transfers, where some transfers may be accompanied by more social stigma than others.[6] Although this distinction is likely to be quite important in practice, we abstract from it here for the sake of analytical tractability.

It is likely that an increase in the number of people who receive welfare benefits weakens the social norm to live off one's own work. Moreover, individuals who live off public transfers may over time come to value their leisure more.[7] While the existence of a social norm against living off other people's work is taken as given here, the intensity of the norm, as perceived by the individual, is endogenous in our model: it depends on the number of people adhering to it. More exactly, we assume that living on transfers becomes relatively less embarrassing when more individuals do likewise. When the population share of transfer recipients is large (small), the individual's discomfort from such a lifestyle is relatively weak (strong).[8] Hence, the intensity of the social norm is viewed as an equilibrium phenomenon which, a priori, allows for the possibility of multiple equilibria (under given taxes and transfers). In this respect our model has some similarity to game-theoretic models in which social conventions are identified with alternative equilibria in coordination games; see, e.g., Young (1993).

In our analysis of the interplay between economic incentives and this social norm, we focus on two types of choice in connection with benefit systems: political and economic. First, the individual expresses her policy preferences as a voter, anticipating the consequences of the chosen policy for her own economic choice and for aggregate behavior – including the adherence in society at large to the social norm. Second, the individual maximizes her utility subject to given taxes, transfers, and the expected population share adhering to the norm.

We assume that every individual in her economic decision has a choice between two, and only two, alternatives: either to work full-time or to live solely on public transfers. Many benefits in the real world do require the individual not to work: examples are unemployment benefits, sick benefits, early retirement, and disability pensions. However, not all individuals are entitled to all benefits, and those who are can usually choose from a variety of combinations of (full or partial) benefits with (part-time or full-time) work. It is not difficult to generalize the model to include entitlements (an extension to include involuntary exclusion from work life is given in section VI).[9] See Sundén and Weibull (1997) for an analysis of the case where individuals can choose hours of work on a continuous scale and where the transfer is means-tested.

Whether the individual chooses to work or not depends on the after-tax wage, the level of public transfers, and the accompanying population share of transfer recipients. The tax rate and the per capita transfer are, in turn, determined in a political process based on majority vote. Each voter is assumed to correctly foresee the share of transfer recipients resulting from any tax/transfer combination on the political agenda, and voters vote earnestly for or against an incumbent policy. We assume that the voters expect the current population share of transfer recipients to persist if the incumbent policy is continued. Moreover, when faced with any alternative policy, they all expect some equilibrium population share of transfer recipients under that policy. The current state of the economy is called a political equilibrium if it balances the public budget and its policy wins against any "opposition" policy.

We show that (generically) there exists at most one political equilibrium. This is either a certain low-transfer policy that is supported by a majority of taxpayers, or a certain high-transfer policy that is supported by a majority of transfer recipients. In the basic version of the model, with no altruism and no risk for involuntary exclusion from working life, the former policy simply means no transfer and no tax. When altruism or the risk of involuntary exclusion from work life is introduced, this policy alternative is replaced by a positive transfer and tax. By way of computer calculations, we show that gradual changes in preferences can result in nonmonotonic and even discontinuous changes in political equilibrium. In this sense, the model can explain a "sudden rise and gradual fall" (or vice versa) of the welfare state in terms of gradual monotonic changes in the exogenous factors.

Income redistribution as a political equilibrium outcome when individual voting decisions are based on economic incentives has been analyzed before; see, e.g., Roberts (1977) and Meltzer and Richard (1981). Our modeling of political equilibrium is similar to theirs. However, while the transfer in their model is granted to everyone, in our model it is granted only to those who do not work. Moreover, in Meltzer's and Richard's model individuals choose their hours of work on a continuous scale while in our model all individuals face a binary choice: full-time work or no work at all. A conceptually more fundamental difference is that social norms are absent from these two models.

An early attempt to incorporate social norms in economic analysis is a study by Akerlof (1980) on the role of social customs in a model of fair wages and unemployment. There are certain similarities between Akerlof's model and ours. However, his model neither deals with welfare-state issues, nor are political decisions analyzed. From a technical viewpoint our analysis of social norms resembles models of interdependent preferences where aggregate behavior – such as average consumption, excess demand, or average hours of work – enter the individual's utility function: see Schelling (1971), Granovetter (1978), Granovetter and Soong (1983, 1986), Basu (1987), Becker (1991), and Blomquist (1993). Social norms have also been analyzed in Bernheim (1994), where adherence to social norms is obtained as an equilibrium outcome driven by the wish of individuals to obtain social esteem. Besley and Coate (1992) analyze welfare stigma in much the same way as we do here. Our analysis differs from theirs in three respects. First, they do not treat political equilibrium. Second, while we consider a continuous wage distribution and identical preferences, they focus on the case of a two-point wage distribution and a continuous distribution of preferences for leisure (our parameter μ). Third, in contrast to the present treatment, they rule out, by assumption, the possibility of multiple equilibrium shares of transfer recipients for given policy parameters. For an informal discussion of the interplay between economic incentives and social norms, see Lindbeck (1995).

The paper is organized as follows. In section II we describe the individual's economic decision problem: whether to work or to live off the transfer. In section III the government's budget constraint is introduced, and section IV examines which balanced budget policies qualify as political equilibria under majority rule. Both sections illustrate some comparative statics properties of the model by way of computer calculations. Section V extends the model to encompass altruism, while section VI generalizes the model to include the individual's risk of being excluded from working life. Section VII discusses the effects on political equilibrium of a time lag in the adjustment of the social norm. Section VIII concludes with a summary and a discussion of some directions for further research. The parametric specification of the model that underlies the graphical illustrations, and the proofs of Propositions 2 and 3, are given in appendices at the end of the paper.

II   The Model

We assume a continuum of individuals with wages distributed according to some continuously differentiable cumulative probability distribution function Φ.[10] There is a positive density $\varphi(w) = \Phi'(w)$ at all positive wage levels w, and no individual has a zero wage ($\Phi(0) = 0$). Suppose also that the wage distribution Φ has a finite mean $\bar{w}$, and let its median be $\tilde{w}$. Let Φ^{-1} denote the inverse function to Φ.

Each individual either works full-time or does not work at all. In the first case, she consumes her after-tax wage earnings $(1 - t)w$ and enjoys some leisure. We normalize this level of leisure to zero. Here t is the tax rate on wage earnings, and w is her wage.[11] In the second case, the individual receives a government transfer T. This transfer is exempted from taxation and is granted to anyone who lacks other income. An individual who receives this transfer thus consumes T and enjoys full-time leisure. Individuals may, however, also experience disutility from accepting the transfer due to embarrassment or social stigma associated with living on public transfers rather than on one's own work. Such embarrassment is likely to be weaker, the greater the number of individuals in society who live on the transfer.[12] Thus, if the population share living on the transfer is x, and the disutility from accepting the transfer is $\nu(x)$, then ν will here be taken to be a decreasing function. Expressed in terms of social norms, if the social norm is that the source of one's subsistence should be one's own work, then the intensity of discomfort when deviating from this norm is a decreasing function of the population share of deviators. Hence, the strength or intensity of the social norm, in comparison with the economic incentive, is determined endogenously in the model.

Each individual chooses to work if and only if that choice results in higher utility than living off the transfer. (Only continuous income distributions are considered, so indifferent individuals can be ignored.) Assuming additively separable utility, an individual with wage w thus works if and only if

$$u[(1 - t)w] > u(T) + \mu - \nu(x), \qquad (1)$$

where $\mu \in \mathbb{R}$ is the utility difference between the leisure of living on the transfer and the intrinsic utility that one may derive from work life.[13]

We assume that the utility from consumption is a strictly increasing and concave function running from minus infinity at zero consumption to plus infinity at infinite consumption, and that the disutility of deviating from the norm is nonincreasing in the fraction of deviators.

A1: $u: \mathbb{R}_+ \to \mathbb{R} \cup \{-\infty\}$ is real-valued and twice continuously differentiable on $\mathbb{R}_{++}$, with $u' > 0$, $u'' < 0$, $\lim_{c \to 0} u(c) = u(0) = -\infty$, and $\lim_{c \to \infty} u(c) = +\infty$.

A2: $\nu: [0, 1] \to \mathbb{R}$ is continuously differentiable, with $\nu' \leq 0$.'

For every tax rate $t < 1$, transfer $T > 0$, and expected population share $x \in [0, 1]$ of transfer recipients, there exists a unique critical wage rate w^* such that all individuals with lower wages choose not to work and those with higher wages choose to work. This wage rate is the unique solution to the equation,

$$u[(1 - t)w] = u(T) + \mu - \nu(x). \qquad (2)$$

Taking the inverse of the subutility function u for consumption, one sees that the critical wage is increasing in the tax rate t and transfer T and nondecreasing in the population share x of transfer recipients:

$$w^* = \omega(t, T, x) = \frac{1}{1 - t} u^{-1}[u(T) + \mu - \nu(x)]. \qquad (3)$$

Note that $\omega(t, T, x) \to 0$ as $T \to 0$. We accordingly set $\omega(t, 0, x) = 0$, and thereby obtain ω as a continuous function on $S = [0, 1] \times \mathbb{R}_+ \times [0, 1]$. We will call a point $s = (t, T, x)$ in S a *state* of the economy, and call a pair $p = (t, T) \in P = [0, 1) \times \mathbb{R}_+$ a *policy*.

If all individuals expect a population share of transfer recipients x, and if this expectation is to be fulfilled, then x must be identical with the population share of individuals with wages below the critical level. Hence,

$$x = \Phi\left(\frac{u^{-1}[u(T) + \mu - \nu(x)]}{1 - t}\right). \qquad (4)$$

Mathematically, this is a fixed-point equation in x, with exogenous parameters t and T. The right-hand side of the equation is a continuous function of x, mapping the unit interval $[0,1]$ into itself. Hence, there exists at least one population share x^* satisfying equation (4), for any policy $p = (t, T) \in P$. (In particular, $x^* = 0$ if and only if $T = 0$.) Whether there exists more than one such population share when the transfer is positive depends on the subutility functions u and ν as well as on the wage distribution Φ. A solution x^* to (4) will be called an *equilibrium population share* of transfer recipients, and a state $s = (t, T, x)$ such that x satisfies equation (4), an *equilibrium state* of the economy.

The right-hand side of equation (4) is a constant in the special case when the disutility from deviating from the norm is independent of the population share of transfer recipients. Hence, the equilibrium population share is then unique; see figure 20.1a. Figure 20.1b shows a case when the disutility $\nu(x)$ of deviating from the social norm decreases rapidly from a high to a low value at some intermediate value of x. As seen in that diagram, equation (4) then has three solutions. The intuition for this multiplicity of equilibria is that if the population share of transfer recipients is low (high) then the disutility from living on the transfer is high (low). Consequently, few (many) individuals live on transfer.[14] Thus,

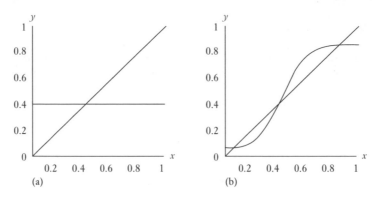

Figure 20.1 The fixed-point equation (4), under "nonsocial" (a) and "social" (b) preferences, respectively

economies with the same tax rate and transfer, factor incomes, and preferences may differ in terms of the share of transfer recipients and the social stigma associated with the transfer. (See Appendix 1 for a specification of the parametric forms used when generating the figures in this study.)

There is a natural class of dynamics in the expectation formation that underlies the fixed-point equation (4). Suppose that a policy $p = (t, T)$ has been decided upon, and that all individuals, when deciding whether or not to work, predict a population share x^e of transfer recipients. The resulting, "true," population share of transfer recipients then becomes $x = \Phi[\omega(t, T, x^e)]$. If x equals x^e, then the aggregate of individuals has succeeded in making a correct, or self-fulfilling, prediction – the above case of "rational expectations." However, suppose that $x < x^e$; i.e., fewer individuals than predicted opted for the transfer. It is then plausible that some individuals who opted for the transfer will now opt for work, since the embarrassment was greater than expected. Likewise, if $x > x^e$, some individuals who opted for work will now shift to the transfer. In such an adaptation process x^e will increase (decrease) if $\Phi[\omega(t, T, x^e)]$ exceeds (falls short of) x^e. Geometrically, x^e will increase (decrease) where the curve in figure 20.1 lies above (below) the 45-degree line. Hence, fixed points where the curve intersects the 45-degree line from above (below) are stable (unstable) under such dynamics. In particular, the intermediate fixed point in figure 20.1(b) is unstable, while the two other fixed points are stable.

III   Balanced-Budget Equilibrium

So far, no connection has been assumed between the tax rate and the transfer. We restrict the subsequent analysis to policies that balance the government budget.[15] This balance requirement simply equates public transfer spending with public revenues from the wage tax.

The aggregate income from all individuals who work can be conveniently expressed in terms of the *truncated expected-value* function Ψ defined by $\Psi(w) = \int_w^\infty w' d\Phi(w')$, representing the wage "sum" for individuals with wages above w, normalized to per capita units.

The *tax base* in state $s = (t, T, x)$, normalized to per capita units, is simply the function Ψ evaluated at the associated critical wage rate: all individuals with higher wages work and pay the income tax, and no individual with a lower wage works. In an *equilibrium* state, the critical wage equals $\Phi^{-1}(x)$, and so the aggregate per capita tax revenue is $t\Psi[\Phi^{-1}(x)]$. Similarly, aggregate per capita government expenditure on transfer payments is the transfer times the population share of transfer recipients, Tx. An equilibrium state $s = (t, T, x)$ thus balances the government budget if and only if

$$Tx = t\Psi[\Phi^{-1}(x)]. \tag{5}$$

Equilibrium states that satisfy this equation will be called *balanced*. For instance, the "zero-tax zero-transfer" state $s^0 = (0, 0, 0)$ is such a state: it satisfies both equation (4) and equation (5).

An examination of the equation pair ((4),(5)) reveals that for *every* population share $x \in (0, 1)$ of transfer recipients there exists exactly one policy $(t, T) \in P$ such that the triplet (t, T, x) constitutes a balanced equilibrium state.[16] To see this, let $x \in (0, 1)$ be given, and first note that the budget equation (5) defines the tax rate t as a linear increasing function of the transfer T. In particular, $t = 0$ when $T = 0$. Second, we note that the equilibrium equation (4) may be rewritten in the form,

$$t = 1 - \frac{1}{\Phi^{-1}(x)} u^{-1}[u(T) + \mu - \nu(x)]. \tag{6}$$

This equation defines the tax rate t as a continuous and decreasing function of the transfer T, with $t = 1$ when $T = 0$. Hence, the graph of this function intersects the graph of the linear increasing function at exactly one point, proving the existence and uniqueness claims. Note also that this intersection is a continuous function of x, the given population share of transfer recipients.

We noted earlier that $x = 0$ is an equilibrium population share if and only if $T = 0$. Budget balance then requires that $t = 0$. Moreover, it follows from equations (5) and (6) that $t \to 0$ and $T \to 0$ as $x \to 0$, and that $t \to 1$ and $T \to 0$ as $x \to 1$.

In sum, we have established

PROPOSITION 1   For every population share of transfer recipients $x \in [0, 1)$, there exists exactly one policy (t, T) such that the triplet $s = (t, T, x)$ constitutes a balanced equilibrium state. The pair (t, T) is continuous in x, with $(t, T) = (0, 0)$ when $x = 0$, and with $(t, T) \to (1, 0)$ as $x \to 1$.

Thus, any population share of transfer recipients uniquely determines a balanced policy and thereby a balanced equilibrium state. Conversely, for any policy there exists *at most* one equilibrium population share that balances the budget. To see this, suppose that x is such that the state $s = (t, T, x)$ is a balanced equilibrium, and let x' be another population share such that $s' = (t, T, x')$ is an equilibrium state. Then s does not meet the budget requirement (5). For if $x' > x$, public spending is higher in s, and public revenues are lower, and similarly if $x < x$.

Expressed in more operational terms, Proposition 1 states that there exist two continuous functions, $f:[0, 1] \rightarrow [0, 1]$ and $F:[0, 1] \rightarrow \mathbb{R}_+$, that map any population share $x \in [0, 1]$ of transfer recipients to the unique tax rate, $t = f(x)$, and transfer, $T = F(x)$, that make the triplet $s = (t, T, x)$ a balanced equilibrium state. Moreover, $f(x)$ and $F(x)$ are zero if and only if $x = 0$, and $f(x) \rightarrow 1$ and $F(x) \rightarrow 0$ as $x \rightarrow 1$.

Equations (5) and (6) enable straightforward comparative-statics analyses of the tax and transfer functions f and F. For instance, an increase in the taste μ for leisure results in a pointwise reduction of both f and F; a lower transfer is needed for each population share x of transfer recipients, and hence the tax rate is also lower. Moreover, if the utility from consumption is logarithmic, then a shift in the whole wage distribution Φ such that all individuals' wages are multiplied by the same factor λ results in no change in the tax function f but a proportional pointwise change in the transfer function F: $F(x)$ is replaced by $\lambda F(x)$ for all x.[17]

In a model based on purely economic incentives, one would expect the tax rate to be higher when the population share of transfer recipients is higher. Indeed, if individuals' preferences are "nonsocial," i.e., independent of aggregate behavior x, then f can be shown to be increasing. See figure 20.2 for an illustration of the functions F and f in this case. (All figures are based on the parametrization given in appendix 1.)

However, in the presence of a social norm with endogenous intensity, f need not be monotonic. The reason is that if the embarrassment of living on the transfer decreases drastically for a small increase in the population share of transfer recipients, say from x to $x + \varepsilon$, then transfers become much more attractive, and thus T must decrease in order for $x + \varepsilon$ to be an equilibrium population share. If the compensating reduction in T is large enough, then budget balance requires the tax rate t to decrease as well.

The model does not preclude, at least a priori, the possibility that for certain tax rates t there exists more than one pair (T, x) that balances the public budget. If both (T, x) and (T', x') are compatible with balancing the budget at the same tax rate t, and the transfer T' is higher than T, then the population share x' must be smaller than the population share x. This is because public spending would otherwise be higher in (T', x') while the tax base would be smaller (the tax rate is by hypothesis the same). Such multiplicity, at a given tax

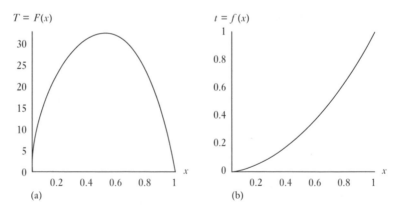

Figure 20.2   A transfer function F with associated tax function f

rate, clearly implies that if fewer individuals choose the higher transfer T' then the social norm against living on transfers is stronger in (T', x') than in (T, x).

Figure 20.4(a) illustrates that a multiplicity of transfer/recipient pairs (T, x) is indeed a real possibility. The curve represents the set of balanced policies, and is based on the same numerical specification as in figure 20.3. Note the folding of the curve above an interval of tax rates near 20 percent. For each of these tax rates t, there are three values of T such that the policy $p = (t, T)$ belongs to the curve (at the end-points of this interval there are two such values of T). Let these three policies be denoted $p = (t, T)$, $p' = (t, T')$, and $p'' = (t, T'')$, respectively, with $T < T' < T''$. As argued above, the corresponding unique population shares must satisfy $x > x' > x''$. In sum, for such tax rates t there exist three transfer/recipient pairs.

It turns out that there are connections between multiplicity of solutions to the fixed-point equation (4), as illustrated in figure 20.1(b), and folds in the balanced-policy curve,

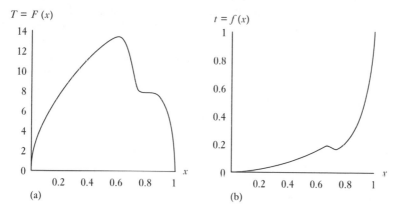

Figure 20.3 A nonconcave transfer function F and the associated nonmonotonic tax function f

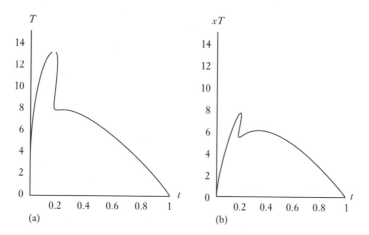

Figure 20.4 (a) The set of balanced policies; (b) the associated "Laffer curve"

shown in figure 20.4. First, policies p on upward sloping segments of this curve correspond to fixed points in equation (4) where the curve in figure 20.1(b) intersects the 45-degree line from above (the lowest and highest fixed point). Second, policies on the backward running part of the fold correspond to fixed points where the curve in figure 20.1(b) intersects the 45-degree line from below (the middle fixed point). Third, all points on the initial upward sloping segment of the balanced-policy curve in figure 20.4, starting at the zero-transfer policy $p^0 = (0, 0)$, correspond to the lowest fixed point in equation (4) – the smallest population share of transfer recipients compatible with the given policy p on that segment of the curve. Note also that policies p on the backward running segment of the fold in the balanced-policy curve in figure 20.4 correspond to unstable fixed points x in the expectations dynamics discussed in the context of figure 20.1. Hence, it seems implausible that such policies can be maintained. (See appendix 2 for a proof of these three claims.)

Multiplication of a transfer payment T by an associated population share x of transfer recipients determines total government expenditures (per capita), xT. See figure 20.4(b) for a plot of xT against the tax rate t; a "Laffer curve." Note that the fold in figure 20.4(a) is carried over to this new curve.

As a brief detour, let us do a dynamic thought experiment regarding the case when certain tax rates t are consistent with more than one combination (T, x) of transfer level and population share of transfer recipients. Suppose that the government gradually increases the tax rate t and the transfer T so as to maintain budget balance, starting from a point to the left of the fold in figure 20.4(a). If expectations concerning the population share x exhibit inertia, then the policy $p = (t, T)$ continues to slide smoothly along the fold, until it turns vertically down. There, a marginal increase of t results in a downward jump in T and a switch by a sizable population share from working to living on transfers. Further increases of t lead to gradual reductions of the transfer. The switching individuals accept a lower transfer because the increased share of transfer recipients reduces the disutility associated with not working. A gradual policy shift has resulted in a shock to the social value attached to work. Reversing the thought experiment, gradually reducing the tax rate from a point above the fold interval, results in a policy p that slides along the lower side of the fold, and then jumps up accompanied by a sudden fall in the share of transfer recipients. This jump takes place at a lower tax rate than the downward jump described before – a case of hysteresis.

The fact that a policy $p = (t, T)$ may be accompanied by multiple equilibrium population shares x of transfer recipients implies an indeterminacy. When a policy is decided upon, the accompanying share of transfer recipients, and accordingly public revenues and expenditures, may take on alternative equilibrium values. This indeterminacy is due to the endogeneity of the intensity of the social norm. It can, for instance, lead to budget imbalance, although the policy in question is consistent with budget balance equilibrium.

IV   Political Equilibrium

We define a *political equilibrium* as a balanced equilibrium state such that no other balanced equilibrium state is preferred by a majority of the population.

The voting situation facing each individual may be thought of as a vote for or against an incumbent policy (t, T), where the current population share x of transfer recipients is such that $s = (t, T, x)$ constitutes a balanced equilibrium state. Assume that all voters expect the population share x to persist if the policy (t, T) is continued, and when faced with any alternative policy (t', T'), they all expect some equilibrium population share x' under (t', T'). Consider a majority vote between (t, T) and (t', T'), and suppose that the opposition policy (t', T') receives no votes unless the expected state $s' = (t', T', x')$ constitutes a balanced equilibrium. Then the incumbent policy (t, T) wins against any opposition policy if and only if $s = (t, T, x)$ constitutes a political equilibrium state as defined above.[18]

In order to render this notion of political equilibrium more precise and operational, we first note that the utility to an individual with wage $w > 0$ in a balanced equilibrium $s = (t, T, x)$ is the highest of two utility levels, one for each of the two economic choice alternatives that are available to the individual:

$$U(s, w) = \max \{u[(1 - t)w], u(T) + \mu - v(x)\}. \tag{7}$$

Accordingly, it may be said that the individual *prefers* state s' to state s if $U(s, w) < U(s', w)$. A balanced equilibrium state s is a *political equilibrium* if there exists no balanced equilibrium state s' such that more individuals prefer s' to s than there are individuals who prefer s to s'. (Indifferent individuals are thus split evenly between s and s'.)

In the present basic version of the model, without altruism and without any risk of being involuntarily excluded from working life, no state $s = (t, T, x)$ with a population share $x \in (0, 1/2)$ is a political equilibrium, since any such policy would "lose" against the "zero-transfer" state $s^0 = (0, 0, 0)$. Individuals who work in such a state s are better off under s^0, and they constitute a majority. Consequently, a political equilibrium is either the zero-transfer state s^0 or a state that has a majority of transfer recipients.

It turns out that there is only one such alternative to the zero-transfer state, namely, the balanced equilibrium state s^+ that requires the lowest tax rate among states that are optimal from the viewpoint of transfer recipients. Any other optimal state for transfer recipients can be "beaten" by this tax-minimizing state since transfer recipients would be indifferent between the two states but taxpayers would prefer the state s^+ with the lower tax rate. The states that are optimal from the viewpoint of transfer recipients are those with population shares x of transfer recipients in the subset,

$$X^+ = \arg \max_{x \in (0, 1)} (u[F(x)] + \mu - v(x)). \tag{8}$$

Let x^+ be the smallest population share in this set: $x^+ = \min X^+$, and let $s^+ = (f(x^+), F(x^+), x^+)$ be the associated balanced equilibrium state. It can be shown that the population share x^+ results in the lowest tax rate among all population shares x in X^+.[19] On the basis of this observation, it is not difficult to show that the state s^+ is the only alternative political equilibrium to the zero-transfer state s^0.

PROPOSITION 2   If $s = (t, T, x)$ is a political equilibrium and $t > 0$, then $s = s^+$, and $x^+ \geq 1/2$.

(See appendices 3 and 4 for proofs of this and the following proposition.) In particular, if the wage distribution and preferences are such that the population share x^+ is less than one-half, then the only potential political equilibrium is the zero-transfer state.

Proposition 2 leads to the question regarding the conditions under which each of the two candidate states, s^0 and s^+, emerges as a political equilibrium. It turns out that this depends on whether or not the median wage $\tilde{w}$ is higher or lower than the wage $\bar{w}$ that makes an individual indifferent between living off her untaxed work, and living off a transfer that maximizes her utility level across all balanced equilibria which have a (weak) majority of transfer recipients:

$$\bar{w} = u^{-1}\left[\max_{(1/2)\leq x<1}(u[F(x)] + \mu - v(x))\right]. \tag{9}$$

PROPOSITION 3   The zero-transfer state s^0 is the unique political equilibrium if $\bar{w} < \tilde{w}$. The positive-transfer state s^+ is the unique political equilibrium if $\bar{w} > \tilde{w}$ and $x^+ > 1/2$. No political equilibrium exists if $\bar{w} > \tilde{w}$ and $x^+ < 1/2$.

When $\bar{w} < \tilde{w}$, then the median wage earner prefers to live off her untaxed wage over the best transfer possible among those that result in a majority of transfer recipients. Accordingly, s^0 is a political equilibrium, while s^+ is not. When $\bar{w} > \tilde{w}$, then the median wage earner prefers the best transfer possible among those that result in a majority of transfer recipients to living off her untaxed wage. Therefore, s^0 is not a political equilibrium. If the optimal state for transfer recipients, among *all* balanced equilibrium states, results in a majority of transfer recipients, then s^+ is a political equilibrium. In the opposite case, when $x^+ < 1/2$, no political equilibrium exists. In that case, there is a balanced equilibrium state with a majority of transfer recipients, which median wage earners prefer to working at their untaxed wage. Hence such a state gains a majority over the zero-transfer state s^0. However, the only remaining alternative for political equilibrium, s^+, results in a minority of transfer recipients (since $x^+ < 1/2$) and is therefore not a political equilibrium either.

As has just been shown, the nature of political equilibrium is determined by the three numbers $\tilde{w}$, x^+, and $\bar{w}$. While $\tilde{w}$, the median wage, is obtained directly from the basic data of the model and thus is easy to track when the data are changed, x^+ and $\bar{w}$ are obtained only indirectly from the data and are accordingly more difficult to track. Since we know from the preceding analysis that only two distinct states, s^0 and s^+, are possible as political equilibria, a marginal change in the data of the model may, a priori, result in a discontinuous switch from one of these states to the other: a sudden "rise" or "fall" of the welfare state.

In order to substantiate this possibility in the simplest possible setting, let us focus on the comparative-statics effects of a change in the "leisure" taste parameter μ. (Recall that μ represents the utility difference between, on the one hand, leisure as a transfer recipient and, on the other hand, the intrinsic utility that one may derive from working life.) Since the social norm plays a subordinate role in this experiment, we impose the simplifying assumption that the intensity of the social norm is constant across states: $v(x) = 0$. This assumption implies that the set X^+ consists of those population shares at which the transfer function F obtains its maximum.

According to Proposition 3, the state s^+ is unbeatable if $x^+ > 1/2$ and if the median wage earner rather lives on the maximal transfer $T^+ = F(x^+)$ than works under the zero-transfer policy. Figure 20.5 illustrates the utility difference, ΔU, between these two alternatives for the median wage earner as a function of μ. Figure 20.5(a) is based on a more dispersed wage distribution than figure 20.5(b). Not surprisingly, both graphs show that the transfer becomes more attractive as the value of leisure, increases. Indeed, for a sufficiently high valuation of leisure, the median wage earner prefers to live on the transfer ($\Delta U > 0$). It is also evident that the associated critical value of μ depends on the wage distribution. In figure 20.5 the critical values are approximately 0.6 and 1.7. Hence, the transfer is attractive to the median wage earner for a wider range of μ-values in the more dispersed wage distribution (a). Since an increase in μ also increases x^+, this suggests that the positive-transfer state s^+ is more likely to be a political equilibrium in the case of a more dispersed wage distribution.[20] This observation conforms qualitatively with the Meltzer and Richard (1981) result that a larger difference between the mean-value and median of the wage distribution results in larger redistributions.

The effect of an increasing valuation μ of leisure on political equilibrium is shown in figure 20.6, using the same wage distribution as in figure 20.5(b). For μ-values below the critical value, 1.7, the zero-transfer state is the unique political equilibrium. At the critical value, the political equilibrium flips to the positive-transfer state s^+. Above the critical value, a higher valuation of leisure further increases the political support for a positive transfer (see figure 20.6a). Moreover, an increase in μ simultaneously leads to a lower per capita transfer (a), accompanied by a decreasing tax rate (b). Thus, starting from the zero-transfer political equilibrium, a gradual increase in the valuation of leisure

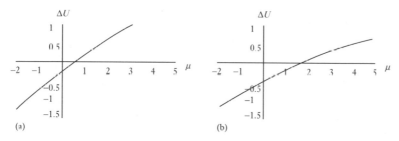

Figure 20.5   The difference in utility for the median wage earner between living off the transfer and off her untaxed wage, as a function of the utility of leisure, μ

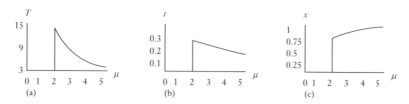

Figure 20.6   The unbeatable policy, and the associated population share x, as functions of the utility of leisure, μ

eventually induces a sudden shift in the political equilibrium to the positive-transfer equilibrium – a highly redistributive policy. Further increases in μ result in a lower transfer, albeit to an increasing fraction of the population.

Having considered the comparative-statics effects of a change in the taste for leisure, let us briefly study the comparative-statics effects of a change of Φ, the wage distribution. Suppose that all individuals' wages are multiplied by the same factor $\lambda > 0$, and suppose also that the utility from consumption is logarithmic, while the disutility function v is kept general – satisfying (A2). As was noted in section III, such a change has no effect on the tax function f, while the transfer function F is point wise multiplied by λ. In terms of the relevant data for political equilibrium – the three numbers $\tilde{w}$, x^+, and $\bar{w}$ – we find consequently that x^+ is unchanged while both $\tilde{w}$ and $\bar{w}$ are multiplied by λ. Hence, if initially $\bar{w} < \tilde{w}$, then s^0, the political equilibrium when $\lambda = 1$, remains the unique political equilibrium for all $\lambda > 0$. On the other hand, if $\bar{w} > \tilde{w}$ and $x^+ > 1/2$, then the unique equilibrium depends on λ: it is $s^+(\lambda) = (t^+, \lambda T^+, x^+)$, where $t^+ = f(x^+)$ and $T^+ = F(x^+)$; i.e., the tax is independent of λ and the transfer is proportional to λ.

V   Altruism

The above model is half-hearted concerning the social nature of preferences. It does allow for preferences to be social in the sense that an individual's economic decision may be influenced by the choices of others. However, an individual's voting decision is assumed to be independent of the policy consequences for other individuals in society. Presumably, most individuals have preferences that are also social in this respect. Here we provide an extension of the model in this direction.

We focus on "Rawlsian altruism," i.e., an altruistic concern for those who are worst off in society. Since all individuals have the same preferences over their own consumption and leisure, the minimal "private" utility, across all individuals in a state with a positive share of transfer recipients, is $u(T) + \mu - v(x)$. We now add the assumption that all individuals in society are equally altruistic, and that they have additively separable utility functions that combine private utility from own consumption, leisure, and source of subsistence, with "altruistic" utility from others' welfare. Since the altruistic term is the same, irrespective of whether the individual chooses to work or live off the transfer, altruism has no effect on the individual's economic decision: all individuals with wages above (below) the critical wage still choose to work (live on the transfer).

However, altruism does potentially affect the political choices made by individuals. Consider again an individual with wage $w > 0$, now faced with a voting decision between an incumbent (balanced-budget) policy $p = (t, T)$ with accompanying population share x of transfer recipients, and an alternative policy $p' = (t', T')$. Let the current state be denoted s, and suppose that x' is such that also $s' = (t', T', x')$ is a balanced equilibrium state. In section IV we defined $U(s, w)$ and $U(s', w)$ as the individual's private utility from these two alternatives. Let $\bar{U}(s', w)$ and $\bar{U}(s', w)$ be her total (private and altruistic) utility from the alternatives, and let a nonnegative weight α be attached to the altruistic component. Then

$$\bar{U}(s, w) = U(s, w) + \alpha[u(T) + \mu - v(x)], \tag{10}$$

and likewise for $\bar{U}(s', w)$, granted that both x and x' are positive.

The (total) utility to a working individual in a balanced equilibrium state can be written as a function of x, the resulting population share of transfer recipients, and w, the wage of the individual. For if $s = (t, T, x)$ is a balanced equilibrium state, then $t = f(x)$ and $T = F(x)$, and the utility to a working individual with wage $w > 0$ is

$$G(x, w) = u([1 - f(x)]w) + \alpha(u[F(x)] + \mu - v(x)). \tag{11}$$

By (A1) and Proposition 1 we have that $G(x, w)$ tends to minus infinity as $x \to 0$ and as $x \to 1$. Hence, all working individuals prefer shares of transfer recipients that lie strictly between zero and one. Consequently, $T = F(x) > 0$ in any unbeatable policy. A necessary condition for a positive population share x (or, equivalently, a positive transfer) to maximize $G(x, w)$ is the first-order condition $(\partial/\partial x)G(x, w) = 0$, which can be written as

$$u'([1 - f(x)]w)wf'(x) = \alpha[u'(F(x))F'(x) - v'(x)]. \tag{12}$$

In general, this equation depends in part on w, the individual's wage. However, if the subutility from consumption is logarithmic, then the wage w cancels out, and thus all taxpayers prefer the same population share $x^a > 0$. Suppose that the solution x^a is unique, and let $p^a = (t^a, T^a)$ be the associated policy; i.e., $t^a = f(x^a)$ and $T^a = F(x^a)$.

Now the logic of section IV kicks in. The set X^+ is still the ideal set for transfer recipients: their utility has only been multiplied by the constant and positive factor $1 + \alpha$. Proposition 2 is modified only in that the condition $t > 0$ is replaced by $t > t^a$, and Proposition 3 remains intact if s^0 is replaced by s^a, $\tilde{w}$ by $\tilde{w}^a - (1 - t^a)\tilde{w}$, and $\bar{w}$ by

$$\bar{w}^a = u^{-1}[(1 + \alpha)u(\bar{w}) - \alpha[u(T^a) + \mu - v(x^a)]].$$

The qualitative features of the analysis of political equilibrium in section IV thus remain intact.

VI Involuntary Exclusion from Work

In practice, many individuals who would prefer to work are excluded from working life. This may be due to unemployment, bad health, etc. We now proceed to include this possibility in the model. Suppose that some fraction λ, where $0 \le \lambda < 1$, do not have a choice whether or not to work; they are *forced* by external circumstances to live off the transfer. For the sake of analytical simplicity, we assume here that this fraction is the same for all wage levels, and that the fraction is known by all individuals.

If x is the total population share of transfer recipients, voluntary and forced, then the fixed-point equation (4) that determines x is generalized to

$$x = \lambda + (1 - \lambda)\Phi\left(\frac{u^{-1}[u(T) + \mu - v(x)]}{1 - t}\right). \tag{13}$$

Here $v(x)$ represents the embarrassment of deviating from the social norm to live off one's own work, given the population share x of transfer recipients.[21] Clearly, any equilibrating population share x in equation (13) will be a number $x \in [\lambda, 1)$. This equation has at least one solution, for the same reason as in the case of equation (4). Thus, the discussion and analysis in section II remains intact once (4) has been replaced by (13). This is also true for section III, dealing with the governmental budget balance, *mutatis mutandis*: the tax base is now reduced by the factor $1 - \lambda$, so the budget equation (5) is generalized to

$$Tx = (1 - \lambda)t\Psi[\Phi^{-1}(x)].$$ (14)

Turning to political equilibrium, the range of possible information scenarios is spanned between two polar cases. In the first case, all individuals know before they vote whether they are forced to live on the transfer. In this case, this population share, which has size λ, will vote for the policy that is best for transfer recipients (irrespective of whether these voters are altruistic or not). The other voters will have policy preferences, as in the basic model version, given by equation (7). In the opposite case, on which we focus here, no individual knows prior to voting whether or not she will be forced to live on the transfer.

Under the maintained hypothesis that all individuals face the same probability λ of being forced to live on the transfer, the expected utility in a state $s = (t, T, x)$ to an individual with wage $w > 0$ is

$$V(s, w) = \lambda[u(T) + \mu - v(x)] + (1 - \lambda)U(s, w),$$ (15)

where $U(s, w)$ is the utility level defined in equation (7). In other words, individuals have the same policy preferences as if they were Rawlsian altruists with the weight $\alpha = \lambda/(1 - \lambda)$ given to the welfare of the worst-off individual in society (see section V).

Hence, the formal analysis of political equilibrium is analogous to that in section V. Indeed, these two elements can be combined. If all individuals face the same (post-voting) risk λ of being forced to live off the transfer, and all individuals are equally altruistic, with weight α, then their economic decisions will be made as indicated in the present section, and their political behavior will be as indicated in section V, with the altruism weight $(\alpha + \lambda)/(1 - \lambda)$.

VII   Lagged Adjustment of the Social Norm

The decision facing the individual voter is quite complex. It concerns a comparison of the current state of the economy with alternative and yet unrealized tax rates and transfer levels with accompanying population shares of transfer recipients. Once a policy has been adopted, each individual's economic decision is based on her prediction of the accompanying population share of transfer recipients. In our model, we have assumed that all individuals are capable of correctly making these predictions. Moreover, we have assumed that the anticipated welfare stigma is fully adjusted to the predicted future population share of transfer recipients. However, both the rational expectations and the "full adjustment" assumptions may be unrealistic. Consequently, there are good reasons to relax them.

At the end of section II we discussed a dynamic adaptation process for individuals' expectations concerning the population share of transfer recipients, when the policy is given. Here we reconsider the second assumption. We now assume that there is a time lag in the perceived disutility from deviations from the social norm. Indeed, we find it quite plausible that individuals' attitudes toward beneficiaries change only gradually over time, and may be experienced only gradually. We consider this modification of the model while maintaining the rational expectations assumption concerning predictions of the population share x of transfer recipients.

It is likely that in practice the intensity of social norms is subject to some inertia. In order to incorporate this in our model, we follow Granovetter and Soong (1983), who use a one-period time lag when they model how individuals are influenced by the aggregate behavior of others. In this spirit, we assume that if the current state, in period τ, is $s_\tau = (t_\tau, T_\tau, x_\tau)$, then voters in period τ evaluate alternative policies for period $\tau + 1$ in terms of the current welfare stigma $v(x_\tau)$. More exactly, all voters reason in the same way as in the original model, but with the "long-run" disutility function v replaced by the constant "short-run" disutility function $v_\tau : [0, 1] \to \mathbb{R}$ defined by $v_\tau(x) = v(x_\tau)$ for all $x \in [0, 1]$. Accordingly, when considering other policies $p \in P$, voters expect a smaller increase in the share x of transfer recipients from an increase in the transfer than if the stigma had been fully adjusted. Similarly, a reduction of the transfer is now expected to result in a smaller decrease in x. In other words, voters perceive it to be cheaper to increase the transfer when the stigma is perceived as constant, and there is less to be gained, in terms of reduced taxes, by cutting transfers. A time lag in the adjustment of the social norm may thus destabilize the political equilibria in our model and may result in budget imbalance.

Let us explore this possibility in somewhat greater detail.[22] Since the stigma is now perceived to be constant in the short run, we may use our original model to generate a "short-run transfer curve" $T = F_\tau(x)$ representing the balanced-budget transfer accompanying any alternative population share x in equilibrium, for a stigma given by the current state s_τ.[23] At the current population share x_τ, the "long-run transfer curve" $T = F(x)$ is intersected by the short-run transfer curve, $F_\tau(x_\tau) = F(x_\tau)$, and the short-run curve is more upward-sloped than the long-run curve: $F_\tau(x) > F(x)$ for all $x > x_\tau$, and $F_\tau(x) < F(x)$ for all $x < x_\tau$. In the lagged version of the model, voters consider alternative points (x, T) on the short-run transfer curve, and may prefer another point than the current point (x_τ, T_τ) even if the current state is a political equilibrium in the original model. If such an alternative policy wins, then a "welfare cycle" may begin, with a sequence of changes in the tax and transfer accompanied by budget imbalances.

The question then arises whether such a process can come to a halt, or, in other words, if the lagged version of the model can have a political equilibrium. In order to discuss this issue, we first need to define a relevant concept of political equilibrium. We suggest the following definition: a state $s^* = (t^*, T^*, x^*)$ is a *political equilibrium* in the lagged model if it is a balanced equilibrium in the original model and if it is a political equilibrium (as defined in section IV) in the model that one obtains by replacing the disutility function v by the constant short-run disutility function $v^* : [0, 1] \to \mathbb{R}$ defined by $v^*(x) = v(x^*)$ for all $x \in [0, 1]$. In other words, the point (x^*, T^*) must lie on the long-run transfer curve, and there should exist no other point (x, T) on the short-run transfer curve through (x^*, T^*) that would be preferred over (x^*, T^*) by a majority when they take the welfare stigma as fixed.[24]

This equilibrium criterion can be illustrated in the (x, T)-plane in terms of taxpayers'
and transfer recipients' indifference curves when all individuals take the welfare stigma as
fixed. A candidate pair (x, T) for political equilibrium is either the zero-transfer pair $(0,0)$,
or it is a point on the long-run transfer curve where the indifference curve of an individual
with the median wage is tangential to the short-run transfer curve through the point. The
median wage earner may be a taxpayer or a transfer recipient. Under the present assumption of a time lag in the adjustment of the norm, the indifference curves of the transfer
recipients are straight horizontal lines since they perceive the disutility from living off the
transfer as being independent of their population share. Taxpayers who are neither
altruistic nor exposed to the risk of being excluded from working life prefer points (x, T)
that lead to low taxes. Since the tax rate t needed to support a transfer T to a population
share x is increasing in both x and T, taxpayers have negatively sloped indifference curves
in the (x, T)-plane. However, altruistic taxpayers or taxpayers who are exposed to the risk
of being excluded from working life may have indifference curves that are at least locally
upward sloping, since they may be prepared to accept some increase in the number of
transfer recipients in return for higher transfers; see figure 20.7.

The two graphs in this figure illustrate two candidate pairs (x, T) for political equilibrium in a numerical specification of the lagged model where taxpayers are altruistic and
have logarithmic utility from consumption. For low transfers and population shares x of
recipients, their indifference curves are gently upward sloping. As x and T increase along
an indifference curve, this becomes steeper and eventually bends backward. The long-run
transfer curve underlying both graphs is the same: the only difference being the fixed
stigma level. The left-hand graph shows a point (x^*, T^*) satisfying the tangency condition
for a taxpayer. It can be verified that a median-wage individual prefers this point to the
highest transfer on the short-run transfer curve (indicated by the horizontal line). Thus,
this point is a political equilibrium in the lagged model. The right-hand graph shows a
point (x, T) satisfying the tangency condition for a transfer recipient. It turns out, however,
that this point results in a lower utility to a median-wage individual than if she had lived off

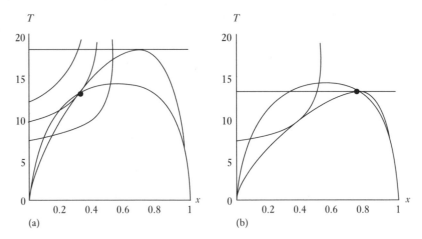

Figure 20.7 The long-run and short-run transfer curves: (a) evaluated for a point with a
majority of taxpayers; and (b) for a point with a majority of transfer recipients

her own work under the best low-tax policy for taxpayers. Consequently, this point does not correspond to a political equilibrium in the lagged model.

How do the political equilibria in the lagged model relate to those in the original model? For instance, is the population share of transfer recipients higher or lower? While it seems difficult to make general statements of this sort, some observations can be made. For example, if the zero-transfer state is a political equilibrium in the original model, then it is also a political equilibrium in the lagged model. The reason is simply that to live off transfers in the lagged model is perceived to give even less utility than in the original model, since the stigma is fixed at its maximal level ($v(0)$).

If individuals are altruistic, and the low-transfer state s^α is instead a political equilibrium in the original model, then a lag in the welfare stigma may well turn s^α into a non-equilibrium state. There are two effects at work here. First, the short-run transfer curve through the point (x^α, T^α) is steeper than the long-run curve, suggesting that political equilibrium with a lag requires a larger share of transfer recipients. Second, for the same reason as given above, the indifference curve for a taxpayer through (x^α, T^α) is steeper in the lagged model, suggesting that political equilibrium may then require a smaller share of transfer recipients. From an altruistic taxpayer's point of view, increases in x become less attractive when the stigma is constant since transfer recipients do not benefit from a reduced stigma. If the effect via the indifference curve predominates, then we may also in this case expect a reduction in the political equilibrium share x of transfer recipients.[25]

In a political equilibrium with a majority of transfer recipients in the original model, the long-run transfer curve slopes downward. In fact, the short-run transfer curve must also be downward sloping at that point. Since transfer recipients have horizontal indifference curves, one may hence expect that the introduction of the lag in the model (under suitable regularity conditions) leads to a reduction in the equilibrium share x of transfer recipients. This allows for a higher transfer in political equilibrium.

We conclude by briefly discussing two comparative-statics experiments. First, consider a positive productivity shock that increases all wages proportionally by a factor λ, and assume that the utility of consumption is logarithmic. As was pointed out at the end of section IV, this leads to a proportional upward shift of the long-run transfer curve. The same is true for all short-run transfer curves. As in section IV, it turns out that the political equilibrium share x of transfer recipients is unaffected by such proportional changes in the wage distribution, while the equilibrium transfer, however, increases by the factor λ. In the short run, however, one may speculate about the effects of a surprise shift in wages. The immediate impact of an increase in wages, prior to the adjustment of economic and political decisions, may be a budget surplus as the tax base increases. The surplus is then further strengthened by the fact that it becomes more attractive to work in comparison with living on the transfer, before this has been increased.

Second, a rise in altruism, i.e., in the taste parameter α, means that the indifference curves for altruistic taxpayers become flatter in the (x, T)-plane since they are prepared to accept more beneficiaries and pay higher taxes for a given increase in T. Suppose that the incumbent equilibrium policy is supported by a majority of taxpayers. An upward shift in α is then likely to lead to a new political equilibrium with higher transfers and more transfer recipients. The indifference curves of transfer recipients, however, are unaffected and remain straight horizontal lines. Consequently, a shift in α does not affect transfer recipients' votes. Suppose that there is a surprise increase in α. Heuristically, an adjustment path could be as follows. First, in the very short run, voters will perhaps choose a new point on the short-run transfer curve that runs through the initial political equilibrium point. With flatter indifference curves, taxpayers prefer a point with higher T and x. Second, when the stigma has been fully adjusted, x will increase further, which leads to a budget deficit under the adopted policy. Thus, even if there is "microeconomic equilibrium" in the sense that the stigma is fully adjusted and x is stable under rational expectations, there is "macroeconomic disequilibrium" in the sense of a budget deficit. Eventually such a budget deficit would have to be removed. This may be achieved by a reduction of the transfer and an increase in the tax rate, bringing the economy to a point on the long-run transfer curve. In sum, such a process can be described as an initial "overshooting" of welfare state spending followed by a "retreat."

VIII   Conclusions and Directions for Further Research

When social norms are introduced into an analysis, one might fear a plethora of possible outcomes – that "anything can happen." However, in the present simple model, this fear turns out to be unjustified.[26] The range of possible outcomes is in fact highly restricted. Essentially, there are only two alternatives: a low-tax society supported by a majority of taxpayers or a high-tax society supported by a majority of transfer recipients. Which of these two potential equilibria will materialize depends on preferences and on the wage distribution.

If the disutility from deviating from the social norm is highly sensitive to the fraction of deviators and the norm is important to the individual – in comparison with her preference for consumption and leisure – then certain tax rates are consistent with multiple combinations of per capita transfer levels and shares of benefit recipients. These combinations imply fulfilled expectations but not necessarily political equilibrium. Given a low proportion of transfer recipients, the disutility of living on the work of others is high. On the other hand, a high proportion of transfer recipients will be associated with a low level of disutility. Because of this potential multiplicity, there is a certain indeterminacy even when the tax rate and per capita transfer level have been determined: the economy may become locked into any of the accompanying equilibrium population shares of transfer recipients.

The present analysis suggests several avenues for future research. First, it might be valuable to further elaborate and formalize the above discussion about a time lag in the formation of welfare stigma. In particular, we have not investigated conditions for the existence of political equilibrium in this case. Second, an obvious modification of the model is to relax the restriction on individuals' work/leisure decision from being binary – full-time work or no work – to a choice from a continuum of hours of work. Sundén and Weibull (1997) show that if individuals have Cobb-Douglas preferences (and, as here, lack non-labor incomes), then the present limitation to a binary choice is not binding. Another extension is to allow the model to encompass supplements to labor income reflecting benefits such as child allowances, day-care subsidies, and housing benefits. It may also be relevant to allow for individual differences in preferences and in the access to benefit systems. For instance, individuals may differ in their evaluation of leisure (see Besley and Coate 1992), and in their sensitivity to social norms, and they may evidently also have differing entitlements to transfer payments. An aspect that we have merely touched upon (in connection with figures 20.5 and 20.6) but that would be worth analyzing further, is the impact of the wage dispersion on the nature of political equilibrium. Moreover, it might be valuable to model a more realistic political process than the simple majority rule used in this paper: for example by studying political institutions such as representative democracy and political parties.

Finally, the approach taken here, to place social norms on an equal footing with economic incentives, may of course be applied to a variety of issues. One such issue, which also concerns the welfare state, is tax evasion.[27] On top of the risk of being caught, tax evaders may experience embarrassment and perhaps also social disapproval.

Appendix 1   Parametric Specifications

The computer calculations behind the figures in this essay are based on logarithmic utility from consumption and Weibull-distributed wages.

Assuming that $u(y) = \log(y)$ for all $y > 0$, equations (5) and (6) yield the following closed-form expressions:

$$f(x) = \frac{x\Phi^{-1}(x)}{x\Phi^{-1}(x) + \Psi\left[\Phi^{-1}(x)\right]\exp\left[\mu - v(x)\right]}$$

$$F(x) = \frac{\Phi^{-1}(x)\Psi\left[\Phi^{-1}(x)\right]}{x\Phi^{-1}(x) + \Psi\left[\Phi^{-1}(x)\right]\exp\left[\mu - v(x)\right]}.$$

The Weibull distribution is governed by three parameters. One, a, determines the lower end of its support; another, b, the "scale" along its support. The third parameter, c, determines the concentration of the distribution, with high values of c corresponding to a high degree of concentration (here wage equality). More precisely, a random variable X is *Weibull* (a, b, c)-distributed if, for all $x > a$,

$$\Pr(X \le x) = 1 - \exp[-((x-a)/b))^c].$$

We here set $a = 0$ and $b = 90$. Hence, $\Phi(w) = 1 - \exp[-(w/90)^c]$.

Appendix 2   Proof of Claims in Connection with Figure 20.4

It remains to prove the three claims made in the discussion of figure 20.4. For this purpose, first note that, as we move along the balanced-budget curve from the zero-tax, zero-transfer policy $p^0 = (0, 0)$ toward the unit-tax, zero-transfer policy $p^1 = (1, 0)$, the population share x of transfer recipients increases monotonically from zero to one. (This implies the earlier observation concerning the fold in the balanced-policy curve that $x > x' > x''$.) This follows from the continuity of the functions f and F, that together map population shares x to policies p, in combination with the fact that for each $x \in [0, 1]$ there corresponds exactly one point p on the curve (one balanced policy). Next, since the critical wage $w(t, T, x)$ is increasing in t and T (for each x), the curve in figure 20.1(a) shifts up (down) if both t and T increase (decrease). This implies that segments of the balanced-policy curve in figure 20.4 where both t and T increase (decrease) correspond to fixed points x where the curve in figure 20.1(b) intersect the 45-degree line from above (below). This proves the first two claims. The third claim follows from the first claim in conjunction with the observation that when $p^0 = (0, 0)$ the unique fixed point is $x = 0$. Hence, by continuity, policies p on the initial segment of the balanced-policy curve correspond to the lowest fixed point (if multiple fixed points exist) that is compatible with p.

Appendix 3   Proof of Proposition 2

Suppose that $s = (t, T, x)$ is a balanced equilibrium with $t > 0$.

If $x < \frac{1}{2}$, then individuals who work constitute a strict majority. Their utility is clearly higher in the zero-transfer state $s^0 = (0, 0, 0)$, since $u(w) > u((1 - t)w)$ for all $w > 0$. Thus, s is not a political equilibrium. Hence $x \geq \frac{1}{2}$ if s is a political equilibrium with $t > 0$.

Suppose now that $x \geq \frac{1}{2}$, and $x \notin X^+$. Let $x' \in X^+$ and $s' = (f(x'), F(x'), x')$. Then the weak majority of transfer recipients in s obtains higher utility in s'. While their utility in s is $u(T) + \mu - v(x)$, the utility in s' to any individual with wage $w > 0$ is

$$U(s', w) = \max \{u(T') + \mu - v(x'), u((1 - t')w)\}$$
$$\geq u(T') + \mu - v(x') > u(T) + \mu - v(x).$$

Moreover, by continuity some wage earners in s (those with wages just exceeding the critical wage) have higher utility in s'. Thus, s is not a political equilibrium. Hence $x \in X^+ \cap [\frac{1}{2}, 1]$ if s is a political equilibrium with $t > 0$.

Suppose finally that $x \in X^+ \cap [\frac{1}{2}, 1]$ and $x \neq x^+$. Then the (possibly weak) majority of transfer recipients in s obtains at least the same utility under s^+ as under s, since both x and x^+ belong to X^+, and any transfer recipient in s has the option to remain a transfer recipient in s^+. Moreover, the positive population share of workers in s obtains higher utility in s^+, since the tax rate in s^+ is lower than in s (see note 19). In s, the utility to a worker with wage $w > 0$ is $u([1 - f(x)]w)$, while in s^+ his utility is

$$\max \{u(F(x^+)) + \mu - v(x^+), u([1 - f(x^+)]w)\} \geq u([1 - f(x^+)]w) > u([1 - f(x)]w).$$

Consequently, s is not a political equilibrium.

Appendix 4   Proof of Proposition 3

First, suppose that $\bar{w} < \tilde{w}$. Let s^0 be the zero-tax state, and let $s' = (t', T', x')$ be any balanced equilibrium with $t' > 0$. Clearly, s' is not preferred over s^0 by a majority if $x' \leq \frac{1}{2}$, since then taxpayers in s' constitute a (possibly weak) majority and pay a positive income tax in s' and no tax in s. Thus, assume that $x' > \frac{1}{2}$. The critical wage in s' exceeds the median: $w - \Phi^1(x') > \tilde{w}$. We thus have $u(T) + \mu - v(x') = u(w) > u(\tilde{w}) > u(\bar{w})$, contradicting the definition of $\bar{w}$ (since we assumed that $x' > \frac{1}{2}$). Thus, s^0 is a political equilibrium. In order to show that no balanced equilibrium state $s \neq s^0$ is a political equilibrium, it suffices, by Proposition 2, to show that s^+ is not a political equilibrium when $x^+ \geq \frac{1}{2}$. But $\bar{w} < \tilde{w}$ implies that $u(\bar{w}) < u(\tilde{w})$, and thus median-wage individuals, along with all individuals with higher wages, and, by continuity also some individuals with slightly lower wages, prefer s^0 to living off the transfer in s^+. Since the income tax in s^+ is positive, they prefer s^0 over s^+.

Second, suppose that $\bar{w} > \tilde{w}$ and $x^+ > \frac{1}{2}$. Then, s^0 is not a political equilibrium, since median-wage individuals obtain less utility from living off their untaxed wage than living off the transfer in s^+. This is also true for all individuals with lower wages, and, by continuity, for individuals with wages slightly above $\tilde{w}$. Hence, a strict majority prefers s^+ over s^0. To see that s^+ is a political equilibrium, note that the utility to a transfer recipient in this state is $u(T^+) + \mu - v(x^+) = u(\bar{w}) > u(\tilde{w})$. Can any balanced equilibrium state $s = (t, T, x)$ secure a majority against s^+? If $x \notin X^+$, then the transfer recipients in s^+, a strict majority, obtain more utility in s^+ than in s, and hence s^+ does not lose against any such state s. If instead $x \in X^+$, then the transfer recipients in s^+ obtain the same utility in s as in s^+. However, all taxpayers in s^+ obtain more utility in s^+ than in s, since the tax rate is lower in s^+ than in s (see note 19). Thus, s^+ is a political equilibrium.

Third, suppose that $\bar{w} > \tilde{w}$ and $x^+ < \frac{1}{2}$. From Proposition 2 the only state that can potentially be a political equilibrium is s^0. By definition of $\bar{w}$, there exists a population share x such that the utility to a transfer recipient in state $s = (f(x), F(x), x)$ equals $u(\bar{w})$. Since $u(\bar{w}) > u(\tilde{w})$, all individuals with wages below the median prefers s to s^0. By continuity this is also true for individuals with wages slightly above $\tilde{w}$ and thus s^0 is not a political equilibrium.

Notes

* The authors are grateful for helpful comments from two anonymous referees, Sören Blomquist, Tilman Börgers, Avinash Dixit, Tore Ellingsen, Nils Gottfries, Jean-Michel Grandmont, Joseph Harrington, Ulf Jakobson, Yeongjae Kang, Alan Kirman, Yvan Lengwiler, John Roemer, Peter Birch-Sörensen, Richard Swedberg, Karl Wärneryd, and the participants in seminars at the IUI (The Research Institute of Industrial Economics), at Cornell, Humboldt, Stockholm, and Uppsala Universities, at the Swedish School of Business Administration in Helsinki, and at University College London. We thank David Sundén for excellent assistance with computer illustrations. This essay is based upon an earlier working paper (Lindbeck, Nyberg, and Weibull 1996). Financial support from the Heddius and Wellander Foundation is gratefully acknowledged.

1 A classic sociological treatment of social norms is Parsons (1952). His views have since been criticized for leaving little scope for individual choice: see Gouldner (1970). The rational choice school of sociologists recognizes the joint influence of social norms and economic incentives; see Coleman (1990).

2 Alternatively, one could view social norms as equilibria in repeated games, where individuals derive utility from consumption and leisure, and where the disutility from a deviation is caused by punishments by others.

3 Statistics Sweden (SCB) and National Social Insurance Board (RFV).

4 For instance, in Sweden the corresponding figures in 1960 were 17 percent including the old-age pensioners and 8 percent excluding this group.

5 Moffitt (1983) could reject the hypothesis that the stigma depends on the size of the welfare transfer. He did not analyze the possibility that the stigma might depend on the participation rate itself.

6 Certain transfers, such as pensions, are usually regarded as entitlements and may not be accompanied by any social stigma at all; see Romer (1997) for a discussion.

7 In an empirical study from the Netherlands, Engbersen et al. (1993) found that a majority of long-term unemployed had stopped looking for work and that more than half of these had done so because "they had found other activities to give meaning to their lives: hobbies, voluntary work, or working in the informal economy."

8 This assumption conforms to some empirical evidence concerning public goods provision. In a study based on laboratory experiments, Gächter and Fehr (1997) found, among other things,

that the marginal social approval gained from contributing to a public good increases with the average contribution level of other individuals.

9   One can easily extend the present model to the case of three categories of individuals: those who are not entitled to transfers, those who can choose between work and the transfer, and those who have no choice but to live off the transfer. The model is extended to include the last group in section VI.

10   We take this distribution to be fixed and given, thus neglecting the possibility that taxes and transfers may (at least in the long run) influence factor incomes. Moreover, an individual's wage is assumed to be independent of others' work decisions. We thus neglect the possibility that the productivity of an individual depends on other's work inputs.

11   Taxes are assumed to be linear for the sake of analytical simplicity. However, for many countries nowadays this is not a bad approximation.

12   In a more elaborate model the disutility $v(x)$ may be group specific, as norms are likely to be formed between individuals who are in close contact with each other. In such a model, groups may differ in their equilibrium behavior even if preferences and wages are the same. Recent empirical support for the notion that individual behavior is contingent on group-belonging is given in Bertrand, Luttmer, and Mullainathan (1997).

13   Of course the utility of leisure may depend on aggregate leisure in society, where leisure may be a positive or negative social externality. In the present model, aggregate leisure is monotonically related to the share x of transfer recipients. The sum of the two utility terms μ and $v(x)$ may thus together represent the compound effect of social norm adherence and such an externality – granted that their joint utility effect is not negative.

14   The cause of the multiplicity of equilibrium population shares is logically similar to that observed in Granovetter and Soong's (1983, 1986), Basu's (1987), Becker's (1991), and Blomquist's (1993) analyses of preferences which depend on aggregate behavior.

15   In reality, government budgets are of course not always balanced. Budget balance is assumed here in order to define a trade-off between taxes and transfers. An analysis of unbalanced budgets would be quite interesting but requires an intertemporal extension of the model.

16   The authors are grateful to one of the referees for suggesting the following argument leading to this conclusion – a much simpler argument than we had developed.

17   See appendix 1, and note that $\Phi^{-1}(x)$ and $\Psi[\Phi^{-1}(x)]$ are then replaced by $\lambda\Phi^{-1}(x)$ and $\lambda\Psi[\Phi^{-1}(x)]$, respectively.

18   In light of the discussion in section III, if the current state $s = (t, T, x)$ is a balanced equilibrium, then x is uniquely determined from the incumbent policy (t, T). However, there is nothing in our model that theoretically prevents voters to expect and act in accordance with a shift in x to an unbalanced equilibrium value. We thank Tilman Börgers for drawing our attention to this phenomenon.

19   The set $X^+ \subset (0, 1)$ is nonempty and compact since the maximand is continuous and goes to minus infinity as x goes to 0 and to 1. Hence x^+ is well defined. Moreover, suppose that $x, x' \in X$ and $x < x'$. Then transfer recipients obtain the same utility levels in the two associated states. However, the critical wages under x and x^+ differ: $w - \Phi^1(x) < \Phi^1(x') - w'$. From the noted indifference, we have accordingly $[1 - f(x)]w = [1 - f(x')]w'$, implying that $f(x) < f(x')$.

20   From equations (5) and (6) it is easy to see that the maximal transfer decreases in μ. Consider the effect of an increase in μ for any given x. Then t must decrease, which, for a given x, means that T decreases in the same proportion. Since this holds for all x between zero and one, both functions F and f shift pointwise down in μ. Consequently, the maximal T-value, T^+, decreases. To show that the corresponding population share (or political support) x^+ is nondecreasing in μ is straightforward but somewhat tedious.

21 It could be argued that this embarrassment should be a function of the share $x - \lambda$ of individuals who *voluntarily* choose to deviate from the norm (see Besley and Coate 1992). However, one may then instead define v by $v(x) = \tilde{v}(x - \lambda)$ for all $x \geq \lambda$, where $\tilde{v}(y)$, for any $y \in [0, 1 - \lambda)$, is the embarrassment of deviating from the social norm when the population share of voluntary deviators is y. Hence, without any loss of generality with regard to the basis for the embarrassment, we may still take v to be as in (A2).

22 We here assume that the disutility function v is decreasing.

23 The function F_τ is obtained in the same way as the function F, but with the long-run disutility function v replaced by the short-run disutility function v_τ.

24 Recall from the budget equation (5) that the balanced equilibrium tax rate t is uniquely determined by T and x.

25 An alternative specification of altruism is to assume that altruistic individuals only care about the consumption utility, and possibly the value of leisure, of the least well off. After all, that is all they may be capable of observing. In such a case the indifference curves of taxpayers are independent of whether stigma is constant or not. The number of transfer recipients in a political equilibrium where taxpayers constitute a majority is therefore likely to be higher. In such a case the lag in stigma leads to a too generous welfare state from the taxpayers' viewpoint.

26 Moreover, if social norms in reality do support a plethora of outcomes, then the fear of such a plethora is no justifiable reason for excluding norms from our models.

27 See Allingham and Sandmo (1972) and Srinivasan (1973) for models of tax evasion driven by purely economic incentives.

References

Akerlof, G., "A Theory of Social Custom, of Which Unemployment May Be One Consequence," *Quarterly Journal of Economics*, LXXXIV (1980), 749–75.

Allingham, M., and A. Sandmo, "Income Tax Evasion: A Theoretical Analysis," *Journal of Public Economics*, 1 (1972), 323–38.

Basu, K., "Monopoly, Quality Uncertainty and 'Status' Goods," *International Journal of Industrial Organization*, V (1987), 435–46.

Becker, G. S., "A Note on Restaurant Pricing and Other Examples of Social Influences on Price," *Journal of Political Economy*, XCIX (1991), 1109–116.

Bernheim, B. D., "A Theory of Conformity," *Journal of Political Economy*, CII (1994), 841–77.

Bertrand, M. E., Luttmer, and S. Mullainathan, "Network Effects and Welfare Cultures," mimeo, Harvard University, 1997.

Besley, T., and S. Coate, "Understanding Welfare Stigma: Taxpayer Resentment and Statistical Discrimination," *Journal of Public Economics*, XLVIII (1992), 165–83.

Blomquist, N. S., "Interdependent Behavior and the Effect of Taxes," *Journal of Public Economics*, LI (1993), 211–18.

Coleman, J. S., *Foundations of Social Theory* (Cambridge, MA: Harvard University Press, 1990).

Elster, J., *The Cement of Society: A Study of Social Order* (Cambridge: Cambridge University Press, 1989).

Engbersen, G. K., Schuyt, J. Timmer, and F. Van Waarden, *Cultures of Unemployment: A Comparative Look at Long-Term Unemployment and Urban Poverty* (Boulder, CO: Westview Press, 1993).

Gächter, S., and E. Fehr, "Collective Action as a Social Exchange," mimeo, University of Zürich, 1997.

Gouldner, A. W., *The Coming Crisis of Western Sociology* (New York: Basic Books, 1970).

Granovetter, M., "Threshold Models of Collective Behavior," *American Journal of Sociology*, LXXXIII (1978), 1420–443.

Granovetter, M., and R. Soong, "Threshold Models of Diffusion and Collective Behavior," *Journal of Mathematical Sociology*, IX (1983), 165–79.

Granovetter, M., and R. Soong, "Threshold Models of Interpersonal Effects in Consumer Demand," *Journal of Behavior and Organization*, VII (1986), 83–99.

Lindbeck, A., "Welfare State Disincentives with Endogenous Habits and Norms," *Scandinavian Journal of Economics*, XCVII (1995), 477–94.

Lindbeck, A., S. Nyberg, and J. W. Weibull, "Social Norms, the Welfare State, and Voting," IUI Working Paper No. 453, 1996.

Meltzer, A. H., and S. F. Richard, "A Rational Theory of the Size of Government," *Journal of Political Economy*, LXXXIX (1981), 914–27.

Moffitt, R., "An Economic Model of Welfare Stigma," *American Economic Review*, LXXIII (1983), 1023–35.

Parsons, T., *The Social System* (London: Tavistock Publications, 1952).

Roberts, K., "Voting over Income Tax Schedules," *Journal of Public Economics*, VIII (1977), 329–40.

Romer, P., "Preferences, Promises, and the Politics of Entitlement," in V. Fuchs (ed.), *Individual and Social Responsibility* (Chicago and London: University of Chicago Press, 1997).

Schelling, T., "Dynamic Models of Segregation," *Journal of Mathematical Sociology*, I (1971), 143–86.

Srinivasan, T., "Tax Evasion: A Model," *Journal of Public Economics*, II (1973), 339–46.

Sundén, D., and J. W. Weibull, "A Note on Social Norms and Transfers," IUI Working Paper No. 478, 1997.

Young, P., "Evolution of Conventions," *Econometrica* LXI (1993), 57–84.

Index